Grea[…] ers in European History

To Joel and Katie
Best wishes

Paul Marston

Front cover image: Eyre Crow's painting of Jeremiah Horrocks, Walker Gallery, Liverpool.

First published by: The University of Central Lancashire, 2014

Produced for The Universty of Central Lancashire by Canopus Publishing Limited
15 Nelson Parade, Bristol BS3 4HY
Director: Robin Rees
Cover Design: James Symonds
Editor: Sarah Tremlett
www.CanopusBooks.com

A catalogue record for this book is available from the British Library.

ISBN: 978-1-901922-97-4

Printed in the United Kingdom by Short Run Press, Exeter.

Table of Contents

About the Author

Paul Marston began an interest in the history and philosophy of science in the classes of Karl Popper, Imre Lakatos and Paul Feyerabend as a masters student at LSE. His PhD concerned a topic in the 19th century interaction of science and religion/metaphysics, and his teaching over many years at the University of Central Lancashire has included courses on both the history and the philosophy of science. He also has an MA in theology. His various solo and jointly authored books have been mostly theological, but include *Reason, Science and Faith* (1999 and 2000) with Roger Forster which contains some material relevant to the present topic.

Introduction

This book is about some of the great astronomers in the history of astronomy up to about 1900. It is not some kind of a catalogue of discoveries, nor does it try to be a comprehensive history of astronomy. Its interest is in the dynamics of discovery and how this interacted with the social and psychological features of some of the seminal figures. There are no 'fathers of', for this is a mistaken understanding of how science works, but there have been some fascinating, innovative, and brilliant characters in astronomy history. Seen in this way the history of science is *fun*!

The first chapter looks at the nature of knowledge, history and science. In the course from which this book arose, it was found that sometimes students were puzzled about why they were reading this. Usually, however, it became clear to them as the course progressed – and one particular distance learning student may be remembered who began by making vociferous complaints about the first section and finished the year so fascinated by it that he was looking to do a masters in the area!

The other chapters mostly concern individual astronomers, though some later chapters have to be more topic focused.

1. History and Science

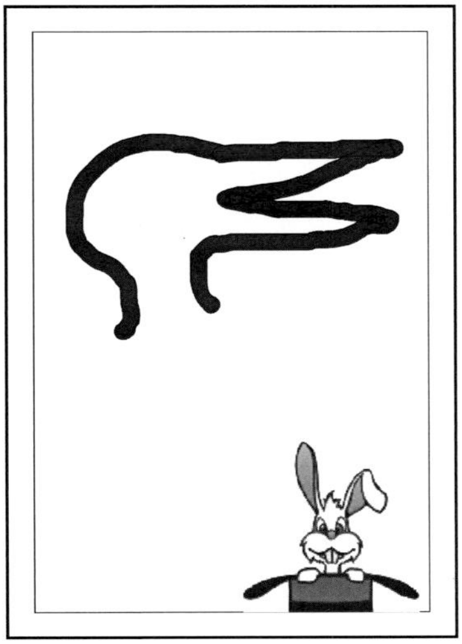

'How am I to Persuade Sir Karl [Popper], who knows everything I do about scientific development, and who has somewhere or other said it, that what he calls a duck can be seen as a rabbit?'

T.S.Kuhn in *Criticism and the Growth of Knowledge* (1970), Imre Lakatos and Alan Musgrave (page 3).

Thomas S. Kuhn became known as a leading philosopher of science in the twentieth century, largely on the basis of his book *The Structure of Scientific Revolutions* (1st ed. 1962, 2nd ed. 1970). Fewer people know that his first book, published in 1957, was called *The Copernican Revolution*, and he came to it as a historian of science with especial interest in the historical events central to this present book.

Kuhn's words quoted above were said in a conference attended by most leading philosophers of science in the early 1970s,[1] and they conveniently raise a number of key issues. This present book concerns the history of science, and to get the most out of studying this it is useful to have thought about both the nature of history and the nature of science. This chapter will therefore raise the following issues:

- The interpretive nature of perception
- The implications of this for the nature of history

---

[1]I attended courses at LSE by Popper, Lakatos and Feyerabend in the late 1960s, when these issues were being debated.

- The implications of this for the practice of science
- Different views taken of the nature of science
- The approach this leads to in studying the history of science

Parts of the material may be new and not easy to some readers, but it is worth persevering with it. The more of the ideas which become clear, the greater depth the actual historical study can have.

One assumption behind Kuhn's words quoted above is that people who assume that the nature of history and/or the nature of science are 'straightforward', and involve just 'getting the facts', miss one central point about knowledge. This is that *all* knowledge (whether historical or scientific) is *interpretive.* Human beings never make 'pure' observation. We *interact* with our sensory experience, using concepts that we both learn and invent. This is the point of the duck/rabbit. Kuhn was applying the idea to the *philosophy of science*, but the notion applies to science, history and any other area of cognitive knowledge. Our visual field detects a particular shape; our minds make it into a duck or a rabbit depending on our previous experiences. Generally we are not conscious of this process – we do not see and *then* interpret, we 'see' it as a rabbit. If we change from one interpretation of the shape to the other, it is usually as a 'gestalt switch', i.e. it does not happen gradually but as a sudden change of 'seeing'.

You may be aware of other similar objects. Is this, for example, a chalice or two people? If it is two people, are they in confrontation, close conversation or about to do a nose-rubbing ceremony?

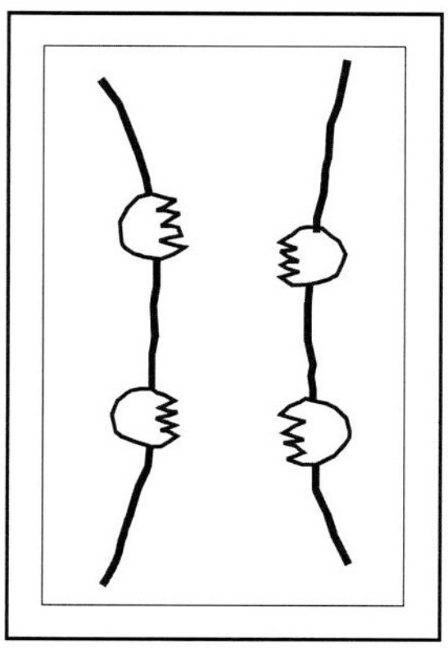

In lecture courses I often draw up something like the picture on the left and ask students what they think it is. The answer is almost invariably a bear behind a tree – though one student thought she saw a female Koala bear behind a tree! People interpret visual clues according to prior concepts and conditioning. An Eskimo familiar with bears but not trees would not 'see' the same thing at all.

What all this is saying is that seeing and interpreting are generally part of the same process. Sensory perception without concepts would be like a kaleidoscopic image of shapes and colours without meaning – and this is not what we 'see'. With some mental effort, of course, we may be able to distinguish aspects of the picture from the concepts, but normally we don't do this.

There is also a further aspect, in that any cognitive knowledge (i.e. knowledge about 'facts') has to be expressed in human language. Words have *lexical fields* (including closely associated words) and also have *semantic fields* (which include their synonyms, antonyms, homonyms and homophones). An early French writer estimated, for example, that the French word *chat* had some two thousand associated words. Using a different word or different language (e.g. *cat* or *pussycat*) alters the meaning. To say of someone 'She's a real cat' is rather different from 'She's a real pussycat'!

All this amounts to adopting a viewpoint that is presently the most common amongst both philosophers of science and philosophers of history, which is called 'critical realism'. This affirms that there *is* a *unique* reality, but that this reality may be experienced and perceived *differently*. Critical realism stands between two extremes:

1. **'Relativism':** a view that there is no absolute truth, but different truths for different observers. A modern form of this is what is now generally called 'postmodernism', – the view that there are multiple realities and so multiple 'truths' (i.e. that truth is different for different observers).

2. **'Positivism':** a view which sees knowledge as purely objective with no influence from the observer. One form of this was a naïve realism or crude positivism which assumed that:

    a. objects

    b. sensory experiences of them

c. terms used of them

had a simple one-to-one-to-one relationship and were somehow inevitable and equivalent.

Critical realism stands between these extremes of relativism and positivism. It assumes that there may be different but 'valid' perceptions, but that there are limits between a different perception and a delusion or hallucination.

The Nature of History

These ideas can be applied to the study of history. John Tosh puts it:

> The word history carries two meanings in common parlance. It refers both to what actually happened in the past and to the representation of that past in the work of historians.[2]

By 'history' we mean here not just what happened in the past, but the actual subject matter of history as written in history books. This means that 'history' is a human artefact – albeit an intellectual one.

To the proverbial person in the street 'history' may seem to be just a matter of 'collecting the facts'. Surely either Caesar did or did not cross the Rubicon? Surely either Galileo did or did not show that the Earth moved? Surely Herschel either did or did not discover Uranus? The basic problems with this naïve view, as we shall see, concern selection, perception and language.

But first let us take a historical perspective. Classically, historians tended to have one eye on the ruling authorities: 'history', as someone has said, 'is written by the winners'. It would have been a brave historian who produced a 'true' history of Richard III in the age of the Tudors, even if recent findings have shown that he did indeed have a crooked back as Shakespeare wrote! It also tended to be nationalistic. The battle of Waterloo was won by Wellington according to the British, Blucher according to the Germans, and the French would perhaps like to think of it more as a draw! Leopold von Ranke, working from the 1830s, wanted to get away from this nationalistic strain, away from the evaluation of historical figures in terms of 'good guys' and 'bad guys'. He therefore saw the task of the historian as 'simply to show how it really was' (*wie es eigenlich gewesen).* The 19th century (and some may remember Gradgrind in Dickens' *Hard Times*) was strong on facts – and in

---

[2] *The Pursuit of History*, preface to the fifth edition (2010).

the early 20th century positivism (as defined above and also below) added its impetus to this approach. In Britain this had especial appeal because of a tradition of empiricism (i.e. an emphasis on the objectivity of observation since John Locke). Lord Acton, in undertaking *The Cambridge Modern History* at the turn of the 20th century, told contributors that the account of the battle of Waterloo, for example, should be one which satisfies all nationalities and where one cannot tell which nationality is the writer. Acton was optimistic that:

> Ultimate history we cannot have in this generation, but we can dispose of conventional history, and show the point we have reached on the road from one to the other, now that all information is within reach, and every problem has become capable of solution.[3]

In the early part of the 20th century, figures like the Italian Benedetto Croce and American Carl Becker were beginning to challenge this. Croce in particular influenced the British historian R. G. Collingwood, who held that history is 'the attempt to answer questions about human actions done in the past …'[4] and involves interaction between the past and the historian. The historian: '[is always selecting, simplifying, schematising, leaving out what he thinks unimportant and putting in what he regards as essential …'[5] History proceeds 'by the interpretation of evidence …'[6] Collingwood also writes, as we shall see, about the need to get inside the thoughts of historical figures.

In 1957, in the second edition, historian Sir George Clark was critical of the earlier edition's notion of ultimate history:

> Historians of a later generation do not look forward to any such prospect …knowledge of the past has come down through one or more human minds, has been 'processed' by them, and therefore cannot consist of elemental and impersonal atoms which nothing can alter … The exploration seems to be endless, and some impatient scholars take refuge in scepticism, or at least in the doctrine that, since all historical judgements involve persons and points of view, one is as good as another and there is

---

[3] *The Cambridge Modern History: Its Origin, Authorship and Production*, 12.

[4] R. G. Collingwood, *The Idea of History* (1946, 1993), 9.

[5] R. G. Collingwood, *The Historical Imagination* (1935) in The Idea of History (rev. edn), 236.

[6] R. G. Collingwood (1946), 10.

> no 'objective' historical truth.[7]

Clarke was still hopeful that the 'facts' could be established and that judgements could then be more personal. E. H. Carr in the classic *What is History?* (1961) is very critical of this. The number of 'facts' available to the historian is very large – the point is to select the *significant* facts. Carr says that we can accept that Caesar crossed a stream known as the Rubicon – but so what? A lot of people have done this. The reason that the 'fact' is of interest to historians is its significance. And then we have to ask 'significant for whom?' Thus William Dray[8] argued that selection as such is not distortion but that 'historical accounts (are) relative to the value scheme which is brought to them by the historian'.

It is not only, however, that selection may differ. Carr also wrote that 'History means interpretation'. Language is involved in this, Carr says: 'the use of language forbids (the historian) to be neutral' (25). Language reflects and moulds concepts.

What about value judgements? In *The Whig Interpretation of History* (1931), Herbert Butterfield was critical of the practice of historians 'dividing the world into the friends and enemies of progress'. He adds:

> Real historical investigation …is not reached by assuming that our own age is the absolute to which Luther and Calvin and their generation are only relative, it is only reached by fully accepting that their generation is as valid as our generation.

There is, he says, no verdict *of* history, only that of historians. Impartiality is impossible and the 'appearance of having achieved it is only the greatest of illusions' (68). There is much in this, and the problem is not eased by projecting (as Carr did in his later work) the 'verdict' to future generations.

One of the current most commonly used books on the nature of history is *The Pursuit of History* by John Tosh. He emphasises the divergence of approach by historians on the 'objectivity' issues, contrasting the perspectivism of Theodore Zeldin with the views of G. R. Elton.[9] Elton wrote:

---

[7] *The New Cambridge Modern History I,* xxiv-xxv.

[8] William Dray, *Perspectives on History,* (1980).

[9] *The Pursuit of History* (5th edition 2010), 176.

> The independent and real existence of historical events implies that, in theory at least, they can be observed absolutely, and for a very large number of basic facts this holds true.[10]

It has to be said, however, that Elton does not answer the basic point at issue. This is that, for any 'fact' considered of importance to record in history, it is the significance of the action rather than its bare occurrence which is important. As Carr says, getting 'the facts' right is a duty, not a virtue, in a historian. It is understanding their *significance* which is crucial. It has to be said that this is reflected in marking history essays. Simply 'getting all the facts right' is certainly a necessary condition to obtain a first class mark, but by no means a sufficient one.

History cannot be purely objective. Neither, however, can it be purely subjective. Even someone accepted as a classic spokesperson for relativism, Charles Beard, wrote:

> If all historical conceptions are merely relative to passing events, to transitory phases of ideas and interests, then the conception of relativity is itself relative. When absolutes in history are rejected, the absolutism of relativism is also rejected.

Any pure relativist view of knowledge[11] is self-contradictory because anything it says must itself be relative. Carr also defends some kind of objectivity:

> ...it does not follow that, because interpretation plays a necessary part in establishing the facts of history, and because no existing interpretation is wholly objective, one interpretation is as good as another, and the facts of history are in principle not amenable to objective interpretation.

A British court in 2000 decided that historian David Irving's version of the holocaust (in which it largely didn't happen) was not a valid perspective on events. This decision must surely in principle be right, perspective is not the

---

[10] G. R. Elton, *The Practice of History* (1967).

[11] One form of relativism is called 'post-modernism'; my son once playfully remarked that at a post-modernist conference 'the toilet is wherever you want it to be'. See the literature if you are interested in a more serious critique! 'Decontructivist' approaches, which are likewise self-destructive, can also be explored if you want.

same as distortion, and the fact that historians may differ in perspective does not mean that 'anything goes'.

Two other suggestions on history should be briefly looked at. The Idealists (such as Collingwood) see understanding ideas as central. The neo-Marxists have thought virtually the opposite – ideas are thrown up as a by-product of concrete physical and economic circumstances. This can be applied to the history of science. Thus Margaret Jacob's work on Newton emphasises his position as a Whig, and the general Cambridge Academics' antipathy at that time to monarchy. This kind of thing is supposed to affect (or in some cases) determine someone's science. I have to confess great scepticism about such explanations – they seem to me to demonstrate ingenuity on the part of the historian rather than reflect any reality.

A second suggestion (particularly from Carl Hempel and Karl Popper) is called 'covering law theory' i.e. looking for repeatable patterns in history.

So where does all this leave the history of science?

Firstly, it is possible to simply get the facts *wrong*. When Patrick Moore stated that John Calvin shared a general opposition to Copernicanism on religious grounds, he was simply wrong.

Secondly, historians inevitably *select* the facts they think are important. Why is Galileo so well known and not (say) Nicole Oresme or Thomas Diggs or Thomas Marriott? Why does the Corel Mega gallery contain a cartoon of Galileo but not one of Kepler? Why does Professor Hoskin omit to mention Horrocks when Professor Turner[12] mentions him and the University of Central Lancashire course includes him? These involve issues of 'significance' – and are perspective-based.

Thirdly, what we are interested in is not a list of who 'discovered' what where but the psychology and dynamics of discovery and scientific development. General histories of science (or astronomy) often, sadly, once tended to be little more than lists with nice pictures but little insight. This is why the present book makes no pretence at being a comprehensive history. Its aim is not to be comprehensive but stimulating.

---

12 H. H. Turner (Savillian Professor of Astronomy at the University of Oxford), *A Voyage in Space* (1915).

Fourthly, I share Collingwood's interest in the thinking of those involved. He writes that, for example, in studying the code of the Emperor Theodosius the historian:

> Is re-enacting in his own mind the experience of the emperor; and only in so far as he does this, has he any historical knowledge, as distinct from a merely philological knowledge, of the meaning of the edict.[13]

History, says Collingwood, is about human actions, and is incomplete if we have not got inside the thinking of those involved. We need to imaginatively recreate their states of mind and set of ideas.

This seems to me to be especially true in studying the history of science, and it can be more difficult for us with Mediaeval or Renaissance figures whose thinking was different from ours. There is a temptation for us to try to see through their eyes *in modern terms* – and it simply will not do. A part of this is to note the concepts available at that time. The Newtonian concept of inertia, for example, was simply not available to figures before Descartes. We will look more at this after considering the nature of science.

Fifthly, we should definitely avoid the 'cowboys and indians' approach to science.[14] We should not divide up scientists into the 'enlightened' and 'unenlightened' according to who 'got it right' according to modern theory. This can be an especial temptation in the history of astronomy, with opponents of Galileo seen as bigoted fools. This point is tied to the previous one – we need to think ourselves back into the situation and concepts available at that time. We should also resist any temptation to 'canonise' scientists like Galileo or Darwin, and should recognise their fallibility. Galileo's comments on comets, for example, were misguided and against known evidence – but those who quote the book containing them as setting out the basis of scientific method often fail to mention this![15] Michael Hoskin rightly remarks that:

---

13 Collingwood, *History as Re-enactment of Past Experience* (1936) reprinted in The Idea of History.

14 An extensive criticism on this score of Neil Gillespie's book *Charles Darwin and the Problem of Creation* is in my *Reason, Science and Faith* ch. 9.

15 *The Assayer* in 1623 asserts that there is as yet no evidence comets are further than the Moon (Tycho had produced evidence much earlier), and 'proves' with great sarcasm that objects moving rapidly through air are cooled not heated (we now recognise meteorites burn up from just such friction).

> Today's historians of astronomy see it as their duty not to award medals to past astronomers whose opinions coincided with those of their modern counterparts, but to take their readers on an exciting journey. This journey introduced them to lands that are conceptually foreign – to past cultures, that sought as we do to make sense of the heavens, but did so by asking questions often very different from those we take for granted …[16]

Finally, we should be wary of the 'father of' approach to the history of science. This is the approach where so-and-so is declared to be the 'father of xology'. Very seldom were there any discoveries or developments which were not part of a more general process than the work of just one scientist.

The Nature of Science

John Tosh's book *The Pursuit of History* notes the connection in the nineteenth century between 'objectivist' views of history and those of science. He summarises the latter as:

> The basis of all scientific knowledge was the meticulous observation of reality by the disinterested, 'passive' observer, and the outcome of repeated observations of the same phenomenon was a generalisation of 'law' which fitted all the known facts and explained the regularity observed.[17]

What we shall see is that just as the understanding of history has moved to a critical realist position, so has the understanding of science. We will therefore look briefly at the development of the philosophy of science – what is the nature of science in the 20th century. Readers need not worry if they do not follow all the details of this, but it will be useful to get us thinking about the nature of science. What is essential is to understand the gap between the unreflective view given immediately below, and my concluding suggestions on science at the end of this chapter.

Naivety and Positivism

To begin with, then, an unreflective view of scientific methodology might be something like this:

---

[16] Hoskin, *The Cambridge Illustrated History of Astronomy* vii.

[17] This is from an earlier edition. The fifth edition explores the ideas in Chapter Seven.

1. A scientist first observes objectively, making sure he or she has no presuppositions or prejudice.
2. His or her observations accurately represent what really is 'out there', and general patterns of cause and effect which necessarily operate.
3. These patterns are formulated into scientific laws, which, once verified, are certain truth.

In actual fact the logical positivism (or the more moderate logical empiricism) which dominated Western philosophy in the 1940s–1950s was not much removed from this – although it dealt with knowledge in general and not just science. The circle included Moritz Schlick, A. J. Ayer, Gustav Bergmann, Rudolf Carnap, Herbert Feigl, Philipp Frank, Kurt Gödel, Otto Neurath, and Friedrich Waismann.

The movement's basic tenets might be summarised thus:

1. Any statement (other than a definition) had meaning *only* if it were capable, at least in principle, of complete verification.
2. Verification implied specifying an observation which demonstrated its truth.
3. Neutrality of observation and the language used to describe it was a desirable aim.
4. Knowledge was actually about human sensations. A table was real in the sense that it expressed a continual possibility of a sensory experience. Non-directly observable concepts, like atoms, were real only in the sense that they were words useful as a shorthand way of speaking of possible sensations (e.g. of seeing chemical reactions).

A. J. Ayer (who cited Carnap as the one to whom he owed most) was fairly clear on all these points in 1936.[18] There is argument as to how far others in the group held all of them – particularly (4), though some think it essentially true of all logical empiricism.[19]

There were obvious immediate problems. No empirical observation could be specified which would 'verify' the principle itself – which was therefore meaningless. Historical statements, statements about what

---

[18] See A. J. Ayer, *Language Truth and Logic* (2nd edn 1946).

[19] See e.g. R Boyd, *The Philosophy of Science* (1991) 7. Also especially our own *Reason, Science and Faith* ch. 10.

others were thinking, etc, could not be 'verified' by any present observation. One of its chief critics, Sir Karl Popper, also raised problems concerning science. Scientific laws are generalisations (e.g. 'Electric current always produces a magnetic field'); but we never *observe* generalised laws as such, we observe only specific instances of them (e.g. 'In 1000 observations, in each case an electric current produced a magnetic field'). How, then, can we make the logical jump from specific instances – however numerous – to the universal statement that it always happens? To do so we need to make two assumptions. The first is that nature always behaves uniformly or consistently – which is not self-evident. Early attempts such as that of J. S. Mill to defend it rationally look very much like circular arguments[20] and it requires an act of faith. In a logical sense, a universal law (or more correctly set of laws) can be falsified (as we have only to observe one counter instance) but never verified.

The second more pragmatic problem is that we can never be sure that there is not some qualifying condition which we have missed. Inevitably, in making observations we are selective: we could not note the total state of everything in the universe at the moment of observation. Thus, for example, electricity might behave differently under conditions of super-cooling. The experience of the leading English positivist, A. J. Ayer is noteworthy. In 1936 Ayer wrote his *Language, Truth and Logic,* setting out in great clarity this wonderful new system. Problems like the above led Ayer in the second edition of his book in 1946 to a long preface, full of special pleading and tortuous logic, in which he tried to argue that single observations might be totally objective, neutral and verifiable with certainty, whilst universal scientific laws were 'weakly verifiable' rather than strongly so. It was unconvincing. By 1956 (in *The Problem of Knowledge*) Ayer was fighting to preserve any sense for knowledge, and by 1978 he said of positivism: 'I suppose that most of the defects were that nearly all of it was false.'[21]

Observing, Selecting and Interpreting

Logical empiricism's demise had also been caused by a further problem. This was, in essence, that all seeing also involves interpreting – there is

---

[20] J. S. Mill, *A System of Logic* (1843).

[21] Interview in *The Listener*, 2nd March 1978.

no such thing as pure objective observation. Books by Hanson (1958), Polanyi (1958) and Kuhn (1962)[22] emphasised this and heralded a new phase in the philosophy of science, but it had been explored in some depth over a century earlier by William Whewell – a Cambridge Professor who actually invented the word 'scientist' in 1834. Whewell was critical of the naive empiricism derived from Locke and Hume, which viewed the mind as a kind of blank sheet passively receiving objective reflections of reality. 'There is,' wrote Whewell, 'no sensation without an act of the mind.'[23] The mind is active. In observing we interpret, though we may not be aware that we are doing so.

Is there such a thing as 'pure observation'? N. R. Hanson (in *Patterns of Discovery*) argued that all observation was 'theory-loaded' – that even in the act of observation we assume theory. Figures like Ian Hacking (in *Representing and Intervening)* were critical of this, but accepted that '*noticing* is theory-loaded' (179), that if there is no theory then visual elements may be ignored e.g. people 'saw' the tracks of positrons only after there was a theory. But this is the point. *Scientific* observation fits observations into paradigms, and observations are reported and recorded in terms of paradigms. Usually, unless there is a new and better paradigm available, a paradigm is kept even when there are observational anomalies – and these do arise because observation may be shaped by but is not determined by belief.

Try this (or imagine it) with a group of friends. Ask them to observe and *write down* what you do. Then raise your hand and drop a piece of chalk from between thumb and forefinger. Look at the variation in answers, and also consider what theory may be involved in them. They have to assume what is 'relevant' – but without a theory or context to guide them they have no idea what is. What different details did they think 'relevant' to record?

When I have done this with diverse groups of students I have found that, especially as they have been given no specific context, they all notice different things: the height, the position of my hand, how the chalk bounces, etc. I may ask them what they noticed: I raised my little

---

22 N. R. Hanson,, *Patterns of Discovery*; M Polanyi,, *Personal Knowledge*; T. S. Kuhn,, *Structure of Scientific Revolutions.*

23W. Whewell, *The Philosophy of the Inductive Sciences* (1840, 1847), 28. Whewell also wrote a *History of the Inductive Sciences I* in 1837, ad we will meet him later in context of the plurality of worlds debate.

finger; my left hand was in my pocket, what was the phase of the Moon …Noticing 'relevant' connections is one way science progresses – but it is the theory itself which teaches us *what* is relevant. The exact size, shape and thickness of a test tube, for example, are seldom if ever noted in a chemistry experiment. They are assumed irrelevant because the theory tells us this is so. Actually, observing 'repeated' events (which most consider the heart of experimental science) is itself a process of *abstraction.* We *abstract* out the 'relevant' common features in two instances of experiment – ignoring any 'irrelevant' differences like, for example, time, place, colour of hair of experimenter, etc.
Sometimes, when I drop the chalk (though in more recent years it has to be a white board or smart board marker if I forget to especially take in some chalk) someone writes as part of what they see that 'the force of gravity operated'. This makes the point that scientific theory about free fall (a topic relevant to the development of physics and astronomy) affects how we 'see'. They were not aware of seeing and interpreting here as separate exercises.

Three entirely different major scientific *paradigms* (or ways of looking at phenomena) have operated historically:

ARISTOTLE (4th Century BC)

Aristotle believed that solid matter was one of the four 'elements' making up the world – and left to itself would return to its natural place near to the centre of the universe (i.e. at the Earth's centre). He did not 'see' a force making it fall. A force would be needed to *stop* it from falling. A force would be needed to *stop* it from returning to its natural place. In my experience one may have to make undergraduates come to classes, but not to the pub – they gravitate there naturally!

NEWTON (17th Century)

Newton 'saw' that there was a force of attraction (gravity) between all pieces of physical matter. This force operating between the chalk and the Earth would have a lot more effect on the chalk (being rather smaller!) which would therefore move towards the Earth. This is the familiar world which we all live in. We 'see' the force of gravity operating – yet in reality all we observe is the fall itself. Observing very closely, of course, one would see the Earth move up slightly to meet the chalk …

EINSTEIN (20th Century)

Newton's idea of 'gravity' meant that objects had to be able to act on each other when they were separated by space. Einstein's theory of relativity denies the possibility of this. For various other reasons also, he rejected entirely the idea of the force of gravity. Instead, he 'saw' the presence of matter warping space-time and so producing motion. Interpretations of parts of this are controversial, and in any case most of us who are not physicists have not yet risen beyond the Newtonian conception of the world.

There is one last point. Any observer who was a trained and enthusiastic geologist might 'see' the white object I dropped as the compressed debris of millions of tiny organisms that died over 65 million years ago![24] A chemist may see mostly calcium carbonate. If you try it with a set of keys rather than a piece of chalk, then you could also get 'perception' of these as 'keys' – a term which has connotations of locks and opening far beyond the objects themselves.

In 'seeing' the event each also 'interprets' it. If questioned each could probably separate the actual visual stimulus from interpreting it, but in practice in science this is part of the observation. An implication of this recognition that observation is not purely passive is that scientific discovery is creative. It actually involves a mixture of painstaking methodical work together with creative intuition and imagination.[25] Seeing, then, always has context. This does not mean, however, that literally any interpretation is a good one. If Aristotle, Newton and Einstein were joined in looking at a falling piece of chalk by someone

---

24 Strictly speaking this should be traditional 'chalk', modern chalk sticks may be gypsum!

25 See W. I. Beveridge, *The Art of Scientific Investigation* (1968) or P. B. Medawar, *Induction and Imagination in Scientific Thought* (1969).

who 'saw' a pink elephant floating in custard we would call this a hallucination not a 'perception' at all. To accept that observing involves interpreting does not imply that it is arbitrary.

Major figures in the development of ideas of 'perceiving is interpreting' were late nineteenth century pragmatist C. S. Peirce, and in the early twentieth century the Catholic physicist and philosopher of science Pierre Duhem.[26] Logical positivism (or logical empiricism) was in many ways an anachronism. Its proponents' naivety on questions discussed so profoundly by the Christian Whewell nearly a century earlier is hard to explain, except on the grounds that their anti-religious fervour blinded their eyes. The criticisms of Hanson and Kuhn restated these old insights, and contributed to the demise of logical empiricism.

Post Empiricism: Popper, Kuhn, Lakatos and Feyerabend

By the end of the 1960s logical empiricism was dead, but what was to replace it? Karl Popper offered 'falsificationism'. Laws of science could not, he said, be *verified*, but they could be *tested.* A theory was scientific if, and only if, it made predictions specific enough to test. It must, therefore, be possible to specify a set of conceivable observations that would be deemed to have refuted the theory. For example, a general law that 'all electricity produces a magnetic field' would be refuted if we ever found an instance where it did not happen.

It was, of course, pointed out by Duhem in 1906 that no theory can be tested in isolation because other theories are assumed in testing it.[27] Quine in 1951 and Braithwaite in 1953 made similar points.[28] Popper argued for a convention to regard particular observations (and therefore background assumptions) as 'not in question.'[29] To many this seemed somewhat arbitrary and unrealistic – in practice scientists do not in any case regard a single counter-instance as a refutation. Others took

---

26 Pierre Duhem, *The Aim and Structure of Physical Theory*, (1906, 1912).

27 Pierre Duhem, op. cit. (1906, 1912). See also D. Gillies, *Philosophy of Science in the Twentieth Century*, (1993), ch. 5.

28 R. Braithwaite, *Scientific Explanation*, (1953). In modern books it may be called the 'Duhem-Quine' thesis.

29 e.g. K. Popper, *Logic of Scientific Discovery*, (1968), 106 where they are called 'basic statements'.

Popper's ideas just to mean that one was testing a set of theories for consistency – much as Duhem had emphasised.

T. S. Kuhn began from quite a different standpoint. Instead of beginning, as had the positivists and Popper, from a logical construct, he began from a consideration of the way in which science had actually advanced in history, it was 'historical philosophy of science'. A key Kuhnian term was 'paradigm'. Initially he used this word 'paradigm' very vaguely, but later took two main meanings:

1. **Exemplars:** results and ideas known and explicitly recognised in that scientific discipline.
2. **Disciplinary matrices:** a more subtle idea meaning a 'conceptual framework' within which phenomena are perceived.

Kuhn portrayed 'normal science' as development of ideas routinely within a scientific specialist area or discipline. Periodically, however, he suggested that anomalies built up to such a degree that the whole disciplinary matrix had to be changed in a revolutionary way, and phenomena viewed from a new perspective.[30] An example of this might be the change from thinking of the Earth as stationary to thinking of the Sun as stationary – the whole way of perceiving the world changed. Similarly, in the 20th century the change from Newtonian mechanics to those of Einstein involved a major change in the way of looking at things. Those with such radically different paradigms may use the same words, but they view them so differently that a simple test cannot decide between them: the two paradigms are 'incommensurable'. His book *The Copernican Revolution* was intended as an introductory text, but also reflected this philosophy.

Many criticised Kuhn because scientific development does not fall neatly into 'normal' and 'revolutionary' science, but there was a more fundamental question. He had portrayed science as being unlike a building programme, where each new brick is added on to those already built up. Rather he had seen it as a process of building (normal science),

---

[30] Hoskin in his *Illustrated History of Astronomy* (vii) refers briefly to this concept of normal and revolutionary science, pointing out that Einstein's later reconceptualisation of the phenomena of Newton's laws does not mean simply that Newton was 'wrong' and his work unworthy of attention.

but with a periodic demolition and entire reconstruction from a different perspective (revolutionary science). But in what sense, then, could one speak of 'scientific progress', and in what sense could any scientific concepts refer to 'real' things which were 'out there', since they might always be changed by a new perspective? The implication of Kuhn seemed to be that science must ultimately be subjective. Later Kuhnian emphasis was on development of ever more specialised areas of scientific knowledge, which Kuhn compared with the process of evolving ever more specialised organisms in biological evolution.[31] As well as emphasising evolution over revolution, Kuhn in his later works continued to emphasise 'incommensurability'[32] i.e. that earlier theories may 'see' phenomena entirely differently from later ones, and not be strictly comparable. In this context also specialisation may mean that there is no common language to link theories in different areas. The later Kuhn portrayed a 'candidate for true/false' as a statement in which language rules forbid asserting both the statement and its contrary, and accepts that 'the rules of the true/false game are ... universals for all human communities' i.e. that all communities have such statements. But which *particular* statements are candidates for the true/false category depends on the particular community's set of word meanings or 'lexicon', and:

> A statement can be a candidate for truth/falsity in one lexicon without having that status in the others.[33]

This means that he rejects what Suppe called 'metaphysical realism' i.e. the idea that theories increasingly 'correspond' to some kind of external reality. Rather, each community has an evolving language, which implies a particular way of perceiving reality. For those into Kant (which probably narrows it down!), Kuhn compares these to an evolution of different species of Kantian 'categories' seen as 'preconditions of possible experience.'

---

[31] T. S. Kuhn, *The Road Since Structure*, PSA (1990), vol 2, 3–13, reprinted in Tauber, *Science and the Quest for Reality*, (1997).

[32] See Kuhn, *Structure of Scientific Revolutions* (1962), also Hacking, *Representing and Intervening* (1983), ch. 5.

[33] Kuhn, op. cit. (1990), 240.

Reactions to Kuhn varied. Paul Feyerabend and his school thought Kuhn not radical enough. Feyerabend moved from positivism in the 1940s, to his own brand of Popperian anti-positivist realism. By 1968[34] he had moved significantly again. Science, he said, did not develop 'logically' and no ideal methodology was possible. Whilst Feyerabend believed in basing science on observation, he did not believe this would lead, even ultimately, to a single 'One True Theory'.[35] Later this view became more extreme. Science was, some said, simply an 'ideology' like any other, with no special claim to truth. In this school of thought 'objectivity' is simply institutionalised belief.[36] This kind of view has cut little ice with real scientists, and other philosophers of science have heavily criticised it. One of its basic problems is that it leads logically to pure relativism: the assertion that any set of beliefs is as true as any other. The internal inconsistency of this approach is seen precisely in the fact that it makes an apparently absolute assertion concerning the relativity of truth – yet it denies that assertions can be absolute! The apparent inability of its proponents to live with the logical implications of their approach (i.e. that no objective statements at all would be possible) is not surprising. In practice it is unliveable, like the trendy 'postmodernism', 'deconstructivism' and other forms of extreme relativism.

A view, which stood somewhere between Popper and Kuhn, was that of Lakatos.[37] Lakatos asserted that:

> For Kuhn scientific change – from one 'paradigm' to another – is a mystical conversion.[38]

He saw what he called 'sophisticated falsificationism' (the later view of Popper) as accepting both that theories could not be tested in isolation,

---

[34] The year the present writer attended a seminar series Feyerabend gave at LSE.

[35] Paul Feyerabend, *Against Method* (1975), also A. F. Chalmers, *What is This Thing Called Science*, (1982), ch. 12; Lossee, *A Historical Introduction to the Philosophy of Science*, (1993), ch. 13 and Preston, 'Feyerabend's Retreat from Reality' *Philosophy of Science*, 64 (1997).

[36] See Bloor, *Knowledge and Social Imagery*, (1976), and Stanesby, *Science, Reason and Religion*, (1985), ch. 3.

[37] Lakatos & Musgrave, *Criticism and the Growth of Knowledge*, (1970), also Chalmers op. cit. (1982), ch. 7; Lossee, op. cit, (1993), ch. 14; D Mayo, (1996) revisited the Kuhn-Popper debate in 'Ducks, Rabbits and Normal Science', *British Journal of Philosophy*, Sc 47, (1996), 271–290.

[38] Lakatos & Musgrave, op. cit. (1970), 93.

and that they were not considered 'refuted' until a 'better' theory was available. But how could one tell if a new set of theories were 'better'? Even sophisticated falsificationism, he thought, had to come back to some kind of Duhemian reliance of 'good sense'. In Lakatos' own view this was better conceived in terms of a succession of research programmes. In each programme there would be a 'hard core' of assumptions accepted as basic to that programme.[39]

Nothing, of course, is straightforward in philosophy! Most clearly stated views have to be modified in the small print, and this brings unexpected similarities. Later writers have seen similarities between, for example, Lakatos and Kuhn, and claimed that once they have made all the necessary caveats and qualifications to their respective theories, they are not all that different. However, in general distinction from both Kuhn and Lakatos have stood various critical realist schools of thought, reasserting (though usually redefining) objectivity and the view that science follows a reality external to ourselves.

Critical Realism and Instrumentalism

In 1977 Frederick Suppe edited the second edition of *The Structure of Scientific Theories,* a book originally based on a 1969 symposium. In the introduction he stated:

> Much has happened to the philosophy of science in the eight years since the symposium: (1) Positivistic philosophy of science has gone into near total eclipse; (2) the more extreme Weltanschauungen views of Feyerabend, Hanson and Kuhn no longer are serious contenders for becoming a replacement analysis and (3) philosophy of science is coalescing around a new movement or approach which espouses a hard-nosed metaphysical and epistemological realism that focuses much of its attention on 'rationality in the growth of scientific knowledge …'

Suppe was heralding 'critical realism'. In general terms this may be characterised thus:

1. Scientific theories (at least in the 'mature' sciences) are typically approximately true, and more recent theories are closer to the truth

---

[39] For more on Lakatos see *Reason Science and Faith*, ch. 10.

than older ones in the same domain.

2. The observational and theoretical terms within the theories of a mature science genuinely 'refer' (roughly). This means that there are substances in the world that correspond to the 'ontologies' (i.e. presumptions of 'being' and reality) presumed by our best theories.
3. Successive theories in any mature science will be such that they preserve the theoretical relations and the apparent referents of earlier theories, that is, earlier theories will be limiting cases of later theories.
4. Acceptable new theories do and should explain why their predecessors were successful insofar as they were successful.[40]

Suppe thought Lakatos not 'realist' enough. Suppe also attacked 'Instrumentalism' which sees scientific theories as *nothing more than* instruments for prediction, and not about 'truth' (a view he ascribes to Stephen Toulmin and one espoused by Van Fraasen). Suppe claims that this would not account for the success of science.'[41] That is a theme repeated by other realists (e.g. R Boyd) – instrumentalism would not account for the success of science in its prediction. Suppe followed Shapere[42] in believing that the by then accepted 'theory-ladenness' of observation 'does not compromise the objectivity of scientific knowledge.'[43] Suppe accepted Shapere's 1969 concept of different 'domains' in knowledge, introduced as 'fundamental conceptual tools for illuminating the nature of science'.[44] There was, then, no assumption that all kinds of knowledge were the same.

Suppe was right about the well-deserved demise of positivism[45] but his triumphalism concerning critical realism was unfounded. It continued to run into questions and problems. It is, in any event, *not* straightforward, and there is some debate as to who counts as a real

---

[40] The four points are taken from B Laudan, (1981), reprinted Boyd, op. cit. (1990), ch. 12.

[41] F Suppe, *The Structure of Scientific Theories*, (1977), 681.

[42] Writing in Suppe, op cit, (1977),518 etc.

[43] Suppe, op cit, (1977), p. 692.

[44] Suppe, op cit, (1977), section vii, also D Shapere, *Reason and the Search for Knowledge*, (1984), ch. 13.

[45] It exists today only in the imaginations of the authors of seemingly interminable books entitled 'Qualitative Methodology for Xologists'!

'realist'! Few if any in modern times (other than, perhaps, a militant Humanist chemist like Peter Atkins) would espouse 'naïve realism', i.e. the view that our ideas or concepts reproduce exactly the true properties of externally existing objects. Allied to this is 'representative realism' which holds that our ideas *represent* externally existing 'real' things though may recognise that some properties (e.g. the 'tickliness' of a feather) are 'secondary' in the sense that the properties cause particular effects in us.

Central to the demise of such naïve or simplistic realism was the work of 18th century philosopher Immanuel Kant.[46] He suggested that as humans we *cannot* perceive except in terms of particular categories e.g. space, time and cause. We do not know what 'things in themselves' are like, because we can never step outside our human perceptual framework.[47] Thus to Kant space and time are 'empirically real' – they are not illusions and they are *given* to any human experience. However they are 'transcendentally ideal' in the sense that they apply only to human experience and not necessarily to the nature of 'things in themselves'. After Kant, no thinker should have been able to take naïve realism seriously. Not only, as we noted, do non-realists like Kuhn have a debt to Kant, but naïve realism has to give way to '*critical* realism'. *Critical* realism asserts that 'behind' it all there is a unique 'reality' but also recognises that perception always involves interpretation, and aspects of this are inevitable to being human.

Ian Hacking (who is some species of critical realist) gives a useful breakdown of types and aspects of realism, as does Del Ratzsch.[48] Hacking himself believes that 'Experimental work provides the strongest evidence for scientific realism' and added:

> The vast majority of experimental physicists are realists about some theoretical entities, namely the ones they use. I claim they cannot help being so.

---

[46] Kant also affected Collingwood.

[47] This also relates to T. Nagel, (1974), '*What's it like to be a bat?* – the way in which human sensory perception affects conceptualisation and experience.

[48] I. Hacking, *Representing and Intervening*, (1983), ch. 1, Del Ratsche, *Science and Its Limits* (2000), 82–6.

To Hacking 'the lesson is to think about practice not theory'. It is pointless arguing on a metaphysical level for 'realism' – in practice what matters is whether, for example, scientists can manipulate electrons (or presumably quarks), not their metaphysics. A. F. Chalmers (in a book which gives a useful summary of philosophy of science[49]) outlines his own 'unrepresentative realism' too briefly for us to make much of it, though it seems similarly pragmatic.

In a very helpful summary of scientific realism, David Papineau suggests that it consists of:

(1) An **independence** thesis (there is a world which exists independently of our awareness or perception of it).

(2) A **knowledge** thesis (by and large, we can know which of our beliefs about that world are true).

Papineau points out that one can doubt the existence of an external world:

Either: (1) taking an idealist or phenomenalist view that knowledge is *just* about sensation (or experience of phenomena) and that a notion of a world 'behind' sensation is incoherent.

or (2) taking a sceptical view that we cannot know the truth about the world.

No one, of course, outside philosophy seminars, doubts that normal elephants or mail-boxes are 'real' in the sense that pink elephants 'seen' by inebriates are not. In this context, 'phenomenalists' are just questioning what 'real' means, and sceptics refer to other levels of 'knowledge'. 'Realism' more commonly refers to concepts found in physics (electrons, muons etc) – though these are, of course, foundational to any physical reality. Anyway, with the welcome demise of phenomenalism in early logical positivism, Papineau rightly points out: 'In contemporary epistemology of science, scepticism is the main alternative to realism.'

All this may seem far from the history of Astronomy, but it isn't. How, for example, are we to approach the issue between Galileo and Bellarmine (or Kepler and Ursus) as to whether the Earth 'really' moves? Is it enough to take an instrumentalist approach to the motion of the planets and 'save the

---

49 A. F. Chalmers, op. cit. (1982).

phenomena' (i.e. produce a mathematical model which works)? Should planetary astronomy just have been about locating the planet in the sky, or about how it 'really moves'? In the light of Einstein's relativity is the issue of whether the Earth 'really moves' a question with meaning?

The Public Understanding of Science

So much has been thought and written about what science is and how it works, that it came as a surprise that one of the anomalies in academia was the appointment in 1995 of an academic with little knowledge of metaphysics and the philosophy of science to a prestigious Oxford Professorship of the 'Public Understanding of Science'. This seemed to be a bit like appointing Formula One driver Lewis Hamilton as a professor of mechanical engineering. Richard Dawkins writes fluently, and became famous for his popularisations of the ideas of R. A. Fisher, William Hamilton, and George Price. But for thirteen years he then presented a confused picture of the nature of science and truth, a lack of understanding that all science is done within some metaphysical framework and set of epistemological assumptions, and an increasingly hysterical attack on religion. This was a shame, because some of his actual scientific presentations could be good; when he came to give the annual Darwin lecture at UCLan one year, he gave a mellifluous and erudite presentation on the idea of evolutionary convergence – although not really emphasising that most of it was taken from a Christian Professor of Evolutionary Palaeobiology at 'the other place' – i.e. Simon Conway Morris of Cambridge. But it is symptomatic of the illusion that someone who is a scientist must therefore understand the nature of science and scientific history.

Some Conclusions about Science

It is certainly *not* necessary to understand all the views in philosophy of science in order to study scientific history. The above has been put in to stretch the thinking a little, but some key points are worth noting:

- Views today still vary between the extremes of:
  - **Instrumentalism:** scientific theories are nothing but instruments for prediction (e.g. Bas Van Fraasen)

- **Critical Realism:** theories involve perspective and diverse domains of knowledge but approach ever more closely to 'truth' (e.g. Richard Boyd)
- **Relativism:** theories are 'true' only for particular observers, there is no objectively true 'big picture' (e.g. late Paul Feyerabend/ postmodernism)

- In general, however, it is recognised that science is about some kind of reality, but that the form and concepts it takes are inevitably affected by the nature of human perception and thinking.
- It is also recognised that ideas are formed not by scientists passively receiving impressions that are turned into scientific concepts, but by actively creating concepts and seeing if they work in practice. Scientific discovery is essentially interactive – but most of us believe that there is some reality which is being explored by scientists.

Studying the History of Science

Doing this kind of study *well*, turns out to be less straightforward than many assume. The process of history itself involves selection: who is 'important' in the development of astronomy? It also involves perspective, for example, is Copernicus a radical lion of science, or a timid cleric? Is Newton the 'last of the magicians' (as Keynes said) or the 'first of the moderns'?[50] It involves trying to think as they thought, for example, Renaissance thinking about an orbiting earth without any concept of either inertia or a force (of gravity) acting at a distance.

It is, however, in some ways more *interesting* than other kinds of history. One has ideally to understand much of the social, political and philosophical background of the times – as for other forms of history. But one also has to understand how the development of theory was interacting with observation and instrumentation. How far and in what ways, for example, was Kepler prepared to drop various of his starting assumptions? How far did Tycho's observations *force* new non-Aristotelian models on any reasonable contemporaries? Were Galileo's opponents bigoted to refuse to accept evidence from an instrument the workings of which he was (at the

---

[50] Even the husband and wife Oxford historians Mary Boas Hall and A. Rupert Hall also seemed to arrive at rather different pictures of Newton!

time) unable to explain? How did Galileo convince anyone (and he still does!) that any of his observations gave the slightest evidence for the motion of the Earth? Was Newton right in believing that mathematics was everything, or Hooke that qualitative ideas were crucial? How far can we blame practical astronomers for their scepticism of Adams' calculations of a new planet?

Here are some things to think about or do

➢ **Historical Myths:**

(1) Ask some friends/family whether the following historical statements are true or false:

- 'People in general didn't at first believe it when Columbus said the world was round.' (F)
- 'Galileo proved that the Earth went around the Sun, but the church said it was heresy and locked him up.' (F)
- 'The first known public presentation of Copernicus's idea that the Earth went around the Sun was in the Vatican gardens.' (T)
- 'Newton was sitting under an apple tree when an apple fell on his head.' (F)
- 'One of the famous things which happened at the leaning tower of Pisa was that Galileo dropped two objects from it to see if they fell at the same rate.' (F)
- 'Darwin challenged the idea that the Earth was created around 4004 BC, and was attacked by the church for this.' (F)
- 'The idea that time and space were created together was first put forward in the first century.' (T)
- 'The idea that the Earth was not the centre of the universe was a shattering blow to human pride and theology.' (F)
- 'The modern theory of the 'big bang' origin of the universe was put forward by a priest, against initial opposition from Einstein.' (T)

(2) Look up any key figure on the internet (e.g. Google Copernicus or Galileo). See how many naïve statements you can find about opposition they experienced.

- **Significant Facts/Perspective:**

1. Get a group of friends/family to write down the events they think the most significant during the last year, last decade, and last century. Compare these and reasons given for them.
2. Ask a group of friends/family what they know about, for example: Henry VIII, Michael Faraday, etc. (you could ask them to name the wife/wives of these!). Who has had more effect on our lives? Think about all the things today which depend on electricity.
3. Obtain for one day a copy of the *Guardian, Times, Independent,* and *Daily Telegraph.* Take a common story and compare what details are included or left out, and how far the stories are 'slanted' without actually being inaccurate.

- **Abstraction in Science:**

  Think about any scientific work you have done at any time, and how far repetition involved abstracting out what was 'relevant'.

Further Reading

Obviously the potential reading in this area is vast!

This chapter began with reference to the two books by T. S. Kuhn: *The Copernican Revolution* (1957 Harvard University Press) and *The Structure of Scientific Revolutions* (1962, 1970 University of Chicago Press), and these are still well worth reading. On the nature of historical study, E. H. Carr's *What is History?* (1987) remains an important marker, and the classic R. G. Collingwood *The Idea of History* (1946 – many reprints) worth looking into. The John Tosh *The Pursuit of History* (5th Edition 2010), Longman) contains some relevant chapters, but much of it is more generally about how to *do* history. Tosh's *Historians on History* (2000) is a useful anthology as is Keith Jenkin's *The Postmodern History Reader* (1997) There are also works e.g. by Richard J Evans, David Cannandine, Arthur Marwick and M.C. Lemon which try to update the 'What is History' debate, discuss postmodernism etc.

General books on the philosophy of science are not usually easy to read without some background, but A. F. Chalmers *What is this thing called Science?* (1978, 1982 Open University) is fairly readable, and John Losee's *A Historical Introduction to the Philosophy of Science* (1972, 1980, 1993, Opus) gives a historical perspective though may be harder without any philosophical background. It can be useful to dip into anthologies such as Ian Hacking's (ed.) *Scientific Revolutions* (1981 OUP) which relates to Kuhn and Popper's ideas, David Papineau's (ed.) *The Philosophy of Science* (1996, OUP) or Richard Boyd's et al. (eds.) *The Philosophy of science* (1991, MIT). Robert Klee's *Introduction to the Philosophy of Science* (1997) unusually begins with a microbiology example. Alexander Bird's *Philosophy of Science* (1998) and James Ladyman's *Understanding the Philosophy of Science* (2nd ed. due 2014) are reasonable introductions. There are anthologies edited by Yuri Balashov and Alex Tosenberg (2002) and Marc Lange (2007). The third edition of *Philosophy of Science A Contemporary Introduction* by Alex Rosenberg came out in 2011.

My own work with Roger Forster *Reason, Science and Faith* (1999, Monarch, 2000 Wipf and Stock) contains a slightly larger version of some of the nature of science materials, though the book as a whole has, of course, a different focus as indicated by the title.

2. The Beginnings of Cosmology

It is rather pointless trying to give a 'date' for the beginnings of astronomy and/or cosmology. Who knows when humankind first studied the stars, noticed stellar, lunar and solar patterns, or speculated about their causes? What does seem clear is that detailed observation began with the Babylonians in great antiquity, and geometrical models with the Greek or Hellenistic culture around the sixth century BC.

Pre-Greek Astronomy

It is very hard for those of us brought up in modern society to recapture or imagine the thinking of people of pre-history and early history. All the interconnecting modern matrix of scientific ideas: astronomy, physics, chemistry, biology, geology etc., were simply not there. People were, of course, aware that, for example, objects fall, the Sun rises, and stars move across the sky. But there was no 'perception' of a force of gravity, earthly globe etc. However, many of their *motives*, where such things were considered, were in a sense surprisingly parallel to ours today:

- The desire to control their environment, and so their fortunes and misfortunes in life.
- The desire to understand reasons for particular things happening.
- The desire to 'make sense' of the world in which they lived.

The human invention of settlement (probably first only in the Natufan culture around 12,000 years ago) brought increasing tendencies to develop a priestly caste specialising in such study.

It was, in general, conceived in terms which included gods as part of nature, powerful figures and forces which needed to be placated, invoked etc. How far the myth and saga, in which terms much may be represented, was taken 'literally' by the ancients is a point of discussion – but in any event much was put in such terms. The study of the stars associated what we would call astronomy (study of celestial bodies as observable objects) and astrology (their role as portents and influences on humankind) as a single entity. There was, in this sense, no distinction between 'observation' and 'interpretation'.

Most people in modern societies have never really seen the stars. If they find time to look up at all (apart from to decide whether to take an umbrella that day), reflected city light drastically reduces perception of the brightness of stars. Anyone, however, who has been able to get out into an area of desert, will have experienced something quite different.[51] The stars seem very bright, extend right down to the horizon, and the Milky Way runs as a great silver stream in a band across the sky. To ancient people this must have given a great impression of power, splendour, and order. If we imagine ourselves back in their situation, what would they have observed? We can divide the observation into obvious, moderate, and advanced:

1. **Obvious:** The Sun rises and moves across the sky during the day. Throughout a period of about 365 days there are different seasonal weather patterns and lengths of solar day. Twice in the year day and night are about equal around March 21st and September 23rd (called equinoxes).

   Moderate: The trajectory of the Sun alters through the year with this cycle. It is highest (in northern latitudes) around June 21st and lowest around December 21st (called the solstices).

2. **Obvious**: The Moon rises and sets by night and sometimes is visible during the day, going through a cycle of about 28 days from a near circle to a crescent.

---

[51] My own experience of this was in Masada, near the Dead Sea.

3. **Obvious:** The stars in general have a fixed pattern, and move across the sky in a nightly rotation.

   Stars differ in brightness and across the sky is a great band of light.

   Advanced: As one moves north or south, different star patterns become visible.

4. **Obvious:** In the evening and morning one star seems to be particularly bright, and generally appears first, usually in roughly the direction of the rising or setting Sun.

5. **Obvious:** Some stars are shooting stars that appear very briefly as flashes of light.

   Moderate: Some stars wander across the background of the 'fixed stars' moving across the sky, then retrogressing, then moving forward again.

As you read this, of course, almost certainly you tried to 'translate' this observation into what you know of the Earth and Solar System. But try to forget it! All you have (as an ancient priest or observer) is the observation. The notion that the Earth (by which I do not mean a globe but simply the solid thing on which we stand) actually moves in space and spins probably would not occur to you, and if it did would rightly be dismissed as absurd.

Civilisation before the Seventh Century BC

Babylon: One of the earliest centres for 'civilisation' was the land between the Euphrates and Tigris – the Sumer. Settlements began as early as 8000 BC, and in time irrigation methods produced more than enough grain to enable leisured and priestly classes to develop. Writing also developed, with marks on clay tablets becoming increasingly stylised and symbolic rather than pictorial. By 3000 BC it was the bronze age, with cities along the banks of the

The Great Sphinx and Pyramids

rivers. One such was Ur (Ur of the Chaldees to Abraham), a city with a sprawling central temple complex to the Moon gods Nanna and Ningal. From 2400 BC great rulers (beginning with Sargon) rose and fell, and cuneiform writing was fully developed. Around 1800 BC the famous Hammurabi code was developed, though by 1500 BC the Hittites had destroyed Babylon. From around 1200 BC the new Babylon arose under Nebuchadnezzar, with fortunes rising and falling (and conflict with Assyria) until the great library of Assyrian Nineveh was destroyed in 612 BC along with Assyrian power. Thereafter Babylon again enjoyed power until conquered by the Persians and finally Alexander in 321 BC.

Egypt: The other great civilisation to develop in this period was the Egyptian. In many ways this developed in parallel, though settlement here didn't start until about 5000 BC. They too developed irrigation and by around 3200 BC had two kings (of upper and lower Nile) and a writing system that was developed into a phonetic system. It was consolidated into one kingdom around 3000 BC, and the great pyramids and Sphinx started around 2570 BC. The gods of Egypt had a brief fright in 1365 BC when Amenhotep IV (or Akhenaten) tried to install a single Sun-god Aten – but the old gods and new Amun soon regained control after his death. By about 1000 BC (around the time King David was writing Psalms) Egypt was in comparative decline, and by the seventh century no longer a world power.

Cretan Palace: Dolphins

Mediterranean: The first great Mediterranean civilisation began with the Minoans in Crete. This began later, perhaps 3000 BC, and the Minoans were traders rather than conquerors. Their buildings are painted with dolphins and less military pictures than Egypt or Babylon. The great Palace dated around 1900 BC, with Linear-A writing from around 1700 BC. A tidal wave around 1450 BC brought a demise in Minoan fortunes, and the Greek world developed with the great citadel at Mycenae (home of the King Agamemnon who invaded Troy), which itself fell around 1140 BC. By 1000 BC the Dorians had

Cretan Bull

overrun the Peloponnesians, and many Mycenaeans took refuge in and built up the city of Athens. By 900 BC they had settlements on other shores, including Miletus, Ephesus and Samos (becoming known as 'Ionians', after the area in Anatolia). Homer was a ninth-century poet from this culture, writing of the good old days in the *Iliad* and the *Odyssey*. These works of saga, resourcefulness and heroism became models for the Greek ideal of life. By the seventh century BC we have reached the period of classical Greece: the familiar picture of city states (Athens and Sparta as the best known), uneasily allying against the Persians but later getting into a disastrous 'Peloponnesian war' In this book reference will be made to 'Greek' culture, rather than the more technical 'Hellenic' after their own word for Greece: *Hellas*.

England: Did Neolithic observers (such as those who built Stonehenge) have a model that predicted astronomical events? When people wonder at the 'marvels' or construction of Stonehenge, they do not always contextualise its period. Carbon dating in 2008 showed that the first bluestones were erected *c.*2400–2200 BC (though the site itself was very much earlier) and the large Sarsen stones are thought to be later. This is after palaces in Sumer and Egypt, fortified cities in Troy and Syria, and a megalithic temple on Malta. They invented writing and established a civil system of government in southern Iraq more than 5000 years ago, and had a great city in Ur (where Abraham came from!) just before the bluestones were erected. No great civilisations seem to have arisen in England at that time, and even cricket had probably not yet been invented![52]

Stonehenge

Scientific Work

What kind of work in physics and astronomy did these various civilisations achieve?

Practical mathematics had to be developed to build stone monuments, especially the magnificent palaces. Building engineering techniques were

[52] The more observant will have noticed that Stonehenge lacks the middle stump!

advanced – though not much 'technology', as we would think of it. But what about theoretical astronomy and/or physics?

Michael Hoskin[53] presents a well-balanced view of Stonehenge and similar monuments – veering towards the sceptical. It would be surprising if many of the stone monuments and ley lines were not in some way connected with the Sun and stars, though Hoskin's scepticism about the extent of their detailed knowledge is probably justified. In any event, this knowledge cannot form part of our story as it seems not to have been transmitted, and no written records were kept.

The Mediterranean peoples do not seem to have left much record of astronomy either. When it did come, it seems to have been through Babylonian ideas.

For the peoples of Egypt and Sumer, reliant as they were upon irrigation which itself was dependent on river flooding, the seasons were important. The Egyptians, for whom the date of the flooding of the Nile was crucial, tried to develop an accurate calendar. The problem is that with 29.5 days in a lunar month, 12 of them make 354 days whilst 13 make 383.5 days. 12.38 was not a convenient number of months for the year! The Egyptian priests and bureaucrats struggled with this, and star constellations were recognised as a part of the way of telling time - but we have no evidence of them having systematically developed astronomy.

The real commencement of astronomy seems to be with the Mesopotamian civilisations. Their particular interest in the stars was in terms of omens – features of the stars which warned those who could read them of what was to come and what could be done to avoid misfortune. In the second millennium BC the Enuma Anu Anlil were a great series of seventy tablets containing thousands of omens. These refer to the celestial bodies including Sun, Moon, planets and meteors, foretelling, for example, success or failure in battle according to the stars. To aid the application of this process of omens, the scribes began to keep star records: 'Astronomical Diaries'. One modern writer comments:

> ...the Diaries, originally extending from the eighth or seventh to the first century (BC), are by far the longest continuous scientific record, or should we say the record of the longest continuous

---

[53] Hoskin, *The Cambridge Illustrated History of Astronomy*, (1997), ch. 1.

> scientific research, of any kind in all of history, for modern science itself has existed for only half as long. And of course it is the Diaries, or the records from which the Diaries were compiled, that provided the observations that were later used as the empirical foundation of the mathematical astronomy of the ephemerides, in which the same phenomena of the Moon and planets recorded in the omen texts were reduced to calculation.[54]

The ephemerides, or tables of celestial bodies, were increasingly accurate, but the predictive systems were made without geometry. Babylonians seem to have used a different approach from the Greek astronomers who formed geometric models. Their focus was on the periods between various phenomena, and one of the motives seems to have been to know when various events happened if the weather prevented observation!

A synodic period is a time between two points where the Earth, Sun and a planet or the Moon are in the same geometric relationship. For the Moon this might be measured when in conjunction or opposition, and it would give the lunar month.

The Babylonians used an accurate sexagesimal system to calculate these periods using their tables of observations. To understand this we may think of our own time measurements, themselves derived from the Babylonians. When we write a time e.g. as: 13:32:24 we mean 13 hours, 32 minutes and 24 seconds. In hours this is:

$$13 + \frac{32}{60} + \frac{24}{60 \times 60}$$

We are effectively using a base of 60 (a sexagesimal system) rather than of 10 as we do in normal decimals. This system still, however, offers a true place system, easier to use for calculations than (say) roman numerals. Our time divisions come from the Babylonians who used this system in calculating various periodic values to great accuracy.

Their figure for the length of the lunar month, for example, was: 29:31:50:8:20. If you do the calculations you will find this comes to 29.530594136 (the modern figure is 29.53059027). Calculations were made a bit more complex because there were 30 'tithis' in a synodic month.

---

[54] N. M. Swedlow, *The Babylonian Theory of the Planets*, (1998), 17.

The scribes also applied this to planets. The synodic period for a planet can be measured at times of successive conjunctions, but it can also be based on heliacal risings. This is when the angular distance between the Sun and planet (e.g. Jupiter) is just enough to see the planet rise. The mean synodic period for Jupiter is around 399 days. This second heliacal rising, however, will be when Jupiter is at a different place in the zodiac – about 33° further on in fact. This gives a 'mean synodic arc'. This arc was not measured with precision but against the zodiacs which varied in size, and only crudely positioned in them (towards the beginning, or towards the end). Longer term periods were also found, for example, that it takes 427 years for Jupiter to return to its original zodiac position for a helical rising. It seems likely, then, that the high degree of accuracy for some of the periods was obtained from the period observations alone, and not from precise positional observation. Since the rediscovery last century of the Babylonian system, there has been exploration by mathematicians of the complexities of the mathematics they used.[55]

For convenience, I have run on with the Babylonians into the third and even second centuries BC (Halley's comet being observed, by the way, in 164 BC). But from the seventh century BC there arose another tradition, which utilised the Babylonian data in a rather different way from that of the Greeks.

The Greeks

First a diversion to ponder. Why is it that so many people regard 'science' as having started with the Greeks? Swerdlow, unusually, is fiercely partisan for his Babylonians:

> They have left no record of their theoretical analysis and discussions, but to judge from the works they have left us …the discussions of two scribes of *Enuma Anu Enlil* contained more rigorous science than the speculations of twenty philosophers speaking Greek, not even Aristotle excepted …it is due precisely to the scientific and technical character of Babylonian astronomy that most historians and philosophers remain without comprehension of it, still preferring to dote upon childish fables

[55] See: O. Neugebauer, *Astronomical Cuniform Texts* (1955), and *A History of Ancient Mathematics Astronomy*, (1975), N. M. Swerlow op. cit.

> and Delphic fragments of the Pre-Socratics, requiring no knowledge of mathematics and less taxing to the intellect ...The origin of rigorous, technical science was not Greek but Babylonian ...[56]

There cannot be a simple 'truth' about whether the Babylonians or Greeks 'invented science', since science is itself multi-faceted. But you may like to think about this one, in the light of some of the views given in the previous chapter about the nature of science. Think, perhaps, in practical terms of:

1. A curiosity concerning the causes of natural phenomena.
2. The determination to find explanatory causes in terms of repeatable natural sequences which enable prediction of natural phenomena.
3. The acceptance that any such explanations can be subject to question and review, and that explanations which better fit the phenomena or enable a wider range of prediction should be sought.
4. The quantification of such natural sequences which enables greater precision of prediction.
5. The separation out of issues of theology and the actions of the God or gods from issues of natural causality.

In some senses the Babylonians were doing much of this in astronomy. Their efforts, for example to find a model for lengths of months etc. to fit the solar year, show much of the above. Perhaps a main difference may be the place of the deities, and the association of scientific ideas with religion. Aristotle, of course, retains a god as his 'unmoved prime mover' without which the system collapses. However (as we shall see) at least he distinguished efficient cause (which is what we would call natural cause) from final cause (the end object of it all). The issue is not a god-free system (the Greeks, Tycho, Kepler, Galileo, and Newton all lacked this), but the separation of issues of natural sequences. It is speculation about causality, and ultimately looking for a level of explanation in terms of forces and objects.

---

[56] Swerdlow, op. cit. 181–182.

The Issues Faced

The Greeks speculated about a much wider class of phenomena than astronomy. So what kinds of things might excite the curiosity of an ancient Greek, apparently demanding explanation?

Imagine that you are a Greek (male) in the leisured classes. You have had a good dinner, the entertainers and flute girls have been on, and you are thinking about what might be the explanation of various natural phenomena. What kinds of things might you consider?

1. *Change and Permanence*

How is it that one can feed green grass to a brown cow and get out white milk (with various other products)? Where does the whiteness in the milk *come from*? It does not seem to be in the grass – and crushed grass does not produce milk. Where do the new properties appear from?

2. *Free Fall*

Most objects released above the surface of the land (we can't say 'in mid air' since we haven't invented air yet) move downwards. On the other hand steam, smoke, and fire rise upwards. Why do these movements occur?

3. *Development*

Natural objects seem to move through some natural cycle towards an apparent end (or *telos*)[57]. How does the acorn *know* it is supposed to develop into an oak tree?

4. *Regularity of Sun/Moon/Stars*

We listed above various observable puzzles concerning the regular movements of the heavenly bodies. *Why* do they move in this way?

5. *The 'Vagabonds'*

You are also aware of the 'vagabonds' (the Greek word for planet) that wander to and fro in the sky. What makes them do this and how can we predict where they will be?

---

[57] From this word '*telos* we get our word 'teleological'.

6. What is Beneath the Land?

I could have used the term 'Earth' but to most of us this immediately implies a near spherical planet. The term 'land' (including the sea but in distinction from the sky) refers to what we walk and sail over. What is it and what does it rest on (i.e. what would we find 'underneath' if we were to keep going downwards)?

How could you begin to *explain* such things? How go about trying to find explanations? How should reason and observation be linked?

Most of the elements finally adopted in science appear in early Greek thinkers (around sixth–fourth century BC). The 'Greek' (or Hellenic) world then, of course, went far beyond modern Greece and Macedonia.

I shall adopt a schematic approach, focusing on the main contributions made in the approaches of various different groups – each of which could merit further study in its own right.

Naturalism - Forces and Mechanisms

The first group was located on Ionia, what is now the West coast of Turkey. At this time (and indeed even into the present century) this was a 'Greek' area. The Ionians included:

- Thales *c.*624–565 BC – MILETUS
- Anaximander *c.*611–547 BC – MILETUS
- Anaximenes *c.*570 – ? BC – MILETUS
- Heraclitus *c.*540–465 BC – EPHESUS

Their contribution was to begin to speculate about the world in such a way that:

(a) Their speculations were divorced from religious dogma.

(b) Their speculations were 'mechanistic', mechanisms were sought to explain what they saw – not capricious deities. Mechanical processes were suggested e.g. *condensation and rarefaction* (Anaximenes) or *tension of forces* (Heraclitus).

They sought underlying unity of material and structure behind the apparent inconsistency of experience, suggesting that the basic 'material' of the universe was:

- *Water* (Thales)
- *Indeterminate Substance* (Anaximander)
- *Mist / Air* (Anaximenes)
- *Fire* (Heraclitus)

Thales

Thales was a figure of great prestige – the only philosopher before Socrates to be numbered by Plutarch among the Seven Sages. We can be sure of little about his life, as we are dependent on later figures who were as prone as modern writers to credit legends. There are some nice personal stories about him using his knowledge to predict a bumper olive crop, buying up the olive presses, and making a fortune. His involvement in practical capitalism went along with political involvement, reputedly dissuading his city from a disastrous alliance. Another endearing tale is that one night he was walking along staring at the stars and so fell into a ditch – to the amusement of a servant girl.

Thales

Writers like Diogenes Laertius, Pliny and Plutarch (all, of course, over six centuries later) ascribed to him a method for measuring the height of pyramids using shadows – which may have involved the idea of similar triangles. He is said to have travelled in Egypt (which seems reasonable if he was measuring pyramids), and may have obtained some of the rule of thumb methods engineers there used (he was an engineer himself). There is controversy about how much geometry he knew or invented, and how far it was theoretical.

Our main source of information about Thales' cosmology and physics is Aristotle who does not seem to have seen any actual works of Thales and gives an interpretive account. In one place he refers to Thales' view that the Earth:

> stays in place through floating like a log or some other such thing (for none of these rests by nature on air but on water) – as though the same argument did not apply to the water supporting the Earth as the Earth itself. (*On the Heavens:* B 13, 294, a, 28)

In his *Metaphysics* Aristotle gives the reasoning (as he saw it) behind the approach of all the Ionians:

> Most of the first philosophers thought that principles in the form of matter were the only principles of all things: for the original source of all existing things, that from which a thing first comes-into-being and into which it is finally destroyed, the substance persisting but changing in its qualities … (*Metaphysics:* A3, 983 b6)

The Ionians were attempting to explain the problems of change and permanence as mentioned above: the basic substance is unchanged but assumes different forms. We do not know where the floating Earth idea came from. The Egyptians saw the Earth as a flat floating disc, and the Babylonians had a story of Eridu (dating at least from the seventh century BC) in which 'in the beginning all land was sea' on which Marduk built a land raft which became the Earth.[58] This was not a Greek idea, but Thales may have adapted it from travels in Egypt and Babylon. Thales left out Marduk, though it seems that Thales retained some idea of a soul-force in

[58] cf. also Psalm 24:2, Genesis 49:25 – dating from at least 1000 years BC.

the world – possibly pantheistic in type. Available details of this are insufficient to make much comment.

How can we assess all this in terms of science? Patrick Moore contemptuously remarked 'There is no true science in this'[59] but we need to think about this. The suggestion that all things were a variation on one basic substance was an attempt to get over the problems of change and permanence as explained. One of the drives of science has been to try to establish some underlying building blocks (atoms, electrons, quarks etc.) quite different from the appearances of the objects which they make up. Is, moreover, the notion of the Earth as a floating disc inherently irrational? Is it less intrinsically rational than (say) the notion of wave-particle duality or that we are standing on a spinning globe in a space which is expanding but has nothing 'beyond' it? Or the idea that most of the energy and matter in the universes is unobservable? *If* Thales adapted it from (say) Babylon, he *did* at least eject Marduk – is it unscientific to seek physical explanations for commonly held beliefs about nature?

More specifically on astronomy, Thales is reputed by several sources to have predicted a solar eclipse in 585 BC though how he could have done so is unclear since not even the Babylonians had a theory for such predictions at this time. Possibly Babylonian methods might have established times at which eclipses *might* occur, and Thales was lucky in predicting from this when one did. There is also a source (Eudemus[60]) claiming that Thales predicted solstices, and various writers ascribe to him vaguely worded discoveries about their features.

Moving on from Thales

The same basic approach was taken and expanded by the other Ionians. That there was more to matter than appeared was also the thought of Anaximander. He suggested, though, 'indeterminate substance' (*epeiron*) because there was no particular reason to pick water as basic, as ice-water-steam transformations are two-way. Anaximander also held that the Earth was poised in space staying where it was 'because of the equal distance from everything'. For Anaximenes the basic material was gaseous ('mist/air'). This material formed different substances by processes of becoming more

---

59 P. Moore, *The Great Astronomical Revolution* (1994), 30.

60 See Kirk and Raven, *The Presocratic Philosophers* (1957), 81 etc.

condensed or more rarefied. Heraclitus sought to account for the constant change around us within this tradition. His basic substance was fire, something both ever changing and active. To him the surprise was not change but permanence – and even this was a kind of illusion. He is reputed to have said that one could never step twice into the same river. This was not because of ancient pollution, but because, of course, although the river looks 'permanent' the water in it is constantly changing. Some modern physics comes close to a similar idea with constant particle movement under apparently stable macro phenomena. To Heraclitus there was a tension in things 'like the bow and the lyre',. It is very difficult to conceptualise how people like Heraclitus were really perceiving reality – it is too easy to read modern concepts back when they were not there.

Pythagoreans – Numbers and Mathematics

The second great 6th century BC movement was based in Greek Italy. This was the secretive cult of Pythagoras. We know little detail about Pythagoras' life. His early life was on Samos, which he reputedly left to escape the tyranny of Polycrates. He settled in Croton where he rose to great influence until ousted in a coup, moving to a nearby city – Metapontium – where he died.

The Pythagorean school seems to have been a religious community, with a belief (made famous to us in *Twelfth Night*) in the transmigration of souls and the necessity for dietary regulation.

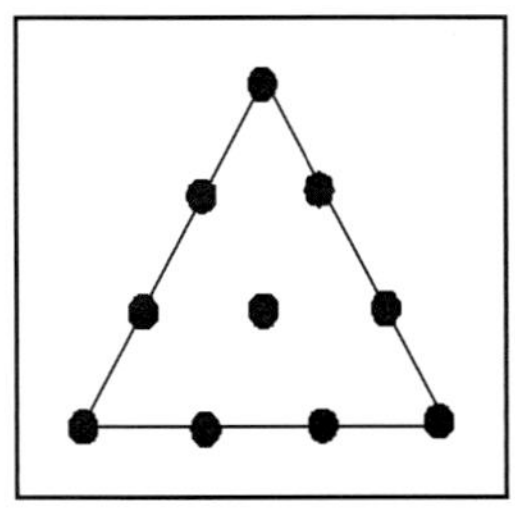

Reality apparently consists of *number*, and this itself is conceived geometrically. Thus ten is a triangular number.

The school believed in experimentation to bring out the basic numerical relationships underlying all reality. (Alcmaeon of Croton did experimental physiology and psychology).

Number also related to music and harmony – with Pythagoras himself credited with discovering the relationship between musical intervals and numbers (e.g. on string length).

A key point which distinguished Pythagoreans from number mysticism in e.g. Orphic cults, was the development of Euclidean geometry. Pythagoras most famous theorem (in a right angled triangle the square on the longest side is equal to the sum of squares on the other two) illustrates this. Geometry seems to provide information about the real world from pure thought. The 'proof' of the theorem is purely rational – one does not go out and measure a triangle. On the other hand it works 'in the field' in a literal sense! Use ropes to mark out a field with straight sides of 3 and 4, and equal straight diagonals. These diagonals will be found to be 5. No need to measure them! In fact, the actual measurement is only an approximation to the 'real' figure which is obtained by thought. In other words, the actual measurable world may only approximate to the ideal one.

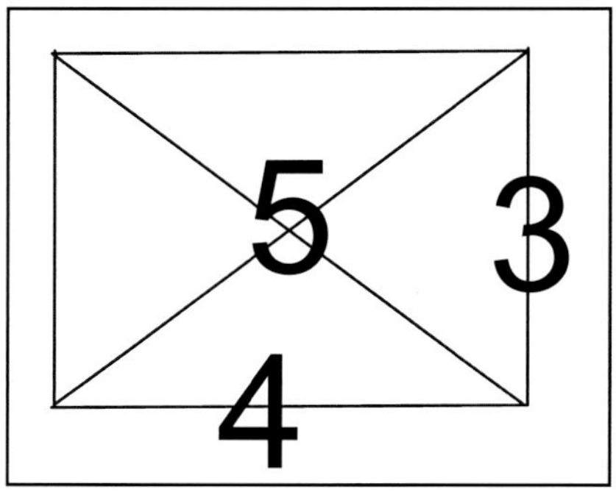

This relates to some very basic issues in science. Firstly, measurement and metrication have been central to much of its development. Secondly, there is a whole 'reality' (some would claim ultimate reality) which is numerical – modern physics describes reality in terms of mathematical equations.[61]

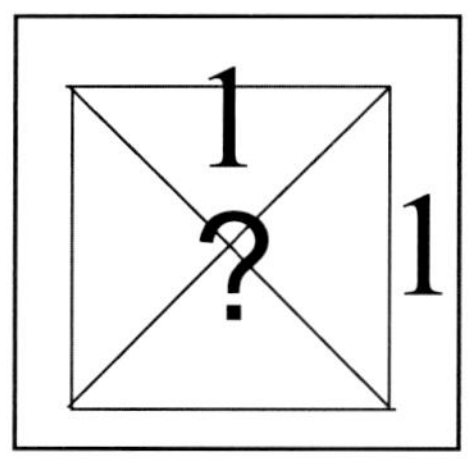

The Pythagoreans had, however, their problems. Construct a square field and what is the length of the diagonal? It is the square root of 2, but this is not a number representable by the ratio of any two integers – it is 'irrational' . To a group believing that reality *consists* of number, the discovery of irrational numbers was a disaster! Some suggest that the one who first revealed this scandal to the world was assassinated!

Pythagoreans associated harmony and mathematics, and had a great sense of the beauty of mathematical theories. This is actually common amongst physicists, and 20th and 21st century figures have remarked on the 'beauty' of the mathematics of physics, or speak of an 'elegant' proof. If the mathematics is elegant and beautiful the theory 'looks' true. To the Pythagoreans this was much stronger. Thus, for example, Aristotle says of them:

---

61 Arthur Eddington (in his classic *The Nature of the Physical World*) even speaks of 'two realities' ie the everyday world and that of mathematical physics. Modern Oxford Chemist Peter Atkins has spoken in terms of translating all reality into mathematics.

> As the number 10 is thought to be perfect and to comprise the whole nature of numbers, they say that the bodies which move through the heavens are ten, but as the visible bodies are only nine, to meet this they invent a tenth – the 'counter earth' (*Metaphysics*, A5, 986 a8).

> Most people say that the Earth lies at the centre of the universe …but the Italian philosophers known as Pythagoreans take the contrary view. At the centre, they say, is fire, and the Earth is one of the stars, creating night and day by circular motion about the centre. They further construct another earth in opposition to ours to which they give the name 'counter Earth'. In all this they are not seeking for theories and causes to account for observed facts, but rather forcing their observations and trying to accommodate them to certain theories and opinions of their own. But there are many others who would agree that it is wrong to give the Earth the central position, looking to theory rather than to the facts of observation. Their view is that the most precious place befits the most precious thing: but fire, they say, is more previous than Earth…it is not the Earth that lies at the centre of the sphere but fire …(*On the Heavens*, B13, 293 a18).

> Some thinkers suppose that the motion of bodies of that size must produce a noise, since on our Earth the motion of bodies far inferior in size and in speed of movement has that effect…from this argument and from the observation that their speeds, as measured by their distances, are in the same ratios as musical concordances, they assert that the sound given by the circular movements of the stars is a harmony. Since, however, it appears unaccountable that we should not hear this music, they explain this by saying that the sound is in our ears from the very moment of birth, and is thus indistinguishable from its contrary silence …(*On the Heavens*, B9, 290 b12).

These are quoted at length because of the profound influence the Pythagoreans had on both Copernicus and Kepler (both of whom could, in some senses) be called 'neo-Pythagorean'. They also show the great contrast between them and Aristotle – the thinker of common sense empiricism. This raises issues of the proper relationship between observation and theory. Was John Couch Adams in theoretical prediction of Neptune, or Stephen Hawking in the theoretical prediction of black holes, in a sense acting in a Pythagorean tradition of theory before observation?

Rationalism – the Role of Thinking

Geometry had raised the issue of the proper relationship of thought and rationality to observation. A group of thinkers called the Eleatics raised further issues about this:

- Parmenides (c.510–? BC) of ELEA
- Zeno (c.487–? BC) of ELEA

Parmenides was (according to Diogenes Laertius) a pupil of Xenophanes who was a pupil of Anaximander, but seems to have come to identify more with the Pythagoreans. Although his subject matter is prosaic, Parmenides wrote in hexameter verse, which tends sometimes to obscure the meaning. Good luck, then, with the following(!):

> One way only is left to be spoken of, that it is; and on this way are full many signs that what is is uncreated and imperishable, for it is entire, immovable and without end. It was not in the past, nor shall it be, since it is now, all at once, one, continuous; for what creation will you seek for it? How and whence did it grow? Nor shall I allow you to say or to think, 'from that which is not'; for it is not to be said or thought that it is not. And what need would have driven it on to grow, starting from nothing, at a later time rather than an earlier? Thus it must either completely be or be not. Nor will the force of true belief allow that, beside what is, there could also arise anything from what is not; wherefore Justice looses not her fetters to allow it to come into being or perish, but holds it fast; and the decision on these matters rests here: it is or it is not. But it has surely been decided, as it must be, to leave alone the one way as unthinkable and nameless (for it is no true way), and that the other is real and true. How could what is thereafter perish? And how could it come into being? For if it came into being, it is not, nor if it is going to be in the future. So coming into being is extinguished and perishing unimaginable.

Clear enough? His basic argument seems to be that change must come either from *being* or *not-being*. It cannot come from *being* (as this already is) and it cannot come from *not-being* (for nothing comes out of nothing). It cannot arise at one particular point in time, for why this point rather than another. So change is an illusion. Reality is a motionless, unchanging, eternally present sphere.

Parmenides' follower, Zeno of Elea, faced with the perhaps rather confused objections of contemporaries, also propounded various riddles to 'show' that motion was impossible. One of the most famous we can formulate in

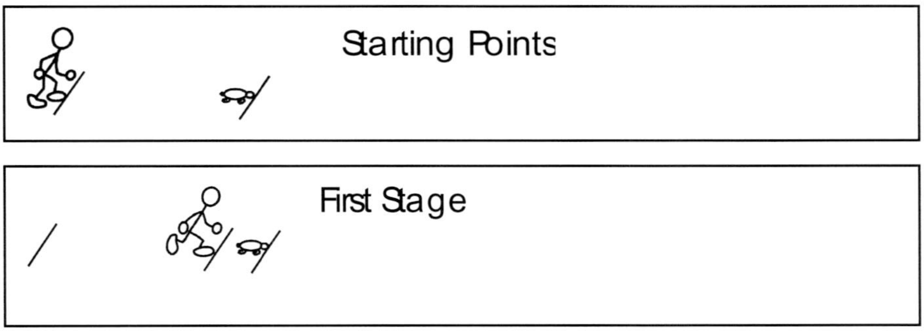

terms of Achilles and the tortoise. Achilles and the tortoise were to have a race and, since Achilles was regarded as somewhat fast, in order to avoid him simply showing a clean pair of heels (as it were) to the tortoise, the latter would be given a start. The race started, but when Achilles came up to where the tortoise had started (called 'the first stage' in my sketch) the tortoise had moved on a bit. When he reached the tortoise's new position, the tortoise had moved on a bit more. Every time Achilles got up to where the tortoise was, the latter had moved on. Achilles could therefore never catch the tortoise. This and various other conundrums (impossible to explain in days before it was recognised that the sum of an infinite series could be finite) 'demonstrated' that motion was impossible.

Obviously no one believed either Zeno or Parmenides – but they did raise a key question. What is the relationship between reason and observation, thought and experience? Geometry seemed to show the power of pure thought to arrive at truths more certain and more precise than those merely of observation – but Zeno's conundrums seemed to show that pure reason could also err. Now we know, of course, that the sum of an infinite series can be finite, but this kind of mathematics was then a long way off.

The Final Pre-Socratics

The final stage in 'Pre-Socratic' philosophy (i.e. before Socrates) consisted of eclectic pluralist systems such as those of:

- Empedocles *c.*490–430 BC – AGRIGENTUM
- Anaxagoras *c.*500–428 BC – CLAZOMENAE
- Democritus *c.*470–400 BC – THRACE

The Ionian tradition was carried on by Empedocles and later by the atomists Leucippus and Democritus. Here again an underlying unity was sought to explain what was observed. But, as before, *reason* is used to reconstruct and defend what 'must be' happening behind actual experience. Empedocles, like Parmenides, wrote in hexameter. Unlike Parmenides, his system defended the basic reliability of the senses. By the time of Empedocles there had emerged the idea of four basic elements: 'earth', 'water', 'air' and 'fire'. We must, of course, beware of taking these in a modern sense. By 'earth' they did not mean something to grow tomatoes in, but anything solid. In our terms 'solid' , 'liquid' , 'gas' and 'active principle' might better convey their thought. Empedocles had a cyclic cosmology, with the elements slowly sorting themselves out into layers (earth-water-air-fire) and then remixing. The rule of *love* (when all the elements were mixed) was at one pole, and *strife* (when all were separate) at the other. We were at an intermediate phase. Again, we must beware the terminology. If we used 'modern' words like 'attraction' and 'repulsion' it sounds so much more reasonable[62] - even though these are also words used in personal relationships! However, we should also beware of making it too modern! To Empedocles 'love' and 'strife' are not purely impersonal forces, but are part of the same thing as the human experiences of these. Since Greeks could not conceive of something being non-material but spatial, these are also considered as material in kind. Empedocles had an evolutionary system, in places coming near to describing a theory of evolution by natural selection. He was also interested in explaining consciousness, and other issues. Democritus came from Thrace (just north of Macedonia), and addressed the problem of permanence raised by the Eleatics by suggesting that atoms were permanent, it was their *rearrangement* (within the void) that led to new properties.

---

[62] There has, of course, been a controversy in the 20th century as to whether our universe was flat or not – i.e. whether forces of expansion would one day be overcome by gravity and return to a 'big crunch'.

Athens and the Path to Plato

Acropolis reconstruction

Pythagoras, and to some extent Empedocles, had set their philosophy within a general mystical view of the human condition. It was, however, in Athens that there came the flowering of a more complete view of education, knowledge and the end-aim of mankind.

Acropolis today

Anyone who has been to Athens, even today, cannot fail to be impressed by the splendour of the Parthenon.

The Athenians were, as St Paul said, 'altogether religious', and yet philosophy and freedom of thinking was prevalent rather than enforced dogma.

Art was also a great forum of questioning. Euripides (484–406 BC), a figure contemporary with Socrates, wrote various plays (e.g. *Helen*) addressing deep questions about fate, the gods, and whether there was any meaning to the human condition.

Epidaurus theatre

Aristophanes' plays were bitingly satirical – and very rude and crude!

Democracy involved all the citizens playing a direct part in the political process, so education was important.

Euripides

Several aspects, then, form a background to the philosophical development:

(a) the pre-classical Greek idea of the pursuit of 'excellence' *arete*

(b) the genuinely democratic nature of the Athenian Polis

(c) the system of education

Up to the age of seven the child merely played at home. From seven to 14 there was school education which included music, recitation, reading, writing and simple arithmetic. At 14+ the more wealthy would use the gymnasium (running track etc.) and receive introduction to the civic and cultural life of Athens and its laws. In recognition of the need for something more, 'higher education' developed as a reaction to the rather haphazard system – with several schools of thought developing as we shall now explore.

Sophists – Practical Wisdom

This was one response to the need for higher education. Some 'sophists' were simply sophists in the modern sense of the term – clever speakers and quibblers. The best known, however, were more than that. They were disinterested in ultimate spiritual questions of philosophies of human nature, but taught a kind of practical wisdom. Protagoras disclaimed intention to teach arithmetic, astronomy etc, claiming 'Man is the measure of all things' and teaching management of home and state affairs citizenship. In 393 BC the sophist Isocrates opened what could be seen as the first 'university' teaching astronomy, geometry and dialectics (as mind training activities). The aim was to produce the educated, wise, all-round man.

Socrates

Socrates (470–399 BC) had a remarkable influence on philosophy. For him, knowledge began with the admission of ignorance!

Like sophists he thought the key question was humankind's situation rather than physical science. Like them he also believed in higher education for citizenship beyond the gymnasium. He differed, however, in believing philosophic education necessary as part of a training for participation in government (i.e. as citizens). He believed government should be in the hands of specialist philosophers – so developed a theory of the nature of knowledge. He also believed knowledge began by admitting ignorance – asking questions. He was executed in 399 BC on charges of atheism and corrupting the young.

Socrates

Plato – Levels of Reality and Knowledge

Socrates' disciple, Plato (c.428–347 BC) founded his academy in Athens in 388 BC, having turned in disgust from politics after Socrates' trial. Many of his works (produced over nearly half a century) survive, largely in the form of 'dialogues'.

Protagoras' 'Man is the measure of all things' could imply:

1. truth may be 'relative' i.e. there may be no unique truth.
2. knowledge must be about perception for this is *all* we actually experience (cf. later ideas of Locke, Hume and empiricism).

Plato rejected both ideas (cf. his *Thaetetus).* The relativistic view of truth is self-contradictory. Knowledge is absolute and relates to what is. Perception is neither absolute nor an infallible guide to what is – it varies between persons and perspectives – so it is unreliable!

His own theories involved a general philosophy of the nature of learning and the *arete* or goal of mankind. He thought there were various knowledge types:

Objects of Knowledge		**Type of Knowledge**	
archai:	THE GOOD	*noesis:*	INTELLIGENCE
ideas:	FORMS	episteme ~~*epitome:*~~	KNOWLEDGE
mathematica:	MATHEMATICS	*dianoia:*	THINKING
	VISIBLE OBJECTS	*pistis:*	BELIEF/OPINION
eikones:	IMAGES/REFLECTIONS	*eikasia:*	CONJECTURE

Starting from the bottom: some things were mere fleeting images, and only conjecture could be made about their real nature.

To us, visible objects may seem things about which we can be certain. Plato, however, was struck by the unreliability of the senses. We can easily be mistaken about particular visible objects.

Mathematical ideas, in contrast (found through the use of reason) could be known with certainty.

There was, moreover, a higher form of knowledge, that of the 'ideal forms' such as those of beauty and justice. Thus, whilst optical illusion might make us err over beauty in an individual physical object, it could never make us mistake the truth or nature of the 'ideal form' . We might, for example, be mistaken in a belief that justice had or had not been done in a particular case, but not about the nature and reality of justice as an ideal form. We might make a mistake about a particular instance of humanity (mistaking a hologram or an android for a human), but not about the reality of an ideal form 'humanity'. Plato thought of real objects as somehow (though he is vague)'participating' in the ideal forms.

Untutored people were like those who mistook shadow for reality – mistaking the physical world for what is 'real' rather than the ideal forms. A long process of philosophical education enabled a person to see the reality behind the physical world – and ultimately to see *the good* which gave rise to that reality.

Some of these questions recur throughout the history of science and knowledge – even until today.

Plato's actual scientific world-view fused together a number of things:

- From Parmenides a rationalistic approach to knowledge.
- From Socrates (& Xenophanes?) a view of God, or the Good as *one* and the world as designed rationally and optimally.
- From Pythagoreans the importance and centrality of number, and the harmony of the heavenly spheres (i.e. the spheres which bear planets etc.).
- From Empedocles the four elements: earth, air, fire and water. (in Plato's Academy a fifth element *aether* was added to the four, being thought to be the element of which the heavens were made).
- From Democritus a form of atomism (though Plato's atoms were *geometrical,* made of abstract geometrical faces).

Actually his specific ideas on astronomy are mentioned almost in passing.

In *The Gorgias* he casually remarks that astronomy concerns 'the movements of the stars and of the Sun and of the Moon, and their speeds relative to each other'.

In *The Phaedo* Plato has Socrates relate how he read Anaxagoras hoping to find whether the Earth is flat or round, whether it is at the centre of the universe and why; to find information about the Sun 'and the Moon and the other stars and their speeds relative to each other and their turnings and characteristics' (*Pheaedo* 97–8). Socrates was disappointed with the mechanical explanations of the Ionians.

In a startling passage in *The Republic* Socrates (Plato's mouthpiece) remarks:

> Those intricate traceries in the sky are no doubt, the loveliest and most perfect of material things, but they are still part of the visible world, and therefore fall far short of the true realities – the true movements in the ideal world of numbers and geometrical figures which are responsible for these rotations. These, you will agree, have to be worked out by reason and thought, and cannot be observed …Accordingly we must use the embroidered heaven to illustrate our theories – just as one might use exquisite diagrams drawn by some fine artist such as Daedelus. An expert in geometry, faced with such designs, would admire their finish and craftsmanship, but he would not dream of studying them in all earnest, expecting to find all angles and all lengths conforming exactly to theoretical values ... So if we mean to study astronomy in a way which makes proper use of the soul's inborn intellect, we shall proceed as we do in geometry – working at mathematical problems – and not waste time observing the heavens.

So what he is saying is this:

- The stars are material and therefore they cannot be expected to exactly conform to the 'true realities' (i.e. the ideal forms).
- We should therefore take the stars we see merely as a model to 'illustrate' our study of 'realities' (i.e. the forms) just as a diagram imperfectly illustrates geometry.

- The basis of our study of astronomy should be (like geometry) by means of thought and reason.

This may also be connected to Socrates' idea that mathematical proofs were 'perceived' because of a soul's pre-birth state of knowledge being brought back to memory. This explained why an untutored slave, asked suitable questions, could 'see' a geometrical proof for himself without being told it.

Later, in *The Timaeus*, Plato explains that the physical world only approximates the ideal one because the creator (or 'demiurge') impressed form and order on things found in a state of chaos. Thus 'the generation of this cosmos was a mixed result of the combination of Necessity and Reason'.

The notion that the study of astronomy should not begin from 'the intricate traceries in the stars' but from *reason and thought* seems to many so absurd that they wonder why Plato was so influential. However, much in later thinking also questioned the role of 'pure' observation against reason. Descartes, for example, pointed out that if we melt wax it changes texture, smell, colour etc – so how do we know that it is 'the same wax' – *by reason*. Reason tells us the *kinds* of explanation which are acceptable, and so the *kinds* of interpretation-observation which make sense. To Descartes and Einstein action at a distance (as Kepler and later Newton suggested for gravity) did not *make sense.* Moreover, the idea that the real world only approximates the ideal may also strike some as absurd. But what is the status of Newton's law:

> Every body continues in a state of rest or uniform motion unless acted on by a force

Did Newtonians take this law to be 'true'? The problem is that even in Newton's own terms there *were no such bodies* since every body in the universe acted by gravity all the time on every other body. In a sense it was a limiting case projected from what we know – but in this sense the law is an ideal form of what can never (even in principle) be observed!

In *The Politicus* Plato goes even further and pictures the universe after a time as 'winding down' and God having to rewind it! Some readers may be reminded of one of the early episodes of *Red* Dwarf! However, Plato expressly says that no one should take everything literally in the mythical form in which he casts his cosmology!

In *The Phaedo* the Earth is recognised as very large with only a small part inhabited. It keeps its place because of equiformity and equilibrium.

In *The Republic* the 'myth of Er' pictures the Earth as a sphere, and around it spinning on a spindle are eight whorls or spheres carrying the Moon, Sun, five (known) planets and stars. These turned from 'necessity', each whorl having a 'siren' (Harmony of the spheres?).

In *The Timaeus* the system of spheres on which the Sun and planets rotate include one rotating on the other (an X to account for the difference between the equator (at right angles to Earth rotation) and ecliptic (plane of rotation around the Sun). Others later developed this idea of additive motions.

The Earth is stationary according to Plato because 'If there were any solid body at the centre of the universe, there would be nothing to draw it to this extreme rather than to that …' Moreover, with regard to the four basic elements there is a 'tendency of each towards its kindred element'. This idea was developed in Aristotle.

The idea of a 'force' seems not to be present in his system.

Eudoxus

Eudoxus (c.400–350 BC) was born in Cnidus in Asia Minor, and a wealthy patron paid for him to go to Plato's Academy. Sometime between 380 and 363 BC he also spent 16 months in Egypt, learning priestly wisdom including some astronomy. He wrote there his first major work, which was a calendar based on an eight year cycle. He eventually returned to Athens where he became a respected legislator. Some of Euclid may have been taken from Eudoxus. He contributed particularly in the area of irrational numbers and measurement theory.

Eudoxus seems to be the first to have constructed a geometric model to predict the positions of the heavenly bodies. His own work has not survived, but the system can be reconstructed from Aristotle's references and some other early commentaries on this.

His basic idea was that one could have:

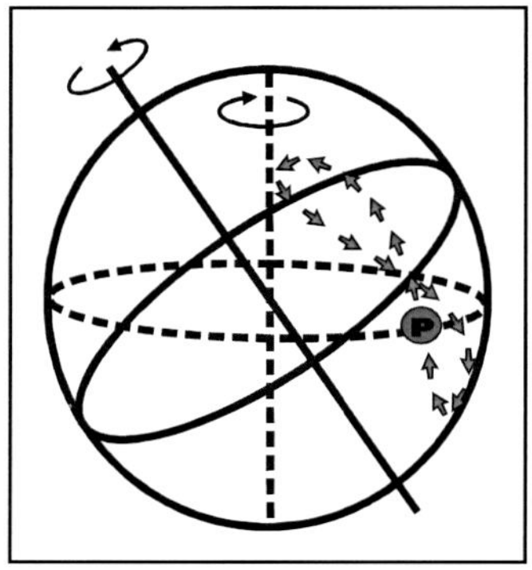

- two rotating spheres, nearly the same size
- one inside the other with its axis fixed to the surface of the other
- rotating in opposite directions at near the same speed

This would produce a net effect of a kind of figure of eight or 'hippopede' as shown in this diagram. The Earth sits, of course, at the centre of both spheres. The planet is fixed to the side of the inner sphere at a point on its circumference furthest from its axis. But this inner sphere (dotted) has its axis fixed to the walls of the outer one (at points in this diagram at top and bottom of it). The combined motion is a figure of eight – a hippopede.

Eudoxus used four such spheres for most planets, producing a much more complex motion. Each sphere had its axis fixed to appropriate points on the inner surface of the next. Eudoxus had the following spheres overall:

Moon 3 Sun 3 Mercury 4 Venus 4 Mars 4 Jupiter 4 Saturn 4 Stars 1

= 27 homocentric spheres (which includes in each case one for 24-hour motion).

The sets for each body could be conveniently placed inside each other if desired, but the system meant, of course, that each celestial body would remain at the same distance from the Earth at the centre.

Advantages:

- Major planetary retrogressive movements could be explained and predicted.
- A geometrical model enabled more flexible prediction of position than the Babylonian periodic approach.

Problems:

- No explanation of varying brightness of the Moon, Venus and Mars
- No explanation of difference between total and annular solar eclipses.

The features of Eudoxus' system which differ from ours today are:

1. It is Earth-centred and not Sun-centred
2. Celestial bodies stay the same distance from the Earth
3. Speeds are built from orbits with uniform angular momentum

Annular eclipse showing ring

The adoption of a Sun-centred system instead would remove only the first of these – so what advantage would it have and which 'problems' would it solve?

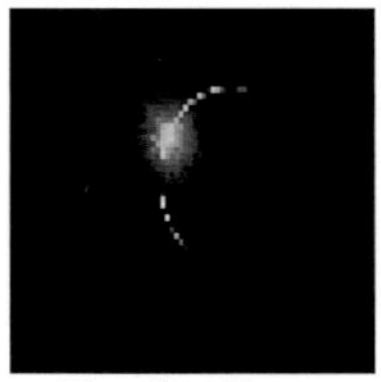
Total eclipse

Retrogressive planetary movements might be more intuitively 'obvious', but prediction was not really improved. The relative motions of Moon and Sun to the Earth, of course, would be unchanged by a Sun-centred system. The distance away of the Moon determines whether an eclipse is total (the Sun totally obliterated) or annular (a visible ring is left around the Moon at full eclipse). A Sun-centred system would not help this at all – even assuming that with naked eye and non-photographic techniques a difference could be noted. Eudoxus needed two spheres (plus the 24-hour rotation one) for the Moon and Sun which *are* (in relative terms) Earth-centred, because the motion is *not* circular. Variations in brightness can be caused by phases – this is actually the main reason for variations in light from Venus. Since the Moon (which does go around the Earth) has phases, obviously phases are not a problem as such for an Earth-centred system. Variations in brightness of Mars could be more of a problem – how would you explain it away if you were Eudoxus? Galileo's telescope, of course, showed *very much later* that the phases of Venus had a full range of *shapes* which would be impossible if it were always in the general direction of the Sun and always between the Sun and the Earth.[63] This would be a problem for Eudoxus' model (though for Ptolemy's only if one assumes orbits cannot intersect).

---

[63] So, for example. Kitty Ferguson, *Measuring the Universe* (2000), 85.

Did Eudoxus think of his spheres as physical? Probably not, though Aristotle did. This actually brings us to a fundamental difference in approach between scientists. Some seem to assume that once phenomena have been brought under the 'rule' of a mathematical system which enables prediction, then the work is done. Others feel that some kind of visualisable 'model' is also a necessity. This issue is not as simple as it might seem. A lot of modern physics is 'unimaginable' if not 'unthinkable' – though it proceeds by loose analogy and rigorous mathematics. So should we regard as 'more scientific' the approach of Aristotle, who wanted a machinery, or Plato-Eudoxus-Ptolemy who focused on getting a viable mathematical method?

Aristotle

Aristotle was born in Stagira, Macedonia, in 384 BC. His father was court physician to Amyntas – father of Philip, father of Alexander the Great. Aristotle's entrée to science was probably therefore through medicine, and this may explain his focus on biology rather than physics. Aristotle was logical rather than mystical and did not write poetry. He went to Plato's Academy in Athens when he was 17 and stayed 20 years. He left Athens after Plato's death around 347 BC, possibly because of anti-Macedonian sentiments in the city after Philip of Macedon sacked the city state of Alynthus in 347.

Aristotle

With him went Xenocrates and also Theophrastrus of Eresus who was Aristotle's pupil, colleague, and eventual successor as head of the Lyceaum and with whom experimental science reached its pinnacle in the ancient world. He set up an academy at Assus in Asia Minor, and then settled on the island of Lesbos for a time. He went to Philip's court to act as tutor to the young Alexander (though the latter seems to have followed little of his specific advice in later life!). After three years and a brief stay at home in Stagira, Aristotle returned to Athens in 335 to found the Lyceum, a rival academy to the Platonic one. The Lyceum's focus was

Mytilene Lesbos today

on biology, history and physics rather than the mathematical interests of the Academy. His instruction was informal, under the *Peripatos* (or a covered walkway), so he is sometimes called the Peripatetic philosopher. The syllabus, however, was rigorous, and some of Aristotle's extant works may be notes for it. He left Athens towards the end of his life, again to avoid anti-Macedonian feelings, and died in 323 BC.

His differences from the approach of Plato were profound:

1. He was interested in *becoming* rather than *being*. Aristotle's 'essences' were not static but dynamic as in living things. He did not see (as Plato) 'chance' as being corruption but as part of life.

2. **ESSENCES** were in objects themselves – not in any external ideal form – and were teleological rather than static. As befits a biologist, he saw for example the 'essence' of an acorn to be to develop into an oak tree – unless it met with an 'accident' (e.g. being eaten by a pig).

3. **SHAPE** and geometry were not basic: 'It is evidently not shapes that mark the different elementary substances off from one another. The most important distinctions between different bodies lie in the properties and functions and capacities which we recognise as characteristics of every natural creature …' **QUALITIES** not shapes were important. Aristotle's atoms – unlike Plato's were distinguished by what combination they had of the active[64] properties (hot/cold moist/dry). They did not have shape. If atoms had rigid shapes then (since a void is impossible) they would all fit together exactly with no possibility of any of them moving as it would be 'locked in' by all the others.

4. Aristotle began from **OBSERVATION** rather than **THOUGHT.** He was more interested in biology than in mathematics, and

[64] 'Active', because heat or moisture is transferred from one object to another, whereas for example, shape or colour do not transfer in this way.

inductive rather than hypothetico-deductive[65] in his approach to knowledge. This is why (as mentioned above) he was critical of the Pythagoreans starting from theory.

5. He was concerned with **MECHANISM** in terms of material, motion and essences not with mere mathematical description.

Aristotle identified four types of cause:

(a) MATERIAL CAUSE (e.g. the marble out of which a statue is made)

(b) FORMAL CAUSE (the form to be realised – the shape of the statue)

(c) EFFICIENT CAUSE (the cause as we know it, the sculptor who shapes it)

(d) FINAL CAUSE (the purpose for which it is made)

Aristotle (in common with the later Academy) distinguished five elements: FIRE, AIR, WATER, EARTH and AETHER. He saw a fundamental (observable) difference between phenomena above and below the Moon:

Above the Moon:

– heavenly bodies were made of unchanging aether

– natural motion was circular

– heavenly bodies were carried on sets of homocentric crystalline spheres

– bodies were moved by the prime mover (whose essence implies existence) who draws them

Below the Moon:

– bodies were made of four elements: fire, air, earth, water

– these were made when 'form' is impressed on basic matter

– properties: fire: hot/dry
water: cold/moist

---

65 'Induction', begins from observation and derives general laws. The hypothetico-deductive method begins with a hypothesis, deduces what would be its consequences, and observes to see if these happen. In practice, of course, all knowledge involves both aspects of process.

earth: cold dry
(all communicable properties, hot/dry
air: hot/moist are active and cold/moist passive)

- elements were transmutable but all matter must be in one or other form

On Motion

Aristotle used the term 'motion' to mean a number of phenomena, but in what we would call motion distinguished:

- natural motion (vertical below the Moon, circular above it)
- violent motion (produced by a force acting); thus:
  - a body does not move unless a force is exerted on it. (NB projectiles could continue to move because of the air propelling them)
  - its speed is proportional to the force exerted
  - its speed is inversely proportional to the resistance of the medium
  - the speed of a body falling under natural motion increases as it nears its natural place

Being, Not-Being and Potentia

He also distinguished:

- POTENTIA:[66] which gives something power (*dunamis*) to be something else
- ENERGIA: process of becoming something else
- ENTELECHY: state of self realised essence

This was Aristotle's solution to the old Parmenidean puzzle of *being* and *not-being*. So, nature involves the movement of things under their own essences towards a *telos* (end), which they achieve unless (in the chaotic state under the Moon) there is a clash of different natures (e.g. when an acorn gets eaten by a pig).

Aristotle is the philosopher of sense and observation, as we shall reconsider at the end of this present chapter. Michael Hoskin rightly says of his system:

---

[66] The key 20th century physicist Werner Heisenberg in *Physics and Philosophy* (1958), ch. 3 reintroduces the term *potentia* to describe the potential for observing a particle. In ch. 4 Heisenberg looks at early Greek philosophy!

> It is important to recognise that this Aristotelian cosmology drew strength from being an intellectual formulation that reinforced common sense, in contrast to modern science, which contradicts what seems self-evident. Aristotle tells us that the Earth is at rest beneath our feet, that we are on *terra firma,* whereas today's astronomers would have us believe that we are hurtling through space at an almost unimaginable speed. Aristotle confirms that there is indeed a fundamental contrast between Earth and sky, whereas post-Copernican astronomy insists that we must disregard the plain evidence of our senses, and accept the Earth as a heavenly body like Venus and Mars and the rest. The history of cosmology is not the easy story of the rejection of absurd ideas in favour of what (perhaps after a little thought) is seen to be patently true, but the heroic saga of the hard-won rejection of the patently true in favour of the absurd. It is this that gives the history of cosmology its fascination.[67]

In astronomy Aristotle inherited the systems of Eudoxus and also the late fourth century Callipus. They had utilised homocentric spheres with the numbers used to explain the movement of each celestial body as follows:

	Eudoxus	Callipus
Saturn	4	4
Jupiter	4	5
Mars	4	5
Venus	4	5
Mercury	4	5
Sun	3	5
Moon	3	5
TOTAL	26	33

Aristotle adopted the scheme with little refinement – but added a further 22 spheres to prevent interaction as his scheme was mechanical rather than mathematical

[67] Hoskin, *Cambridge Illustrated History of Astronomy* (1997), 32.

Between Aristotle and Ptolemy

Various figures are important for the next phase in Greek thinking:

- Heracleides *c.*390 – 322 - PONTICUS
- Aristarchus of Samos *c.*310 — 230 BC – SAMOS
- Apollonius of Perga fl. *c.*200 BC – PERGA
- Eratosthenes *c.*276 – 195 BC
- Hipparchus fl. *c.*141 – 127 BC

Heracleides was really a contemporary of Aristotle. He was also involved at the Academy and may have had charge of it for a while. Little of his work remains, but he apparently put forward a system in which:

- The Earth was at the centre of the universe but rotated (to explain the 24 hours day–night cycle).
- The Moon, Sun, Mars, Saturn and Jupiter went around the Earth.
- Venus and Mercury (which 'dance attendance' on the Sun) go around the Sun.

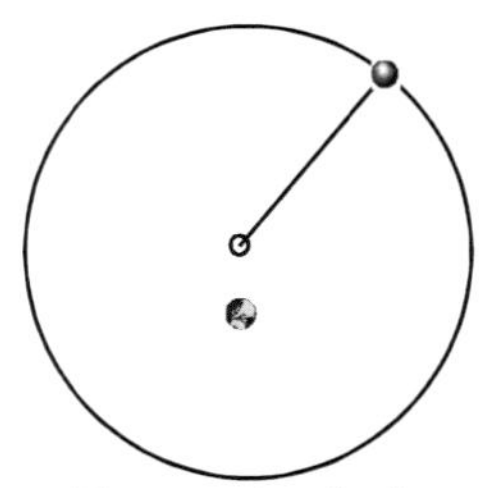
Eccentric circle

Aristarchus is credited with first putting forward a fully heliocentric system. He also attempted to measure the distances of the Sun and Moon from Earth. His method was correct, but the data were flawed and his figures were not very accurate. We actually know little else about him. We do not have any details of a mathematical system, nor how he overcame the massive physical problems his system would entail. Copernicus (see Chapter 3), famously first inserted and then deleted Aristarchus's name from the preface of his work. Copernicus would not, of course, have had to go right back to Aristarchus to find the idea – it was talked about by others (and rejected on rational grounds) well within Copernicus's early life and likely reading material.

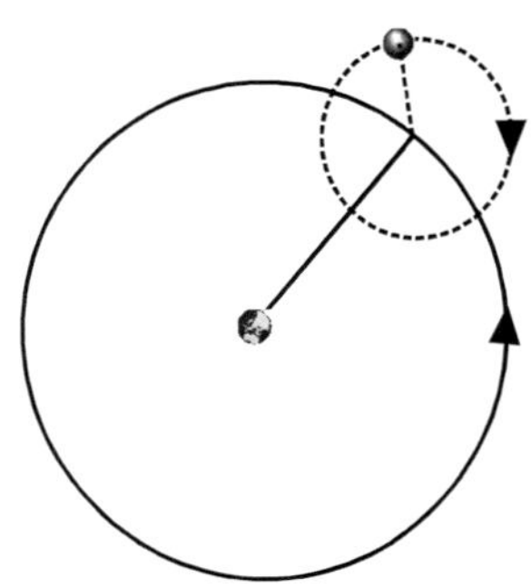
Epicycle and deferent

Apolonnius has left little record, but seems to have lived for a while in Alexandria – the city that was by then a major centre of Greek learning. He may have invented the devices of eccentric and epicycle. The *eccentric* simply means that the centre of the orbit of a planet is not at the Earth, but a point some way from it. An **epicycle** is a circle the centre of which is located on a point on the moving circumference of a larger circle called the *deferent*. The net effect is a kind of spiralling motion, and if a number of epicycles are added one on another a complex motion can be found which allows for the retrograde planetary motions.

Eratosthenes came from Cyrene (North Africa – some may remember Simon of Cyrene in the gospels) but studied in Athens, and then stayed as librarian in the Museum at Alexandria. By this stage the latter was possibly more renowned for learning than Athens itself. He developed a method for measuring the size of the Earth (see Hoskin[68]) which brought remarkable accuracy.

> Contrary to what many modern people think, early Greek astronomers all knew not only that the Earth was an approximate sphere, but that it was *very* small in comparison with the distance to the stars.

Hipparchus is the final figure in our series. He was an observer who also derived a model to explain the unequal angular velocity of the Sun. Hipparchus's model was the one used and adapted by Ptolemy, and whose data Ptolemy may have copied.

Ptolemy

Claudius Ptolemy (c.100–170 AD) made the synthesis of Greek astronomy which came down to the middle ages. He flourished in Alexandria, the undisputed centre for Greek (Hellenistic) learning in the second century, but little is known of his life.

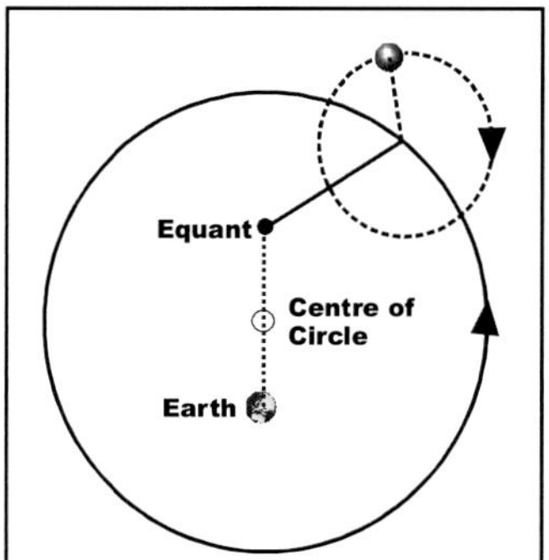

Equants

Ptolemy wrote a series of books, apparently intending to compile some kind of mathematical encyclopaedia, but extant work is incomplete. Ptolemy was a renowned mathematician, and also wrote on geography, optics, and, of course, astronomy. Ptolemy's

[68] Hoskin, op. cit. ch. 2.

book on astronomy was modestly entitled Megale Syntaxis (the Great Composition), translated into Arabic as al-Majisti, and hence into Latin in what became known as the Almagest.

Ptolemy extended the work of Appolonius and Hipparchus, using the same device of epicycles and deferents. He tried to complete Hipparchus' work on the Sun, Moon, and fixed stars (all of which do, in relative terms, circle the Earth). The planetary theories (in Books ix to xi of the Almagest) are his own re-computation.

One of the axioms of Greek super-lunar motion was that it was circular and with equal angular velocity about the circle or orbit centres. Ptolemy himself declared it to be the only kind of motion 'in agreement with the nature of Divine beings'. Yet he also reputedly invented the **equant.** This is a device which not only locates the centre of an orbit at a point in space separate from the Earth (the eccentric) but also has the angular velocity uniform about yet another point, the equant, rather than the centre of the orbit.

Kepler's laws would much later establish that planets go about the Sun as one focus of an ellipse, sweeping out equal areas in equal times and therefore going faster when nearer the Sun. The equant has the same kind of effect, angular velocities no longer have to be equal.

Some more mathematical details of Ptolemy's system can be found elsewhere[69], but one or two things about it may be noted. Firstly, since everything was viewed from the Earth, in principle the sets of epicycles for any particular body could be placed as near or far away as desired. In other words, the system gave no unique order for them. In practice he ranged them as:

- Moon
- Mercury
- Venus
- Sun
- Mars
- Jupiter
- Saturn

---

69 e.g. in Hoskin op. cit., or Olaf Pedersen, *Early Physics and Astronomy*, (1993); Robert Newton, *The Crime of Claudius Ptolemy* (1978).

He placed the system for each one just beyond that of the previous, and so obtained an order and ratio for orbits. Parts of his reasoning (for example to put three bodies either side of the Sun as earlier astronomers had done) were not very convincing to our understanding. Secondly, this raises the issue of whether he thought his spheres were physical or not. This is hard to say, though there seems no point in 'stacking' them in the way he does (to give an order for the planets) if they are not. Thirdly, his system was a bit ad hoc in other ways. Mercury and Venus bore an especial relationship to the Sun but (unlike in Heracleides' system) there was no obvious reason for this.

Great or Fake?

There have actually long been some puzzles about Ptolemy's observations and their relationship with his theoretical models. The Almagest became known in Europe in the (Latin) version of Gerard of Cremona (1114–1187) in 1175 (and an alternative version by the Spaniard Johannes de Luna in the same century). Copernicus used the Ptolemaic general approach minus the equants and of course centred on the Sun. But Copernicus, although he grew suspicious of the accuracy of ancient measurements, was not an observer. Tycho, who shared Copernicus's aversion to equants, was the first to offer a newer non-Ptolemy based star catalogue, and also to have three sets of detailed observations: Ptolemy's, the arab astronomers, and his own. Tycho established figures for the precession of the equinoxes using the latter two and without Ptolemy. This enabled him to discover that actually Ptolemy had made a systematic error in longitude. Tycho could suggest several possible reasons for this:

- Inadequate solar and lunar theory
- Effects of refraction on sunset
- Neglect of lunar parallax
- Factors in Ptolemy's conversion of earlier stellar positions from Hipparchus using a low Hipparchian figure for precession

Tycho himself concluded that Ptolemy was basically an encyclopaedist who derived his figures from Hipparchus, rather than an original observer.

An astrolabe relates star positions to the Sun[70], and in fact Ptolemy had used a spherical astrolabe which he describes in the first chapter of the Almagest. He claims to have used this instrument in the year 137 to catalogue the stars 'as many stars as we could sight down to the sixth magnitude'. Positions of bright stars to act as reference were determined with the help of the position of the Sun and Moon, and the other stars positioned relative to them. This sequence means that any solar errors would be reflected systematically in all the star positions.

Laplace in his 1796 System of the World refers to a general view that:

> Ptolemy's star catalogue is merely the one prepared by Hipparchus adjusted to the time of the former through a yearly precession of 111.

Laplace did not accept this, and thought the systematic error more likely to have been the result of solar errors affecting real observation. In contrast, a memoir presented by Lalande to the French Academy in 1757 noted that:

> [Ptolemy] attached emphasis to hypotheses which could not yet be very exact, attempted to make everything agree with them … nearly all the astronomers have found Ptolemy in default, each in that part of astronomy that he has examined thoroughly …[71]

Lalande (who wrote the standard text of the time) later claimed in it that:

> Astronomers are persuaded that Ptolemy was a bad observer, and that he drew from Hipparchus and others who preceded him all that is good in his work.[72]

Lalande's pupil and successor J. B. Delambre took the opposite view again! He thought that:

> Ptolemy compared only *Regulus* and *Spica* directly with the Sun … he took the distances of the other stars with respect either to each

---

[70] Hosking beautifully describes and illustrates the flat astralobe in his *Illustrated History of Astronomy*.

[71] See Curtis Wilson 'Essay Review: The Sources of Ptolemy's Parameters' *Journal for the History of Astronomy*, xv, (1984), 37.

[72] ibid.

other, or to *Regulus* or *Spica* ...[73]

An error in the mean Sun position, not noticeable to Ptolemy, could produce systematic error.

The controversy has continued – with commentators seeing Ptolemy either as essentially an encyclopaedist who was economical with the truth concerning the extent of his own contributions, or as a genuine observer making an unfortunate systematic error.

In the 1970s, geophysicist Robert Newton produced much more detailed mathematical evidence/arguments that Ptolemy actually fabricated most of his data. The method Newton used was this:

> First we locate genuine observations made by other astronomers that are relevant to the theories that Ptolemy wants to establish with the aid of his own observations. Next we find the parameters in Ptolemy's theories by using the observations made by others, and we calculate the circumstances of Ptolemy's alleged observations from his theories, using these parameters to do so. Finally we compare the calculated circumstances with those which Ptolemy claims to have observed. In many cases, the calculated and 'observed' circumstances agree to every digit that Ptolemy writes down.[74]

Such agreement would be extraordinarily unlikely if the measurements were really independent, and since the theory itself was needed to make the calculations Newton concludes that it was Ptolemy himself (not an assistant) who cheated. Newton argues that Ptolemy not only fabricated nearly all his own data and much attributed to others, but that Ptolemy's own theoretical work was also poor. He claims that Ptolemy's fabrications led to more confusion than light for later writers including Copernicus. His conclusion is:

> [The Almagest] has done more damage to astronomy than any other work ever written, and astronomy would be better off if it had never existed.

---

[73] J.B. Delambre, *Histoire de l'astronomie ancienne* vol II, 250.

[74] Robert Newton, *The Crime of Claudius Ptolemy* (1978), 343.

In his later work, *The Origins of Ptolemy's Astronomical Parameters* (1982), Newton even doubts (on the grounds that Ptolemy was an incompetent liar) that Ptolemy himself invented the equant as is popularly believed.[75]

Some later writers argue strongly against Newton's assessment. Owen Gingerich (an eminent astronomer before becoming an eminent historian of astronomy) reacts to Robert Newton by reasserting of the Almagest:

> Altogether it is a remarkable achievement, combining in a brilliant synthesis a treatise on theoretical astronomy with a practical handbook for the computation of ephemeredes.[76]

Gingerich concedes various points often before noted, e.g. that Ptolemy may have fabricated an equinox observation which he in fact projected from Hipparchus. Gingerich accepts that the reported positions of celestial bodies reported by Ptolemy agree well with his theory, but not with modern computations of the actual bodies. But he puzzles because Ptolemy's model seems more accurate than his data-base. Gingerich's conclusion is that Ptolemy used many more observations, for example, to establish his lunar theory, than reported in the Almagest, so that the end result is much more accurate than those observations reported. Ptolemy shared the ancient conviction that nature only approximated the ideal theory anyway (and many modern scientists ignore 'inconvenient' data points or results). Challenged that he had not really rebutted Newton, Gingerich admits that Ptolemy claimed for himself a star catalogue probably originating with Hipparchus, but is critical of many of Newton's calculations.[77]

Grasshoff robustly attacks the assumptions behind Newton's methodology.[78]Newton basically argues that to get so many observations in such precise agreement with theory would be very very unlikely. For Spica, for example, the allegedly measured longitude is exactly in accord with its theoretical value but out from modern recalculated values – and 3.5 times

---

75 op. cit.158. Newton again concludes that Ptolemy is not the greatest astronomer in antiquity but the 'most successful fraud in the history of science'.

76 Owen Gingrich, 'Was Ptolemy a Fraud?', *Quarterly Journal of the Royal Astronomical Society* (1980), 21, 253.

77 Owen Gingrich, 'Ptolemy revisited: A reply to R.R. Newton,' , *Quarterly Journal of the Royal Astronomical Society* 22 (1981), 40–44.

78 Gerd Grasshof, *The History of Ptolemy's Star Catalogue*, (1990), 79–92.

the standard error of observation. This would be incredibly unlikely by chance. Gasshoff, however, is more sympathetic to the conclusion of Pannekoek rejected by Newton[79] that Ptolemy had only selected favourable data out of a much larger real data set of observations. He is also critical of many of the technical details of Newton's analysis.

So how far was Ptolemy following normal scientific practice in relating theory to observation, and how far was he simply a fraud? How far was he a great systematiser and astronomer and how far a mere plagiariser? You will have to decide for yourself if you want to follow it up!

The Legacy of Ptolemy and Aristotle

We will not be tracing the path of the cosmology of Aristotle and Ptolemy through Islamic scientists and the Middle Ages. Apart from some development of impetus theory (for which see Pedersen op. cit.) the essentials remained similar. The mathematics were fearsomely complicated, of course. The scholar king Alfonso X 'the Wise' (1221–1284) of Castille and Leon, patronised astronomy (and had both a set of tables and much later a Moon crater named after him). After initiation into the Ptolemaic system he reputedly sighed and said: 'If the Lord Almighty had consulted me before embarking upon the Creation, I should have recommended something simpler'. Generations of science students may identify with this! A personal irony is that the garden of Alfonso in Seville is near the cathedral housing Columbus' magnificent final tomb. Whilst standing in the garden I overheard a conversation which went along the lines of 'Well of course it was natural enough for everyone in the days of Columbus to believe the Earth was flat'. Alfonso died over 150 years before Columbus was born – and knew perfectly well it was a sphere! Such is the power of myth.

The system, however, had other strands than the purely mathematical. One strand was the neo-Pythagorean/neo-Platonic idea relating celestial movements to harmony and looking for beauty in the mathematics. We will return to this in the next chapter. The other was in the highly commonsensical physical and astronomical Aristotelian system, which had both depth and breadth of explanatory and observational base. Any new cosmology (in particular a heliocentric one) would have to find some kind

---

[79]Newton, op. cit. 222.

of replacement physics. This is an outline of what, in the Aristotelian system, it would have to replace:

(i) Its Unifying Effect

The function of science is to explain and predict dissimilar facts from the same basic premises, postulates and laws. The laws of motion of (say) Galileo covered just a small area of dynamics – those of Aristotle covered biology, physics, chemistry and human enterprise.

(ii) The Size of the Earth

The Earth is of small size compared with the size of the universe, for more stars become visible as one travels the globe.

(iii) The Sub-lunar/ Super-lunar Distinction

As the Earth is so small, it is unreasonable to expect laws to apply all over the universe merely because they apply here. In point of fact we observe quite a different motion in objects above the Moon – compare, for example, the predictability of the motion and form of clouds as against that of the stars. On Earth 'accidents' may be observed to prevent objects pursuing their teleological paths. The heavens, in contrast, are predictable and unchanging. It therefore stands to reason that the heavenly bodies are made of an eternal aether, different from the materials on the Earth.

(iv) Motion

Super lunar motion cannot be vertical (like sub lunar) for if it were then stars could shoot off into infinity – and the universe (see below) is finite. Motion, therefore, must be for the heavenly bodies what we observe – circular. Natural sub-lunar motion is vertical. To make anything move in another direction (e.g. a Greek cart) requires a force. Projectiles might seem to be an exception to this rule, but, for example, an arrow whilst still being pushed by the bow creates a disturbance, a vortex in the air, which has the power to keep it moving. As this power gradually diminishes the projectile slows and so stops. (Note the power of air to move objects in hurricanes etc – there is no irrationality in assuming air can be a powerful motive force.)

(v) The Four Elements

Since change is observed in the world, it must be possible for motion to be transmitted. The basic elements of the world, must therefore also be capable of transmitting motion and receiving it – for motion can be impressed only from outside. What qualities can be *transmitted*? Not, for example, hardness or colour – but wet/dry and hot/cold. The binary combinations of these give the four Aristotelian elements: earth, air, fire, water. Left alone, these will sort themselves out into the natural order.

(vi) Vacuum

A vacuum is impossible because:

(a) it would presuppose a position for an object but not relative to anything else – in which case position and therefore motion become meaningless

(b) projectiles would be impossible as there would be nothing to keep them going

(c) since speed is proportional to the inverse of resistance, objects acted on by a moving force would arrive instantaneously (i.e. have infinite speed)

Since a vacuum is impossible atoms with specific *shape* can have no vacuum through which to move, and so are impossible.

(vii) Spherical Earth

The Earth is spherical because:

(a) we observe more stars as we traverse it

(b) it must be stable

(c) it is the natural shape (maximum volume in minimum surface area) assumed by an accretion of deposits of earth falling from all directions.

(d) It casts a circular shadow on the Moon during eclipses.

(viii) Finite Universe

The universe must be finite because:

(a) otherwise a line could be drawn of infinite length. If this were divided into two then we should have two lines each of infinite length but smaller than the first – which is absurd

(b) the Earth is at its centre point, and infinity has no centre

(c) the daily turning of a crystalline sphere of infinite size is inconceivable

(ix) Spherical Universe

The universe must be spherical because:

(a) the sphere is the perfect shape – to imagine protuberances in a finite universe is absurd

(b) super-lunary bodies travel in circles – a sphere is the logical shape for the whole

(x) Stationary Earth

The Earth must be stationary because:

(a) If we jump in the air friction will cease to act on our bodies. As there will be no force acting on us the Earth would spin by underneath and we would hit the wall.

(b) Common experience of an object placed on a spinning top is that it is flung off.

(c) If the Earth moves, its speed must be very large – which would imply that clouds etc move at enormous speed.

(d) Since there is no vacuum, if the Earth moves then friction will operate– which would make it very hot (the crystalline spheres are, of course, frictionless – but we know that the Earth is not).

(e) If the Earth moved then (i) the stars should increase and decrease in size (ii) there would 'of necessity be passings by and turnings of the fixed stars, but we find that none such appear' (i.e. no parallax). If it is countered that the stars are too far away to see this, then how come we can see them at all?

(f) The natural motion of Earth is vertical. To keep it rotating would need a large force – which would make it disintegrate.

(g) If the Earth did move then its motion would be vertical and we would be left behind – but in any case this is absurd since there can be no absolute up or down if the Earth is not central.

Imagine you are Copernicus facing all this. Scary isn't it?

Further Reading

There is no obvious overall book for this chapter though Olaf Pedersen's *Early Physics and Astronomy* (1974, 1993, CUP) may be useful. Hugh Thurston's *Early* Astronomy (1994) outlines the technical side. The Pre-

Socratics can be found in their own words in G. S. Kirk, J. E. Raven & M Schofield *The Presocratic Philosophers* (1957,1982: CUP). Books on Plato and Aristotle are myriad, and their primary works in translation easily available on the internet. I am not presently aware of any ideal book on Ptolemy, though Gerd Grasshoff's *The History of Ptolemy's Star Catalogue* (Springer-Verlag, 1990) is a fascinating perspective on how Ptolemy has been viewed through history. N.M. Swerdlow *Ancient Astronomy and Celestial Divination* (1999, MIT) is a useful compendium on early astronomy, whilst Allan Chapman's *Gods in the Sky* (2002, Channel 4) was made into a flamboyant TV series in 2003 and gives a distinctive slant on early astronomical issues. A book that focuses especially on the Greeks is *The History and Practice of Ancient Astronomy,* 1998) by James Evans; *The Eye of Heaven: Ptolemy, Copernicus, Kepler* (Masters of Modern Physics) by Owen Gingerich (1993) is also accurate and useful. Ptolemy's *Geography* and *Tetrabiblios* (on astrology) are available (the latter in a 2012 paperback or free download). The Almagest itself (if you feel up to it!) is available in an American edition (1998) by G. J. Toomer and Owen Gingerich. Finally there is the very expensive *Episodes From the Early History of Astronomy* by Asger Aaboe (2001).

3. Nicholas Copernicus

In 1543 two books were published which are regarded as heralding a new age in science. One was a lavishly illustrated book 'On the fabric of the human body' by Andreas Vesalius (1514–1564). The other was called 'Revolutions of the heavenly spheres' a book placed into the hands of its dying author in May of that year. That Author, Nicholas Copernicus (1473–1543) is the subject of this chapter.

The end of the fifth century saw the final disintegration of the Roman Empire. Christendom was divided into the Orthodox East (centred on Constantinople the city of Constantine), and Latin West (centred on Rome). In the West, Greek learning was largely lost. Scholars relied on works in Latin, some translated by the tragically martyred Boethius (c.480–524), which tended to focus largely on logic. Sadly, many of the best ideas of Plato and Aristotle (who differed so much but became the 'twin suns' of philosophy) were lost. Yet, astronomy still remained of interest for practical reasons. To the medieval scholars 'practical reasons' included astrology, the need to tell the time for monasteries to perform their offices, the setting of the date for Easter which was linked to the spring equinox, and navigation. Scholars like the Venerable Bede (c.673–735) and Alcuin of York (732–804) kept alive ancient learning, whilst individual rulers like Charlemagne (768–814) and Alfred the Great (849–899) encouraged such scholars. It is probably fair to say, however, that during this period any *development* in astronomy took place in the Islamic world – though we will not be covering this in this book. There were at least three translations of Ptolemy's *Almagest* into Arabic in the ninth century, as well as a translation of his *Planetary Hypothesis.* The astronomer Al-Farghānī (c.800–807) wrote a popular summary that was influential in later mediaeval Europe.

In 1085 Toledo was taken from the Islamic Moors by King Alfonso VI and became a centre for transmission of Islamic learning. This introduced some of the previously unknown works of Aristotle, and fostered a revival of interest in sciences. The University of Paris barred English students from about 1167, and Oxford was modelled on the University of Paris, with initial faculties of theology, law, medicine, and the liberal arts. Local difficulties also sometimes caused new universities; thus, for example, Cambridge was formed from Oxford in 1209 and Padua from Bologna in 1222. During the 13th century, the university system spread throughout Spain, France and Italy. During the 14th century cities north of the Alps like Prague and Crakow (1364) followed. Also during this period real science was carried on particularly in Oxford and Paris. In Oxford the massive learning of Richard Grosseteste was followed by Franciscans Roger Bacon (1220–1292), (who reputedly blew himself up in his cell whilst experimenting with gunpowder!) and William of Ockham (c.1285–1347) (famed for his razor) who did work on dynamics as well as chemistry. In France, Jean Buridan (c.1295–1358) and Nicole Oresme (c.1323–1382) did work on dynamics and theories of the Solar System.

Average Distances for Ptolemaic Systems (assumes 1 stade = 600ft)

	Ptolemy		**Al-Farghānī /Roger Bacon**		**Copernicus**
	min-max e.r.	***miles***	**min-max e.r.**	***miles***	**max e.r.**
Moon	33-64	*108-208th*	33-64	*109-209th*	<65
Mercury	64-166	*208-541th*	64-167	*208-543th*	<1695
Venus	167-1079	*541th-3.52m*	167-1120	*543th-3.64m*	<2020
Sun	1160-1260	*3.78-4.11m*	1120-1220	*3.64-3.97m*	1179
Mars	1260-8820	*4.11-28.73m*	1220-8876	*3.97-28.85m*	<3081
Jupiter	8820-14187	*28.73-46.22*	8876-14405	*28.85-46.82m*	<7412
Saturn	14187-19,865	*46.22-64.72m*	14405-20110	*46.82-65.36m*	<12252
Stars		*65.51m*	20110	*65.36m*	immense
e.r.		*3258*		*3250*	

The "e.r." means earth radiuses, earth radius was assumed to be about 3250 miles (the modern figure is about 3960). The max/min distances of celestial bodies from earth were known to vary greatly.

The Ptolemaic system, virtually unchanged, became the standard model in Europe. Since the system is simply viewed from the Earth the order in which planets are 'nested' is to some extent arbitrary, but in practice the order and magnitudes tended to follow Ptolemy. Compare, for example,

Ptolemy with Al-Farghānī and the virtually identical Roger Bacon's *Opus Maius* (1266).[80]

We will look later at the effect of the Copernican system on distances, but should note that they did not think the universe 'small' . Think of the average 13th century person imagining 65 million miles. We will look later in more detail in ideas in institutions more immediate to Copernicus.

The late 15th century, however, saw the rise of Christian humanism, of which the leader and greatest star was Desiderius Erasmus (c.1469–1536). Christian humanism was an assertion of the value of human life and culture, but without any denial of the reality of God and the need for salvation. It was a mixed blessing for science. It encouraged the acceptance and value of secular learning, but it tended to focus on literature, and could also tend to magnify the work of the ancients (Plato, Aristotle, Ptolemy, Galen etc.) to the detriment of empirical science.

Myths

There are a number of myths about the mediaeval period. One is that medieval scholars thought the world was flat (one version of this myth having this belief continue until Columbus!) Scholars, of course, had known from the times of the Greeks that the Earth was roughly spherical and was small in relation to the universe. A second is that the church was somehow repressive of ideas, and science was persecuted on dogmatic grounds. Generally this was not true. Augustine (354–430) came to dominate Western theology, and although he generally advocated persecution of non-Catholics he was insistent that science should be empirically based and not tied in with dogma. Grosseteste was likewise adamant, whilst Oresme as a Master in Paris and then Bishop of Lisieux saw no problem in speculating that the planets might be centred on the Sun in his famous *Livre du ciel et du monde*.[81] The church may have incidentally fostered disinterest by focussing on theology and logic rather than science, but there was no air of fear that scientific speculation was dangerous.

---

[80] These are my estimates, largely based on Albert Van Helden's *Measuring the Universe* (1985).

[81] *Reason, Science and Faith*, Paul Marston & Roger Forster, ch. 9.

In 1517 Martin Luther (who had studied in the universities of Leipzig and Wittenberg) nailed his 95 theses to the door of the castle church in Wittenberg. Many of the criticisms had already been made by Erasmus, and Luther initially had no idea of forming a separate church. It led, however, to the Protestant Reformation, which saw Western Europe divided into three basic groups. The Protestants formed their own state churches, often persecuting non-conformists and Catholics as ruthlessly as some of the Catholics had done. The Catholics continued to be ruled from Rome, again fostering state churches, but began their own 'Counter-Reformation' with various orders culminating in the Jesuits as an educational order in 1540. The Catholic Counter-Reformation Council of Trent (1545–63) came after Copernicus's death. The third group, who feature little in the present study, were the 'anabaptists' ,who eschewed both state churches and persecution. To them the 'Church' was a voluntary body of freely associating believers.

Martin Luther

Copernicus's Life

The quaint town of Torun (Thorn) on the River Vistula was over 200 years old when Copernicus was born there on 19th February 1473. It was on the border between the Duchy of Prussia and Poland, a walled town with watch towers, founded by the Teutonic Knights who were often in conflict with Poland. The River was an

Torun today: Vistula and Cathedral

Torun (Thorn) from an old print

important trade route at that time (the Vistula going down to what is now the port of Gdansk) and Nicholas was the youngest of four children born to a merchant – who died when Nicholas was ten. The family was soon adopted by their mother's younger brother, Lucas Waczenrode. Uncle Lucas had studied at Cracow and Bologna, and was Canon of Frauenburg (Frombork) when he adopted Nicholas. In 1489 he became Bishop of Ermland, a small area surrounded by the lands of the Teutonic Knights. Copernicus showed some interest in astronomy whilst still at school, but went in 1491 to study at the University of Cracow – a major centre for European learning, which had especial links with Italy. Copernicus stayed four years and studied: Euclid, philosophy, astronomy, astrology, geography, and disputatious method (in Latin). Cracow was famous for its astronomy, and Copernicus met two renowned astronomers Wojciech of Brudsew (Brudzewski) who was critical of many aspects of Ptolemy[82] and Jan of Glogow. He also began to collect books on astronomy.

Copernicus's statue Cracow

After a brief recall to Frauenburg, Copernicus went to Bologna, one of Europe's oldest universities and the place where uncle Lucas had studied law. Italy was then the centre of Greek Humanist study. Bologna was under a Seigniory independent of Venice and the Papal States, Giovanni II patronising arts and sciences.

It had strong student tradition (it still does!) and was governed by the students who elected a Rector every two years. Study took place between 7–9 a.m. and for two and a half hours in the afternoon. The code for lecturers was as follows:

Archiginnasio today – erected 1563 on the site of previous academic sites

[82] See Armitage, 58.

> A teacher had to swear to obey the Rector or be deprived of the right to teach at all. He was fined if he fell behind schedule in the course of his lectures, or if he left anything out, or if he was late in starting his lecture or went on speaking too long. He was also fined if attendance at his classes fell below a certain number. He must not take a day's leave without special permission from the Rector and students … If he married, his honeymoon was limited to one day.[83]

Nicholas was supposed to study Canon Law, but actually studied everything! He started in autumn 1496, enrolling in the German (not the Polish) 'nation' or student faculty – as had his uncle Lucas (perhaps the beer was better). Bologna had a long tradition in astronomy going back at least to Guido Bonati who referred to Ptolemy's work in the late 12th century. Dante Alighieri got his own astronomical knowledge from the same source in 1287 – though he placed Bonati amongst magicians, soothsayers and astrologers who slowly proceeded backwards:

> … along the hollow vale … so that the countenance was from the reins averted; and because none might before him look, they were compell'd to advance with backward gait.

Bonati and later figures laid down possible uses for a horoscope, and rulers in general extended patronage because astrology was thought a useful art. In 1334 astrology became the ninth salaried discipline under a reshaped funding from the municipality. The oldest statutes of the *Universita degli Artisti* we have are from 1405, and their detailed astrology/astronomy programme states this:

Mediaeval housing in Bologna today

> During the first year of the astronomy course the Algorismi de minutis et integris are read, after which the first book of Euclid's geometry is read, with the commentary of Campanus. When this latter is read the Tabulae Alphonsinae with the Canons is read.

[83] From Armitage, 63.

> After which the Theorica Planetarum is read. During the second year the Tractatus de Sphera is read for first, after which the Canons for the use of the geometric tables are read. Once these are read the treatise on the astrolabe of Messehallah is read. During the third year Alcabitius is read for first, after which the Centiloquium of Ptolemy with the commentary by Haly is read. After which the third book of Geometry is read, after which the Tractatus Quadrantis is read. During the fourth year all the Quadripatitus is read for first, after which the book De urina non visa [on urines unseen] is read. After which the third edition of the Almagest is read.

The study began with a classic book on calculations (algorithms), and of Euclid. The first year astronomy included the Alphonsine Tables codified in the *Canons* of John of Saxony in 1370. The second year tractate on the spheres was probably that written by the Englishman Johannes de Sacrobosco[84] as a summary of Ptolemaic and Arabic astronomy and perhaps the first such written by a western author. The version used could have been that written by the first lecturer at Bologna on Astronomy Bartholomeaus de Parma in the late 12th century *Tractatus Spherae,* though more probably was that of Cesco d'Alscoli who wrote a commentary for Bologna students in 1322. Also in the second year was Jean de Lihnieres' *Canons* produced in Paris in 1321, and known in Bologna from 1344 when Astrology became a salaried discipline. The treatise on the astrolabe dated from the early ninth century and was translated from Arabic by Johannes de Luna in 1153. The third year study included a treatise on the quadrant – probably from Montpellier by Robertus Anglicus in 1274. In the fourth year the third section of the *Almagest* dealt with the motion of the Sun along the ecliptic, the length of the seasons and variations in lengths of days and nights. The other works were astrological. Firstly, *Alcibitius* was a mid-tenth century work translated from Arabic again by Johannes de Luna and usually including a 15th century commentary by John of Saxony. The *Centriloqium* and *Quadripartitum* date from Ptolemy. Finally, the insertion of a study on the astrological approach to unseen urines[85] is rare in a modern

[84] Apparently a literal translation of 'John of Holywood', though film rights are unlikely.

[85] This was a study written in Marseilles in 1219 by Guilielmus Anglicus to help physicians in dealing with a distant patient whose urine could not be examined. The Sorbonne condemned it as a work of black magic in 1494.

astronomy course (!) and indicates that the target group were actually *Artisti* or medics!

This shows the rich inter-European background in the subject which was available at Bologna. Astrology actually had its critics. Around 1260, for example, the friar Gionanniv Schio de Vincenza had been a vigorous opponent. In the 15th century the Humanistic swing was against ideas of fortune and towards ideas of human choice and virtue. Human destinies were not an inevitable result of fate as read in the stars, but of human reaction to circumstances. This attitude is reflected in Johannes Pontanus's later 15th century commentary on Ptolemy's *Centriloqium*. Nicolo Leoniceno (1428–1524) publicly expressed doubts on the value of medical astrology. A papal bull in 1586 actually condemned judicious astrology, and Pico della Mirandola around 1494 wrote *Disputationes adversus astrologium divinatricem* highlighting the contradictions in astrology as well as criticising it on general philosophical grounds.

This, then, was the atmosphere into which the young Nicholas Copernicus came. The ideas of heliocentricism were well known in Italian scholarly circles, and the thought of Nicholas of Cusa (1401–1464) was well known throughout central Europe including in Cracow from which Copernicus had come. He was a truly Renaissance scholar, a Cardinal learned in theology, mathematical and experimental sciences and philosophy.

Copernicus began a friendship with the professor of astronomy Dominico Maria Novara, became a paying guest at his house, and effectively became a kind of assistant. Novara was also professor of astrology, which assumes a central Earth, though we have no indication of when Copernicus's change of mind began. Novarro criticised Ptolemy over a presumed shift in the axis of terrestrial rotation which Novarro put forward to explain differences in latitude of some Mediterranean cities in his time as against the time of Ptolemy. Nicholas also studied Greek, and may have come across Archimedes' work *Arenarius* in which Aristarchus's heliocentric system is described. In his 1543 book, Nicholas mentioned measurements made with Novarro of a lunar occultation[86] in 1497 and a conjunction of Saturn and

[86] An occultation is the hiding of one celestial body by another interposed between it and the observer, as the hiding of stars and planets by the Moon.

the Moon[87] of 1500. Lunar parallax[88] may have affected his thinking. Navarro's neo-Platonism may also have influenced him.

In 1498 Nicholas was joined by brother Andreas. Student funds were (as ever) insufficient, and at one point in 1499 (if I may put it in terms many of us may find familiar!) the young students Nick and Andy ran out of money, and uncle Lucas came to the rescue. They left in September 1500, going to Rome and recording a lunar eclipse on the sixth of November. It was the year celebrating the 1500th anniversary of Christendom – the Pope (Alexander VI) being one of the charming Borgia family. Rheticus claimed that Nicholas lectured on astronomy in Rome to large audiences, but we have no independent proof of this.

They returned to Frauenburg and Nicholas was installed as a Canon, but was then given leave to go to Padua to study Canon Law and medicine, for which Padua was renowned.

Padua was a part of the Venetian Empire, where scholars had considerable freedom and prestige. Astronomy was highly regarded, the clock on St Mark's Square in Venice (completed 1499) has zodiac signs, and in the main Senate Chamber are huge astronomical clocks.

St Marks Square Venice

Clock in St Marks Square

[87] A conjunction is when two celestial bodies have the same apparent geocentric longtitude.

[88] Parallax is described later in these notes.

Nicholas achieved some fame as a doctor (later attending his uncle). Here is one of his remedies:

> Take two ounces of Armenian clay, a half ounce of cinnamon, two drachms of tormentil root, dittany, red sandalwood, a drachm of ivory and iron shavings, two scruples of ash and rust, one drachm each of lemon peel and pearls; add one scruple each of emerald, red hyacinth and sapphire; one drachm of bone from a deer's heart; sea locusts, horn of a unicorn, red coral, gold and silver foil – all one scruple each; then add half a pound of sugar, or the quantity one usually buys for one Hungarian ducat's worth.

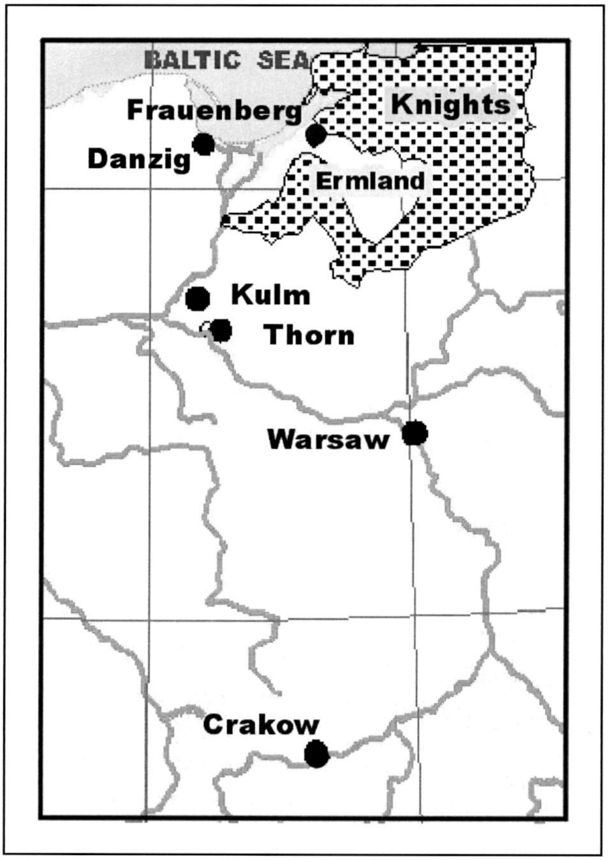

I wonder if it worked if one couldn't find a unicorn! All fairly conservative stuff.

In 1503 (aged thirty) Nicholas graduated from nearby Ferrara University rather than Padua (we don't know why, perhaps it was less expensive) and returned to Poland where he lived the rest of his life.

Nicholas became a kind of personal assistant and doctor to his uncle, and spent the next few years busy in administration.

He published in 1509 a Latin translation of the Greek epistles of the 7th century Byzantine historian Theophylactus Simonatta. This was the golden age of humanism, before the problems of the Reformation – but Copernicus picked a work which was 'safe' (i.e. from Christian Byzantium) although Greek.

He also may have written around this time (perhaps 1515) a short resumé of his heliocentric ideas and their motivation. This work (then called the *Commentariolus*), was later circulated in manuscript form.

Uncle Lucas died in 1512, and his brother Andreas was forced to leave because he had 'lepra' (probably syphilis). Nicholas was invited by Pope Leo X to join a distinguished group of scholars in making needed adjustments to the calendar, which had accumulated because the solar year is actually 365.25 days not 365. He was urged by fellow Canon Sculteti (the domestic chaplain to the Pope) to come, but declined on the grounds that the problems of the calendar could only really be solved when the motions of the Sun, Moon and stars were solved.

In the next few years there was conflict between Poland and the Knights, with Nicholas playing an active role on the Polish side and being besieged

Frauenburg from an old print

in Olsyrn castle from 1516–19.

After 1520 he was involved only in quieter administration duties in Frauenburg – and had time for his astronomical work. His friend Tiedemann Giese (a fellow cleric in Frauenburg from about 1505) wrote a book in 1525 pleading for Catholic–Protestant toleration and saying Copernicus agreed with him. From 1538 Giese became bishop of Kulm and Dantiscus bishop of Ermland. Dantiscus had been a man of affairs, a Humanist scholar and priest who doted on his illegitimate daughter. He seems to have sent Copernicus a couple of invites but received negative replies which Koestler calls 'pathetic' and 'in the style of an obsequious clerk'.[89] During the Counter-Reformation, as the Catholic Church responded with measures of reform to the Protestant challenge, a cleric keeping a 'focaria' (a kind of housekeeper with some extra duties) was frowned on. Dantiscus seems to have mostly gone through Giese to make Nicholas get rid of his, the pretty and apparently astronomically informed Anna Schilling. Some books try to make it a 'persecution' issue, though it was certainly not because of Copernicus astronomical views. Repcheck goes the other way and suggests that Copernicus was a 'womaniser' because of his relationship with this one mistress.

Nicholas did not record many observations (some 30 or so are recorded), and did not publish. His *Commentariolus* was known to some, however, and in 1533 the papal secretary (John Widmanstad) gave an exposition of Copernicus' heliocentric ideas in the Vatican Gardens before the Pope Clement VII and some Cardinals. In 1536 Cardinal Nicholas von Schonberg (whose secretary Widmanstad had become) wrote to Copernicus begging him to publish details of his system. There is no record of a reply, but Copernicus kept the letter and quoted it in his book in 1543.

In 1539 one George Joachim Rheticus arrived with presents of three important scientific books for Copernicus. He was a young and rising professor of Mathematics at the recently founded Protestant University of Wittenberg – the very centre of the Lutheran 'heresy'. He arrived shortly after an edict from the bishop (backed by the Polish king) banning all Protestants from the area. He remained there from 1539–41, and in 1540 published the 'First Account' *(Narratio Prima)* which outlined the

[89] Arthur Koestler, *The Sleepwalkers* (1959, 1986), 182.

Copernican system as taught by 'my teacher'. The title does identify 'my teacher' as Copernicus, though Rheticus omitted his own name.

Perhaps after some hesitation, Rheticus was eventually entrusted with the publication of the full manuscript although (outrageously) his name was omitted from the 'credits'. The actual printing was entrusted to the printing house of Johannes Petrius in Nuremberg – 200 miles south of Leipzig where Rheticus had taken up a new post with the recommendation of Melancthon.

Copernicus' ideas faced two obvious possible sources of opposition. Firstly, there could be theological objection. Rheticus himself composed in 1541 a treatise explaining how the system was not contrary to Scripture. The Bible is not to teach cosmology but things 'necessary for our salvation'. The language it uses is 'accommodated to the popular understanding'.[90] John Calvin took virtually the same approach, and it was common amongst leading Protestants (as we will see later). The Catholic Bishop Guise wanted an edition of *Revolutions* with Rheticus's work as a preface, and at this time the Catholic Church had no formulated view on it – so Copernicus was able to dedicate it to the Pope.

More serious was the opposition of natural philosophers who would regard it as absurd – as indeed it was to all common sense. In Nuremberg there was a leading Protestant Minister, Andreas Osiander, who was also interested in astronomy. Around this time he was in correspondence with both Rheticus and Copernicus. To the latter he wrote:

> I have always felt about hypotheses that they are not articles of faith but the basis of computation. Thus, even if they are false, it does not matter, provided that they reproduce exactly the phenomena of the motions … it would therefore be desirable for you to touch upon this matter somewhere in an introduction. For in this way you would mollify the peripatetics (Aristotelian natural philosophers) and theologians whose opposition you fear.[91]

---

[90] This was printed with translation in R Hooykaas' *G. J. Rheticus Treatise on the Holy Scripture and Motion of the Earth* (1984).

[91] Quoted in Rosen *Copernicus and the Scientific Revolution*, 192.

This was an old tradition of 'saving the appearances' – subjecting them to mathematical systems without worrying if these were true or not. Plainly neither Copernicus nor Rheticus took this view – their works made this plain. Yet when the hefty volume eventually appeared, *The Revolutions of the Heavenly Sphered* contained an *Ad lectorum,* an anonymous preface giving exactly these 'saving the appearances' ideas.

Did Copernicus know that this *Ad lectorum* was going in? Giese wrote to Rheticus describing the deathbed scene of Copernicus where: 'He had lost his memory and mental vigour many days before; and he saw his completed work only at his last breath upon the day that he died'. The author of the preface was unknown, though the printer asserted that it had come to him with the rest of the material. Years later Osiander (who had been a proof-reader of the printing) admitted that he had submitted it as his own idea, so it seems unlikely that Copernicus approved it. Rheticus and Giese were both furious, Rheticus crossed it out with thick red crayon in any copy he possessed or sent out!

Copernicus's Character

The character of Copernicus is paradoxical. By nature he was conservative, and his prime motivation for his system was that the equants broke the approved rational (Greek) cannons of circular motion. Yet he was putting forward a radical system that defied all common sense as well as the most established ideas of natural philosophy (i.e. science). He was a scholar in the age of humanism, the celebration of human knowledge and culture, when Reformed and Anabaptist leaders were wanting to see more knowledge disseminated to the public. Yet in the introduction to his major work he explicitly espoused a neo-Pythagorean idea of knowledge, in which a scholar would pass on high knowledge to selected few disciples, not making it generally known because the masses would not appreciate it and would only mock. With a theory as 'absurd' as supposing that the Earth moved, perhaps his fears of mockery were well founded!

Sometimes he is presented as a bold lion of science, a revolutionary figure bravely facing the possibility of persecution and ignorance of bigots, e.g.:

> … at last the problem was taken up by a man of thoroughly unprejudiced mind and with a clear mathematical head … it is certain enough that Copernicus owed very little if anything to the

> ancients (Dreyer, 1906).
>
> Copernicus … was increasingly left to himself in his declining years. Another reason for this isolation was, of course, the novelty of his opinions concerning the Solar System … The whole story of the man speaks to us of his independence of mind and self-reliant tenacity of purpose (Armitage, 1938).
>
> … he is symbolic of scientific courage evidenced by his opposition to traditional authority and dogma (Soldaczuk, Ed Beer, 1975).

Compare this with the following when in his preface to the Pope in his 1543 book Copernicus explains:

> I may well presume, most Holy Father, that certain people, on learning that in this my book On the Revolutions of the Heavenly Spheres I ascribe certain movements to the Earth, will cry out that holding such views I should at once be hissed off the stage … Therefore I have doubted for a long time whether I should publish these reflections written to prove the Earth's motion, or whether it would be better to follow the example of the Pythagoreans and others who were wont to impart philosophic mysteries only to intimates and friends, and then not in writing but by word of mouth, as the letter of Lysis to Hipparchus witnesses.

The quotation is from the (forged) letter of Lysis to Hipparchus – a neo-Pythagorean work:

> After the death of Pythagoras … it remains our sacred duty to remember the divine teaching of our master and not to divulge the treasures of philosophy to those who have not undergone the preliminary purification of the mind. For it is not proper to divulge to all and sundry what we have learned with such great effort … It is as though one were to pour clean fresh water into a well filled with dirt – for the dirt will only get agitated and the water will be wasted … Thick and dark forests cover the minds and hearts of those who have not been initiated in the proper manner, and disturb the mild contemplation of ideas … Many tell me that you teach philosophy in public, which was forbidden by Pythagoras …

There no evidence that Copernicus felt under any threat from ecclesiastical authorities, from which he experienced nothing but encouragement.[92] His fear was of common ridicule – the kind for which the famous have been targeted throughout history and still are by modern comics and satirists.

Koestler's famous picture of 'the timid Canon' may contain more truth than the 'lion of science' image. Yet, of course in *scientific terms,* rather than in terms of some mythical fear of religious persecution, the system was bold to the point of absurdity. No wonder he was reluctant to open it to the public gaze.

Rheticus, his only student, may have seemed to him the kind of disciple to whom one could confide. Yet, of course, he was well aware that Rheticus took a Humanist and not a Pythagorean, view of science, and would certainly publicise the system.

Did it make sense to believe Copernicus?

In my lecture course I usually 'demonstrate' to students that the Earth cannot move – without even having to leave the room. You can try it yourself:

1. *Does it rotate?* Stand up. Now jump in the air. As the friction no longer operates on your feet, the Earth should whizz by you underneath. It doesn't – so the Earth doesn't rotate.

2. *Does it rotate?* Imagine a top or an old-fashioned gramophone turntable. Put an object on it and start the rotation. What happens? If the object is not stuck on then it will fly off. Surely if the Earth rotated then it would fling us off into space?

3. *Does it orbit?* Imagine that the Earth orbits the Sun. Looking at two stars unequal distances away at the opposite points of the Earth's orbit will have the following effect:

---

[92] The 2001 Institute of Physics/IEE official textbook for A level, *Advancing Physics A2* says: 'In the 16th century the monk Copernicus upset a lot of people with a book. The Catholic Church had adopted a geocentric model. So Copernicus's book was unpopular especially among church people, and eventually his book was banned …' 'Giordano Bruno got into serious trouble with the Catholic Church over this question … He was handed over … and burnt at the stake. Copernicus was right to be cautious.' Virtually none of this is true. Vollman (2006) repeats the same kind of nonsense though more incoherently.

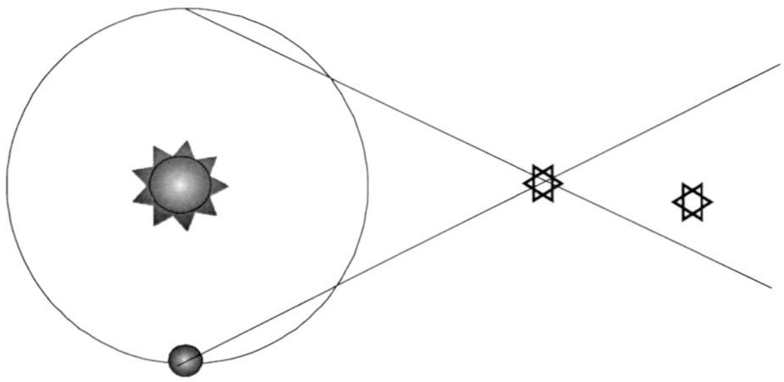

> From one viewing point the nearer star would be on the right of the other, and from the other viewing point on the left. In other words, stars should move relative to each other as the Earth orbits – and no such movement is detectable. In Copernicus's day the limits of naked eye accuracy were about 5 minutes of arc. The stars would therefore have to be over 1000 times the distance of the Sun and 100 times the distance of Saturn. If they are so far away from the Earth then how is it that we can see them at all?

Now we may have physics (if people know it) to answer these issues, but in Copernicus's day there really was none.

Summary of Copernicus's Works

The mathematics involved in Copernicus's theories is complex, and you can obtain the full English translation if you want! The following is a summary of main ideas in the successive works:

Commentariolus (unpublished manuscript privately circulated)

Copernicus states his motives as wanting to get rid of equants and to make the calculations simpler.

He states his assumptions:

- There is no one centre of all the celestial circles or spheres.
- The centre of the Earth is not the centre of the universe, but only of gravity and of the lunar sphere.
- All the spheres revolve about the Sun as their mid-point and therefore the Sun is the centre of the universe.
- The ratio of the Earth's distance from the Sun to the height of the firmament is so much smaller than the ratio of the Earth's radius to its distance from the Sun that the distance from the Earth to the

Sun is imperceptible in comparison with the height of the firmament.

- Whatever motion appears in the firmament arises not from any motion of the firmament but from the Earth's motion.
- What appear to us as motions of the Sun arise not from its motion but from the motion of the Earth and our sphere with which we revolve about the Sun like any other planet. The Earth, then, has more than one motion.
- The apparent retrograde and direct motion of the planets arises not from their motion but from the Earth's.

Narratio Prima

This begins by emphasising respect for ancients – only about one third of the way through do we discover it is a heliocentric system!

According to Koestler, Rheticus gives the number of epicycles here as in Commentariolus (34 or 38). The Ptolemaic system of Peurbach used 40, and Copernicus's *Revolutions* 48.

Rheticus explains why the new system is better:

- The precession of the equinoxes and diminution of the eccentricity of the Sun are better explained (Rheticus does not say why – though the precession would be hard to explain with a static Earth).
- 'The planets evidently have the centres of their deferents in the Sun, as the centre of the universe …' (this is not true of this system). Also it explained the varying brightness of Mars (so did Ptolemy).
- 'My teacher saw that only on this theory could all the circles in the universe be made to revolve uniformly and regularly about their own centres, and not about other centres – an essential property of circular motion' (i.e. no equants).
- The Ptolemaic systems did not make 'the order and motions of the heavenly spheres agree in an absolute system' (?)

- There is some Neoplatonic[93] enthusing about the place of the Sun, and Rheticus says that if Ptolemy and Aristotle could now come back they would agree with Copernicus.
- He notes the absence of parallax so that the sphere of the stars is 'similar to the infinite'.
- Rheticus notes that the system gives a unique order for the planets; 'in addition the large spheres revolve more slowly and, as is proper, those that are nearer the Sun which may be said to be the source of motion and light, revolve more swiftly …'

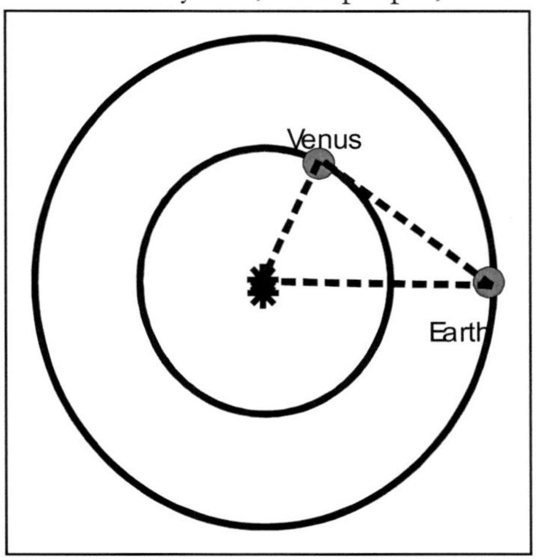

The planets were not only in a unique order but Copernicus could determine their distances relative to the Earth–Sun distance. The procedure for Venus is shown in the diagram. Taking the point at which Venus was at the greatest angle away from the Sun, a simple use of trigonometry gives the ratio of the Earth distance and Venus distance from the Sun using that angle. A similar use of geometry gives relative distances for planets outside our Earth's orbit.

Revolutions of the Heavenly Spheres (1543)

- The book begins with a general treatment and physical defence of his system.
- The universe is spherical either because 'that figure is the most perfect' ,or 'all things tend to assume this shape' .

93 In Plato himself, of course, the Sun was the symbol of The Good. Neoplatonic thinking involved what was 'fitting'. This may seem foreign to us, though major modern physicists refer sometimes to the beauty of their theories.

- The Earth is also spherical because on all sides it tends towards the centre.
- The Earth is primarily earth with some water.
- The motion of the heavenly bodies is circular because: 'Rotation is natural to a sphere and by that very act is its shape expressed … the irregularities themselves are subject to a definite law and recur at stated times, and this could not happen if the motions were not circular …' – nonsense!
- Since the Earth is spherical: 'we now consider whether her motion is conformable to her shape and her position in the universe …' (i.e. it is natural for a sphere to rotate).
- Copernicus notes that one observes only relative motion – cites various authorities who believed in a rotating Earth and asks why it should not move as well (as Philolaus taught).

Copernicus answers some of the traditional objections, as follows:

(A) THE EARTH'S ROTATION

(a) Argument: Centrifugal forces would make it disintegrate.

Counter: This would apply *a fortiori* to any sphere if it existed as it would be so much larger and in any case the natural motion for a sphere was rotation – no force is needed to keep it going and no violent force is involved.

(b) Argument: If it rotated then a strong east wind would occur and cannon balls should fly further in one direction than another.

Counter: Since rotation is natural the air shares it.

(B) THE EARTH'S MOVEMENT

(a) Argument: The Earth must have been formed by a collection of deposits of 'earth' whose natural motion is vertical.

Counter: The Earth's formation is explained by the tendency of all matter to form spheres i.e. gravity (not conceived of as a force but a tendency to form spheres) is localised.

(b) Argument: Falling bodies would be left behind by a moving Earth.

Counter: Falling bodies have an affinity to follow it because they share its nature (not, note, because they share its momentum).

(c) Argument: Aristotle said each elementary body had only one single natural movement – Copernicus gave the Earth three.

Counter: none!

(d) Argument: Stellar parallax should occur if the Earth moves.

Counter: The stellar sphere is too far away for this to notice.

Measurements of Parallax Through History:

Ptolemy had said the Earth was like a fixed point compared with the distances to the stars since no parallax was observed as people moved about the Earth.

In **Copernicus's** day the limits of naked eye accuracy were about 5 minutes of arc. Therefore the stars would have to be over 1000 × distance of the Sun from the Earth, and 100 × distance of Saturn (the furthest known planet – it is actually an average of 9,539 × that of the Earth from the Sun) from the Earth. Since the Earth's orbit was believed to be about 1200 times the size of the Earth, a Copernican system required the stars to be this much further away than previously thought.

Tycho Brahe had accuracy to much higher levels, and the continued absence of observed stellar parallax would imply on early estimates of his accuracy distances of 7000 × distance of Sun or 700 × distance of Saturn.

Bradley (in the 1730s) discovered stellar aberration (caused by finite velocity of light reaching a moving Earth) but in 1742 failed to find parallax with accuracies up to a few seconds of arc. This would imply stars 100,000 × distance of Sun or 10000 × distance of Saturn from the Earth.

F W Struve in 1837 was first to publish details of observed stellar parallax. The largest was for α Centuri, 1 second of arc, implying a distance of 200,000 × Sun.

The Foucault pendulum was introduced in 1851 to show the rotation of the Earth.

This 'proves' the movement of the Earth, doesn't it?

Some Myths

Myth 1: 'Copernicus invented a new idea'.

Actually, Aristotle had considered Sun-centred systems and refuted them – they were well known. Hoskin, in *The Cambridge Illustrated History of Astronomy* points out that Albert of Saxony (sometime Rector of Paris in the 1350s) had summarised heliocentric ideas (and why they were improbable) in his *Questions* which were reprinted six times during Copernicus's lifetime. Copernicus deleted from early in his manuscript a reference to Aristarchus, one of the best known ancient heliocentrists.

Myth 2: 'Copernicus's system was simpler and more accurate'.

Michael Hoskin notes on page 93 of his illustrated history:

> Modern legend has it that by the 16th century, the Ptolemaic models had been elaborated in a desperate search for greater accuracy, to the point where the number of circles required was beyond all reason. The legend goes on to claim that on the Sun-centred hypothesis the number of circles was greatly reduced and that the motion of the Earth was considered an acceptable price to pay for this simplification. In this legend there is no truth. Copernicus's detailed models are every bit as complicated as Ptolemy's.[94]

The Copernican system was *not*:

(a) More simple.

(b) More accurate or a better forecaster.

(c) A strictly Sun-centred system.

(d) Much of a replacement physics.

It *did*:

(a) Abolish the dreaded equants – arguably a backwards step in view of Kepler's later system which *abandoned* constant angular velocity! It did so by introducing extra epicyclets – though this could also have been used to rescue the Ptolemaic system.

---

[94] Gingerich's *The Great Copernicus Chase* makes a similar point.

(b) Remove the need for major epicycles.

(c) On the recognition that planetary paths were approximately circular, explain why Mercury and Venus stayed close to the Sun and give a unique order and relative orbit size for planets.

Actually, Copernicus's own main motivation may have been more aesthetic and Neoplatonic – in the middle sits the Sun enthroned!

Myth 3: 'No one read the book'.

Koestler, in particular, fostered this notion, heading a section, 'The Book That Nobody Read'. Actually this has been shown by Owen Gingerich[95] to be seriously mistaken. It was not intended as a popular 'best seller', but major European astronomers *did* read it (and left copious notes in the margins of their copies). There was no strong 'school' of support, but Copernicus's ideas became well known, the mathematics was widely admired, and there were various important full or nearly Copernicans.

Myth 4: 'Protestants and Catholics regarded the system as heretical, and its advocates feared persecution'.

John Donne (who wrote ''tis all in pieces etc.') is often cited to show how devastating people felt the theory was – and we today somehow feel that they *ought* to have felt threatened. In practice, it appeared to them less important than we might think.

Yet the 'religious opposition' myth is one of the most common even today. Thus, for example, the renowned Patrick Moore (in *The Great Astronomical Revolution* (83) cites Luther's 'onslaught', Melancthon as saying it is 'absurd', and adds; 'Calvin was another critic'. In footnote 92 above we noted the historically misinformed A-level textbook published under eminent imprimaturs!

Much of these still common myths may come originally from Andrew D. White's great diatribe against religion – *A History of the Warfare of Science with Theology in Christendom* (1896). This influential book bears the

---

95 Owen Gingerich: *The Eye of Heaven* (1997). In his *The Book Nobody Read* (2004) he charts his compilation of the 400-page reference book in 2002 – *An Annotated Census of Copernicus' De Revolutionibus*. This describes the annotations on the six hundred extant copies of the work.

appearance of scholarship but is littered with inaccurate and simply wrong 'facts'. Having claimed that Copernicus feared Catholic persecution even in Ermland, White continues:

> All branches of the Protestant Church – Lutheran, Calvinist, Anglican – vied with each other in denouncing the Copernican doctrine as contrary to Scripture; and at a later period the Puritans showed the same tendency (126).

Technically this could be described as 'poppycock', as we may now briefly explore. White first quotes Luther's remark about 'this fool who wishes to revise the entire science of astronomy'. In fact, this comment of Luther was reported in a book of after-dinner conversations decades later (after Luther's death) – none of Luther's voluminous published works mention the issue. Luther tended to biblical literalism, was generally rude, and probably said it after a good dinner and some wine – but he had no anti-Copernican crusade in mind.

White then quotes Melancthon in his general objections to the theory and adds: 'he suggests severe methods to restrain such impious teachings as those of Copernicus'. White does not explain Melancthon's continued support and patronage for Rheticus who was the foremost advocate of Copernicanism in the world, but tells us that though Rheticus and Rheinhold became Copernicans 'neither was allowed to tell it to his students'. In reality Melancthon thought it absurd rather than heretical, and did write to a correspondent in 1541, just after Rheticus came back and was promoted: 'Many hold it an excellent idea to praise such an absurd matter like that sarmatic (i.e. Polish) astronomer who moves the Earth and lets the Sun stand still'. Danielson notes this but also Melancthon's continuing generous patronage of Rheticus.[96] There is no evidence that Rheticus felt compelled to 'keep it quiet'.

Then White turns to the Reformed church:

> Calvin took the lead, in his commentary on Genesis, by condemning all those who asserted that the Earth is not the centre of the universe. He clinched the matter by the usual

---

[96]*The First Copernican,* 91ff. He also makes clear the real position of Rheticus and Rheinhold as lecturers.

> reference to the first verse of the ninety third Psalm and asked 'Who will venture to place the authority of Copernicus above Holy Scripture?'

This is simply made up. There is no such reference in Calvin's commentary on Genesis, and he nowhere mentions Copernicus. What Calvin does say in his commentary on Genesis is:

> He who would learn astronomy, and other recondite arts, let him go elsewhere. Here the Spirit of God would teach all men without exception; and therefore what Gregory declares falsely and in vain respecting statues and pictures is truly applicable to the history of the creation, namely, that it is the book of the unlearned.[97]

Calvin goes on to exemplify this in that the Bible calls the Sun and Moon 'lights' because that is what they appear to us – even though we now know that the Moon is really giving *reflected* light. Genesis speaks the language of appearances. It would be tedious to wander through White's equally inaccurate attacks on the Anglicans and Puritans. Even poor John Wesley (the Anglican founder of my own Free Methodist church) is claimed by White to have said that the new ideas 'tended towards infidelity'. Actually, in his work *A Survey of the Wisdom of God in the Creation* Wesley correctly outlines the history of Copernicus, Tycho, etc, and concludes that Newton:

> … found out the true system of the universe, and confirmed the Copernican system. He demonstrated by unanswerable arguments, that it could not possibly be otherwise, without the utter subversion of all the laws of nature (V.i).

There are other wrong statements White makes on other astronomers, which are still reflected today in the 'persecution' myths, but enough has been said to illustrate why similar myths are still too frequent amongst those today who do not bother to check their facts – and not just to the late and rightly respected Patrick Moore.

---

97 The printed versions have this, or it has been available on http://www.ccel.org/ccel/calvin/calcom01.pdf My friend the late Professor Colin Russell in the OU book Unit 16: *The Copernican Revolution*, 15, exploded these myths in 1972, and more recent work confirms his line of approach.

There is no denying the crimes of state-enforced churches, and the 16th–17th centuries were *religiously* intolerant times – but *scientific* theories were seldom if ever a basis for persecution, and 'natural philosophers' (as scientists were called) were generally venerated. Figures like Rheticus and Kepler, committed Protestants, both received protection and patronage from powerful Catholics – their fame in natural philosophy (science) protected rather than endangered them.

Did Osiander's preface claiming that it was just a mathematical construction actually protect the book? Gingerich tends to think so, though it was always clear that figures like Rheticus, Maestlin and Kepler did not regard Coprnicanism in such a light but as a physical system, and they seem not to have felt threatened.

Distances

Above we looked at the distances in the standard geocentric model. How did Copernicus affect this? In that table was placed the Copernican equivalent of the geocentric distances from Earth. Three key things are apparent:

1. The Ptolemaic system has the celestial bodies nesting fairly well without 'gaps' between one 'sphere' and the next.
2. The Copernican system has 'gaps' and an immense empty space between Saturn and the stars.
3. The Copernican system has more distant 'inner' planets (Mercury and Venus) because the Sun-Earth distance has to be added to their orbit at maximum distance, but the overall size of the Solar System (i.e. Saturn) is much *smaller* than the Ptolemaic system.

Averages for Copernican Systems

	Copernicus			Modern	
	av e.r.	a.u.	miles	a u	miles
Mercury	430	0.38	1.4m	0.39	36m
Venus	821	0.72	2.7m	0.72	67m
Earth	1142	1.0	3.7m	1.00	93m
Mars	1736	1.52	5.7m	1.52	142m
Jupiter	5960	5.22	19.4m	5.20	778m
Saturn	10447	9.17	34.0m	9.54	1427m
Stars			Immense		2.3m m.

The comparison between Copernican and modern distances is shown in the table. Here 'a.u.' stands for number of times the size of Earth orbit, whilst 'e.r.' as before is Earth radii. What is noticeable is that whilst the relative ratios were fairly good, Copernicus greatly underestimated the actual sizes of orbits. Copernicus, then, left us with a shrunken Solar System and a huge wasteful gap to the stars.

Questions

Here are some questions to ask as you think about Copernicus:

- In what sense was Copernicus a 'conservative' and in what sense a 'radical' ?
- What kind of opposition did Copernicus expect, and how far was he justified in his expectation?
- Supposing that you were presenting a case for the truth of the Copernican system to his contemporaries – what positive evidence would you present?
- Could a real empiricist accept the Copernican system in 1544?
- What are the sources and motivations for the many myths that are still repeated about Copernicus and his system?

Further Reading

I have not found a definitive biography of Copernicus, though the following may be relevant:

Andronik, Catherine M., *Copernicus: Founder of Modern Astronomy* (2002)

Armitage, A., *Copernicus* (1957) a classic but limited book

Banville, John., *Doctor Copernicus* (rp 1999) is a novel, a Kafkaesque perception of what he regards as a modern figure in a nightmare Renaissance era, which tells us more about Banville than Copernicus.

Beer A & Strand K., *Copernicus* (1975) tends to canonise

Biekowska, B. (trans. C, Cenkalska). *The Scientific World of Copernicus* (1973); Dobrzycki, J. (ed.) *The Reception of Copernicus's Heliocentric Theory* PRO, Proceedings of a Symposium Organized by the 'Nicolas Copernicus Committee' of the International Union of the History and Philosophy of Science, Torun, Poland, 1973.

Danielson, Dennis, *The First Copernican: Georg Joachim Rheticus and the Rise of the Copernican Revolution* (2006) is interesting and informative both for Copernicus and Rheticus.

Gassendi, Pierre & Thill. *The Life of Copernicus* (Fairfax: Xulon) (2002) consists of Gassendi's 17th century biography with extensive 21st century notes from Thill. It is a useful source book, though perhaps patchy in places.

Henry, John. *Moving Heaven and Earth* (2001);

Owen Gingerich was Harvard Professor of the History of Science and a world authority on Copernicus. He especially traces the influence of *The Revolutions*, through existing annotated copies. *An Annotated Census of Copernicus's De Revolutionibus* (Nuremberg, 1543 and Basel, 1566)(1999) is his magnum opus - good luck! His book with James MacLachlan, *Nicolaus Copernicus* (2005) is good as is the more specialist: *The Book Nobody Read* (2004) looking at the story of his quest. His more general book: *The Eye of Heaven: Ptolemy, Copernicus, Kepler* is also good.

Repcheck, J., *Copernicus's Secret* (2009) is not at all technical, but has some well written biographical details of Copernicus, Rheticus etc. It has a few loose statements, and the final chapter on Brahe-Kepler-Galileo reflects some common misconceptions.

Rosen, Edward & Hilfstein, Erna., (ed.): *Copernicus and His Successors* (1994)

Sobel, Dava., *A More Perfect Heaven: How Copernicus Revolutionised the Cosmos* (2011) was disappointing. A 75-page biography of Copernicus is followed by 178 pages of a play she has written.

Swerdlow, N.M., and Neugebauer, O., *Mathematical Astronomy in Copernicus's De Revolutionibus* (1984) is technical but contains a good short biography.

Vollmann, William., *Uncentring the Earth: Copernicus and the Revolution of the Heavenly Spheres* (2006) (Library Binding), a rambling and inaccurate book, devoid of proper referencing, is an attempt to expound Copernicus's *Revolutions of the Heavenly Spheres* in some kind of context. However, the author himself truly writes: 'In my own case the result was an autodidact's exercise in explicating a subject slightly beyond my intellectual competence.'

4. Tycho Brahe

Amongst the larger than life characters in the history of Astronomy, none was more so than the Great Dane Tycho Brahe (1546–1601). Here was someone whose life was so romantic it sounds like fiction, and also the person who brought his great wealth, influence, and patronage to place observational astronomy on a new plane. Without Tycho's accurate observations Kepler could not have founded his system.

On December 14th 1546, in Knudstrup castle in Denmark, twin boys were born to Beate Bille, wife of Otte Brahe. One was stillborn and remained unnamed, the other was named Tyge (or Tycho) after his grandfather. What kind of world did the young Tycho come into?

Astronomy and Physics

In terms of astronomy, the Ptolemaic geocentric still predominated. Ptolemy's system of epicycles, deferents and equants could predict the positions of planets fairly well, and had been preserved and in places improved by the Arab astronomers. We may distinguish several aspects of this astronomy.

Firstly, there was the pure mathematics of it: the business of 'saving the phenomena'. This was complex, and we must remember that coordinate geometry had not yet been invented.

Secondly, there was the relationship of theory and observation. Plato, of course, had taught that the physical world could be expected only to imperfectly reflect the ideal (or 'real') world derived mathematically. Faced with a range of possible parameter values, it was therefore natural to choose one that was mathematically pleasing. Ptolemy (as discussed in the second chapter) at the very least had done this – if he did not actually rig the 'observations' to fit his theory. This is, in practice, what scientists tend to do – though usually we pretend that they don't.[98]

There was also, as a third element to consider, a strong tradition that associated some kind of 'harmony' with nature and particularly the planetary motions. From Pythagorean times music and mathematics were assumed to be connected. It would be misleading to call this 'mystical' – any more than (say) modern discussion of the 'anthropic principle' or the 'nature and meaning of consciousness'. Certainly, however, it made assumptions. Science itself is, of course, based on the assumption that physical reality is both rational and susceptible to understanding by human reason. The latter assumption is no more *a priori* and self-evidently true than the former. We have no more inherent reason to expect that reality will be reducible to laws than that musical harmonies will be involved. This will be important when we come to contrast Tycho and Kepler in their approaches to astronomy. In any event, if observation permitted a range of parameter values to be assumed, then if someone selected a value which was in line with ideas of musical harmony this would be perfectly natural. Plato, in the *Timaeus*, had adopted some ideas of harmony, though not very developed. Ptolemy actually caused to be engraved on a stele set up near Alexandria not only his early astronomical parameters, but a system of harmonics.[99] The existence of some kind of music of the heavens was a normal assumption made, for example, by Boethius (c.480–524 AD) who developed harmonic theory. Later, medieval writers also followed this. Boethius, incidentally, held some profound Neoplatonic views on space and time that prefigured some elements of Einstein and Minowski, and his *Consolation of Philosophy* was widely read.

Finally, there were aspects of the physical system. Since the Earth was at the centre, and no parallax was observed, any of the planetary sets of deferent-epicycles could be any distance away – the effect viewed from Earth would be the same. Ptolemy's assumption that each system of spheres nestled just inside the next gave some kind of ratio for the sizes of orbits around the

---

[98] Galileo almost certainly 'fiddled' his observations of balls rolling down inclined planes, but was fortunate to pick the right formula. In more modern times, there is a lovely entry in Milikan's notebooks in his work on electrical charge, something like 'this one doesn't fit, leave it out'.

[99] Bruce Stephenson describes this in *The Music of the Heavens* (1993), 29.

Earth. This made sense only if one had the twin assumptions that the system was physical (and so any given system had to be outside the previous), and economical (leaving no unnecessary space between them). Along with the supposedly crystalline spheres there was Aristotelian physics. His theories of natural motion had been somewhat challenged by developing theories of 'impetus' . This was a kind of property like heat, which seeped away over time, but kept an object in motion for a while by a kind of internal motive force. It is not inertia (the idea that a body continues to move unless acted on by a force), but it departs from the Aristotelian idea that a continually applied force is needed to keep any 'violent' motion (i.e. motion other than natural up and down motion).

In 1543, three years before Tycho's birth, Copernicus had finally published his *Revolutions of the Heavenly Spheres.* This was not a popular book, but one for professional astronomers, and in that fraternity it was becoming known. Mathematically it was not dissimilar to the Ptolemaic system – except that the equant was replaced by an extra epicycle and the 'centre' was not the Earth but a point in empty space at the centre of the Earth's orbit and near the Sun. The physical problems involved in accepting the system as 'real', however, were stupendous, and it had no well-known advocates.

Religion and Politics

Luther

The Protestant Reformation began (insofar as one can speak in such terms) with Luther's 95 theses in 1517 and his writings of 1520. King Christian III of Denmark and Norway had been brought up as a Lutheran in a state that tolerated both Catholicism and Lutheranism, and defeated Catholic forces (which tried to install his younger brother) to become king in 1534. The Diet of Copenhagen in 1536 confiscated episcopal property, established a state Lutheran religion, and confirmed the rights of nobles in the state council (Rigsråd) to rule with the king. Christian III modernised the church (new bishops were of bourgeois origins), modernised the administration, and, after concluding a brief war with the Spanish Hapsburg Holy Roman Emperor Charles V, tended to take a neutral international political position. The Denmark-Norway state was therefore prosperous, officially Lutheran, and ruled by King and Rigsråd.

The Counter Reformation was just beginning in Europe in 1646, but would little affect Protestant Denmark.

The influence of the moderate Reformer Phillip Melanchthon[100] was particularly important in Denmark, and he remarked shortly before his death in 1560 that no realm in Christendom outshone Denmark in learned men. His influence led to an emphasis in higher education on fluency in Latin, Greek, and Hebrew, familiarity with church fathers, and also music, mathematics and astronomy (which led to contemplation of the wonders of creation). This reflects an academic interest in astronomy not so much present in either Catholic Spain or Protestant England. Melanchthon (unlike Luther) retained an idea that the stars influenced human life. This was a kind of sanctified astrology, which looked back at the Magi as astrologers. Astronomy and astrology were at that time distinct, but were associated together and some Italian universities actually had chairs for astrology. The focus tended to be on great events, and the influence of the stars on human experience and emotion. 'Phillippism' was the predominant force in Danish theology in this period (though came under attack in the 1580s).

Prior to the Reformation, learning tended to be associated with clericalism which implied 'celibacy' (i.e. not being married). With a Lutheran regime, university learning went just as well with family life, and the Danish nobility were coming to see it more as a general education than as a training for ordination.

One of the points essential to understanding Tycho concerns the stratification in society at that time. The structure of royalty | nobility | middle-classes | peasants was much more rigid than we can now imagine. Nobles simply could not marry commoners, at least not in an official church wedding. Only offspring from official marriages between nobility could have the recognition of title or position. Nobles did not enter academic careers, or publish on science. There may be here some contrast even to England at this time, where Francis Bacon (1561–1626) became a barrister before being a Baron and then a Viscount – as well as writing on science. Robert Boyle (1627–1691) was the son of the Earl of Cork.

---

[100] This is therefore sometimes termed 'Phillippist'. Melanchthon was also less enthusiastic than Luther about enforcing state religion.

Family

Tycho's parents were from two great noble families. All his great grandfathers and grandfathers had been in the Rigsråd. His paternal grandmother was descended from Rosencrantz and Gildenstern – real noble families placed by Shakespeare in his play about the legendary tenth century prince Hamlet.[101] The Brahe's supported the Lutheran cause (Tycho's great uncle carried the sceptre for Christian III's coronation). On the maternal side the Bille's had been Catholics, but the marriage of the 18-year-old Beate Bille to the 26-year-old Otte Brahe in 1844 marked a new direction. When Tycho was born, his uncle Jørgen was governor of Tranekaer Castle, and his father Otte of Helsinborg. The Brahe's were apparently known as *de lystige Braher* or 'the jolly Brahes'. They were able, intelligent, and well cultivated though not academically educated.

Tycho's Early Life

Tycho reported in later life that his uncle Jørgen:

> … without the knowledge of my parents (took) me away with him while I was in my earliest youth [and] brought me up and thereafter supported me generously during his lifetime … and always treated me as his own son.

Gade (followed by Koestler) perhaps overdramatises the picture of a recently born infant being galloped back to a castle and the drawbridge raised, but it *is* still fairly dramatic. Adoption was fairly common amongst Danish nobility, but we don't know why the still young Jørgen and his young wife Inger Oxe[102] were unable to have their own children. Perhaps it was something they didn't care to leave us records about. Probably the adoption/kidnap occurred after the birth of Tycho's younger brother Steen, and when Tycho was between 1–2 years old.

Uncle Jørgen was a practical man of action, his wife Inger Oxe a person of charm and social grace, from a family committed to culture and education. Jørgen was promoted to govern first Nesbyhoved Castle in 1549 and then

---

101 Elsinore was the name of the castle Frederick built around this time. Shakespeare seems to have met in 1592 Tycho's relatives Frederick Rosenkrantz and Knud Gildernstierne.

102 Estimated by Thoren in *The Lord of Uraniborg* p. 4 as 20. Incidentally, Danish noble ladies commonly retained their maiden names after marriage.

Vordingborg Castle in 1552. Danish fiefdoms, like modern corporation posts, often required the ambitious to move.

Between the ages of 7–12 Tycho went to a 'grammar school'. This was probably an episcopal school in a cathedral town, and he probably boarded with a bishop. A Danish Lutheran bishop was of middle-class not noble origin, had probably studied under Melanchthon and/or Luther at Wittenberg, and was married. The gathering of pupils, family guests and clergy at meal tables afforded educational table talk. Studies included Latin, Lutheran theology, drama and poetry, and sometimes Greek and mathematics. By their early teens, pupils were supposed to be ready for university.

Tycho entered Copenhagen University in April 1559 when he was 12. The university started in 1474, but in 1537 had been remodelled based on Wittenberg, and located in the old palace and grounds of the Catholic Bishops. In our terms it was more of a high school with students aged 12 upwards, but it also had some illustrious scholars there as tutors. The education would have been a broad one, based on Melanchthon's ideas, though discipline was probably strict. We know little of the detail of Tycho's studies. A popular story (repeated by Tycho's first biographer Gassendi in 1653) has him agog at the predicted partial eclipse of the Sun on August 21 1560, though some recent writers have cast doubt on this.[103] In any event there is nothing improbable in the story; a general interest in astronomy was not uncommon.

The general process of education for the Brahes (for example Tycho's younger brothers) was as page – squire – courtier/knight, followed by marriage and hopefully the award of a fiefdom. Perhaps through the influence of his aunt/foster-mother's family[104], Tycho was the first Brahe to go through the university system rather than this court system of training. When, in 1561 at the age of 15, Tycho left the university he continued along the 'alternative' path. For a nobleman this meant gaining understanding of foreign languages and cultures. Education, in those days, was much more 'European' than it is today. Even with the Reformation division of Europe, foreign experience was essential. In February 1562 Tycho left for Leipzig

---

103 So reports Thoren op. cit. 12.

104 Inger Oxe was sister to Peder Oxe, who became a dominant figure in Danish politics and had himself spent five years travelling European universities.

university (Prague, Heidelberg, and Wittenberg had also been considered) together with the 20-year-old Anders Sørensen Vedel. The latter was a middle class youth who would act as a *Hovemester* – a kind of guardian who would oversee the studies of the young Tycho whilst himself a student. There were few Danes at Leipzig but the teaching was all in Latin, the religion Lutheran, and the ethos influenced by Melanchthon – so it would have seemed all very familiar. Tycho was supposed to be studying classical culture not astronomy, but as he claimed later he 'bought astronomical books secretly, and read them in secret'. He had a small globe, and the tables (*Epimerides*) based both on Ptolemy and Copernicus. Tycho then obtained a pair of compasses, and by late August was keeping a log of observations, and realised that even the Copernican tables were quite a way out. In later life he claimed that at this time he formed the ambition of rectifying this affair based on a large body of observation. Tycho's first commissioned instrument was a cross-staff, used for sighting the angles between stars. Sights on the cross part and scales entered on the instrument, allowed these angles to be read off.

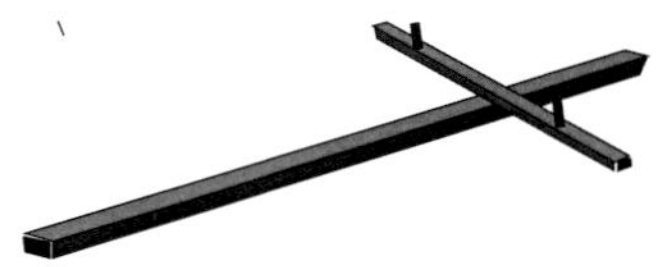
Principles of Cross-Staff

Gade suggests some friction between Vedel and his charge over the latter's interest in astronomy, and certainly Tycho could work up little enthusiasm for law. In any event both were recalled in 1565 by uncle Jørgen who was about to leave as vice-admiral to sail on his flagship in a war with Sweden. By this time Tycho's father Otte was a member of the Rigsråd. Shortly after Tycho's return, the king Ferdinand II (then 31) fell from a Copenhagen bridge and Jørgen died of pneumonia contracted whilst saving his monarch. Accounts vary as to whether or not both were drunk at the time! Gade and Koestler mark this as a time of financial independence when Tycho inherited his uncle's wealth, but the reality seems to be that Jørgen had not completed the necessary paperwork to benefit Tycho, and his wife Inger Oxe retained the estates until her death in 1591. Tycho was 19 and still a minor, and guardianship of him now reverted to his natural parents.

What was Tycho to do now? He writes in a letter of the time with contempt of those who 'play in pride and luxury … with wine, dogs and horses. May God, as I trust he will, grant me a better lot'. He was not, however, trained or fitted for the kind of military career most Brahe's had pursued, and had little interest in administration or court life. We don't know how much opposition his father had to the notion of him taking an academic direction. For his mother's side this would be likely to be more acceptable, and there is some evidence Tycho got moral support from his maternal uncle Steen Bille, and perhaps from his aunt/foster-mother. In any event Tycho left in spring 1566 for Wittenberg, and hence to Rostock.

It was whilst in Rostrock in December 1566 that, at a party, Tycho had a dispute with a third cousin Mandurup Parsberg. The story that it was over who was the better mathematician seems apocryphal[105], though it could have been to do with Tycho's astronomical interests. A duel followed – a common cause of injury and death amongst Danish noblemen who usually carried swords! Most of Tycho's nose was sliced off in the duel. When it healed, he eventually replaced it with a metal piece – probably of copper for everyday use and perhaps precious (and heavier) metal for special occasions! The suggestion of his enemy Bär that he sighted stars down it is implausible(!) – but it is an obvious feature in portraits.

Young Adulthood

Around this time the brother of Tycho's foster-mother/aunt (Peder Oxe) was beginning his rise to great power in Denmark. Inger and Steen Bille obtained in May 1568 a royal undertaking that Tycho should be granted a lucrative sinecure in the form of a canonry in Roskilde Cathedral when one was available. Tycho could well have opted for a diplomatic future with such strong connections – and there was evidently from his letters some conflict with his family over his decision instead to focus on scientific interests. Tycho left again before any canonry came through, and travelled through various cities to

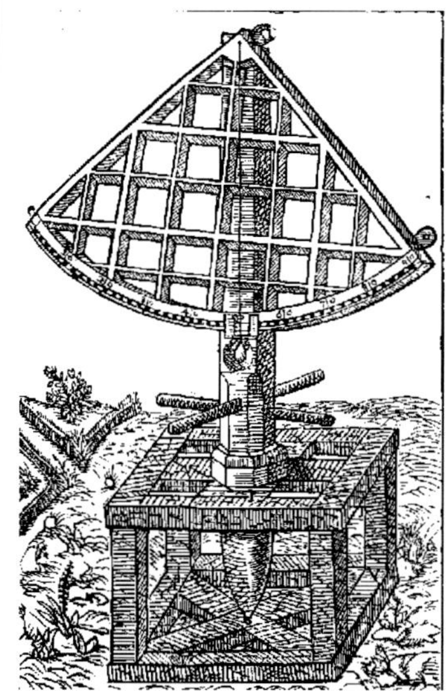
Augsberg Quadrant 1570

[105] See Thoren op. cit. 23 citing Norlind. Parsberg (a Rigsrad member from 1580) became a friend and supporter of Tycho in later years, and was very sensitive about the 'mishap' in their youth (op. cit. 343).

Augsberg where he stayed 14 months. Whilst there he inspired an Augsberg alderman Paul Hainzel to pay for the construction of a huge quadrant. This was made in 1570 of seasoned oak, and was 5½ metres in radius! Tycho also ordered a sextant, and commissioned a large (5 foot) globe to map stars on. Tycho spent as much time at Augsberg on alchemy as astronomy, natural philosophers at this time tended to be more 'all round' than today. Around this time Tycho also met the famous French Philosopher and Hugenot Petrus Ramus who had taken as his MA thesis that everything Aristotle said was wrong!

Tycho returned home again, perhaps because his father was ill. The letter which Tycho wrote to Vedel concerning his father's death incidentally shows that he had a genuine Lutheran piety:

> I have received and read your letter filled with sweet words of consolation, which raised my spirits no small amount from my distress and great sorrow over my father's departure from this life … There are certainly many theological grounds for consolation that can be extracted from the divine expressions of the Holy Scriptures, and philosophical ones that can be derived from the common fate of humanity and from the inconsistency and unceasing alteration of everything earthly, on which I draw for support in my distress and sorrow. But I also take no slight consolation from the fact that my father passed from this wretched life of mortality so peacefully and quietly to the heavenly and eternal realm of our father, where we, according to Paul's testimony, have a secure home and city …

Other letters of Tycho's refer to God, and the references seem to show a more than formal commitment to his Lutheran faith.

Tycho stayed on at Knutstorp after his father's death, though it took some time for affairs to be sorted out under complex Danish inheritance laws. Sometime in late 1571 Tycho probably moved to quarters in or near Herrevad Abbey where his uncle Steen Bille lived. Steen arranged for a chemical laboratory, and also a small observatory to which was to be brought the Augsberg sextant. Nothing of Tycho's science remains from this time, though his thoughts may have been elsewhere.

Two Key Decisions

The story of Tycho reads like a mixture of a Hollywood movie, a Tolkein novel, and a fairy tale. It was at this point that he fell in love and married what Gade, Koestler, etc. call a 'woman of low caste', 'peasant girl' or 'bondswoman'. Gade suggests it was a 'social catastrophe', and that Tycho was motivated by a pragmatic wish for a wife who would:

> … never bother him or be in his way, and who would not be nagging him to take her up to court in Copenhagen or to give her dresses and jewellery. She was to work and not to be seen. Kirstine, he thought, would cause him no trouble. She would on the contrary, agree smilingly to all he said, purr over his socks and never remonstrate at his eccentricities … Tycho seldom mentioned her in his voluminous correspondence and surely did not prize her as highly as he did his irreplaceable instruments or books …[106]

The Gade-Koestler picture may bring to mind a ruddy cheeked, complaisant if dim, peasant girl, picked purely as good breeding stock by a pragmatic Tycho devoted to nothing but his work.

The dictionary defines a 'morganatic' marriage as 'between a person of high rank and another of lower rank, the spouse and children having no claim to the possessions or title of the person of higher rank'. Under Jutish (i.e. Danish) law, a church wedding with full rites and rights between noble and commoner was unthinkable, but a woman who lived with, ate with and slept with a man for three years, functioning as a wife and carrying the keys of the house, would be deemed to be in a morganatic marriage. Tycho, generations of whose ancestors were Rigsråd members, would bear children who (although legitimate) would inherit none of his lands, titles, or nobility. No wonder if his family were less than enthusiastic.

So why did he do it? Tycho often showed contempt for the empty-headedness of court life and the pastimes of the nobility. Tycho valued his noble descent but wrote:

> what I myself have not personally accomplished, but have received by descent and ancestry, I would not count my own. My

[106] J. A. Gade, *The Life and Times of Tycho Brahe*, 48.

> mind is set on much greater things, in which there is real work … few, yes, all too few, are those to whom God has given the faculty to see what is above them.[107]

But why marry a 'peasant'? The notion that a noble wife would have got in the way of his work seems rather far-fetched. Tycho's connections were the highest in the land. The brother of his foster-mother/aunt virtually ruled the country. He could surely have found some lower ranking but still noble girl who would do as she was told?[108] Likewise with the contemporary (mostly foreign) suggestions that a noseless noble could not find a noble wife. Plenty of families would have been only too keen to ally themselves with the powerful Brahe-Bille-Oxe clan – with nose or not. Moreover, being in a morganatic marriage was likely to bring both difficulty and slander – this was not a match made for Tycho's better convenience. Unless he was a complete nincompoop Tycho must have realised that marrying Kirstine would cause much more trouble than it would avoid, so why do it?

Romantic Tycho?

One problem is that the picture of a complaisant if dim 'peasant' wife is very probably a mistake. What seems more likely is that Kirstine Jørgensdatter was the daughter of Pastor Jørgen Hansen, the clergyman of Knutstorp's village church since the year of Tycho's birth. Tycho would have seen her not in bright peasant garb with ruddy cheeks and big rough hands, but the white lace collar and cuffs of a Lutheran clergyman's daughter. Tycho had, after all, imbibed his learning at the tables of Lutheran bishops who were themselves not from the nobility but the same middle classes as Kirstine. The contrast between the high minded and learned mien of clergy in the mould of Melanchthon, contrasted in Tycho's mind with the banal triviality and earthly focus of many of the lives of nobility. Had Kirstine been daughter of a bishop she would still (we need to remind ourselves) have been a commoner – and perhaps her personal qualities

107 To Pratensis 1572.

108 One may be reminded of Jane Austen's Darcy and Elizabeth Bennett. Challenged on her lowly estate she reminds Lady de Burgh that she too is a gentlewoman – for Darcy to marry a *commoner* would be unthinkable even to the romantic Jane Austen!

outweighed those of any bishops' daughters Tycho met! As a Lutheran minister's daughter in the Melanchthon milieu she may have been comparatively well educated, interested in Tycho's work, and for all we know was graceful, witty and charming to boot. Tycho and Kirstine certainly regarded themselves as married (Tycho's sister also insisted on this after his death), and if there was Court criticism it may be that King Frederick quashed it. He himself had suffered at a higher level, having to marry his niece the Swedish Princess Sophia rather than the lady he loved (Anne Hardenberg) who was noble but *not* royal. Unfortunately for Tycho, later ordinances of 1580 and 1584 moved away from the Melanchthon Phillippist concept of marriage as at base mutual commitment, and insisted that only church weddings were valid. Tycho's enemies used this against him at the time when he was, effectively, forced into exile in 1597.

The other big event in Tycho's life in these years came on the evening of November 11th, 1572. Walking back from his laboratory, Tycho saw a *new* bright star in the constellation of Cassiopeia. What was it and where was it? Aristotelian physics said that only below the Moon was there change and decay. Comets had often been seen, but the Aristotelian system said these were Earthly and sub-lunar exhalations. Astronomers throughout Europe saw the star (they could hardly miss it). They saw that it apparently moved across the sky with the other 'fixed stars'. But could it be proven to be superlunar? The star remained visible for 17 months, until March 1574, though Tycho probably did not need that long. To make the observation Tycho used the sextant he had invented to improve on the cross staff. Now two stars could be sighted along movable arms of his sextant (so called because 60°, a sixth of a circle).

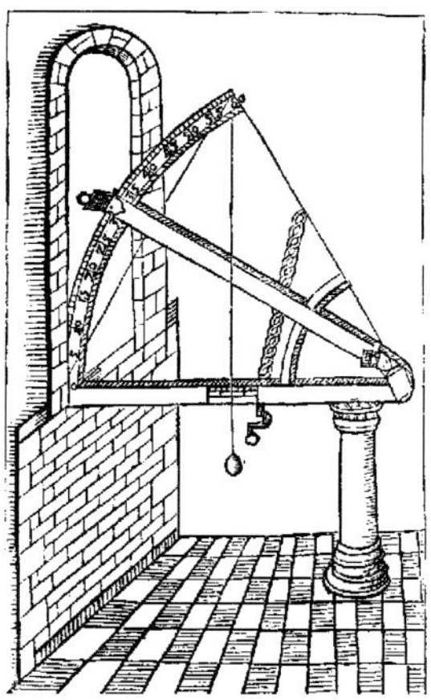

'New Star' sextant

The central issue was parallax (as explained above in chapter 2). The Moon changes apparent position against the stars depending on from where on the Earth it is observed. If an object (like the new star) fails to do this, then it cannot be nearer than the Moon. Tycho showed that the new star did not move relative to the fixed stars, and since this was true over a period of time and at all angles it could not be that it was moving in exactly a path to counteract apparent parallax. In other words, it was definitely above the Moon.

1572–4 was a critical time for Tycho. Between the ages of 26–28 he was doing two decisive things that would signal a definite rejection of the path of civil service or professional courtier. One, as already noted, was to set up the basis of a morganatic marriage with a commoner. The other was to publish a work on astronomy.

Myth

Was the idea that there could be change in the heavens a shocking one? Koestler wrote:

> The sensational importance of the event lay in the fact that it contradicted the basic doctrine – Aristotelian, Platonic and Christian – that all change, all generation and decay were confined to the immediate vicinity of the Earth, the sub-lunary sphere.[109]

This raises issues of the position of the incorruptible heavens within the church and society at that time. Concerning the church, here are two quotations:

> Usually even a non-Christian knows something about the Earth, the heavens, and the other elements of this world … and this knowledge he holds to as being certain from reason and experience. Now, it is a disgraceful and dangerous thing for an unbeliever to hear a Christian, presumably giving the meaning of Holy Scripture, talking nonsense on these topics, and we should take all means to prevent such an embarrassing situation, in which people show up vast ignorance in a Christian and laugh it to scorn. (*Augustine of Hippo)*
>
> Two rules are to be observed, as Augustine teaches. The first is, to hold the truth of Scripture without wavering. The second is that since Holy Scripture can be explained in a multiplicity of senses, one should not adhere to a particular explanation, only in such measure as to be ready to abandon it if it be proved with

---

[109] Koestler, *The Sleepwalkers* (1959), 292.

> certainty to be false; lest Holy Scripture be exposed to the ridicule of unbelievers, and obstacles be placed to their believing (Thomas Aquinas).

The adoption of Aristotelian physics by the church was, according to its two key influential theologians, conditional and *not* part of the theology. A common myth is that theologians saw attacks on Aristotle's physics as attacks on the church.

Concerning society, within Tycho's Phillippist form of Lutheranism Aristotle was not a sacred cow. The Huguenot philosopher Petrus Ramus had (as noted) taken an extreme anti-Aristotle view, but was well respected. Within the Danish and German universities there just does not seem to be the kind of attachment to Aristotle in this generation that would make Tycho's discoveries shocking. Amongst the nobility, the main problem was disinterest and disdain for such activities – not commitment to Aristotle.

There are divergent views on the extent of the reluctance Tycho may have felt to publish his manuscript on *The New Star*. Certainly he received great encouragement from several people. One was Charles Dancey, the French envoy to the Danish court, a Calvinist and a renowned thinker. The other was Johannes Pratensis, the Professor of Medicine at Copenhagen (who was actually about Tycho's age). It is also possible that Peder Oxe himself may have given encouragement. Tycho's reluctance was not about the contents but the propriety of a noble publishing on science. Overall the evidence is that Tycho had decided to publish anyway, but liked to be thought to have been persuaded to it. It was, in fact, a convention amongst Humanists of the time to appear to publish only with modest reluctance, at the insistence of their friends. By the time the work actually reached the press in late 1573 Tycho had decided to 'go for it', dropped any pretence of anonymity, and even included a withering attack on the emptiness of nobility pursuits (as cited above). Probably he had decided by then to emigrate to pursue his researches. The work also included much discussion of the *meaning* of the star. This was both in astrological terms, but also because God must have some purpose in creating it – and the assumption (common at the time) was that this purpose would be to do with human affairs.

The Career Move

In 1573–4 we find Tycho designing new instruments, but otherwise involved in just everyday administrative tasks. In the summer of 1574 Tycho's growing reputation was recognised by engaging him to lecture at the university in Copenhagen. This was tricky for a noble and special arrangements had to be made regarding location and requests for such a series. Tycho duly delivered, however, his initial oration on 23rd September. In the audience were renowned Professors in Theology, Law etc., from the Phillippist brand of Lutheranism.

Tycho's oration set the whole of human enterprise within a theological framework. His outline of astronomy began with Adams' son Seth, then Moses, the Greeks, and to Copernicus. Tycho recognised Copernicus's genius, though thought his theory contrary to sound physical principles. He then launched into a long defence of astrology as consistent with Christianity. Lutheran opinion was divided on this. Tycho argued that the stars influenced, but did not negate either divine or human free will – and this seemed to reconcile the Professors that his astrology was not unchristian (which is not to say that they all accepted it).

Tycho's lectures proper apparently dealt with theories of the Sun and Moon 'according to the models and parameters of Copernicus'. He presented the general model of Copernicus's planetary theory, and showed how this could be amended to allow for a stationary Earth. Effectively, this is the 'Tychonic' model, where the other planets go around the Sun, which goes around a stationary Earth. Mathematically it is identical to a Copernican model – except as regards movement relative to the stars. Ironically, Tycho shared Copernicus's dislike of the equant, and his system avoided it, using extra epicycles instead.

Myth

Koestler entitles a section on Copernicus's work 'The Book That Nobody Read', and proclaimed it 'an all-time worst seller'.[110] This was, as already noted, misleading. It was not aimed at a popular audience, but the evidence is that it was widely known and respected amongst

---

[110] Koestler, op. cit. 194.

'professional' astronomers[111] – Tycho is a case in point. Tycho even sent someone to Frombork in 1584 to find out more about Copernicus – the servant returning with an instrument of the great man that Tycho kept and treasured. Ironically, Thoren claims that the widespread use of Copernican rather than Ptolemaic tables is hard to explain as their improved accuracy would be undetectable to the vast majority of users.

Tycho had a further period of European travel, but, back in Denmark in 1575, was definitely contemplating how to emigrate abroad, probably

to Basle. King Frederick offered Tycho a castle and fiefdom, but Tycho prevaricated. Finally, probably through Steen Bille, the king divined what was in Tycho's heart and thinking and summoned him to an audience on 11th February 1576. Whilst building his castle (Elsinore) the king said, he noticed the island of Hven (or Hveen) lying off the coast. Would Tycho like to have means to build an observatory there, where he could have a fiefdom free from the general administrative and

Hven

[111] Owen Gingerich ironically entitled his 2004 book *The Book Nobody Read* – detailing hiswork that showed how carefully the leading astronomers of Europe read and annotated Copernicus's work.

defence ties? The King would sail over occasionally 'to see your work in astronomy and chemistry, and gladly support your investigations, not because I have any understanding of astronomical matters … but because I am your king and you are my subject, you who belong to a family which has always been dear to me, and you who are said to have considerable insight into such matters…' Why, asked the king, should Tycho go to Germany? Why not make Denmark the centre to which those interested in such things would come?

Tycho was stunned, and after discussion with his various friends and advisers accepted. Frederich II's offer not only provided for Tycho (immediately doubling his income), but also gave Royal approval in a very tangible way to Tycho's scientific interests. This was not only from personal affection and esteem for the Brahe-Bille-Oxe clan, but in recognition of the prestige brought to Denmark. So was built the extraordinary observatory on Hven.

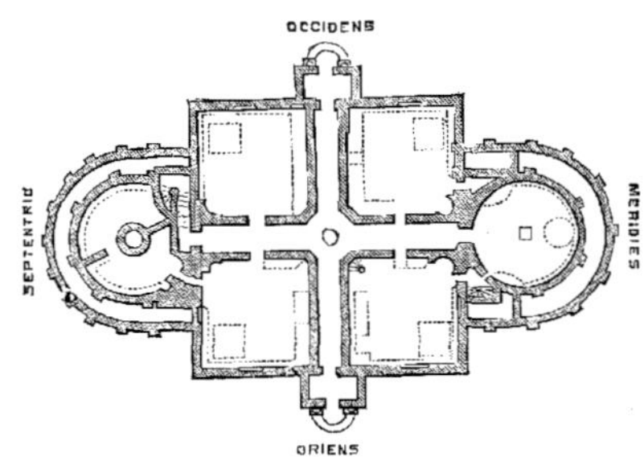

Plan of Uraniborg

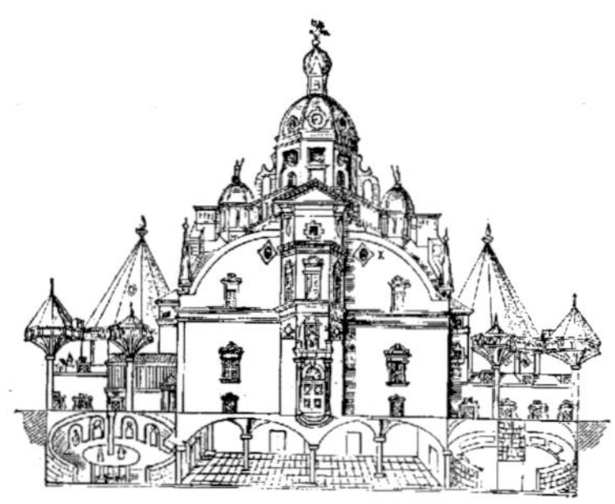
Uraniborg

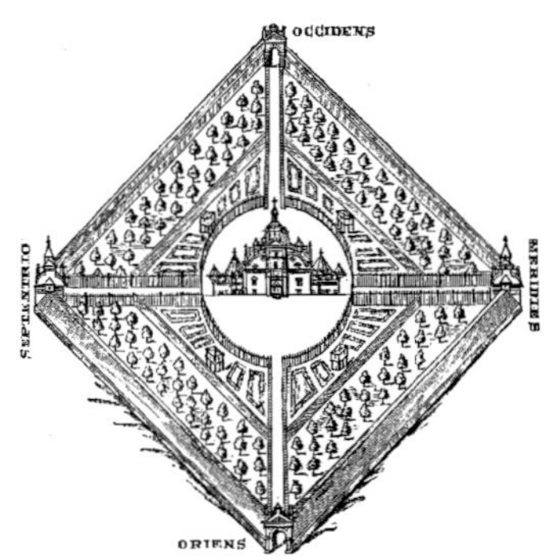

Grounds of Uraniborg

Tycho met some resistance from the peasants of Hven, who were freehold farmers and had not previously had any overlord. The document from Frederick proclaimed Hven the Fief of Tycho, but added 'he shall observe the law and due right towards the peasants living there …' The farmers paid dues, but also labour dues to Tycho. Christianson denies any 'particular malice or tyrannical inclination' of Tycho or his bailiff. This was just the system coming into Denmark. The freemen of Hven, however, were unused to it, and there was often friction between Tycho and his islanders.[112]

Stjerneborg recontructed

The actual building was not large or ostentatious, but (according to Thoren) reflected 'in its proportions the order of heaven and earth. The house had running water, a fountain, and various other contrivances, which must have made it seem (for example to the young Prince Christian on a visit) like Disneyland. To Uraniborg was added the nearby observatory Stjerneborg around 1584. This had five chambers built separately and mostly underground to avoid wind-shake on the instruments. The instruments were large and increasingly accurate, and only a selection is shown here.

Tycho began his work of systematic observation, aided by various assistants over a number of years. Often different assistants would observe separately but at the same time to average out for greater accuracy. Thoren lists and describes the various instruments and times of manufacture and we will consider their accuracy later.

Steel sextant c. 1574

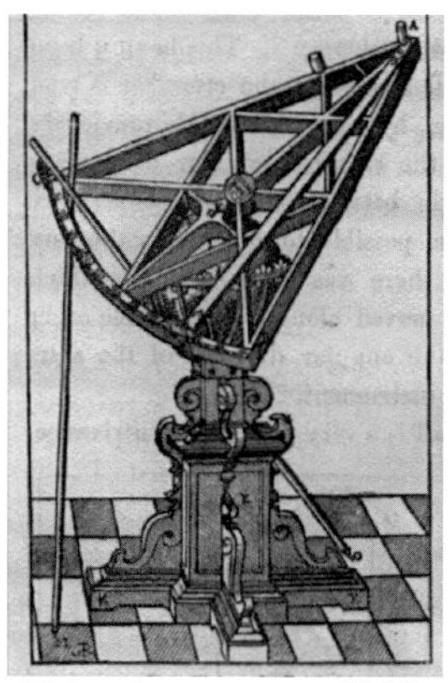

Trigonic sextant c. 1582

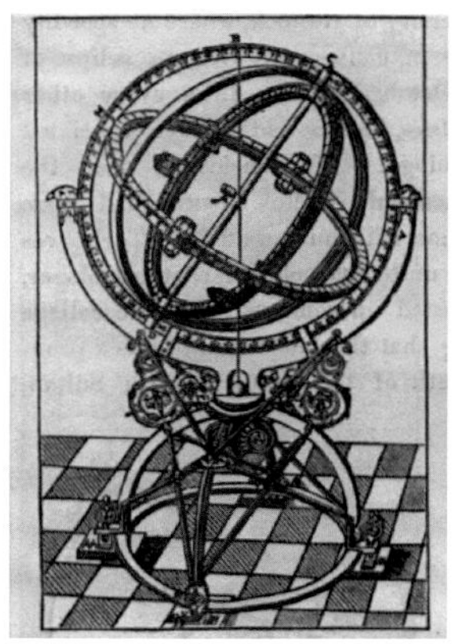

Equatorial armillary 1584

[112] J. R. Christianson, *On Tycho's Island* (2000), 36. The book chronicles much of the conflicts etc., though it is not very relevant to us.

Mural quadrant

Basically, sextants like cross-staffs) are used to find angles between bodies, quadrants to find angles of altitude. One of the most important innovations Tycho made was in the sights used. His parallel sights got over the problem of sighting a star really accurately rather than judging when it was at the centre of a hole big enough to find it.

One the most famous and most pictured instruments was his great 'mural' quadrant mounted on a north-south wall. This involved a quarter circle of brass over six feet in radius, with intervals of ten seconds of arc marked. On the left, built into the wall, is a fixed foresight. The two backsights slide on the arc itself. The mural of Tycho (plus dog) is purely for decoration, – and possibly inspiration!

The Comet

The second important Tychonic observation came in 1577. On 13th November 1577 at dusk, Tycho noticed a bright star in the West. As darkness fell, it was obvious that the star had a tail – it was a comet. The comet was near the Sun, and observation was not easy, but, again, Tycho persevered and demonstrated that there was no parallax. The comet had horizontal parallax of less than 15 minutes of arc, so the comet had to be at least four times as far away as the lower bound of the Moon. Tycho also showed that the motion of the comet seemed to

Bayeaux Tapestry comet

strongly indicate an orbit round the Sun. Finally, the path of the comet seemed to cut across several planetary spheres. They could not, in this case, be physical. Sadly, his later and more accurate instruments were not available at the time – though his observations were still very good compared to (say) Michael Maestlin (Kepler's mentor) who used a piece of string.

Modern photo of a bright comet

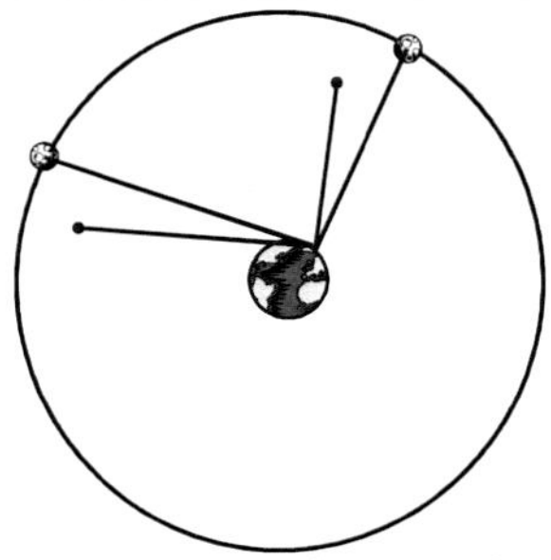

Showing how because of Earth's size the angle would change (allowing in practice for motion) were a comet below the Moon

Tycho had to deal with alternative theories about the comet – particularly astrological ones predicting disaster. He did his own astrological analysis in depth, but in the Phillippist tradition of prediction that could be circumvented by human freewill. The publication of his results, however, had to wait some years.

Tycho's System

Tycho was also reconsidering the nature of the planetary system itself, and had his own distinctive system by the mid 1580s. This had a long gestation period. When Tycho had first lectured at Copenhagen he had taken up an idea already 'in the air' of utilising essentially Copernican parameters without making any assumption of a moving Earth. The idea was to avoid 'both the mathematical absurdity of Ptolemy and the physical absurdity of Copernicus'.

In 1573 Valentin Naboth's book *Primarum de coelo et terra* adopted the system of the fifth-century Martianus Capella. The Capellan system has Venus and Mercury circle the Sun, whilst the other planets circle the Earth. When Tycho drew his diagrams relating to the comet of 1577, Venus is shown as in a heliocentric orbit, and in a report to the King he mentions this Capellan system. It seems also to have affected a mathematician Paul Wittich who in 1580 came to work at Hven for a few months, and his annotations of a copy of *The Revolutions* contained diagrams with such a system. A final diagram contained the outer planets on epicycles similar to the size of the Sun's orbit. Had this been converted to the equivalent system of eccentrics, it would have given a system where all the planets orbited the Sun. There is no evidence that he or Tycho did so.

In 1582–3 Tycho became convinced that the parallax he obtained for Mars was smaller than that for the Sun and so Mars must be further away. In 1588 Tycho described this early sketch as a mistake (Kepler later ascribed it to an assistant.[113]) and his final system has the Mars and Sun celestial spheres intersecting.

But why did he delay publication? In a letter to Caspar Peucer, Tycho later remarked:

> I was still steeped in the opinion, approved and long accepted by almost all, that the heavens were composed of certain solid orbs that carried around the planets … I could not bring myself to allow this ridiculous penetration of the orbs, thus it happened that for some time this, my own discovery, was suspect to me.[114]

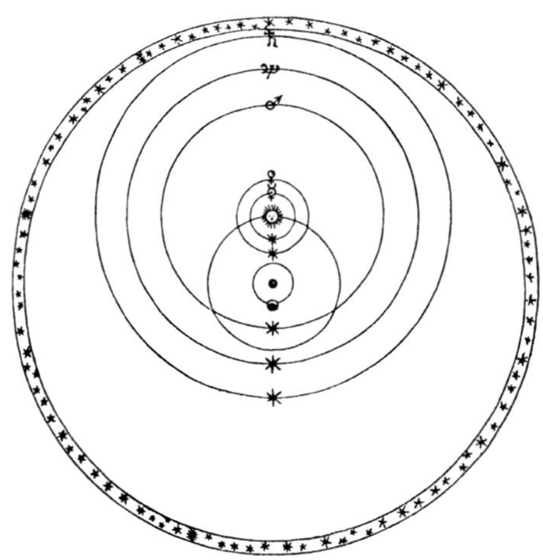

Tycho's diagram: *De Mundi* 1588

Dreyer remarks that: 'The idea of the Tychonic system was so obvious a corollary to the Copernican system that it almost of necessity must have occurred independently to several people'.[115] This is not necessarily so. The problem of intersecting spheres made it less obvious.

In 1579 Tycho had received Maestlin's work on the comet, in which he calculated and plotted the comet's daily distances as well as the angular coordinates Tycho had given. The comet

113 Krisitan P. Moesgaard in *The Reception of Copernicus Heliocentric System* (Ed Dobrzychi).

114 Quoted in ibid. 76.

115 Dreyer, *A History of Astronomy from Thales to Kepler*, 167.

clearly went through the Ptolemaic spheres of Mercury and Venus, but at that time it seems not to have struck Tycho.

Tycho was in friendly correspondence with the Langrave William (1532–1592), the son of Phillip of Hesse (Luther's patron). Like his father, he sought consensus amongst Protestants, and favoured toleration. His mathematician, Christoph Rothman had long and friendly correspondence and discourse with Tycho (visiting Hven in 1590). In 1586 Tycho received some independent observations from William, made with instruments that included the various latest Tychonic inventions. A treatise by Rothman (together with earlier observations by Kepler's mentor Michael Maestlin) seemed to show that the comet went through several supposed planetary spheres which could not therefore be solid. Comets of 1580, 1582, and 1585 backed up his ideas. In his *Apologia* (see below) Kepler states that it was this discovery of comets located above the Moon and penetrating the spheres that 'dissipated those solid orbs and removed the hindrances from the Tychonic hypotheses'. So, in a letter of 1587 Tycho expressed his first open doubt about the solidity of the spheres.[116] Once decided Tycho was, as often, decisive. He added a final chapter on the system of the world to his book *De mundi aetherei recentioribus phaenomenis* (usually just called *De mundi*) in 1588. Rothman himself had his own 'inverted Copernican' system in 1587, but after reading Tycho's 1588 work concluded 'I cannot help inferring that no hypothesis can be true except the Copernican one'. His reasoning is interesting and can be summarised:

1. The Tychonic system does not really *explain* the major retrograde motions.
2. It seems incredible that the major solar epicycle could be so powerful – given there is no material connection.
3. The Tychonic system reintroduces the ambivalence on the order of the spheres.
4. It is less economic than the Copernican scheme.
5. A variation in solar eccentricity would affect all the other planets systems.

116 Thoren, op. cit. 258.

Moesgaard describes Tycho's counter to these and how it seems to have convinced Rothman.[117]

The Ursus Controversy

Nicolai Reymers Bär (Ursus – Nicolaus Raimarus) visited Tycho in 1584. He was a German self-taught mathematician/astronomer, a former swineherd, so it is hard to imagine a greater contrast with the noble Tycho. Tycho suspected him of snooping around his data, and had him searched whilst asleep – to Ursus's ire! In any event, after he published his system, Tycho found that Ursus had just published a variation of the system under the title *Fundamentum astronomicum.* This book contains a lot of trigonometrical and geometric methods used in astronomy, including those derived from Paul Wittich (and maybe Jorst Bürgi) using addition *(posthesis)* and subtraction *(aphaeresis*) in trigonometry, but also a fold-out chart of Ursus planetary system. This was like Tycho's except that:

1. Ursus had the orbit of Mars outside the orbit of the Sun whereas in Tycho they were intersecting.
2. Ursus also had the Earth rotating though static, in Tycho the heavens rotate daily.

Ursus also took a very instrumentalist view, mathematical systems were simply to enable prediction, and he was unconcerned that some of his other planets' orbs intersected (though he is not altogether consistent on this). Thoren suggests that Ursus may have picked up (and probably plagiarised) an earlier version of Tycho's, especially as in earlier thinking Tycho had Mars outside the Sun, though he could also have derived ideas from Wittich. As by this time Tycho knew that Mars does come closer than the Sun, this idea is flawed.[118]

To Tycho, Ursus had plagiarised him but misrepresented his system, and in his book Ursus had notably omitted any recognition of Tycho. In 1596 Tycho published a selection of his letters, in some of which Ursus was denounced as a dirty scoundrel. Unfortunately, also, Ursus was styling himself 'Mathematician to Rudolph II' and may have become aware that Tycho might be trying to move in on his patch with the Emperor Rudolph.

---

117 Moesgaard, op. cit. 53.

118 It varies between 35 million and 240 million – the Sun is consistently about 93 million miles.

Ursus produced a furious book 'refuting' Tycho's accusations, and accusing Tycho of plagiarising anyway. Ursus actually went very much further than this, heaping personal abuse on Tycho and his family, implying that his wife (referred to as a concubine) and daughter were of loose morality, etc. It was unfortunate that at the same time as Tycho received Ursus's scurrilous book *De astronomicis hypothesibus* which contained an apparent Ursus fan letter from Kepler, Tycho also received his own fan letter from Kepler with the latter's *Mysterium Cosmographicum* (of which more later). As we shall see, Kepler became involved in the dispute, and Tycho and Ursus traded insults until Tycho successfully sued Ursus, and most of the copies of the latter's tract were destroyed (Ursus died in October 1600 a year before Tycho).

Tycho was possessive about his system, but was it really original? In such priority disputes there are often two questions (i) is the *idea* the key, or the full mathematical system? (ii) is having it enough or does it have to be *published* – and what constitutes 'publication'? Copernicus was certainly not the first to think about heliocentricity, but his was the first mathematical and published system. Others in Tycho's generation, like Rothman, were also working on 'inverted' Copernican systems. Ursus published a diagram first, though it differed in key respects from Tycho's. So maybe we can say Tycho was original but exaggerated the originality.

During the 1590s Tycho continued to do work on the other successive comets, he did some important work on the Moon, and he continued to plot his star catalogue so that it was up to nearly a thousand stars by 1597. Then his life radically changed, for reasons we will now explore.

Troubles in Denmark

In 1588 Tycho's royal patron King Frederick died. Anyone familiar with the modern problem of research scientists who need expensive equipment and have to keep filling in applications and lobbying for funding (when what they really want to do is to get on with the research) may warm to Tycho's 16th century predicament! Wanting to be working on Hven and resenting having to go off to court to protect his interests periodically, Tycho must have tried Frederick's patience at times with his demands for more and more income. In the immediate aftermath of Frederick's death, Tycho continued to receive substantial income with the realm under Regency during the minority of prince Christian (IV). The prince himself (aged 15) made a visit to Hven in July 1592 and was fascinated with a wind-up globe showing the Sun and Moon going around the Earth – with which he was duly presented by Tycho.

Some shadow came later between the young Christian IV and Tycho, over Tycho's insensitivity in repairing the Chapel of the Three Wise Men at Roskilde, in which Frederick had been entombed. Tycho was negligent in obeying a royal command to rapidly fulfil his duty to repair the chapel roof, and then wanted to do it on the cheap. Tycho was undiplomatic over this; the resting place of his royal patron did deserve better, and the young Christian IV was quite understandably genuinely miffed. Tycho was also involved in various disputes with tenants and peasants on Hven – though this was not all that unusual for a Danish nobleman. Real problems arose, however from his marriage to Kirstine. Danish law and Phillippist Lutheran theology regarded Tycho and Kirstine as married. Tycho's dream was that his offspring – probably his sons – would continue his work at Hven. However, in June 1580 an ordinance condemned the kind of liaison Tycho and Kirstine had, and from 1582 a Royal ordinance clarified that any children of such a liaison could not have noble privileges. They would not, therefore, be able to inherit Hven, and would be very unlikely to be able to marry Danish nobility. The Regency made a special recommendation that if no suitable nobles could be found then Hven could pass to suitable commoners.

But to whom could Tycho marry off his children? His daughter Magdalene was 20, and could not marry a noble. Tycho arranged for her to marry one of his long-time assistants, Gellius Sascerides. Gellius had studied at Copenhagen and Wittenberg, became skilled in medicine and astronomy, travelled abroad to study in Marburg, Basle, and Padua, and returned (aged 31) to Denmark in 1593 as one of the rising intellectual lights. His betrothal to Magdalene, however, turned into a catastrophe, he seems to have taken fright at what Tycho expected of him, covered his own change of mind by increasingly wild accusations about Tycho and Magdalene, and the affair resulted in a long drawn out calumny and slander trial.[119]

Tycho's real troubles, though, stemmed from changes that arose after Christian IVs coronation in 1596. The new inner circle (including chancellor Christian Fris) wanted to centralise the government (i.e. assert

---

119 This is chronicled in depth in Christianson, *On Tycho's Island.*

royal power over the nobles) and cut down on expenses. Tycho (in their terms a bit of an 'odd ball' anyway) was probably an obvious target. He received notification that his income was to be cut drastically, and that the young king had no interest in providing funds for Tycho's instruments. Tycho (possibly either in huff or bluff) removed nearly all his instruments to his house in Copenhagen. At this point, after a further cut in funds, and a few days after the exit from Hven, the king issued a warrant to look into the charges that Tycho had mistreated the Hven peasants and 'dared to act against the ritual'. As Thoren says, it seems unlikely that the peasants would complain just as Tycho was leaving – it was probably part of a wider plan to discredit and humble him. The 'ritual' referred to the exorcism of babies during christening – a practice disapproved by Phillippist Lutherans, but supported by some other Lutherans and the official church liturgy. The likelihood, however, that the king's close advisors really cared deeply about the omission of exorcism from christenings seems remote – the ploy was to 'get Tycho'. The civil charge came to nothing, but the priest on Hven went to prison. The real target *was* Tycho his patron, and the priest was also a proclaimed subject of 'royal disfavour' for 'failing to punish and admonish Tycho Brahe on Hven, who for 18 years has not taken Holy Communion but lived an evil life with a concubine'. Those who issued this judgement knew well enough that Tycho *was* morganatically married to Kirstine according to Jutish (Danish) law, and had voluntarily withdrawn from communion to avoid any difficulties as church practice had hardened against admitting any but the church-married to communion.

Tycho really had no option but to leave Denmark. His income was cut, he could not attend Holy Communion in his church, his wife was branded a mistress, his children could not inherit, finding marriage partners for them in Denmark would be difficult, and there was even the possibility that Hven (and his instruments) might be given to someone else. The nobility, whose banal occupations and lifestyles Tycho had so long despised, and whose conventions and values (e.g. on marriage) had flouted, had finally struck back! In June 1597 he sailed for Rostock in Germany.

Into Exile

Tycho would have found Rostock a civilised Lutheran city, and for the first time in 18 years could take communion with all his family in St Mary's Church. From Rostock Tycho wrote a last appeal to Christian IV. His letters to the king may have lacked due grovelling (as Koestler and others have suggested), but they were probably born from a real sense of injustice and lack of recognition. Tycho did feel that the importance of what he was doing gave him some kind of moral right to be funded; though he did 'humbly state' that he 'would not refuse' to continue to work in Denmark if funded, and that otherwise he would remain a loyal subject of the king wherever the Lord Almighty might send him. From Christian IV's point of view this was insubordination. The king could have no one question anything he decided to do with his largesse, and 'if you (wish to) serve as a mathematicus and do what he ought to do, then you should humbly offer your service and ask about it as a servant ought to do'. The king took offence (or at least pretended to) at Tycho soliciting support abroad, but was unwilling 'to trouble ourselves' in the future about whether Tycho left or stayed.[120]

Christian's letter missed Tycho at Rostock as he had gone on to stay as a guest of Heinrich Rantzov who was a very wealthy viceroy of Schelswig-Holstein and an old friend of King Frederick. Temporarily settled in Rantzov's Wandesbeck estate, Tycho produced a book with pictures of his instruments, describing his life and work. Tycho also produced in early 1598 a catalogue of 1000 star positions, dedicating it to the Holy Roman Emperor Rudolph II. Rudolph (or Rudolf) was a Habsburg who spent his early years in Spain and reversed his father's tolerant approach to Protestants. King of Bohemia and Hungary, by 1598 he was increasingly mentally depressive and unstable, living fairly reclusively in Prague and patronising arts and sciences. The constant Catholic-Protestant friction would soon lead to the thirty years war. Prague had a history of interest in astronomy, as shown by the town hall clock. Like those in Italy (but unlike England and Spain) it was astronomical.

Tycho lived in some luxury with Rantzov, near Hamburg, and was widely recognised by the German intelligentsia, a number of whom pondered the strange 'shortsightedness' of the Danish treatment of Tycho. In the two years he was there he had, however, large expenses, and really needed a patron. Rudolph was the obvious choice. Unfortunately, Ursus was styling himself 'Mathematician to Rudolph II', as we noted, and this apparent attempt to invade his patch may have increased Ursus's fury.

---

120 The full (translated) text of Tycho's and Christian IV's letters is available. The tone and tenor of both is of interest.

Prague today: Charles Bridge etc.

Tycho was continually using channels to negotiate with various potential patrons, and spent six months in Wittenberg on the way to Prague. Finally arriving in June 1599, he found temporary lodgings.[121] Tycho had a splendid reception at Rudolph's court including an audience with Rudolph who promised support, and Benatky Castle, 22 miles north-east of Prague, was set aside for his adaptation and use. He entered it in August 1599.

Prague and Kepler

Used to the absolute power of Danish monarchs, Tycho took a little while to get used to the ways of a regime in which the Emperor (who was finally deposed for mental instability) could make financial promises the treasurer (Mühlstein) either would or could not honour. The Bohemian aristocracy, of course, were not altogether sympathetic to a foreigner (however eminent) coming in and commandeering large

---

[121] In was in these early weeks that a report by the visiting Flemish astronomer Adrian van Roomen said Tycho seemed to be doing more drinking than science at Prague!

sums of money. Tycho, however, managed to extract a fair amount of money, and adapted the castle to form an adequate observatory. Around May 1600 a visitor reported that there were thirteen rooms with large instruments, and twelve assistants. Unfortunately some of his best instruments had to be left at Hven or stored elsewhere, though Tycho already had a wealth of observational data.

The initial correspondence between Tycho and Kepler seems to have been a catalogue of missing letters and letters that crossed in the rather lengthy processes of letter carrying. Kepler was mortified that his innocent fan letter to Ursus had been quoted in an attack on Tycho, and nervous that two further letters sent to Ursus (and he had not kept copies of any of the three and could not remember exactly what he had said!) would turn up to further embarrass him. He initially heard of the problem through Maestlin. An abject letter to Tycho contained apologies but also the rather tactless suggestion that such issues didn't really matter because Tycho's reputation was secure. Priority issues did not seem to matter much to Kepler, but he could perhaps have understood better Tycho's concerns. In the

The astronomical clock (Orloj) in the Town Hall of the Prague Old Town. The clock attracts a constant stream of admirers and, as the hour comes around, a substantial crowd gathers. The clock strikes and then the show begins, reminding all of the steady passage of life and time. The Apostles, together with Christ himself, turn and turn around. Death waggles his hour glass, Turk, Jew and Vanity Fair perform their parts, and a cockerel pops out cuckoo-like to bring the parade to an end. It was first installed by royal clockmaker, Nicholas of Kadan, around 1410, repaired and improved by Master Hanus around 1490, and perfected by Jan Taborsky in the mid-16th century. Legend has it that the proud burghers were so protective of secrets of the mechanism that Hanus was blinded lest he reveal them. His revenge was to have himself led up the tower by a boy, then plunging his hand into the works, immobilising them for a long time afterwards. The central dial of the clock has three hands to indicate not only the passage of the hours but also the position of sun, moon and planets according to late medieval cosmology. [cf. Michelin Guide]

Town Hall clock

circumstances Tycho's could be called a generous response:

> Even though I have not yet met you face to face, most learned sir, nevertheless I love you very dearly on account of the excellent qualities of your mind … What you say in the beginning at great length for the purpose of exculpating yourself with regard to that misplaced Ursus would not indeed have required so many words and so elaborate an explanation, since I myself regard you as sufficiently excused on other grounds. Nor do I hold it against you at all that he inserted your letter without your knowledge or consent in that defamatory and foul-mouthed writing which he published. As I now learn from you, he chopped up your letter and distorted it for the purpose of making himself look good, for this is perhaps what he had to do.[122]

Kepler was looking for a job because he had no private income and was likely shortly to be ejected from Catholic Graz. Why was Tycho so keen to recruit Kepler as an assistant? The 'traditional' view (e.g. in Gade and Koestler) is that he recognised Kepler's brilliance as a mathematician, and (perhaps subconsciously) knew that only Kepler would be able to do the mathematics to utilise Tycho's data in establishing a system for the celestial bodies. The more recent suggestion (e.g. from Thoren and Stephenson) is that it may have been more because Kepler was the ideal person to refute Ursus's slander. It is difficult to judge this. All Kepler had actually published was the *Mysterium cosmographium* which tried to map a Copernican system on the five perfect Greek solids (we will look at this later). The mathematics in this was not profound. On the other hand, Kepler was known as the protégé and (in some senses) disciple of Michael Maestlin, with whom Tycho was in correspondence and whose work and judgement he valued. It would therefore be reasonable to suppose that Tycho had both motives. Kepler would be a good ally against Ursus, and would also make a very able assistant – Tycho was usually in need of these.

The relationship consisted of three months working together at Benatky in 1600, and ten months after Tycho moved back to Prague in 1600–1601. Longomontanus arrived in Benatky castle by 17th January (and was set to work on lunar orbits), Kepler on 4th February 1600. Arriving at the castle,

---

122 Quoted e.g. in Thoren, op. cit. 436.

Kepler seems overwhelmed by the bustling household, with Tycho, Kirstine, two sons, four daughters, and assistants like Logomontanus, Tengnagel, Fels and Eriksen. Kepler's reaction was mixed. He was pleased that Tycho seemed keen to provide for him (and his wife and stepdaughter), but was irritated at being regarded as a kind of hired hand and second after Logomontanus and probably Tengnagel. This is understandable, but Tycho could hardly be blamed. He recognised the brilliance of Kepler, but Logonmontanus was a proven worker with an MA in spite of peasant origin. He had been with Tycho for eight years in Hven, a warm and steady man of whom Tycho was fond. Kepler also found it hard to speak with Tycho except at the convivial lunch table over which discussion might be astronomical. Tycho probably hoped that eventually he would be able to persuade Kepler, as he apparently had been able to with Christopher Rothman, to abandon the foolishness of the Copernican system.

Prague: Novy Svet

There were several bust-ups between Kepler and Tycho, and Tycho seems to have been fairly patient with Kepler. Kepler was, of course, under stress at having to uproot his wife from her home and reasonable holdings in Graz. Kepler's exile, even more than that of Tycho, was totally involuntary.

In June 1600, however, Rudolph returned and ordered his Mathematicus Tycho to return to Prague – probably so that he could have astrological analysis on tap. First lodgings were in a rooming house called the Golden Griffin. Tycho reputedly complained that the cloister bells of the local monastery kept him awake, and Rudolph expelled the monks though later seems to have relented. In the records they added the item that an alchemist called Tycho had complained that their 'their prayers and services disturbed him'. The records add, however, when the Emperor started to have cramps during the times the monks were praying (caused by the sorcery of the alchemist!) he reversed the order. Tycho later denied having influenced Rudolph against them in any way, but in any event Tycho was then moved to a private residence near Baron Hoffmann's house.

Why did Rudolph want Tycho near him? Rudolph had a lot of problems. He had no heir, he suffered fits of depression, and his Catholic but tolerant stance was under threat from his more militantly Catholic brother Matthias who eventually supplanted him. He might have valued Tycho's general advice as a foreign noble, but more likely he wanted astrological predictions.

Longomontanus left Tycho's service amicably on 4th August 1600, making Tycho the more anxious to have Kepler back. It was Rudolph's brother the Archduke Matthias who (September 1600) finally forced all Protestants to leave Graz. Kepler's hopes of a post at Wittenberg seemed unlikely to be fulfilled and so (despite his realisation that even an officially paid post with Rudolph left one with the difficulties of actually getting the money!) he had no choice but Prague and Tycho. Kepler was set to work on a 'Defence of Tycho Brahe against Ursus'.[123] Ursus had inconsiderately died (from syphilis, asthma or tuberculosis or all three) just before Tycho could prosecute his case of libel, refusing to recant his calumnies against Tycho and his family. Tycho at least hoped to salvage his professional reputation, demonstrating that the Tychonic system was indeed his. Kepler did not comment on the personal attacks, but showed that Ursus had misunderstood Copernicus and was wrong in suggesting that Tycho had copied his system from Apollonius anyway. Kepler was still at this enforced task the following spring when he had to go back to Graz in 'fruitless effort of four or five months to salvage his wife's … holdings'.[124] Kepler did receive some sort of 'recognition' from Rudolph, though it's real benefit was that he was appointed to Tycho's post after the latter's death.

Tycho's Death

Tycho never quite got through the process of seeking Bohemian citizenship, but he did get official recognition of his marriage to Kirstine and the legitimacy of his children by a document published in Prague. This meant that when he died Kirstine (although by her daughter's testimony she was often 'melancholy' after Tycho's death)

---

123 This is examined in *The Birth of History and Philosophy of Science: Kepler's 'A Defence of Tycho against Ursus' with Essays on its Provenance and Significance* by Nicholas Jardine (1988).

124 cited in Thoren, op. cit. 460.

could utilise his legacy (a good sum in view of a recalled loan) to live comfortably. She was eventually buried next to him in Prague's Tyn Cathedral.

It meant also that Tycho's son Thyge (Tycho) could marry a noble (if 'not particularly rich') widow and Tycho's daughter Cecelia a 'handsome hereditary baron' the Swedish Gustaf Sparre.

Tycho's health had not been very good of late, and he was affected by the death of his younger brother and wondering how long he would live. Yet he was comparatively young (54), and had no obvious life threatening ailment. At his funeral oration, his friend Jessenius (who was a medical doctor) finished with the words:

Tycho's grave: Prague

> … at the dinner of an illustrious man, dining with others as a guest, he suppressed his urine, which, having been increased by the drawn out assembly, so distended his bladder that, as if displaced, afterward it did not obey any more the wanting to cleanse it …

Kepler also describes this, and how, on his death-bed, Tycho during his eleven days of illness repeated several times '*Ne frustra vixisse videar!*' (I hope I will not appear to have lived in vain.) He beseeched Kepler in particular to finish the tables to be named after Rudolph, and to vindicate Tycho's system. He bequeathed, however, his log books and instruments to his heirs in the family; though later Kepler deftly 'liberated' the log books before the heirs could lock them away! Another doctor, Johannes Wittich, who was in Prague but not in attendance on Tycho concluded (in an account found in 1876) that:

> A stone caused him not to be able to urinate, And he dies of a burst bladder.

However, though many gave this credence, had this been the cause of the difficulty in urinating then contemporary doctors like Jessenius knew well how to use a catheter to relieve the pressure. In 1955 the Danish Urologist Edvard Gotfredsen looked at the theory, dismissed it, and suggested rather that an enlarged prostate led eventually to uremea through kidney failure. This idea, however, also seems implausible because Tycho's symptoms came on so suddenly.

In 1901 his crypt in Tyn Cathedral was refurbished, and some of his head hair and part of the hair from his long moustache were preserved. In the early 1990s a forensic scientist Bent Kampe was given some hair to analyse using a modern absorption spectrometer. He found no significant traces of arsenic (a common poison) or lead, but found high levels of mercury. In his report to the International Association os Forensice Toxicologists in 1993 Kempe concluded:

> Tycho Brahe's uremia can probably be traced to mercury poisoning, most likely due to Brahe's experiments with his elixir 11–12 days before his death.

The assumption is death from uremia – kidney failure. Uremia can be caused by blockages of the flow of urine due to urinary stones or, in males, enlarged prostate glands. It can also, as Kempe suggests, be caused by mercury poisoning, and Tycho was known to use elexirs containing mercury. Kempe's conclusions, however, were made suspect because mercury compounds could have been used in embalming the corpse.

In 1996 another scientist, Jan Pallon, used PIXE (particle-induced X-ray emission) to analyse a strand of hair from Tycho. Pallon concluded:

> One of the hair strands, which also contained the root, exhibited a very high local concentration of mercury (Hg). The location of the mercury was close to the hair root. Careful investigations of the Hg distribution across the hair strand also show the Hg is situated inside the hair … studying the Hg concentration along the hair from the root towards the tip is then actually a study in time. It can also be seen that the rise in concentration of Hg was very quick, maybe five to ten minutes … Assuming that the hair was growing up to the point of death, the Hg must have been

> given to Tycho Brahe only one day before he died. The Hg-exposure had a duration of less than one hour.[125]

The 2004 book by Joshua and Anne-Lee Gilder took this evidence and concluded that Kepler murdered Tycho using his alchemical knowledge of poisons. They combined the results of Pallon and Kempe to conclude that there were *two* administrations of mercury, one around the time of the party 11 days earlier, and one 13 hours before his actual death. The Gilders claim that this clearly shows it was murder – Tycho himself was too experienced an alchemist to have accidentally poisoned himself attempting a cure, and his mercury compounds were (as he claimed) not toxic. They claimed that there were no other suspects who would have had both motive and opportunity to poison Tycho. Kepler certainly had things to gain from Tycho's demise. But would so apparently devout a soul, whose life's work was 'thinking God's thoughts after him', really have decided to murder someone in cold blood, even in the cause of science? Various commentators were sceptical.[126] There was no proof that the hair concentration represented blood concentration nor that the dosage would have been fatal.

In November 2012 a study was published which seems now to have shown that Tycho was not poisoned after all![127] The levels of mercury in Tycho Brahe's beard were investigated by Dr Kaare Lund Rasmussen, associate professor of chemistry at the University of Southern Denmark and Dr Jan Kučera, professor of nuclear chemistry at the Nuclear Physics Institute in Prague. The online summary states:

> 'We measured the concentration of mercury using three different quantitative chemical methods in our labs in Odense and Řež, and all tests revealed the same result: that mercury concentrations were not sufficiently high to have caused his death' says Dr Rasmussen.

---

[125] A summary is on http://nuclearphysics.nuclear.lu.se/docs/historic.pdf (Accessed August 15th 2013) – also quoted in Joshua Gilder and Ann-lee Gilder's *Heavenly Intrigues.*

[126]http://www.pachs.net/blogs/comments/dawn_of_the_living_brahe/

[127]Kjaergaard, Anja, 2012, *Mercury Poisoning Ruled Out As Cause of Tycho Brahe's Death*, Aarhus University, published online 14 November 2012.

http://cas.au.dk/en/currently/single/artikel/mercury-poisoning-ruled-out-as-cause-of-tycho-brahes-death/ (accessed 15th August 2013)

> 'In fact, chemical analyses of the bones indicate that Tycho Brahe was not exposed to an abnormally high mercury load in the last five to ten years of his life', continues Dr Rasmussen, who analysed the bone samples using cold vapour atomic absorption spectroscopy at the University of Southern Denmark.
>
> 'Analyses of hairs from the beard were performed using radiochemical neutron activation analysis and proton microprobe scanning in Řež. They reflect the mercury load in the last approximately eight weeks of Tycho Brahe's life, and these analyses show that mercury concentrations fell from the high end of the normal level eight weeks before death to the low end of the normal level in the last two weeks before death' explains Dr Kučera.

So what was the cause of his death? In the online published resume the researchers make no suggestions – so you can formulate your own theory! I don't know why he died, but the story makes a fascinating study in how history is reconstructed. Maybe in ten years' time another scientific study of another hair using even more impressive sounding apparatus will conclude that he died from some other previously unsuspected form of poisoning. Who knows?

In any event, Tycho Brahe died on 24th October 1601. Rudolph, much affected, ordered and largely paid for a magnificent funeral. When Kirstine in 1604 followed Tycho to the grave, their children erected over it an imposing monument with Tycho in his armour. Back in Denmark the king received back the fief of Hven, and eventually gave it to one of his mistresses: Karen Anderslatter. Neither he nor she had much interest in astronomy, and have generally sunk into a well-deserved oblivion.

Character

The character of Tycho Brahe can be portrayed differently for all kinds of reasons. Thus to Gade Tycho was 'unapproachable, irritable, unsparing and even vengeful' and:

> Unfortunately Tycho and Kepler, though both men of genius, were of such hopelessly different temperaments that amicable, daily labour in common was out of the question. Tycho never worked with equals, only with assistants and pupils whom he had commanded and ordered around as if they were servants. The

> sensitive, pure and truly noble character of the younger man was wounded by being treated as a beginner and an inferior by the irritable and violent elder, who evidently made no attempt to master his temper.[128]

This contrast with Kepler is of interest, and Koestler likewise contrasts the two but is less inclined to canonise Kepler:

> Tycho was fifty-three, Kepler twenty-nine. Tycho was an aristocrat, Kepler a plebeian. Tycho a Coresus, Kepler a church mouse. Tycho a Great Dane, Kepler a mangy mongrel. They were opposites in every respect but one: the irritable, choleric disposition which they shared. The result was constant friction, flaring into heated quarrels, followed by half-hearted reconciliations.[129]

Koestler does remark that in regard to Kepler 'Tycho acted with unusual diplomacy and restraint' but his picture is of a high-handed Danish noble, generally intolerant and bombastic.

Thoren and Christianson are even less inclined to canonise Kepler, and recount Tycho's patience when Kepler (who was understandably edgy in this period) several times flew off the handle.

So was Tycho contemptuous and high handed in dealing with Kepler? Several things need to be remembered here. Firstly, Tycho had imbibed his learning at the tables of middle class Lutheran Bishops in Germany, spoke good high German as well as Latin, and had flaunted convention and risked ruin to marry a Lutheran pastor's daughter. He enjoyed living the grand style, but expressly pronounced that inherited title and riches were of no credit to a person compared with knowledge and learning. His daughters were aimed to marry his assistant/scholars – Gelilius Sascerides with disastrous failure but Frans Tengnagel van der Camp with great pomp – even if a little after the actual consummation of the match! The notion seems unlikely, therefore, that he would have lacked respect for the brilliant Lutheran scholar – a star from exactly the circles Tycho respected, and recommended by Maestlin whose work Tycho admired. His sympathies for

---

128 Gade op. cit. 189, 176.

129 Koestler op. cit. 306.

Kepler as an exile and victim of politics outside his control must also have related to his own misfortunes. At the same time, when Kepler came to him it was as a comparative unknown and unproven scholar, a man exiled because of his faith and without means of financial support other than what Tycho could arrange for him or give him. For Tycho to have received Kepler more as a social 'equal' than he did – even had Tycho himself not been preoccupied with slanders and problems – would have been virtually unthinkable in the context. Whether this fully explains Kepler's lament: 'Tycho is a man with whom no one can live without exposing himself to the greatest indignities' is hard to say.

Was Tycho otherwise high handed? Towards his Hven freemen he probably was, although that would not have been unusual at the time. Some of Tycho's litigation e.g. against Gellius Sascerides and Ursus, was virtually forced upon him by the extraordinary slanders both made not only against Tycho but his wife and daughters. If one reads through the accounts[130] it is hard to believe that anyone else would have behaved with much more restraint had they had a wife and daughter so vilified. Tycho seems quick-tempered, though could also be tolerant – especially in the case of Kepler. He also became very touchy about his priority and intellectual property – and in the instances of his one-time associate Wittich's development of the prosthapharetic method in mathematical astronomy Tycho rather over inflated about his own contribution. Again, however, a man who has had to endure enormous personal slander – some of it from the Danish court which proclaimed him an evil man living with a mistress – may well feel a bit more professionally touchy than otherwise.

Tycho as a man was 'high-minded' for his age in regard to what he valued. He was someone who shared with some foreign nobles a vision for science and its importance, but who found few in his own country to share this view. He despised the values and frequent lifestyles of the nobility, but enjoyed both the lifestyle and the potential for expensive instruments that a noble income provided. Tycho is a romantic, a tragic, yet a visionary and impressive figure. Koestler remarks that he did not have the 'creative genius' but by this he must surely mean *mathematical* or *theoretical* genius. It must surely be a kind of genius to see the need for accurate regular observation, and that expense is needed for this. If the Largrave Willhelm

---

130 Christianson op. cit. treats Gellius at length, Thoren op. cit. treats Ursus.

and others might have followed Tycho's lead, nevertheless he was doing something that the richest of previous astronomical sponsors had not seen a need for.

Tycho's Work

It may be of interest to have some idea of the size Tycho thought the universe. He thought that the Sun was (on average) about 1150 Earth radii away (which is about the same as Copernicus). Actually the Earth is about 93 million miles away from the Sun, and has a radius of about 3964 miles, which makes it by modern calculation about 23,500 Earth radii away. The stars Tycho thought about 14,000 Earth radii away, which (assuming a reasonably accurate figure for the Earth size) would be around 51.7 million miles (the more 'traditional' view in his time according to Thoren would amount to over 79 million miles). Our modern figure for (say) Sirius, the brightest star (actually a binary star) in the sky, is about 50 trillion miles, and to the nearest star (apart from the Sun) 25 trillion.

Tycho's main contributions as generally recognised were:

❖ The New Star

1573 *De nova Stella* (on the new star of 1572) demonstrated with his instruments that this was definitely a fixed star and was new. There could be changes in the sphere above the Moon.

❖ The Comet

1588 *De mundi …* included observations of the 1577 comet. Tycho showed that this was definitely above the Moon, yet it intersected the 'spheres' of several planets and its motion did not look very circular.

❖ His System

1588 *De mundi …* also included his planetary system, with a stationary Earth and orbiting Sun but the planets going around the Sun. This became a common view, for example, amongst the Jesuits.[131] It was the most

---

[131] Rocky Kolb's statement 'Tycho's cosmology offended everyone. He demanded an acceptance of Aristotelian physics by astronomers … Most academics of the time ignored Tycho's model' (*Blind Watchers of the Sky*, 36) seems to be a mixture of hindsight, unwarranted assumption and anachronism. There *was* no other available physics, and Tycho was far from

empirical system, and by the time of Galileo few if any astronomers were Ptolemaic – they had a Tychonic system, a semi-Tychonic system with the earth rotating, or a Capellan system with Venus and Mercury orbiting the Sun.

❖ His Instruments

Tycho, as we saw, invented the sextant in 1569, as a better alternative to the traditional cross staff for determining angles. The mountings were developed and the observer relocated at the end which had to be moved or adjusted. Finally, his new parallel sights replaced the traditional pinhole. Tycho was continually amending and updating them in the search for the most accurate observation humanly possible. His *Astronoimie instauratae mechanica* (1598) describes and pictures his instruments.

❖ His Data

Tycho's data became increasingly accurate. His instruments before 1581 had errors of about 4 minutes of arc. Walter G. Wesley in a modern study based on twenty star positions estimates that by 1585 Tycho was using averaging and improved instruments to get much smaller errors.[132] Wesley estimates individual instrument (averaged) errors as follows:

Instrument	Average error
Mural Quadrant	34″·6
Revolving wooden azimuthal quadrant	32″ ·3
Revolving steel quadrant	36″ ·3
Portable quadrant	40″ ·1
Small brass quadrant	48″ ·8
Astronomical sextant	33″ ·2

slavish in following Aristotle. His system was not a 'hybrid' but the most sensible and empirical system available given the lack of stellar parallax.

132 Walter G. Wesley 'The Accuracy of Tycho Brahe's Instruments' *Journal for the History of Astronomy* IX (1978), 42–53.

Large equatorial armillary	38″ ·6

Wesley concludes:

> The overall consistency of Tycho's major instruments is impressive. His often expressed confidence in the design and construction of his instruments seems to have been justified.

Wesley states in a later article based on solar figures:

> This study of solar observations coupled with the earlier one involving those of stellar positions indicate that Tycho's mature instruments were capable of producing positions of celestial bodies accurate to within about 30 seconds of arc.[133]

As is well known, the accuracy of this data was crucial to Kepler's arrival at his final system via Mars (the observable planet with the highest eccentricity of elliptical orbit).

❖ His Star Catalogue

In his introduction to his 1598 work *Stellarum Interrantium Restitutio* and the incomplete *Astronomiae Instauratae Progymnastata* (1602) Tycho describes the origins of star catalogues and presents his own. The mediaeval Arab astronomers made their own observations, but had to rely on Ptolemy's figures to examine, for example, the precession of the equinoxes. Copernicus's star catalogue is based just on Ptolemy's Almagest, so although he was suspicious of the accuracy of this he could progress no further. He made few observations. Tycho had the Arab data, and his own meticulous observations including over 700 stars (though Thoren points out that the fainter ones are not all that accurately positioned). Tycho discovered that there is a systematic error of longitude in Ptolemy which accounts for an incorrect figure for precession of the equinoxes.[134]

Tycho and The Copernican System

Tycho respected Copernicus as an astronomer, and helped to make his mathematical system known. Why did he reject the Copernican system? Dreyer calls the Copernican system the 'logical sequel' to the Tychonic

---

133 Walter G. Wesley 'Tycho Brahe's Solar Observation', *Journal for the History of Astronomy*. X, (1979), 96–101.

134 See Gerd Grasshoff, *The History of Ptolemy's Star Catalogue* (1990), 24, etc.

one, and several writers call Tycho's system a 'half-way house' or as Repcheck (2009) a 'hybrid'. This is misleading. Our present view of the Solar System is a 'half-way house' , since in it the Moon still goes around the Earth. Tycho adopted his system because it was the logical induction from the observed data, not because he was frightened to 'go the whole hog'.

How far were Tycho's objections to Copernicanism *theological*? Thoren suggests that for Catholics (in the late 16th century) Copernicanism was no problem, but amongst Protestants 'Luther and Melanchthon both unhesitatingly ruled out the possibility that the Earth could be in motion on the basis of biblical reference to the diurnal motion of the Sun …' [135] As we have already noted, Luther only gave an uncouth growl about 'that fool' in an after-dinner chitchat, and Melanchthon promoted Rheticus and thought Copernicanism absurd rather than heretical. Thoren does concede, however, that Rheticus, Maestlin, Rothman[136] and Kepler seemed to have experienced no problems – and, we might add, seemed to feel under *no* pressure or threat from theologians or their own pious patrons. Such theologians may have felt that the tenor of Scripture was against Copernicanism (just as they felt that the physical evidence was), but this was far from being an article of faith. Tycho listed the theological issues – but the kernel of the objection was more its physical absurdity. Not only would it necessitate a whole new physics for a moving Earth which simply did not exist, but the lack of any stellar parallax in spite of the great accuracy of Tycho's instruments placed the Copernican stellar sphere an immense distance away. In Tycho's scheme the stars were 14,000 e.r. i.e. 45.61 million miles. By Tycho's measurements the Copernican scheme would make the stars something like eight million times the distance of the Sun, 700 x the distance of Saturn, i.e. 7850,000 e.r. or 2623 million miles (the nearest in modern ideas is about 23 million miles). A third magnitude fixed star would have a diameter over 200 x that of the Sun, Sirius would be over 400 x. Tycho made this point to the Copernican Rothman, and Rothman

[135] Thoren op. cit. 276. The evidence on Luther is actually very flimsy, he does not seem to have been much interested. Melanchthon was more explicit, though much of his reasoning is physical.

[136] Christopher Rothman (1550–c.1608) studied at Wittenberg c.1570 where he wrote a manuscript on astronomy combining Aristotelian and Copernican ideas.[136] He was astronomer to Landgrave William VI of Hesse-Kassel.

replied that there was no obvious inherent absurdity in so large figures if God wanted such a system! Van Helden comments:

> Although as a Copernican Rothman was willing, by necessity, to let the evidence guide him, he had to appeal to a higher authority to balance the weight of tradition. Tycho's objection was based on a notion of cosmic sizes and distances that was deeply etched into the collective consciousness of educated Europeans. Therefore his objection was a very serious one: no answer was in sight.[137]

The measurements and Solar System mathematics in Tycho's scheme were identical to the Copernican ones – the only difference being the immense distances to, and immense sizes of, the stars in the Copernican scheme. Note that this was *not* really a religious issue – Tycho and Rothman shared the same Phillippist Lutheran tradition and faith, and Tycho's system also became popular with Jesuits. Around the end of the 16th century, then, the three systems (and some variants) were all well known to astronomers, and all had advocates. As previously indicated, leading astronomers were mostly with Tycho (or a variant), whilst the Copernican system was widely respected but had fewer direct adherents as it just did not make physical sense of earthly physics or stellar phenomena.

Further Reading

There are not all that many books specifically on Tycho. By far the best is still that of Victor E. Thoren *Lord of Unraniborg,* (1990 CUP). This does tend to jump around a little in time, and has a few implausible aspects, but it's generally well documented and detailed.

The later book *On Tycho's Island* (2000 CUP) by John Robert Christianson (who also contributed to Thoren's book), contains some interesting insights, but is not much good as a biography.

Older works, e.g. J. A. Gade *The Life and Times of Tycho Brahe* (1947 Greenwood) lack some of the insights of modern scholarship and are not altogether reliable.

---

[137] op. cit. 53.

The best general book on Tycho is now probably Kitty Ferguson's *The Nobleman and his Housedog* (2002). This contains some nice colour pictures and a generally sound and balanced view of Tycho and his relationship with Kepler.

Gilder, Joshua & Anne-Lee: *Heavenly Intrigue: Johannes Kepler, Tycho Brahe and the Murder Behind one of History's Greatest Scientific Discoveries* (2004) contains much biography, but focuses on arguing that Tycho was murdered by Kepler as described above.

Dreyer, J.L.E. *Tycho Brahe: A Picture of Scientific Life and Work in the Sixteenth Century* (1890 repr. 2009) is a Victorian perspective, recently reprinted, and you can also get the 1923 edition with a co-author.

5. Johannes Kepler

Johannes Kepler 1571-1630

Johannes Kepler (1571–1630) was myopic and sometimes saw double and was not an obvious candidate to revolutionise astronomy and optics and invent astrophysics. He had, however, one of the most original and brilliant minds in history, and his mathematics and physics were unique to his genius. Kepler's science and faith moulded seamlessly into a world-view in which he said he was 'thinking God's thoughts after him' and those thoughts were mathematical and musical.

The Protestant Reformation had been going just over half a century when Kepler was born. Western Europe was divided. Catholicism and various brands of 'Protestant' or 'Reformed' churches vied to form state churches, and often persecuted each other and the pockets of more radical groups like the Anabaptists who did not believe in state religious enforcement at all. Conflicts were not only between countries, but also often within – as rulers increased or decreased toleration of alternatives within their boundaries. The great French philosopher-mathematician Peter Ramus died in the infamous 'St Bartholomew's day massacre' of Huguenot Protestants in Paris the year after Kepler was born. Francis Drake (and the British weather!) defeated the Armada of militantly Catholic Spain when Kepler was 17. Things did not improve, and the more conciliatory Phillipist brand of Humanistic Lutheranism, to which Kepler was drawn, began to lose out in Germany and Denmark to sterner views. The Thirty Years War began when Kepler was 47 – and raged throughout the region in which he lived and moved. These were turbulent times and

Kepler, who would not compromise his own religious beliefs, led a life that reflected this.

Paradoxically, the world of science-scholarship remained European. Traditional Catholic universities in Italy were joined by the new Protestant ones in Wittenberg, Copenhagen etc. in an interest in science.

Myths

Very common today are two associated myths:

1. That scientific controversies divided along religious lines.
2. That scientists feared persecution for their scientific interests.

In reality, scientific controversy seldom divided along religious lines. Thus, for example, the (correct) view of the comets taken by Lutherans Tycho and Kepler was espoused by leading (Catholic) Jesuits – but opposed by the Catholic Galileo.

Far from fearing 'persecution' for their science, leading natural philosophers (i.e. those we would call 'scientists') were sometimes given specially protected status in areas where those of their faith were being persecuted. This happened to Rheticus in visiting Copernicus. Kepler got special protection during the extreme Catholic persecution of Protestants in Graz, Linz, Ulm, and Sagan, and was employed as Mathematicus by successive (and increasingly militant) Catholic Holy Roman Emperors. An interest in science did not *necessarily* protect someone from general persecution (as noted with Peter Ramus), and occasionally someone like Giordano Bruno was singled out for execution – but Bruno was burned for his theology, not his scientific speculation. These were dreadful, savage, times, but scientific fame was more likely to be an *advantage* (as certainly with Kepler) than to *endanger*.

Astronomy, Physics and Lutheranism

Much of the background on this has already been given in the chapter on Tycho, which refer to the mathematical ideas, concepts of 'harmony', and the various systems. The Ptolemaic system was still popular, but the Copernican system was becoming well known to astronomers. Copernican mathematics was preferable, but as a physical system it had horrendous problems making it seem absurd.

As a devout German Lutheran, Kepler moved in the circles of Tübingen University. As we have previously noted, whilst Luther may possibly have made an after dinner remark against Copernicus, and Melanchthon argued against the system, there was never any move from the Lutherans to try to suppress or restrict the Copernican ideas. Gingerich states:

> In fact, Copernicus's book was highly regarded in Lutheran circles and extensively studied throughout their university system, beginning in the first place with the efforts of Rheticus to have the work published, and especially continuing with the analysis by Erasmus Reinhold, a leading professor at Wittenberg.[138]

The preface by the Lutheran Osiander, which offered an instrumentalist slant to the work, also helped. Gingerich has followed up all the known early copies of Copernicus's work (some 500, 180 of the first edition), and noted the heavy annotations in the margins (left especially wide for such purposes). Not only does this show (as we saw in a previous chapter) that Koestler was profoundly wrong in calling it 'The Book Nobody Read' , but it tells us how it was viewed. The Wittenberg Professor of Mathematics, Joachim Rheticus, who had sent the book to printing, crossed out the preface written by Osiander, and also deleted 'of the Heavenly Spheres' from the title – evidently it too was added at the printing stage. The book was studied carefully at Wittenberg – as witnessed by the heavily annotated copy of Erasmus Reinhold, the Professor of Astronomy at Wittenberg at the time Copernicus's book was published (Reinhold died in 1553). Reinhold published his own *Prutenic Tables* in 1551, in which he said:

> All posterity will gratefully remember the name of Copernicus, by whose labour and study the doctrine of celestial motions was again restored from its near collapse. Under the light kindled in him by a beneficent God, he found and explained much which from antiquity till now was either unknown or veiled in darkness.

Reinhold's tables were based on the Copernican scheme (with equants eliminated), but made no commitment to the Earth's motion. He may have taken the Osiander instrumentalist view of the system.

---

138 Owen Gingerich, *The Eye of Heaven* (1993), 270.

In the 1560s, as Gingerich shows, the introductory astronomy course was based on Sacrobosco.[139] Considerable commentary was, however, added, in which: 'Copernicus's name appears often in print, but his heliocentric system is never discussed'. As an actual physical system it seems to have been seen (in the few mentions) as 'absurd' rather than heretical. Perhaps the silence on the literal system was a mixture of protection for Copernicus's own reputation, and a prevailing instrumentalist view of mathematical astronomy.

Michael Maestlin (1550–1631)

Michael Maestlin (or Mästlin) was the Professor of Astronomy at Tübingen when Kepler went there, and became something of a sponsor and almost father figure to the young Kepler. Caspar says of Maestlin:

> … in his public lectures, as well as in all the editions of the *Epitome* (he) sided completely with the system described in Ptolemy's *Almagest,* because the Copernican theory was strictly prohibited amongst his theological colleagues, due to its supposed contrariness to Holy Writ …[140]

Michael Maestlin
1550-1631

Some have even suggested that he would have feared for his position had he openly espoused Copernicanism – others simply state that he taught Copernicanism. So what do we know?

- Maestlin was a technically able astronomer, and Maestlin's copy of *Revolutions* is 'one of the most thoroughly annotated copies in existence'[141] and was in his possession in 1573 when he commented on the new star.
- His *Epitome of Astronome* (which went through seven editions 1582–1624) mentions Copernicanism several times, but only on technical not

---

[139] cf. chapter 4 on Copernicus.

[140] Max Caspar, *Kepler.*

[141] Gingerich, *The Eye of Heaven*, 177.

cosmological issues. But the *Epitome* (as Rosen points out[142]) was an elementary textbook, and Maestlin explained to the local Duke: 'To be sure, in all schools the familiar ancient hypotheses are retained for the young and, being easier to understand, are taught as correct; but all specialists as a body agree with Copernicus's demonstrations'.[143]

- Kepler famously wrote that: 'partly from Maestlin's utterances, partly by my own efforts, I gradually made a collection of the superiorities of Copernicus over Ptolemy from a mathematical point of view'.[144]
- Kepler also says that he joined the Copernican party: 'not without the extremely weighty authority of my teacher Maestlin, a most renowned astronomer'.[145]
- Maestlin advised the Senate of the Tübingen University that Kepler's openly Copernican work *Mysterium Cosmographium* should be published in 1596, and he wrote the customary eulogy in the preface.

Clearly Maestlin held that Copernicus's mathematical system was superior to Ptolemy's, though perhaps too complex to expound much at an elementary level. He was also willing to put his name to it as a 'true' system – as Kepler clearly held and thought from the beginning, even if less willing than Kepler to proclaim this assertively.

What was the attitude of the Tübingen theologians? Rosen points out the 1596 Tübingen Senate's 'unanimous endorsement of Copernicanism as expounded by Kepler and recommended by Maestlin'. This implied the silence of the philosophy professor Muller, who had objected three years earlier to the arguments of Kepler and a friend about the *physics* of Copernicanism. Maestlin himself wrote to Kepler that on the issue the pro-rector, the theologian Matthias Hafenreffer, has 'time and again … assailed me (jokingly, to be sure, although serious tones too seem to be intermingled with the jests)'.[146] Maestlin responded likewise jokingly to the pro-rector – though would have responded more seriously if necessary.

---

[142] In Arthur and Peter Beer, *Kepler, Four Hundred Years* (1975), 318.

[143] Johannes Kepler, *Gesammelte Werke* XIII, 68: 45–48.

[144] Caspar, op. cit. 49.

[145] Kepler, op. cit. I, 16: 39–40.

[146] Kepler, op. cit. XIII, 151: 19–32.

Maestlin's basic picture is of one where the theologians were uneasy about Copernicanism, but although 'otherwise fine and very scholarly' actually 'have no adequate grasp of the fundamentals of these subjects'. Hafenreffer had also corresponded directly with Kepler (whose exceptional talents he clearly acknowledged) advising him to omit a chapter dealing with the theological issues and speaking to him with a 'strong and sincere brotherly affection'. Kepler's impression was that Hafenreffer was not truly opposed to Copernicanism, but wished to see him spared unnecessary controversy. Caspar suggests that Kepler's Copernicanism 'cast a shadow on his otherwise excellent qualities and achievements in the eyes of his professors of theology'.[147] This is probably misleading. The theologians were apprehensive and nervous of the possible controversy, but any notion that they therefore wanted to pack Kepler off to Graz, or had any less regard for him, seems to be mistaken. Nor is there any indication that Maestlin felt under serious threat. He had no especial reason to be *aggressively* Copernican, but nor did he have any especial reason to keep it quiet.

Kepler's Life

On 27th December 1571, after a gestation period of 224 days, 9 hours, and 53 minutes, was born one of the greatest geniuses in human history. The child was baptised Johannes, and later called himself Kepler, Keppler, Khepler, Kheppler or Keplerus with the characteristic casualness towards names of the era.[148]

Weil der Stadt

His place of birth was in the Swabian town Weil-der-Stadt. This was a small and crowded place, but a free imperial city gathered around a Gothic church from which Kepler's parents soon moved to neighbouring Leonberg. He was from craftsman stock, though there is some hint of an earlier fall from minor nobility. His paternal

[147] Caspar, op.cit.

[148] The works already cited by Koestler, Caspar and Beer are all useful for biographical details.

grandfather Sebald was a furrier and was mayor for a while, and Johannes later described him as 'arrogant … short tempered and obstinate … eloquent … ignorant …' and of declining substance and reputation after 1578. Johannes' grandmother Katherine was 'restless, clever and lying, but devoted to religion; slim and of a fiery nature; vivacious, an inveterate troublemaker; jealous, extreme in her hatreds, violent, a bearer of grudges … all her children have something of this'. His father, Heinrich, married another Katherine – who sounds even sharper and more vivacious than the grandmother, with just a hint of witchcraft! It was not a happy marriage, but Johannes was born after about seven months as the first of six children. Heinrich was a soldier of fortune, spent much time away

Europe Around 1600 (modern states are outlined)

(during some of which Johannes was with his grandparents), and disappeared finally in 1588. Though the town church remained Catholic, Sebald was a Lutheran and Johannes was probably christened as a Lutheran in the neighbouring town of Magstadt.

Johannes' picture of his own childhood is tempestuous and illness-ridden. He attended a local school intermittently, and was also sent to one of the

Latin schools that had been established since the Reformation to help poor but talented children learn the language of scholarship. He records just two interesting incidents in this period. When he was six:

> I heard much of the comet of that year, 1577, and was taken by my mother to a high place to look at it.

When he was nine:

> I was called outside by my parents especially, to look at the eclipse of the Moon. It appeared quite red.

Koestler remarks: 'When he had passed the elementary Latin school, Johannes' good brains, bad health and interest in religion made the career of clergyman the obvious choice'. He passed the competitive examination, and between ages 13–17 attended the (free) school/seminary which would prepare him for Tübingen university. The regime was hard, at four or five in the morning the day began with psalm singing, and there was no 'time off' during the day. Kepler studied the classics, rhetoric, dialectics and music, spherics and arithmetic, and Bible reading. Kepler later pictures himself as a tortuously introspective lad, impulsive, garrulous and sometimes sarcastic, and falling in and out of friendships. He adds: 'though morally he was the worst amongst his contemporaries … he was religious to the point of superstition'. The picture is of a brilliant, creative, but guilt and angst-ridden lad, and, even if exaggerated, gives some idea of his youth.

In 1589 he entered the seminary of the university of Tübingen. Initial studies were in ethics, dialectics, rhetoric, Greek, Hebrew, astronomy and physics and, after two years, a master's examination in which (in 1591) Johannes came second out of 14. He was seen as a diligent, sedate and pious young man – and his continuation to study theology was warmly endorsed by the senate.

We know little about the details of his university studies, but we do know that he there met and befriended Michael Maestlin, as described above. Theologically he seems to have struggled with the Reformed version of predestination, doubted the certainty of the Lutheran (as against the Calvinist or Catholic) view of the Eucharist and the person of Christ, and in particular could not accept the Lutheran notion of 'ubiquity' i.e. the universal *corporeal* presence of the body of Christ.

Graz (1594–1600)

On April 11th 1594, aged 22, Johannes Kepler came to take up a month or two's trial as teacher of mathematics (which included astronomy) at the Protestant seminary at Graz, a lovely city on the river Mur with a castle topped hill.[149] This was a land under Roman Catholic rule which, having once granted freedom to Protestants, was slowly taking back these concessions. In 1586 the Jesuits (an educational order of Roman Catholics) had set up a university there, in opposition to the Phillipist (Lutheran) Protestant seminary. Kepler's subject was unpopular, and he had few students the first year and none the second – though the school inspectors apparently did not blame Kepler for this! Kepler was drafted in to teach other subjects like history and ethics, and was well regarded. He did tend, however, to speak fast and deviate from subjects if a new thought struck him.

On 19th July 1595 Kepler drew for his class a diagram of a triangle inscribed inside two circles. He suddenly had the idea that perhaps this could be used to relate the orbits of Jupiter and Saturn the outermost known planets.[150] The idea did not work, but from it he

developed his idea that the ratio of orbits of the six planets (Mercury,

---

[149] There is no evidence for the view of Berthold Sutter in Beer op. cit. 140 that Tubingen has 'cast out this rash young man' who espoused Copernicanism. Even Caspar pointedly denies it (51).

[150] The diagram in *Mysterium Cosmographicum* has a series of rotating triangles showing the conjunctions of Jupiter and Saturn.

Venus, Earth, Mars, Saturn, Jupiter) related to the sizes of the five perfect convex solids. i.e. the *only* solid figures which have all faces the same and are convex. Kepler's basic idea was that if you inscribed one inside the other inside the other of these then (allowing for a reasonable thickness) this might correlate with the orbit sizes of the six planets. He wrote up this idea in mathematical detail in a book titled *Cosmographic Mystery* (*Mysterium Cosmographicum).* This is the work, already mentioned, which Michael Maestlin saw through publication with the Tübingen Senate's full approval. Kepler dashed off copies (with fan letters) to various people, including Tycho, and copies found their way to Galileo in Italy.

Whilst in Graz, Kepler married in 1597 Barbara Muehleck, a twice-widowed daughter of a rich mill owner. Barbara was (according to Kepler) fat, stupid, religious, often ill, forgetful and melancholic, and she eventually died after 14 years of apparently less than idyllic marriage.

Graz now: red roofs, green hill

In summer 1599 the Catholic Archduke Ferdinand closed down Kepler's college, and in September all Lutheran preachers and collegiate teachers were required to leave. After one month Johannes Kepler, apparently the only exception, was allowed to return because (he said) the Archduke liked his work. Koestler also seems probably right in suggesting that the powerful Jesuit order and some of their friends like Herwart von Hohenburg and Johan Baptist Fickler, with whom Kepler corresponded, were active on Kepler's behalf. He had, of course, no class, but could continue his work and speculation in mathematical astronomy.

Kepler had sent his *Cosmographic Mystery* to various people including both Tycho and Ursus – who published the letter in an attack on Tycho in 1597.

Tycho Brahe (as we saw in chapter 4) left Denmark in 1597 and was then in Prague. This was the period of letter exchange between Kepler and Tycho. Tycho had expressed his displeasure that Ursus (Nicolaus Reimers) had bound up the fan letter from Kepler with a virulent attack not only on Tycho's astronomy but his family. So Kepler was working on his *Apologia,* exposing Ursus and defending Tycho.

Kepler too, was reading, and working on various other ideas including biblical chronology and the effects of stars on weather. At this time too the central idea of *harmony* emerges – later reflected in his *Harmony of the World.* The whole of reality was bound up in a harmonious whole, with mathematics as a key to it (an approach, as we shall see, with parallels in the later Newton).

The Catholic screw was tightening in Graz. All Protestant clergymen were now expelled, and effectively the *practice* of the Protestant faith was forbidden. Kepler still received his teaching salary and was free to pursue his astronomy, but his position was becoming untenable. On 1st January 1600 he left for Prague to meet Tycho.

Prague (1600–1612)

When they met on February 4th 1600 Tycho was 53, Kepler 28. We saw in the Tycho chapter how Kepler, understandably stressed, impetuously fell out with Tycho, but was reconciled and stayed five months. When he returned to Graz, his employers (unimpressed it seems with Tycho's warm commendation) suggested Kepler would be better employed in studying in Italy the useful art of medicine, rather than developing the aesthetic but impractical art of astronomy in such turbulent times. Kepler saw that any hope of returning to Prague on extended leave of absence was impractical. What could he do? He had some hopes of becoming to the Catholic Archduke Ferdinand what Tycho was to his cousin the Catholic Holy Roman Emperor Rudolph. He dedicated to Ferdinand an essay on the Moon in which he introduced amongst the complex mathematics a revolutionary notion 'There is a force in the Earth which causes the Moon to move'. Ferdinand thanked him with a gift, but nothing more was muted.

Finally, in August 1600 all Protestants were banished from Graz. Kepler, although granted some concessions, had to leave with wife and child. His father in law had converted to Catholicism and so retained his lands, but the glut of attempted land sales had reduced their value and Kepler had little money of his own. Having failed to obtain a place in Tübingen, Kepler arrived in Prague on October 19th.

Kepler's House: Prague

Tycho genuinely did his best for Kepler. After a brief (and apparently unmolested) return to Graz in spring 1601 at the death of his father in law, Kepler finally settled in Prague. Tycho died in 1601 and Kepler became the Imperial Mathematician until Rudolph's death in 1612. This was the period of greatest productivity for Kepler.

In 1602 he produced *On the More Certain Foundations of Astrology (De fundamentis astrologiae cerioribus).* This was to satisfy the emperor, though Kepler was always very guarded in his approach to astrology – even if, like Tycho, most of his detailed predictions turned out to happen!

In 1604 Kepler produced his *The Optical Part of Astronomy* (*Astronomiae pars optica),* the first of a set of writings on optics which comprise about a quarter of his work – and alone would have made him a great scientist.

In 1604 a new star (commonly known as 'Kepler's nova') appeared, and Kepler wrote about it in a detailed book of 1606 dedicated to the emperor – a book in which he also suggested that the star of Bethlehem was actually a conjunction in four BC.

His work on the difficult Mars continued until 1606, and led in 1609 to the work containing the two basic planetary laws concerning the elliptical orbits and varying speeds of planets around the Sun.

Remarkably, Kepler left us a detailed account of how he reached these laws, but we will leave this until we look at his actual works. We should, however, note that the full title was *New Astronomy, Based upon Causes, or Celestial Physics, Treated by Means of Commentaries on the Motions of the Star Mars, from the Observations of Tycho Brahe.* Kepler was unique in that he was not attempting just positional astronomy, but a *physics* of the celestial bodies.

Kepler now had high renown, both in court and in scientific circles. Amongst other things, he was a member of the Italian *Accademia dei Lincei.* In April 1610 Kepler received a work by a man who valued his own membership of that body highly – with a request for his opinion. The book, *The Starry Messenger*, was the first work of Galileo Galilei, announcing his discovery with the telescope of the moons of Jupiter. Galileo could not explain *how* the telescope worked or why some stars appeared in double, and this makes it the more understandable that some of his countrymen remained sceptical. Kepler's high reputation at this time made the more important his immediate support for Galileo's discovery in a pamphlet *Conversations with the Starry Messenger.* Unfortunately, Galileo thanked him but ignored Kepler's urgent request for a telescope to check the observation for himself. Kepler only finally got his hands on one in August – borrowed from the Elector Ernst of Cologne. Kepler then published (1611) his own *Account of Jupiter's Satellites.*

Kepler also completed for 1611 his important *Dioptrics* in which he both explained Galileo's telescope and described the theory of a new design with two convex lenses instead of Galileo's earlier model. Whereas Galileo's telescopic discoveries were or would have been made around the same time by other astronomers (and he was not the first to observe celestial bodies through a telescope), Kepler's contributions were unique – his genius was unparalleled in his age. Kepler's, not Galileo's, is the model for the standard telescope – and Kepler developed and explained the optics of it. He added, however, a long preface to the book extolling Galileo's discoveries (which by this time included the phases of Venus).

In 1611 Kepler's son and wife Barbara both became ill and died. His patron the Emperor Rudolph II, increasingly under military and political threat and mentally unstable, first abdicated and then finally died in January 1612. The new Emperor Matthias, Rudolph's brother, confirmed Kepler in his post as Imperial Mathematician, but also gave him leave to move to Linz.

Linz Town Hall

Linz (1612–1626)

Kepler made a last attempt to get a post in Tübingen. The basic problem was his earlier refusal to accept the

Lutheran 'Augsburg Confession' as enshrined in the ironically named 'Formula of Concord' . This was not only attacked by Catholics but excluded Calvinists who rejected the doctrine of 'ubiquity' (as mentioned above). Kepler still had serious doubts about this doctrine of ubiquity (which Lutherans later abandoned anyway), and could accept the formula only with reservations. He also still rejected the 'barbarous' views of both Calvin and Luther on the meaning of divine predestination and the bondage of the human will (although it has to be said that Melanchthon himself had also leaned to a softer, more Erasmian view on these issues). Kepler always regarded himself as a member of the *catholic* (though not of course the *Roman Catholic)* church, and disliked exclusivity. This was not from some kind of postmodern fuzziness, but because he sought Christian communion with all sincere Christians irrespective of doctrinal differences. Alas for Kepler, this was an age with Lutheranism increasingly seeing 'faith' as adherence to a creed rather than a spiritual bond-link with the risen and living Christ. Kepler's views were certainly more Lutheran than anything else, but if 'faith' is seen as creedal then even tiny divergences become crucial. It was Kepler's theology, not his Copernicanism, which made the Lutherans see him as an 'unhealthy sheep' and block his appointment.

Linz was a provincial capital in upper Austria, a small but ancient town on the upper Danube. Kepler came, aged 41 and with a high European reputation, to be district mathematician and schoolteacher (in a school even less important than the one in Graz in his first job!). A humble post in an intellectual backwater seems to have been selected not for his own benefit but for that of his wife – with whom he had little rapport and who died before he got there. The population were mostly Lutherans in the Tübingen mould, and the local minister refused Kepler communion. Kepler appealed, but the appeal was turned down – the theologians telling him to get on with the mathematics and stop meddling in theology!

Other parts of the picture in these early Linz years are of a great man of undoubted total personal piety suffering a series of petty annoyances from local small-minded self-important officials. There was even an attempt in 1616 (he found out later after the more powerful Barons on the council blocked it) to terminate his employment because he was too expensive.

Kepler was a widower with two children aged 6 and 11. He sought a wife – eleven 'candidates' being considered (and recorded in tortuous detail as Koestler and others indicate). He finally plumped for number five, Susanna

Reuttinger, a twenty four year old spinster from nearby Eferding. Kepler was a widower with two children aged 6 and 11. Susanna was an orphan, adopted by Baroness Elizabeth von Starhemberg – though she did not offer a big dowry and Kepler was considered (like Tycho) to have married in a love-match beneath his stature. His self-analysis reveals he had indeed fallen head over heels for her, but was struggling between love and the prudence of 'giving her up' and marrying instead any of various available noble and/or well-off ladies. He seems to have been blissfully happy with her, and they had seven children (few of whom survived to adulthood). She provided the peaceful home for his work on the Rudolphine tables and other works of this period – though money worries were never far away.

During this period Kepler addressed in tracts and letters the date of the birth of Christ – arriving at the (now generally accepted) view that it was around 4 BC.[151] He was also involved in a controversy on the reform of the calendar, wisely recommending the Lutherans to follow the example of other Protestants in accepting the papal proposals that would bring Easter back to its proper place in the calendar. Their refusal meant that, for 17th century Lutherans, Newton was born in 1642 rather than 1643!

In 1613 Kepler produced in Latin a work which grew out of his own domestic ownership of wine barrels: *Nova sterometria doliorum vinariorum* (the gauging of wine casks). This, with a more popular (and humorous) version in German, was actually an important treatise on geometry and conic sections, forming a bridge from Archimedes to later integral calculus.

An unwelcome interlude occurred with the protracted trial for witchcraft of his near septuagenarian mother Katherine. It began (and one can think of modern counterparts) as an action for slander that backfired, and resulted in a catalogue of invented accusations and raising of popular spectres.[152] Katherine fled to live in Linz with Kepler, but disliked Austria and returned to Württemberg in October 1617. Kepler went with her and

---

151 With apologies to any of you who celebrated the new millennium some years after the event! There are some today, however, who have reverted to the 1 AD date.

152 If we are tempted to smugness we may remember the corrupt goings-on and mutual denouncement in some local and national politics – but the spectres now sometimes falsely raised are e.g. 'being PC' and accusations of harassment! Gingerich calls the trial 'a showcase for human fears, greed, and stupidity'

stayed two months. Legal actions ground on, and she was eventually arrested in August 1620. Kepler set out again for Württemberg, and was active in the complex procedures of her defence. After 14 months in prison and an unfulfilled threat of torture (which Lutherans used as freely as the Inquisition), she was acquitted by the Duke of Württemberg in 1621.

Meantime, in 1619 Emperor Matthias died and was replaced by his cousin Ferdinand II, an absolutist and fanatical Catholic who began the forcible Catholicisation of areas including upper Austria. However, also in 1619 the leader of the Protestant faction in the Thirty Years War was proclaimed King Frederick I of Bohemia in Prague, and Kepler's salary as an employee of Ferdinand was under threat. Kepler's departure from Linz to Württemberg (the reason for which he understandably kept secret!) was seen by some as flight, and rumours circulated. However, Ferdinand II's Catholic army defeated King Frederick I decisively in November 1620, and some of Kepler's friends in Prague were amongst those executed in the ensuing carnage in June 1621. Nevertheless, the Catholic Ferdinand II immediately confirmed the devout Lutheran Kepler as Imperial Mathematician in December 1621! In the following year when all 'preachers and non-Catholic schoolmasters' were banished from Linz, Kepler once again was made an exception. Perhaps, again, his Jesuit contacts (who were influential with Ferdinand) were active for him, and Ferdinand's own regard for him seemed unabated. In any event, once again, Kepler's scientific standing (including his Copernicanism) was a protection – not a danger to him.

Kepler was surrounded by wars, the savage death of friends, exclusion from his own church, and the deaths of his children. How much the more extraordinary, then, that he could produce in 1619 the amazing work *Harmony of the World* (*Harmonices mundi*) – although he himself says he turned to it as relief from sadness at his little daughter's death. It is a vision of the unity of all reality as creation of God, a mathematical and musical harmony. The work included the third planetary law relating times of planetary orbits to their distances from the Sun. He also completed in three parts (1618, 1620 and 1621) his *Epitome of Copernican Astronomy* (*Epitome Astronomiae Copernicanae*). The work contained many of his ideas on the Sun as motive force for the orbiting of planets, and (although 'wrong' in important aspects) was also a precursor of later Newtonian ideas on gravity.

In 1625 the Catholic screw tightened further in Protestant Linz, but once again Kepler was largely exempted. His library was briefly sealed, but released after the intervention of his friend the Jesuit Paul Guldin. The wars, and particularly peasant uprisings, caused great suffering and a brief siege of Linz. Kepler and his printer were safeguarded, but the printing press and some of the printed material went up in flames with part of the city. In 1626 Kepler finally decided to leave Linz for Ulm via Regensburg (where he left his family over winter).

Ulm, Sagan and Regensburg (1626–30)

In Ulm, Kepler had various troubles with arranging the printing of his Rudolphine astronomical tables. He also had a son at university whose expenditure exceeded his parental allowance (a situation some of us will recognise!) The system of logarithms newly invented by Napier and with improved arithmetical explanations from Kepler was also described in the work – the tables involving, of course, a great number of multiplications. It finally appeared in a stately folio volume in 1627. The frontispiece is elaborate. Five people meet as though in an academy: an ancient Babylonian, Hipparchus, Ptolemy Copernicus and Tycho. Kepler is on one of the side panels looking out anxiously whilst the imperial eagle (hint hint!) drops money onto the astronomer's writing table. There were still some wrangles with Tycho's heirs about the introduction and dedication, so there are several alternative early versions of these. The work included a fold-out world map (with longitudes of major cities), a chronology of world history, etc. The tables, although not totally accurate even at the time of printing, remained important for a century. The tables marked the completion of his main work as Imperial Mathematician. Kepler was still cherishing hopes of publishing Tycho's observations, and meantime returned to Prague. His standing with the Emperor is shown in the warm welcome he received as virtually a lone Protestant in a Catholic

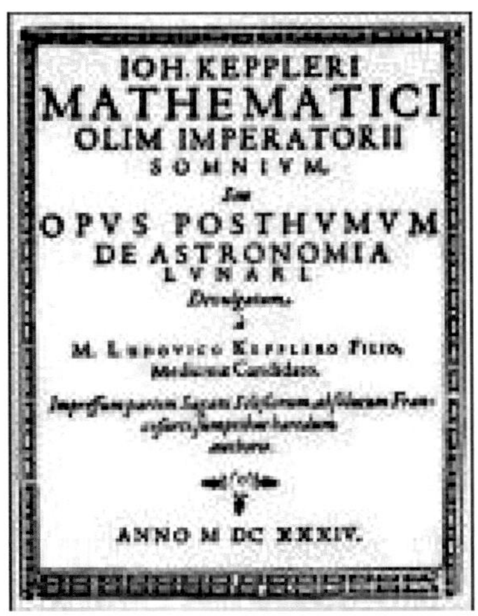
IOH. KEPPLERI
MATHEMATICI
OLIM IMPERATORII
SOMNIVM,
OPVS POSTHVMVM
DE ASTRONOMIA
LVNARI.
ANNO M DC XXXIV.

city. Kepler was pressed by his friend the Jesuit Paul Guldin to convert, but was under no threat. In Prague Kepler also renewed contact with the powerful Albrecht Wallenstein (whose horoscope he had cast in 1608 supposedly without knowing who was the subject).

Frontispiece Rudolphine Tables

Another cautious horoscope secured him the offer to settle with a generous salary and a printing press on Wallenstein's estates in Sagan (or Zagan) in Silesia. He arrived there with his family in July 1628. Kepler was a lonely foreigner in Sagan, and, yet again, arrived in a location just as the pressure was applied on all Protestants to convert or leave in a regime organised by the Jesuits. Kepler, as usual, was exempt, but it made his life more difficult.

It was at this time that Kepler, incidentally as it were, invented science fiction with his production of *The Dream, or Astronomy of the Moon* (*Somnium seu astronomia lunari*), which involves a supposed round trip to the Moon. An early manuscript version of this had already been circulating since 1611 (which may not have helped his mother's case in the witch trial). The work reflects both an interest in lunar geography and a desire to show what a 'Moon's eye view' would look like – to render more credible the idea of an 'Earth's eye view' as part of Copernicanism.

Huge sums remained owed to Kepler by the Imperial treasury, along with various other sums – and he continued to have money concerns. In summer 1630 the Electors were meeting with the Emperor at Regensburg to discuss, amongst other things, the dismissal of General Wallenstein. Kepler called there on his way to Linz, and fell ill of a fever. He died, aged only 58, in Regensburg on 15th November 1630. His last work *Dream of lunar astronomy* appeared in a final version posthumously in 1634.

Character, Religion and Science

It is hard to read much about Kepler without feeling some sympathy for this petulant, sensitive, almost child-like character. Critics may portray a bombastic noble hauteur in Tycho, an arrogant sarcasm in Galileo, and a certain cold aloofness in Newton – but many seem to fall under the charm of Johannes Kepler. Kepler was impetuous and sometimes tempestuous, but open, forgiving, and not selfish by disposition. To go deeper, one can hardly separate his character from his world-view, so this too will need to be considered here.

There are a number of ways in which science and religion can relate in a scientist's thinking:

1. A scientist could be antireligious.
2. A scientist could be disinterested in religion.
3. A scientist could be formally or conventionally religious – going through the forms with no depth of feeling.
4. A scientist could be devoutly religious but with this largely separate from his/her science.
5. A scientist could be devoutly religious with this central within her/his scientific world-view.

Kepler was supremely in the fifth of these categories, and had a world-view that to him was Christian, rational, unified, and scientific. How far one sees this depends on one's own world-view. The sympathetic agnostic Arthur Koestler was charmed but mystified by Kepler, for example, writing off as 'crankish' the *idée fixe* of the five perfect solids as a 'delusion' which luckily stimulated real discovery. To Koestler, some of Kepler's questions were 'inspired by a medieval brand of mysticism' and the roots of his inspiration were 'purely mystical'.[153] More recently Bruce Stephenson[154] adamantly states:

> Kepler was not a mystic. He was, understandably, an astrologer, but in that age astrology was not yet entirely irrational … Their origin was no more mystical than a sincere belief in God, a belief

[153] Koestler, *The Sleepwalkers* (1959), 263.

[154] Bruce Stephenson, *Kepler's Physical Astronomy* (1987) and *The Music of the Heavens* (1994).

> that certainly was neither abnormal nor irrational at the beginning of the seventeenth century.[155]

Stephenson holds that Kepler believed, for example, in the plurality of worlds for 'ordinary, down to earth reasons'. Stephenson grasps the breathtaking overall vision of Kepler of a unified and rational reality – but he does so wistfully, from the outside. The interest today is, he says, because we wish that:

> … he had in some way been right. Our detailed knowledge of the world forbids us from imagining that the heavens embody harmony in the usual, everyday sense…Living in a world… that knows no recognizable purpose, we are intrigued by the thought that a scientist like Kepler pursued a truth beyond reason … He had the good fortune to be born at a time when it was still possible to believe … that the Creator of the world had employed a design, and that he could by himself discover that design.[156]

Owen Gingerich is associated with the Christian, evangelical American Scientific Affiliation, and so likely to be more sympathetic to a view that sees coherent design in the universe.[157]Gingerich points out that Kepler's third law – itself an unexplained mathematical harmony, was the foundation for Newton's gravitational synthesis:

> Kepler's great cosmic vision of celestial harmony – part fantasy and chimera – had indeed ultimately brought him closer to the eternal architecture of his Creator.[158]

Jesuit Job Kozhamthadam S.J. is also sympathetic, seeing Kepler as 'an ardent believer in the mystery of the Holy Trinity' but also as one who:

> ... had serious reservations about several other Christian doctrines (e.g. the real presence of Christ in the Eucharist, Calvinist predestination, infallibity, etc.) …[159]

---

155 Stephenson (1994), 249.

156ibid. 251–22.

157 Owen Gingerich, *The Eye of Heaven* (1990).

158ibid. 404.

159 Job Kozhamthadam, *The Discovery of Kepler's Laws* (1994), 16.

To a modern Jesuit, then, Kepler appears as a theological radical rejecting 'traditional' doctrines – though others may accept Kepler's own view that in all such matters he is simply going *back* to the Christianity of the New Testament and the early Fathers. Our own world-views, then, very much affect our perspectives of Kepler.[160]

Kepler's theology was essentially 'evangelical' (the word Lutherans' generally used) with a neo-platonic flavour. God is pictured as personal, rational, mathematical and musical. Human beings are made in God's image, and so are able (in his famous phrase) to 'think God's thoughts after him'. The universe also reflects the nature of God, with a direct symbolism as well as in more general terms. Kepler repeatedly symbolises the Trinity as a sphere: The Father is the centre, the Holy Spirit is Space, and the Son the surface. God is One, rational, musical, a mathematician and geometer, an active force, and a source of illumination. Thus:

> The souls of Christians are copies of the creator and are sustained as such by him through a certain 'irradiation' of the divine countenance unto them.[161]

Both the souls of Christians and physical nature reflect the attributes (as listed above) of the Creator. The Trinity is (to Kepler) also reflected directly by the Solar System. In the centre the Sun represents the Father, providing both illumination *and* the motive force for all the motion. The power is transmitted through space, representing the Holy Spirit. The Earth sits as the mid planet, reflecting the intermediate positions of humans, as one of whom the Son was incarnated.

Kepler thought that God created the world in this way because the self-unfolding God 'wishes to be known through this Book of Nature'. God has written two books: the Book of Scripture and the Book of Nature. The book of Scripture is read through theology, and that of nature through science. This was a belief common to other figures like Francis Bacon (1561–1626) and Galileo. In Kepler, however, the division between the two is less clear cut as the physical *symbolises* the spiritual. In common with

---

[160] The lack of any uniquely 'objective' historical perspective was explored in our first notes. The present writer, in case you wonder, holds theological views very sympathetic to those of Kepler!

[161] See Kozhamthadam (21 etc.) for this and other quotations.

Bacon, though, Kepler held that the study of science was sacred – it was exploring the works and mind of God. This also brought Kepler an element of humility:

> I am of the opinion that since astronomers are priests of Almighty God with respect to the Book of Nature, we should concern ourselves not with praise of our cleverness but with the glory of God.[162]

If by 'mystic' then, we mean that Kepler was irrational, this is not so. Kepler believed in a rational creator-God, and he thought that his world-view was both empirical and made overall sense of the human experience.

Kepler was at fundamental odds with the Aristotelian focus on qualities (as represented in a famous controversy with Robert Flood[163]) and in favour of a mathematical approach. On the other hand he departs from Platonism in being a scientific *realist* and not just interested in 'saving the phenomena'. He is interested in the *physics of the skies* – not just in mathematical stratagems to predict planetary positions. He also believes in *precision* – abandoning an earlier planetary theory because it was eight minutes of arc out. Plato had believed that the actual physical world only approximates to the ideal one, and a true Platonist might not have been much bothered about the odd eight minutes or so. So Kepler is a kind of Platonic/Pythagorean *realist.* Like Bacon, he was also applying ideas of concomitant variation (e.g. looking for a cause as the sole factor always present). He sought in nature harmony, economy, rationality, simplicity etc. His physics involved forces and mechanisms – and the assumption that there must be reasons for any apparent coincidence (e.g. that the further away a planet was from the Sun the slower it moved).

So how should we regard Kepler today? Is Stephenson right in assuming that we can only look wistfully back at an age when such an approach of looking for overall coherence was possible? Are there parallels between his age and ours? This is one of the most interesting questions we can ask, so here are some pointers.

Firstly, Kepler assumed that the universe was rational and the human mind rational enough to comprehend it. This is not self-evident, yet today scientists continue to make this assumption – even when they

---

[162] Letter to Hewart March 1598 cited in Kozhamthadam op. cit. 41.

[163] See the appendix to book V of *Harmonies of the World.*

have no theistic belief upon which Kepler (and others like Descartes) founded such assumptions.

Secondly, let us note a certain unity in Kepler's aims:

- to reduce phenomena to a rule of mathematical ratios.
- to see some 'fittingness' and 'beauty' in the mathematics involved.

Why *should* physical reality be reducible to mathematics? Why *should* the mathematics be elegant? There is no *a priori* reason, but physicists and cosmologist still tend to assume that both are true. Given a lack of any underlying theory, there was no more irrationality in Kepler looking for a ratio of planetary orbits matching five perfect solids, than in looking for a ratio of orbit sizes linking the squares of the sizes to the cubes of their semi major axes.

Did Kepler work *a priori*? Ironically, Kepler's theory of the perfect solids was at least susceptible to some kind of test. Max Tegmark today has seriously suggested that there *must be* universes corresponding to all the mathematically possible ones.[164] Multiple universe theories are perfectly scientifically respectable suggestions made to account for the otherwise inexplicable inhabitability of our own.

This is reflected, for example, in a 1999 work by the Cambridge Professor and Astronomer Royal, Martin Rees. Having noted the extraordinary 'fine tuning' of six basic constants (without which any universe would be uninhabitable) Rees entitles his last chapter *Coincidence, providence – or multiverse?* He suggests that we either have to believe that it was all amazing coincidence, or that God designed it thus (as does Cambridge cosmologist/clergyman John Polkinghorne), or that 'our universe is "one atom" selected from an infinite multiverse'.[165] Rees remarks:

> Some people may be inclined to dismiss such concepts as 'metaphysics' (a damning put-down from a physicist's viewpoint). But I think the multiverse genuinely lies within the

---

[164] 'all structures that exist mathematically exist also physically' – his famous 2003 article can be accessed through his website currently http://space.mit.edu/home/tegmark/technical.html

[165] Martin Rees, *Just Six Numbers* (1999). See also Rees with John Gribben, *Cosmic Coincidences* (1990).

> province of science, even though it is no more than a tentative hypothesis.

So is Rees a 'mystic'? This same kind of amazing 'coincidences' in cosmic constants led Fred Hoyle from militant atheism to something like theism, and to Freeman Dyson famously remarking 'It looks as though someone knew we were coming'. Stephen Hawking once said:

> The odds against a universe like ours emerging out of something like the Big Bang are enormous. I think there are clearly religious implications.[166]

These odds led to cosmologist Paul Davies (who is not a Christian) remarking that science is a surer road to God than the Bible.[167] In his 1998 work he concludes that there *is* an alternative to the view of a purposeless universe:

> … undeniably romantic, but perhaps true nevertheless. It is the vision of a self-organising and self-complexifying universe, governed by ingenious laws that encourage matter to evolve towards life and consciousness …[168]

In a later work *The Goldilocks Enigma: Why is the Universe Just Right for Life?* (2006) he explores how the universe is 'just right' – like baby bear's porridge!

Alternatively, Stuart Kauffman has written a work – again not from a Christian position – arguing that the universe is such that we are 'at home' in it.[169] This is not to mention those like Sir Anthony Hewish (who won a Nobel prize for the pulsar discovery) whose world-view is specifically Christian. Hewish has remarked:

> … many people have an idea that science is common sense, nuts and bolts theory, if you can see how all the bits and pieces link together, you understand it all, but in fact modern physics isn't like that, it's way beyond common sense, and the way that the particles behave, and the sort of language you have to use to describe this, is so far removed from all that, it requires acts of

---

[166] Quoted in John Boslough, *Stephen Hawking's Universe* (1985), 121.

[167] These and similar materials are contained in our own *Reason, Science and Faith*, ch 3.

[168] Paul Davies, *The Fifth Miracle* (1998), 256. Davies also repeats the Freeman Dyson quote.

[169] Stuart Kaufmman, *At Home in the Universe* (1995).

faith that are almost harder than having a religious faith.[170]

Hewish, too, uses words like 'mystery' of physics, and believes that 'It looks to me that the universe was designed for human beings to arrive.'

No one is suggesting that cosmologists are all religious mystics! But there *is* some reason to doubt Stephenson's apparent assumption that they are nowadays all hard-headed materialists who believe the universe to be pointless, accidental, and without rational explanation. Of course many of the *particulars* in the Keplerian vision turned out to be misguided. But it is arguable that many of the same principles can still be found in modern Christian, deistic or secular versions.

Was he a murderer?

In the previous chapter we noted how Tycho died fairly suddenly. *The Heavenly Intrigue* made out a good case that he was poisoned, and identified Kepler as the obvious suspect. This led to much thinking about whether one so apparently devout could have done such a thing, even in the interests of science. Sadly for speculation, as we saw in the previous chapter, empirical testing done in the year 2012 seems to have shown that Tycho was not poisoned after all. A pity really, it made for such interesting speculation!

Kepler's Work

We have found it necessary to describe much of his work either in his biography or in describing his character. There is, indeed, a sense in which his work was a coherent whole, fitting within his intense world-view. Here, however, we may outline his astronomical works chronologically.

1597 Cosmographic Mystery

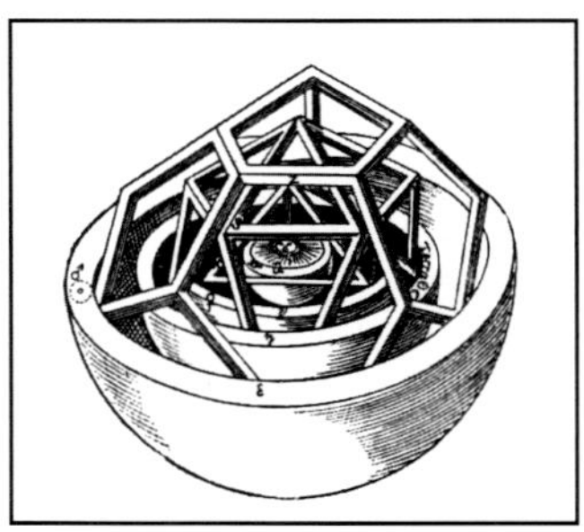

This work (as already mentioned) suggested that the ratios of the orbits of the planets were according to the five regular solids. The table given below shows how Kepler's figures correlated with the Copernican ones for the orbits.[171] Stephenson gives much of

[170] Antony Hewish on a CSIS (Christian Students in Science) video *Encounter* (1999).

[171] Stephenson, *The Music of the Heavens*, chapter v.

Kepler's thinking process on this as he wrote in consultation on the mathematical details with Maestlin.[172] The latter seems to have initially made various calculations for Kepler based on the assumption of some kind of epicycle machinery – but Kepler decisively rejected the idea of including rigid-sphere machinery in the figures.

Kepler noticed the following basic points about planetary orbits:

1. There are six planets.[173] The outermost planets not only have further to go in a complete orbit, but actually travel slower – so taking a *more than proportionate time* to orbit. (To put it in terms of modern probability, the 'chances' of this happening in the exact order purely *by chance* would be 6-factorial to1, i.e. 120–1).
2. For any given planet it is sometimes nearer the Sun (the perihelion) and sometimes further away (the aphelion). It goes fastest when it is near the Sun.

Get a group of friends who don't know much modern physics or astronomy, and present them with these basic facts. Ask them what the obvious conclusion would be.

My students in such groups generally would guess that the Sun is providing the motive force to move the planets (remember also, at the time of Kepler inertia had not yet been invented).

This is exactly what Kepler concluded. In his 1609 work he calls

Relative sizes of the adjacent planetary orbits (assuming the innermost part of the outer orbit to be 1000)

Planet	Intervening regular solid	Computed by Kepler	From Copernicus
Saturn			
Jupiter	Cube	577	635
Mars	Tetrahedron	333	333
Earth	Dodecahadron	795	757
Venus	Icosohedron	795	794
Mercury	Octahedron	707	723

172 ibid.

173 This is, of course, as known at the time of Kepler.

it a 'preconceived opinion' – we would probably call it a logical hypothesis.

Kepler pictured the Sun as the only 'moving soul' at the centre (though he later amended 'soul' to 'force'). This gives a *physical* reason for the Sun being at the centre, the Sun is the motive force and the further out they are the slower it pushes them around. Kepler developed formulae for these that led to ratios of orbits, and these ratios were tolerably accurate.[174]

We should note that this assumes both that a force is necessary; and also that the heavenly bodies are similar in kind. It expands on Copernican ideas in a way that leaves no doubt that the system is actual and physical, not merely mathematical and hypothetical. Whereas Copernicus himself left the real centre as not the Sun but the centre of the Earth's orbit. Kepler insisted that it really had to be on the Sun, which is the driving force. Gingerich rightly remarks:

> This idea, which was to be much further developed in the *Astronomia nova,* establishes Kepler as the first scientist to demand physical explanations for celestial phenomena. Although the principal idea of the *Cosmographic Mystery* was erroneous, never in history has a book so wrong been so seminal in directing the future course of science.[175]

1600A Defence of Tycho Against Ursus

This *Apologiapro Tychone contra Ursum* was not published at all until 1858. In 1988 the Latin original and a translation was published by the Cambridge philosopher of science N. Jardine. It shows up Ursus's shortcomings as an astronomer in terms of understanding Copernicus and Apollonius as reported in Ptolemy. It defends Tycho's originality. More interestingly, it contains ideas on the nature of science. Ursus had argued that mathematical hypotheses were merely instruments for prediction on four basic grounds. With Kepler and then Jardine to help us with Ursus's unclear style, these could be reformulated as:

1 Hypotheses = *aitermata* which Aristotle takes as being false, so by implication hypothesis are not meant to be 'true'.

---

[174] This table is also given by Gingerich, ibid 57, and by Dreyer, *A history of Astronomy from Thales to Kepler*, 378.

[175] Gingerich, *The Eye of Heaven*, 309.

2 True conclusions can result from false hypotheses, so true predictions do not imply the truth of the hypotheses.

3 In algebra, one can start out from a false number and by iteration approach the true one.

4 All systems so far have proven to be incorrect so we have no reason to suppose any present one is not.

Kepler counters each of these arguments, but here we will just consider some key points. Jardine takes Kepler to be implying that the Copernican and Ptolemaic systems may be mathematically equivalent (within the bounds of observational accuracy) because the motion is relative.

> … if however we insist on an account of the form of the universe which 'contains the causes' of the phenomena then there are … ample grounds for preferring the Copernican system.[176]

False hypotheses can give true predictions, but sooner or later will give false ones when applied in different circumstances. Kepler demolishes Ursus's argument 3 by showing that this is not an instance of using false hypotheses. Basically, Kepler has a 'realist' view of science, though Jardine is careful to note that his concern is not with the anti-realism of the 20th century but with scepticism in the 17th:

> Kepler is not defending realism in science but rather the claims of one particular science, astronomy, to have attained some truths about the world and be capable of attaining more such truths.[177]

Kepler's use of the word 'hypothesis' at times approached modern usage, and Jardine summarises:

> … in (the *Apologia*) there emerge, apparently for the first time in European literature, concepts that have remained central to our understanding of science and scientific enquiry: the concept of a scientific theory as a definite and consistent body of propositions systematically related to each other and to some domain of practice; the concept of a rational methodology for the

---

[176] Summary in Jardine, *The Birth of the History and Philosophy of Science*, 218.

[177] Jardine, 223.

> resolution of theoretical conflict; the concept of scientific progress mediated by a rational method and evincing an ever more accurate portrayal of the world (289).

Francis Bacon's *Advancement of Learning* appeared in 1605, and of course Kepler's work had no influence because it was not published at the time. But this does indicate how Kepler in this, as in much else, was an extraordinarily innovative figure. His scientific realism led him also to look not simply for positional accuracy but a *physics of the skies*. The Sun was not merely the centre of the Solar System but its motive force.

1609 New Astronomy

In this work are announced the first two laws of planetary motion:

(1) Planets orbit in ellipses with the Sun at one focus of the ellipse and with the planes for the ellipses passing through the Sun but only near to and not identical to each other.

(2) The line between the planet and the Sun sweeps out equal areas in equal times.

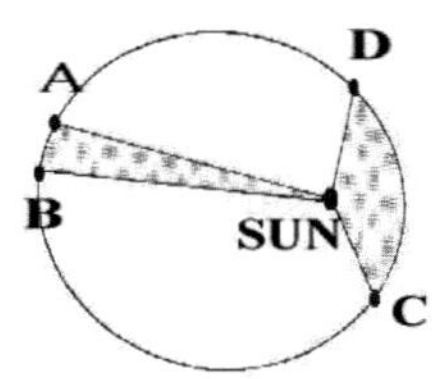

Planetary motion (but note that the orbits are actually not so far from circles)

There are several key points to bear in mind about Kepler's system:

- Copernicus's work was widely known and respected. Copernicus himself obviously believed his system 'true' but astronomers always had the option of treating it in the Osiander manner purely as a means to 'save the phenomena' Kepler's system was unavoidably physical, it was a physical system of the universe, not just a mathematical one.
- As a physical system it demanded (and partly provided) an entirely new and radical physics – both terrestrial and for planetary motion.
- Kepler's system departed radically in mathematical terms from the Copernican one, and actually overturned completely Copernicus's main motivation for his work! In Kepler's system:

1. Planets went in *ellipses* – not in some combination of *circles* as 'true motion' required.

2. Planets did *not* move with equal angular velocity about their centres – as Copernicus had insisted they should – planets went faster or slower depending on their distance. Kepler's orbits are more reminiscent of equants than the Copernican system, which slipped in extra epicycles to avoid that very thing.

Kepler's system was *neither* Ptolemaic *nor* Tychonic *nor* Copernican!

This may help explain the structure of the book. It is not a sober summary of results, but a record of a journey with all its blind alleys and difficulties, to getting these. Kepler presumably hopes that the reader (following his own experiences) will be caught along with it all, and experience the relief and joy which Kepler himself may have on reaching a sensible solution. Having said this, however, it has to be added that his naturally introspective nature seems to have carried him away, and the work contains a detail excessive to this basic 'carrying along the reader' purpose.

Kepler focused on Mars – the planet that in fact turns out to have the most pronounced elliptical orbit. He showed near the start that actually the Tychonic, Copernican (and Keplerian) models will all be mathematically equivalent. Kepler actually prefers the equant model to Copernicus's strategy of adding an extra epicycle – though again in Chapter Four shows their equivalence mathematically. The main point in his first six chapters, however, was to assert that the central point of the orbits really *is* and has to be the Sun and not a point in empty space. Astronomers were able to locate the position of a planet (e.g. Mars) as viewed from the Sun by waiting until the Earth was between the Sun and the planet. But should planetary positions be located relative to the Sun, or to the centre of the Earth's orbit?

For old Ptolemaic astronomy, there was the option that the spheres really existed, so the planets ran on clockwork, and all that was needed was some *anima* or motive force to keep them going. By this time, however, to 'cutting edge' Copernican or Tychonic astronomers the idea of solid spheres was effectively dead because any 'spheres' would have had to *intersect* and be whizzed through by comets. So *what* kept the orbiting planets in their courses? Something had to both keep them moving *and* keep them in their particular orbits. To follow complex epicycles and eccentrics would require multiple movers acting together. Copernicus had rejected the equant because, using the wheels within wheels approach, it made sense for each wheel to go at uniform speed. In Copernicus's system the Sun simply sat at the centre to illuminate. But if the Sun were seen as illumination *and* motive-force *and* holding the bodies in orbit, it made perfect sense for planets to go faster when they were near it. Uniform rotation was then *not* self-evidently logical. Moreover, it was also important to relate orbital distance to the actual Sun and not the 'mean Sun' (or centre of Earth orbit in empty space) as Copernicus had done. If the speed at which the planet travelled were indeed inversely proportional to its distance from the actual Sun, then using the 'mean Sun' would produce errors.[178]

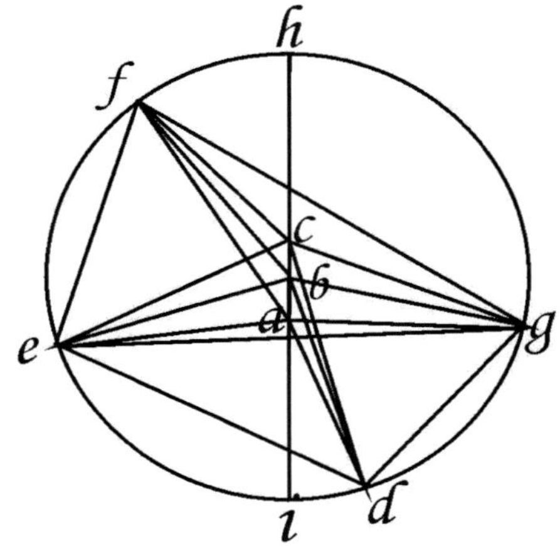

a = sun *b* = orbit centre

c = equant

d e f g = opposition points of Mars orbit

ih = apsidal line

i = aphelion *h* = perihelion

The first six chapters, then, explored all these various hypothetical implications of the different models available. Then Kepler had to turn to Tycho's actual data. Unfortunately, Tycho's assistants had not only related the data to the mean Sun, but made various other errors. These Kepler had to laboriously correct.

Another problem was that the planetary orbital planes through the Sun are close but not precisely aligned. Copernicus had these planes passing not through the Sun but through the mean Sun – which meant that to get accurate figures for Mars he had to make it oscillate in time with Earth's orbit. But why on Earth (as it were) should Mars be dependent on Earth, which, as Kepler says, 'is no business of Mars'? Kepler showed that if the

178 Stephenson, in *Kepler's Physical Astronomy* well describes all details of such issues summarised here.

plane of Mars were at about 1°50 to that of the Earth then there would be no need for oscillation. He remarked that 'the observations took the side of my preconceived ideas, as they often did before'.

This brings us to chapter 16 of the work. Kepler attempts, having adjusted the plane of Mars' orbit and corrected Tycho's figures, to establish a circular Martian orbit using an equant. Kepler assumed (and it is actually an implication of his view that the speed must depend on distance from the Sun) that the Sun (a), orbit centre (b), and equant (c) were in a straight line. He then found four points d e f g when Mars was in opposition (i.e. the Earth was exactly between Mars and the Sun) so that he could place Mars as viewed from the Sun. From the four points he had to find:

- the radius of the orbit
- the position of the line ih
- the distances ab and bc

He laboriously tried at least 70 different values, and eventually arrived at the best fit. Gingerich makes the general point that Kepler could not simply go and observe Mars at some particular point, and often had to interpolate from Tycho's actual observations. Anyway, this took months, the draft calculations covered 900 pages of close-written folio, and his work contains a number of arithmetic errors and misreading of his own writing. He included the six other opposition positions of Tycho and two of his own made after Tycho's death – coming finally to accuracies of just two minutes of arc which were then well within observational accuracy.[179]

Then he started book 3 ch. 17:

> Who would have thought it possible? This hypothesis, which so closely agrees with the observed opposition, is nevertheless false.

Kepler had realised that different models could predict the same heliocentric longitudes without predicting the same heliocentric distances. The Martian latitudes would give an indication of whether the distances were correctly predicted. Had Kepler been merely 'saving the phenomena' then different models for longitude and latitude would have been possible. But Kepler was seeking a *physical* system. His model did not work, and adjusting it left an eight minutes of arc deficiency – more than the inaccuracy in Tycho's figures. So the second book in the work closes with

---

[179] A table of the twelve values is given by Gingerich in Taton and Wilson, op. cit. 63.

the abandoning of this model (which he calls the 'vicarious hypothesis') – a 'punishment for having followed some plausible, but in reality false, axioms of the great men of the past'. Kepler presumably hoped to take the reader with him – something new and more radical must be attempted.

If a circular orbit will not work, and Kepler does not want to use epicycles, the task becomes that of determining orbit. Unfortunately, whilst a circle is determined by just three points, a non-circular orbit needs a lot more – and in this instance the problem is confounded because of unequal angular velocities. Kepler therefore turns to the issue of the Earth's motion as a prerequisite to determining that of Mars. Earth, as just another planet, must have the same kind of orbit with varying speeds depending on solar distance; but how to find the distance? One way might be apparent size – and Kepler spent a year or so on optics to try this. The method didn't work because the differences were too small to measure, but he transformed the science of optics!

Kepler solved the Earth problem by imagining an observer on Mars, which was known to return to the same point in space every 687 days. The Earth's apparent position could be plotted at this point, and Kepler was thus able to show that the Earth also varied in speed and at the furthest and nearest points (aphelion and perihelion) its speed was proportional to distance. Kepler concluded:

> … the centre of the Earth's revolution is at an intermediate place between the body of the Sun and the equant point of that revolution: that is, the Earth moves non-uniformly in its orbit; it becomes slow where it withdraws from the Sun, swift where it approaches; which is agreeable to physical considerations and to the analogy of other planets.

Starting in Chapter 26 he explored again the equivalence of the Ptolemaic, Tychonic, and heliocentric systems. It was, he showed, *possible* to achieve an equivalent Ptolemaic model, but it became extremely complex compared to a heliocentric one. In Chapter 32 he notes that at the perihelion and aphelion speed is proportional to distance from the Sun. This is in fact true, though it is *precisely* true *only* at those two points and it was *not* valid for Kepler (as he later did) to assume it true throughout the orbits.

From Chapters 33–38 he turned, however, to physics. If planets go faster when near the Sun the implication is obvious. A 'soul' which resided in some way *in* the planet would surely not vary in intensity in this way, even if one could imagine such a force. It was far more reasonable to suppose that a force emanated from the Sun itself. Tycho's model explained the other planets going around the Sun, but offered no explanation for the Sun's orbit.[180]

Kepler pictures this motive force as analogous to light:

> just as light … is an immaterial image of that fire which is in the body of the Sun, so this virtue, grasping and carrying the bodies of the planets, must be an immaterial image of that virtue which resides in the Sun itself …

Kepler had pictured light as travelling out from a source in an (infinitely fast) expanding spherical surface.[181] He compared the Sun's emanating force with this, and also with magnetic forces. Gilbert's recent demonstration that the Earth as a giant magnet supported this and gave more credibility to the Earth having the motive force to keep the Moon orbiting. This might not be a force of attraction, but a force that (like terrestrial magnetism in some situations) brought alignment. The Sun itself rotates faster than Mercury orbits, and it is logical to think of its emanating force sweeping round the planets as it spins. The spinning Sun creates a kind of vortex or whirlpool. Planets have a natural resistance to motion, and the further away they are the less rapidly this whirlpool can drag them around.

Kepler had, however, to explain why the planets did not travel in simple circles and why (as he would later indicate) their ellipses varied in eccentricity. The logic of this was that each planet had some 'virtue' in itself that moved it towards and away from the Sun. The variation in orbital speed was then a secondary effect caused by it moving from a stronger to a weaker point in what we would call the Sun's field of emanating force. The individual planetary virtue could imply first magnetic attraction and then repulsion – producing an approach towards or movement away from the Sun.

---

[180] This,of course, left Kepler with a similar problem regarding the Moon (and Jupiter's moons)!

[181] Stephenson takes it thus, Gingerich as an emanating plane.

To find the orbit of Mars was still a headache. The equals sign had only been invented in the previous generation, and co-ordinate geometry (in, for example, the form later developed by Descartes) was not generally available. Kepler could not simply plot a graph. He began with an epicycle, and developed onto a kind of ovoid or egg shape. In the course of his calculations he repeatedly used ellipses, and referred (in letters at the actual time of doing the work) wistfully to a desire that it might be something simple like an ellipse – but he never thought it was. Finally, he seems to have blundered with a series of lucky assumptions and compensating errors[182] into getting the correct path. But even then he didn't recognise what it was, explaining that he:

> … laid it aside, and fell back on ellipses, believing that this was quite a different hypothesis, whereas the two, as I shall prove in the next chapter, are one and the same …

Kepler's work was crucial to astronomy, but it also involved a type of mathematics that pointed towards the infinitesimal calculus of Newton and Leibniz.[183] The introduction to the work also contained some of the following comments on gravity:

> It is therefore clear that the traditional doctrine about gravity is erroneous … . Gravity is the mutual bodily tendency between cognate bodies towards unity or contact (of which kind the magnetic force also is), so that the Earth draws a stone much more than the stone draws the Earth … . Supposing that the Earth were in the centre of the world, heavy bodies would be attracted to it, not because it is in the centre but because it is a cognate body. It follows that regardless where we place the Earth … heavy bodies will always seek it … . If two stones were placed anywhere in space near to each other, and outside the reach of force of a third cognate body, then they would come together, after the manner of magnetic bodies, at an intermediate point, each approaching the other in proportion to the other's mass …
>
> If the Earth and the Moon were not kept in their respective

182 Koestler, Gingerich and Stephenson all record these steps in their own ways.

183 Newton, who first clearly laid out what we call differentiation and integration, built on the work of others – including Kepler, Descartes, Frans Van Schooten (1615–1660), John Wallis (1616–1703) etc.

> orbits by a spiritual or some other equivalent force, the Earth would ascend towards the Moon one fifty-fourth part of the distance, and the Moon would descend the remaining fifty-three parts of the interval, and thus they would unite.
>
> If the Earth ceased to attract the waters of the sea, the seas would rise and flow into the Moon … . If the attractive force of the Moon reaches down to the Earth, it follows that the attractive force of the Earth, all the more, extends to the Moon and even farther …
>
> Nothing made of earthy substance is absolutely light; but matter which is less dense, either by nature or through heat, is relatively lighter … . Out of the definition of lightness follows its motion; for one should not believe that when lifted up, it escapes to the periphery of the world, or that it is not attracted by the Earth. It is merely less attracted than heavier matter, and is therefore displaced by heavier matter, so that it comes to rest and is kept in its place by the Earth …

Kepler is describing universal gravitation, and developed a theory of the tides based on lunar (and later also solar) attraction. As we shall see, Galileo totally rejected this part of Kepler's ideas, thinking them (aptly enough) 'lunatic'.

1618 Three Tracts on Comets

1625 Hyperaspistes

Kepler's 1618 work on the 1607 and 1618 comets contained his usual blend of astronomy, physics and astrology. In the later work, Kepler defended Tycho's view of comets against views of them as atmospheric held by Galileo[184] and Scipione Chiaramonti. He also pointed out that the phases of Venus could be as well explained by the Tychonic system as by a heliocentric one.

1619 Harmony of the Universe

Since his idea of the five regular solids in 1595 he had long been meditating on a deeper harmony, which brought mathematics, science, and music into one resonant and meaningful whole. All this meant a kind of inspiration:

---

184 Galileo somewhat disrespectfully called them 'Tycho's monkey planets'.

> I feel carried away and possessed by an unutterable rapture over the divine spectacle of the heavenly harmony.

But Max Caspar has well said:

> However, nothing would be more wrong than to assume that by his harmony speculations Kepler lost himself in a nebulous reverie. He did not enjoy the resounding tinkling of words or the torrential flow of vague speech. What he presents to us is an edifice of thoughts, well-proportioned in all parts, built according to a clearly recognisable plan, whose uniform organisation and unbroken lines bear witness to the mathematical stamp of the architect's mind. His rapture is not the exaltation of a dreamer; it is the enthusiasm of the discoverer, of the mathematician, of a mathematician, of course, who does not want to play with self-created notions in accordance with self-created rules, but recognises the foundation of the mathematical notions in the highest and ultimate existence and knows of what he talks. His enthusiasm borders on sublime rapture, even on the ecstasy of mysticism; mysticism, indeed, in the lucid brightness of its contemplation, comes closer to the transparency of mathematical observations than is known to or suspected by the many representatives of an eager and obscure interpretation of that intellectual domain. What comes first is not emotion seeking expression, but the clear thoughts, which rouse and fire emotion. It is only in the background that one senses the warmth, the fullness of feeling, the exaltation and happiness, the knowledge of being allowed to pull aside the veil before the divine plan of creation.[185]

The *Harmony* begins with geometrical figures (especially polygons) that underlie harmony. This progresses by Book IV to the soul's faculty for perceiving harmonies. This is also a kind of astrology – but purely theoretical, not a guide to horoscopes. From Book V he turns to the issue of planetary spacings. The five perfect solids were by now not enough – they could not be made accurate enough. He had to explore God's secondary means – based on harmonics.

---

185 Max Caspar, *Kepler* (1959), 267–8.

Kepler finished the work p.m. 27th May 1618. On 15th May, however, after a three month gestation period, he fully recognised the third planetary law.

(3) The squares of their period of revolution are proportional to the cubes of their mean distances from the Sun.

He then frantically revised book V over the next nine months, whilst type was being set. The third law, however, was not really given any star billing. It was stated in Book V Chapter Three as the eighth of 13 points in a 'Summary of astronomical doctrine necessary for speculation into the celestial harmonies'. Kepler went on to describe in detail the musical associations of planetary movements. Since their distances vary, one might expect their harmonies to reflect this. Kepler transposes to fit onto the staves.

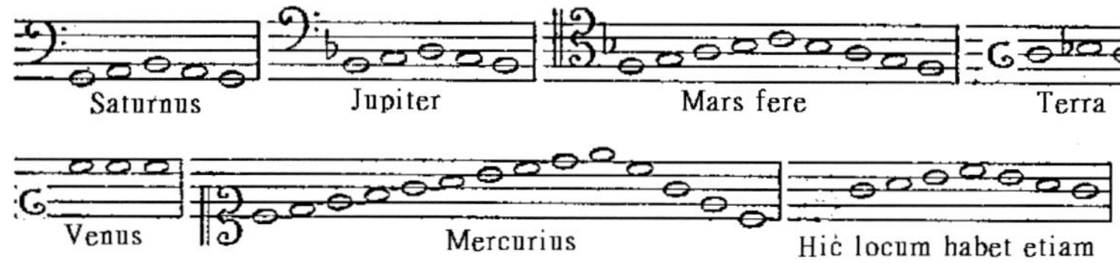

The silent notes of planets in their eccentric courses

Harmonice Mundi (1619) p. 207.

In modern terms Bruce Stephenson states that it would look like this:

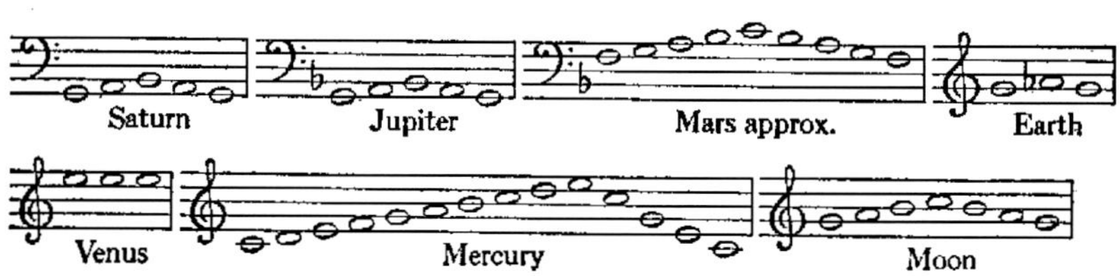

Anyone interested in the voluminous details of the system, should look at Bruce Stephenson's 1994 work *The Music of the Heavens.*

1618–21 Epitome of Copernican Astronomy

As he was working on the planetary tables and the *Harmony*, Kepler was also working on a textbook in question and answer style for Copernican astronomy. This was written in seven books. The first three (on spherical astronomy) were in early 1618. The fourth (theoretical astronomy) was in 1620, and the last three (practical geometrical astronomy) in 1621.

The work actually began with Kepler's analogy of the world to Father, Son and Holy Spirit, and quite a lot of similar material. Since the nub of the astronomy starts in book IV we will start there.

The three 'principle parts' of Book IV are:

1. The bodies and regions in the universe and their respective places.
2. The 'revolution of the Sun around its axis, and its effect in making the planets revolve … the revolution of the Earth around its axis and its effect in making the Moon revolve; the additional help in moving the Moon by the light of the Sun …'
3. The 'causes of the threefold irregularity of the altitude, longitude, and latitude in the single planets – and how these regularities are doubled in the Moon by the force of illumination from the Sun'.

Referring back to Book I Kepler explains:

> … there are three regions, symbols of the three persons of the Holy Trinity – the centre, a symbol of the Father; the surface, of the Son; and the intermediate of the Holy Spirit …

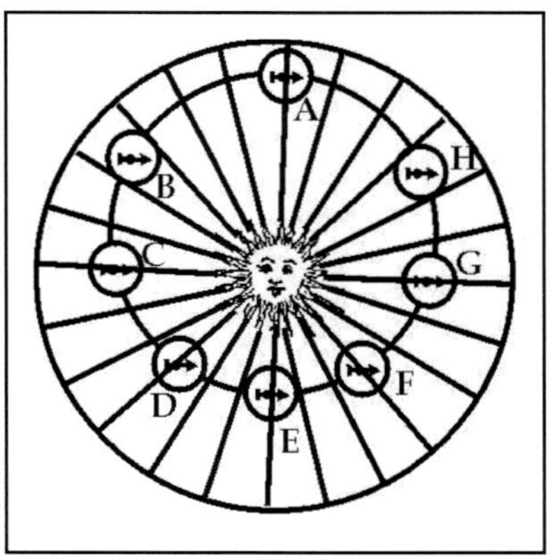

This early section mixes Pythagoras, David in the Psalms, and Trinitarian ideas – all in the interests of portraying a harmonious universe that 'makes sense'. Within this, however, we are also told what (to the modern mind) are the empirical bases for the world-view. Thus Tycho has 'disproved' the existence of solid spheres, etc. The five regular solids are here again introduced (recognising the 'small deficiencies' in their ratios). A diagram shows how the balancing forces of Sun and planet produce the compound motion. The 'Magnetic threads' of the planets are shown by an arrow. The arrow point is attracted to the Sun and operates between A and E drawing it in, whilst the back of the arrow repels the Sun and repels the planet from E back up to A.

The *Epitome* contained all the basic Keplerian ideas and arguments, and includes reference to Galileo's discoveries, for example, the phases of Venus (discovered *after* the publication of Kepler's *New Astronomy* in 1609). It included all his laws, and also, for example, 'Kepler's equation' E = M – e sine (E) which relates orbital eccentricity, mean angular momentum and angles – an equation of practical use in computations.

The *Epitome* was easier to read than Copernicus's book, it contained all the relevant evidence, and it contained much mathematical detail. We shall see that in contrast Galileo's *Dialogue* (1633) was easy reading, but had no mathematics, no planetary laws, and was effectively 24 years out of date. Kepler's work was reprinted in 1635 as Copernican ideas spread, and his reputation was enhanced by the Rudolphine Tables in 1627.

Rudolphine Tables 1627

Finally, they arrived. In undertaking the vast numbers of calculations needed, Kepler developed his own brand of geometrically based logarithms after hearing of the newly invented Napierian ones. Kepler's (according to Gingerich) related to modern ones as $10^5\ln(10^5/x)$. The tables were the first book to actually require logarithms in a scientific application. We now know that his tables were some thirty times more accurate than predecessors – and soon began to prove their accuracy even then.

Dream or Astronomy of the Moon 1634

This work was published after Kepler's death, and it is perhaps the first real work of science fiction. It tells the story of a boy Duracotus whose father dies when he is three and whose mother is involved in some kind of herbalism. When aged 14 Duracotus is given by his angry mother to a seafaring captain, and left on the island of Hven where he studies until 19 with Tycho. Returning home, his now repentant mother makes arrangements for daemons (or wise spirits) to take him to the Moon. This has to be during a lunar eclipse because the daemons dislike sunlight. Some of Kepler's descriptions are amazing:

> The initial shock [i.e. of take-off] is the worst part of it, for he is thrown upward as if by an explosion of gun-powder … Therefore he must be dazed by opiates beforehand; his limbs must be carefully protected so that they are not torn from him and the recoil is spread over all parts of his body. Then he will meet new difficulties: immense cold and inhibited respiration …

> When the first part of the journey is completed, it becomes easier because on such a long journey the body no doubt escapes the magnetic force of the Earth and enters that of the Moon, so that the latter gets the upper hand. At this point we set the travellers free and leave them to their own devices: like spiders they will stretch out and contract, and propel themselves forward by their own force – for, as the magnetic forces of the Earth and Moon both attract the body and hold it suspended, the effect is as if neither of them were attracting it – so that in the end its mass will by itself turn toward the Moon.

These are the Keplerian equivalents of space-suit and firing-rockets to escape the Earth's gravity. Arriving on the Moon, we hear of the Moon's inhabitants, dwellings and lifestyles, seas and marshes, animal and vegetable life etc. Woven into all this, however, are exact astronomical descriptions as seen from the Moon. The movements of stars, the apparent earthrise etc., are all given – drawing the reader into realising that what is seen from the Earth may likewise be a result of relative motion etc. Finally, Ducatus finds himself woken from what turns out to have been a dream. The book is an amazing product of fantasy and science – a kind of Asimov for the 17th century. No wonder Kepler's mum nearly got burned as a witch!

Kepler's Genius

Kepler is one of the most original and brilliant figures in the history of science, and if I believed in 'fathers of' he would surely be a candidate to be the 'father of' several things! Apart from his optics and his radical elliptical planetary motions, he virtually invented astrophysics, invented science fiction, and gave some of the earliest modern (if unpublished) analyses on the philosophy of science.

Questions

Here are some questions to ask as you think about Kepler:

- Kepler's ideas of the Sun as motive force of planetary motion turned out to be 'wrong' in the light of Newton's ideas on gravity and momentum. Newton's ideas on gravity and momentum turned out to be 'wrong' in the light of Einstein's theories of special and general relativity. Is it logical for Koestler to portray

Kepler's 'wrong' ideas as cranky but lucky delusions, but Newton's 'wrong' ideas as a breakthrough?

- How far today does (or should) science and cosmology seek a 'unified' view of a reality that makes sense?
- The following is a quotation from John Gribbin and Cambridge astronomer Martin Rees: 'This combination of coincidences, just right for resonance in carbon-12, just wrong in oxygen-16, is indeed remarkable. There is no better evidence to support the argument that the Universe has been designed for our benefit - tailor made for man'[186] Is this evidence of a Keplerian-type acknowledgement of 'harmony' – the 'resonance' is just right!?

Further Reading

Koestler's section in *The Sleepwalkers* (1959) is entertaining, though perhaps exaggerates somewhat. The classic work is *Kepler* by Max Caspar (1959 repr. 1993), and there is a short reasonable biography *John Kepler* by Angus Armitage (1966). The massive compendium by Arthur and Peter Beer *Kepler: Four Hundred Years* (1971) is a mixed bag of the good and less good, one needs to be discerning, but it does have useful detail. Bruce Stephenson's two works Kepler's *Physical Astronomy* (1987) and *The Music of the Heavens* (1994) are both detailed and good. Owen Gingerich's *The Eye of Heaven* (1993) is excellent on Kepler and Copernicus, and contains new material not given elsewhere. Job Kozhamthadam's *The Discovery of Kepler's Laws* (1994) gives a modern Jesuit view of Kepler, and it also seems technically sound. Although mostly about Tycho, Kitty Ferguson's *The Nobleman and his House dog* (2002, Review) does given some insight into Kepler at a general level. N. Jardine's *The Birth of History and Philosophy of Science* (1984 repr. 2009) looks in detail at his unpublished *Apologia pro Tychone contra Ursum* and its implicit philosophy of science. John Banville's *Kepler* won the Guardian fiction prize in 1981, and in 2011 Banville also won the Franz Kafka prize, which seems appropriate as his fictional works on Copernicus and Kepler reconstruct a Kafka-esque world. Just don't read it as biography.

---

[186] Gribbin & Rees (1990), op.cit. 247.

6. Galileo Galilei

Galileo Galilei (1564–1642)

'Contrary to statements in even recent outlines of science, Galileo did not invent the telescope, nor the microscope, nor the thermometer, nor the pendulum clock. He did not discover the law of inertia; nor the parallelogram of forces or motions; nor the sun spots. He made no contribution to theoretical astronomy, he did not throw down weights from the leaning tower of Pisa, and did not prove the truth of the Copernican system. He was not tortured by the Inquisition, did not languish in its dungeons, did not say "eppur si muove"; and he was not a martyr of science. What he did was to found the modern science of dynamics …' [Arthur Koestler: *The Sleepwalkers*].

Italy in the late 16th and early 17th centuries was divided into different states. Unlike the northern European countries (e.g. Holland, Germany, and Bohemia) where Protestant and Catholic armies fought bitter wars, all the Italian states remained Catholic. The three states of central importance to us here are:

Tuscany

Pisa Cathedral and Tower

Tuscany occupied the northwest part, including Florence and Pisa. After 1406 Pisa was ruled by Florence. Pisa's famous Cathedral and leaning tower were built in its heyday in the 12th century, though work continued until the 14th.

In 1434 the wealthy Médici merchant family came to power in Florence. After 1530 Florence was no longer a Republic but with the support of Pope and Emperor was converted into a hereditary Duchy. The Pope granted Cosimo I de Médici the title of Grand Duke of Tuscany from 1569, and he and his descendants governed it in general alliance with the Habsburgs and the Papacy. Ferdinando I, who ruled Tuscany from 1587–1609, was a strong ruler, generally favouring religious freedom. Cosimo II (1609–1620) and Ferdinando II (1620–70) were less strong and more open to Papal influence. Pisa contained the main university for Tuscany at this time and had faculties for law, theology, and 'arts' i.e. medicine.

Rome

Rome: St Peter's Square

In Rome the Pope was also temporal ruler of a large central Italian state. Popes were elected from powerful Italian families, usually moving relatives and friends into positions of power and influence during their rule. In the 1520s Protestantism supplanted Catholicism as state religion in various states, and the Humanist Pope Paul III (1534–49) moved in various ways to combat this.

First he recognised in 1540 the Society of Jesus (Jesuits) set up by Ignatius Loyola as a military style priestly order offering him total obedience, discipline, and a willingness to go to all parts of the world to spread the true Catholic faith. By 1600 there were 372 Jesuit colleges in Europe, and a prestigious Jesuit university the *Collegio Romano* in Rome itself. In 1586 the Jesuits issued its *Ratio Studiorum* (revised 1599) laying down a general syllabus that followed Aquinas's theology and Aristotelian science as interpreted by Aquinas. It also dealt with issues of allowable variation. Sharratt suggests that this should be compared with 'contemporary university syllabuses rather than with the writings of pioneers like Galileo who turned out to be successful'[187] In 1607 the Pope drew a line under a twenty-year controversy between Jesuits and Dominicans on freewill, and the Jesuit order was increasingly directed by its generals to a 'solid and uniform doctrine' which meant less variation. This led to a tension for a number of leading Jesuits who were at the cutting edge of the sciences, and had to choose between their scientific knowledge and obedience to their

---

[187] Michael Sharratt *Galileo Decisive Innovator* (1994), 40.

order. Leading figures had by then accepted much of Tycho's work and his system too. This kept a static Earth and had no Biblical implications, but it was *not* Aristotelian. Of significance at the *Collegio Romano* were Professor of Mathematics Christopher Clavius (1537–1612) and his successor Christopher Ginberger (1561–1636). The Jesuit Cardinal Roberto Bellarmine (1542–1631) was recognised by around 1600 as the pre-eminent Catholic theologian of the day, respected for his learning and erudition even by his theological enemies.

Pope Paul III also established a central Congregation of the Inquisition or Holy Office in 1542 to investigate alleged instances of heresy – with the possible use of torture that was common to Lutherans, Calvinists and Catholics.

Finally, Pope Paul III set up the Council of Trent (1545–1563), which failed to reunite Catholics and Protestants, but did initiate far-reaching reforms in the Catholic Church and spelt out the nature of orthodoxy. The Council asserted that God's revelation was contained *both* in the Bible *and* in tradition – without being specific on their respective roles. In 'matters of faith and morals' no one was to 'rely on his own judgement and distort Holy Scripture'. But the resulting Tridentine profession of faith also included the following:

> I most firmly accept and embrace the Apostolic and ecclesiastic traditions and the other observances and constitutions of the Church. I also accept Sacred Scripture in the sense in which it has been held, and is held, by Holy Mother Church, to whom it belongs to judge the true sense and interpretation of the Sacred Scripture, nor will I accept or interpret it in any way other than in accordance with the unanimous agreement of the Fathers.

Where all the saints and fathers were in agreement, even if something was not explicit in the Bible, that thing was to be regarded as Catholic truth. In practice, leading Trent theologian the Dominican Melchior Cano (1509–60) recognised that saints and fathers might disagree – in which case only probable rather than certain truths could be ascertained. He also said:

> When the authority of the saints, be they few or many, pertains to the faculties contained within the natural light of reason, it

> does not provide certain arguments but only arguments as strong as reason itself when in agreement with nature …[188]

Neither the Council of Trent nor the Jesuits were crudely literalist. Bellarmine, for example, followed a traditional view of Biblical interpretation distinguishing levels of meaning – so that (as, for example, in Augustine) the 'literal' meaning might in fact be figurative. He distinguished:

I Literal or Historical

(a) Simple (proper meaning of words i.e. literal in our sense e.g. 'Abraham had two sons').

(b) Figurative (words are used figuratively e.g. 'I have other sheep which are not of this fold').

II Spiritual or Mystical

(a) Allegorical (pertaining to Christ or the church e.g. the allegory of Sarah and Hagar).

(b) Tropological (pertaining to morals).

(c) Analogical (signifying eternal life).

Bellarmine, however, took it as 'essential to faith and morals' to believe that something literally (in our sense) was true if it was plainly meant in this way – e.g. that Abraham really did have two sons.

The Council of Trent never addressed Copernicanism. Father Clavius in his massive tome on astronomy, rejected Copernicanism primarily for physical reasons, concluding:

> All this is contrary to the common teaching of philosophers [i.e. scientists] and astronomers and seems to contradict what is taught in many places in the Sacred Scriptures, as we have extensively discussed in Chapter 1. Therefore it seems that Ptolemy's opinion should be preferred over Copernicus's invention.[189]

---

188 All this material is in Richard Blackwell's *Galileo, Bellarmine and the Bible* (1991).

189 Cited in Blackwell op. cit. 25.

He uses phrases like 'seems to' and 'it seems that' which is not very dogmatic – Clavius was fundamentally an empiricist not a dogmatic Aristotelian. Bellarmine himself was not even an orthodox Aristotelian[190] in astronomy (rejecting the idea of solid spheres). His comments on Copernicanism are likewise cautious – though it has to be said that not everyone was similarly wary.

All this forms a complex background to Galileo. The repeated warnings to him, for example, to stay out of theology and Biblical interpretation were not because he was necessarily wrong, but because *if* a change in Biblical interpretation was to be done it should be worked out and agreed by the professional church theologians. Galileo could teach Copernicanism 'hypothetically' and might possibly even discuss physical pros and cons. But *if* he did come up with a real *proof* that the Earth moved he should produce it, and then leave it to the theologians to adjust the interpretations of the Bible.

Venice

The Venetian Republic was ruled by an elected Doge with a balance of powers between himself, the Venetian Senate, and the judiciary.

St Marks with Astronomical Clock

St Mark's Square and Campanile (rebuilt on original design)

Venice was a longstanding maritime power, again based on merchant riches but much less under Papal influence. The pre-eminent Venetian theologian, the Friar Paolo Sarpi, had rejected any idea that temporal government was subject to Papal authority

---

[190] A point missed e.g. by David Goodman in Goodman and Russell *The Rise of Scientific Europe* (1991) who has him as ensuring 'there would not be the slightest deviation' from Aristotelian cosmology.

– holding that it was responsible only to its people. In general there was more religious toleration in the Republic, and Sarpi did not believe that theological orthodoxy was necessary to make a person a good scientist. To recognise a heretic as a good scientist or medic does not 'prejudice the Catholic faith' – any more than recognising Hippocrates and Galen who were infidels does so. The Venetian university was at Padua, and a Jesuit rival institution set up there was suppressed and expelled (after the Padua Aristotelian philosopher Cremonini pointed out to the senate that the Jesuits were also handing out degrees). Bellarmine tried to claim temporal authority for the Pope, Venice resisted and as a state were excommunicated in 1605. The Pope (Paul V) was, however, soon forced to climb down, and Venice retained its autonomy. Galileo was a friend of both Cremonini and Sarpi.

Perspectives on Science

What we would call 'scientists' could come in several forms:

1. Professors in universities.
2. Those in various religious orders: particularly Jesuits or Dominicans.
3. Noblemen with private means.

All three of these groups could range between extreme scientific conservatism to positions like those of Galileo himself. Galileo's earliest opposition came from a group with several Pisan professors led by the Florentine Ludovico delle Colombe. Galileo, in an anonymous response, sarcastically referred to him as Signor Colombo (Mr Pigeon) – an insulting variation on his family name delle Colombe (of the Doves). The group was then nicknamed 'the pigeon league' – a kind of equivalent to 'the birdbrains'.

Variation amongst Dominicans is illustrated by the attack on Galileo in December 1614 by the junior Dominican friar Caccini – and the Dominican Preacher-General in Rome who wrote shortly afterwards to Galileo apologising for his subordinate's stupidity. The Jesuits were cautious in reaching any new opinion, but fairly soon accepted, for example, Galileo's work on the moons of Jupiter. On the roughness of the Moon they varied – without denying what the telescope showed. The phases of Venus were rapidly accepted, and they may have seen them before Galileo. They had a number of well-informed scientists amongst them, and their concern in the Copernican debate was mainly that Galileo should not be involving himself in theology. We should, however, distinguish issues of *heresy,* which relate to Scripture, from adherence to the physics of Aristotle. Someone might argue that a moving Sun and stationary Earth were taught in the Bible. However, the phases of Venus, moons of Jupiter, and unevenness of the Moon were equally explicable under the Tychonic static-earth system. Any issues arising with these for Jesuits was more about the need for a uniform teaching syllabus – we need to make a distinction between everyday syllabus setting and cutting-edge science.

Galileo's Early Life

Galileo's father Vincenzio Galilei came from a one-time important Florentine family, but earned a modest living as a lutenist and music teacher in Pisa. As a musician, he contributed to the major change from polyphony to harmony. He refuted some ancient ideas of relationships between string length and harmony by his own experimentation, and remarked in an essay on counterpoint:

> It appears to me that those who try to prove an assertion by relying on the weight of authority act very absurdly.[191]

In 1562, aged 42, Vincenzio married 24-year-old Giulia, and their first child Galileo Galilei was born on 15th February 1564. In 1572 the parents returned to Florence, whilst Galileo stayed on with an aunt and uncle in Pisa. Aged ten, he rejoined his parents, was given basic Latin education, and learned drawing and lute playing. Galileo was interested in becoming a priest, but his father wished him to enter a lucrative career. Initially he intended Galileo for a merchant (a respected profession in Tuscany) but then decided on medicine. Galileo was unable to obtain a bursary or scholarship for this (though many were available[192]) but in 1581 returned to Pisa (and his aunt and uncle) to enrol for medicine in the university.

In late winter of 1583 (and stories vary about how exactly it happened) Galileo discovered Euclidean geometry. This was probably through the Tuscan court mathematician Ostillio Ricci rather than the Pisan Professor Fillipo Fantoni. Mathematics did not seem to offer much of a career, and his father needed some persuading that Galileo had any chance of earning

---

[191] cited in F Sherwood Taylor, *Galileo and Freedom of Thought* (1938), 1.

[192] Early biographies improbably explain this as due to heterodox views.

much. Eventually, however, Galileo was allowed to stay in Pisa until 1585. He seems effectively to have dropped out from studying medicine, and eventually left (as many did) without graduating. In his second year there Galileo reputedly discovered that for short swings of arc a pendulum's period of swing is independent of the length of arc. He may at this time also have used this to invent a pulsimeter to time patients's pulses – though did not invent the pendulum clock as sometimes reported. There is no evidence of any radical physics in his student days, or of any interest in astronomy (which was not important at Pisa).

In spring 1585 Galileo spent a time helping his father with musical researches, getting odd jobs in private tutoring, and continuing studies of Archimedes. Reconstructing Archimedes famous 'Eureka' solution to the problem of determining the alloy proportions in King Hiero's crown, Galileo invented a hydrostatic balance. This used the ratios of weights of pure metals in air and in water to compute their proportions in alloys – effectively using the concept of specific gravity. His manuscript booklet on this in Italian was circulated in 1586, and included details of calibration using wound wire along the balance arm. This kind of area, combining mechanical skill with a small mathematical content, was always Galileo's forté. In 1587–8 he continued work on the centre of gravity of solids.

Galileo, a 24-year-old university dropout with a couple of unpublished papers, managed in 1587 on a Rome visit to meet the principal mathematician at the Jesuit college – Christopher Clavius. Clavius (already mentioned above) had been chief instrument in the reform of the calendar in 1582, and was building up the importance of mathematics in the college. He apparently received Galileo very kindly, writing to him in 1588 that he was unconvinced himself by Galileo's treatise but was not in touch with that area of study and should not be taken as an oracle. However, Galileo's attempt to secure the vacant Professorship at Bologna was not surprisingly unsuccessful (the post eventually went to Magini) and he likewise failed in his attempt shortly after to obtain the Professorship at Padua.

Galileo did manage to impress an Urbino noble interested in mathematics Guidobaldo del Monte, who sent his own work on Archimedean mathematics to Galileo for perusal. Guidobaldo enlisted the help of his brother Cardinal del Monte who was involved in Florentine politics, he in turn seems to have caught the ear of Ferdinand I de Médici, and Galileo obtained a Professorship of Mathematics at Pisa in 1589.

Pisa (1589–1592)

R. S. Ball in *Great Astronomers* (1906) tells us that Galileo got the idea of a pendulum from a chandelier in Pisa Cathedral (which was put up some years later) and constructed a pendulum clock. Then he says:

> The summit of the Leaning Tower of Pisa offered a highly dramatic site for the great experiment. The youthful professor let fall from the overhanging top a large heavy object and a small light body simultaneously. According to Aristotle the large light body ought to have reached the ground much sooner than the small one, but such was found not to be the case. In the sight of a large concourse of people the simple fact was demonstrated that the two bodies fell side by side, and reached the ground at the same time. Thus the first great step was taken in the overthrow of that preposterous system of unquestioning adhesion to dogma, which had impeded the development of the knowledge of nature for nearly two thousand years (71).

On the 1971 Apollo 15 moon mission an astronaut dropped a feather and a geological hammer in the airless conditions and, after they landed together, said: 'Mr Galileo was correct'. An OU video later carried the same title with its odd use of Mr Galilei's forename.

Modern biographers do not credit the leaning tower stories, at least not in the simplistic approach of Ball. Sharratt, generally sympathetic to Galileo, points out the general unreliability of Galileo's early biographer Vivani from whom such tales come. He adds:

> First of all we should forget any later ideas about showing that in a vacuum a golden guinea and a feather will fall together. Whatever else Galileo could demonstrate during his days as a Pisan lecturer it was not Newtonian ideas on free fall, as can be seen from Viviani's restriction of the demonstration to bodies of the same material.
>
> Galileo was not the first to show that Aristotle was mistaken in thinking that the speed of falling bodies was proportional to their weight. John Philoponus had pointed this out over a thousand years earlier, as had several medieval philosophers. More recently Benedetti had done the same, as had Simon Stevin in the

> Netherlands in 1586. Yet many Aristotelian philosophers were still content to pass on what they found in Aristotle's Physics.[193]

Galileo was certainly not taking 'the first step' since Aristotle, and did in his early works indicate a belief that the objects' rates of fall would depend on specific gravity. Only later did he come to believe (as stated in his last *Discourses*) that in a medium devoid of resistance all bodies would fall at the same speed. If he did indeed drop anything from the tower it was not the first such demonstration, and was more likely to have been just to his students. The problem was that if such experiments did not prove a strict version of Aristotle they did not (then or later) show what Galileo expected either. Galileo reports that his repeated experiments showed that releasing a lead and wood weight simultaneously led to the wood at first going faster but being overtaken by the lead. His main later arguments concerned thought experiments – what happened if two different weights of the same material were connected by a thin thread – at what speed would they then fall? David Wootton, in *Galileo Watcher of the Skies* (2010) is inclined to believe that Galileo did more actual experiments than commentators have credited him for. He cites the various weight-dropping experiments performed, the difficulties of doing the experiment accurately, and the divergent results obtained.

Our view of how much research Galileo did whilst at Pisa depends on when we date some of his unpublished manuscripts, in particular *De Motu*. Traditional Aristotelians made speed proportional to distance travelled for falling objects. In 1545 Dominigo de Soto extended work of the 14th Century Oxford Merton School to a clear statement that speed was proportional to time. Whilst today we can see clearly that these are contradictory laws, in those days when the equation had barely been invented this was not at all clear – and Galileo may well have been the first to realise this and eventually plump for the second (though he dealt in ratios not formulae). Even in 1604, however, he seems to have still his own earlier model that suggested that objects rapidly reached a maximum speed depending on the medium in which they fell. By 1615 he had arrived at the speed proportional to time and to square root of distance.[194]

---

[193] Sharratt, op. cit. 47.

[194] See Stillman Drake, *Galileo Studies* (1970), Essay 11, or Sharratt, op. cit. ch. 3.

At Pisa, then, he had no clear idea of acceleration in free fall, and showed no sign of any concept of inertia. His ideas on projectiles were purely qualitative, and projectiles explained on a basis of impressed force not momentum. Drake argues that he had already accepted Copernicanism by 1591 at least as a calculating device, but the evidence is flimsy. More recent evidence (given, for example, in Sharratt) is that Galileo's early ideas owed something in their logic and scientific methodology to Jesuit Aristotelianism[195] in the 1590s, and applied this to cosmology first before motion. In any event, in 1592 Guidobaldo and Paduan Giovanni Pinelli managed to obtain for him the chair of mathematics at Padua.

Galileo's house, Padua

Padua (1592–1610)

Professors at Padua had prestige but did not earn much, and Galileo was expected to give paid tuition on the side. Like Kepler, he struggled throughout his life to meet financial obligations of family.[196] Wootton and Heilbron suggest that finance and the oppressive obligations resulting from friends supplementing his income in Padua, were much to do with his later move back to Tuscany.[197]

---

[195] This is worked out also in W. A. Wallace, *Galileo and His Sources* (1984).

[196] Lest we feel too smug today we might note that a would-be maths/mechanics professor in England would now probably need to pay £9000 p.a. fees plus living costs to do a 4-year degree, 3-years on low or no income mostly working long hours on joint research for a PhD, several years on long hours low income as a post doc, and if lucky then work up from a starting lecturing salary equivalent to a good hairdresser in Hammersmith. Then, as now, the money was in law and commerce. Even Stephen Hawking reputedly earned more in a year from a glasses advert than his professorial salary. Oh, and incidentally, most classical musicians today probably earn little more than the impoverished Mozart!

[197] Wootton, *Galileo Watcher of the Skies*, 69. Heilbron, *Galileo*, 146.

Galileo was a good engineer, and was consulted about oar arrangements by Venetian shipwrights, and patented an irrigation device. In 1597 he received a copy of Kepler's *Cosmographic Mystery*, and wrote on 4th August:

> … So far I have only perused the preface of your work, but from this I gained some notion of its intent, and I indeed congratulate myself on having an associate who is a friend of Truth. For it is a misery that so few exist who pursue the Truth and do not subvert philosophical reason … I will only add that I promise to read your book in tranquillity, certain to find the most admirable things in it, and this I shall do most gladly as I adopted the teaching of Copernicus many years ago, and his point of view helps me to explain many phenomena of nature which certainly remain inexplicable according to the more current hypothesis. I have written many arguments in support of him and in refutation of the opposite view – which so far I have not dared to bring into the public light, frightened by the fate of Copernicus himself, our teacher, who though he acquired immortal fame with some, is yet to an infinite multitude of others (for such is the number of fools) an object of ridicule and derision …

The full letter contains four references to devotion to Truth, and later announces his intention to suppress it. This, indeed, he did. His lectures in Padua alternated between Sacroboso's standard Ptolemaic system, and Peurbach's Aristotelian cosmology. Galileo's first public Copernicanism came 16 years later, and he here states his reasons for this. At that time he had as little reason (especially living in the Venetian Republic) to fear persecution as Copernicus – his fear is of ridicule. Viewed cynically, this is a pretty no-risk letter. The book was not sent to him specifically, he had published nothing and Kepler had never heard of him. Kepler was a rising if Protestant star whose support might one day be useful, and Galileo can flatter without fear of rivalry and without even bothering to read the book. As for the 'many proofs' he claims to have, he may well by then have formulated his tide theory – an idea which may have arisen from watching the water in Venetian canal barges as they accelerated and reached constant speed. A note in the diary of his Venetian friend Paolo Sari for 1595 contains material which sounds as though Galileo may have told him about it.[198] Wootton suggests that the other 'proofs' were Galileo's discovery of

---

[198] See e.g. James MacLachlan, *Galileo Galilei First Physicist*, (1997), 34, and later in these notes.

the relativity of motion, and also the phenomena of 'earthshine' that others had observed (i.e. the illumination of the Moon by the light reflected from the Earth).[199] Maybe Galileo saw them like this, but of course the relativity of motion does not prove that the Earth moves, and earthshine is just as explicable by the Tychonic model (to which Wootton elsewhere refers). Mountains on the Moon (which again he may have seen even with the native eye) disprove Aristotelianism, but are not evidence for a moving Earth.

Kepler wrote back commending Galileo's 'clever secretive manner' but politely urging him to stand up and be counted. Failing this, could he tell Kepler privately what the 'many proofs' were or at least join him in some observations looking for stellar parallax. Galileo did not reply and did not contact Kepler for another twelve years.

On a visit to romantic Venice, the 40-year-old Professor began a ten-year relationship with the young Venetian Marina Gamba. They had three children Virginia (1600) Livia (1601) and Vincenzio (1606). Galileo never married, and kept his mistress (though Heilbron[200] seems to regard her more as a kind of high class courtesan) in her own house near his in Padua. Their birth certificates did not name Galileo, but he adopted Vincenzio and provided for him.

Vincenzio Galilei was baptised in the beautiful, plain, early 12th century church of Saint Sofia – not in the famous Cathedral or a more ornate setting. Galileo – in spite of having a long-term mistress – always claimed to be religiously orthodox by the Catholic standards of the times. He never, privately or publicly, ever expressed any doubt about his Catholicism, did not see any of his ideas as undermining it, and never doubted the inspired truth of all of the Bible – his divergence was on its proper interpretation. David Wootton rightly

St Sofia Church Padua

[199] David Wootton, *Galileo Watcher of the Skies* (2010), ch.11.

[200] J. L. Heilbron, *Galileo*, (2010), 84.

Vincenzio's Baptismal Font

points out that Galileo's writings do not contain any naturally pious Christian expressions (such are found, for example, in Kepler and Tycho – though of course they were Protestants). Wootton also argues that 'three types of evidence establish … that Galileo was not a Christian' (241). The first is evidence that Galileo was an atomist and a believer in central physical fire in the Earth rather than Dante's hell. Atomism was considered inconsistent with *transubstantiation* – though this is of course a Catholic rather than a Christian doctrine, and Wootton later says that the Catholic Castelli was an atomist though 'always a pious Christian'. Anyway, Wootton admits that this is 'at best indirect evidence'. Much of the rest of his chapter seems to me to be little less 'indirect', and his only actual quotation from Galileo is from a letter of 1615 which ironically contains uncharacteristically pious statements from Galileo. Wootton's 'decisive' evidence is a letter to Galileo in 1639 from a close friend Castelli rejoicing that he (Galileo) has finally 'given his soul to Christ' at the close of his life. This, Wootton claims, proves that Castelli always knew Galileo had been an unbeliever and also proves that Galileo faked his supposed new piety to his friend to gain advantage. Castelli, however, rejoices that Galileo has 'given his soul to Christ' – it is not about any particular change of *belief*. We really cannot know what had passed between the friends concerning the *experience* of God, and of course much depends on what one considers a 'good Catholic' or a 'Christian'. In the end even Wootton admits that it is inconclusive, and that Galileo always presented himself as a Catholic.

The university was by then situated in the present site called 'The Bo' (i.e. the ox). The reputed plain wooden lectern there is still shown to visitors and then, as now, the student body had strong traditions. Lecturers who were late or failed to deliver lectures were fined.

In 1604 a bright new star appeared – the one called Kepler's nova. Galileo lectured on it, but published nothing. Galileo seems to have placed the object well beyond the Moon, but was not sure if it was really a star, or even what a star actually was. Perhaps it was just some kind of condensation of Earth originating vapours far out in space. Ironically, this is much more like an Aristotelian explanation, and attempts of defenders of Galileo like Michael Sharratt are unconvincing in their attempts to explain this away. The object looked like all the other stars, lacked parallax like all the other stars – so if it looks like an elephant and smells like an elephant then … . The Aristotelian, Ludovico del Colombe, actually accepted it as a star, but suggested that it had merely been invisible until heavenly motions brought some kind of lens amongst the spheres to make it visible to us. Galileo was disdainful of such an *ad hoc* explanation – printing his ridicule in an anonymous work under the pen name Mauri and insulting Colombe by calling him Mr Pigeon.

Galileo's Lectern ?

'The Bo' Spring 2000 on a students-award doctoral day: on this they give funny (often crude) orations written by friends who dress them up bizarrely

Whilst at Padua Galileo also worked on improvements to various gadgets, something he was very good at doing. His 'Geometric and Military Compass' consisted of two arms each about a foot long and an inch wide, hinged at one end. The inscriptions on these, together with dividers, could be used either to measure angles or to do calculations – a kind of pre-logarithm slide rule. Galileo's first actual publication was a manual for this compass, which he had a craftsman turn out at a rate of one a month.

Manuscript copies were also circulating of Galileo's work on levers – a continuation of Archimedes's famous work in Syracuse. Work was proceeding, off and on, researching into pendulums, motion and free fall. By 1608 Galileo knew that projectiles (e.g. cannonballs) went in parabolas – useful information for a military Republic.

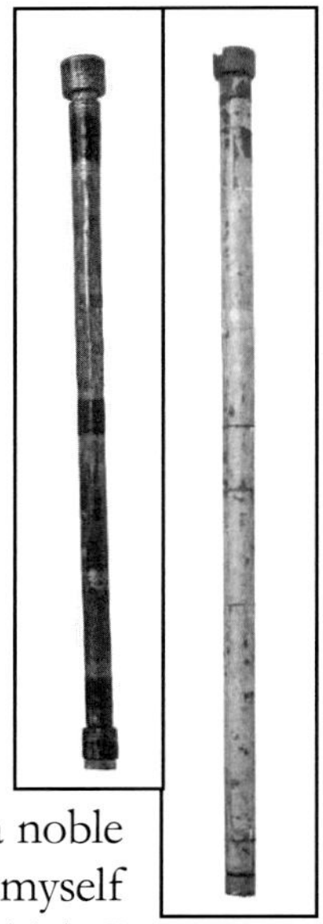

Spectacle lenses had been used for about three centuries when, in September 1608 a new invention using two such lenses in a tube was offered for sale in a Frankfurt fair. In October Dutch spectacle makers were disputing licenses, and in April 1609 Paris shops offered them for sale.

In March 1610 Galileo published his first astronomical work *The Starry Messenger*. In it he recounted how:

> About ten months ago a report reached my ears that a certain Fleming had constructed a spyglass by means of which visible objects, though very distant from the eye of the observer, were distinctly seen as if nearby … A few days later the report was confirmed to me in a letter from a noble Frenchman in Paris … which caused me to apply myself wholeheartedly to inquire into the means by which I might arrive at the invention of a similar instrument. This I did shortly afterwards, my basis being the theory of refraction. First I prepared a tube of lead, at the ends of which I fitted two glass lenses, both plane on one side, while on the other side one was spherically convex and the other spherically concave. Then, placing my eye near the concave lens I perceived objects satisfactorily large and near, for they appeared three times closer and nine times larger than when seen with the naked eye alone. Finally, sparing neither labour nor expense, I succeeded in constructing for myself so excellent an instrument that objects seen by it appeared nearly one thousand times larger and over thirty times closer than when regarded without natural vision.[201]

The Paris telescopes were probably about a foot long and magnified perhaps up to at most seven times. The rumours Galileo had heard were probably confirmed by a letter of his former pupil Jacques Badovere to Paolo Sarpi when Galileo was on a visit to Venice in late July 1609. It is possible that Badovere actually described the instrument – though Galileo's later comments in *The Assayer* deny this. Anyway, just after Galileo's return to Padua, an enterprising foreigner (who refused to let

---

[201] Galileo, *Starry Messenger* (1610), in Stillman Drake, *Discoveries and opinions of Galileo* (1957), 29.

anyone examine his instrument) arrived offering one to the Venetian Senate for 1000 florins in August 1609. Paolo Sarpi advised procrastination, and wrote to Galileo in early August confident that he could work out how to make one. In *The Assayer* Galileo explains:

> … in Venice, where I happened to be at the time, news arrived that a Fleming had presented to Count Maurice [of Nassau] a glass by means of which distant objects might be seen as distinctly as if they were nearby. That was all. Upon hearing this news I returned to Padua, where I then resided, and set myself to thinking about the problem. The first night after my return I solved it, and on the following day I constructed the instrument and sent word of this to those same friends at Venice with whom I had discussed the matter the previous day. Immediately afterward I applied myself to the construction of another and better one, which six days later I took to Venice, where it was seen with great admiration by nearly all the principal gentlemen of that republic for more than a month on end, to my considerable fatigue. Finally, at the suggestion of one of my patrons, I presented it to the Doge at a meeting of the Council. How greatly it was esteemed by him, and with what admiration it was received, is testified by ducal letters still in my possession. These reveal the munificence of that serene ruler. In compensation for the invention presented to him I was reappointed and confirmed for life in my professorship at the University of Padua with double my previous salary, which was already three times that of some of my predecessors.

Campanile seen from Doge's Palace

The 'theory of refraction' Galileo used seems to have been little more than choosing between the limited number of possible lens shapes, finding a combination (not the best one in fact) which worked, and playing with ratios and rules of thumb until a good result was obtained.[202] Even Drake seems to accept this. The instrument presented to the Senate magnified about nine times. Galileo's claim to have spent a month demonstrating it is economical with the truth (no such prolonged visit occurred according to his contemporary records), though a letter he wrote describing aged senators hiking up the Campanile for a look is likely enough. Venice was a city built on an island in a lagoon, a major maritime power, and both the city and the ships would especially value a telescope. The Campanile (or bell tower) was a high vantage point in the heart of the city (the present one was built to exactly the same design after the original collapsed suddenly in 1902). Galileo's audience with Doge and Senate probably took place in the large Senate room in the fabulous Doge's Palace, a room with a huge astronomical clock on its wall.

Galileo continued to work on the instrument later called a 'telescope', and produced one with 1000 magnification – bringing objects some 30 times nearer. This is about the limit using such a design.

Looking at celestial bodies through telescopes was a fairly obvious thing to do. The earliest reports from the Hague indicated that they revealed many more stars than are visible with the naked eye. The Englishman Thomas Harriott (1560–1621)[203] had attempted to use a very early one to draw the Moon in summer 1609 well before Galileo thought of it.[204] Even Emperor Rudolph II had looked at the Moon through a telescope before he had heard of Galileo. Modern fans of Galileo admit this, but see his 'decisive innovation' as the *scientific* use of the telescope in astronomy. The real point, in my view, was that Galileo's telescopes (like William Herchel's years later) were *much more powerful* than any others at that time. Even then, only one in ten of his products could spot Jupiter's moons. Manipulating a three-to-four-foot tube with no mountings and a small field of views was difficult. But it seems highly unlikely that astronomy would have long been without systematic scientific observation even had Galileo never lived. Tycho and Kepler, in contrast, brought innovations and theory that were *not* 'in the air' as it were.

---

202 This is pretty well Galileo's description in *The Assayer.*

203 Harriott was more into mathematics and optics than Galileo, and corresponded on these with Kepler cf. John Whirley (ed.), *Thomas Harriot Renaissance Scientist* (1974).

204 Harriott's accurate drawing is published in the *Journal of the British Astronomical Association,* vol 75,102.

Galileo's first scientific publication 'Starry Messenger' came out in March 1610. It is a 24-page booklet in terse Latin. Its main observations were:

1. The Moon has an uneven surface, with mountains and valleys.
2. The Milky Way is nothing but innumerable stars in clusters.
3. Nebulae (e.g. of Orion and Praesepe) are in fact star clusters.
4. Around Jupiter there are four planets orbiting.

The introductory dedication to the Grand Duke Cosimo II of Tuscany refers to the Medician planets:

> Variously moving about most noble Jupiter as children of his own, they complete their orbits with marvellous velocity, at the same time executing with one harmonious accord mighty revolutions every dozen years about the centre of the universe; that is the Sun.

This is Galileo's first printed indication of Copernicanism.

Over Easter Galileo returned to Florence, wishing to cement relationships with this new Duke Cosimo II, his former pupil. Galileo received immediate support from Kepler, though he steadfastly ignored Kepler's pleas for a telescope to be able to see for himself. Writing back after returning to Padua Galileo records not only this but that in three public lectures he was so convincing that former opponents were won over. The rather triumphalist letter (to Florentine Secretary of State Belesaio Vinta) proclaims his own refusal to be browbeaten and the ultimate triumph of truth.

At the end of May 1610 Galileo was appointed to a chair of court mathematician and chief mathematician in a non-teaching Professorship at Pisa. His salary, 1000 florins, was to match that given for life by Venice. The Venetian Senate were distinctly miffed at his departure. Galileo perhaps was homesick, and perhaps wanted to have more time for research. He obviously didn't want 'more time with the family'. His son and mistress remained in Padua (she eventually married an employee of a rich family), and his daughters were packed off to a convent at the earliest time possible (or actually rather earlier than was legal). Some biographers explain that being illegitimate they could not have married satisfactorily – though this did not stop his son Vincenzio. Probably he just did not want to pay the Dowry. The convent concerned was Franciscan (of St Clare), and the sisters there lived very meagrely indeed. One daughter was chronically unhappy at being packed off unconsulted to be a nun, the other became Sister Marie Celeste – a name which reflected her affection for and near adoration of her famous father.

Galileo can, at this time, have felt no threat from the Inquisition. Drake remarks that: 'historians are generally agreed that Venice would never have offered Galileo up to the Inquisition'.[205]

Pisa/Florence (1610–1612)

On July 25th 1610 Galileo noticed something strange about Saturn – thinking at first that it had two moons. Galileo protected his priority in a private letter five days later Secretary Vinto intended for his new employer, but Saturn continued to puzzle everyone until after Galileo's death.

The Jesuits had begun telescopic examination of Venus in November, and certainly knew of the phases by December. The Copernican Castelli (then living in Brescia) wrote to Galileo on 5th December 1610 informing him of this and asking for Galileo's opinion. On 11th December Galileo sent an anagram message to Giulano de Medici in Prague 'Venus has phases like the Moon'. Sometime during December the senior Roman Jesuit Clavius became convinced that Galileo's *Starry Messenger* discoveries were true, and wrote to Galileo to say so. Galileo, delighted, wrote back on 30th December, mentioning also his discovery of the phases of Venus, which he had been observing (he said) for three months.

Florence

So did Galileo discover them independently, or did he just react to Castelli's letter and claim it for himself? Drake argues that it would have taken too long for Castelli's letter to travel some 150 miles to Pisa/Florence to allow Galileo enough

---

[205] Drake, *Discoveries and Opinions of Galileo*, 69.

time to compose an anagram to send to Prague on 11th December. However, others (particularly Richard Westfall) have pointed out that an anagram was a safe way to preserve priority without being explicitly committed. He would not have had much time for protracted observation, but may have taken a chance on one night's sighting. Gingerich sides with Drake, suggesting that Galileo probably had been observing, the letter may have precipitated the anagram, but his observation could not make him sure until later.[206] In practice it does not make much difference. It is a very obvious thing to point a telescope at the brightest object in the evening/morning sky, and any serious observation would in time have led to spotting the phases. It is not important whether Galileo, the Jesuits, or, indeed, someone else first noticed it.

The implication of phases was that Venus was sometimes between the Earth and the Sun, and sometimes on the far side of the Sun. This was plainly in contradiction with a strict Aristotelian system, but it was equally compatible with Copernican epicycles, Tychonic epicycles, or Keplerian ellipses (published in 1609). Why did Galileo entirely ignore the last two? Sharratt suggests:

> To Galileo, Tycho's system was no system at all and could never be turned into one, whereas Copernicanism was a system and one which held out hope of a celestial mechanics. To Galileo it was intuitively obvious that somehow the Sun must cause planetary motions, so it would be physically absurd to insist on a special status for a fixed central Earth. Hence the discovery of the phases of Venus was a wonderful vindication of *Copernicanism*; the fact that it fitted Tycho's arrangement equally well was to be brushed aside as irrelevant. [207]

Sharratt really sees things from a 'Galileo viewpoint'. Thus Sharratt always describes Tycho's system as a 'compromise system' – when it is no more a 'compromise' than the Copernican system which has the Moon go around the Earth but everything else around the Sun. Sharratt refers to Galileo's lack of sympathy for 'heady and mystical Pythagoreanism' (70) and 'strange

---

[206] Owen Gingerich, *The Great Copernicus Chase* (1992), ch. 13, previously Sky and Telescope 68 520–2, 1984.

[207] Michael Sharratt, op. cit. 89.

preoccupations' (182). Elsewhere, however even Sharratt hints at the *real* reason for Galileo's silence i.e. Tycho was primarily famed as an *observational* rather than a mathematical astronomer – and would therefore be a real rival to Galileo himself. Sharratt's view that the Sun was 'obviously' the cause of planetary motion is not true. Kepler reached this conclusion, but it is not explicit in Galileo's works, nor would it be necessary if inertia really were circular as Galileo thought. Galileo was dismissive of action at a distance as nonsense – and how else could the Sun hold objects in orbit? Most of this paragraph from Sharratt is implausible if not untrue. Galileo didn't want to offer Tycho any credit or publicity, and probably hadn't got around to ploughing through any of Kepler's works. He ignores them both.

In Spring 1611 Galileo left Pisa for a visit to Rome. By December, as already noted, Jesuits in Florence and in the *Collegeo Romana* had been able to confirm all Galileo's work in *The Starry Messenger,* and were perhaps extending his puzzling work on Saturn and his and their work on the phases of Venus. Galileo arrived in Rome on 29th March 1611. He went to meet with the science-inclined *Jesuits* at the *Collegeo* the next day. Cardinal Bellarmine took an interest, apparently looking at Venus and the Moon himself (with Galileo?), and asking those at the *Collegeo* for their views whether:

1. were there really many stars invisible to the naked eye?
2. was Saturn composed of three stars?
3. did Venus really have phases?
4. was the Moon really uneven?
5. did Jupiter really have four moons?

Their response was yes to 1, 2 , 3, and 5, and a report of divergence on 4 with one (the venerable Clavius) thinking that the marks could just be markings under a smooth surface. In April Galileo attended a banquet given by Frederico Cesi and was made a member of the then semi-moribund *Academy of the Lynxes* (which at that point had four members). Galileo had a friendly audience with Pope Paul V and around the middle of May a special reception was held for him in the *Collegeo Romano* at which Galileo was feted and honoured. We should note that all these things happened *after* his Copernican views were made explicit in the introduction to *The Starry Messenger.*

Back home in July 1611 Galileo became embroiled in a dispute about floating bodies. It apparently began with another philosopher at a banquet asserting that ice was condensed water. Galileo claimed that it was actually *rarified* water because it floated. His opponents claimed that it was shape that made things buoyant. Ludovico delle Colombe pointed out that ebony chips would float on water. Galileo knew nothing, of course, about surface tension, but noticed a slight impression in the water surface around them, and claimed that this air then formed part of the body and so reduced its average density. This also explained why a point-down cone may float whilst a point-up cone of the same material sinks – it can include less air in its weight. Part of the dispute involved a banquet for Cardinals on 2nd October 1611. Two Cardinals debated, the side of Galileo being taken by a visiting Cardinal from a noble Florentine family, Maffeo Barbarini – the future Pope Urban VIII. Galileo's *Bodies in Water* was published in 1612.

In early 1612 Galileo also received a letter from Mark Welsner, a German official and amateur scientist. He enclosed a pamphlet by an anonymous local Jesuit (in fact Christoph Scheiner) on sunspots. MacLachlan remarks:

> Galileo had already seen sunspots for himself. He had shown them to people in Rome a year earlier.[208]

The basis of this plain statement is Galileo's claim (made 3–4 months after receiving Scheiner's work[209]) that he had shown sunspots to 'many prelates and gentlemen in Rome' – though actually Galileo names not a single one of these. So did Galileo or Scheiner 'discover' sunspots? First, we should note that in Galileo's own *Letters on Sunspots* he points out that the spots are sometimes large enough to see by eye, and had already been noticed in the time of Charlemagne etc. The point was not just to *see* one, but to study them systematically. Galileo's claim to have shown them to various Roman odd bods (even if true) is hardly, then, a claim to first 'discovery'. Moreover, he gives Welsner, as reason for not responding sooner, not only a protracted illness but a lack of sufficient number of continuous observations to make him sure enough to publish. This sounds much as though even if he had seen them earlier, his stimulus for serious study could well have come from receiving Scheiner's work.

[208] James MacLachlan, *Galileo Galilei IRST Physicist* (1997) p. 67.

[209] Galileo's first letter is dated May 4th 1612.

Actually, Thomas Harriott was probably the first to see them using the telescope – his first observation is dated 8th December 1610.[210] The first systematic published study was from the Wittenberg-based Johannes Fabricius on 13th June 1611. Fabricius stated they were neither clouds nor comets, but were on the solar surface. From their pattern and behaviour, Fabricius concluded that the Sun was probably rotating on its axis.

Scheiner and his assistant first noticed them in March–April 1611, but did not publish at that time. In October Scheiner's interest was reawakened. If he had seen Fabricius's paper then he was unconvinced, thinking the spots were minor planets. On 12th November, 12th December and 26th December 1611 Scheiner sent letters to Welsner on the sunspots, which were collected and published as a pamphlet. Galileo received a copy asking for his opinion sometime in January.

Galileo's response was the *Three Letters on Sunspots*. Their tone towards 'Apelle' (Scheiner's pseudonym) was respectful and polite throughout. The work has the tone of one scientist sharing a different perspective with another – you can read less polite controversy in scientific journals today. Galileo described everything in the patterns of the spots that would indicate a rotating Sun with patches in or near the surface.

On 1st June 1612 Welsner thanked Galileo for his first letter, and proposed its printing. Galileo and his friend Sagredo had already circulated it in manuscript form. Cardinal Maffeo Barbarini had received one and praised Galileo for his perspicacity and accepted his view over Apelle's. Galileo had asked Cardinal Carlo Conti if any Biblical issue was involved, and modern author Fantoli well summarises the response:

> The cardinal answered in July 1612 and stated that Scripture did not support the Aristotelian theory of the incorruptibility of the heavens but that, on the contrary, the common opinion of the Fathers of the Church was that the heavens were corruptible. As to the circular motion of the Earth, Conti stated that it was not very consistent with Scripture and that, therefore, the Copernican hypothesis could be reconciled with Scripture only if one held that the Bible spoke the ordinary language of the common people, a thing, however, which (the cardinal added) 'should not

[210] In John Shirley (Ed.) *Thomas Harriot Renaissance Scientist* (1974) opposite page 118.

> be admitted unless it is really necessary' (XI, 355). Despite his personal caution, Conti did not hesitate to inform Galileo in complete honesty of the existence of [a Spanish Dominican friar] Diego de Zuiliga's opinion in support of the possibility of a reconciliation between Scripture and Copernicanism.[211]

Apelle produced three new letters in 1612, and through Welsner had them published. Meantime Galileo wrote a second letter via Sagredo in August, but it reached Welsner only in October. Welsner had on 28th September sent the Apelle publication to Galileo, who was disappointed to find Apelle unconvinced by his first letter. Galileo accepted that in writing his letters not in Latin but in Florentine Italian he had made it difficult for Apelle to read them. His excuse, that they should be more accessible to Florentine dignitaries, indicates a focus on possible patronage rather than communicating with the scientific community. Apelle, like all European scholars, could read Latin fluently but as a German struggled with Italian. Galileo is prickly about the notion that his 'Medician planets' (i.e. Jupiter's moons) are anything but real, and denies Apelle's suggestion that there is a fifth (certainly not detectable by telescopes of that period). Galileo was clearly irritated that his clear arguments had been ignored, but maintained a respectful tone. He disagreed with Apelle but did not ridicule him.[212]

An interesting aside is that Galileo here reflected on the role of eccentrics and epicycles, concluding that they are a useful calculating tool but little more. This is three years after Kepler's *New Astronomy* – Galileo makes no mention of elliptical orbits and presumably had not read Kepler's work.

A second point of interest is that in these *Letters on Sunspots* Galileo stated that his Saturn discovery:

> … harmonises with the great Copernican system, to the universal revelation of which doctrine propitious breezes are now seen to be directed towards us, leaving little fear of clouds or crosswinds.

---

211 Annibale Fantoli, *Galileo: For Copernicanism and for the Church* (1994), 141.

212 Van Helden (in Taton &Wilson, op. cit., 93) claims 'Scheiner's claim' (to priority) was 'ridiculed'. It is contested, though does not read to me like 'ridicule'.

This second open avowal of the Copernican system brought him no opprobrium, and the book won wide acclaim. Cardinals Boromea and Maffeo Barbarini wrote expressing their sincere admiration. The senior Jesuit Grienberger confided to Galileo his agreement with him and against his fellow Jesuits on this issue. Galileo was still riding high.

Pisa/Florence 1616: The Church and Copernicanism

In 1610 or 1611 Mr Pigeon (Ludovico delle Colombe) wrote an anti-Copernican tract citing Scripture and science – but not mentioning Galileo. Galileo, as already noted, asked Cardinal Conti about this in a letter.

Then on 2nd November 1612 Galileo heard that a Dominican friar Niccolo Lorini had made an attack on him. Galileo wrote to Lorini who was a septuagenarian Professor of ecclesiastical history. Lorini replied that he had no interest in such matters and had merely chipped into a conversation, to prove he was still alive, and that Ipernicus, or whoever he was, seemed to hold an absurd idea!

On 14th December 1612, Galileo's former pupil and friend (then a Professor at the generally hostile Pisa) wrote telling him of a dinner at the table of the Grand Duchess Christina (mother of the present Grand Duke Cosimo II) during which both Castelli and the philosophy professor Boscaglia had assured the Duchess that the Jupiter planets named after her were real as were Galileo's other discoveries. Boscaglia doubted only the Earth's motion, and seems to be privately explaining to the Duchess the Scriptural and physical problems. It was Christina herself who after dinner plied Castelli with Scriptural questions, and eventually after further debate was won over with most others to Galileo's views.

Galileo sought to press home the advantage in writing to Castelli a 'Letter to Castelli' which was later expanded into the 'Letter to the Grand Duchess Christina' with the subtitle 'Concerning the Use of Biblical Quotations in Matters of Science'.

Santa Maria Novella

Little of note happened throughout 1614, but on 20th December a Dominican friar Tommaso Caccini used his turn as Scriptural lecturer in the large 14th century Dominican church Santa

Maria Novella in Florence to denounce Copernicanism, Galileo and mathematicians in general. The Dominicans were proud of the pun on their name 'hounds of the Lord' – sniffing out and suppressing heresy. In January 1615 Galileo received an entirely sympathetic letter of apology from Father Luigi Maraffi the Dominican Preacher-General in Rome, adding wearily: 'Unfortunately, I have to answer for all the idiocies that thirty or forty thousand brothers may or actually do commit!'

Shortly afterwards, however, Caccini and also Lorini became concerned at a copy Lorini had received of the *Letter to Castelli*. Lorini wrote to the holy office in Rome complaining:

> … it asserts that the language of Holy Scripture does not mean what it seems to mean; that in discussions about natural phenomena the last and lowest place ought to be given to the authority of the sacred text; that its commentators have often erred in their interpretation; that the Holy Scriptures ought not to be mixed up with anything except matters of religion … I, who hold that those who call themselves Galileists are orderly men and good Christians all, but a little overwise and conceited in their opinions …

Unfortunately Lorini's copy had been subtly altered in a couple of places. The Holy Office agreed that these particular phrases sounded bad, but that they were acceptable in context. The accusation was dismissed.

Roberto Bellarmine

Galileo, however, had sent a true copy of his *Letter to Castelli* to his friend Cardinal Dini and Monsignor Ciampoli. At the end of February Ciampoli wrote back saying he had talked with Cardinal Maffeo Barbarini, who advised sticking to the arguments used by Copernicus: 'For to explain the Scriptures is claimed by theologians as their field …' On March 3rd Dini wrote back having spoken at length with Bellarmine. The latter said that there was no question of Copernicus's work being banned, at worst a few marginal comments on the use of the theory to save the appearances would be added:

> And with a similar precaution you may at any time deal with these matters. If things are fixed according to the Copernican system, [he said], it does not appear presently that they would have any greater obstacle in the Bible than the passage '[the Sun] exults as a strong man to run his course,' etc., which all expositors up to now have understood by attributing motion to the Sun. And although I replied that this also could be explained as a concession to our ordinary forms of expression, I was told in answer that this was not a thing to be done in haste, just as the condemnation of any of these opinions was not to be passionately hurried …[213]

Dini also consulted Grienberger who evidently thought Galileo's arguments plausible rather than proven, and (like Bellarmine) would have preferred Galileo to have given his proofs and *then* asked for a reinterpretation of Scripture by the experts.

In January 1615 a Carmelite friar Paolo Antonio Foscarini wrote a book claiming that Copernicanism was compatible with Scripture. This he sent to Bellarmine who replied in a famous letter. This thanked Foscarini cordially and praised the ingenuity and learning of the work, but added:

> But since you ask for my opinion I shall give it to you … First I say that it appears to me that Your Reverence and Sig, Galileo did prudently to content yourselves with speaking hypothetically and not positively as I have always believed Copernicus did …

Bellarmine knew perfectly well that this was barely true, but was cleverly disguising his advice as praise! His first two real points were:

1. He doubts it is all that easy to reinterpret Scripture.
2. He affirms his belief that the Council of Trent forbids interpretations differing from all the Holy Fathers – and responds to those who claim it is not a 'matter of faith' that the *veracity* of Scripture is *always* such a matter.

His third point is:

---

[213] These various letters are in Koestler op. cit. amongst other works.

> I say that if there were a true demonstration that the Sun was in the centre of the universe and the Earth in the third sphere, and that the Sun did not go around the Earth but the Earth went around the Sun, then it would be necessary to use careful consideration in explaining the Scriptures that seemed contrary, and we should rather have to say that we do not understand them than to say that something is false which had been proven. But I do not think there is any such demonstration, since none has been shown to me. To demonstrate that the appearances are saved by assuming the Sun at the centre and the Earth in the heavens is not the same thing as to demonstrate that in fact the Sun is in the centre and the Earth in the heavens. I believe that the first demonstration may exist, but I have very grave doubts about the second; and in case of doubt one may not abandon the Holy Scriptures as expounded by the Holy Fathers …

Bellarmine had been asked for an opinion and had given it, but showed no intention to take any action. Whether Galileo was given any other verbal injunctions at that time is a subject of hot dispute – in the later trial he claimed not to remember.

Galileo rewrote his work as *Letter to the Grand Duchess Christina.* In doing so he went against all the advice given by friends and admirers. The book is clearly not about astronomy but about Biblical interpretation. In today's climate (when anyone can write a book claiming that Jesus was a sacred mushroom or recovered from crucifixion to marry again and have three children – and have the books carried by Waterstones!) it is hard for us to imagine the vanity and folly of a layman at that time publishing a book setting straight leading Catholic theologians on how to interpret the Council of Trent decisions! Bellarmine had set out the stall: give us the proof (that is the scientist's business) then we will reinterpret Scripture (the theologian's business). Sharratt admits that there *was* no proof, but claims that Bellarmine would never have accepted any anyway. This is not very convincing. In any event, Galileo denied that the opinions of all the church fathers implied geocentricity because:

1. They never really considered it as a serious issue.

Pope Paul V

2. Augustine (and others) held as an opinion that such issues should not be determined from Scripture.

Galileo also offered his own interpretation of the supposed long day in Joshua when the Sun 'did not go down'.

By February 6th 1616 Galileo was sure his own name had been cleared, but wished to clear Copernicanism. He induced Orsini to raise the issue with Pope Paul V, mentioning his theory of the tides. The Pope, however, referred it to the Inquisition's eleven consultors who considered two propositions:

(1) The Sun is the centre of the world and consequently immobile with local motion.

(2) The Earth is not the centre of the world nor immobile, but moves as a whole, also with diurnal motion.

The consultors agreed that the first was foolish and absurd in philosophy and formally heretical in that it expressly contradicted many sentences of scripture, taken in the proper meaning of the words and according to the common exposition of the Fathers and learned theologians. The second was given the same philosophical (i.e. scientific) censure and theologically was 'erroneous in faith'. This was, of course, only *advice* from the consultors, and *not* a formal Catholic pronouncement of heresy. The formal decree of 5th March 1616 did *not* contain the word 'heresy' – and Cardinal Maffeo Barbarini later claimed credit for its omission. It simply said that the views were 'false and completely contrary to the divine Scriptures'. Foscanini's work was banned, and de Zuniga's *Commentary on Job* and Copernicus's *Revolutions* suspended until corrected. The alterations to *Revolutions* consisted of a few lines, and (as Gingerich has shown) were in practice made in only some copies in Italy and in none elsewhere in Catholic Europe. Elsewhere it was regarded as some kind of local Italian wrangle.

No public mention was made of Galileo, but Pope Paul asked Bellarmine to call in Galileo and make the implications clear. Bellarmine, received Galileo cordially, and duly made the points. Galileo, fearing for his reputation, shortly afterwards asked Bellarmine for something declaring that he had not been censured and Bellarmine wrote:

> We, Robert Cardinal Bellarmine, hearing that it has been calumniously rumoured that Galileo Galilei has abjured in our hands and also has been given a salutary penance, and being requested to state the truth with regard to this, declare that this man Galileo has not abjured, either in our hands or in the hands of any other person here in Rome, or anywhere else as far as we know, any opinion or doctrine which he has held; nor has any salutary or any other kind of penance been given to him. Only the declaration made by the Holy Father and published by the Sacred Congregation of the Index has been revealed to him, which states that the doctrine of Copernicus, that the Earth moves around the Sun and that the Sun is stationary in the centre of the universe and does not move east to west, is contrary to Holy Scripture and therefore cannot be defended or held. In witness whereof we have written and signed this letter with our hand on this twenty-sixth day of May, 1616.

There unfortunately existed in the records an unsigned unauthorised note that bore a rather different account of the meeting – perhaps the result of rather sloppy recording. Galileo's note, however, is definitely genuine. We have also to note the suggestion of Pietro Redondi in *Galileo: Heretic* (1983) that the controversy was 'really' about Galileo's atomism – though it is one I personally find implausible.

Galileo actually had at this time a friendly audience with the Pope, and apparently retained the support of Jesuits like Grienberger and Guildin for example.

Florence 1617–1632

In Autumn 1618 three comets appeared in the sky in quick succession, the last and brightest remaining visible until January. Galileo was ill at the time and made no personal observation, and Drake seems to cast about a bit to explain Galileo's interest in the comet issue. Clearly Galileo was jealous of Tycho who had shown in 1577 that the parallax on comets showed them to be as distant as Venus. The Roman Jesuits, and in particular their now senior mathematician Father Orazio Grazzi, published their views that the recent comets were indeed well outside the lunar orbit, and crediting Tycho with the original discovery (in 1577).

Galileo covered the margins of his copy of the Grazzi lecture with 'piece of asininity' , 'elephantine' , 'buffoon' , 'evil poltroon' and 'ungrateful villain' . Quite what Galileo was cross about is uncertain, as his only previous 'work' on comets is a side-comment in his *Letters on Sunspots*: 'a host of observations come to teach us that comets are generated in the celestial regions'. Drake and Koestler (unusually!) agree that this is an oblique grudging tribute to Tycho. However, 'generated in the celestial regions' seems to me just as compatible with Galileo's later suggestion that comets were 'generated' by vapours in the superlunar atmosphere. In any event, Galileo published an attack (under the name of a close associate Mario Guiducci) on Grazzi. Galileo suggested that comets might not be real objects but could be sunlight reflecting on vapours just outside the lunar orbit – vapours that might emanate from Earth. Galileo also mocked Grazzi for suggesting that since comets (like stars and unlike planets) were not enlarged by telescopes, they must be far away. Just to add to his bid for popularity, Galileo then went out of his way to insult Scheiner as a plagiarist of Galileo's priority on sunspots (which showed that smoky vapours could exist in the heavens).

On 12th August Ciapoli reported from Rome that the Jesuits were rather miffed and preparing a reply. Grazzi wrote this reply, like Galileo, in the name of a supposed pupil Lothario Sarsi. So anxious is Drake to exonerate his hero that (according to Sharratt) he translated Grazzi's obscure Latin as 'my whole desire is nothing less than to champion the conclusions of Aristotle' instead of 'the least of my wishes is to contend for Aristotle's opinions' .[214] This latter rendering certainly makes more sense given that actually Galileo's suggestion is a modified form of Aristotle, and Grazzi's radically breaks from it. Sharratt also assesses that Grazzi's work 'in general is quite dignified' .

Finally, Galileo's *The Assayer* came out in 1623. One's view of Galileo generally affects whether it is seen as 'plaintive', 'magisterial' and a 'masterpiece' (all phrases used by Drake and Sharratt) or bitching, pompous, and hypocritical (which others of us might find more appropriate!). It begins with lots of self-praise, bewailing the criticisms

---

[214] Sharratt, op. cit. 135.

others had made of his previous masterpieces. Then Galileo proceeds to hurling insults at any who have disputed his absolute priority in observations of sunspots and Jupiter's moons. Scheiner (though not specifically named) is frontally accused of dishonest plagiarism, and Simon Mayr of falsely claiming to have seen the moons of Jupiter before Galileo himself – shock horror! Galileo modestly asserts at one point:

> You cannot help it Mr Sarsi, that it was granted to me alone to discover all the new phenomena in the sky, and nothing to anyone else. This is the truth which neither malice nor envy can suppress.

This is part of a series of sarcastic and insulting jibes at 'Sarsi' (whom he knows perfectly well is Grazzi). Galileo argues, for example that Galileo's own use of the word 'infinite' (to which objection had been made) plainly did not *really* mean infinite but only a large number. Galileo objects to the telescope being called his 'foster child' – minimising the impact of its previous discovery because (he claims) he did not actually hold one before making his own.

To those sickened by Galileo's overgrown ego, a lot of the sarcasm and nit-picking becomes tedious. Galileo's basic argument about comets is that since we do not yet know what they are, we cannot be dogmatic about their position. Tycho's observations are 'alleged observations' and comets are 'Tycho's monkey-planets'.

Two passages in *The Assayer* are generally hailed as masterpiece statements of a new scientific methodology. One is where he notes Sarsi's statement that Babylonians could cook eggs from friction by whirling them in slings. Since, Galileo, says, we cannot now achieve the same effect it must be because they were Babylonians that the eggs cooked. It is not much noted that this revolutionary 'method of differences' in fact goes back to the 14th century Franciscans at Oxford. Even less often noted is that, whilst Sarsi chose a poor example, in actual fact meteorites *do* get so hot from atmospheric friction that they burn up as 'shooting stars'. Since Galileo himself believed there is an atmosphere out in space (hence the vapours can rise to form comets), such bodies should indeed have become very hot from friction.

The second famous paragraph is Galileo's proclamation:

> Philosophy is written in this very great book, which always lies open before our eyes (I mean the universe), but one cannot understand it unless one first learns to understand the language and recognise the characters in which it is written. It is written in the language of mathematics and the characters are triangles, circles and other geometrical figures, and without these means it is humanly impossible to understand a word of it …

Grand stuff! Often quoted. Unfortunately it comes in a work in which Galileo professes (largely on the basis of a parable about a man listening to different sources of sound) that the mathematical parallax demonstrations of Tycho should be ignored, and which also ignores Kepler's views (published in 1619) which prefigure the now accepted view that the curving tails of comets are caused by composite motions in materials driven from them by the Sun. Galileo shows no sign of having read anything of Kepler beyond non-mathematical introductions, and, indeed, it may be doubtful whether his mathematics was up to it. Even his copy of the Copernicus Magnum Opus *Revolutions of the Heavenly Spheres* (according to Gingerich) is very unusual in having almost no marginal notes – indicating that he probably had not read it!

One person who was delighted with the *Assayer* and had it read to him over dinner, was a man who had sent Galileo a Latin poem in his praise in August 1620 – Cardinal Maffeo Barbarini. In 1623 this same man was elected as the new Pope Urban VIII. In 1624 Galileo visited Rome and was granted six audiences by the new Pope even though the latter was busy (in the manner of the time) promoting friends and relatives to positions of power in the state. In 1625, reassured by Pope Urban VIII that he could write an even-handed dialogue 'hypothetically' about Copernicanism, Galileo began on such a work.

Though interrupted by work on magnetism, recurring illness, etc., he finally finished it in 1630. In 1631 he received permission to print it in Florence. In February 1632 it was finally published.

1632–3 Dialogue and Trial

Galileo's most famous work *Dialogue Concerning the Two World Systems* (1632) is a discussion between three people:

- *Giovannio Francesco Sagredo* – a noble Venetian who was a pupil and friend of Galileo at Padua. In the dialogue he represents the intelligent layman.
- *Philippo Salviati* – a noble Florentine who may also have been a pupil of Galileo at Padua and became a friend and patron. In the dialogue he represents Galileo himself as a scientific expert.
- *Simplicio* – a naïve Aristotelian. Galileo says that he often talked with him in the presence of the other two, and so pseudo named him for this devotion to Simplicius the sixth-century commentator on Aristotle (though the double meaning is obvious). Simplicio's arguments follow those of Colombe in *Against the Motion of the Earth* (1611), but in a Venetian setting (Sagredo's palace on the Grand Canal) it could be Cesare Cremonini. Perhaps the character is a compendium.

First edition Dialogue

The dialogue is a long book, and is scripted over four days. It assumes, of course, that there are only *two* 'great world systems' – the Tychonic one is steadfastly ignored. The first day sets the basic scene. It also replaces the Aristotelian ideas of natural motion as circular above and straight line below the Moon with Galileo's idea that all natural motion is circular. There is, moreover, change both in the heavens and on Earth. In this Tycho is naturally mentioned with the new stars but Salviati airily remarks he has 'never set much store by Tycho's verbosity', so unsurprisingly Simplicio's simple dismissal is not contested. The 'real' proof is in the sunspots – discovered by guess who! To the long explanation of this, Simplicio professes himself defeated and he will have to study this more. Telescopic examinations of the Moon (by guess who!) are equally convincing.

The second day begins with a lot of irrelevant digs at the stupidity of Peripatetic (Aristotelian) philosophers. Salviati also (fairly implausibly) explains that he is only adopting the *persona* of a Copernican – in real life he may take a very different view. When he eventually gets on with it, it mostly concerns the rotation of the Earth. Salvati simply asserts that it is 'more reasonable' to suppose the small Earth rotates than the immense heavens – somewhat missing the point that according to Aristotle the heavens are made of an easily movable element, whilst the Earth is not. Then Salviati argues that *no* natural motion can be linear since no such motion could be eternal – the only natural motion therefore must be circular/rotational. The Earth's motion is therefore rotational. This is really a development of Aristotelian thinking, it is *not* Newtonian inertia. Salviati demonstrates the fallacy in the argument that, for example, an object falling from the top of a mast of a moving ship would not be left behind. His reasoning is based on the idea that the circular motion of the rock as it descends is natural to it. Simplicio is forced to admit that he has never tried the ship-mast thing … but then sometime later Salviati admits that neither has he – but 'without experiment I am sure that the effect will happen as I tell you'! A real advocate of empirical science! At the end of the day, however, he has only shown that either schema is *possible,* not that the Earth really moves.

The third day deals with astronomical arguments. Galileo uses the phases of Venus and moons of Jupiter to show Copernicus is superior to Ptolemy (Tycho is, of course, ignored). Then Salviati explains that Ptolemy had to introduce 'very great epicycles' which Copernicus was able to exclude 'with one single motion of the Earth'. There is no mention of all the ferris wheels in the Copernican system, nor of the real problems of positional astronomy that Tycho and Kepler battled through to arrive at ellipses twenty-four years earlier. In Galileo's system all the planets go in simple *circles* with uniform motion around the Sun – a system which would be wildly inaccurate as a model of our system. Galileo really liked circles, and they fitted his ideas of circular conservation of motion. Towards the end of the day we find a spurious claim of Galileo to be the 'discoverer' of the 'new and great wonder' of sunspots and to have discovered that the Sun rotates at an angle – which was actually discovered by a former member of the pigeon league! Even then, however, there is no actual *evidence* that the Earth moves.

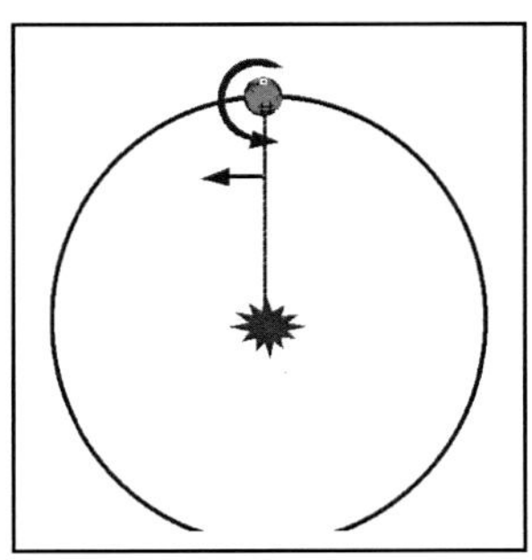

So, to the fourth day and Galileo's special contribution. A barge on a Venice canal when it accelerates causes the water to pile up at the rear – it only flattens when constant speed is reached. As the Earth rotates *and* goes around the Sun this means that its surface is constantly accelerating and decelerating depending on which side one looks at. This, therefore, causes the water to slosh around like water on a barge, and the irregularities in the ocean basins, together with this acceleration, causes the tides. This all seems very odd in some senses, since Salviati/Galileo has already established that actually there is a conservation of circular velocity – so one might expect the water (like the stone dropped from the mast) to share the continuing rotation. The modern view seems to be that if there is such an effect (given that we do not believe in the conservation of *circular* motion) it is negligible. The major causes of tides – a combination of the gravity of the Moon and Sun – was correctly put forward by Kepler; and Galileo referred to it thus:

> I am more astonished at Kepler than at any other. Despite his open and acute mind, and though he has at his fingertips the motions attributed to the Earth, he has nevertheless lent his ear and his assent to the Moon's dominion over the waters, to occult properties, and to such puerilities.

You can basically take your choice. Galileo's *Dialogue* is either an incredibly brilliant defence of empirical science, or it is an out of date, confused, and egotistical piece of special pleading. In either event, it finishes with the following words put into the mouth of Simplicio, who has been shown over and again to be a buffoon, an ignoramus, and a 'thicko'. He admits himself browbeaten and convinced by the arguments, but adds:

> I do not consider them therefore true and conclusive; indeed, keeping always before my mind's eye a most solid doctrine that I once heard from an eminent and learned person, and before which one must fall silent, I know that if I asked whether God in His infinite power and wisdom could have conferred upon the watery element its observed and reciprocating motion using some other means than moving its containing vessels, both of you

On the gondola

> would reply that he could have, and that He would have known how to do this in many ways which are unthinkable to our mind …

Sagredo proclaims the both of them silenced by such a gem, and proposes that they all go off for an hour on the gondola. What the readership may or may not know is that this 'angelic' argument in the mouth of the simpleton was the favourite argument of Pope Urban VIII, which he had advised should be put into the *Dialogue* to avoid criticism.

Strangely, some of the fans of Galileo appear much puzzled as to why Pope Urban VIII seemed at this point to swing from being a friend, admirer and protector of Galileo to manifest an incensed fury and determination to humble him. One wonders, in the apt phrase in the circumstances, what planet they are on.

Trial and Post-trial

Pope Urban VIII

Urban had received Galileo in 1630, and accepted the publication of the book provided it was hypothetical and included his argument. He suggested changing the title from *Dialogue on the Flux and Reflux of the tides* (which seemed too physical) to *Dialogue on the Two Great World Systems.* Some jiggery had gone on about obtaining the imprimatur. At the end of it all, the only real censor was Galileo's Florentine friend Father Stefani who was 'moved to tears at many passages of it, by the humility and reverent obedience' of the book. In February 1632 it came off the presses.

By August Urban VIII had read it, and it was confiscated, and Galileo summoned to Rome in October. Urban was exhibiting what Koestler calls 'the fury of the betrayed lover' – suspecting even that Simplicio was intended to represent himself. All the various conspiracy theories of Jesuit plots are superfluous in spite of Galileo's plaintive letters three years later bewailing that nothing had been further from his mind than 'perpetrating so sacrilegious an act as to make game of his holiness'. Urban not only had personal fury, but was also in a ticklish political situation. He had sided with Catholic France against Catholic Spain, and the Spanish (who dominated the Neapolitan Kingdom). Spanish claims were made that Urban was not a loyal defender of the faith. Galileo had plainly defied the earlier papal decree and written a book advocating Copernicanism – so would the Pope as a known friend of the miscreant – bring him to account?

Pope Urban rejected all Galileo's pleas of age and infirmity (which were true enough – he was seventy and had a severe hernia amongst other things). To Rome he must go – though actually he stayed in some luxury. Initially he stayed with the Tuscan ambassador, and then in a five-room flat overlooking the Vatican gardens – he never languished in the dungeons. The hearing began on 12th April 1633.

The main issue actually turned on whether or not Galileo had deliberately contravened an instruction given him by Bellarmine in 1616. Gingerich tends to the view that there was such an injunction, and Galileo had 'misremembered' – though it seems hard to understand how such a thing could have slipped his memory! To be fair to the Commissary of the Inquisition, they seem to have been doing their best for Galileo. Initially he was making the claim that 'really' it was a *refutation* of Copernicus[215] – a claim so absurd that one wonders what he was thinking. Next he stated that he had reconsidered and reread his work and felt that perhaps it had come across as too much in favour of Copernicus. At the end of it all, Galileo made a rather grovelling disclaimer of Copernicanism. One cannot be over critical of this. He was old, sick, in pain, and had realised that they knew as well as he did what he had been up to. The inquisitors accepted his obviously untrue statement that he had never held Copernican views after 1616 – though they, as well as he, knew he was lying. The role of Urban VIII in it all is disputed. In spite of his fury he gave permission for Galileo to be treated well, and no one expected that the ritual threat of torture if Galileo didn't tell the truth would be carried out. How much of this was respect for Galileo and how much for his Florentine patron is hard to say. Urban never described Copernicanism as 'heresy' but as 'contrary to Scripture' as in the 1616 decree. Some suggest that Urban scotched an

---

215 See e.g. Fantoli, op. cit. 424.

earlier attempt at a plea bargain, but the evidence on this is inconclusive. The final sentence proclaimed:

- Galileo was 'vehemently suspected of heresy' (*not* pronounced heretical).
- 'namely, of having believed and held the doctrine which is false and contrary to the sacred and divine Scriptures …'
- he had to 'abjure, curse and detest before us the aforesaid heresies …' (the latter phrase being part of the general formulary used in such cases).
- the *Dialogue* was prohibited.
- Galileo was condemned to 'formal prison'.
- he had to repeat once a week for three years seven penitential Psalms.

In practice 'formal prison' meant living in luxury (in the Duke's Grande Villa or the Archbishop's palace) but with restrictions on who could visit him, and the Psalms were said by his daughter Sister Marie Celeste on his behalf. Heilbron actually shows how Galileo was given extraordinary leniency in this respect, even though his former friend the Pope was very angry with him. Three of the ten cardinals (including the Pope's brother) did not sign it. Copernicanism was never officially declared a 'heresy' by either the Pope or Ecumenical council. The prohibition of the *Dialogue* was ineffectual, since it was printed in a Latin translation in Northern Europe and widely disseminated.

In the year following the trial Galileo turned back to writing the work which contained his really original contributions to science: *The Discourses … Concerning Two New Sciences.* It was completed in 1636, but published in Leiden, Holland, in 1638. It was popular in France and Germany, and in 1639 was on sale in Rome with official permission. The same characters are in it as before – but now the figure of Simplicio is a more serious one without appearing the complete muffin. Galileo's beloved daughter Marie Celeste died in 1634 – at just the time when he was told by the holy office that he would never be free from house arrest – and by the time he received his new book he was blind. Galileo died, aged 77, in 1642, the year that (according to our English calendar) Isaac Newton was born.

Galileo – Victim or Self-Destroyer?

As explained in the References section below, biographers of Galileo differ wildly in their assessments of his character. To Koestler Galileo's personality is 'unattractive' and he is egotistical, proud, and obstinate. Santillana[216] or Drake, on the other hand, offer us a whitewashed version, largely an innocent victim. You will find many sympathetic accounts, mine is near the hostile end! Heilbron, in his most recent biography, seems to get a good balance of judgement, with Galileo's character failings and imprudence balanced by an understanding of the concerns and also foibles of those who came to oppose him.

My own view is that he was a fundamentally proud man, with an inflated idea of his own importance. He was dismissive not only of the ignorant, but of Tycho (as verbose) and even Kepler (as a 'luney'). Galileo worsened with age – though recurrent illness and a painful hernia may partly explain this. The *Starry Messenger* and *Letters on Sunspots* were fairly polite, *The Assayer* was largely an outburst of unjustified conceit with little of value in it, and his first *Dialogue* treated all opponents (and his friend the Pope) as idiots. His treatment of various Jesuits (particularly Scheiner and Grazzi) and Urban VIII probably deserved much greater enmity than he actually received. Other friends could only look on as good prudent advice was ignored and Galileo painted himself (and his church) into a corner.

How should we view the 'trial'? As Koestler said in his classic book, we cannot see it as a kind of 'showdown' between enlightened reason and blind faith. Galileo himself never wavered in his Catholic faith; he was advocating science which was at least 24 years out of date and had no proof at all that the Earth moved apart from a bogus one which contradicted his own dynamics.

Were the actions of the Church inherently immoral? This may depend on one's ultimate priorities. In today's context, is 'academic freedom' the ultimate value? Suppose, for example, that someone formulates a theory (for which they have no real evidence) that one particular race is inherently inferior? Should they be allowed to publish in *New Scientist*? Suppose that a historian has a theory that the holocaust was a myth – should he be allowed to publish pamphlets in Germany? Supposing that someone has a theory (with poor evidence but some scientific opinion behind him) that AIDS is not in fact caused by a virus but by poverty – should he be allowed to widely publicise it in South Africa?

---

216 Giorgio de Santillana, *The Crime of Galileo* (1962).

Suppose that one doctor believes, without any real evidence, that the MMR vaccine causes autism – should he publish and stimulate a campaign in the Daily Mail which indirectly leads a number of children to deafness or blindness through contracting measles? So do we *really* believe in absolute academic freedom? To 16th-century Catholics, the veracity of the Bible was something that, if undermined, would produce bad social as well as religious effects. Figures like Bellarmine, Maffeo Barbarini, Grienberger, etc., wanted to avoid any pronouncement on Copernicanism (and regretted Galileo forcing the issue), but had a higher overall commitment to maintaining society. None of these were ignorant, and none were 'bigots' by standards of their times – or arguably by ours.

We may all today share abhorrence of the savage religious repression (not only by the Inquisition but also in France, and Protestant Germany, Switzerland and England) in the 16th century. But, as we have seen, Kepler led a charmed, protected life (although an open Copernican), and Galileo was given as much comfort and as gentle treatment as his self-destruct attitude allowed within the system. Generally, great scientific fame brought protection rather than danger.

Was everything Galileo's fault? We have to recognise that he did face a certain problem. If Copernicanism was being attacked on theological grounds, then Galileo felt he had to answer this before he could argue physically for heliocentricity. However, the clear message from friends and advisors was to avoid theology, and stick to the astronomy couched hypothetically. Obviously the latter was impossible given that Galileo was looking for *physical* proofs. One can sympathise with the difficulties he faced, but Galileo certainly did handle things badly, and precipitated a reaction that Bellarmine and others sought to avoid. Putting his former friend the Pope's key argument in the mouth of the simpleton was, by any account, not a good career move.

Galileo's Work

We have found it necessary to describe much of his work during the biographical part above. Here will be attempted some brief additional comments on the nature and value of his work:

Galileo's Telescopic Work

In a 1998 book Noel Swerdlow asserts:

> In about two months, December and January [1610] (Galileo) made more discoveries that changed the world than anyone has ever made before or since. He began with the irregular surface of the Moon, went on to the uncountable number of the stars, and then in early January found the satellites of Jupiter … He continued his observations, and in the course of the year discovered the peculiar shape of Saturn, the phases of Venus, and the irregular spots on the Sun … Within a year of publishing *Sidereal Messenger,* Galileo was the most celebrated natural philosopher in Europe …[217]

This kind of adulation is not uncommon, so let us look at his telescopic work.

Making Telescopes

Galileo did not invent the telescope, nor work out its optics. His unusual abilities in mechanical ingenuity and fabrication enabled him to improve it practically, though the optics for Galileo's telescope and for better models were worked out by Kepler and Newton.

Sunspots

Galileo did not first discover these, was not the first to publish that their patterns indicated solar rotation, did not notice first the inclination of the angle of the axis, and did not invent the screen method to observe them. He did rudely attack a respected Jesuit scientist (Christopher Scheiner) who became the century's biggest expert on sunspots.

Jupiter's Moons

Galileo was probably the first to see the moons of Jupiter. He observed them systematically, and calculated orbital periods for them that are close to modern figures. This required a good telescope and patient observation, but not a great deal of mathematics.

The Moon

Galileo was not the first to observe the Moon through the telescope[218], and it was an obvious thing to do. His arguments for an irregular surface were

---

[217] Peter Machamer (Ed), *The Cambridge Companion to Galileo* (1998), 246.

[218] Heilbron notes (151) the details of Thomas Harriot's observations.

good, and relevant to the demise of Aristotelianism. Assessing the accuracy of his actual sketches is made more difficult by the haphazard and sometimes misleading treatment in contemporary books.[219] Wootton argues that 'The illustrations of the Moon were remarkably accurate'.[220] He criticizes Feyerabend for producing pictures from a pirated edition rather than Galileo's original (which showed more shadow) and reproduced both pictures. He tells us that 'if they are placed side by side with a modern photograph their accuracy is apparent' – but he does not actually do this. Well, below are some comparisons with the images as you would see them in the sky, and you can judge for yourselves:

Galileo's sketches do indeed bear some resemblance to the photo, but the big crater about two thirds way down (which he compared to Bohemia) just is not there. Wootton suggests that Galileo exaggerated it because he had observed it with his naked eye and thought it must be large. This, however, is not my idea of being 'remarkably accurate'. We can identify reasonably on his maps the smaller craters now called Deslanders Walter, Orontius, Peurbach, and Regiomontanus.

Invisible Stars

Galileo was not the first to notice that many more stars became visible with a telescope than the naked eye. It had little immediately obvious implication.

The Phases of Venus

Galileo probably saw these around the same time as leading Roman Jesuits, but probably heard of their discovery when he was not quite sure enough to 'go public' (hence the anagram mentioned earlier). The phases of Venus were impossible to explain under the Ptolemaic system, but fitted either the Tychonic, Copernican or Keplerian systems.

---

[219] Moon pictures can be inverted (i.e. mirror image) or rotated. Hoskin (1997) gives six small Galileo sketches upright in colour; Taton & Wilson (1989) compare an upright Galileo sketch and photo of last quarter; Ronan (1974) gives Galileo sketches rotated; Goodman & Russell (1991) compare an upright 1st quarter Galileo sketch with a rotated last quarter photo; MacLachlan (1997) gives four inverted Galileo sketches; Moore (1994) compares upright Galileo sketch and photo of the first quarter. Confusing?

[220] *Galileo Watcher of the Skies*, 100.

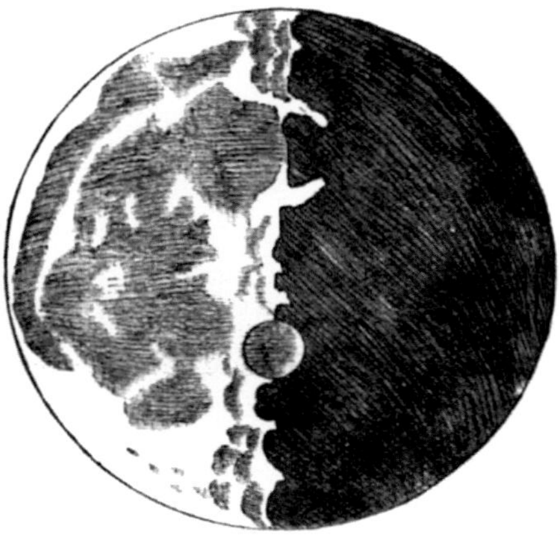

Galileo Sketch: last quarter

Modern photo

Galileo Sketch: first quarter

Modern photo

Saturn

Galileo was perhaps the first to observe something odd about Saturn, but, like the Jesuits and others, was puzzled about what he was observing.

Comets

Galileo's ideas on comets were completely wrong, and were closer to

Aristotle's than were those of the Jesuits he virulently attacked.[221] In his vitriolic and bile-ridden attacks, Tycho is an 'idiot' and the leading Jesuit scientist and architect Grassi a swindler as well as an idiot. Both had correctly, and contrary to Aristotle, put comets beyond the Moon. To Galileo comets were earthly exhalations.

Galileo and Copernicanism

As already mentioned, when the *Dialogue Concerning the Two Chief World Systems* came out in 1632:

- It ignored all Kepler's planetary laws, two of which had come out 24 years earlier.
- It ignored Copernicus' epicyclic system (Galileo probably could not plough through it anyway) and presented simple circles.
- It ignored the Tychonic system altogether.
- It berated Aristotelians for not doing experiments, but later Salviati admitted not doing them either because he 'knew what would happen' .
- It offered a bogus 'proof' from the tides (which seems to contradict his own circular preservation of velocity), and it explicitly derided Kepler's more correct ideas on the tides.

Galileo offered no plausible evidence that either his own Mickey-Mouse circular system, nor a Copernican one, nor even Kepler's (which he ignored) was better than the Tychonic system adopted, for example, by leading Jesuits.

Scientific Method

The work *The Assayer* is sometimes hailed as a breakthrough in methodology. This seems often to be based on two basic ideas:

1. *The process of elimination* by which he sarcastically arrives at the conclusion that eggs whirled in slings cook because the whirlers are Babylonians. This, of course, was an idea well worked out by Franciscans or their sympathisers like Roger Bacon and Grosseteste in the 14th century – it was not new. Ironically, he was wrong in both his rejection of significant friction in air, and his notions of comets.

---

[221] Amazingly, Galileo fan Santillana in *The Crime of Galileo* (1961)) presents Grazzi as reaching his highly empirical and correct ideas because the sly old Jesuit had ulterior religious motives!

2. *His advocacy of the language of mathematics in science.* This is, in a sense, a recommitment to Plato, Archimedes, and Ptolemy, against Aristotelian emphasis on qualities. Galileo then ignored the detailed mathematical and measurement work of Tycho on comets, and adopted an argument for uncertainty. This seems to be because in practice comets clearly did not go in anything like circular motion, and so did not fit his dynamics theory.

Philosophers argue over Galileo's scientific methodology. Was he a champion of empiricism and observation, or of the use of reason and thought experiment? It all depends on which quotation one uses. Koyre's picture of a Platonic rationalist seems as forced as Drake's of him as a mathematically-minded empiricist. Certainly he did believe that geometry should be central in science, but any idea of geometrical essences does not seem to be systematically worked out. Actually, even in his final *Discourse,* Galileo never portrays himself as attacking Aristotle's *approach* to science. Galileo does, as Losee indicates, sometimes use idealisations, and his fundamental approach seems to be that empirical observation tests/confirms mathematical explanations which are only loosely 'derived' from observation.[222] The tensions in his various divergent comments – never worked into a single explicit methodology but arising as he deals with specific topics – explain how so many observers have been able to read into him their own conception of science.

Hydrostatics – Dynamics

Galileo extended the Archimedean ideas of hydrostatics, but this does not concern us here. His work on dynamics, however, was important. Classically, Mach argued in the mid-19th century that Galileo virtually invented empirical dynamics, but Duhem's work in the early 20th century showed that much or even most of the approach was rooted in the 14th-century work in Paris and Oxford. Acceleration was described as 'difform motion'. At Oxford was developed the 'Mertonian Rule' or 'Mean-Speed Theorem' that in a given time uniformly accelerating objects travel the same distance as if travelling with uniform motion at the speed of the middle instant of travel. The 'odd-number rule' relating distances under uniform acceleration in equal time-intervals to the odd numbers beginning

---

222 See also McMullin in Butts & Pitt, *New Perspectives on Galileo* (1978), ch. 9.

from one, and the relationship of the distance travelled to the square of the time both follow from this. Bishop Nicole Oresme (1320–1382) in Paris, seems to have known of both. He also actually developed an idea of like-objects (e.g. Earth) attracting, which would counter the notion that objects would be flung into space by a rotating Earth! His work tended, however, to be theoretical.

What Galileo did was to roll balls about an inch diameter down increasingly steeply inclined planes of about six foot long, and so link his theory to an idealisation of free-fall. His work did set forth the ideas of motion clearly, and does have to be seen as a key work in the area. The *Discourse* is mostly in Italian, but includes Latin treatises introduced by Salviati – the 'dialogue' format often becomes nominal.

Galileo did not use algebra or formulas, and though his results are now often given in modern form, he gave them in ratios. Thus *implicit* in his work were:

$v = gt$ [v= velocity, t=time, g=gravitational constant]

$d = \frac{1}{2} gt^2$ [d=distance, t=time, g=gravitational constant]

Galileo, however, did not find the gravitational constant g, nor, of course, use calculus.

There was at some time doubt as to whether he could have in fact even checked (let alone *derived)* his implicit formula experimentally, though modern reruns seem to imply that he might have done so.

A controversy has existed over whether Galileo had a principle of inertia. Basically he concluded that:

- The only 'natural' motion is circular at uniform angular velocity.
- Any body will continue in a state of rest or uniform circular motion unless acted on by a force.

To Drake, Galileo has the 'essence' of the theory of inertia[223], to Koyre he does not. Shapere pertinently points out that the notion that there is an 'essence' of the theory is itself Aristotelian![224] Drake struggles to make Galileo consistent in his treatment of motions, and his success is doubtful. Whilst there is a superficial resemblance to the ideas of linear inertia later

---

223 A. Koyre *Etudes Galileenes* (1939), 246–7. Drake, *Galileo Studies* (1970), 247–251.

224 Dudley Shapere, *Galileo A Philosophical Study* (1974), 125.

developed in Descartes and Newton, a brief consideration shows that it gives rise to an altogether different kind of dynamics. Indefinite straight-line motion cannot be natural. In some ways it is actually more profoundly Aristotelian than some of the Impetus theorists.[225] Ronan is therefore misleading in suggesting that Galileo made the really radical break with Aristotle to show that 'motion does not require the constant application of a motive force'. Rotational motion, including that of the spheres, required no such force (apart from the prime mover) in Aristotle – Galileo just extended this 'natural' motion to free orbits. Nevertheless, the implicit laws in Galileo's work did stand as a base for Newton's much more profound analysis.

Questions

Here are some questions to ask as you think about Galileo:

- How far does Galileo (in any particular paragraph in his work) convince by a kind of mental 'sleight of hand' and how far are his arguments sound?
- Was any particular piece of work (i) Original? (ii) Significant? (iii) Unlikely to have been discovered quickly by someone else?
- Is his present reputation and fame related to his actual contribution, or to his double-edged knack of self-publicity?

References

The books on Galileo vary wildly.

Arthur Koestler's section in *The Sleepwalkers* (1959) achieves the near impossible by exaggerating the conceit and malice of Galileo.

Giorgio de Santillana *The Crime of Galileo* (1962) presents a slanted picture of the trial that vaguely resembles history.

Stillman Drake, in various works e.g. *Galileo Studies* (1970) attempts a whitewash that is convincing only if you are determined to be convinced – though also some useful translations. Drake has affected works like *Galileo Decisive Innovator* by Michael Sharratt (1994) and *Galileo First Physicist* by James MacLachlan (1997) – though neither follow Drake entirely. Pietro Redondi, *Galileo Heretic* (1987), takes a particular line on the reasons for opposition to Galileo, which has not found much support.

---

[225] See e.g. Shapere op. cit.

Annibale Fantoli, *Galileo Copernicanism and For the Church* (1994, 1996), is detailed and seems fairly even-handed.

For a good understanding of the religious issues Richard Blackwell, *Galileo, Bellarmine and the Bible* (1991), is good and contains some original material e.g. of Foscarini.

Maurice Finocchiaro (ed.), *The Galileo Affair: A Documentary History* (1989), contains a number of translations of original documents.

There are compendia like R. E. Butts and J. C. Pitt (eds.), *New Perspectives on Galileo* (1978) and Peter Machamer (ed.), *The Cambridge Companion to Galileo* (1998), which seem mostly to contain specialised papers.

Dava Sobel, *Galileo's Daughter* (1999), gives us his daughter's letters, though the accompanying commentary varies in accuracy.

Colin Ronan, *Galileo* (1974), has lots of lovely colour pictures, but is not always perceptive on the church figures involved.

Michael White's 2007 book *Galileo Antichrist: A Biography* gives some useful biographical description, though tends towards the apologist rather than the critic scale of the man. Simon Callow's review in the Guardian, by the way, says that Galileo was 'unquestionably the greatest scientist of his age', which only goes to show that the Guardian should get more expert people to write their reviews.

David Wootten's *Galileo, Watcher of the Skies* (2010) states that 'Galileo was the first modern scientist, arguable the first true scientist'. Evidently neither Tycho nor Kepler count as 'scientists', but Wootten seems to have a particular view of science. The book is informative and has a wealth of detail, though is thematic rather than strictly chronological. One of its main hypes, that Galileo was not a 'good' Catholic/Christian, turns out to be based on rather flimsy evidence – at least insofar as a 'good' Catholic was then defined.

A major biography of Galileo published in 2010 is *Galileo* by J. L. Heilbron. This is chronological and deals well with both the scientific ideas and the interplay of personalities.

There are a few other books on Galileo published over the last decade, but anything with a title as silly as 'Galileo: Father of Modern Science' seems hard to take seriously. It is not that I think science is illegitimate, but it certainly doesn't have a father – nor a mother in case you ask …

7. Jeremiah Horrocks[226]

Jeremiah Horrocks (1618-1641)

'Jeremiah Horrox possessed one of the most original minds of the seventeenth century. A follower of Tycho, Horrox combined a gift for instrumentation with a theoretical genius that later won the acclaim of Hevelius and Flamsteed. His contributions to the lunar theory were the first significant advances on the subject since antiquity, and earned the praise of Newton himself in the pages of Principia.'
Allan Chapman[227]

Gloriana, Elizabeth I, died in 1603, and James VI of Scotland became James I of England.[228] This first Stuart monarch incompatibly combined autocratic royalist views with a Protestantism that was instinctively Presbyterian. The peculiarly English brand of Protestantism had begun with Henry VIII, and settled under his daughter Elizabeth. As James travelled to England in 1603, he received a petition from about 1000 ministers, asking for a conference to decide on church reforms. They objected to the sign of the cross in baptism, wanted less liturgical music, no bowing at the name of Jesus, no profanation of the Lord's Day, reform of church courts and various other things. In January 1604 James himself chaired the resulting Hampton Court Conference. Most of the 'Puritan' demands were rejected, though James did agree to some liturgical changes, and also agreed to authorise a bible translation from which came the 'King James' version of the Bible in 1611.

---

226 'Horrocks' is an East Lancashire name. He Latinised his name to Horrox for his 'official' name e.g. on the Emmanuel College Register and his Latin manuscripts. No one knows what he looked like – the picture was painted much later (and has Venus in the wrong place!)

227 Allan Chapman, *Dividing the Circle* (1990), 26.

228 In view of this, by the way, some of us think that England should be holding a referendum as to whether to leave the United Kingdom, not Scotland!

Charles I tries to get his head around his problems with Parliament.

James died in 1625, and his son Charles I was crowned. The House of Commons was now dominated by 'Puritans' who advocated extempore prayer and preaching in Anglican churches, whilst the king favoured the 'High Church' party, which stressed the value of ritual and prayer book. Charles promoted William Laud to be Archbishop of Canterbury, and he encouraged the reintroduction into churches of stained glass windows, crosses, railed altars, bowing at the name of Jesus, and making the sign of the cross in baptism – all things Puritans hated! The king was also in conflict with Parliament over the conduct of various continental wars. From autumn 1641 the tensions between King and Parliament were rising, and the civil war started in September 1642. Royalist forces dominated in the North and the South West, but also in Oxford. The rise of the New Model Army in 1645 led to Royalist defeat in 1647, and eventually the execution of the still-intriguing king in 1649. The Commonwealth then ruled until the Restoration with Charles II in 1660.

In the England of the early 17th century there was little of the strong traditions of astronomy in continental centres like Cracow, Venice, Padua or Bologna. Francis Bacon (1561–1626) was writing to encourage the development of science and scientific communities – but this was a vision not a reality. Bacon's almost exact contemporary Thomas Harriot (1560–1621) was one of few who sprang to his mind in seeking to further his projects.[229] Harriot was interested in a whole range of scientific issues, including the making of lenses that he was using to make telescopes at the same time as Galileo. He was viewing the Moon through one on 26th July 1609, three weeks before Galileo showed his to the Venetian Senate, and he was one of the first to observe and study sunspots. He did this in great detail though apparently left no theory about them. Harriot received

[229] See John W. Shirley (Ed), *Thomas Harriot* (1974), 29.

patronage from various nobles (including Raleigh), but held no academic post. William Gilbert had published his influential work on magnetism in 1600, and (like Harriot, Digges, and the other small number in this set) favoured Copernicanism. None of these, however, were involved in Keplerian type mathematical astronomy. The universities generally neglected science and astronomy not so much from hostility (there is no evidence of any religious threat to Copernicanism for example) but indifference. It was not part of the curriculum, and if students were interested in the subject then it was as a hobby or pastime. This changed a little in 1619 when a Chair of astronomy was founded at Oxford (more traditionally a science centre than Cambridge), but there was still none at Cambridge.

In religion Cambridge was, of course, exclusively Anglican, and Oxford and Cambridge were the training centres for future ministers in the Church of England which itself (as noted above) was generally Puritan in sympathy – this continued throughout the civil war and even after the Restoration.[230]

Horrocks's Life

Details of Horrocks's brief life are scant and sometimes uncertain. He died on January 3rd 1641, and Dr John Wallis, who entered Emmanuel College with Horrocks and edited his *Opera Posthuma* in 1673, says that he was in his 23rd year. However, Horrocks matriculated at the University of Cambridge on 5 July 1632, and for this he had to be 14 according to the regulations. His birth was therefore between January and July 1618.[231]

His family home was at Toxteth Park, now a suburb of Liverpool but then a country hamlet of some two dozen houses with an area called 'Otterspool' (heigh ho!). It was once believed that his father was a farmer – William Horrocks – and such a man did indeed live in Toxteth[232], but the evidence points more to his father as James Horrocks, a watchmaker. The main evidence for this is a remark made by Horrocks's friend William Crabtree (1610–1644[233]) in a letter to William Gasgoigne (1612–1642) that

---

[230] Thus e.g. the great naturalist John Ray refused to assent to the conditions of the Restoration and was unable to hold a post at Cambridge – this leading to his comparative poverty.

[231] The DNB wrongly stated 1817, but see e.g. S. B. Gaythorpe, op.cit. on Horrocks' birth etc.

[232] Thus e.g. Robert Brickel, *A Chapter of Romance in Science* 1639–1874.

[233] A later date of death of 1652 seems improbable as a will is extant applied in 1644.

Jeremiah's father 'died May 3, 1641, grief for his son hastening his own death' . Flamsteed (the first Astronomer Royal) transcribed this letter in the 1670s, and the Bishop's transcript records the burial of a James Horrocks of Toxteth on May 4th in St Nicholas Church, at the Liverpool pierhead. Unfortunately the baptismal records at this church for 1618 (the probable year of Horrocks's birth+ christening) are missing. There is also a possibility that the family had come originally from the Deane district of Bolton, where some have suggested Jeremiah was born. A Jonas Horrocks was baptised in Bolton in 1622 – and Jeremiah refers to a brother Jonas of whom there is no other record.[234] Assertions of his birth in Toxteth were made in the 1832 Emmanuel College register itself, in 1859 by fellow Emmanuel student John Worthington (who later preserved his papers), and in 1773 by Emmanuel Fellow George William Bennet in a register of students in 1773 referring to Horrocks as a 'very curious astronomer'. Toxteth therefore seems the almost certain birthplace.

Lower Lodge Toxteth: possible birthplace

The actual *place* of his birth and childhood is a subject of some dispute. Toxteth Park was a former deer park, and had two lodges when it was de-parked in 1591. By the first years of the 17th century some twenty houses and a couple of mills had been built, causing a contemporary reference to Toxteth as a 'Hamlet without a chapel'.[235] One of the lodges, Lower Lodge, is the most likely place of Horrocks's birth and upbringing though the evidence is inconclusive[236]. The Lodge was demolished around 1862 to make way for a railway station now itself derelict, and the reputed brass plate commemorating Horrocks's birth disappeared.

[234] These and a lot of other details are in W. F. Bushell's 'The Keats of English Astronomy', *The Mathematical Gazette*, xliii, 343, 1–16.

[235] Lawrence Hall, *Toxteth Park Chapel in the 17th Century*, 7.

[236] Lawrence Hall, *The Birthplace of Jeremiah Horrocks in Toxteth Park.*

The Chester register of marriage licenses records the marriage on January 17th 1615 of Jeremiah's parents James Horrocks and Mary Aspinwall. His mum's brother (as various contemporary documents make clear) was Edward Aspinwall (1567–1632) a prominent watchmaker.[237] Edward had matriculated from Brasenose College Oxford in 1585. Though they did not own much in the immediate area, the Aspinwalls were a family of standing and property.

Jeremiah Horrocks is today comparatively unknown, but there was a flurry of interest in Victorian days, and various myths abounded. He was often viewed as both poor and sickly e.g. 'There can be no doubt that Jeremiah came of impecunious parents and that the whole of his brief life was a struggle against poverty'[238] Though he went up to university as a sizar or poor scholar, and obviously did not have great wealth, it seems unlikely that he suffered great pangs of poverty. Lower Lodge – described as 'snug' by Victorians – was a substantial dwelling for the early 17th century, and not a labourer's cottage!

Richard Mather

Richard Mather came to teach in the new school in Toxteth in 1611, apparently living with Edward Aspinwall. Mather went up to Brasenose, Oxford, but returned at their invitation to begin preaching at the chapel (which had now been added to the school) in November 1618. He quite probably also acted as schoolmaster until his marriage in 1624 – by 1625 we know a George Whaledale was schoolmaster.[239] Richard Mather had Congregationalist ideas (i.e. saw the church as a body of covenanting believers rather than the expression of

Toxteth Ancient Chapel today

[237] See S. B. Gaythorpe: 'Jeremiah Horrocks: Date of Birth, Parentage and Family Associations.' *Trans Hist Soc of Lancashire & Cheshire* 106 (1954) 23-33.

[238] W. H. Watts, 'Jeremiah Horrocks and the Transit of Venus of 1639" (1910)

[239] Lawrence Hall, *Toxteth Park Chapel in the 17th Century* gives these and other details.

state religion in a locality). He was, however, ordained into the Anglican Church, probably in 1619. At this time (as mentioned above) the 'Puritans' hoped that the state church itself would go in their direction. Mather, however, practised extempore prayer and steadfastly refused to wear a surplice, so was eventually suspended in 1633 for not keeping to the proper ceremonies. He left for America in 1635 to join other 'Pilgrim Fathers' (who had sailed in 1620). The Chapel itself was never officially 'consecrated' (although at one time it was recommended to be), and Congregationalists and Presbyterians continued to share it, comparatively unmolested, under a sympathetic refusal to suppress them by the Earl of Derby. The Ancient Chapel today has a brass plaque from 1856 transferred from a floor tomb to the wall, commemorating 'Edward Aspinwall' – though this is a different man of this name and Jeremiah's uncle clearly seems to have died in October 1632.

Chapel interior now; lower benches c.1650

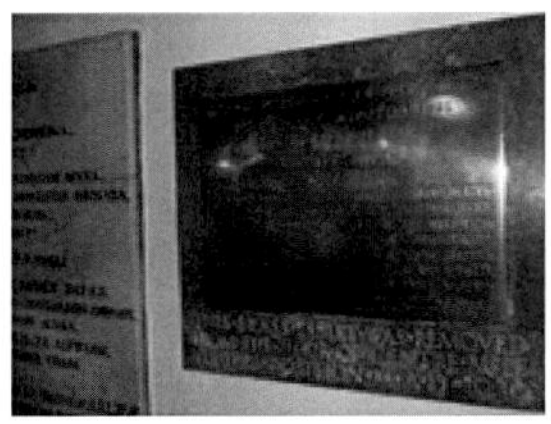

Brass Plaque 1856 Edward Aspinwall

Jeremiah, then, was born into an artisan family of some standing, probably comfortably if not well off. The picture of him struggling with poverty is implausible. Instrument making was in the young lad's family, and dexterity in making and dealing with instruments a feature of his upbringing. Tradition has it that his uncle Ted first interested the young Jerry in astronomy. He may have studied at Mather's school up to the age of seven years, and his family and friends' connections were all Puritan in sympathy. An early reference to his uncle Edward Aspinwall speaks of 'a learned and religious gentleman'[240] The title 'gentleman' may have been honorific – he was probably technically a 'yeoman'.

[240] Samuel Clark, *The Lives of Sundry Eminent Persons in this later Age* (1683) cited by Hall.

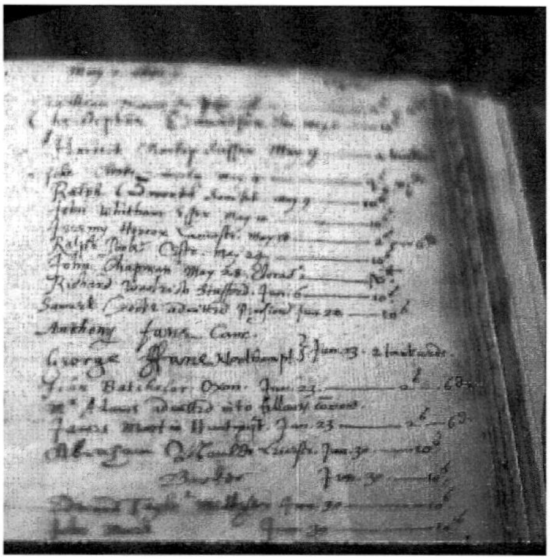

Emmanuel Register

Brought up in a hamlet with perhaps few children, and surrounded by studious relatives and schoolmasters, we may wonder less at the serious-mindedness of the young Jeremiah as he set out, aged only 14, for Cambridge university.

Jeremiah Horrocks (registered Horrox) entered Emmanuel College, Cambridge, as a Sizar on May 11th 1632. A Sizar or poor student might have to wait on tables or perform other chores, and probably survived on very low funds, but this route could offer a way to a degree and an appointment as a minister. Emmanuel College was founded by Sir Walter Mildmay in 1584 on the site of a Dominican priory – and would (after Horrocks's death) be graced with its present lovely Wren chapel. It was very much a Puritan college, and its first Master

Lawrence Chadderton was a distinguished Puritan biblical scholar and preacher. In the year Horrocks entered, there graduated one John Harvard whose family later went with the New England Settlers and eventually formed Harvard University. For Jeremiah to enter at age 13–14 was not noteworthy – his friend Worthington was 14 when he entered Emmanuel in the same year. Both, in fact, 'matriculated' together (i.e. were sworn before the Vice Chancellor into the university which was distinct from the college) on July 5th 1632.

1588 Portrait of Sir Walter Mildmay

John Harvard and Emmanuel Master Lawrence Chaderton (chapel window of 1884)

Study at Cambridge was, of course, very different then from today. The curriculum was mostly arts, divinity and classical languages (particularly Latin). A few scraps of geometry and even classical astronomy would be included in the arts course, but nothing thorough and certainly nothing of the latest scientific works of Tycho, Galileo or Kepler. Kepler had, of course, published his three laws in 1609 and 1619, and the telescopic discoveries of Jupiter's moons, phases of Venus, and sunspots were known. None of this was in the syllabus, but there was plenty of time spare and undergraduates could study such things if they wished. There were other European centres where astronomy was taught, but Horrocks had no means to study there. He resolved to teach himself, even though it was the difficult *mathematical* astronomy that interested him:

Emmanuel – an ancient doorway

Emmanuel 'Old Chapel' (now 'Old Library'), there in Horrocks time, is in puritan style

> There were many hindrances. The abstruse nature of the study, my inexperience, and want of means dispirited me. I was much pained not to have any one to whom I could look for guidance, or indeed for the sympathy of companionship in my endeavours, and I was assailed by the languor and weariness which are inseparable from any great undertaking. What then was to be

Emmanuel Pond – result of waterway there in Horrocks' day

done? I could not make the pursuit an easy one; and yet to complain of Philosophy [i.e. science] on account of its difficulties would be foolish and unworthy. I determined therefore that the tediousness of study should be overcome by industry – my poverty (failing a better method) by patience – and that, instead of a Master, I would use Astronomical books. Armed with these weapons I would contend successfully; and having heard of others acquiring knowledge without greater help, I would blush that anyone should be able to do more than I …[241]

What background was there in astronomy when Horrocks entered Emmanuel? Kepler had died in 1630, having predicted a transit of Venus and Mercury in 1631, and Venus not again until 1761. The 1631 Venus transit was visible in America but not in Europe and was not observed, but Pierre Gassendi observed the transit of Mercury. On this, Kepler was out by only 6 hours, and his Rudolphine Tables were generally the most accurate available. The Belgian astronomer Philip van Lansberge (1561–1632), however, was a follower of Copernicus and wanted to show that the ancient observations were accurate and could be incorporated into a Copernican model.[242] Lansberge's *Tabulae motuum coelestium perpetuae: ex omnium temporarum observationibus consentientes* (1632) was a polemic against the 'Tychonici' (Tycho, Longomontanus and Kepler), and an attempt to explain the difficulty of the precession of the equinoxes à la Copernicus. Lansberge's friend and co-worker Matinus Hortensius wrote a similarly anti-Tychonic account in *De Mercurio in Sole Visa* in 1632. Horrocks, beginning his serious study of astronomy (still, remember, only 14–15 years

[241] This was in a retrospective letter to his friend Crabtree.

[242] On all these points see Surtis Wilson in ch. 10 of R. Taton and C. Wilson (Eds), *Planetary astronomy from the Renaissance to the rise of astrophysics, Part A: Tycho Brahe to Newton* (1989).

old) acquired Lansberge's works[243] after noting the praise of them in a treatise by 'D. H. [Henry] Gellibrand, a Professor of Astronomy, in London'[244] and began to compile his own tables (Ephemerides) from the Flemish mathematician/ astronomer's work. Horrocks did acquire other works: in the Trinity College library in Cambridge there is his annotated copy of Philip Lansberge's *Tabulae Motuum,* in which he lists 24 astronomical authors he has read – of which, incidentally, only the medieval Sacrobosco was from his own country![245] Lansberge, however, must have seemed to be the 'latest and best', and his trenchant criticism of the 'Tychonists' including Kepler led Horrox to focus on Lansberge to the detriment of the latter. At some point (the chronology is uncertain) he testifies that, having realised the inaccuracies 'I broke off the useless computation, and resolved for the future with my own eyes to observe the positions of the stars in the heavens'.[246]

In 1635 Horrocks returned to Toxteth, aged about 17. He did not graduate, although this was not all that unusual. Sometimes the expense of graduating was delayed until it might be used to gain a curacy or some preferment. We do not know what he did back in Toxteth, but he must have spent much spare time on astronomy.

Amongst Horrocks's contemporaries at Emmanuel were not only Worthington (later Master of Jesus College) but also the mathematician John Wallis, and the Cambridge Platonist Ralph Cudworth (who influenced Newton[247] in his mechanical philosophy). Perhaps it was Worthington who, shortly before Horrocks left Cambridge, mentioned him to the young Salford cloth merchant William Crabtree who was to be

---

243 These were the *Uranometriam*, the *Tabulas Perpetuas* and the *Proggymnasmate de motu Solis.*

244 A. R. Whatton, Memoir (1859), 17.

245 Albategenius, Alfraganus, J. Capitolinus, Clavii Apolog. Cal. Rom., Clavii Comm. in Sacroboscum, Copernici Revolutioones, Cleomedes, Julius Firmicus, Gassendi Exere. Epist in Phil. Fluddanam., Gemmae Frisii Radius Astronomicus, Cornelii Gemmae Cosmocritice., Herodoti Historia., J. Kepleri Astron. Optica. – Epit. Astron. Copern. – Com. de motu Martis. – Tabulae Rudoplhinae, Lansbergii Progymn. de motu solis, Logomontani Astron. Danica., Magini Secunda Mobiliae, Mercatoris Chronologia., Plinii Hist. Naturalis., Ptolemaei Magnum Opus., Regiomontani Epitome, – Torquentum. – Observata., Rhenoldi Tab. Prutenicae – Com. in Theor. Purbachii, Theonis Comm. in Ptolom., Tyc. Brahaei Progymnasmata. – Epistl. Astron., Waltheri Observata.

246 Horrocks, *The Transit of Venus*, 110.

247 See e.g. Richard Westfall *Never At Rest* (1980), 304.

his main scientific correspondent from 1636–40. Crabtree had not been to university, but had learned Latin at school and had means to buy astronomical books so would not have been in a much different case from Horrocks. Crabtree mentions Brahe, Kepler, Galileo, Lansberge, Descartes and Gassendi – and by 1635 realised that Lansberge's planetary tables were inaccurate. This is parallel to Horrocks and also William Gascoigne who independently made the same discovery.[248] Crabtree wrote to Horrocks, probably at Worthington's suggestion, begging that he will excuse the liberty that he, a stranger, was thus taking, but hoping that his love for those astronomical pursuits in which Horrocks so greatly excelled would be deemed a sufficient apology. So there was formed in 1636 the circle of the Keplerri – a tiny group of those in England interested in Keplerian astronomy, but committed to astronomy as a mathematical and empirical science. Crabtree confirmed Horrocks's suspicions that Lansberge was unreliable, and his later references (e.g. in *The Transit of Venus*) to Lansberge are very critical – in contrast to his admiration of Kepler.

We have to get out of our minds the picture that Horrocks was an 'amateur' astronomer, for such categories applied anachronistically can only be misleading. Cambridge had no department and no professor, there were no official observatories in England, there was no obvious scientific society or group, and certainly nothing like a degree/career structure in astronomy. Lack of funds and lack of any rich patron were obvious problems, but that Horrocks had no recognised 'post' or qualification was almost inevitable.

Near the end of 1637 he commenced a treatise: *Jeremiae Horroccii Anti-Lansbergianus, sive disputationes in astronomiam P. Lansbergii, quibus perspicue demonstratur, hypotheses suas nec caelo nec sibi consentire,* later retitling and rewriting it as *Astronomiae Lansbergianae censura et cum Kepleriania comparatio.* One does not even need to be able to read Latin to get the gist – Lansberge NO! Kepler YES! Various other treatises were compiled in this time. Horrocks was writing not only on planets, but on the Moon on which his work was original and important. He published nothing, however, lacking both the means and probably a circle of potential buyers

---

248 See Allan Chapman, *Three North Country Astronomers* (1982) and *Dividing the Circle* (1990) ch. 1.

to do so. The *Keplerri* were a tiny group in England, and not personally in contact with continental scholars.

That he was compiling tracts in Latin, the common scholarly language of Europe, seems to indicate an intention at least to publish. These were not purely personal notes, but were intended to enter upon the world at some stage. What plan he may have had in mind we cannot now tell.

In this period Horrocks was working on his lunar theory – eventually showing that the Moon's orbit was elliptical. Horrocks also had an interest in comets, concluding that they 'move in an elliptical figure or near to it'. He commenced a series of observations on the tides, working on this for three months. He wrote to Crabtee about this, but no papers survive relating to his observations or theories.

On 1st June 1639 Horrocks wrote to Crabtree: 'Next week I remove to Hoole, a village about 5 miles from Preston'. Much Hoole was a small, damp country village, set between 'the Moss' to the east and north, the wetlands of the coast and down to Martin Mere on the west and south. We have no certainty about what he did in Hoole, but the strong tradition is that he was tutor to the children at Carr House. The latter was built in 1613 (as noted in an inscription on the stone porch lintel) by Thomas Stones of London Habersdasher and Andrewe Stones the Amsterdam merchant, for their brother John who was a farmer and landowner. Thomas also built (of similar, probably Dutch, bricks) a chapel of ease (St Michael's) in 1628 – a date carved on its wooden lintel. An octagonal font was given by John Stones in 1633, and when the chapel became a parish church in 1641 Stones was given its patronage. The curate there during this time was

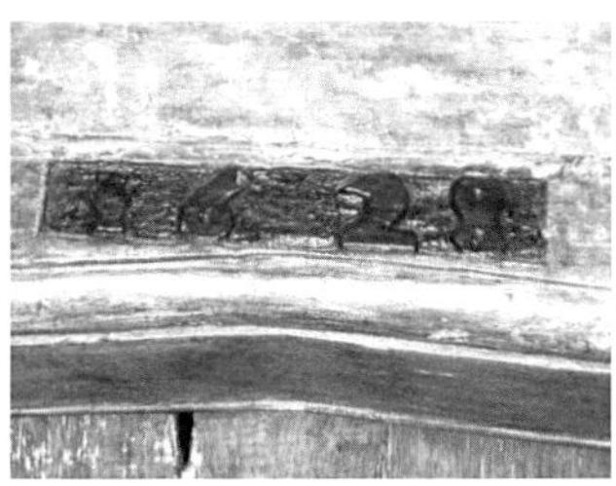

St Michael's lintel

probably[249] Robert Fogg, who was given the new living in 1641. The font and two 1631 pews are still in the church, but the pulpit, West tower, tower clock, and various memorial tablets, all date from later.

Was Horrocks a curate at Hoole? He is so named on the plaque now in St Michael's Hoole (erected in 1859 by the 19th century Hoole Rector Robert Brickel), and on the (1874) plaque in Westminster Abbey. In the Memoir attached by Rev A. B. Whatton to his 1859 translation of *Venus in Sole Visa*, he accepts that to become ordained 'young men are now required to be 23 years of age'. Whatton notes, however, a mention of Reverend Mr Horrox in a treatise by John Gadbury (which he does not date), also one by the early 18th century astronomer Costard, and by Hearne in the 1720s. He suggests that in the 1630s the Bishop could simply exercise discretion without any special dispensation, and ascribes the work to 'Reverend Jeremiah Horrox'. Is there other evidence? In his work *Venus in Sole Visa* Horrocks states

> I watched carefully on the 24th from sunrise to nine o' clock, and from a little before ten until noon, and at one in the afternoon, being called away in the intervals by business of the highest importance which, for these ornamental pursuits, I could not with propriety neglect.

---

249 Bushell op. cit. states that Fogg was mentioned as Curate in 1632 and 1639 but does not state his source, and Chapman (in 'Jeremiah Horrocks and the New Astronomy' Quarterly Journal of the Royal Astronomical Society (1990) 333–357 note 90) says he cannot find any such references.

What were these duties to which Horrocks refers? The Victorians thought they were duties of a curate. Actually, if the duties really were those of a curate their apparent brevity would be very surprising. Moreover, Horrocks was too young to be ordained as he was not yet 23.

More probably the duties were to do with being tutor at the house, or perhaps his 'business' as any serious Christian would be to attend the church. Most crucially, *none* of Horrocks's friends or contemporaries mentions any ordination or refer to him either as 'Revd Mr Horrox' or 'Revd Jeremiah Horrox'. Crabtree, for example, sadly wrote the memorandum: 'Letters of Mr Jeremiah Horrox to me of the years 1638, 1639, 1640, until his death on the morning of 3rd January …' No title of 'Revd' is given as it surely would have been. It seems virtually certain that Horrocks's supposed ordination/curacy was a myth. He was probably called upon to pray, catechise or say grace for the Stones family, and may even have been some kind of lay reader (or 'Bible Clerk' as Chapman puts it) though we cannot be certain.

Carr House, where Horrocks was probably a tutor, still stands, and now has a plaque up outside to mark the local view that Horrocks observed the transit of Venus on 24th November 1639 (put up by Chorley Civic

Society – an event in which the University of Central Lancashire was involved in the late '90s). Kepler had calculated a transit in 1631, but Horrocks realised that in fact the transit occurs twice with an eight year gap

Epidaurus Theatre

Parthenon Today © Guillaume Piolle

Ptolemy

Archiginnasio today

Frombork Cathedral © Schneider Ludwig

Torun Cathedral © Tilman Berger

Nicholas Copernicus

Map of Hven c.1663

Reconstructed Stenborg Observatory

Tycho Brahe

Tycho's Great Quadrant

Graz © Matthew Field

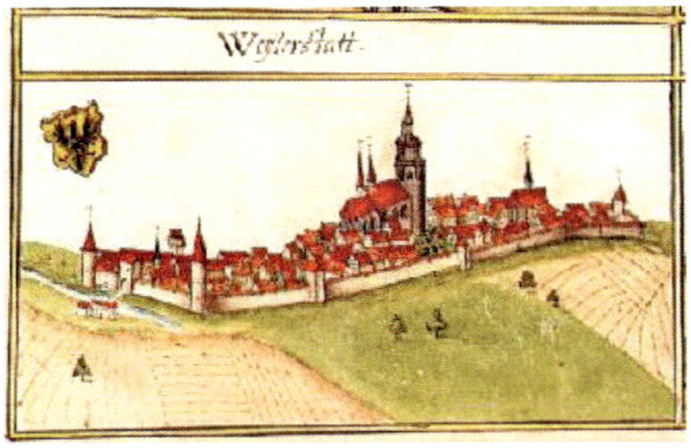

Weil der Stadt c.1682

Johannes Kepler

Prague Astronomical Clock

St Marks Square Clock © Waysider 1925

Doges Palace and Campanile

St Marks Square Venice and Campanile

Galileo Galilei

Replica of Galileo Telescope

Carr House

Much Hoole Church

Hoole Plate and Chalice

Hoole Plain Font

Toxteth Chapel

Woolsthorpe Manor House with Apple Tree

Newton's School

Colsterworth Parish Church

Trinity College with Apple Tree

Tower and Royal Mint

Principia

Isaac Newton 1689

Isaac Newton 1702

William Herschel

King's Street Workshop

King's
Street
House

Geroge Biddell Airy

John Couch Adams

(by permission of the Master and Fellows of St John's College, Cambridge)

William Whewell

Percival Lowell

(by permission of the Lowell Observatory)

William Huggins

– so would occur in 1639 but then not again until 1761/69 and then 1874/82 etc. Horrocks realised it was coming only weeks before the event – an amazing 'coincidence' unless you have a Puritan view of providence.

I and a group from the University of Central Lancashire were kindly allowed by its owners in 2004 to go to Carr House to observe the transit of Venus from the location, and probably the actual room, where Horrocks observed it. For us, as for him, the clouds cleared 'as if by divine interposition', and we had a clear view of the black dot of Venus against the Sun. There was another transit in 2012, not visible from Much Hoole, and the next one is in 2117 so I don't think I'll be there to see it!

Carr House is a listed building and retains a beauty that is not well conveyed in a black and white picture. The most probable room for his observation (assuming it was made here) is in the window on the first floor above the porch. This is, in fact, the only window from which the Sun would have been observable during the whole of the relevant day 24th November. Horrocks had also written to his younger brother and to Crabtree in Manchester advising them to observe on this day. Crabtree did so and Horrocks says that: 'Rapt in contemplation he stood for some time, scarcely trusting his own senses, through excess of joy'. Crabtree, however, was not able to make any actual measurements – it was cloudy in Manchester as so often! No one else in Europe seems to have known about the event and observed it.

Details of the observation will be given under his works below. At this point it is useful just to say that he observed on the day before he had calculated the transit would come, and seen nothing. He then says:

> I watched carefully on the 24th from sunrise to nine o'clock, and from a little before ten until noon, and at one in the afternoon, being called away in the intervals by business of the highest importance which, for these ornamental pursuits, I could not with propriety neglect. But during all this time I saw nothing in the Sun except a small and common spot … This evidently had nothing to do with Venus. About fifteen minutes past three in the afternoon, when I was again at liberty to continue my labours, the clouds, as if by divine interposition, were entirely dispersed, and I was once more invited to the grateful task of repeating my observations. I then beheld a most agreeable

> spectacle, the object of my sanguine wishes, a spot of unusual magnitude and of a perfectly circular shape, which had already fully centred upon the Sun's disc on the left, so that the limbs of the Sun and Venus precisely coincided, forming an angle of contact. Not doubting that this was really the shadow of the planet, I immediately applied myself sedulously to observe it.[250]

View from Carr house window

Horrocks had about thirty-five minutes to observe the transit before apparent sunset at 3.50 pm, making three careful measurements at 3.15, 3.35 and 3.45. Hoole residents may not be altogether flattered by Horrocks's comment at this point that the observation was made in 'an obscure village … about fifteen miles to the north of Liverpool'. Liverpool itself, of course, in those days, was not a centre of industry, but a place (as Whatton remarks) of 'comparative insignificance'.

Horrocks's letters from Hoole cover 8th June 1639 to 12th April 1640 after which he returned (by summer 1640) to his family in Toxteth. We do not know what his employment was, but he continued to write to his friend Crabtree concerning astronomical matters. He died very suddenly on 3rd January 1641, we do not know what from. Crabtree lamented this sudden loss, on the very day before Horrocks had planned a trip to see him. Horrocks is believed to have been buried in an unmarked grave in (possibly actually inside the building) the old Toxteth chapel, which is pictured. Both Crabtree and Gascoigne died shortly afterwards in 1644 – we do not know how Crabtree died but Gascoigne died in the Royalist cause, probably at Marston Moor.

Horrocks's Christian Beliefs

Allan Chapman says:

> … as an English Protestant, Jeremiah Horrocks would have found far fewer restrictions to scientific research than a continental Catholic would have felt after 1633. Quite simply, the Church of

[250] Jeremiah Horrocks, *On the Transit of Venus* (Trans. Whatton, 1859), 124.

> England had no policies on science whatsoever, and during the 1630s, the English bishops were more concerned with the theology of the Divine Right of Kings than they were with the shape of the orbit of the Moon.[251]

The extent to which Catholics were, in practice, restricted even after 1633 is debateable – the Cartesian followers of the devout Catholic Descartes managed to hold Copernican views. What is true is that, whilst the devout Lutheran Kepler was free to be a Copernican but felt the need to speak about reconciling it with Scripture, the devout Anglican Horrocks seems not even aware that there might be any Biblical problem with his heliocentricity.

What was Horrocks's personal religion? Chapman rightly says:

> What shines through Jeremiah's writings is a sense of awe and praise for the Deity who could make a universe that was so intricate and so beautiful. One also perceives his sense of privilege at being the first human creature to learn of certain things - such as the shape of the Moon's orbit – or to see the transit of Venus.

Horrocks's motivating force is shown in his prayer as he started the arduous task of correcting Kepler's tables:

> And may he, who is the great and good God of Astronomy and the Conservator of all useful Arts, bless my unworthy efforts for his mercy's sake, and cause them to redound to the eternal glory of His name and the advantage of mankind.

In his context this was neither unctuous nor empty. But where was he likely to have stood in the spectrum of Anglicanism of his day? Allan Chapman claims:

> We can suggest, however, that if Jeremiah was in any way employed by the Stones family during his stay in Much Hoole, he was not a Puritan. For the Stones family had presented a font to the parish church of St. Michael, along with a communion chalice and platen. These were sacramental vessels, and as such,

[251] Allan Chapman, *Jeremiah Horrocks and Much Hoole* (1994), 10.

strongly disapproved of by many Puritans, who regarded these sacraments as 'Popish'. The Stones family also endowed Much Hoole as a new parish in the Anglican Communion in 1641, with Robert Fogg as the first rector. It is unlikely that a family that displayed such marks of loyalty to the sacramental offices of the Anglican Church would have employed a theological radical.

St Michael's Font

St Michaels cup and plate

This seems a dubious argument. Puritans were Calvinist/Reformed in theology, and not part of the Radical Reformation or Anabaptist movement that practised only believers' baptism by immersion. Puritans wanted to use extempore rather than liturgical prayers and objected to Archbishop Laud's reintroduction of crosses, crucifixes and surplices, so had the family dedicated some crucifixes and fancy surplices then Chapman's argument might have been valid. A controversy did arise, particularly in the 1640s, as to whether an infant should be dipped (using a font) or sprinkled (which could be done from a basin). Many 'Presbyterians' in the church favoured sprinkling and the Westminster Confession of 1646 finally favoured sprinkling, yet in the 1643 Westminster Assembly of Divines actually 25 voted for sprinkling, and 24 for immersion. The suggestion that anyone tolerant of 'Puritan' sympathies (itself a somewhat fluid term) would be against having a plain church font seems exaggerated. Cranmer had retained the two sacraments of baptism and the communion, and presumably some kind of vessels had to be used to administer them by

any Anglican minister. Horrocks was, after all, not even a clergyman, and moderate Puritan sympathies in an upright young Christian man of about 20 years of age do not seem incompatible with working for a family who gave the basic equipment to an Anglican church for the two Prayer Book sacraments to be lawfully administered.

Horrocks's family associated with the Puritan Richard Mather, and Horrocks went to the Puritan college Emmanuel, but this would not necessarily indicate his own views. Horrocks, however, makes the following comment in the chapter on Kepler – whom he calls 'the most learned astronomer who ever lived':

> Kepler's astronomy differs from mine as his religion: he gives the planets a divers nature (good and bad) that they may either come to the Sun, or fly away at their pleasure, or at least (as his second thoughts are) so dispose themselves (in spite of the Sun's magnetical power) that the Sun is bound to attract or repel them according to that position, which themselves defend against all the Sun's labouring to incline their fibres. I, on the contrary, make the planet naturally to be averse from the Sun and desirous to rest in his own place, caused by a material dullness naturally opposite to motion and averse to the Sun without either power or the will to move to the Sun of itself. But then, the Sun by its own rays attracts and by its circumferential revolution carries about the unwilling planet, conquering that natural self-rest that is in it; yet not so far, but that the planet doth much abate and weaken this force of the Sun, as is largely disputed afore … So just do the papists, whose free will to do good or bad, can by its own strength go to God or fly from Him, or at least frame their own actions, as that God is bound to save them or damn them, *volens, nolens*. But I will confess myself not equally composed of good and bad, that myself may give either to flesh or spirit the upper hand; but rather wholly desirous to rest in myself, and

> wholly averse from God, and therefore justly deserve (as the fixed stars from the Sun) to be blown away from God in infinitum; but that God, by his Son's taking on Him man's nature and the undeserved inspiration of His spirit, doth quicken this dullness, nay, deadness, of my nature, yet still, ah me! How doth it choke and weaken their operation.[252]

Kepler, indeed, thought that the orbits were affected by the planets' own magnetic forces – Horrocks's slightly different theory places all the determinative action in the Sun itself. But, on the theology, we know that Kepler – otherwise a fairly orthodox Phillipist Lutheran – rejected the Reformed view of predestination and advocated freewill. A major point of disagreement between Puritans and their arch-enemy Archbishop Laud, was exactly over the freewill issue. Horrocks here, then, is advocating classic Reformed Puritanism – he believes that every part of the conversion/salvation process in individuals is divinely controlled and ordained. Horrocks was, basically, a Puritan – this much was not part of any later Victorian myth. How *extreme* he may have been in this view is not apparent from his comments. The Stones family, however, can hardly have been surprised that a man who came from Emmanuel College held such views – and there is no reason to suppose that they would have objected to them. The font presented by John Stones in 1632 is a perfectly plain and serviceable one, with neither ornate decoration nor even a cross on it. The chalice is actually dated 1629, and was presented by Margaret Walker. The platen was inscribed as 'The gift of Katherin Stones ye wife of Andrew Stones' and on the bottom is inscribed 'The Chappell of Hoole in the Parrish of Crostom Lancashire'. Both are very plain, serviceable, silver coloured utensils. None of these indicate high-church commitment, let alone favour towards Laud.

Having, however, made some criticism of Chapman (to whose work this present account is so much indebted) it seems appropriate to quote appreciatively his further comment in the same work on the more general science-religion issues of Horrocks's times:

[252] This (from *Philosophicall exercises* Part 1 para 26) is quoted in Brickell, op. cit., who rightly concluded that Horrocks was a Puritan.

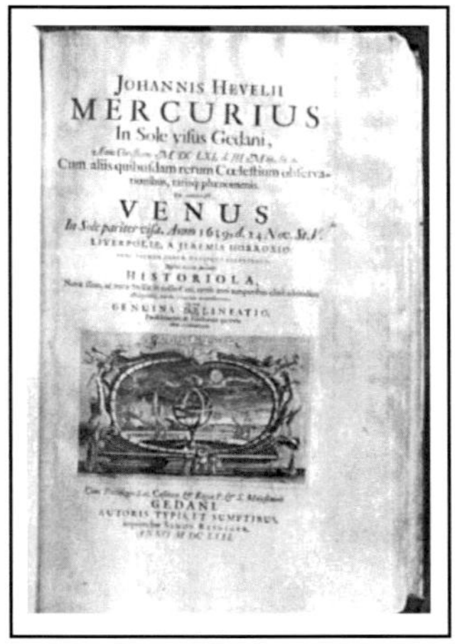
JOHANNIS HEVELII
MERCURIUS
In Sole visus Gedani,
VENUS
HISTORIOLA,
GEDANI

Horrocks's attitude towards science – as the great revealer of God's design to the human intellect – was shared by the following generations of English scientists who came to form the Royal Society in 1660, and published his surviving letters and treatises in 1672. John Wallis, who edited Horrocks's *Opera Posthuma*, was a clerical mathematician who refused a Deanery to remain a professor. The Royal Society's effective founder, the Oxford astronomer John Wilkins, became Bishop of Chester in 1668, and would have come thereby to have spiritual supervision over Much Hoole which was then in the diocese of Chester. Seth Ward moved from an astronomical professorship at Oxford to the Bishopric of Sarum at Salisbury, while the man who wrote the first history of the Royal Society and its work in 1667, Thomas Sprat, became Bishop of Rochester. The 'father of English Chemistry', the Hon. Robert Boyle, was invited by King Charles II to take Holy Orders so that he could receive preferment in the Restoration Church, but refused, arguing that he felt more able to promote the Christian faith if he were not obliged to do so by law. These men represented the intellectual cream of Horrocks's generation, and show how powerfully they unified the investigations of science not only with their Christian faith, but also with the holding of ecclesiastical office. Had Jeremiah lived into his fifties rather than dying at 22, he could well have been one of their number.

Horrocks's Work and Reputation

After the death of the three friends, some of the relevant Horrocks's papers disappeared with his brother Jonas. Some passed into the hands of Lancashire historian Christopher Townley where they were consulted appreciatively by Jeremy Shakerley, who wrote three books on astronomy in the mid 17th century.[253] Some of the Horrocks's papers passed into the care of John Worthington who had been at Emmanuel with Horrocks.[254]

Johannes Hevelius (1611–07)

Huygens saw a copy of *Venus in Sole Visa* and the work was published (still, of course, in Latin) in 1661 by his friend the self-financed Danzig astronomer Johannes Hevelius (1611–1697). He added his own explanations to the work (though in fact Flamsteed thought that these were of dubious value), and appended it to his own parallel work on Mercury.

In the year 1666 the Royal Society became interested in the Horrocks's papers, commissioning Dr John Wallis (who entered Emmanuel with Horrocks) to collect and edit what he could. After many difficulties (some papers lost in the great fire and the Royal Society generally cash strapped!) he published in 1672 *Jeremaie Horrocci Liverpoliensis Angli ex Palinate Lancastiae Opera Posthuma* – letters and papers of Horrox in Latin.

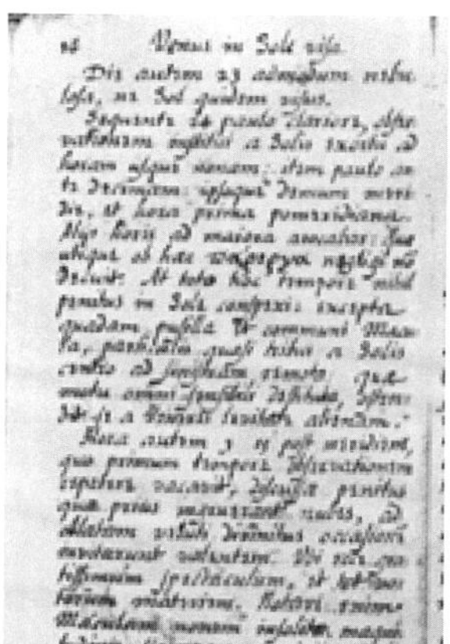

Venus in Sole visa

Venus in Sole Visa
Mansc. RGO1.68C

Chapman also suggests:

Sir John Moor, the motivating force behind the founding of the Royal Observatory, may have known Horrocks as a young man in Lancashire, and was certainly a friend of Christopher Townley, who preserved the Horrocks's papers after Crabtree's death in 1644 … Flamsteed, whose appointment as Astronomer Royal in 1675 owed much to Moor, had seen and transcribed some of Horrocks's correspondence at Towneley

---

253 Allan Chapman, 'Jeremiah Horrocks, the transit of Venus …' Journal of the Royal Astronomical Society (1990), 31 333–357.

254 See e.g. Allan Chapman, *Three North Country Astronomers* (1982) and *Jeremiah Horrocks* (1994).

> Hall in the 1670s.[255]

Horrocks's work may well have highlighted the paucity of observation facilities in England compared with those for example in Italy or Germany. Flamsteed, although Astronomer Royal at the new Royal Observatory, was receiving insufficient funds from the government (so what else hasn't changed!), and having to supplement his funds with a church living. Perhaps this helped him sympathise with Horrocks with his financial limitations! Certainly he valued highly Horrocks's work. Newton's first edition of the Principia (1687) said:

> I am not quite certain about the diameter of the Earth as seen from the Sun. I have assumed it to be 40 inch, because the observations of Kepler, Riccioli and Vandelini do not allow of its being much greater. The observations of Horrox and Flamsteed make it somewhat less.

Newton continued to write of the ideas of Flamsteed-Horrox. In fact, Flamsteed took what Westfall describes as a 'fatherly pride' in Horrocks's lunar theory, writing (perhaps not with great tact) to Newton on third November 1694:

> when you have determined what corrections or additions are to be made to that theory which it was my Good fortune to meet with & usher into ye light, I doubt not but you will import them to me as freely as I did the observations whereby you limit or confirme them to you.[256]

The second (1713) edition of the *Principia* left all this out. Newton, however, continued to value Horrocks, noting in this edition that Horrocks was the first to show the Moon as moving in an ellipse with the Earth at one focus. In his separate work *The System of the World* he describes Horrocks's lunar system as 'the hypothesis of Horrox which is the most ingenious, and, if I do not deceive myself, the most accurate of all'

Horrocks was a natural link between Kepler and Newton, but we should not overestimate his influence. Exaggerated 19th century claims (e.g. in

---

[255] Chapman, 'Jeremiah Horrocks, the transit of Venus …', note 2.

[256] Richard Westfall, *Never At Rest* (1980), 542. Westfall has little sympathy with Flamsteed.

Whatton's and Brinkley's *Memoirs* in 1859) that Newton derived his idea of gravity and/or inertia from him are mistaken. Horrocks speaks still of 'impetus', and Kepler's ideas on gravity are probably closer to Newton's.

Horrocks's Memorials

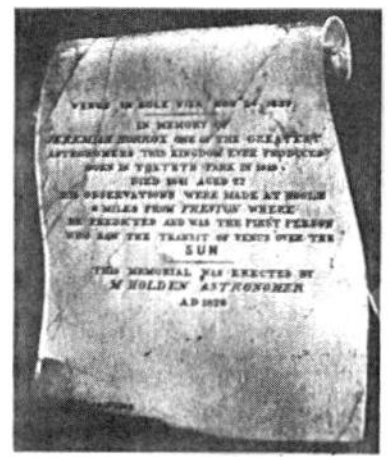

From the point of view of the history of science it is interesting to follow the waxing and waning of interest in Horrocks – especially in his home country. In the nineteenth century there was a surge of interest in and memorials to Horrocks in England.

St Michael's Church Toxteth Park

A new Parish Church of St Michael (with iron pillars) was built in Toxteth near to the ancient chapel (now Unitarian), and in 1826 a white marble scroll on a black slab commemorating 'Jeremiah Horrox' as 'one of the greatest astronomers this Kingdom has produced' was mounted prominently at the front of the church.

Whatton's Memoir

In 1859 Whatton's translation of 'Venus in Transit' was published – this was the first English version. With it was published Whatton's Memoir, showing Horrocks as poor and also as almost certainly ordained – in spite of acknowledging that he was officially too young.

St Michael's Hoole; Horrocks's Memorials

The church has a memorial plaque on the inside wall of its 'Horrocks's Chapel', erected by the Rector, Rev Robert Brickel, in 1859 – apparently officially ordaining Horrocks!

Prominent at the front of the church is a stained-glass picture of Horrocks, in a lovely window with the crucifixion above Horrocks, above which is the Sun. The actual picture is pure Victorian imagination as it shows the Sun projected on a sheet, whereas Horrocks actually used a piece of paper with degrees drawn on it. We do not know what he really looked like.

There are also two very attractive 'roundel'-type commemoration windows. The 1874 window shows a book and telescope, and a new window was installed in 2004 designed using the ideas suggested by local Hoole school children.

THE WORD OF OUR GOD SHALL STAND FOREVER

1639 RELIGION AND SCIENCE IN FELLOWSHIP 1874

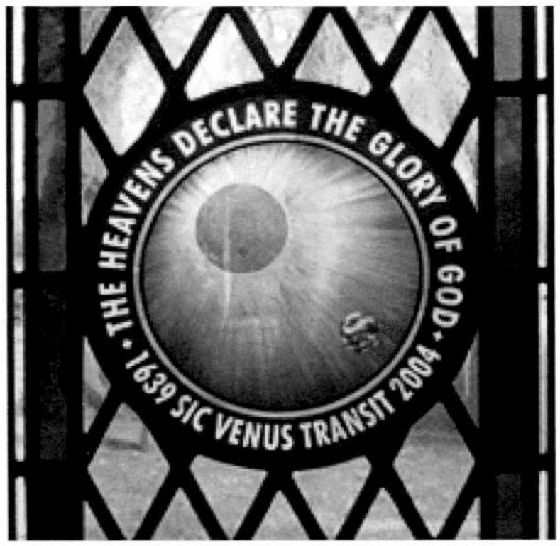

THE HEAVENS DECLARE THE GLORY OF GOD. 1639 SIC VENUS TRANSIT 2004

Westminster Abbey

In 1874, after much lobbying, a memorial was mounted in Westminster Abbey opposite that to Newton. It reads:

In memory of Jeremiah Horrocks Curate of Hoole in Lancashire who died on the third of January 1641 in or near his 22nd year. Having in so short a life detected the long inequality in the mean motion of Jupiter and Saturn,

> discovered the orbit of the Moon to be an ellipse, determined the motion of the lunar apse and suggested the physical cause of its revolution and predicted from his own observations the transit of Venus which was seen by himself and his friend William Crabtree on Sunday the 24th of November (O.S.) 1639.[257]

This tablet facing the monument of Newton was raised after the lapse of more than two centuries on the 9th December 1874.

The Eyre Painting

Presently on loan from the Walker Gallery and hanging in the Liverpool Museum Planetarium is a famous painting by Eyre Crowe BA. The painter said that he modelled the room on that in Carr House, which he claimed in 1891 to have visited, though the Puritan outfit seems unlikely and elaborate equatorial telescopic apparatus unhistorical. The painting is now very dark, and is unclear without computer enhancement.

The Ancient Chapel Memorial – Toxteth

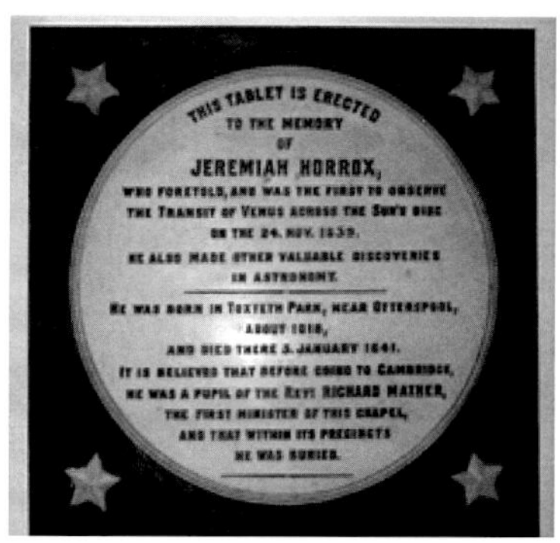

In 1891 a tablet was put up in the (now Unitarian) Ancient Chapel of Toxteth (pictured page 64). Horrocks is still Horrox, but has been defrocked again. The tablet finishes: 'It is believed that before going to Cambridge he was a pupil of REV[D] RICHARD MATHER the first minister of this chapel, and that within its precincts he was buried'.

---

[257] O.S. = 'Old Style' i.e. before ten days were added to adjust the calendar in England.

Nineteenth century and early 20th century English academics tended to make much of Horrocks. This seems, however, to have faded during the twentieth century. Kitty Ferguson, in her popular book on *Measuring the Universe* (1999) mentions Harriot and Gascoigne but leaves out the Englishman who first measured accurately our nearest planetary neighbour, and pushed up the key measurement of solar distance to nearly 60 million miles. Michael Hoskin, sometime Head of Department of History and Philosophy of Science in Horrocks's *Alma Mater,* leaves him out of his compendious *Cambridge Illustrated History of Astronomy* (1997). However, Allan Chapman, who is from the 'Other Place' (Oxford), argues that what Horrocks (and his friends Gascoigne and Crabtree) did was original and innovative.[258] He notes that Newton 'sang the praises' of Horrocks in *Principia* (1687), whilst John Herschel called him 'the pride and boast of British astronomy'. To Chapman what is crucial is the innovative use of the telescope in measurement, together with a high level of mathematics.

Horrocks's Work

Some Technical Background

Some comment has already been given on technical background, but we need here to expand this (which may involve some slight repetition). To determine the distance and amount of solar parallax Ptolemy[259] had worked as follows:

a. The Earth's radius was known.

b. The Moon's distance was found by parallax (i.e. observing at different points on the Earth's surface against fixed stars assumed very distant) and at apogee (i.e. furthest away) is 64.17 Earth radii (= 209 thousand miles).

c. The Moon's apparent diameter is equal to the Sun's in total eclipse at apogee distance – with figures 31 20″ (the modern lunar figures are 29′ 22″ at apogee and 33′ 31″ at perigee giving mean 31′ 5″, the mean for the Sun is 32′).

---

258 In particular in D.W. Kurtz, *Transits of Venus: New Views of the Solar System and Galaxy* (2005).

259 See Albert Van Helden, 'The telescope and cosmic dimensions' in R. Taton and C. Wilson (eds.), *Planetary astronomy from the Renaissance to the rise of astrophysics Part A: Tycho Brahe to Newton.*

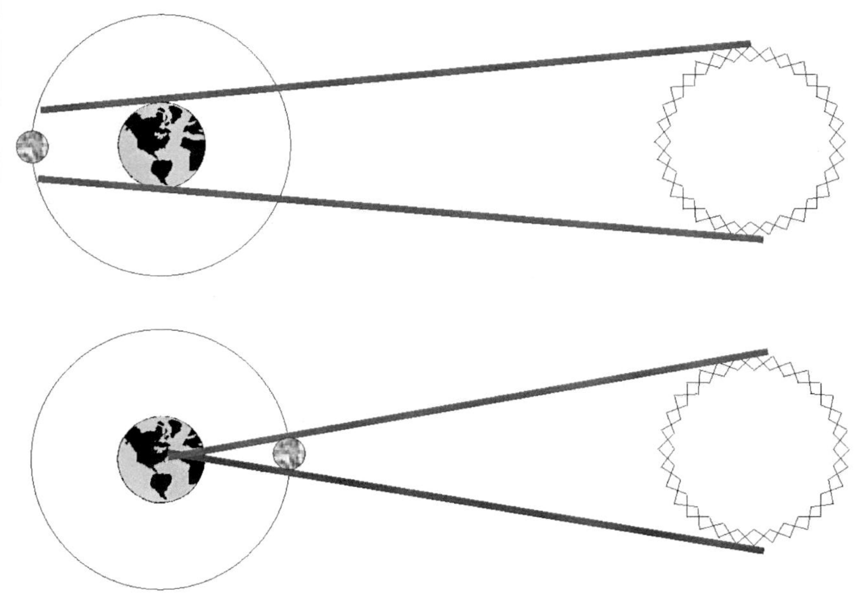

Illustrations of Ptolemy's reasoning (not to scale!!)

d. The width of the Earth's shadow cone as the Moon passes through it is a little less than 2.6 times the Moon's width.

This produced a solar distance of 1210 Earth radii (about 3.9 million miles). Ptolemy also estimated that Venus was about one tenth of the Sun's angular diameter. The Arab/mediaeval distances differed little, and Copernicus (as we have seen) adopted similar dimensions. Galileo insisted in his *Dialogue* that these apparent diameters and distances were wrong, but did not say what they should be.

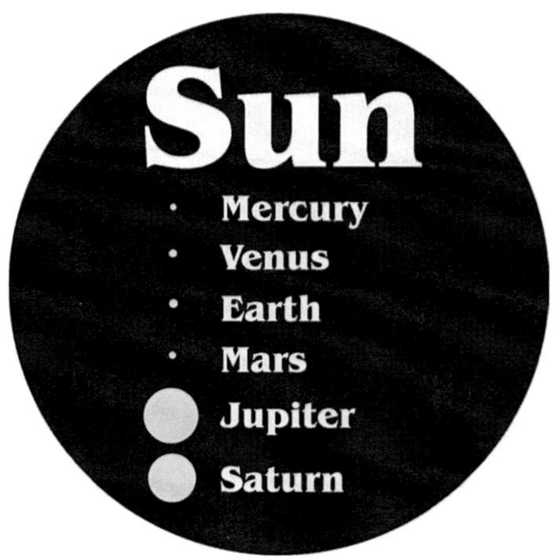

Modern view of sizes

Kepler gradually lost faith in the traditional Ptolemaic method for estimating the parallaxes and distances. He had, however, no obvious alternative, and resorted to considerations of harmony. By the introduction to his *Ephemerides* in 1617[260] he arrived at a solar parallax of 2′ and a distance of about 1800 e.r. i.e. 7.1 million miles. By 1618 Kepler had fairly accurate relative distances of orbits for the planets – relating, of course, to his planetary laws and in particular the third law discovered that year. Actual distances, however, were elusive. By now the only method for measuring parallax/distance he thought useful was consideration of the time between lunar dichotomy (when the Moon appears as exactly a half) and quadrature (when it forms an angle of 90° in relation to the Sun). Kepler hoped that the telescope would now enable these times to be measured more precisely – though he was disappointed when he tried it. Kepler's system is a mixture of the empirical and ideas of the harmony (in mathematical terms) which must exist.[261] It is important to remember (and this was explored in the notes on Kepler), that one cannot separate Kepler's mathematical astronomy from his supposed 'number mysticism'. Kepler began from a belief that the world was made by a rational God, committed to mathematical harmony, and that therefore would finally be decipherable in terms of beautiful mathematics. His third law was no more inherently rational or less 'mystical' than his theory of orbits based on the five perfect solids. Horrocks's approach was virtually identical in all respects. Details were changed, and the same approach led to slightly different conclusions, but he too was looking for mathematical harmony. In some ways, as was argued in the Kepler notes, mathematical astrophysicists may be looking for analogous 'beautiful' mathematically based systems today – with or without reference to any God.

In any event, by 1618 Kepler had concluded that solar parallax was nearer 1′ than 2′, and this gave a solar distance of 3469 Earth radii which (using a mean Earth radius of 3960 miles) gives about 13.7 million miles (the modern figure is, of course 93.0 million). The lunar distance Kepler found to be 59 Earth radii giving 198 thousand miles (the modern figure for the mean lunar distance is 240 thousand miles). Kepler held that the volumes of the planets were proportional to their mean distances from the Sun, their densities proportional to the inverse root of their mean distances, and the solar 'push' (anima motrix) to make them orbit was therefore equal. If

---

260 See Albert Van Helden, *Measuring the Universe* (1985), ch. 8.

261 His *Harmonice Mundi* came out in 1619.

planetary densities were equal then this would lead to their orbital periods being proportional to their distances. Kepler's third law gave a different result, and so he deduced that this was because of their varying densities.

Transits of Mercury are more common than of Venus – about a dozen occur each century. Kepler had greatly overestimated the apparent planetary diameters, with Venus expected as about a quarter of the Sun and Mercury similarly scaled – he therefore thought that a *camera obscura* would reveal the transit. In the event only three astronomers (Remus, Cysat and Gassendi) observed this November 1631 Mercury transit, all by projecting with a telescope. Pierre Gassendi (or, as Horrocks calls him, 'illustrious Gassendi' ![262]) made the best observations, and was astonished at how small the planet was. He made the apparent diameter only 20″ instead of the 15′ he had expected. Gassendi, in fact, observing through intermittent clouds, almost missed it altogether until he realised that the motion of this tiny dot across the solar disc meant that it could only be Mercury. Remus made it 18″, which fitted well his own schema that supposed that apparent diameters when seen from the Sun were the same.

Philip van Lansberge, who as noted, was Copernican rather than Keplerian, reverted to the Hipparchic-Ptolemaic approach on measuring distances, and was critical of Kepler's results. His colleague and follower Hortensius, however, defended Gassendi's view of the smallness of Mercury against various critics who claimed that it was some kind of optical illusion.

When Horrocks entered Emmanuel, then, in 1632, there were exciting new theories and observations, but also many open questions. Kepler had been dead less than two years, Galileo's *Dialogue* was about to create a stir in Italy (although about 24 years out of date since it ignored even Kepler's first two laws let alone the third), and the amazing telescopic discoveries of the previous two decades had been crowned by Gassendi's bombshell that Mercury was *tiny*. We need to note that in terms of planetary prediction (and therefore predictions of transits) very small errors could make a big difference. It was, in fact, wrong assumption about solar parallax and refraction that had led to Kepler (and his assistant Jacob Bartsch) missing

---

262 Actually he says: 'though to illustrious Gassendi, above all others, hail! thou who first didst depict Hermes changeful orb in hidden congress with the Sun ... etc.' (*Venus in Transit*) Poetic stuff – modern astronomy journals cannot match it!

the fact that a second Venus transit would occur in 1639. Astronomers were struggling to find new ways to improve accuracy.

Horrocks's Work on the Moon

Lunar theory is, of course, inherently complex, for the Moon reacts not merely to the Earth's gravity but also to that of the Sun, and the Earth-Moon system itself reacts complexly in orbiting the Sun. This should be borne in mind.

In his early letters to Crabtree in Autumn 1636, Horrocks (still only 18 years old) indicated that he had found Lansberge's lunar theory faulty, and inaccurate in predicting the durations of lunar eclipses (which were, of course relevant to Lansberge's method for solar parallax as above).[263] On 14th January 1637 Horrocks informed Crabtree that he now had his own lunar theory. Only in May that year did he get a copy of Kepler's *Rudolphine Tables.* He wrote:

> I judge it to be a most perfect work … Embracing his hypothesis as true, I have undertaken to correct his tables.[264]

Horrocks had concluded by 1838 that the Moon went around the Earth in an ellipse, the first application of this idea outside of planetary movement.[265]Wilson explains[266] how Horrocks tried various ways of adapting Kepler's lunar theory. He suggests that Horrocks was using the duration of lunar eclipses to measure eccentricity:

> From the apparent angular, semi-diameter of the Sun, and the horizontal parallax of the Earth, he can calculate a value for the semi-angle of the cone of the Earth's shadow; the calculation is relatively insensitive to the value of the horizontal parallax, and since Horrocks has reduced this to a lower and thus more correct value than any of his predecessors, namely 25″, his value for the semi-angle of the cone is almost exactly right.

---

263 Curtis Wilson 'On the Origins of Horrocks's Lunar Theory' *Journal of the History of Astronomy,* xviii (1987), 77–94, which also noted Horrocks' notes in his copy of Lansberge's tables which is in Trinity College Library.

264 ibid., 85

265 In D.W. Kurtz, *Transits of Venus: New Views of the Solar System and Galaxy*, 9.

266 ibid. 86–90.

The duration of a lunar eclipse obviously depends on both the Moon's speed and its distance from the Earth (the shadow being less when nearer), and in doing careful measurement and calculation Horrocks found (effectively) that when the Moon is in between the Earth and the Sun (i.e. in syzygy) its ellipse is elongated (i.e. eccentricity increases). In Horrocks's final lunar theory, then, both the eccentricity of the lunar orbit and the apogee (its furthest point from the Earth) oscillate. This, in effect, was similar to an earlier model of Kepler's, which the latter had abandoned.

Wilson suggests that the reason for the divergences between Kepler and Horrocks lay in the issue on which Horrocks was quoted above. Kepler had suggested that magnetic fibres within the planets themselves might cause alternate attraction and repulsion, which, operating with the basic motive force of the Sun, would cause the elliptical orbits. In his *Philosphicall Exercises* Horrocks explains that this seems irrational for:

> … if the Sun be able to carry about the whole body of ye planet, questionless it will be much more able to turn ye friendly part to itself and so unite it to itselfe.[267]

Horrocks, in contrast, finds in the conical pendulum a partial model for elliptical orbits. The pendulum bob moves in an oval and the apsides of this oval advances just as with planetary ellipses. It is worth quoting here from Wilson's conclusions to his study:

> Horrocks assumes that, just as the pendulum bob is attracted to the centre of its oval, so is the planet attracted to the Sun; and contrary to Kepler's conception, it is never repelled. Both pendulum bob and planet must receive a transradial impulse if they are to move in rounded orbits instead of directly toward the centre of attraction, and in the planet's case Horrocks locates the source of this impulse in the rotation of the Sun. A certain imbalance between the transradial and central forces is responsible for the forward motion of the apsides.
>
> The only discrepancy is that the conical pendulum produces a concentric oval, while the planetary oval is eccentric. A wind, Horrocks suggests, could cause the oval orbit of the conical pendulum to become eccentric; in the case of the planets, the

---

[267] Quoted in ibid., 92

> displacement must be due to an internal propensity. The internal propensity, Horrocks conjectures, is a tendency for the planets to rest in the place where they were first placed, namely, their aphelia. He devotes considerable effort to the attempt to locate the moment of the creation of the planets, on the fourth day of some past week, in which all the planets would be at their aphelia.
>
> If the explanation seems unbelievable to post-Newtonians, we should yet recognise that it is an important step beyond Kepler. It relies, not on a complicated internal structure of the planet and Sun, but on the Sun's attraction and on properties of matter thought of as inertial …
>
> Thus, where Kepler had explained the planetary motions by special mechanical contrivances, designed by a providential artificer and arranger, Horrocks now saw them as the result of the Sun's force combined with the inertial properties of matter … He could not, of course, account for the oscillations …
>
> But then, even the explanation of the evection that Newton offers in the Principia is less than satisfactory, since in accounting for the oscillations of eccentricity and apse he uses only the radial component of the Sun's perturbing force, and leaves the transradial component out of account. And without Horrocks's lunar theory as a starting-point, he would have had available neither a correct statement of the facts of the Moon's second inequality, nor one inviting any manner of Newtonian explanation.[268]

Horrocks was hailed in some 19th century eulogies as having almost invented Newtonian gravity and inertia.[269] This is exaggerated, and some of the things cited are actually already in Kepler's work. However there *are* aspects in which Horrocks *does* form a kind of bridge between Kepler and Newton. All three men, of course, were absolutely convinced that the

---

268 ibid., 92–3.

269 Newton himself in *Principia* 2nd–3rd edns Scholium to Prop. 35 of Book II says 'our Horrocks was the first to state that the Moon revolves in an ellipse about the Earth placed at its lower focus.' Kepler had already done this.

cosmos was the work of a great and mathematical designer, all three looked for a mathematical harmony in physical nature, and all three were great *mathematical* and *empirical* astronomers.

Horrocks's Solar and Planetary Work

Improved solar theory was essential for improved planetary theory and especially planetary prediction. Horrocks therefore worked on solar parallax, rejecting the old Ptolemaic method (still used by Lansberge) as too full of inherent errors to be of use. Horrocks's reasoning was that parallax for Venus is undetectable, yet must (when Venus is near to inferior conjunction) be four times that of the Sun.[270] Horrocks's figure of 14–15″ was much smaller than Kepler's, and Horrocks came to believe that many of Kepler's errors were due to his inflated figure of solar parallax. Horrocks also calculated an eccentricity of around 0.01735 – the modern figure is 0.0167[271]. Horrocks's figure for equation of centre (relating to the angle of the major elliptical axis) was out by only +3′ – he had arrived at a more accurate solar theory than anyone else so far.

Wilson points out that improvements in solar theory led to improvements in planetary theory.[272] In a letter to Crabtree of 19th January 1638 Horrocks suggests increasing Kepler's figure for the eccentricity of Mars of 0.09265 to 0.09292 (the present value put on it is 0.09303). This made Horrocks's predictions (and he made many of his own observations to check them) accurate to within 1–2′ of arc.

For Venus, parallel improvements were of great significance, as they led to his recognition (in Autumn 1639) that transits of Venus occurred *twice* in each of the major cycles Kepler had found, with a gap of eight years between the pairs of occurrences. Horrocks wrote to Crabtree on 5th November 1639:

> The reason why I am writing you now is to inform you of the extraordinary conjunction of the Sun and Venus which will occur on November 24. At which time Venus will pass across the Sun.

---

270 See Wilson in Taton and Wilson, op. cit. 168 etc.

271 These and other figures are taken from William J. Kaufman's *Universe* and/or *Encyclopaedia Britannica*..

272 Wilson, op. cit. 167.

Which, indeed, has never happened for many years in the past, nor will happen again in this century. I beseech you, therefore, with all my strength, to attend to it diligently with a telescope and to make whatever observation you can, especially about the diameter of Venus, which, indeed, is 7' according to Kepler, 11' according to Lansberge, and scarcely more than 1' according to my proportion.

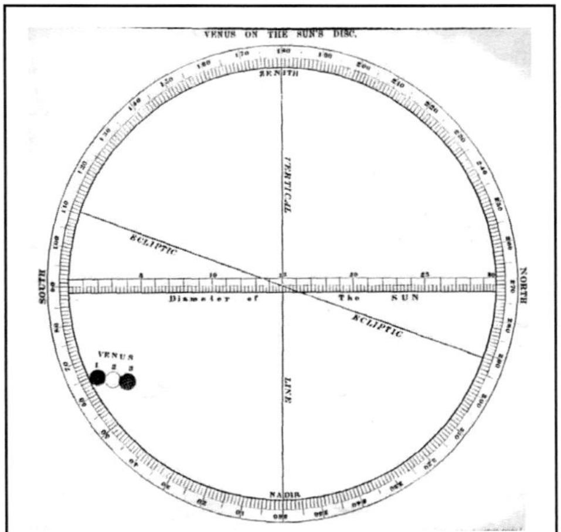

From *Venus in Transit* (Tr. Whatton)

The telescopic projection method was essential because a *camera obscura* (as Kepler had suggested) would not work with a Venus as small as Horrocks expected.

To observe the transit Horrocks says he: 'described on a sheet of paper a circle whose diameter was nearly equal to six inches, the narrowness of the apartment not permitting me conveniently to use a larger size'.[273] Onto this he projected the image of the Sun using a telescope. The kind of telescope he used was probably Galilean rather than Keplerian in design. During the transit he took three measurements at 3.15, 3.35 and 3.45 pm. He found that Venus's diameter was about 1/25th of that of the Sun. Horrocks found the longitude and latitude of Venus from the centre of the Sun, and demonstrated that his estimate was robust i.e. not altered much if there were observational errors.

Horrocks calculated Venus's apparent diameter during the transit as 76″ and accepted Gassendi's 20″ for Mercury. Critics had claimed regarding Gassendi's observation of Mercury that it appeared over small because of the Sun's rays shining around it. Horrocks also tried other means to check the smallness of planetary diameters. On 7th and 29th January 1640 he

273 *Venus in Transit*, 121.

used a pinhole and moved an iron needle back and forth until it just covered the planet to observe the exact size of Venus (and other planets). The diameter of the needle was measured by winding a thread around it numerous times. In arguing for a small diameter Horrocks utilised general arguments in Galileo's *Dialogue*, but apparently had not see his *Letters on Sunspots* which gave estimates generally confirming Horrocks's figure.

From Gassendi's and Horrocks's measurements, Mercury and Venus would have apparent diameters of about 28″ as seen from the Sun. Horrocks extended this mathematical harmony to other planets – though it has to be said that the measurements made of them were by methods far less reliable. He then asserts as a 'probable conjecture' [274] that the Earth may also appear as 28″ from the Sun. So he challenges his fellow Copernicans ('for I esteem not the opinions of others'):

> … what prevents your fixing of the Earth as the same measurement, the parallax of the Sun being nearly 0′14″ at a distance, in round numbers, of 15,000 of the Earth's diameters?

This figure would make the Sun 59.4 million miles away – larger than anyone had previously suggested.[275]

Horrocks rejected Kepler's speculations which related planetary distances to planetary volumes. For one thing, the discoveries of Gassendi on the size of Mercury and Horrocks himself on the size of Venus would not fit this. Horrocks made a suggestion (which he did not know had already been made by Remus) that is that their distances were proportional to their diameters. He had suggested this in 1639 to Crabtree before the transit, and now felt that it was confirmed. Horrocks was, however, well aware that his measurements were speculative, asserting:

> I demonstrate in round numbers a very great distance, outstripping all senses. I shall, therefore, not consider someone to dissent from me if he adds to or subtracts from the distance of the Sun even a thousand semi-diameters of the Earth. And the same is to be said much more of the size, with which, if you were

[274] *Venus in Transit*, 213.

[275] Van Helden (op. cit. 112) notes that the Belgian Priest Gottfried Wendelin (1580–1667) had written to Gassensdi in 1635 suggesting planetary diameters proportional to distances, apparent diameters of 28" from the Sun, and a solar distance amounting to some 58.3 million miles – but this was unpublished!

> to double it, you would not find me disagreeing very much. For a small and imperceptible change in the Sun's parallax would produce all this and more ...[276]

Horrocks was, to some extent, 'lucky' in the particular set of assumptions he made, assumptions that made him come closer to certain figures (e.g. the distance of the Sun) than anyone had done previously. The 'luck', however, went along with some careful observational and mathematical work. Horrocks was very much in the Keplerian tradition – he recognised the difference between speculation and reliable measurement even though he mixed the two in an attempt to find a system that reflected the mathematical harmony of a universe made by a loving and rational Creator.

Post Horrocks

Horrocks's lunar theory was, as we have noted, taken up by Newton, who never arrived at a theory he found satisfying on it. On more general issues of the measurements made of planetary and solar parallaxes Van Helden traces some of these in the years after Horrocks's death. By 1650 the old sizes were discredited, but no agreed method was available to get better figures. Convex eye pieces had by now replaced concave, and various micrometers were being tried. Christiaan Huygens (1629–1695) made various estimates which gave rise to a solar distance slightly *higher* than the modern estimate – though some of his assumptions were arbitrary:

(diameters)	**Sun**	**Venus**	**Earth**	**Mars**
Huygens	111	1.32	1	0.67
Modern	109	0.95	1	0.53

Thomas Streete (1622–89), in his 1661 *Astrononomia Carolina*[277], used Huygens's micrometer measurements but Horrocks's parallax figure. He also seems to have followed Horrocks in asserting the exactitude of Kepler's third law. By the time of Flamsteed in the 1670s figures fairly close to modern ones were arrived at, though they remained uncertain.

---

[276] Quoted in Van Helden, op. cit. 112.

[277] Curtis Wilson suggests that Newton probably first read Kepler's third law in this work 'Horrocks, Harmonies, and the exactitude of Kepler's third Law', *Studia Copernica* 1978, 16, 235–259.

Halley tried using the transit of Mercury in an expedition in 1676–78 to determine parallax, but remained dissatisfied. Ironically (in view of Horrocks's work) he concluded that the *only* reliable method would be to observe the transit of Venus – but he was unable to await the next one in 1761! Others did, however, make careful measurements in 1761[278] and 1769, getting the first accurate measurements for parallaxes of Venus and the Sun. Finally, *Venus in Sole Visa* established the size of our Solar System, as Horrocks had believed it would.

Some Questions

[1] The years 1630–1633 show the overlap of the three great Copernican pioneers Kepler (a German Lutheran), Galileo (an Italian Catholic) and Horrocks (an English Puritan):

- Kepler died in 1630, having received general sympathy if not support from his Lutherans for his astronomy, and unique protection from powerful though otherwise 'fanatical' Catholics like his patron the Emperor.
- Galileo was tried in 1632 on account of his *Dialogue,* in a Counter-Reformation suspicious of private re-interpretation of Scripture.
- Horrocks entered Cambridge in 1632, without apparently even a thought from himself or co-Puritans that Copernicanism (whether of the Lansberge or Kepler variety) caused any problems with his Christian beliefs, and a belief that the only sensible astronomers were Copernicans.

Did, then, the rise of Copernicanism *really* cause the kind of 'soul searching' about 'man's place in the universe' which is often supposed with hindsight?

[2] What would have happened to English (and world) astronomy had Horrocks and his two friends lived?

---

[278] Bushell, op. cit. reports that Le Gentil was sent to India to observe the 1761 transit but war delayed his arrival. He stayed out there eight years for the next one, but it was cloudy on the day. Coming home he was twice shipwrecked and when he got home found he had been proclaimed dead and his property divided up. And you thought you had problems! Others, fortunately for science, had more success.

References

The primary sources for Horrocks are:

Jeremiae Horrocci Liverpoliensis Angli ex Palinatu Lancastriae Opera Posthuma, edited by John Wallis (London 1673).

A copy of this is in Liverpool Central Reference Library, and another in the Bodleian Library – but be warned that it is all in Latin even if the diagrams are pretty!

Memoir of the Life and Labours of Jeremiah Horrocks, To Which Is Appended A Translation of His Celebrated Discourse The Transit of Venus across the Sun by Arundell Blount Whatton BA LLB (London 1859).

This classic translation of the *Discourse* is being placed on our website.

Jeremiah Horrocks: *The Transit of Venus Across the Sun 1639* (trans. A. B. Wharton, 1859) has also been republished in January 2010 and is on Amazon.co.uk – though the publisher is not stated.

Secondary Sources

The Transit of Venus, Peter Aughton, (Weidenfield, 2004). This contains great detail of the materials available on Horrocks. Its faults are that it tends sometimes to present speculation as virtual fact, and its presentation of both the general religious and the general astronomical background are patchy and sometimes misleading. Aughton's later book *The Story of Astronomy* (2008) has a chapter on Horrocks, but its general history is seriously flawed.

A Chapter of Romance in Science 1639–1874: In Memoriam Horroccii. Brickel's work on Horrocks, to commemorate the Building of the Brickel Vestry 1998 – available from St Michael's Church, Hoole.

J. E. Bailey, 'Jeremiah Horrocks and William Crabtree, Observers of the Transit of Venus, 24. November 1639', *The Palatine Note-Book II* (Manchester 1882), 253–66.

J. E. Bailey, 'The Writings of Jeremiah Horrox and William Crabtree', *The Palatine Note-Book III* (Manchester 1883), 17–22.

W. F. Bushell, 'Jeremiah Horrocks; the Keats of English Astronomy', *Mathematical Gazette* 43, 343 (February 1959), 1–16; reprinted in the North-West Astronomers Series by the *Liverpool Astronomical Society*, 1992.

Allan Chapman, *Three North Country Astronomers* (Richardson, 1982).

Allan Chapman, 'Jeremiah Horrocks, the Transit of Venus, and the 'New Astronomy' in early seventeenth-century England', *Quarterly Journal of the Royal Astronomical Society* 31 (1990), 333–571.

Allan Chapman, *Dividing the Circle* (Horwood, 1990 / Wiley, 1994), ch. 2.

Allan Chapman, *Jeremiah Horrocks* (1994: available from St Michael's Hoole).

S. B. Gaythorpe, 'Horrocks' Observation of the Transit of Venus 1639, November 24, O.S.' *Journal of the British Astronomical Association* 47, 2 (December 1936), 60–8.

S. B. Gaythorpe, 'Jeremiah Horrocks: Date of Birth, Parentage and Family Associations' *Transactions of the Historical Society of Lancashire and Cheshire* 106 (1954), 23–33.

S. B. Gaythorpe 'Horrocks' Observations and contemporary Ephemerides' *Journal of the British Astronomical Association* 47 (1937) 156–7.

Lawrence Hall, *The Birth-place of Jeremiah Horrocks in Toxteth Park* [In Liverpool Central Reference Library].

Lawrence Hall, 'Toxteth Park Chapel in the 17th Century' [Rewritten for the *Transactions of the Unitarian Historical Society* from a paper in July 1933. Copy in Liverpool Central Reference Library].

Eli Maor, *Venus in Transit* (Princeton, 2004). A reasonable book looking at the transits in general – not so much on Horrocks.

H. C. Plummer, 'Jeremiah Horrocks and his Opera Posthuma' *Notes and Records of the Royal Society of London* 3, (1940) 39–52.

David Sellers, *The Transit of Venus* (Magavelda Press, 2001). A good overall book on the Venus transits, including some material on Horrocks.

W. F. Spalding, 'A Country Curate' *Quarterly Journal of the Royal Astronomical Society* 12 (1971), 179–182.

R. Taton and C. Wilson (Eds), *Planetary Astronomy from the Renaissance to the rise of Astrophysics Part A: Tycho Brahe to Newton* (1989), ch. 10.

Curtis Wilson, 'Horrocks, Harmonies and the Exactitude of Kepler's Third Law' *Studia Copernicana*, 16 (1978), 235–259.

Curtis Wilson, 'On the Origins of Horrocks's Lunar Theory' , *Journal for the History of Astronomy* xviii (1987), 77–94.

Albert Van Helden, *Measuring the Universe* (Chicago, 1986), ch. 10.

In 2008 *The Diary and Correspondence of Dr. John Worthington, Volume I* was published, though I have not personally looked at this book.

David Sellers, *In Search of William Gascoigne: Seventeenth Century Astronomer* (2012).

8. Isaac Newton

Newton (1642-1727) age 46

'By the time of his death in 1727 Newton stood as the representative figure of modern science ... He became a key figure in the Enlightenment of the eighteenth century, and his work correspondingly aroused unease among Romantics who saw his science as inhuman and reductive. A mythical Newton, a new Adam born on Christmas Day and nourished by an apple from the tree of knowledge, came to obscure the real man who had worked in dynamics, astronomy and optics, and less successfully in chemistry, to synthesize the work of great predecessors.'

David Knight[279]

The English civil war started in September 1642, the Royalists were defeated in 1647, and King Charles I was executed in 1649. The Commonwealth under Cromwell then ruled until the Restoration of Charles II in May 1660.

Francis Bacon (1561-1626)

Francis Bacon died in 1626, well before the Commonwealth was established, but many of his ideas were influential throughout the period. Bacon advocated a radical break with earlier scholastic approaches to science. He says:

> Those who have handled sciences have been either men of experiment or men of dogmas. The men of experiment are like the ant: they only collect and use; the reasoners resemble spiders, who make cobwebs out of their own substance. But the bee takes a middle course; it gathers its material from the flowers of the garden and

---

279 From the preface to Rupert Hall's *Isaac Newton Adventurer in Thought* (1992).

> of the field, but transforms and digests it by a power of its own. Not unlike this is the true business of philosophy; for it neither relies solely or chiefly on the powers of the mind, nor does it take the matter which it gathers from natural history and mechanical experiments and lay it up in the memory whole, as it finds it but lays it up in the understanding altered and digested. Therefore from a closer and purer league between these two faculties, the experimental and the rational, (such as has never yet been made) much may be hoped.[280]

Bacon's empiricism recognised that observation was not haphazard, and that it needed to go along with reason. He emphasized methodical, empirical work, in which experimentation would be used to interrogate rather than to simply observe nature. Hypotheses should not be jumped to quickly for:

> The human understanding is of its own nature prone to suppose the existence of more order and regularity in the world than it finds. And though there be many things in nature which are singular and unmatched, yet it devises for them parallels and conjugates and relatives which do not exist. Hence the fiction that all celestial bodies move in perfect circles; spirals and dragons [*dracos*] being (except in name) utterly rejected.[281]

Bacon was probably not aware of Kepler's ellipses (published in 1609), but he is wary of prior assumptions as part of the 'dols' he describes, which can prevent science reaching the truth. The title page of his *Novum Organum Scientiarum* shows a ship symbolically setting out through the pillars of Hercules, into the uncharted waters of new knowledge. This 'millennial' aspect of his work (sometimes linked to a kind of religious millennialism) found a resonance in the Commonwealth. New knowledge and science, linked to technology, would improve the general lot of humankind. In his last work *The New Atlantis*

280 Bacon, *Novum Organum* (1620) xcv.

281 ibid. xlvi

(1626) he elaborated on the kind of scientific community which would be instrumental in bringing in this new age.

The reality was less exhilarating. We have noted the dearth of much astronomy in the times of Horrocks, and the next generation of astronomers saw little improvement. Figures like Thomas Streete (1622–89) and Jeremy Shakerley, carried on some of the Horrocks material and traditions, but are not well known. The nearest anything came to Bacon's vision was Gresham College, founded in London in 1598 with professors in music, rhetoric, divinity, law, physic, astronomy and geometry. [282] Puritan in tone, their work did encourage experimentation, and it was the professor of astronomy Henry Gellibrand whose commendation had focused Horrocks on Lansberge as we noted. Gresham College was in decline in the 1630s but revived in the 1640s and from 1645 a group was meeting which later (under the leadership of Christopher Wren, Professor of Astronomy from 1657–1661) provided a basis for the foundation of the Royal Society in 1660. The other major root for the Royal Society was a group meeting in Wadham College Oxford from about 1645. Under the Commonwealth, Puritans received preferment in Oxford, including as Savillian Professor of Geometry from 1649 John Wallis (who had matriculated with Horrocks and later edited his papers). Wallis, as we shall see, was a major figure in mathematics and mechanics, being described as the 'most influential English Mathematician before Newton'.[283] All branches of the sciences were pursued experimentally. Robert Boyle led this Oxford axis after some of its leaders left in 1558 to revive the Gresham group. Members of these groups favoured religious toleration and were permeated by a Baconian spirit which was both anti-authoritarian and deeply Christian. Even when not actual Puritans, they tended to have deep religious convictions and led ascetic lives.[284] John Wilkins, for example, was central. A leading figure at Gresham College, he became Warden at Wadham College from 1648, reconnected with the Gresham group from 1654, married Cromwell's sister, was one of the first secretaries of the Royal Society (which he was a driving force in founding), and later

---

[282] See David Goodman and Colin A. Russell, *The Rise of Scientific Europe 1500–1800* (1991) ch. 8.

[283] From the entry in *Encyclopaedia Britannica*.

[284] This includes Robert Boyle at Oxford who, though like Newton, remained nominally Anglican.

became bishop of Chester. He also wrote about possible space travel to meet inhabitants on the Moon![285]

The Royal Society[286] was founded on 28th November 1660 at an informal meeting after an astronomy lecture at Gresham College. Since scientists in Gresham, in Oxford and in Cambridge[287] tended often to be either Puritans or Anglican Whigs, the newly restored Charles II was unenthusiastic about giving his support. The society received a Royal charter in 1662, but, unlike its foreign counterparts, received little or no Royal patronage. The Society, however, became a focus for science across all disciplines. It was also practical, the sometime Professor of Astronomy Christopher Wren and the Royal Society Curator of Experiments Robert Hooke doing much to help design the rebuilding of London after the great fire in 1666.

Newton's Life

Formative Years

Isaac Newton was born in the year Galileo died, on Christmas day 1642.[288] At least, if you are English he was born that year. Italian friends of Galileo would have placed it as 4th January 1643, since on the Continent (unlike in England) they had accepted the reformed calendar. Any account like this can hope only to outline some key points in such a long productive life, and leave those interested to seek more detail in the various secondary works on Newton.[289]

Like Horrocks's, Newton's family were 'yeomen' rather than either gentlefolk or peasants. The place of his birth was the substantial farm house at Woolsthorpe, Lincolnshire. This was sturdy and spacious, though its title of 'Manor House' should not bring to mind a picture of a stately home! His father, also Isaac Newton, was a prosperous though illiterate

---

285 *Discovery of a World in the Moone* (2nd edn 1640).

286 Full title: 'Royal Society of London for the Promotion of Natural Knowledge'

287 The great naturalist John Ray (1627–1705) lost his fellowship at Trinity College Cambridge for refusing to sign the Act of Uniformity.

288 For great detail of Newton's background etc. see Richard Westfall, *Never At Rest* (1980).

289 Copious footnotes will be avoided, but the account is mostly indebted to Richard Westfall *Never At Rest* (1980) and A. Rupert Hall *Isaac Newton (1992)* – though also to various other books as in the bibliography.

farm owner, and had married Hannah Ainscough who was from a more genteel and educated but less prosperous background. Isaac senior died two months before Isaac was born, leaving the house, lands, and also goods and chattels worth £459 12s 4d – quite a sum. By his own later account, the baby Isaac was premature, tiny, and the general view was that he would be unlikely long to survive. He was baptised on 1st January 1643 (O.S.)[290] in Colsterworth Parish Church. The area is about seven miles south of Grantham, a market town.

Woolsthorpe – with apple tree!

Colsterworth parish church

Smith's church and the rectory today

Three years later Hannah Ainscough-Newton, aged thirty, remarried to a 63-year-old minister Reverend Barnabas Smith, rector of the next parish about a mile and a half away. Smith was the son of a minister, an Oxford graduate, and owned a large library particularly of the early fathers (which Isaac later inherited). Reverend Mr Smith was well off, but did not want young Isaac with his mother, so from age three until Smith's death in August 1653 Isaac was brought up by his grandparents in the Woolsthorpe house. Biographers sometimes link Newton's later neuroses with this traumatic maternal separation (albeit only to a distance of under two miles), and in a list of his

[290] O.S. means the 'Old Style' Julian calendar. Since then England too has added ten days to bring us back into line with Europe's new calendar as noted above.

Grantham now

sins he compiled nine years after being reunited with his mother he reported one as:

> 'Threatening my father and mother Smith to burne them and the house over them.'[291]

At age twelve Isaac went to the Free Grammar School of King Edward VI of Grantham – lodging with the apothecary Mr Clark. Previous pupils included the Cambridge Platonist Henry More, and the school was a respected institution. We presume it covered the standard curriculum, which was mostly Latin with some Greek and not a lot else. At least this made him fluent in the language of scholarly Europe, and (as with Horrocks) opened up possibilities of self-learning in subjects like mathematics. He apparently left his mark on the school – a graffiti carved on a windowsill. This was normal at that time, however, and was not 'vandalism'!

School – and graffiti

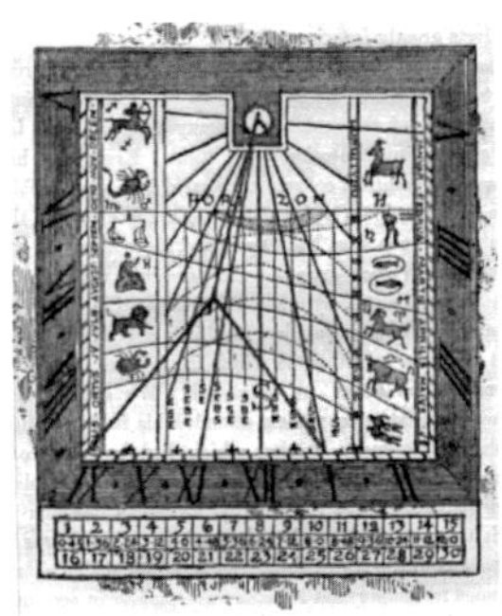

A Newton sundial

[291] Quoted e.g. in Westfall, op. cit. 53.

Colsterworth sundial

Young Isaac enjoyed making mechanical contrivances, many of them found in a book by John Bate *The Mysteries of Nature and Art.*[292] An early interest in the heavens was manifested in an interest in sundials. One, reputedly made by Isaac, is on the wall of the Colsterworth church. He seems to have got on better with girls than lads, and the girl with whom he came closest to a romance in these adolescent years remembered him as a 'sober, silent, thinking lad'.[293] He seems also to have had a great ability to teach himself, and a high level of concentration on what interested him.

Newton left the school at just 17, his mother's intention apparently being that he would now learn to manage the farm. By all accounts he was pretty hopeless at it! The sheep got out, the pigs trespassed on other people's corn fields, and the fences fell down! Mercifully, by the intervention of his old schoolmaster Mr Stokes and his uncle Reverend William Ainscough, his situation was altered. He had a brief period back at school, and then he was off – at the rather late age of 18 – to Trinity College, Cambridge where his uncle had also studied. Ironically (in view of the suppositions of poverty made for Horrocks in a similar case and the undoubted affluence of Newton's mother), he entered as a subsizar.[294] It was June 1661, and he was joining a community of some 400 scholars and students in the richest college in Cambridge where he was to spend most of the next 35 years. Socially (perhaps especially in the heady days of the Restoration of the monarchy) the university was very stratified, with sizars and subsizars socialising little with the gentry. Newton, whose home background was affluent, must have found it galling to be classed in such a group. He seems to have been friendly with a number of pensioners (the middle ranking group), and shared a room with one, John Wickins, from the beginning of 1663. His room-mate also helped Newton with his various experiments – though later they seem not to have maintained much contact.

[292]ibid. 61.

[293]ibid. 59.

[294] Westfall in *Never At Rest* explains the difference between sizar and subsizar – which were of equally low status (71).

Trinity College Great Court (the chapel opposite now contains Newton's statue)

In his personal life, biographers differ about the extent to which they portray Newton as the tortured melancholy lonely genius. He was certainly ascetic in his personal life, and devout in his faith which was Puritanical in aspect. Some kind of religious crisis in the summer of 1662 was related to his near obsession with listing his sins. Manuel, followed in this by Westfall, sees all this as indicative of a 'sense of guilt, doubt and self-denigration'.[295] In a sense this is self-evident, but we must also be aware of any implicit assumption (in a Freudian religious world which sees Newton's root problem as separation from his mother) that such guilt is a 'Bad Thing' . In Newton's religious circles it might not be so seen, depending on what it led to. From his second year Newton was also influenced by the Cambridge Platonists, especially Henry More. On *mind* their view was that it was definitely *not* like a blank sheet – a *tabula rasa* – as later asserted by Locke. Perception was interactive. On *matter*, Descartes' version of the mechanistic philosophy seemed to More to remove the need for a God.[296] More (and later Newton) moved away from this to a form of Christian

[295] Frank E. Manuel, *The Religion of Isaac Newton* (1974) 15–16, Richard Westfall, *Never At Rest*, 78.

[296] Descartes himself was, of course, a devout Catholic, and God is basic to his system in underwriting the reliability of human sense/intuition – but the mechanical system itself seemed self-contained.

Platonism that saw the spiritual as permeating all things. Newton's early notes on atomism refer to the More version of it. This approach is quite central to Newton's science, and also pervades his astronomy.

Modern writer Michael White[297], who has little empathy for any such religious views and emphasises the 'alchemy' aspect of it all, opines that 'mainstream modern atomism could not be further removed from More's idea of a personal, all-pervading deity' and to unite faith and quantum theory is a 'strange marriage'. Yet central 20th century physicists like Arthur Eddington[298] seem to have taken a not dissimilar 'spiritual' view. Is it so strange?

The curriculum was out of date and addressed almost none of the scientific concerns of the previous half-century. Learning outcomes were to understand Aristotelian logic, ethics, physics and cosmology, and the fundamental object was to be able to dispute successfully in Latin about these. The still-operative Elizabethan statutes prescribed rhetoric (in effect classics) for the first year, logic for the second, and third and philosophy for the fourth. Mathematics (along with logic and moral or natural philosophy) could provide the matter for the third year disputations in the run up to the final public 'Acts' which concluded the degree. Tutors varied in the mathematical content offered, but John Ray lamented in 1660 the lack of both experimental science and mathematics in the curriculum.[299] The system became increasingly empty and fairly pointless, but academics whose lives have been focussed on such a system are not always quick to change it – either then or today! In 1663 Henry Lucas founded a Lucasian Professorship of Mathematics, and Isaac Barrow (a fellow of Newton's own Trinity College) moved from the chair of Greek to that of Mathematics.

Newton's notebooks show the usual undergraduate preference for pre-digested works, but also a growing interest in mathematics and experimental philosophy. His interest was reflected in his notebook after a heading (probably late in 1664) *Questiones quaedam Philosophcae.* This and

---

[297] Michael White, *Isaac Newton, The Last Sorcerer*, 57.

[298] Arthur Eddington, *The Nature of the Physical World* (1928).

[299] Hall (1992) 15; Hall notes also e.g. that More used Descartes' *Dioptics* at Christ's.

other notes show him reading carefully e.g. Descartes[300], Galileo[301], Gassendi[302], Boyle[303], and John Wallis.[304]

Newton's interest in mathematics was obvious, and, in April 1664 he was required to pass an examination to register for his BA degree to be taken the following Spring. According to his early biographer Conduitt, Newton's Trinity tutor, Benjamin Pulleyn, referred him to the newly appointed Lucasian Professor Isaac Barrow (also a Trinity Fellow) for examination. Unfortunately Barrow examined him on Euclid, which Newton had neglected, and it never occurred to Barrow that Newton could have read the more advanced material without Euclid, so he obtained no high view of Newton's abilities. In spite of this Newton was made a 'scholar'[305], but he resolved to go back and remedy the deficiency. In fact, his elevation from subsizar to scholar meant a path to the MA degree and possible Fellowship beyond this, which seems to have confirmed Newton in his pursuit of natural philosophy. His interest in mathematics increased, and Newton's experiments on optics seem to have begun after he bought a glass prism at a fair in 1664 – by his own later account to try out some of Descartes ideas on colours. Newton graduated BA in January 1665 – though he seems to have done little formal study on the official curriculum and achieved only a second-class degree.

In summer 1665 plague hit Cambridge. The problems of sanitation and crowding in cities made them unhealthy places to be during plague, and Newton left for Woolsthorpe in June or July. He returned in March 1666 (no deaths having been reported for six weeks), but plague broke out again in June and he went back to Lincolnshire until April 1667. Later Newton looked back:

---

300 Descartes, *La Geometrie* (1637) and *La Dioptrique* (1637)– Descartes had died in 1650.

301 Galileo, *Dialogue on Two World Systems* (1632).

302 Walter Charleton's epitome and translation of Gassendi – possibly some Gassendi in Latin too.

303Boyle, *History of Colours* (1664).

304Newton noted his debt to *Arithmetica Infinitorum* (1655), and *Opera Mathematica* (1656). *Mathesis Universalis* (1657) and *Tractatus de Sectionibus Conicis* (1659) were also important works.

305 Westfall suggests at the intercession of some powerful fiend, perhaps Babbington. Hall seems to discount Conduitt's account, and speculates that Barrow himself spotted Newton at his lectures.

> In the beginning of the year 1665 I found the Method of approximating series & the Rule for reducing any dignity of any Binomial into such a series. The same year in May I found the method of Tangents of Gregory & Slusius, & in November had the direct method of fluxions & the next year in January had the Theory of Colours & in May following I had entrance into ye inverse method of fluxions. And the same year I began to think of gravity extending to y'orb of the Moon & (having found out how to estimate the force with which [a] globe revolving within a sphere presses the surface of the sphere) from Kepler's rule of the periodical times of the Planets being in sesquialterate proportion of their distances from the centre of their Orbs, I deduced that the forces which keep the Planets in their Orbs must [be] reciprocally as the squares of their distances from the centres about which they revolve: & thereby compared the force requisite to keep the Moon in her Orb with the force of gravity at the surface of the Earth, & found them answer pretty nearly. All this was in the two plague years of 1665–1666. For in those days I was in the prime of my age for invention & minded Mathematicks & Philosophy more then at any time since.[306]

The years from about 1664–1668 were fertile times for Newton.

Manuel's 'psychological' account of Newton[307] fostered the idea that Woolsthorpe and the 'bosom of his mother' were crucial to an *anna mirabiles* of scientific breakthrough. Westfall seems rightly to cast some doubt on this, since the productivity predated his departure north and continued after his return. His BA may have been more to do with it. What, however, about the most famous incident in scientific history? Did a falling apple really inspire him, and if so where? The story circulated

Woolsthorpe: present view of the orchard from Newton's window

[306] Quoted in Westfall, 143, also Hall,19.

[307] Frank E. Manuel *A Portrait of Isaac Newton* (1968).

early, but was related best by his friend William Stukeley:

> After dinner, the weather being warm, we went into the garden and drank tea, under the shade of some apple trees, only he and myself. Amidst other discourse, he told me, he was just in the same situation, as when formerly, the notion of gravitation came into his mind. It was occasion'd by the fall of an apple, as he sat in a contemplative mood. Why should that apple always descend perpendicularly to the ground, thought he to himself. Why should it not go sideways or upwards, but constantly to the Earth's centre? Assuredly, the reason is, that the Earth draws it. There must be a drawing power in matter … If matter thus draws matter, it must be in proportion of its quantity. Therefore the apple draws the Earth, as well as the Earth draws the apple. [And thus] there is a power, like that we here call gravity, which extends its self thro' the universe.[308]

Few people would be brave enough to sit under an apple tree in Lincolnshire when the apples were falling – not from fear of being struck but from fear of being stung by wasps. At Woolsthorpe he could, of course, have been sitting nearer the house, and an account given by his half-niece and longtime housekeeper Mrs Conduitt to Voltaire has him *walking* in the garden.[309] On the other hand Hall suggests it may all have been in Babbington's orchard in Boothby Pagnell. Michael White says the whole story was 'almost certainly fabricated by Newton to disguise the truth' i.e. that his ideas derived from disreputable alchemy.[310] In any event, the idea of gravity as mutual attraction did not spring out of nowhere. The works of Kepler and others contained more than a germ of the idea. Newton's genius was not merely to universalise it, but to be able to work out the mathematics. Some, like Robert Hooke, might do the former but could not do the latter. Others, like John Wallis, may have been able to develop the mathematics, but did not get interested in quite the same mechanical problems. Newton once said that he could see further

---

308 William Stukeley, *Memoirs* (1936), 19–20.

309 Rupert Hall, *Isaac Newton Eighteenth-century Perspectives* (1999), 18.

310 Michael White, *Isaac Newton the Last Sorcerer*, 214 – seemingly linking Newton's ideas with alchemy.

because he stood on the shoulders of giants. Too often people have magnified his undoubted genius as though his ideas sprang almost from nowhere – ignoring the brilliant men on whose ideas he drew. The history of science almost always shows development rather than any sudden revolution or total novelty in ideas.

Established in Cambridge (1667–1702)

Newton was just 24 years old when he went back to Trinity College in 1667. He was elected to a minor Fellowship in 1667, and following his MA, a major Fellowship in 1668. Newton's wardrobe and his social engagements increased. Although he could forget to eat when he was engrossed on some experiment or thought, he was still a youth who could enjoy a game of bowls or an evening at the tavern.

In 1668 we find Newton high in Barrow's esteem. Barrow was a part of that group of communicating scholars developing with the Royal Society. John Collins was an FRS and government clerk in London, acting as a kind of mathematical interchange. He sent Barrow a copy of a new book published late 1668 by Nicholas Mercator: *Logarithmotechnia,* and in July 1669 Barrow wrote to Collins saying that he had a friend who had written an unpublished paper on similar issues but more general.[311] Newton was apparently reluctant to allow his work to venture into any public domain – but was persuaded to let Barrow send it to Collins. Only after Collins had indicated his approval was Barrow allowed to reveal the name of the author:

> His name is Mr Newton; a fellow of our College & very young (being but the second year Master of Arts) but of extraordinary genius & proficiency in these things.[312]

Newton always seemed to hate having to defend ideas which he thought obvious and proven, and not for the first time friends had to urge publication or public exposure. Collins recognised the genius of the paper *De analysi*, copied it, and through him others came to know of the young Newton. Newton, however, resolutely refused to allow its publication as an

---

[311] For this episode see Westfall, op. cit. 202 etc., Hall (1992),79 etc.

[312] Barrow to Collins, 20 Aug 1669 *Corres* 1, 14–15 quoted in Westfall op. cit.

appendix to Barrow's forthcoming optics lectures which he helped edit. Over the next couple of years Newton revised it as *De methodis serierum et fluxionum* – fluxions was his version of calculus.

By around 1668 Newton, probably influenced by More and Gassendi, had reacted against the Cartesian version of the mechanical philosophy. By separating the worlds of matter and spirit Descartes seemed to Newton to open the way for atheism. Westfall[313] suggests that Newton's interest in alchemy comes from around this time, believing spirit to permeate the universe.

In 1669 Isaac Barrow resigned his Lucasian Professorship of Mathematics. Why did he do it? At the extremes are the theories of the 'grand gesture' (that he 'recognised his master') and of selfish motive (that he was 'angling

Trinity College: The apple tree (right centre) was grown from a Woolsthorpe pip, and the rooms Newton occupied are behind and to the rear of it.

for a higher post'). The answer is probably more complex. He *was* ambitious, but his ambition was probably more ecclesiastical, and his rise to King's chaplain and then Master of Trinity within three years fulfilled his hopes. He need not, however, have resigned his Professorship to seek such positions, so his motive cannot have been pure selfish ambition. On the other hand he was as able and active a scientist as Cambridge possessed at the time, and no one (in Restoration Cambridge) would have been

[313] Westfall, op. cit. 301.

bothered even if he knew little mathematics at all, let alone have expected him to resign for a young MA. In my view Barrow had a genuine interest in sciences and, having found a worthy successor (a rare find in that context) wanted to resign to devote himself more to his direct Christian calling. Coupled with this may well have been a desire to push Newton into a more public exposure of the science which so far he was withholding from publication. A Lucasian Professor had to expound 'some part of Geometry, Astronomy, Geography, Optics, Statics, or some other Mathematical discipline' weekly during term time. Barrow knew that effectively he could ensure Newton's appointment, and as Lucasian Professor Newton would be *forced* to break cover!

To Newton, who had needed to be careful to make ends meet but had spent lavishly on his BA/MA academic gown, the prospect of £100 per year and a resplendent scarlet Professorial gown must have outweighed any reluctance to 'go public' Newton, aged 27, became Lucasian Professor on 29th October 1669.

Cambridge itself, under the Restoration, was in decline, with patronage, seniority and empty procedure replacing any pursuit of academic excellence. Professorships became empty sinecures, and fewer and fewer gave lectures.[314] Little was required of Newton, then, either as a Fellow or a Professor. Newton was supposed to give tutorials, though only to the affluent 'fellow-commoners' few of whom were interested. He began a course of lectures on optics in 1670, a subject on which Barrow had previously lectured, apparently with some input from Newton. Newton referred back to Barrow's course and had no hostile intent, but his own lectures were novel and dealt with geometrical optics rather than *qualities* of colour and light. Barrow himself recognised their outstanding value, though Newton's two courses deposited with careful dates (possibly for preservation or priority) appear to contradict at various points.[315] These lectures, however, were upon his current researches, and given the almost total lack of knowledge of mathematical basics amongst Cambridge students few indeed would have been able to understand them even if they went. Fifteen years later Humphrey Newton recorded quaintly:

---

[314] Only at the turn of the 19th century did this tendency start to reverse, and lecture courses became expected of Professors again.

[315] One set had 31 the other 18 and the dates are dubious – see Hall (1992), 99 etc., for details.

> So few went to hear Him, & fewer understood him, yet oftentimes he did in a manner, for want of Hearers, read to ye Walls.[316]

Fellows had to avoid crime, not to fall into heresy (fairly broadly defined), and not to marry. A Fellowship was supposed to be a stage in a path to an ecclesiastical calling, not a career grade. Newton had no criminal tendencies, kept his unorthodox theological leanings quiet, and had no desire to marry (though actually he could have married and remained Professor had he so wished).

During this time Newton was working not only on mathematics and optics but also on chemistry. He apparently had an alchemical laboratory set up, which he used (for some reason) particularly during spring and autumn. We will say little about his alchemy in this period, as in general he did not publicise or publish it.

In 1671 the Royal Society heard of Newton's six-inch reflecting telescope and asked to see it. Various reflecting models had been tried before, but without much success. Newton's was based on mirrors of hard white bronze – which it took much skill to make. Barrow took it to London where it aroused interest – but no instruments of workable size could be made at that time with existing technology.

Newton was, however, elected to the Royal Society in 1672, and, being well pleased, sent off to Oldenburg his first printed work – a letter on his new theory of light and colours. It described experiments (some of which seem to be fabricated in the form described) showing that prisms separate pre-existing different coloured beams of light, rather than qualitatively alter the light itself. We may look at some detail in his works, but Newton made high claims for his new theory:

[316] Quoted in Westfall, op.cit. 209.

> A naturalist would scarce expect to see the science of [colours] become mathematicall, & yet I dare affirm that there is so much certainty as in any other part of Opticks. For what I shall tell them is not an Hypothesis but most rigid consequence, not conjectured by barely inferring 'tis thus because not otherwise or because it satisfies all phenomena (the Philosophers universall Topick,) but evinced by the mediation of experiments concluding directly and without any suspicion of doubt.[317]

The excited young professor was claiming two things. Firstly, his theory was *mathematical*. Different colour light beams were refracted by different amounts – each colour could be associated with a *number*. Secondly, it was not some vague *hypothesis* (e.g. about swirling unobservable vortices), it was simply empirically observed *experimental fact*. He 'feigned no hypotheses' about *how* it worked – but experiment and mathematics showed that it *did*.

Unfortunately, under normal working conditions actual experiments tend to refute Newton's theories! His own sight of the elongated spectrum was in his 22-foot-long room in Woolsthorpe – most experimenters used a smaller scale in which it was much less apparent. His new theory did not win immediate universal acceptance as he expected. Warmly received by the Society on 8th February, it was given to Robert Hooke the Curator of Experiments to review and print. Hooke accepted the experiments but denied the theory and focussed on the corpuscular part that, to Newton, was incidental. Hooke's draft critique reached Newton on 20th February. Hooke's own idea was of light as 'nothing but a pulse or motion, propagated through a homogenous uniform and transparent medium' To Hooke, light was able to be *changed* e.g. by a prism as the pulse pattern was altered, to Newton it was only separated. Huygens, with whom Newton was also in contact, first (June 1672) thought Newton's new theory 'probable', but then wondered whether Hooke might not be nearer the truth and every colour made of mixtures of yellow and blue. To Newton, all this was reversion to vague hypotheses with no basis in observation, rather than what he had demonstrated empirically. He came near to resigning from the Royal Society, which, in turn, embarrassed at Hooke's criticisms, declined to print them for fear of offending Newton. Newton's response, sent the following June, was devastating in its critique of Hooke

---

[317] Newton, *Correwspondance* vol 1, 1959, 96–7.

and fairly insulting – and Hooke was forced to hear it read and see it published in the *Transactions.* Huygens, however, wryly remarked to Oldenburg (Secretary of the Royal Society) of Newton that 'seeing he maintains his doctrine with some warmth, I do not care to dispute'. The gift to Newton of a copy of Huygens's *Horologium oscillatorianm* at the same time in summer 1673 restored cordial relationships.

As noted above, Fellowships were generally a stage in an ecclesiastical career, and most were for ordained men. In 1675 his lay Fellowship at Trinity would expire, and Newton did not want ordination. He perhaps told Barrow that he felt no calling, but in reality his developing Arian views may have been a strong reason. In any event, Newton applied for and obtained Royal dispensation not to take holy orders – almost certainly helped by Barrow who was King's chaplain and had the King's ear. In February 1675 a visit to London in connection with this application also led to formal entry to Fellowship of the Royal Society to which he had been elected three years earlier, and he probably also met Robert Hooke as well as Robert Boyle face to face for the first time.

At the end of 1675 Newton sent another optics paper, even in it making some friendly overtures to Hooke. However the paper again emphasised that in his work 'the science of colours becomes a speculation more proper for mathematicians than naturalists' The theory of interference colours went into Newton's later *Opticks* part II. An apparent claim of Hooke's that Newton had stolen ideas from him was patched over.

By 1676 Newton was corresponding with Leibniz, who expressed admiration for Newton's work. On his way through London in October 1676 Leibniz met John Collins, who allowed him to see Newton's *De Analysi* and work on tangents. Leibniz made notes on infinite series, though not on the method of fluxions.

Newton was also heavily involved at this time both in alchemy and in theology – though neither of these was made public.

In 1679 his mother died, and he spent some months back in Woolsthorpe settling affairs. Newton also began an extensive correspondence with Boyle, associated with a continuing interest in alchemy/chemistry. He was continually also interested in mathematics. Around this time he reread Descartes's *Geometry* – this time writing very critical comments in the margins. He was reworking his method of fluxions to remove from it any traces of Cartesian approach.

In 1679 Newton was also corresponding with Hooke concerning how a body would fall to the centre of the Earth. Hooke actually asked Newton for an opinion of his theory of planetary motions. Hooke had outlined this in his *Attempt to Prove the Motion of the Earth* (1674, reprinted 1679):

> This depends upon three Suppositions. First, That all Celestial Bodies whatsoever, have an attraction or gravitating power towards their own Centres, whereby they attract not only their own parts, and keep them from flying from them, as we may observe the Earth to do, but that they do also attract all other Celestial Bodies that are within the sphere of their activity … The second supposition is this, That all bodies whatsoever that are put into a direct and simple motion, will so continue to move forward in a streight line, till they are by some other effectual powers deflected and bent into a Motion, describing a Circle, Ellipsis, or some other more compounded Curve Line. The third supposition is, that these attractive powers are so much the more powerful in operating, by how much the nearer the body wrought upon is to their own Centres. Now what these several degrees are I have not yet experimentally verified.[318]

This passage is significant in view of Hooke's later claims of plagiarism. Westfall argues that Hooke did not 'truly hold a concept of universal gravitation' The idea of each body having a *localised* sphere of influence is perhaps not universal gravitation, but it is not far off. The gravitational idea is, of course, in nascent form in Kepler – Newton hardly needed to look to alchemy as some have suggested. But the idea of linear (and therefore tangential) inertia bent by gravity does not seem to appear in Newton's papers before this time. In later controversy, of course, Hooke would regard the key part of the system as the concepts – Newton would regard the key as the mathematics without which it remained a mere hypothesis. Others, such as Wren, had also thought about how to combine dynamics with an inverse square law to obtain planetary motion. None had a mathematical system.

---

[318] Quoted in Westfall, op. cit. 382.

In this present Hooke-Newton interchange, Newton sent some less than carefully worked out calculations about potential falling patterns. Westfall notes that Hooke:

Halley (1656-1742)

> Couched his correction in the mildest of terms, and though he did read this letter and his next one (which also corrected Newton) before the Royal Society, he did not depart further from his promise of 1676 to keep their correspondence confidential.[319]

This seems a bit disingenuous. Newton was wary at the best of times of controversy and jealous of his reputation – to read two letters and then expose their errors to the Royal Society was frankly asking for it. In a later letter Hooke referred to the inverse square law of gravitation – though his way of relating this to planetary velocity is mistaken.

The correspondence irritated Newton, but it also stimulated him to think about the problems of forces of attraction, inertia etc. We do not know if this was a reconsideration of ideas started earlier or not, but he had reformulated his ideas on the philosophy of nature by the mid-80s.

Another stimulus to this was the comet that appeared in 1681, recognised by Flamsteed (now Astronomer Royal) as having turned around the Sun. Flamsteed contacted Newton, who wrote him long letters about the comet correcting some of Flamsteed's views. The comet we now call Halley's comet appeared in 1682, and Newton was also in contact with Halley from this time.

As mentioned, Wren as well as Hooke had thought about an inverse square law in some kind of planetary orbit explanation. In January 1684 Hooke boasted to Wren and Halley that he had demonstrated all the laws of the celestial motions, but did not produce the evidence. In August Halley, admitting his own inability to solve problems of planetary motion,

---

[319] Westfall, op. cit. 384.

visited Newton in Cambridge and asked if he could calculate what the path would be of a body moving under the action of a central force which varied as the inverse square of its distance from the centre. Newton told him that he had already calculated it and it was an ellipse. Newton claimed to have lost the calculations (from over a decade earlier)[320] but promised to recalculate them and send them down to Halley. They came shortly afterwards in the form of a manuscript *De Motu.* This derived Kepler's three laws from the starting assumptions of inverse square law. After another hasty visit to Cambridge, Halley registered it with the Royal Society. It did not, however, state any of Newton's three laws of motion, and it is a snapshot of half-formed ideas.

Newton's room-mate and amanuensis John Wickins left Cambridge in 1683, and it was a new assistant Humphrey Newton who helped Isaac over the next few months as he worked on the larger version of *De Motu* which eventually became *Principia.* This was the period of which Humphrey later wrote telling of Newton's single mindedness and self neglect – though there may be some doubt as to whether this in fact applied to all of Newton's scientific life. Alchemy as well as dynamics occupied him. From December 1684 to January 1685 Newton was also in correspondence with Flamsteed, getting data he wanted for his theories, especially about comets. Newton mentioned the ptossibility that Jupiter and Saturn might affect each other when in conjunction. Flamsteed apparently thought he meant attraction by magnetism, and pointed out that even the largest magnet could not affect a needle 100 yards away, so this was unlikely. Flamsteed seems to have had an inkling that Newton might be talking of some other force, but could not think what it was!

Parliament

[320] Westfall thinks it more likely he wanted to recheck them, since the paper still exists, though Hall seems to express no such suspicion.

The traditional view is that it was Halley who persuaded a reluctant Newton to publish all his results as *Philosophiae naturalis principia mathematica* or *Principia,* which was published by the Royal Society in 1687 at Halley's expense. More recent scholars cast doubt on this reluctance. There were some problems caused by claims of Hooke that Newton had taken the idea of gravity from him. Newton reacted angrily – his stress made worse by the accession of the Catholic King James after King Charles II's death in February 1685. In Newton's theology the Catholic Church was evil, and he was concerned both at the effects on national life and on the university. However, finally Halley succeeded in getting the Royal Society to publish *Principia.* The first edition contained various errors, but it was an impressive work.

In Spring 1687, as *Principia* was going to print, Newton was highly involved in the refusal of Cambridge to agree to the Catholic King's command that a Benedictine monk be allowed to graduate and become a Fellow. It was as a result of this that, when the Protestant William and Mary arrived for the glorious revolution of 1688, Newton was voted into Parliament as representative for the university in January 1689.

John Locke

In the years 1689–90 Newton spent 55 weeks in London, lodging near Parliament Square. He would have been involved in the legislation against popery – also (ironically) against Arianism. We have no records of speeches (other than a famous request to shut the window!), though he did ask leave to bring in a bill confirming the rights and privileges of his university. Newton was also in contact with Charles Montagu (later Lord Halifax) who had been a Fellow at Trinity, and renewed contact with Huygens (the new King's fellow countryman) who helped seek a preferment for Newton as Provost of Kings (an effort which failed). Also in London, at Hampton Court, Newton met Nicholas Fatio de Duillier, a young Swiss mathematician (also interested in chemistry and alchemy and who had studied divinity and Hebrew). Fatio showed adulation to Newton, he sought (and for a while held) a close friendship with Newton and hoped to edit a second edition of *Principia.*

The wider London circle brought other friends. One of his new friends was the philosopher John Locke (1632–1704). As common in those days,

Locke was also a theologian, a physician, a chemist, and writing on currency as a member of the Board of Trade whilst Newton was at the Mint, as well as becoming one of the key figures in empiricist philosophy. He had long been a member of the Royal Society, had read the *Principia* and moved away from Cartesianism. Locke, a very committed Christian, also admired Newton's knowledge of the Bible and theology. Newton, in fact, sent Locke a long treatise written in 1690, arguing that the Vulgate version had mistranslated some of the Bible and introduced Trinitarian ideas where there were none. He apparently thought to have it published anonymously abroad – we don't know what Locke (whose theology was orthodox) thought of it, though he was willing to help in publication. Newton never did bring himself to publish anything on his Arian views, even anonymously.

In 1693 Newton had a breakdown. He wrote two now famous letters to his friends John Locke and the Royal Society Secretary Samuel Pepys. To Locke he apologised in a letter of 16th Sept 1693:

> Sir,
>
> Being of opinion that you endeavoured to embroil me with woemen & by other means I was so much affected with it as that when one told me you were sickly and would not live I answered twere better you were dead. I desire you to forgive this uncharitableness. For I am now satisfied that what you have done is just & I beg your pardon for my having hard thoughts of you for it & for representing that you struck at the root of morality in a principle you laid down in your book of Ideas & designed to pursue in another book & that I took you for a Hobbist. I beg your pardon also for saying or thinking that there was a designe to sell me an office, or to embroile me, I am your most humble & most unfortunate Servant
>
> Is. Newton

At around the same time an equally strange letter was sent to Samuel Pepys, Secretary of the Royal Society:

> Sir
>
> Some time after Mr. Millington had delivered your message, he pressed me to see you the next time I went to London. I was

averse; but upon his pressing consented, before I considered what I did, for I am extremely troubled at the embroilement I am in, and have neither ate nor slept well this twelve month, nor have my former consistency of mind. I never designed to get anything by your interest, nor by King James's favour, but am now sensible that I must withdraw from your acquaintance, and see neither you nor the rest of my friends any more, if I may but leave them quietly. I beg your pardon for saying I would see you again, and rest your most humble and obedient servant,

Is. Newton

Mr Millington apparently had no idea what this was about, and Newton's two friends were concerned for his mental health rather than affronted. What were Newton's apparent concerns?

- Seemingly his conscience brooded on the idea that he might have been thought to be seeking preferment from the Catholic King James (a copy of *Principia* had been presented to the king, but nothing more).
- What the 'embroilment with women' was about we have no idea.
- He took Locke for a 'Hobbist' – Hobbes was a corpuscular materialist of the 'worst' Cartesian kind, but also in his *Leviathan* both struck at the heart of the meaning of morality and also carried notions of absolute monarchy which would have been anathema to Newton (and also, in fact, to Locke).

None of this makes much sense. What caused it is also uncertain. You can take your choice:

- **Emotional:** Some point to the effects of his recent break with Fatio[321] – though we cannot know how far this was symptom and how far cause. Newton may also have lost some manuscripts in a fire.
- **Overwork:** Newton had apparently been overworking, and his sleep pattern had been destroyed by his own account.

[321] e.g. White, op. cit. 247 'Within weeks [of his break with Fatio] his caged emotions overflowed into temporary insanity'

- **Poisoning:** Like many alchemists he worked with heavy metals and an analysis of a lock of hair has apparently shown contamination.[322] He seems, however, not to have shown usual symptoms of mercury or lead poisoning, and made an apparently full recovery.
- **Religion/Repression:** His secret Arianism (known to Locke) may have led to repression of conscience at being in posts (at Cambridge and Parliament) that required orthodoxy.[323]
- **'Normal' Breakdown:** Who knows? Hall, following Ditchburn, suggests that Newton 'suffered from a normal episode of depressive illness'
- **'Distemper' & Lack of Sleep:** Newton himself put the letters down (in a written apology to Locke and a message to Pepys through Millington) to a 'distemper' and lack of sleep.

He seems to have recovered by September or possibly sooner, though on the Continent dark tales circulated about a long-term loss of mind or even Newton's death.

As he recovered, Newton took up a problem not dealt with in the *Principia* – that of the Moon. The problem of lunar motions had not really advanced beyond Horrocks, who died before Newton, now aged 50, had been born. In approaching this Newton required detailed observations from the Astronomer Royal John Flamsteed with whom he had dealt before. Now, however, relationships between the two slowly deteriorated. Newton not only pestered for observations but – as Flamsteed delayed publishing his promised star catalogue – Newton (then President of the Royal Society) used his influence to force the publication of the partly completed catalogue in 1712, edited by Flamsteed's arch-rival Halley. Under Newton's character we will consider this again, but at this point can note that Newton never did arrive at a lunar theory which satisfied him.

The Mint Years (1696–1727)

In March 1696 Newton was appointed Warden of the Royal Mint – through the agency of Newton's friend the Chancellor of Exchequer Charles Montagu (later Lord Halifax).

---

322 See papers by L. W. Johnson et al. in *Notes and Records of the Royal Society* , 34, 1987, 1–32.

323 See e.g. Hall (1992), 245.

In his letter Montagu pointed out that it carried an income of £500–600 p.a. and 'has not too much bus'nesse to require more attendance than you may spare'. It was expected to be a sinecure – but Newton pursued it with great vigour. Probably living at first in the Warden's house, by November Newton was living in a pleasant house at 88, and then 87 Jermyn Street in London, until 1709.

Tower of London – Mint and Warden's House

In 1696–7 his 17-year-old niece Catherine Barton, daughter of his favourite sibling Hannah (whom he supported financially after the death of her husband) came to set up his household. Catherine lived as his housekeeper for 20 years until marrying in 1717 to John Conduitt – an ardent admirer of Newton nine years her junior. Catherine was very beautiful, witty and charming, and became the toast of the fashionable Kit Kat club of which, for example, Jonathan Swift was a member. In 1706 Newton's friend Charles Montagu (now Lord Halifax) made a very generous codicil in his will to benefit Catherine because of 'the great Love and Affection I have long had for her' and the 'Pleasure in her conversation'. Inevitably there was later speculation that they had been lovers or even secretly married, though there is no evidence for

1796-1700 Newton lived in No. 88 (on left, door shown). He then moved to No. 87 - now demolished though two plaques (extreme right) commemorate his stay

St James Church

this and Hall gives strong reason to doubt it. In any event it is very unlikely that Newton's Mint job was anything to do with Catherine offering Halifax sexual favours, as the dates would be wrong for this.

Newton's parish church was now St James, a lovely Wren church, and he seems to have been active as Trustee of the Golden Square Tabernacle, which was built as an overflow. His protégé, Samuel Clark, who sympathised with his Arian views, was rector from 1709–14.

Newton age 59

How did he do as a civil servant? Newton (previously identified by Westfall as some kind of reclusive introvert) is now hailed by that same biographer as a 'born administrator'. Certainly he *was* very able, conscientious, and very effective.

Newton was doing little new science, but was during this time slowly putting disciples into positions of power, acting as a mentor and patron. For example he financed the publication of Edward Lhuyd's 1699 *Lithophylacii britannici ichnographia.*

In December 1699 Master of the Mint, Thomas Neale, with whom Newton as Warden had long been in conflict, died. Newton got the post, adding some £1500 p.a. on average to his other salary of £500–600. At the start of 1701 Newton engaged William Whiston as his deputy as Professor in Cambridge, and at the end of the year resigned to allow Whiston formally the position of professor. Whiston later lost the post in 1710 for Arianism, and the indications are (although Whiston was careful to protect them) that there was a circle associated with Newton who held similar views.

In the early years of the 18th century Newton felt sufficient antipathy to Robert Hooke to absent himself from meetings. Although Hooke in his final years suffered ill health, the society met in his Gresham Chambers. Hooke died in March 1703, and Newton was elected as President later that same year. Again, as President, Newton was both an able administrator and a conscientious worker. Westfall notes that Newton failed to preside at only three meetings over the next 20 years of being President.

In 1704 his *Opticks* was published – much of the material researched much earlier. Newton presented it to the Royal Society from the chair – a reminder of its basic purpose. He may have waited for Hooke's death to proceed with publication – tired of constant wrangling over priority.

From 1709–10 he moved to Chelsea, and from 1710 to 1725 lived in 35 St Martin's Street near Leicester Square. The house was demolished in 1913 for a library, and Newton would be unlikely to recognise the site now (even with the help of a bust of his erected in commemoration!). He continued to work both in the Mint and through the Royal Society throughout this time – though obviously a man of his age was not markedly innovative.

Library and bust in Leicester Square

In 1713 a second edition on the *Principia* was published, and in 1726 the third edition – now in English. Westfall gives copious details of this period for anyone who wants them.

In his last two years of illness (1725–27) he lived in Kensington – in a house also since demolished. Newton died painfully of a bladder stone, and was buried at Westminster Abbey. An elaborate memorial was erected to him there.

Character

Basic Character

Biographical pictures of Isaac Newton have varied wildly. His first biographer was John Conduitt (1688–1737) his successor at the Mint.[324] Conduitt knew Newton personally, married Newton's niece Catherine who had been his housekeeper for twenty years, and also solicited memories from various of Newton's friends after his death. Conduitt, perhaps in slight embarrassment, makes the highly improbable suggestion that Newton's interest in history, chronology, divinity and chemistry were for 'amusement' when he tired of pursuing mathematical sciences! Of Newton's character, Conduitt suggests that his whole life was 'one continued series of labour, patience, charity, generosity, temperance, piety, goodness, and all other virtues, without a mixture of any vice whatsoever' This picture of a super-saint was largely repeated by 18th-century writers – with added (and seemingly sometimes invented) anecdotes about his absent-mindedness in dressing, or patience when a pet dog accidentally burned some key papers. In the 19th century, the work of Jean Baptists Biot[325] brought to light Newton's mental breakdown in the early 1690s, making the implausible suggestion that after this time he was incapable of scientific work and so wrote his material on chronology and theology! Francis Baily in his *Account of the Revd. John Flamsteed* (1835) reflected badly on Newton's treatment of Flamsteed (see below) – giving rise to a picture of high-handedness and autocracy. David Brewster (in works in 1831 and 1855) tried to some extent to reassert the hagiographical approach, but De Morgan in an 1840 biography sought a more balanced picture. He noted Newton's faults, but as Hall puts it:

> De Morgan also made the point that amidst the moral corruption of the age in which he lived, Newton the blameless, efficient Civil Servant and idol of the Royal Society stood out relatively as much as if he had really possessed the superhuman perfections attributed to him by biographers.[326]

---

324 See Rupert Hall *Isaac Newton Eighteenth Century Perspectives* (1999) ch. 1.

325 Biot *Biographie Universelle* (1821) in Hall (1999), 180 etc.

326 Hall (1999), 186.

Twentieth century views of Newton have been more diverse. One school began with John Maynard Keynes and the discovery in 1936 of a number of Newton's papers. Keynes, studying these, proclaimed:

> Newton was not the first of the age of reason. He was the last of the magicians, the last of the Babylonians and Sumerians, the last great mind which looked out on the visible and intellectual world with the same eyes as those who began to build our intellectual inheritance rather less than 10,000 years ago. Isaac Newton, a posthumous child born with no father on Christmas Day 1642, was the last wonder-child to whom the Magi could do sincere and appropriate homage.[327]

This view is essentially restated by Michael White in *Isaac Newton The Last Sorcerer* in 1997:

> Newton was above all a secretive man, a man coiled in upon himself, detached from the world, and for long periods of his life he was secluded from the everyday current of affairs. For much of his working life he experimented alone in his college rooms and in his laboratory nearby … living in self-imposed isolation at university, refusing to take holy orders. He subscribed to Arianism … when public awareness of such beliefs would have wrecked his career. And, most importantly, he was an alchemist.[328]

This passage makes White seem even more extreme than his biography really is, and there is obviously some truth in it as far as White rejects any view of Newton as a supposed Enlightenment rationalist. One cannot help feel, however, that it is overstated. Hall remarks that perhaps he and his wife (Mary Boas Hall) erred in once denying *any* alchemy to Newton but:

> To call Newton a magician because he applied quantitative chemical experimentation to the study of alchemical writings is going too far in the opposite direction.[329]

---

327 Keynes 'Newton the Man' in *Newton Centenary Celebrations* (1957), 27–34.

328 White op. cit. 2.

329 Hall (1992), 200.

The supposedly isolated and withdrawn figure, moreover, also represented Cambridge twice in Parliament, took public office as Master of the Royal Mint, and was an extremely able administrator in that capacity. These are odd activities for an obsessive recluse.

The old myth of a 'rational enlightenment man' can persist. In spite of Keynes, we find, for example, Dijksterhuis in 1950 (though he says nothing about Newton's *personality*) reasserting that 'with Isaac Newton an old period in the attitude of philosophers towards nature ended and a new one began'[330]

To Koestler in 1959, Newton was a 'muddled metaphysician' and a 'crank theologian like Kepler' who 'desperately tried to find a niche for God somewhere between the wheels of the mechanical clockwork'[331] Newton, thinks Koestler, is desperately trying to find room for God when he knows there really isn't any. This picture of a neurotic almost obsessive Newton was extended by Frank E. Manuel in his works between 1963–74. To Manuel, Newton's mother was a fixation in his life. Her loss in his childhood years led to Oedipal relationships accounting for all his complexities and secrecy of character, and this fixation probably 'crippled Newton sexually' so he remained a virgin (the Freudian presumption being that anyone who chooses celibacy must be sexually crippled). Manuel continues the sorcerer tradition in portraying Newton as 'making a last great attempt to keep science sacred and to reveal scientific rationality in what was once the purely sacral. The coupling of the two realms … is the syncretist fantasy of a scientific genius and a God-seeker.' How far one follows all this depends on one's view of Freud and his particular fantasies. Manuel's own fantasies stretch to suggesting that Newton took the Mint job so that he could express his suppressed Oedipal rage against his long-dead stepfather by hanging counterfeiters. Even Westfall is sceptical of Manuel's apparent inability to conceive that Newton could simply have been conscientiously doing a job he regarded as important to his country. In days when people were regularly hanged for trivial offences, Newton's pursuit of coin clippers and counterfeiters was not any kind of mark of particular savagery let alone repressed Oedipal anger.

---

[330] E. J. Dijksterhuis, *The Mechanisation of the World Picture* (1950, trans. 1961), 463.

[331] *The Sleepwalkers* (1959) Epilogue.

Westfall's great biography (1982) really dominated for some time. His picture of Newton at Cambridge is of a silent, conversationless, isolated, even alienated figure who seldom left Cambridge, and often worked steadily neglecting both meals and chapel.[332] Later on Newton turns out to be a 'born administrator' mysteriously transformed into a man of affairs competent in his work at the Mint. At the same time he also turns into an imperious autocratic despot in the Royal Society circles. All this may seem a bit metamorphic for some of us. A Rupert Hall was writing on Newton for decades, and his later works like the 1992 biography tended to temper the early alienation view using all recent resources. One of the problems is that because Newton did tend to have few close friends, and wrote comparatively few 'chatty' letters, because he was somewhat reserved and secretive, so little material survives to give a 'true picture' of him. Even Newton's connection with John Wickins[333] – with whom he shared a room for twenty years – was apparently eventually virtually severed by Newton with little subsequent correspondence (although he paid for Bibles to be distributed to the poor in the parish Wickins eventually took up). The scholarly tomes of both Westfall and Hall are inevitably littered with 'it must be supposed' and 'we may well imagine'.

So what was Newton 'really' like? How can one close to him (Humphrey Newton) say he saw him laugh only once, whilst another (William Stukeley) say 'I have often seen him laugh, and that upon moderate occasions'?[334] How can friends say he was 'affable, courteous, agreeable in company' whilst others portray him as cold, imperious, and unpleasant? This present account can only give one set of perspectives from perusal of the materials. Plainly Newton was a reserved, private person. He was abstemious in personal life, and devout in personal religion (although we do not know much about any personal religious observances). He did not generally form deep, demonstrative friendships, and was not garrulous. He was careful with money, but also generous to relatives and in other ways.[335] His

---

[332] Westfall, op.cit. 192.

[333] Is it a sad reflection on our times that we find it hard to conceive of a non-sexual closeness? In any event White, 245 pops in the suggestion that Newton 'may have had a physical relationship' with Wickins.

[334] See Westfall, 849–850.

[335] See Westfall, op. cit. e.g. 831, 854, 858 etc.

various studies were a passion, pursued at times with a great single-mindedness understood only by those who have themselves been seized with the excitement which an insight into the inner meaning of a particular reality can bring. Obviously anyone observing him at such times might find him 'absorbed' or even morose, but the testimonies of friends to affability surely cannot have been entire lies, even if they were exaggerated?

Gottfried Leibniz

That friends concealed his nervous breakdown is again hardly surprising, but whether or not it arose from heavy metal poisoning it would not necessarily indicate anything about his normal state of mind. His reluctance to publish and then have to defend his works in public arenas seems clear – though (as Hall has pointed out) is often exaggerated. He *did* allow Oldenburg to publish quite a lot in the *Philosophical Transactions,* and he *did* attend some meetings and correspond with many scientists. Though his motivation was pursuit of *truth*, when he thought he had perceived a particular truth he was both impatient with denials of it and jealous of his own priority in discovering it. At risk of over dramatising one might suspect that the *truths* he thought he discovered were like children to him. This, of course, led both to continued breakouts of controversy towards Hooke (who was not the most tactful of men), and towards Leibniz. It now seems almost certain that Leibniz discovered calculus independently, and whilst approaching a different set of problems (mathematical rather than mechanical). Newton, having once become convinced of Leibniz's guilty plagiarism, wallowed in self and patriotic indignation, and behaved badly. But this does not necessarily make him querulous and unpleasant in general. It would have perhaps taken a superman indeed who, when loaded with adulation, flatterers, and his nation's pride, would not succumb to such temptation when it concerned one of his key ideas.

Newton's personal life was 'moral'. Westfall makes dark hints that Newton must have connived at an illicit relationship between his niece and Lord Halifax (hypocrisy/deceit being the ultimate crime in the late-20th century as open licentiousness was in the mid-19th century!).[336] Hall is very sceptical of this.[337] Newton's 'morality' is not relevant to his astronomy, but the tendency today to equate 'standards' with priggishness, neuroses, or hypocrisy, will not help us understand what made the man 'tick'.

Newton as Controversialist

By standards of the time Newton was generally humane – emphasizing, for example, a moral duty to avoid cruelty to animals.[338] He was also conscientious and thorough in everything he undertook. What are we to make, in the light of this, of his various major controversies?

Robert Hooke (1635–1703) was curator of experiments at the Royal Society from its inception, and Gresham Professor of Geometry from 1665. Like Newton he believed in experimentation, and was adept at it. Unlike Newton, he was not a great mathematician. During the controversy Newton did act ungraciously at times (e.g. cutting out all reference to Hooke when the latter claimed he should have had more recognition in a work), but the general picture seems to be that Hooke was provoking. To Newton, Hooke seemed simply not to understand the basic difference between hypotheses and demonstrated relationship. The real point of his optics was not the corpuscular theory, but the demonstrated properties of light as composed of different colours. He patched it up a few times, but it was also irksome to have Hooke read out his letters to the Royal Society in order to point out his errors. That Newton's patience finally broke down is not all that surprising.

John Flamsteed (1646–1719) had an interest in astronomy from his youth, rather than in the business career his father intended. He graduated MA only in 1674, and in 1675 took both ordination and the post of Astronomer Royal, which was newly created. Unfortunately he had to furnish many of the instruments himself out of meagre means, and was given no

Flamsteed (1646-1719)

336 Westfall, op. cit. 595–600.

337 Hall (1992), 305.

338 Westfall, op. cit. ??

Greenwich Observatory: early view

assistants. He took private pupils and in 1684 he took the living of Burstow to supplement his income, which was only £100 p.a. (but unlike the Lucasian Professorship not supplemented by a Fellowship). His major work was on an accurate star catalogue, though he also furnished Newton with Moon data. Early contacts were cordial, but they degenerated. Newton formed a low opinion of Flamsteed's theoretical abilities, and just wanted the data. Flamsteed was suspicious of Newton revealing his data, and wanted to know what it was for. Newton eventually seized Flamsteed's observations and had a section of them edited and published in 1712 by Flamsteed's arch-rival Halley. Are we to see, in this, Newton as an 'imperious autocrat' willing to 'abuse his power'[339] which is the traditional view? Hall seems to see it otherwise:

> Newton started from acceptance of Flamsteed as the finest observer of the time, deferring to him on all astronomical matters until his patience broke. Flamsteed, a man with tremendous confidence in himself beneath a misleading diffidence of expression, had never accepted Newton as the finest natural philosopher of the time. The astronomer entered their relationship, therefore, with the feeling that he did not need Newton's lunar theory and that the world could well wait until his own (founded upon unimpugnable observations) was ready for it … Flamsteed resented being Newton's observational drudge but, since he could hardly refuse co-operation openly, he played a canny part, readily furnishing observations that Newton had not asked for, while passing over those that he wanted. This may well not have been conscious malice. That, in consequence, Flamsteed destroyed Newton's chances of working out a complete and fully satisfactory theory of the Moon in 1694 (as older writers claimed) is doubtful … But only a very close and

---

[339] Westfall (1992), 659–660 etc. Gale Christianson in *Isaac Newton* (1993) speaks of Newton's 'cunning', being 'rankled' that 'for the first time in his professional life someone else was in control', treating Flamsteed in a 'shabby way' etc.

> expert examination of the computations through which Newton went could decide the point. For Newton himself, however, it was clear that Flamsteed must be the scapegoat for his failure: but for his laziness, disobligingness, incompetence – wherever the weakness might lie – the lunar theory might, in Newton's eyes, have made in his hands the decisive advance that for ever eluded him.[340]

Newton probably saw himself as acting as a conscientious civil servant, ensuring public money well spent. Westfall's repeated claim, as though self evident, that the man who had made the observations would be best able to present them, is not at all self-evident. Flamsteed was undoubtedly pious, but could also be pompous and self-justifying (ironically Westfall, if anything, exaggerates this!) Newton could become over zealous – and no one is suggesting he was a perfect angel. But the controversy is not clear-cut, and anyone can read the more full accounts in Westfall and Hall to form their own informed view.

The controversy over priority in calculus with Leibniz, as we have noted above, had a patriotic dimension to it, and neither man was helped by zealous acolytes. The general view now is that Newton found it first, but that Leibniz's method was formed independently – though that was not how Newton saw it. His antipathy may also have been increased by Leibniz's general philosophy, which seemed to him to remove the need for God, other than to design and start things off.

Perhaps few men, given *a chance* to control events to ends they believe right will choose not to. Newton was not among them. But *was* he querulous and autocratic? Is, for example, Kitty Ferguson right to say that:

> It is surprising that he agreed to become head of the Royal Society. Unfortunately he used the position of power in an extremely unpleasant, autocratic manner, bringing misery to other fine scientists (including the elderly Flamsteed).[341]

Hall remarks:

---

340 Hall (1992), 277.

341 Kitty Ferguson *Measuring the Universe* (1999), 120. The 'elderly' Flamsteed was born four years after Newton and had probably attended his lectures, and died aged 73 eight years before him.

> Such recent scholars as Richard S. Westfall speak of Newton's paranoia, his wish to humiliate antagonists, and even his 'complete loss of control that is compatible with a [nervous] breakdown' . Such judgments ignore differences in styles of rhetoric between Newton's age and our own. A tendency to classify Newton as clinically ill might perhaps be diminished by greater familiarity with other examples of coarse and 'brutal' language in 17th century controversies.[342]

On the whole the present account takes the view that he was fairly thin skinned but far from unduly obnoxious by standards of his time. Ferguson's comment above is wrong both in the 'surprise' that he became President, and in the suggestion that he used his power badly. His time as its President was of tremendous benefit to the Society and its reputation at home and abroad. Newton encouraged young scientists and of course put those he approved of into positions of scientific power. As for his personality, on the one hand he could be affable though not gushing amongst friends but on the other hand he was not disposed to see every crank or enthusiast who sought an audience. He was so able as a thinker, mathematician, natural philosopher, and administrator that he could tire of trying to deal with those he felt failing in their duty or insights. A man like Newton is a rare historical phenomenon – we have little data to know whether others would behave more magnanimously in such a position. Much of the criticism levelled at him seems to be either cranky (putting it all down to complexes), unrealistic about human nature, or lacking a feel for what was expected at the time.

Beliefs

Scientific Methodology

Newton distinguished fundamentally between speculative 'hypotheses' and demonstrable fact. On light, for example, Newton regarded the properties he had observed experimentally as demonstrable. Light *was* composed of different coloured lights, separable but not transmutable. This was in contrast, for example, to a hypothesis that it consisted of just two transmutable colours. But it was also in contrast to hypotheses about whether light was corpuscular or wave-like.[343] In early work he veered to

---

[342] Hall (1992), 140.

[343] See Rupert Hall *All Was Light* (1993), 167 etc.

corpuscular views – but was concerned when Hooke took this to be central to his theory, and later speculated that waveforms could also explain the demonstrable properties. On gravity, Newton emphasized that the inverse square law was a demonstrable *mathematical* concept – it was a different question to ask what *caused* it (if anything) mechanically (if, indeed, God chose to use any secondary mechanism). 'I feign no hypotheses' he famously declaimed.[344]

Newton's actual methodology can take two forms. First there is the 'Method of Analysis and Synthesis'. In the tradition of Grosseteste, Roger Bacon, and Francis Bacon, experimentation produced results that through this method gave a special kind of generalisation. Like the bee (in the Francis Bacon quote above), induction involves *transforming* and *digesting* facts by a process of its own – it is more than simply enumerative generalisation. A prism experiment showing elongated beams can by induction lead to a conclusion about the nature of light. A rotating bucket (the water surface in which becomes concave) leads to recognition of absolute space. This is not simply generalisation to repetition of the effect, but a jump to explanation of the effect. Moreover, some generalisations are about idealised situations one can never meet in practice. 'Every body continues in a state of rest or uniform motion unless acted on by a force.' But there *are* no such bodies – since gravity acts always and everywhere! The law is an idealised abstraction, not a simple generalisation from repeated observations.

The other format for Newton's methodology was that of axioms. An axiomatic system is a set of propositions deductively related, in which the *axioms* are basic and not deducible from any other proposition. *Principia* is couched in these terms. There then have to be *rules of correspondence* linking the axiomatic system to observation. Having formulated these, the implications can be tested empirically.

To Newton, it is a mistake to try in Cartesian manner to deduce properties of the universe metaphysically. Truth about the universe is contingent not necessary, although Newton could still wonder at the ingenuity of a

---

[344] See also Alexander Koyre Newtonian Studies (1965) – though Koyre does tend to read his own philosophy of science into Newton!

Creator who designed a system which worked! Famously, he summed up four 'Rules of Reasoning in Philosophy':

1. We are to admit no more causes of natural things than such as are both true and sufficient to explain their appearances.
2. Therefore to the same natural effects we must, as far as possible, assign the same causes.
3. The qualities of bodies, which admit neither intensification nor remission of degrees, and which are found to belong to all bodies within the reach of our experiments, are to be esteemed the universal qualities of all bodies whatsoever.
4. In experimental philosophy we are to look upon propositions inferred by general induction from phenomena as accurately or very nearly true, notwithstanding any contrary hypotheses that may be imagined, till such time as other phenomena occur, by which they may either be made more accurate, or liable to exceptions.

The first two are firmly bedded in the 14th century British Franciscans – including Occam and Roger Bacon, the third is a burial of Aristotelian sub and superlunar cosmology, and the fourth an amazing admission that scientific knowledge is always tentative. It can, however, be doubted whether in his version of the hypothetico-deductive method Newton thought that the inference of basic propositions (or axioms) happened otherwise than by induction.

World View

Newton's world-view tried to *make sense* of the universe and human condition as a whole. Descartes had insisted that the only rationally acceptable cause of motion was a push or impact. Gravity, therefore, was caused by vortices of unseen particles, as also was magnetism. Newton (like More and Barrow) turned away from Cartesianism. Some writers see this as the influence of alchemy, but this is misleading. 'Alchemy' sometimes has a general meaning and sometimes the narrow meaning of seeking transmutation or base metal into gold or the search for elixirs of life. There was no clear cut division between alchemy and chemistry – and of the numerous books Newton possessed on the subjects the full spectrum is represented. Newton himself showed no interest in the goal of riches or extended lifespan by alchemy. Different ideas are, of course, connected. The ideas which Newton came to have, that there was a subtle spirit permeating matter and that a *force* could act at a distance, both had to come from *somewhere.* From a Cartesian viewpoint both were occult and obscurantist – only particles could cause motion. Today, locally acting fields may have replaced simple forces – but our physics looks a lot more Newtonian than Cartesian! Nor is it less mysterious. What would rationalist Cartesians have made of relativity and quantum theory?

Newton, then, had a world view which was *spiritual* rather than *mechanical.* The 'vulgar supposition that gravity is mechanical' was absurd. His own form of atomism (influenced by Gassendi not Descartes) not only operated in a vacuum (Newton's universe was largely vacuum, Descartes's was full!), but had porous matter as well. What filled the vacuums? God was literally omnipresent, and gravity was a direct effect of God acting. But because there was no matter present, light could travel fast, for example through water because it would not meet anything solid. Matter is mostly empty space.[345] The universe is almost matter-less, sustained by the will of God and regulated continually by him operating through immaterial forces. Newton objected strongly to an interpretation of his theory that ascribed some 'inherent' property of gravity to brute matter. 'Gravity' itself is a mathematical not a physical concept to Newton. The ultimate cause of all phenomena is God, not acting as some kind of absentee Deistic landlord, but constantly active all the time. Moreover, absolute space presupposes something beyond what we can actually observe which is relative space. To Newton there is a sense in which space is the sensorium of God. This should not be taken crudely for God is not corporeal. In the *General Scholium* added to the second edition of Principia, he wrote:

> [God] endured forever, and is everywhere present, And, by existing always and everywhere, he constitutes duration and space … He is omnipresent not *virtually* only but *substantially*; for virtue cannot exist without substance. In him are all things contained and moved yet neither affects the other… bodies find no resistance from the omnipresence of God … As a blind man has no idea of colour so have we no idea of the manner by which

---

[345] This was repeated by Priestly in 1777 (cf. Thackray in A.I.B. Cohen & R. S. Westfall *Newton)* and also in the 1930s in Arthur Eddington's works!

> the all-wise God perceives and understands all things. He is utterly void of all body and bodily figures … We have ideas of his attributes, but what the real substance of anything is we know not …

God was the great artificer – and in this Newton agreed perfectly with the great naturalist John Ray, and with Robert Boyle. Newton saw mathematics as the key to everything. In optics light was defined by refractive angles, in physics by mathematical laws, in chemistry by weights, in theology by biblical numerology. Newton never doubted that behind it all was one God, who had made reality mathematical. To say (as one writer does) that the universe was a kind of 'cryptogram' given by God could be to trivialise it, it is better to say that elegant and beautiful mathematics is the language chosen for creation. Actually, the notion that mathematics is a key to understanding physical reality is fairly fundamental to modern physics – and cosmologists still look for mathematical elegance!

Newton was extraordinarily well read in Biblical studies, early Hebrew and Christian studies etc.[346] – though few at the time knew this apart from some close friends like Locke, Clarke and Bentley. His manuscripts contain some one and a quarter million words on theology, church history and prophecy. Actually, until about 1670 there is no indication that Newton's theology was particularly unusual. He had assented to the Anglican 39 articles to graduate and take up his Fellowship – and as Westfall remarks everything we know about Newton tells us he would not have sworn falsely.[347] However, he faced the apparent need to be ordained in 1675 to retain his Cambridge posts, and seems to have begun intensive biblical and theological study in the 1670s. His conclusion was that Arianism rather than Trinitarianism had been New Testament Christianity. Arianism denies the trinity but is *not* the same as Unitarianism. To Newton, Christ was divine and did not even have a human soul. He was subject to the Father, yet was also a fit object for worship and adoration as the Lamb of God, the Redeemer of humankind etc. Westfall is, however, probably right in suggesting that whilst Newton's religion deeply affected his science, the specifically unorthodox parts of his theology were generally not significant to it – so we shall not pursue them here.

---

346 So, in some aspects, was the devout Boyle, who read fluent Hebrew and criticised existing translations.

347 Cohen & Westfall, op. cit. 361.

One final point is that Newton had the idea that originally humankind had possessed much better knowledge of a whole lot of phenomena – and that this had been lost or distorted. Perhaps this is one of the ideas of his that has least resonance today – but there was no *a priori* reason it should not have been true, and it was a common notion.

It is easy to find patronising modern works that begin something like: 'Isaac Newton was, of course, a true son of his age'. The usual implication is that he was a bit of a weirdo in some respects, believing in alchemic nonsense and what not, but we must make allowances for him from our superior 21st century understanding because of his benighted early century of birth. This approach seems highly questionable. The universe which modern physicists/cosmologists present to us is at least as mysterious as the world Newton looked at. Any attempt to formulate an understanding of all reality today would be likely to run into just as many problem issues as Newton faced. If modern 'science' has progressed by fragmenting into smaller and smaller research areas, and if the modern way of organising it means that there is little official space left to ask basic over-view questions, then whether or not this is 'progress' is itself a value judgement.

Newton's Scientific Works

This must be the barest outline – Newton's works are well covered in secondary literature and this Chapter is already long.

Opticks

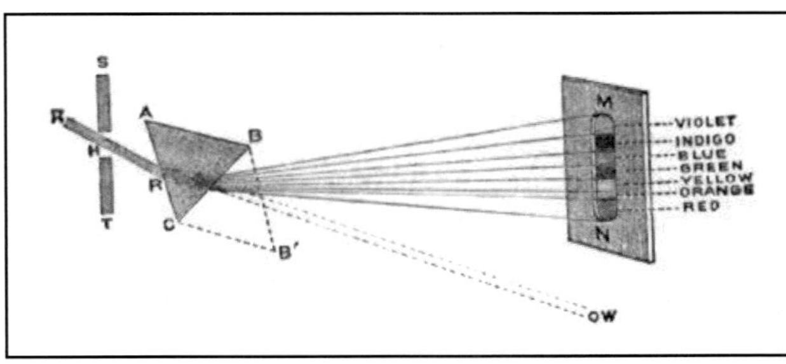

Newton noticed that when a spot of light was passed through a prism, the resulting spectrum was elongated. He gave seven colours, although these were just those we could distinguish and he was well aware that the banding was much finer. The point was, however, that different colours of light had been bent by the prism by different amounts. Newton then tried isolating colours of light from this first prism, and passing the isolated beams through a second prism. The result convinced him again that the light was not qualitatively *altered* by the prism, but that different colours were simply separated by being refracted different amounts. The difficulty of doing this experiment adequately meant that some other observers got different results! The optics are actually amongst Newton's first works in the 1660s – but he delayed full publication until 1704 by which time some of his ideas had developed. In 1669 he also began experiments on 'Newton's rings' – coloured rings in the film of air between a lens and a sheet of glass. To us these are interference fringes caused by the wave nature of light. To Newton, the wave theory was associated with hypothetical qualitative notions of light, and his theory was corpuscular. He later insisted, however, that his work on separation of light was purely empirical, and either a corpuscular or a wave theory was compatible with it. The *Opticks* claims it will not 'explain the properties of light by hypotheses, but propose and prove them by reason and experiments'. Newton was happy to hypothesise and speculate, but thought it separate from his demonstrated properties. Observers note a difference in tone between Newton's earlier lectures when a taut, enthusiastic young discoverer, and the *Opticks* as a retrospective more cautious work. The value of the work was, however, obvious. One corollary was that no refracting telescope (without the advent of achromatic lenses) could get the sharp focus one might expect in a reflecting telescope.

Fluxions

Newton's method of fluxions was an infinitesimal method that he developed not as an abstract branch of mathematics but because of an interest in dynamics. Newton had read Oughtred's *Clavis mathematicae* (1652), Wallis's *Arithmetica Infinitorum* (1656), and Descartes *Geometrica* – almost certainly the second (1659) edition published in Latin and containing material by Schooten. The English mathematicians also included Isaac Barrow, and James Gregory (1638–1675) with whom Newton had contact. All this background was the use of *analytic* geometry, the use (effectively) of algebra, which arose in the 18th century.

Newton was virtually self-taught in mathematics – his effort beginning with Descartes's work. By 1666 he had written what is now called his *Tract*. This uses the now familiar language ('let x and y represent the ordinate and abscissa of the curve') and assumes that an algebraic expression will represent a curve. A line is the path of a moving point and an area is generated by a moving line. The name 'fluxions' comes from the word to flow, and the whole concept was in these terms. Unlike the Leibniz form of calculus, Newton's relates variations to velocities (effectively dy/dt and dx/dt in modern terms). What the self-taught Newton did was to recognise that the method of drawing tangents to curves (fluxions=differentiation) was the opposite of finding areas under curves (inverse fluxions=integration). The now familiar differentiation of polynomials is first given in this tract. Newton's *De Analysi* appeared in 1669 (though not exactly published). The title repeats a central point, that this was *analytic* geometry.

Principia

The *Principia* had to bring together a number of concepts:

- **Inertia**: A concept originating from impetus theories, passing through Galileo's circular inertia, and Descartes's straight line inertia. In Newton it is that every body continues in a state of rest or linear motion unless acted on by a force.
- **Mass:** Defined in terms of quantities of matter. Newton himself saw these in atomistic terms. Mass is distinct from weight, yet weight and inertial mass are related.
- **Gravity**: An inverse square law of attraction – in Newton universal gravitation i.e. that every mass attracts every other, with a force proportional to their masses.
- **Universal Law:** As in Newton's 'Rules of Reasoning' that what operates on Earth operates everywhere including between planets.
- **Kepler's Laws**: These were taken as the basic facts of planetary motion, to be somehow explained by physics.
- **Calculus**: In order to put together gravity and inertia to obtain elliptical orbits, Newton has to use infinitesimal calculus.
- **Fluid Dynamics**: Quite a lot of the *Principia* is involved in showing that the fluid dynamics of swirling particles cannot account for the observed effects of gravity.

The staggering achievement of *Principia* is that it does all of this. Hall explains how in fact both *De Motu* and *Principia* actually developed the laws of Kepler from the inverse square law and inertia not by the algebraic method of fluxions (invented in 1671), but by an equivalent geometric method. *De Motu* struggled with dynamics that were not quite those of inertia. Parallelograms of forces were used to derive the paths – but these assumed that the force or inertia was similar in kind to gravity. By the *Principia,* inertia had reached its modern form, and the concept of mass (as requiring a force to accelerate) became matured.

One of the laws developed was that:

Force = Mass x Acceleration [p = ma]

There has been controversy[348] as to whether this law is a tautology or an empirical law abstracted from observation. For an empirical law each of the three would have to be separately measurable. The view taken here is that Newton, at least, thought it empirical because mass was in principle measured by quantity of matter.

Restoration

Newton's system was very complex, and his cosmology had elements that were cyclical. If material from stars could form other bodies, so stars in turn might be fuelled for example by comets. The motions of the planets, comets, and all the other bodies would need a constant regulation by God – whether or not he chose to use secondary means. This, in fact, was a source of controversy with Leibniz. To Leibniz this constant supervision of God bespoke a bodged job in the first place. What to Newton was part of a dynamic divine interaction, to Leibniz was a flawed system.

Chemistry

Newton's alchemy seems to have had not much impact – if for no other reason than that he did not publish it. But the idea of action at a distance could be applied as much within matter as between bodies. Having rejected Cartesian corpuscles, by the 1713 second edition of *Principia* Newton was more openly atomistic. His particles have extension, shape, solidity and inertia – but they also have attractive forces. Thackray claims that these assumptions, however, militated against any viable concept of a chemical

---

[348] See, for example Mary Hesse *Forces and Fields* (1961) and Dijksterhuis *The Mechanisation of the World Picture* (trans. 1961).

element.[349] What it did, however, was to open up the possibility of inter-atomic forces, and, indeed, valency. Quite new perspectives on matter were possible – though we cannot explore these here. As just one example the French Newtonian Pierre-Louis Moreau de Maupertuis (1698–1759) developed a hypothesis of genetics based on a form of pangenesis which depended upon duplication by attraction.[350] Though it led to no research program, the resemblance to aspects of modern DNA theory is remarkable.

Newton's Legacy[351]

Newton's science was above all mathematical, and the poor level of mathematical education in England made it hard for people to understand it. It made little impact in areas like botany or electrical experiments, and in Chemistry only in so far as weight/mass became crucial. On the Continent, the Low Countries (Holland etc.) were receptive to Newtonian empiricism. Germany, home of Leibniz, was less receptive. In France the authority of Descartes slowed down the acceptance of Newtonianism (though Newton was, of course, admired) – and when it eventually triumphed it was the mathematical *Principia* rather than the more empirical *Opticks* that appealed. In astronomy the work of Pierre Simon Laplace (1749–1827) universalised the work of Newton. It also reduced the system to one that was purely mechanical. Laplace's famous reported words when asked by Napoleon where God was in his scheme 'Sire, I have no need of that hypothesis' (whether mythical or not) showed a version of Newton he would not have liked, one in which Cartesian mechanism could be thought in one sense to have swallowed up Newtonian dynamics!

Questions

Here are some questions to ask as you think about Newton:

- How do the pre-Mint and post-Mint 'Newtons' relate to each other? Was he introspective, reclusive, and retiring, or was he a man of the world, able administrator and self-confident? Or was he all of these things?

---

349 Arnold Thackray *Atoms and Powers* (1970), 16.

350 See Hans Stubbe *History of Genetics* (1972) ch. 5.

351 The clearest analysis of this is Colin Russell's 'The Reception of Newtonianism in Europe' in Goodman and Russell *The Rise of Scientific Europe 1500–1800* (1991).

- Can his view of the distinction between hypotheses and demonstrated theory be maintained?
- Is the brilliant 'scientific' Newton of the Principia a different Newton from the 'Magician' bubbling with his alchemy and poring over cabalistic mumbo jumbo?
- How far was he an isolated genius, arising from nowhere, and how much *primus inter pares* of a set of people working on the same problems as he at the time, but slightly less effectively?

References

Primary Sources:

Obviously works like *Principia* and *Opticks* can be readily obtained. A selection from Newton's works is also in Bernard Cohen and Richard Westfall *Newton* (1995).

Secondary Sources:

In my view A. Rupert Hall's *Isaac Newton Adventurer in Thought* (1992[352]) is the best single secondary source, giving the most balanced view of Newton without undue detail. Hall's essays in *Newton, his Friends and his Foes* (1993) and *All Was Light* (1993) are also useful.

The most complete biography, giving endless detail of Newton's activities, purchases, etc. is Richard S. Westfall *Never At Rest* (1982). In places Westfall seems to me to understand Newton less, but it is an invaluable sourcebook.

Michael White's *Isaac Newton The Last Sorcerer* (1997) is nicely written and easier to read, but tends to view Newton through spectacles bemused by 'alchemy'.

John Fauvel et al. (eds.) *Let Newton be!* (1988) has a mixed bag, chapters on the *Principia* and Newton's religion seem useful.

There are other biographies (by E. N. Andrades (1979) and Peter Jones (1991)), which seem to have no particular advantages.

Gale E. Christenson's *Isaac Newton and the Scientific Revolution* (1996) is easy reading, though seems a bit naïve in places.

---

[352] This was reissued virtually unaltered by CUP in 1996.

For specialist areas there are Bruce Brackenridge (trans. Mary Ann Rossi): *The Key to Newton's Dynamics : The Kepler Problem and the Principia* (1995) Mary Hesse, *Forces and Fields* (1972), Westfalls' 'Hooke and the Law of Universal Gravitation' *British Journal of the History of Science* 1967, and Alexander Koyre's *Newtonian Studies* ch. 5 & Appendices (1962).

A more recent book is James Gleick (2003) *Isaac Newton.*

Some materials in the form of a kind of journal are in Joel Levy (2009) *Newton's Notebook: The Life, Times and Discoveries of Sir Isaac Newton*;

Thomas Levenson's *Newton and the Counterfeiter* (2009) is entertaining and also academic, but Philip Kerr's (2002) *Dark Matter: The Private Life of Sir Isaac Newton: A Novel* is lurid but uninformative.

William L. Harper's *Isaac Newton's Scientific Method: Turning data into Evidence about Gravity and Cosmology* (2011) argues that Newton's approach to science is really still part of science as we see it post-Einstein.

9. William Herschel

W. Herschel (1738-1822) age 46

'What! say your opposers, opticians think it no small matter if they sell a telescope which will magnify 60 or 100 times, and here comes one who pretends to have made some which will magnify above 6000 times! Is this credible? So that by what I can learn, the trade, as well as astronomers oppose your pretensions. Yet, my dear Sir, be not in the least dejected, your facts will be verified and the greater will be your glory.' Dr William Watson

'It cannot be denied that he was given to jumping to conclusions in a way which when it comes off, we describe as profound insight, and when it does not come off, we call wild-cat speculation.' Sir Arthur Eddington[353]

After the death of Flamsteed in 1720, Edmund Halley (1656–1742), was appointed as Astronomer Royal. Halley worked enthusiastically for the dissemination and exploration of Newtonian ideas. A 'proof' of the Earth's orbit would have been found had parallax been established – but this was impossible even with telescopes. What Halley did show (amongst other things) was that comets might sometimes return to our Solar System – in the case of Halley's Comet every 76 years. Their paths, of course, differed from those of the planets in that they were either parabolic or very eccentric ellipses. Halley also showed that all stars were not static but some moved discernibly (or had a 'proper motion' against the others: in 1718 he identified four bright stars that had moved since Ptolemy's day.

---

[353] Arthur Eddington 'Herschel's researches on the structure of the heavens' *Occasional Notes of the Royal Astronomical Society* 1 (1938–41), 30.

When Halley died in 1742, he was succeeded by James Bradley (1692–1762). In earlier work, to eliminate parallax Bradley picked a star (*γ Draconis*) near the zenith (i.e. straight overhead!). This had a slight motion in the *opposite* direction to that potentially from parallax, which Bradley supposed was due to the Earth's motion. He eventually realised that there would be a combined effect due to the velocity of light being finite and the nature of the Earth and its orbit. This effect, ***aberration***, was the *first* real *physical* evidence (in 1728) for Copernicanism. As Astronomer Royal he continued to work on unexplained aspects of the apparent motion of *γ Draconis*, finding a cycle of about 18 years caused by the Moon's effect on Earth rotation.

Bradley

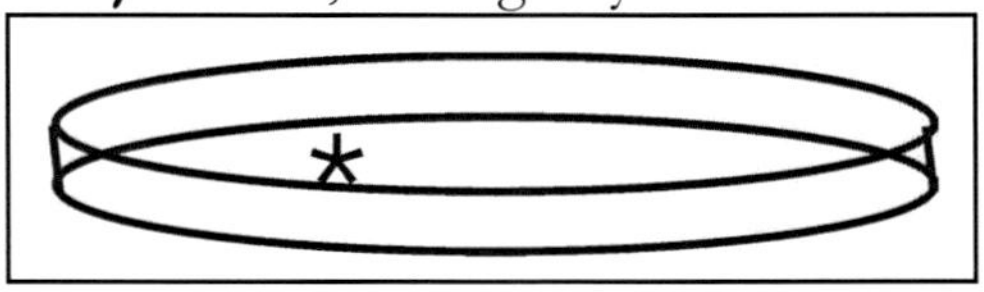

Nathaniel Bliss was Astronomer Royal for a couple of years after Bradley's death, followed by Reverend Nevil Maskelyne (1732–1811).

At this time 'magnitude' of stars referred to *apparent* brightness – all, of course, that could be observed from the Earth. The naked eye can see stars of the first magnitude down to about the sixth, which is some 100 times less bright.

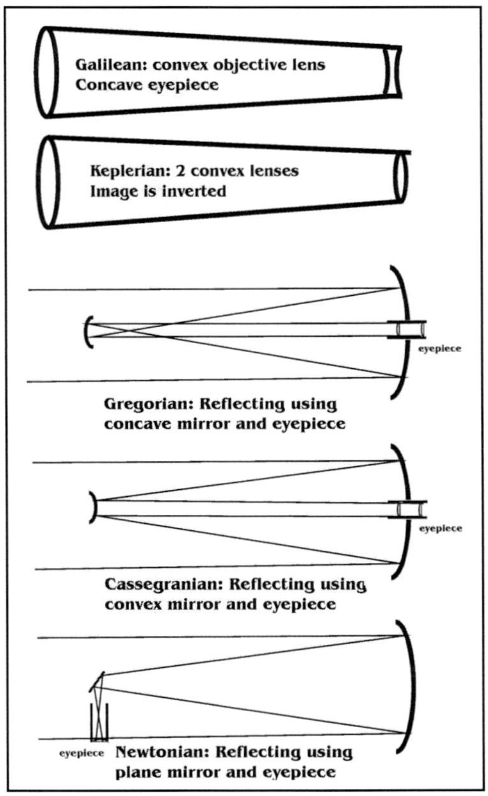

Since the time of Galileo it had been known that telescopes could resolve some fuzzy patches in the sky, and parts of the Milky Way, into star clusters. German philosopher Immanuel Kant (1724–1804)

(following what *he thought* was an idea in a work of Thomas Wright of Durham) suggested in 1755[354] that the Milky Way was in fact a set of stars in a disc-shaped pattern, with our Sun as one of these stars set in the body of the disc. This meant that when we look (as it were) along the length of the disc we see many more stars than if we look crossways – thus producing the great band of the Milky Way in the sky. Kant also suggested that nebulae could be other 'Milky Ways' – an idea later described as 'island universes'.

The telescope had opened up new vistas on the stars, and various designs were available. Refracting telescopes (Galilean or Keplerian) produced chromatic aberration since different colours refract different amounts. Reflecting telescopes of various types (as shown) avoided this. In 1733 the achromatic lens was invented, joining a plano-concave flint glass to a convex crown glass lens to correct the different refractions and avoid chromatic aberration in a refracting telescope. From 1758 an optician (Dolland) was producing high quality achromatic telescopes.

There are several obvious key points about such telescopes. First, in each case the objective lens or mirror brings distant objects to a focal point at its focal length. The eyepiece is placed so that its own focal point coincides with that of the objective lens/mirror, and the magnification achieved is the ratio of the two focal lengths. Secondly, the light from any distant object is collected across the whole of the area of the objective lens/mirror, so the larger it is the more light is collected. Since light diminishes according to the square of the distance, this means that a big lens/mirror enables us to see more distant objects, and to get a brighter image of closer ones. All this would be obvious to Herschel as he came to make his own telescopes.

Through the 18th century interest increased in stellar motion. In 1760, Tobias Mayer pointed out the obvious point[355] in a famous lecture that if our own Sun were moving towards a set of stars then these would appear to be moving apart. Mayer himself listed some 15 stars that had apparently moved, but was unable to detect any discernible pattern that would indicate our own Sun's movement.

---

[354] Immanuel Kant, *Universal Natural History and Theory of the Heavens* (1855 in German).

[355] A point also made in Ferguson's *Astronomy* (1857) – a book read by Herschel as we note later.

Herschel's Life

The Musician

Friedrich Wilhelm Herschel was born in Hanover on 15th November 1738. His mother Anna was a respectable Hausfrau of limited interests, his father an oboist in the Hanoverian Foot Guards who had an interest in subjects like astronomy. Caroline Herschel later wrote of their father:

> I remember his taking me, on a clear frosty night, into the street, to make me acquainted with several of the most beautiful constellations, after we had been gazing on a comet which was then visible. And I well remember with what delight he used to assist my brother William in his various contrivances in the pursuit of his philosophical studies, among which was a neatly turned four-inch globe, upon which the equator and the ecliptic were engraved by my Brother.[356]

Wilhelm attended the Garrison school that then provided a basic education, and in 1753 (still in mid-teens) he became an oboist and violinist in the Guards' band. In 1756 the Guards (and Wilhelm) came to England (with whom Hanover was then allied under George II), where he learned some English and made some contacts which turned out to be useful later. Returning to the Continent in 1757, the Hanoverian Guards were defeated by the French, and Hanover occupied. By November 1757 Wilhem (now calling himself William) was in England – this time to stay. This was just two years before the death in London of another German musician who made a career in England – George Frederich Handel.

> There is a story that Wilhelm was a deserter: 'that the Hanoverian King George III of England duly pardoned his desertion from the army some twenty five years previously. As a further mark of his favour the King proposed to confer on Herschel the title of his Majesty's own astronomer …'[357] This is

[356] Quoted in J. B. Sidgwick, *William Herschel, Explorer of the Heavens* (1963), 15.

[357] R. S. Ball, *Great Astronomers* (1906), 216.

over-romanticised, as his father did procure some kind of discharge paper for him[358], and he never had an official title.

Durham: Cathedral skyline

In England Herschel worked as a copyist and player, and in 1760 Lord Darlington appointed him as music instructor to the Durham Militia band. Herschel lived in Sunderland for two years, then resigned this post and became a fairly peripatetic music teacher and a composer. During this period Herschel retained a general thirst for knowledge, his spare time was taken up with study of Latin and French, and an interest in Harmonics leading to an interest in mathematics. From 1762 he was a concert manager in Leeds, in 1766 he moved to Halifax to be church organist, but then received an offer of the post of organist at the new Octagon Chapel in Bath.

Octagon Chapel (roof)
[Chapel is now used only as a store]

Beauford Square

Bath from about 1760–1790 was at its zenith as a popular winter resort for gentlefolk. From October to Easter Bath was *the* fashionable centre, to which London society repaired to 'take the waters' i.e. to drink the famous warm mineral spring waters, to seek partners, or just to eat, converse, and admire or be admired. The acknowledged architect of this cultural ascendancy 'Beau' (William) Nash, died in 1761. He had ensured that the immorality that was in Bath was *refined* and *genteel* immorality, and was generally humane. Herschel moved in

---

358 This is published in the introduction to Dreyer, *The Scientific Papers of Sir William Herschel*, (1912).

Pump House: today's post-1790 building outside and inside and 1760s orangerie

(joined later by the Bulmans with whom he had stayed in Leeds) to a (now unknown) house in Beauford Square, just round the corner from where Nash had lived and died in his mistress's house.

Herschel entered an increasingly busy lifestyle of public performance, training the Octagon Chapel choir, and teaching private pupils. For a musician/composer it was ideal. Bath society gathered at the Pump House (built next to the spring) to 'take the waters' and then (as the Pump House Trio do now) musicians played as the punters chatted idly. There are now CDs of some of William's own compositions, which sound competent though not outstanding. During the summer Bath emptied, and William was travelling again to teach and play elsewhere.

7 King Street (since renovated)

In April 1770 Herschel rented the house at 7 King Street (for thirty guineas a year). William was joined by various of his musician brothers at times during the next few years, but more significantly he visited Hanover in 1772, and 'rescued' his sister the diminutive Caroline (then 22). Caroline's mother and elder brother Jacob seem not to have shared their father's wider view of education, and had Caroline set for a life of respectable drudgery – from which William rescued her only by offering to pay a yearly sum for a servant to replace her!

Caroline

After a stormy passage and rough trip (during which, however, William had pointed out to her various constellations in the cold, clear night air), Caroline was thrown into the turmoil of English lessons, music lessons, and acting as companion, housekeeper and later collaborator to her idolised but frenetically busy brother William. Caroline's thirst for self-improvement revelled in the singing lessons and prospects of a musical career, but she apparently found the general empty-headedness of female conversation in fashionable Bath society rather trying. Newton's niece, Catherine Barton, a generation earlier, had used her undeniable talents in an approved 'feminine' manner by being charming, witty, and educated in a dilettante way. Caroline had neither the training nor inclination to excel in this fashion, later remarking wryly to the Astronomer Royal Nevil Maskelyne:

> I have too little knowledge of the roles of Society as to trust much to my acquitting myself so as to give hope of having made any favourable impressions.[359]

She also ironically but nicely encapsulated gender stereotypes of the age in a later letter to Maskelyne, expressing pleasure at a compliment he had paid her:

> You see, Sir, I do own myself to be vain because I would not wish to be singular, and was there ever a woman without vanity? – or a man either? – only with this difference, that among gentlemen the commodity is generally styled ambition.

Caroline's singing career as a soloist blossomed until the late '70s when household and astronomical duties slowly extinguished it.

The Astronomer

William's interests turned increasingly to astronomy. Caroline Herschel reported of her first winter months of 1772–3 that she was disappointed in the hope of seeing much of her brother who would retire exhausted to bed

James Ferguson
1710-76

> … with a bason (sic) of milk or glass of water, and Smith's Harmonics and *Opticks*, Ferguson's Astronomy, etc., and so went to sleep buried under his favourite authors; and

[359] Quoted in Sidgwick, op.cit. 43.

> his first thoughts on rising were how to obtain instruments for viewing those objects himself of which he had been reading.

Robert Smith's *A Compleat System of Opticks (*1738) included in book IV a history of telescopic discoveries, and noted that larger apertures would enable more to be seen. This idea was repeated in the popular book by James Ferguson *Astronomy explained upon Sir Isaac Newton's Principles* (1756 2nd ed. 1757, 5th ed. 1772). Ferguson also pointed out that apparent stellar movements could result from the movement of our own Sun, and suggested a plurality of worlds (i.e. that other worlds were probably inhabited). Both these ideas were adopted later by Herschel. Ferguson was a self-taught man, ingenious in making instruments, who had been admitted FRS in 1763. He gave subscribed lectures, and actually gave a series on astronomy (and other subjects) regularly. He gave such a series in Bath in 1767[360] though we don't know if Herschel attended these or any others.

From Spring 1773 Herschel began a series of purchases: a quadrant, a book of astronomy, an object glass of ten-feet focal length, eye glasses, tubes, etc. In September he hired a two-foot reflector telescope, and, deciding to try his own hand at making one, was able to buy up a local man's unwanted tools and workshop for the purpose. Herschel's approach to telescope making was always pragmatic rather than strictly mathematical – he ground the lenses and mirrors and tried them out, rather than relying on purely mathematical calculations.

In Summer 1774 the Herschels and Bulmans moved to a house 'near Walcot turnpike'. The house was inconveniently out of the centre, but had sheds for workshops and a field for observing. By 1774 a five-and-a-half-foot reflector telescope – initially Gregorian in design but later adapted to a Newtonian format – was mounted and in use. He moved to a seven-foot, then ten-foot, and by July 1776 was using a 20-foot telescope mounted in his back garden. He also invented the front-view or Herschelian construction of telescope used in his later instruments. This design involved tilting the main mirror slightly so that it reflected the converging cone of rays to an eyepiece mounted at the edge of the tube. The image was then viewed with one' back to the stars, but there was no need for an

---

[360]E. Henderson *Life of James Ferguson* (1870), 338.

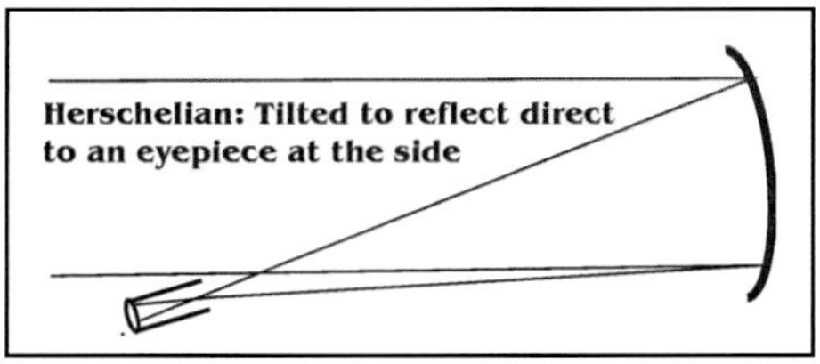

additional mirror that would inevitably cut down the light. The tilt produces a slight astigmatism, but at large focal lengths this was unimportant. Herschel mounted his eyepiece lenses in interchangeable wood tubes (using the same wood as for making oboes!) which meant that he could vary the magnification using the same telescope. He also invented mechanisms to mount his telescopes.

19 King Street: old print: house: garden (with workshop on left)

In 1777 the Herschels (by then without the Bulmans) moved back to central Bath, to 19 New King Street. This is now the beautifully restored Herschel Museum, with elegantly styled Georgian rooms. The basement was converted into a workshop, and the small rear garden used to make observations. The row of high chimneys along the terrace (for both

19 New King Street: Dining room Music room Cellar workshop

number 7 and number 19) makes one wonder at how ideal the conditions would be on cold nights to observe the stars!

Replica 7-foot Newtonian

Bath was a tourist town, and those on holiday made a circuit of any local attractions. It seems that the telescope-making hobbies of the esteemed Bath musician became known. In 1777 he was visited by the directors of England's only two official observatories (i.e. the Astronomer Royal Nevil Maskelyne and the Professor of Astronomy at Oxford Thomas Hornsby). He was also visited by Dr Blagden the President of the Royal Society. This seems, however, not to have led at this time to any integration into the scientific community. Herschel was, of course, an 'amateur' – but this was not essentially the issue. Science was not in general a 'career' in the modern sense, and many accredited scientists (like his later friend Alexander Aubert) were 'amateurs'. The key was integration into the scientific community. This generally began with membership of and activity in a local scientific society, and then could go on to involvement in the Royal Society itself. Herschel was autodidactic and solitary in his interest; he did not even look for a Bath scientific group.

In 1778 Herschel made a mirror with seven-foot focal length, which became part of a favourite instrument as a Newtonian telescope. A beautifully made replica (with the mechanisms) is on display at the Herschel Museum today.

In 1779 he moved again, this time to 5 River Street. This was almost within sight of the highly fashionable Royal Crescent, and a stone's throw from The Circus – but it was a house with no garden. In August he began a second systematic sweep of the stars, and was also regularly observing the Moon.

His 20-foot telescope was set up in a hired garden, but his favourite seven-foot one was often used on the pavement in front of his house. This must have been a fairly busy street, with carriages, sedans, and pedestrians passing by. [The locations of Herschel's houses in Bath are shown on an appended map of Georgian Bath]. Observing the Moon one night in December 1779, he made the acquaintance of a passer-by who turned out to be Dr William Watson, an FRS who introduced Herschel to the Bath Literary and Philosophical Society. Over the next year or so Herschel poured papers into the Society, who forwarded the best material to the Royal Society. Unfortunately Herschel had never learned his science under any accomplished master, and neither (unlike, for example, Horrocks) had he read widely in scientific literature. As he now entered as an already accomplished observer, and was in any case not one to learn from others, he never really learned disciplined scientific writing. His works mix together sober observation, assumption, and wild speculations about inhabitants on celestial bodies.

5 River Street today – with a rare view of an 'un-parked by' pavement!

Early in 1781 Herschel moved back to 19 New King Street. He recorded in his 1781 log an observation in the Gemini constellation:

> Tuesday March 13
>
> ---
>
> in the quartile near ζ Tauri the lowest of two is a curious either Nebulous star or perhaps a Comet.

Actually it turned out later that various astronomers (going back to Flamsteed in 1690) had seen this object, but taken it for a star. Herschel looked at it again four days later on 17th March and noted that it had already moved, so was not a star but probably a comet. On 19th March he concluded:

William Watson

From these observations it appears that the Comet moves according to the order of the signs, or direct; that its orbit declines but very little from the ecliptic, and that it moves at present at the rate of about 2 ¼ seconds per hour.

His friend Dr Watson suggested Herschel write to his father Sir William Watson in London, and on the 22nd March, through this means, his letter was read to the Royal Society. It reported that the body 'was much larger in diameter but less luminous' than any comet, and that 'its body seemed very well defined having neither beard nor tail'.[361] All the known planets more or less followed the ecliptic as this new object did, the object differed in shape and luminosity from comets – but still Herschel did not deduce it was a planet!

Watson also communicated to Maskelyne and Hornsby who both looked for the new object. Hornsby at Oxford needed a second fix from Herschel before he could even find it. Maskelyne, at Greenwich, was observing objects in that part of the sky in the first few days of April, and on April 4th wrote back to Watson:

> I was able last night to detect a motion in one of them, which … convinces me that it is a comet or a new planet, but very different from any comet I ever read any description of or saw …

This is interesting, as little seems to be made of Maskelyne for making this quite revolutionary suggestion: he was suggesting that this might actually be a seventh major planet, the first new planet discovered in human history. That he could even think it seems at least as surprising as the fact that an 'amateur' could first see its un-star-like nature using a homemade telescope. On 23rd April, moreover, Maskelyne wrote to Herschel directly:

361 The best source on these details is Simon Schaffer 'Uranus and the Establishment of Herschel's Astronomy', *Journal of History of Astronomy* (1981), 111–26.

> I am to acknowledge my obligation to you for the communication of your discovery of the present comet or planet, I don't know which to call it. It is as likely to be a regular planet moving in an orbit nearly circular round the Sun as a comet moving in a very eccentric orbit.

Herschel's paper, however, read on April 26th to the Royal Society, was simply entitled 'Account of a Comet' and this was its title when it was later published in the *Philosophical transactions.* He realised his own shortcomings in plotting the orbit of the 'comet' but in March and April thought the diameter of it was 'certainly increased, from which we may conclude that the Comet approaches to us' (actually we now know it was receding at the time). He thought that it was nearer than Mars, whereas, as Hornsby pointed out to him in May, most astronomers placed it outside Saturn. [By October 1781 the Russian Anders Johann Lexell (1740–1784) had computed an orbit about 16 Earth orbits away, and ultimately 18.93 (the modern figure is 19.36)]. From 16th April Herschel also thought he could detect a diurnal (daily) parallax – though no such could have been seen. In other words, though Herschel should be credited for spotting that it was not star-like, his observational powers were by no means perfect. Fortunately for him, the references to the diurnal parallax were omitted from the paper as published in the *Philosophical Transactions.* That paper, called 'Account of a Comet', did, however, include a detailed description of his micrometer. This was important in explaining to astronomers how he was approaching the observations. Herschel's emphasis on the appearance of celestial objects rather than just position was novel, and in fairness to astronomers like Hornsby and Maskelyne, Herschel's evident errors in some of his claimed observations left doubts about his general methodology.

In May Herschel visited London and met Joseph Banks who became a friend, and next month Herschel was elected a Fellow of the Royal Society.

Herschel was now involved both in systematic observation and in serious telescope making – and in late summer 1781 made abortive attempts to cast a three-foot diameter mirror with 30-foot focal length. The first attempt failed, and the second led to molten metal pouring across the flagged floor of Herschel's basement, at which the flags cracked and some blew up so that (as Caroline put it) 'both my brothers, and the caster and his men, were obliged to run out at opposite doors for the stone flagging (which ought to have been taken up) flew about in all directions as high as the ceiling …'

Meanwhile, his 'comet' was tracked over the months after his discovery. Various astronomers tried to find a parabolic path for it, accepting Herschel's identification of it as a comet although it did not look much like one. Anders Lexell, however, concluded that it looked more like a planet, and by summer 1781 computed an approximate planetary orbit of a circle. From this time its planetary nature was widely accepted. Various names were suggested for it. In France, the suggestion by Joseph de Lalande (1732–1807) to call it 'Herschel' was popular, and was still being canvassed by Arago in 1846! By the end of 1782 Herschel himself wanted to call it *Georgiun Sidum* after George III, and this became common British usage. Johann Bode (1747–1826), who edited the *Berlin Astronomical Yearbook*, advocated 'Uranus', which was the most common European name for it. All three names were in use over the next 60 years, though the name 'Uranus' eventually triumphed.

So who discovered Uranus? An interesting question here is what does this really mean. As we have described:

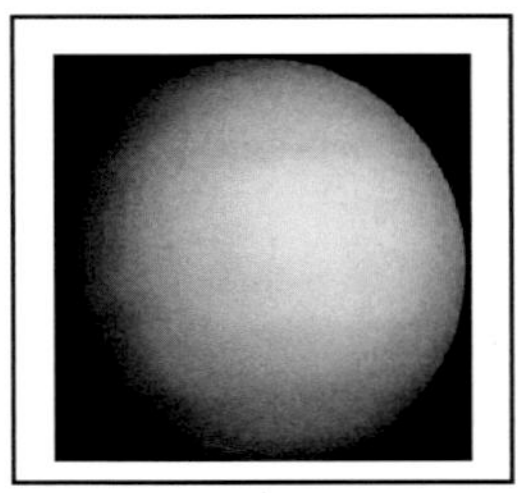

- John Flamsteed had already noted the object on 23rd December 1690 but classified it as a star. Tobias Mayer (1723–62) had likewise misclassified it in 1756.
- Herschel noted in March 1781 that it was not star-like, and noted it was roughly on the plane of the ecliptic, but identified it as a comet.
- Nevil Maskelyne on April 4th/23rd 1781 seems to have been the first to have suggested it might actually be a new planet 'as likely as' a comet, and returned to this view after a time of hesitation.
- Ander Lexell (by late summer 1781) first calculated its orbit as an approximate circle – after which its planetary nature was widely accepted.
- Pierre Simon de Laplace (1749–1827) and Pierre Mechain (1744–1804) published an elliptical orbit in 1783.

So if Herschel was not to the first to *see* it, not the first to *suggest* it might be a planet, and not the one to *demonstrate* that it was *in fact* a planet – in what sense then did he 'discover' the planet Uranus?

On 6th December 1781 his paper *On the Parallax of the Fixed Stars* was read to the Royal Society, and in January 1782 his first *Catalogue of Double Stars* was presented. Herschel's interest in double stars was in particular hope that where a bright star doubled with a faint star the latter might be further away, and, with them so close, parallax might finally be found which would enable star distances to be gauged. This did not happen in his lifetime, but Herschel was moving the primary emphasis away from *positional* astronomy, to seeking three-dimensional astronomy, qualities and development.

The magnifications Herschel was claiming in these papers were far in excess of anyone else at the time, and many doubted him. On 18th December 1781, Dr Watson wrote to him about the reception of his stellar parallax paper by the Royal Society noting the scepticism of the experts. A week later he wrote:

> I have now had a better opportunity of knowing the opinions of astronomers and opticians than I had before and I will now give you the result of my enquiries. Those who are not very much conversant in these studies have in general united their suffrages in your favour. I wish I could say the same with respect to those who are well acquainted with these matters. Of these, I am sorry to say, few are inclined to give you credit for your assertions. Some, however, I have found among these, who from what you have already done and from their personal knowledge are much inclined in your favour. What! say your opposers, opticians think it no small matter if they sell a telescope which will magnify 60 or 100 times, and here comes one who pretends to have made some which will magnify above 6000 times! Is this credible? So that by what I can learn, the trade, as well as astronomers oppose your pretensions. Yet, my dear Sir, be not in the least dejected, your facts will be verified and the greater will be your glory.

Astronomers were not sure whether Herschel was a genius or 'fit for Bedlam'! Watson went on to tell Herschel that astronomers generally were unable to see the stars without aberration, and struggled to see Herschel's 'comet' at all well defined. This was an eye-opener to Herschel, who had previously imagined that other astronomers could see as well as he could with their instruments:

> I am surprised that neither Mr Aubert nor Dr Maskelyne have seen the stars round and well defined. I do not say without the least aberration, for so far I will not go even with Jupiter or Saturn; but that I have a thousand and a thousand times seen them (with 460) as well defined as I ever saw Jupiter (with 227) I am very well convinced of to myself. And I believe till these gentlemen can see them so, they will not be able to find that ζ Cancri, *h* Draconis etc. are double … for the aberration of one of the stars will efface the other star, or make them appear as one … Seeing is in some respect an art which must be learnt. To make a person see with such a power is nearly the same as if I were asked to make him play one of Handel's fugues upon the organ. Many a night have I been practising to see, and it would be strange if one did not acquire a certain dexterity by such constant practice.

Herschel's discovery of the new planet was not just a matter of luck. Firstly, he was making systematic sweeps of the skies – and would have been bound to direct his telescope at it at sometime or another. Secondly, his telescopes really were better than others then in use. Thirdly, he was well aware that 'seeing' is not a passive action, but really involves a trained art. All this meant that when he did 'happen to' train his telescope on the object, he recognised by its appearance that it was not a star. We have, of course, noted that in some other respects what he 'saw' (increasing diameter and parallax) was not there. We also noted that he thought it was a comet, not an event of great interest.

Although still dubious of the exact powers of his instruments, Herschel's friends were pushing his interests at court. These friends included Maskelyne, Alexander Aubert (whose fame as an observer rested on his fine privately owned observatory), Joseph Banks, and William Watson. In May 1782 Herschel had a first Royal audience, and whilst in London said:

Greenwich Observatory

> These last two nights I have been stargazing at Greenwich with Dr Maskelyne and Mr Aubert. We have compared our telescopes together and mine was found very superior to any in the Royal Observatory. Double stars which they could not see with their instruments I had the pleasure to show them very plainly, and my mechanism is so much approved of that Dr Maskelyne has already ordered a model to be taken from mine and a stand made by it to his reflector. He is, however, now so much out of love with his instrument that he begins to doubt whether it *deserves* a new stand.

The observatory's four-foot achromatic refractor and six-foot reflector could not compete with Herschel's home-made seven-foot reflector. One pictures the Astronomer Royal (who to his credit was never anything but supportive of Herschel) facing the stunning fact that an instrument home-made by a professional musician was far better than the best money could buy. How human is the picture of Maskelyne 'out of love' with an instrument that had previously presumably been a regular night-time companion!

The outcome of all this was, however, that Herschel's fellow Hanoverian, George III, offered him an annual income of £200 (two-thirds that of the Astronomer Royal himself!) to move to Windsor and set up an observatory there, conditional only on him attending on the Royal family when they might choose to make some observations. Hershel therefore moved post haste from Bath to Datchet. The income was half that he made as a musician in Bath, but he was able to supplement the income by making telescopes. The king would also give him two grants of £2000 each towards the making of a 40-foot telescope, and £50 per annum to Caroline recognised as his assistant.

20-foot focal length telescope

The Royal Patronage Years

In his first year at Datchet Herschel published his paper *On the proper motion of the Sun.* He had concluded from the way that stars apparently moved that the Sun itself was moving towards the star λ

Hercules. On 4th May 1783 Herschel (and some friends) thought he had observed two 'volcanoes' erupt on the dark side of the Moon – identifying some craters when it was later illuminated as the likely source (our present knowledge assures us Herschel was mistaken in this). The third review of the entire sky was completed in January 1784, and a Second *Catalogue of Double Stars* presented to the Royal Society in December. In October 1783 he mounted his new 20-foot-focal-length telescope, which had an 18.7-inch aperture and was on the Herschelian design rather than the Newtonian. This was the instrument used for all the nebulae sweeps made from 1783–1802.

In 1784 came Herschel's first paper on 'The Construction of the Heavens'.

The paper misleadingly claimed that 'as soon as' he had Charles Messier's 1780 catalogue of nebulae and star clusters: 'I applied my former 20-feet reflector … and saw … that most of its nebulae … were resolved into stars.' Actually, he did not even begin looking at nebulae until he got to Windsor in August 1782. Over the period 1782–1783 both William and Caroline were finding nebulae, and it was then that his interest in resolving them arose.[362]

The paper reports his success in resolving many nebulae into clusters of distinct stars (including some which actually he couldn't have done!). It also gave his shape for the Milky Way i.e. our own galaxy. A second paper in 1785 differentiated types of nebulae.

Herschel's house at Datchet was really in too damp a spot both for observation and for his own health, so in June 1785 he moved to 'Clay Hall' in Old Windsor, and then in April 1786 he moved for the last time to Slough. This house (demolished early in the 1960s) was a small 18th century, red-brick house with a good view of Windsor Castle in an acre of garden.

Herschel House, mid 20th century

[362] See Michael Hoskin, 'William Herschel's Early investigations of Nebulaer: A Reassessment' *Journal of the History of astronomy* 1979, 165–176.

Here it was that Herschel's very expensive 40-foot telescope with a four-foot mirror slowly took shape.

Herschel House Slough - back

Herschel House Slough - front

Caroline Herschel had been conducting sweeps since 1782 for comets and any other unusual sights, and from 1783 was using a Newtonian two-foot reflector with an aperture of 4.2 inches. It had a magnifying power of only 24, but had a very clear image. At the end of 1783 Caroline recorded that her own sweeps were impeded by having to act as William's scribe for his own nebulae observations with the new 20-foot instrument.[363] In Slough, Caroline converted the stable buildings as a private apartment and made her own cometary sweeps using the small Newtonian reflector whenever William did not require her or was away. She found a comet on 1st August 1786 (whilst William was in Germany), another in December 1788 and two more in 1790. From 1791 William gave her a sweeper with focal length of five and a quarter feet, aperture of 9.2 inches and magnified (according to Maskelyne) some 25 to 30 times. She added further comets in 1791, 1793, 1795, and 1797 – though seemed to lose interest after about 1800.

40-foot telescope

The 40-foot telescope finally reached commission in 1788, though William continued polishing it until 1796 when he finally concluded the parabolic shape was optimal. The telescope became a kind of tourist attraction, though it was unwieldy and became

---

363 For all this see Michael Hoskin & Brian Warner 'Caroline Herschel's Comet Sweeps' *Journal of History of Astronomy* (1981), 27–34.

tarnished easily because Herschel had needed to add copper to the metal for strength. It was increasingly neglected. This may also partly have been that within a couple of years of setting it up Herschel had concluded that some nebulae could not be resolved – even with this huge telescope.

Herschel in 1794

William in old age

In 1788 Herschel, then aged fifty, married a wealthy local widow Mary Pitt. For Caroline this was traumatic, as she was no longer mistress of the house and eventually she moved to lodgings.[364] Mary was an intelligent, cultivated, kind-hearted and charming woman, and fortunately Caroline was soon charmed and won over, if not without regret at the change. To William and Mary a son, John William Herschel, was born in 1792, to whom Caroline was devoted.

Caroline in old age

In Westminster Abbey

Herschel continued his work at Slough virtually until his death in 1822. During all this time his particular interest was in the *construction* of the heavens. He was unable ever to obtain a good estimate of the distances of stars (which was achieved only after his death). His instrumentation was not, in any case, designed to give accurate positional measurements that would be needed to use a method of triangulation. The idea of using double stars did not work. Nevertheless, in some ways Herschel invented the science of astrophysics – at least in principle. He was buried in St Lawrence Church in Slough. Both

364 The dress Caroline wore to the wedding shows a slender lady of only about five feet tall – not an ideal physique for moving heavy telescopes.

William and his son John Herschel were later commemorated in a memorial in the floor of Westminster Abbey.

Caroline went back to Hanover after William's death, where she remained to receive respect and honour from the scientific fraternity until her own death in 1848. In 1828 she received the gold medal of the Royal Astronomical Society for her work in manuscript reduction of William's work on nebulae.

John Herschel
1792-1871

John Herschel went to Cambridge University and had the education his father had lacked. He used his father's 20-foot telescope for many of his own observations, and especially extended the work to the southern hemisphere. He became a leading astronomer, and one of the most respected scientists in England – also writing work on the philosophy and practice of science. His initially slighting reference to the apparently 'higgledy piggledy' nature of the science in Darwin's *Origin of Species* (1859) was viewed with dismay by its author, such was the respect John Herschel commanded!

Character

William Herschel is pictured as a kindly man, amiable and obviously talented musically. He was polite to visitors, though was ferociously single-minded in his pursuit of astronomy. He rescued his sister Caroline from drudgery, but then sacrificed her musical career almost without noticing it. He was willing to sit out in freezing weather, all night, night after night, to make his observations – and drove himself harder than anyone else around him. In his science, he was never troubled by inconvenient facts, and had a knack of ignoring them if necessary. He was confident of his own ability and discoveries, and often too slow to find out or take note of what others were doing in his field. At the same time, he seems not to have aroused the kinds of animosity that manifest pride usually causes, and came to be regarded as perhaps a bit singular, but worthy of great scientific respect. Religious beliefs seem not to have particularly affected his science (as far as I can discern), and his belief in the plurality of worlds etc. was perfectly religiously orthodox. His marriage was very happy, and his son devoted to his father's memory.

Herschel's Scientific Works

We will look at these thematically rather than chronologically. The best material on the subject comes in Hoskin's works, to which reference may be made.[365] In actual fact, the discovery of Uranus, although not exactly 'accidental', was incidental to Herschel's main interests. Herschel wanted to add two basic elements to astronomy: three-dimensionality and stellar evolution. In Herschel's day, there were too many technical difficulties for either to be done successfully. Without hefty dollops of assumption, one needed patience to wait until much more data and/or theoretical physics became available. William Herschel was in middle age when he began serious astronomy – and was in no mood to wait!

Scientific Methodology

His own approach to scientific method was stated in his paper of February 3rd 1785:

> … let me mention that, if we would hope to make any progress in an investigation of this delicate nature, we ought to avoid two opposite extremes, of which I can hardly say which is the most dangerous. If we indulge a fanciful imagination and build worlds of our own, we must not wonder at our going wide from the path of truth and nature; but these will vanish like the Cartesian vortices, that soon gave way when better theories were offered. On the other hand, if we add observation to observation, without attempting to draw not only certain conclusions, but also conjectural views from them, we offend against the very end for which only observations ought to be made. I will endeavour to keep a proper medium; but if I should deviate from that, I could wish not to fall into the latter error.

Herschel tried to keep a distinction between the 'certain views' which could be derived from pure empiricism, and the right kind of 'conjectural views' which went well beyond actual observation but not into imaginary phenomena like Cartesian vortices. That he goes on to quote Newton's

---

365 Michael Hoskins (1963) *William Herschel and the construction of the heavens;* (1979) 'William Herschel's Early investigations of Nebulae: A Reassessment' *Journal of the History of Astronomy* x 165–176; (1980), 'Herschel's Determination of the Solar Apex' *Journal of the History of Astronomy* xi 153–163.

Principia in the paper is no surprise – possibly he thinks that what he is doing here is following Newton. His friend Watson was known to have remarked that Newton's famous dictum *Hypotheis non fingo* did not mean that he would not hypothesise but that he would not *feign* any hypotheses. What Herschel then goes on to do in the paper is to begin with a theoretical model of a great number of stars acting under gravity, and to 'deduce' from the model what one might expect. We will look at the actual 'deductions' below.

Stellar Distances

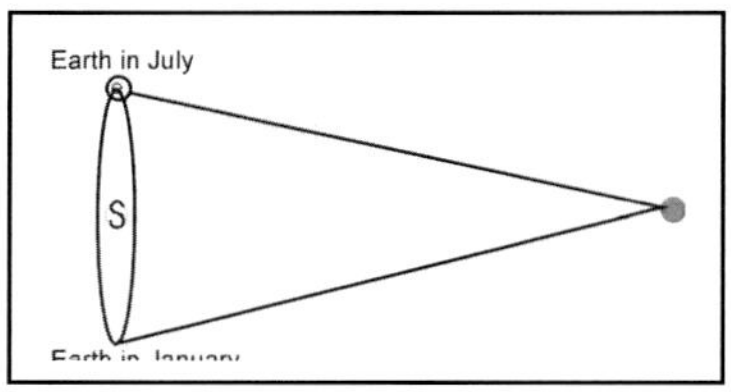

Instruments were not accurate enough to measure stellar distances by methods of triangulation (this only happened at all after Herschel's death). There was, therefore, no way to determine either absolute or relative distances of stars. Herschel tried several ways around this.

Firstly, he simply assumed (in his 1781 paper):

> (1) Let the stars be supposed, one with another, to be about the size of the Sun.
>
> (2) Let the difference of their apparent magnitudes be owing to their different distances …

Maskelyne and the Royal Society committee were unhappy with these assumptions which were unwarranted and probably wrong, and drew his attention to a 1767 paper by the Reverend John Mitchell which made similar speculations (arriving at a distance for Sirius of 20 million miles which is about 40% of the modern accepted value). Mitchell also computed odds against uniform distribution – concluding that the stars were indeed in clusters. Eventually, of course, Herschel's own model of the 'construction of the heavens' assumed star cluster systems – but by then his focus had shifted. Mitchell, however, suggested odds showing that most double stars were probably revolving binary systems. This was a problem to Herschel, whose hopes to get an actual distance for stars were pinned on double stars. If a faint star in a double was far, and a bright star was near, then one might hope to see parallax over the year of the Earth's orbit in space. In practice Herschel was never able to get a good figure for this – and in the end it turned out that Mitchell's work was right – most of them *were* revolving binary systems, and any alterations of position were according to their own periodicity and not the Earth's year.

The Solar Movement

The idea of determining solar motion from apparent stellar movement was in Ferguson's book (as mentioned above) and Herschel raised it in connection with double stars in his 1781 paper. Herschel had one list of stars that had moved from Lallande (derived from Tobias Mayer), and another from Maskelyne.[366] His paper on the Sun's motion was read on 6th March 1783. He speculated that assuming Newtonian gravitation to operate then surely stars would in general move, and ours no less than others. Herschel suggested a motion towards λ Herculis, but then hesitated as some of the most pronounced motions did not fit this well. Hoskin has carefully examined all the data and concludes:

> A solar apex in the region of Hercules and Corona Borealis could reasonably be inferred from the Mayer data; but the extraordinary closeness of Herschel's apex to the best modern values owed much to his illicit use of the listed change of 3″ in the R.A. of Aldebaran.[367]

Herschel was lucky! In company with many epoch making scientists he rigged his evidence towards a good guess! In a later 1805 paper Herschel recalculated the motion, based on a selected six stars from 36 given by a table of Maskelyne, and again in 1806 using more stars from the same table. Again, Hoskins points out the large amount of assumption needed to obtain an actual figure for our Sun's movement (still towards λ Hercules). The only way to disentangle the Sun's motion from motions of stars themselves was to assume figures that would reduce all the motions to become nearer to each other – though there was no particular theoretical reason to suppose that this would be true.

---

366 See Hoskin (1980), 155.

367 Hoskins (1980), 162.

The Shape of the Milky Way

As we noted, ideas of Wright and Kant (and others) suggested that the Milky Way was in fact our own galaxy, which was not uniform in all directions from where we sit. Herschel wanted to begin to quantify this, and so made three assumptions:

1. that (adopting a model of Halley's) stars are distributed more or less uniformly throughout the space of our galaxy
2. that telescopes could see to the edge of the galaxy in all directions
3. that stars of our own galaxy vastly exceed the numbers of bright objects outside the galaxy which could be mistaken for stars.

Making these assumptions, if one then made star gauges, i.e. counts of the numbers of stars in each similar-sized section of sky viewed from Earth, these could be used to estimate the shape of the galaxy. A large number of stars in a particular direction would indicate that the depth of the galaxy in that direction was greater. In a paper read 3rd February 1785 he sets out the basic problem and his assumptions:

> PROBLEM.
>
> *The stars being supposed to be nearly equally scattered, and their number, in a field of view of known angular diameter, being given, to determine the length of the visual ray.*

If, then, we assume that we are in the middle of a block of equally spaced stars, and that any particular cone of telescopic vision sees all the stars to the edge of the block, then simple geometry (effectively a mathematical series) can relate the number of stars visible within the cone to the distance it represents to the edge of the block in that direction. Herschel was confident he *was* seeing to the very edge because:

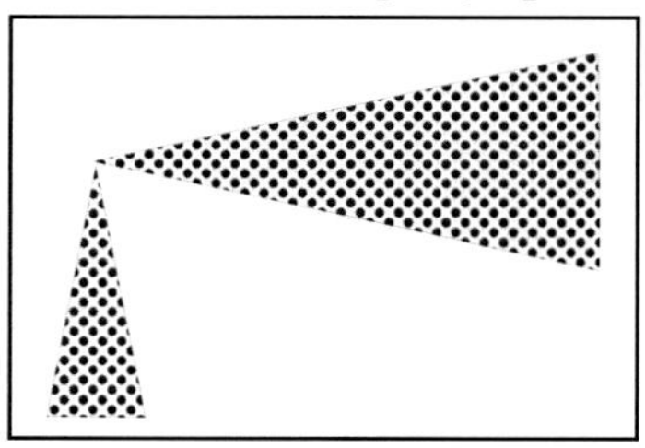

> in those parts of the Milky Way where these high gages were taken, the stars were neither so small, nor so crowded, as they must have been on a supposition of a much further continuance of them, when certainly a milky or nebulous appearance mist ?

must have come on, I need not fear to have overrated the extent of my visual ray …

In counting the stars Herschel attempted to omit any which were apparently distant nebulae or clusters. Herschel used his gages and calculations in conjunction with ideas on shapes of galaxy clusters he had

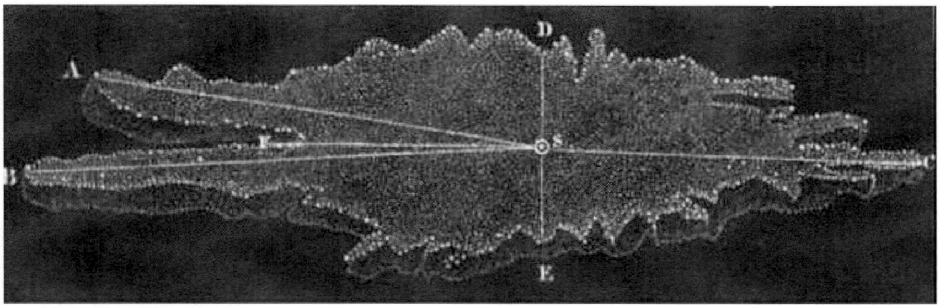

from observing them elsewhere in the heavens. The shape he came up with for our system was as illustrated[368]:

Later on, Herschel recognised that the two first and key assumptions he had made in his exploration of the shape of our galaxy were both wrong. In a paper read on 19th June 1817, Herschel wrote again about the construction and extent of the Milky Way in section IX. He concluded that: 'the utmost stretch of the space-penetrating power of the 20-foot telescope could not fathom the Profundity of the Milky Way.' He added that if the 40-foot telescope were used for the same purpose it would probably 'leave us again in the same uncertainty as the 20-foot telescope'. Herschel also concluded that *all* the stars seen with the naked eye were a part of the Milky Way.

The Nature of Nebulae & Stellar Evolution

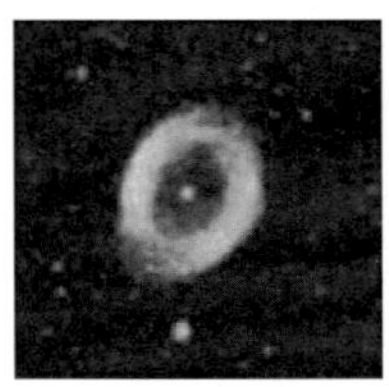

Lyra Ring Nebula

Herschel began observing nebulae (which in his terms included what we would now regard as star clusters and galaxies) in August 1782. Amongst others he saw the Ring Nebula in Lyra, which he suggested would be partly resolvable into a star cluster.

---

368 Our galaxy is, of course, actually a spiral galaxy and really looks nothing much like this.

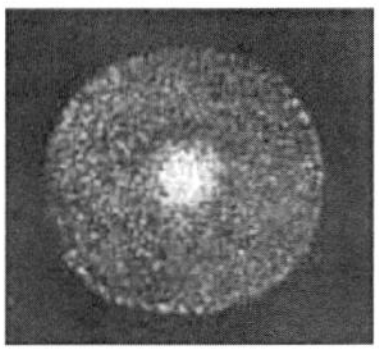

Planetary Nebula
(J. Herschel)

He saw the 'Saturn Nebula' which he termed a 'planetary nebula' because it appeared disc-shaped. This was a term he applied to anything disc shaped – and these include various different types of body/cluster. He also noted by January 1783 that in the Orion Nebula 'the nebulous part is quite different from what it was last year'. By August, with it still changing, he had concluded it must be true nebulosity rather than a star cluster.[369]

In his paper of 17th June 1784 he described nebulae as including those:

> of the cometic shape, with a seeming nucleus in the centre; or like cloudy stars, surrounded with a nebulous atmosphere; a different sort again contain a nebulosity of the milky kind, like that wonderful, inexplicable phenomenon about θ Orionis; while others shine with a fainter, mottled kind of light, which denotes their being resolvable into stars.

Orion Nebula

Five days after this paper Herschel discovered the 'Omega' Nebula, M17, and then the 'Dumbell Nebula' M27. These led him to conclude that all nebulae (though not necessarily including so-called planetary nebulae) were actually star clusters. By his paper of 1785, therefore, he was speculating on the process of stellar evolution under gravity, which would lead stars to cluster in large Milky Way type galaxies which then may fragment into smaller galaxies over time. We began this section on his works with a quotation on methodology from this paper. Herschel suggests that various stages or forms might be expected as stars move under gravity:

Star Cluster

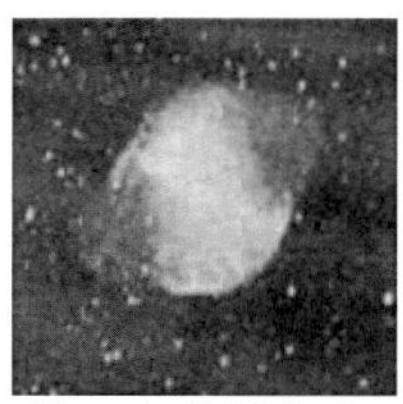

Dumbell Nebula

[369] Hoskins (1963) actually suggests that Orion does not change all that much, Herschel was mistaken!

Form I: As stars differ in size, a large star may attract others which also have mutual attraction, to form a 'more or less regular' globular cluster.

Form II: Stars of more nearly equal shape may come together attracted towards a mutual gravitational centre, but therefore forming an irregular star cluster.

Form III: From a conjunction of numbers of the previous two types, a long extended form with hooks and branches may form [like our Milky Way].

Form IV: There may be mutual attractions of Form III's towards each other.

Form V: There may in view of all this develop cavities or empty parts of space from which stars/galaxies have been drawn away.

This speculative model Herschel then applies to what he actually observes. He explores the shape of our own Milky Way (as above) and then looks at nine other 'Milky Ways' (only three of which apparently are actually galaxies!). Thus he says: 'In the list of these must also be reckoned the beautiful Nebula of Orion'. He thus ignores his own earlier observation of true nebulosity and now proclaims Orion a galaxy comparable to ours.[370] Planetary nebulae, apparently uniform discs of light, still puzzled him. He suggested that they could be 'Stars that are compressed and accumulated in the highest degree' adding that perhaps:

> the stars forming these extraordinary nebulae, by some decay or waste of nature, being no longer fit for their former purposes, and having their projectile forces, if any such they had, retarded in each other's atmosphere, may rush at last together, and either in succession of by one tremendous shock, unite into a new body.

A Nova might, he says, be thus accounted for.

In 1789 he published a second catalogue of a thousand new nebulae and star clusters, and prefaced it with another paper on the construction of the heavens. This simply extended the speculation in the 1785 paper, but

---

[370] See Herschel's papers or in Micahel Hoskin, 'Herschel's Investigations of Nebulae' *Journal of the History of Astrononmy* x (1979), 165–176.

seems more convinced. Thus, for example, on Form I his earlier statements were 'little better than hypothetical reasoning' whereas now 'actual and particular facts are brought to vouch for the truth of every inference'. He now, therefore, regarded his earlier reasoning on formation of globular clusters as empirically corroborated. He also gave a further principle:

> Any force, that acts uninterruptedly, must produce effects proportional to the time of its action. Now, as it has been shown that the spherical figure of a cluster of stars is owing to its central powers, it follows that those clusters which *ceteris paribus*, are the most compleat in this figure, must have been the longest exposed to the action of these causes.

Herschel's 'new kind of light' on the heavens was to view them as a snapshot of heavenly bodies or groups of bodies at various stages of evolution in natural life cycles. The cycle itself could be logically deduced from the relationships of the kinds of thing seen.

Planetary Nebula NGC1514

In this period of 1784–1789, therefore, Herschel was speculating on the nature of stellar and galaxy evolution, with the view that all the nebulae were actually some kind of star cluster.

On 13th November 1790 he saw:

> A most singular phenomenon! A star of about the 8th magnitude, with a faint luminous atmosphere, of a circular form, and of about 3' in diameter. The star is perfectly in the centre, and the atmosphere is so diluted, faint, and equal throughout, that there can be no surmise of its consisting of stars; nor can there be a doubt of the evident connection between the atmosphere and the star. Another star not much less in brightness, and in the same field with the above, was perfectly free from any such appearance.

He was convinced again of the existence of true nebulosity, and he concluded that the star was condensing (under the force of gravity) out of the nebulosity. In the revised approach, the way would be open for the

Andromeda: near nebula or far cluster?

nebula in Orion to be reconsidered: 'a luminous matter accounting much better for it than clustering stars at a distance'. To Herschel then, planetary nebulae were intermediate stages in the formation by gravity of a star out of the nebulous cloud.

His third (and final) catalogue of nebulae and star clusters in 1802 contained another prefatory article on the construction of the heavens. This paper is notable for another passage, Herschel notes:

> …that a telescope with a power of penetrating into space, like my 40-feet one, has also, as it may be called, a power of penetrating into time past. To explain this, we must consider that, from the known velocity of light, it may be proved, that when we look at Sirius, the rays which enter the eye cannot have been less than 6 years and 4½ months coming from that star to the observer. Hence it follows, that when we see an object of the calculated distance at which one of these very remote nebulae may still be perceived, the rays of light which convey its image to the eye, must have been more than nineteen hundred and ten thousand, that is, almost two millions of years on their way; and that, consequently, so many years ago, this object must already have had an existence in the sidereal heavens, in order to send out those rays by which we now perceive it.

Herschel's granddaughter, Lady Lubbock, suggested that:

> …it was natural that there was a certain reluctance to show approval of Herschel's theories, which seemed to run counter to the accepted interpretation of the Biblical Account of Creation.

Hoskin, who cites this[371], rightly expresses scepticism at any supposed clerical opposition. Even today[372] the myth is too often put about that

---

[371] Hoskin, op. cit. 132.

[372] Ironically in a program on the *Discovery* channel in February 2001 as these notes were being compiled!

Darwin in 1859 challenged a prevailing view of an Earth about 6000 years old, or that this was the view taken by his clerical opponents. This is (at risk of lapsing into non-academic language) utter baloney. In the period around 1790–1820 geologists were concluding (with little or no clerical opposition, and many leading geologists were clerics anyway!) that the Earth was very very old. Reluctance to accept Herschel's theories was because he had little or no actual evidence, and astronomers were cautious.

In papers of 1811 and 1814 Herschel continued to speculate on a sequence of stellar/galaxy evolution that included both star clusters and true nebulosity. The 1811 paper describes all the varieties of 'nebulae' Herschel has observed – and arranges them in a supposed sequence of evolution. The sequence – repeated in a paper of February 24th 1814, moves from 'very gradual conversion of the nebulous matter into the sidereal appearance' and thence into star clusters. In the 1814 paper Herschel also began some analysis of the *colours* of light from different stars using prisms. This kind of spectroscopic analysis increased in importance – but Herschel did not develop it much perhaps because he did not know how to interpret the results.

Origins of Infra-Red Observation[373]

On 24th April 1800 Herschel read 'Experiments on the Refrangibility of the invisible rays of the Sun' – the second of two papers at this time. Since Newton's day, a prism was known to transform (or split) a round beam of sunlight into an oblong spectrum. Herschel used three thermometers onto which he directed various parts of the solar spectrum split by a prism. But Herschel also moved the arrangement so that any radiation *beyond* the range of visible light fell on one of the thermometers. He concluded:

> It is now evident that there was a refraction of rays coming from the Sun, which, though not fit for vision, were yet highly invested with a power for occasioning heat.
>
> … A beam of radiant heat, emanating from the Sun, consists of rays that are differently refrangible. The range of their extent, when dispersed by a prism, begins at violet-coloured light, where

[373] This section is mostly taken from E. F. J. Ring, 'William Herschel: Discoverer of Infra-red Radiation' *The Speculum* (2000), 1.1, 27–33.

> they are most refracted, and have the least efficacy. We have traced these calorific rays throughout the whole extent of the prismatic spectrum; and found their power increasing, while their refrangibility was lessened, as far as to the confines of red-coloured light. But their diminishing refrangibility, and increasing power, did not stop here; for we have pursued them a considerable way beyond the prismatic spectrum, into an invisible state, still exerting their increasing energy, with a decrease of refrangibility up to the maximum of their powers; and have also traced them to that state where, though still less refracted, their energy, on account, we may suppose, of their now failing density, decreased pretty fast; after which, the invisible thermometrical spectrum, if I may so call it, soon vanished.

Solar heat, he showed by experiment, could be reflected and refracted. Obviously it had long been known that the Sun's heat could be focused with a 'burning glass', but this extension of the spectrum was a new approach at this time.

Herschel's Work: Conclusions

William Herschel had world recognition: as a telescope maker he was unrivalled, and as a dedicated observer very skilled. However, his 'discovery' of Uranus arose out of these, and not any theoretical understanding. His star maps and observations were valuable, but his own desire was to make fundamental contributions in the areas of *understanding* the construction and evolution of the heavens. He was, however, neither a great mathematician nor a great physicist, and in any case sufficient data did not yet exist to enable the process of stellar evolution to be worked out. Hoskin's 1963 conclusions still stand:

> For all the profound importance of the questions he asked and the methods he developed, his achievement measured in terms of his contribution to established knowledge of its construction bore little relation to his Herculean efforts … His mapping of the Galaxy stood or fell with two postulates, each of which he was later forced to abandon. His confident early work on the distribution of nebulae and star clusters drew its strength from his belief that all unresolved nebulae were distant star clusters. When evidence forced him to reverse this opinion he was robbed

> of his linear dimension of distance: a large unresolved nebula was probably near rather than far, but this was all one could confidently say, and Herschel actually mistook many distant galaxies for small, near-by nebulae. And all this time he had to contend with the methodological problem of inferring change from static evidence.
>
> Still more revealing is his attitude to the 'brightness equals nearness' postulate. Crucial as it was to his work, he clung to it through thick and thin in defiance of the growing body of contrary evidence, from Mitchell's work on star systems, from his own binary stars, from the enormous proper motion of 61 Cygni ...[374]

Herschel was an unusual and individualistic figure. His dramatic 'bursting' onto the astronomical scene in 1781, rapidly moved expectations from telescopes to new levels – not least because he himself was making and supplying instruments to important European observers. He also made some first rate observations, and was a skilled observer. Most of his *theories,* however, were premature, and his belief that they were demonstrable was unrealistic and mistaken. What he did achieve in this, perhaps, was to raise clearly some scientific agenda which have borne great fruit in the one and three quarters centuries since his death. The spatial distribution of stars, and the development and evolution of stars and galaxies have been fruitful studies. We *have* been able to infer star cycles over great time periods and without waiting to see out any cycle – but it has been done through a closer integration with physics. New technology has also enabled development of infra-red astronomy.

Herschel's immediate work with large telescopes was continued both by his son John Herschel and by William Parsons, later the Earl of Rosse. The latter thought that he had resolved distant nebulae into star clusters – and the controversy raged on for decades. Only in the 1860s – using techniques new to astronomy – was it finally established that some nebulae were truly gaseous and not resolvable into star clusters.

---

374 Hoskin (1963), 189. Hoskin's 1997 *The Illustrated History of Astronomy* seems much more positive, saying that 'Herschel had been able to make this [i.e. a knowledge of the Construction of the Heavens] into a true science' though does not expand on the sense in which this was so.

Questions

Here are some questions to ask as you think about Herschel

- Was the great acclaim that he received justified and if so on what grounds?
- What (if anything) was the novelty of his approach to stellar evolution?
- How far were his assumptions brilliant guesses, how far were they purely gratuitous, and how far were they a lucky means to more discovery?
- Should we regret the passing of the age of the maverick 'amateur' in the realms of scientific work?

References

Primary Sources

In 1933 Herschel's granddaughter Constance Lubbock produced *The Herschel Chronicle* – (repr. 2010).

Extracts of his papers are in Michael J. Crowe *Modern Theories of the Universe from Herschel to Hubble* (1994) and Michael Hoskin *William Herschel and the construction of the heavens* (1963).

CUP repr. Mary Herschel's *Memoir and Correspondence of Caroline Herschel* (Cambridge Library Collection – Physical Sciences) in July 2010.

Secondary Sources:

The books cited above by Crowe and Hoskin, and the two papers by Hoskin cited above in footnotes, are good sources on Herschel's work. Hoskin also wrote a short biography *William Herschel: Pioneer of Sidereal Astronomy* (1959), and there is a considerable section in his *The Cambridge Illustrated History of Astronomy* (1997).

J. B. Sidgwick *William Herschel: Explorer of the Heavens* (1953) is a readable biography, and Angus Armitage *William Herschel* (1962) is a bit more analytical.

The book by Tom Standage *The Neptune Files* (2000) actually contains a reasonable summary on Herschel and Uranus. The Herschel Society have reissued short booklets by Patrick Moore on *William Herschel* (new edition

2000) and *Caroline Herschel* (1988), and sell reprints of an 1998 article 'A compendium of all known William Herschel Telescopes'. Their journal *Speculum* started in 2000 with *Issue 1*.

Clair Brock, *The Comet Sweeper: Caroline Herschel's Astronomical Ambition* (2004).

More recent works include:

Michael D. Lemonick, *The Georgian Star: How William and Caroline Herschel Revolutionized Our Understanding of the Cosmos* (2009).

Marilyn Bailey Ogilvie, *Sweeping the Stars: The Story of Caroline Herschel* (2008).

Michael Hoskin, *Discoverers of the Universe: William and Caroline Herschel* (2011) is recent and good, and his *The Construction of the Heavens: William Herschel's Cosmology* (2012) will be great if you can afford it!

10. Finding Neptune

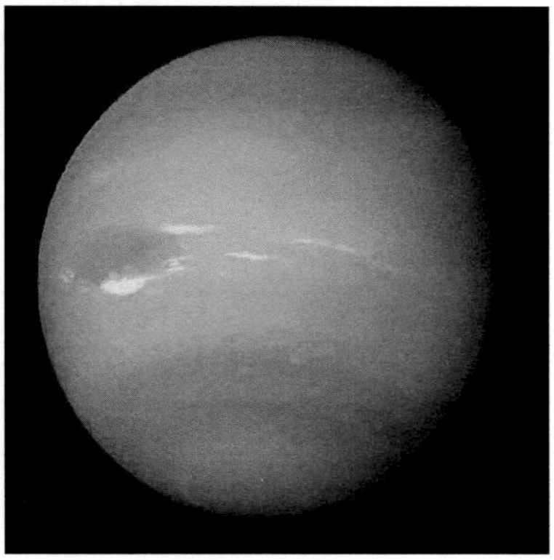
Neptune (aged about 4.5 bn years)

'My attention was first directed to this subject several years since, by reading Mr Airy's valuable Report on the recent progress of Astronomy. I find among my papers the following memorandum, dated July 3, 1841: "Formed as a design, in the beginning of this week, of investigating, as soon as possible after taking my degree, the irregularities in the motion of Uranus, which are yet unaccounted for, in order to find whether they may be attributed to the action of an undiscovered planet beyond it, and, if possible, thence to determine approximately the elements of its orbit, &c., which would probably lead to its discovery. "' John Couch Adams (13th November 1846).[375]

The star, as it were, of this chapter is not an individual but the planet Neptune. The events surrounding its discovery raise a number of interesting points about scientific methodology and the conduct of science, as well as being important to the memory and careers of several important astronomers. The format of this chapter, then, differs from previous sets. In our previous chapter we looked at the discovery of Uranus, we can begin this one with an outline of the wayward behaviour of that planet, which is the background to the discovery of Neptune. Then we will consider the discovery of Neptune in outline and meet the main characters in what became a drama. Then we will look at brief biographies of each of these characters, understanding the approach and perspective of each on what happened. This may involve some amount of repetition, but seems the best way to understand the issues. Finally we will try to draw some conclusions.

375In a paper to the Royal Astronomical Society, vol xvi (1847), included in Adams' 'Scientific Papers'.

Newtonianism and Wayward Uranus

Laplace (1749-1827)

The six ancient planets (Mercury, Venus, Earth, Mars, Jupiter and Saturn) had been shown by Kepler to orbit in ellipses, and Newton had shown that an inverse square law of universal gravity acting as a centripetal force would account for this. Improving telescopes and micrometers enabled more accurate planetary and lunar observations, but various anomalies in orbits remained. Mutual attraction, as Newton himself had recognised, would operate between all the planets, and as Jupiter and Saturn are big planets the effects might be expected to be observable. Pierre Simon de Laplace (1749–1827) had shown in 1785 that slight variations in their orbits were indeed explained by their mutual gravitational attraction. As Jupiter overtook Saturn in its orbit, during its approach it would be pulled forward slightly (and pull back Saturn), and after it had passed it would be pulled back (pulling Saturn forward). By the 19th century therefore, all the six planets were conforming to Newton's laws. Laplace also identified in 1787 a cause for the secular acceleration of the Moon – which had elements in its orbit that had puzzled Newton and others since. Laplace's discovery was that changes in the Earth's eccentricity were affecting the Moon – though actually in 1853 it was John Couch Adams who showed that this was only half the story and another effect on the Moon was caused by friction of tides in shallow seas on Earth. In general, however, Laplace could account for all planetary movements in the Solar System as a self-regulating system; the world was Newtonian, predictable and deterministic.

Bode's Law and Science

'Bode's law' was invented by Johann Titius in 1766 and popularised by inclusion in a work of Johann Bode. It related planetary distances from the Sun according to the formula $[4 + 3(2^n)]/10$, giving ratios of orbits as follows:

Planet	**Mercury**	**Venus**	**Earth**	**Mars**	*{Ceres/ Pallas}*	**Jupiter**	**Saturn**	***Uranus***
Bode	**0.4**	**0.7**	**1**	**1.6**	*2.8*	**5.2**	**10.0**	***19.6***
Actual	**0.39**	**0.72**	**1.00**	**1.52**	*{2.77}*	**5.20**	**9.54**	***19.18***

In 1766 it seemed to work well but with the exception of a missing planet between Mars and Jupiter. Uranus seemed in 1783 to provide a remarkable confirmation – though left this 'missing planet' issue. In 1801, a small planet-like object 'Ceres' was confirmed in about the right orbit – though it had a diameter of only 1000 kilometres so it was stretching it a bit to see it as the missing planet. In 1802 another object, Pallas, with a diameter of only about 600 kilometres was discovered in the same orbit, leading to speculation about a planet that might have broken up – though where the other pieces were no one knew. Only a couple more were found before 1850, and since then many much smaller bodies have been found in the 'asteroid belt' between Mars and Jupiter. Modern theory suggests that perhaps the large mass of Jupiter stopped the original solar nebula debris forming a planet.

But what was the status of 'Bode's law' in the second quarter of the 19th century? We have seen that Kepler's laws were originally mathematical generalisations which worked in predicting orbits, but which were not connected with gravitational *physics* until Newton connected them. We have also seen that Kepler, Horrocks, and others, looked for laws linking planetary distance with mass or volume – but with no physical derivation. Bode's law was a similar mathematical generalisation, it was not derived from or linked with any physics or gravitational theory.

All this raises some interesting issues about the nature of science. Recollecting some of the issues raised in our first chapter, a stringent 'falsificationist' or Popperian view would have seen Newton's gravitational theory meet immediate tests with the Moon, Uranus, and Mercury – all of which it would have failed! As already noted, problems Newton admitted (c. 1727) with lunar motion were solved much later by Laplace (1787) and Adams (1853). Uranus's problems were solved by the mid-19th century as we shall see. Only Mercury's perihelion remained intransigent – and this was explained only by relativity in the 20th century. So at what stage was Newton's theory 'refuted'? What *actually* happened was that scientists looked for explanations of anomalies – either within or outside the Newtonian inverse square law paradigm. The first two problems were solved within it, the third by changing it – but no one could know in advance which would happen. Another interesting 'philosophical' issue is why we somehow find Bode's law more likely to be contingent than the inverse square law itself. Most of us probably do – but in strict terms there is no obvious reason for this.[376]

Uranus

In orbital terms, however, Uranus was *not* a well-behaved planet! Its orbit was first computed by Lexell of St Petersburg, on the assumption that the eccentricity of the orbit was small enough for it to be approximated by a circle. By 1783, further observations had enabled Laplace (and Mechain) to obtain an elliptical orbit, allowing for effects of other planets as well. Johann Bode suggested that earlier astronomers might have seen it, and in 1781 identified a sighting by Tobias Mayer in 1756, and in 1784 one by Flamsteed in 1690 – both on apparent 'stars' which later were not there; (19 earlier sightings were identified similarly in the subsequent period). The period of Uranus is some 84 years, but these provided observations spanning this cycle. In 1784 Placidus Fixlmillner (1721–1791) among others found an elliptical orbit satisfying the 1690, 1756, and 1781–4 observations. In 1788, however, the observed position of Uranus was not even tolerably near that which had been predicted. Fixlmillner tried to fix it, but found that for any extended application he could construct an orbit for the earlier positions, or one for the later positions, but not one for both. Like a true scientist he therefore decided to discard Flamsteed's 1690 value, and construct tables based on the later figures alone!

In 1790, Jean Baptist Joseph Delambre (1749–1822) obtained an orbit that seemed to cover all the observations – and for a while this was apparently successful. Interest in Uranus was, in any case, on a comparative wane.

In 1820, Alexis Bouvard (1767–1843) found ten more early sightings of Uranus mistaken for stars, and tried to find an orbit to match all the figures 'ancient' and 'modern' (i.e. those over the now forty years since Uranus discovery). He could find no such orbit – an orbit fitting the ancient ones did not fit the modern and *vice versa.* He concluded:

> I leave to the future the task of discovering whether the difficulty of reconciling the two system results from the inaccuracy of the

---

376 For the record, modern figures for Neptune are 30.06 (Bode figure 38.8) and Pluto 39.44 (Bode figure 77.2) – but Pluto is an odd planet anyway with a highly elliptical orbit steeply inclined to the ecliptic.

> ancient observations, or whether it depends on some extraneous and unknown influence which may have acted on the planet.[377]

Bouvard opted for the former – though this involved accusing such careful observers as Flamsteed, Bradley and Lemonnier of huge percentages of error some ten times greater than their normal error of observation. Other astronomers like Friedrich Bessel (1784–1864) and Urbain Le Verrier (1811–1877) did not find this credible, and looked for other explanations for Uranus's misbehaviour. Their suspicions were confirmed when, within five years or so, Bouvard's own tables began to diverge from Uranus's observed behaviour.

Errors in Bouvard's tables increased and then decreased over the following years, but it was still obvious something was wrong. In 1832 the astronomer George Biddell Airy (1801–1892) reported to the British Association for the Advancement of Science that Bouvard's tables were now out in geometric longitude by nearly half a minute of arc – a huge discrepancy.

Airy did not suggest an explanation, but different people had suggested various possible reasons for this:

- There might be some kind of Cartesian cosmic fluid.
- Uranus might have a satellite.
- There might have been a radical change that happened to occur to Uranus around 1781, e.g. a big comet impact.
- The inverse square law itself might be only approximate or not apply at greater distances.
- There might be another planet orbiting outside the orbit of Uranus, which was affecting it.

The first lacked any empirical basis, the second would not explain such long-term perturbations, and the third seemed too far-fetched a coincidence and still would not explain later deviations.

By 1836 the climate of opinion was in favour of there being another planet. Morton Grosser logs the changes in the well-regarded popular scientific

---

377 A. Bouvard, *Tables Astronomiques*, xiv.

works of Mary Somerville (1780–1872), culminating in the view in 1836 that if discrepancies still remain in Uranus's orbit after further observation:

> … the discrepancies may reveal the existence, nay, even the mass and orbit, of a body placed for ever beyond the sphere of vision.[378]

The Somerville's close friends in London included the Airys (George having been Astronomer Royal at Greenwich since 1835) and Mrs Somerville's words may reflect his view. There might well be such a body, but if so there would be great difficulties in seeing it.

On October 6th 1837 Eugene Bouvard wrote to Airy stating that his uncle Alexis Bouvard now thought there *was* an external planet. Other astronomers were taking this opinion, and by 1840 it was a well-recognised possibility.

George Biddell Airy (1801–1892)

George Biddell Airy was born in 1801 near the mediaeval market town of Alnwick in Northumberland. He was the eldest of four children of William Airy and Ann Biddell – fairly affluent yeoman farmers. At age ten he went to a school in Colchester, but other than becoming adept at arithmetic and bookkeeping did not distinguish himself (apart from expertise in constructing peashooters which made him popular with his fellows!) At age 12 he came to know his uncle Arthur Biddell, and between 1814–19 spent half his time with his uncle. Through some of his uncle's contacts, George entered Trinity College, Cambridge as a sizar in 1819.

Over the next few decades, Trinity College was central to the rise of Cambridge to a dominant position in British science. Trinity Fellow Adam Sedgwick (1785–1873, 5th Wrangler in 1808) had become Woodwardian Professor of Geology in 1818, began annual lectures in 1819, and went on

378Somerville*Connexion of the Physical Sciences* 3rd edn, 74.

to become a key stratigraphic geologist. The great polymath William Whewell (1794–1866) who invented the word 'scientist' in the early 1830s, became a Fellow of Trinity in 1817 and Professor of Mineralogy in 1828. In 1813 John Herschel (1792–1871) had passed out senior wrangler from neighbouring St John's College and became a Fellow of the Royal Society at the age of 21 – going on to win the Copley medal for mathematical papers by 1822 when he took over his father's telescopes and work. Others in the circle, like Joseph Romilly, John Stevens Henslow, Richard Sheepshanks, and George Peacock, also went on to scientific interest and honour. Sometimes dubbed 'the Cambridge Network'[379], the brilliant group had great effect in science. The British Association for the Advancement of Science (BAAS) was founded in 1831 by a group in which these men were central. George Airy became a part of this group, with Whewell and Sedgwick as particular friends. Airy received a very broad education at Cambridge, theology, classics and advanced mathematics, though in those days part of the examination was still having to have a disputation in Latin! His first publication was a paper on constructing a telescope with silvered glass to avoid aberrations in 1822. Unfortunately when he tried to have one made it didn't work!

Trinity College Cambridge

He graduated as Senior Wrangler in 1823, and was elected as a Fellow of Trinity in 1824 earning £150 p.a. as an Assistant Tutor. Around this time, whilst on a walking holiday, he met and fell in love with a Miss Ricarda Smith (daughter of Reverend Richard Smith the Duke of Devonshire's chaplain). He proposed two days later, but her father did not deem his income and

[379] A term in S. F. Cannon *Science in Culture* (1978) and A. Thackray & J. B. Morell *Gentlemen of Science* (1981). These books wrongly label them as 'Broad Churchmen' i.e. liberal in theology. Actually, there was a strong evangelical/conservative strain in the undoubted piety of Whewell and Sedgwick. Airy, however, was liberal in his theology.

situation satisfactory. In 1826 he was elected to the Lucasian Professorship – which brought only £99 p.a. with some additional income from being on the Board of Longitude. At this time Airy developed (for himself) the first spectacle lenses to correct for astigmatism. In 1826 he also began with Whewell experiments to determine the density of the Earth by comparing pendulum times at the top and bottom of a deep copper mine. In summer 1828 they were joined too by Sedgwick. The natives apparently suspected them of being up to no good, and Airy had been seen to 'stand with his back to the Church and make strange faces' Their lamp box was suspiciously marked Deville, Strand, and to keep up the joke Sedgwick apparently asked one sturdy miner acting as guide how far it was to the infernal regions. The miner, to Sedgwick's great amusement, replied 'let go the ladder sir, and you'll be there directly' . They had a great sense of fun – thinking it hilarious when, arriving in their working dress at the house of their host for the night, they were directed by the butler to the back door.[380]

Earlier in 1828 Airy had applied to become Plumian Professor, a post that carried with it directorship of the newly completed Cambridge Observatory. Most professors (e.g. Sedwick) were ordained and held a living (in Sedgwick's case as Canon of Norwich Cathedral) to supplement an insufficient salary. Airy (who probably also had possible marital union with the lovely Ricarda in mind!) campaigned that the £300 salary was insufficient, and was appointed on 6th February with a salary of £500 p. a. The observatory had two assistants, and instruments for student instruction. Airy began to systematise the work of the observatory, and was able after one year to publish a volume of observations. Meridian work was especially important. Airy's methodical approach was famous, and he kept detailed records of all kinds of things. In 1830 he was at last able to marry Ricarda Smith, to whom he was a devoted husband.

1832 was an important year for Airy. He had been studying the mutual gravitational effects of Venus and Earth. Since they come back to about the same point of relation about every eight years, the effects multiply and are measurable. The calculations involved in this were arduous, but Airy was given the gold medal of the Royal Astronomical society for this in

1832. Reports on this were in Airy's *Report on the Progress of Astronomy* for the second annual meeting of the British Association for the Advancement of

---

[380] See Clark & Hughes, *The Life and Letters of Adam Sedgwick* (1890), I, 32.

Science, which was at Oxford in June 1832. In the same report he referred to the problems of Uranus. In 1828 Airy had found errors in the positions of Uranus of 12 arc seconds, by 1830 it was 30 arc seconds. Thus, even with Bouvard's approach of ignoring the 'ancient' observations of Uranus, there were serious errors. Airy's report concluded:

> I need not mention that there are other subjects (the theory of Uranus, for instance) in which the existence of difficulties is known, but in which we have no clue to their explanation.

There was no particular mention of possible explanations, but on 17th November 1834 a British ('amateur') astronomer Reverend Dr Thomas John Hussey wrote to Airy:

> The apparently inexplicable discrepancies between the ancient and modern observations suggested to me the possibility of some disturbing body beyond Uranus, not taken into account because unknown. My first idea was to ascertain some approximate place of this supposed body empirically, and then with my large reflector set to work to examine all the minute stars thereabouts; but I found myself totally inadequate to the former part of the task … I therefore relinquished the matter altogether; but subsequently, in conversation with Bouvard, I inquired if the above might not be the case: his answer was that, as might have been expected, it had occurred to him, and some correspondence had taken place between Hansen and himself respecting it.

Airy replied:

> I have often thought of the irregularity of *Uranus*, and since the receipt of your letter have looked more carefully to it. It is a puzzling subject, but I give it as my opinion, without hesitation, that it is not yet in such a state as to give the smallest hope of making out the nature of any external action on the planet … if it were certain that there were any extraneous action, I doubt much the possibility of determining the place of a planet which produced it. I am sure it could not be done till the nature of the

> irregularity was well determined from several successive revolutions.[381]

These comments were not made in ignorance, we remember that the effects of one body on another was *exactly* what Airy himself had done for Venus and Earth and Laplace had earlier done it for Jupiter and Saturn. But what was involved here was a problem of *inverse perturbation*. This was not one of calculating the effects on one planet of another of more or less known orbit and mass, but of inferring an orbit and mass for an unknown planet given only the unexplained variations in the effected planet. The orbit of that latter planet was itself, as yet, not determined, and all that existed were a set of apparently inconsistent positions. Logically enough, Airy suggested that until the actual orbit of Uranus was better known (and we remember that its orbital period is about 84 years) the task was hopeless. If he also believed (as Mary Somerville's popular account suggested) that the planet might be too distant even to be visible, then the problem would be even harder.

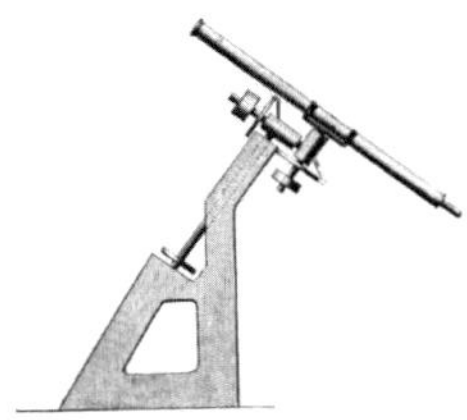
Orbit Sweeper

Airy had been given a special government pension for discoveries, and in 1835 was offered the post of Astronomer Royal to succeed the rather ineffective Pond. More from duty than opportunity for research or hope of any gain, Airy left Cambridge for Greenwich in October 1835. The function of the observatory was to observe, but raw results are of little use until 'reduced' by calculating allowances for various known errors. Airy set batteries of computers (people not PCs!) to work on this, to provide useful accurate observations. He was also inventive, designing improved patterns for instruments, including an orbit sweeper, an equatorial driven by a clock, a meridian circle, etc.

His view of solving Uranus's problems remained pessimistic. In response to an enquiry from Eugene Bouvard he replied in 1837 pointing out the increasing errors in the predictions for Uranus:

> I cannot conjecture what is the cause of these errors, but I am inclined, in the first instance, to ascribe them to some error in the

---

381 Airy, 'Account …' 124.

> perturbations … If it be the effect of any unseen body, it will be nearly impossible to ever find out its place.

In an article in the journal *Astronomische Nachrichten* in 1838, Airy showed that not only were Bouvard's tables out in longitude, but also in the radius vector.

As Astronomer Royal Airy had fought for and obtained a salary of £1100 on the assumption that (as with his professorship at Cambridge), he would not be supplementing his income by taking a living as a clergyman. In his autobiography he says he had 'an aversion to entering the church'. He does not say why, and was liberal in theology rather than irreligious, but maybe he had the vision to see such science posts as proper professional posts not as part-time ones. Allan Chapman also explains:

> He did not see the Royal Observatory as a research institution, or a place where the frontiers of knowledge should be pushed back. This was the duty of the academic and private observatories, operating on independent endowments designed to finance 'philosophical' enterprises. Greenwich, on the other hand, was paid for out of taxation, to provide essential services to the Navy and Empire, and absolute standards to the world in general, and not to squander the citizen's money on abstract projects arising from private investigations. As he reminded the Board of Visitors many years after, '… the Observatory is not the place for new physical investigations …'[382]

It has to be said that perhaps Chapman exaggerates in saying 'Airy was, by instinct an engineer and administrator rather than a research scientist'. His work on astigmatism, the mass of the Earth, the Earth-Venus effects etc. were all theoretical. Nor does Tom Standage seem to have much basis for later asserting: 'Airy was a methodical, unimaginative man …'[383] Various anecdotes are repeated to show that Airy was some kind of obsessive, e.g. because on one occasion he took on a routine labelling task himself rather than call away any of his assistants from their allotted tasks. Plainly he was unusually retentive of documentation, and committed to routine at the observatory. But this does not mean that he thought speculative astronomy

---

382 Allan Chapman, 'Airy and Neptune', *Journal of History of Astronomy* xix (1988), 122.

383 Standage, *The Neptune File*, 58.

pointless or had no personal interest in it. It seems rather that, having accepted a post that was essentially administrative, he was committed to it.

Of 1844 Airy wrote in his autobiography:

> In this year commenced that remarkable movement which led to the discovery of Neptune. On Feb. 13th Prof. Challis introduced Mr Adams to me by letter. On Feb. 15th I sent my observed places of Uranus, which were wanted. On June 19th I also sent places to Mr E. Bouvard.

So Airy promptly sent off the observations made at Greenwich between 1754 and 1830. Though the Observatory was not to conduct theoretical research, he would quickly provide data for those who did.

Airy was kept very busy as a civil servant apart from astronomical duties. Chapman usefully points out that in 1845–46 out of a possible 310 working days Airy spent 90–100 on Railway Gauge business, and 30 on other business unrelated to astronomy. He also travelled on business on the Continent. In fact, it was on his return on 26th September 1845 from Cherbourg to look at the breakwater there, that Airy found a note left him by one of his many visitors. The note was a letter of introduction from his old friend and successor James Challis, recommending 'My friend Mr Adams (who will deliver this note to you) [who] has completed his calculations regarding the perturbations of the orbit of Uranus'. Airy wrote back promptly on 29th September to Challis:

> I was, I suppose, on my way from France, when Mr. Adams called here; at all events, I had not reached home, and therefore, to my regret, I have not seen him. Would you mention it to Mr. Adams that I am very much interested with the subject of his investigations and that I shall be delighted to hear of them by letter from him.

In his autobiography Airy wrote:

> On Sept. 22nd Challis wrote to me to say that Mr Adams would leave with me his results on the explanation of the irregularities of Uranus by the action of an exterior planet. In October Adams called, in my absence. On Nov. 5th I wrote to him, enquiring whether his theory explained the irregularity of radius-vector (as well as that of longitude). I waited for an answer, but received none …

It is a total mystery how Morton Grosser and others could read this and then assert that Airy had 'no confidence in [young people's] abilities' and that Adams' hypothesis 'not surprisingly had a very cool reception'.[384] This letter, remember, was sent almost immediately Airy got back (presumably to a mountain of mail), and if phrases like 'very much interested' and 'delighted to hear' indicate coolness then one wonders what heat would look like.

Airy heard nothing, and received no letter, and on 21st October was out on Railway gauge business in London when again young Adams called unexpectedly and without any prior writing or warning. A card was left, and Adams later said that he had told the servant he would return soon. Whether or not that message was passed on we do not know. Adams gave no reasons for not waiting for Airy's return, but later said that he returned in 'a little more than an hour' and was told by the servant that Airy was at dinner (he often dined early on doctor's orders at around 3.30 p.m.) and there was no message. We presume that Airy was dining with his family including a wife who was near term in her pregnancy and generally experienced difficult births. Should Airy have left a message for this unknown young man who had failed to reply to his request for more written details, had called without warning, and may have left only a vague message that he would return 'soon' (which could means hours, days or weeks)? Should the butler have disturbed the exhausted and overworked Airy who was snatching a precious family mealtime, to announce the unexpected visit of someone Airy had never met and didn't know? We can only leave each person (including Morton Grosser) to decide.

When Airy finished his family dinner he found that Adams had left for him an outline of his results for Uranus, but no calculations.

Actually, the next couple of weeks were horrendous for Airy. Seven of the next ten days were filled by railway business, including one on the 23rd when a deputation came to discuss the problems of vibration on his instruments if a line passed through Greenwich park. On 27th October Airy had to dismiss an assistant Mr William Williamson who was about to face a serious charge for incest and murder. On 29th October Airy's wife

---

[384] Grosser *The Discovery of Neptune*, 91–2. A *Britannica* entry on Neptune asserts 'Airy did not take them (i.e. Adams' results) seriously' – a comment which it is hard to take seriously.

gave birth to a son. Incredibly, on 5th November, Airy found time to write off an encouraging note to the young Adams – whom he had never met and who had called unannounced and uninvited and left an undated note:

> I am very much obliged by the paper of results which you left here a few days since, showing the perturbations on the place of Uranus produced by a planet with certain assumed elements. The latter numbers are all extremely satisfactory: I am not well enough acquainted with Flamsteed's observations about 1690 to say whether they bear such an error, but I think it extremely probable. But I should be very glad to know whether this assumed perturbation will explain the error of the radius vector of Uranus. This error is now very considerable, as you will be able to ascertain by comparing the normal equations, given in the Greenwich observations for each year, for the times *before* opposition with the times *after* opposition.[385]

Adams was Challis's protégé, and Airy saw no need to take further action other than to await a reply from Adams to this encouraging note. He had no way of checking any calculations as Adams had left none. He later reflected:

> I waited with much anxiety for Mr Adams' answer to my query. Had it been in the affirmative, I should have exerted all the influence which I might possess … to procure the publication of Mr Adams' theory.[386]

So was Airy reprehensible at this point for not jumping up during dinner and rushing down to meet an unknown uninvited guest? Should he have followed up the note more vigorously? Should he have publicised Adams' summary?

Morton Grosser's treatment of Airy[387] contains highly implausible suggestions, not to mention (as Allan Chapman does!) some errors of fact. Thus Airy was according to Grosser:

> … a man strongly opposed to theoretical investigations and sceptical of the abilities of younger scientists.

---

385 Quoted in 'The Scientific Papers of John Couch Adams' xxii.

386 Airy 'Account', 397.

387 Grosser *The Discovery of Neptune*, 90 etc.

Grosser suggests the reason he delayed *two weeks* before replying to Adams' hand delivered note was that:

> Perhaps it took that long for him to find some suitable scientific basis for his rejection. He found one, characteristically, in his own past work …
>
> Airy's repeated use of the word 'assumed' in this letter (replying to Adams) indicated that either he did not realise, or was loath to admit, that Adams had not assumed his elements, but derived them from perturbations of Uranus.

Much of this is moonshine. Airy himself had undertaken theoretical investigation of the mutual effect of Venus and Earth – exactly the kind of issue involved here. Far from being 'sceptical' of young scientists, he had been prepared to send off very promptly the information that Adams had asked for (with Challis's backing). He later told Sedgwick he thought Adams a young MA rather than a BA – and assumed the lack of reply due to perhaps some flaw discovered in the calculations rather than inexperience. Adams did not include the calculations but only the results, and in the note itself said that the mean distance had been '*assumed* nearly in accordance with Bode's law' i.e. 38.4. The results were, indeed, based on assumption – it is nonsense for Grosser to suggest that the planet's position could be 'derived' from the few positions available for Uranus. Smart also plausibly suggests that Airy may not even have been sure whether trial and error had been used, rather than any real inverse perturbation method. Airy was, of course, basically right – Adams and Le Verrier succeeded partly through luck, and partly because both assumed Bode's law – a shaky generalisation with no solid physical derivational base. It seems absurd for Grosser to suggest that two weeks was a long time (especially as earlier commentators had pointed out that Airy was involved in all the activity and trauma we saw above in those two weeks). It seems absurd to suggest that Airy needed the time to scrub around looking for excuses to make to Adams.

Coming back (in the modern vernacular) to planet Earth, was Airy's request to Adams for calculations on the radius vector justified? Much later J. W. L. Galisher asked Adams why he had not replied and Adams said: 'I should have done so; but the enquiry seemed to me to be trivial'. From a later letter to Airy (see below) it seems that Adams simply *assumed* that the radius vector would come out right if his theory worked for the positions. Interestingly, Morton Grosser (who as we have seen is very hostile to Airy) quotes Airy's later explanation, which is actually in a letter to Challis 21st December 1846:

> There were two things to be explained which might have existed each independently of the other, and of which one could be ascertained independently of the other: viz. error of longitude and error of radius vector. And there is no *a priori* reason for thinking that a hypothesis which will explain the error of longitude will also explain the radius vector …[388]

Airy goes on to suggest that if the two in fact diverge, then it would be the *laws of gravitation themselves* which would be shown to have failed rather than Adams' figures. Grosser states that this 'was not a widely shared opinion' – but he also goes on to reluctantly admit that actually Airy was right, it was *not* obvious or automatic that correction of the longitude would correct the radius value. Airy was looking for two *independent* lines of corroboration for calculations that were inherently difficult, made assumptions, and could contain slips.

In a letter to Challis (21st December 1846), Airy gave it as his view that the laws of gravitation themselves might turn out to 'fail'. He then expanded on his philosophy of science:

> The progress of science almost always depends on questions of this kind. Thus in Chemistry, the phlogistic theory explained the concurring facts of oxidation of metals and vitiation of air, or gaseous formation in water. But did it *also* account for the increased weight of the metal? No. Then it was false. Laplace's notion of forces gave an explanation of the course of extraordinary pencils of light. But did it or could it give an explanation of the separation of pencils and their polarisation? No. Then it was false. The theory of gravitation *might* have been in the same predicament with regard to Uranus. Adams' answer

[388] The whole is in Adams 'Scientific Papers', xxx.

> would have made this satisfactory … What could be the reason of Adams' silence, I could not guess. It was so far unfortunate that it interposed an effectual barrier to all further communication. It was clearly impossible for me to write to him again.

To Airy, Newtonian gravitation was not sacrosanct. He did not share the confidence of Adams and Le Verrier that it was inviolable. Uranus might have scuppered it. What is ironical is that Airy's modern detractors do not seem to note that this was *exactly* what happened in the end with Mercury. Le Verrier's attempts to explain its misbehaving perihelion in like fashion to Uranus failed – the 20th century brought recognition that Newtonian gravitation was defective and Mercury could be explained only by the theory of Relativity.

Airy's later account emphasized that he considered the issue of the radius vector:

> … would be truly an *experimentum crucis*. And I waited with much anxiety for Mr Adams' answer to my query. Had it been in the affirmative, I should have at once exerted all the influence which I might possess, either directly or indirectly through my friend Profesor Challis, to procure the publication of Mr Adams' theory.

In summary then, from Adams' list of errors Airy could not even tell whether he had arrived at the orbit purely by trial and error or by some kind of genuine inverse perturbation theory. Airy was also looking for *two* independent lines of evidence (e.g. longitude + radius vector) to corroborate the validity of the theory. All Adams had to do was send the relevant calculations. Whether or not in *Adams'* mind leaving the note with Airy was tantamount to publication, whether or not Adams expected its circulation, no experienced person could expect Airy – without the requested detail – to circulate it in this state.

On November 10th 1845 Urbain Le Verrier presented to the French Academy an investigation into the effects of Jupiter and Saturn on Uranus, but noted that discrepancies remained. On 1st June 1846 Le Verrier presented a second paper, *Comptes Rendus*, suggesting a perturbing planet outside Uranus, with a longitude (January 1st 1847) of 325°. This differed by only 1° from the position given by Adams, though neither the elements of the orbit nor the mass of the planet were given. Airy received the paper around 23–4th June, and on 25th replied to an enquiry on Uranus from his friend Whewell (who was revising his work *History of the Inductive Sciences*) stating 'Peoples' notions have long turned to the effects of an external planet', and noting his own receipt of 'two remarkable calculations' from Adams and Le Verrier which 'have arrived at the same result' (i.e. a longitude of near 325°) he added:

> If I were a rich man or had an unemployed staff I would immediately take measures for the strict examination of that part of the heavens containing the position of the postulated planet.[389]

Airy (as he later wrote) was sceptical of working from just one set of results without seeing the calculations – since an arithmetic or legibility slip would be so easy to make. The concurrence of two independently made calculations was more impressive – and Airy's words belie any suggestion of disinterest. But he still would have liked a corroboration from two independent derivations, and wrote to Le Verrier on 26th June, noting his paper and asking:

> It appears from all the later observations of Uranus made at Greenwich … that the tabular radius vector is considerably too small. And I wish to enquire of you whether this would be a consequence of the disturbance produced by an exterior planet, now in the position which you have indicated? I imagine it would not be so, because the principle term of the inequality would probably be analogous to the moon's variation, or would depend on sin 2(v – v′); and in that case the perturbations of the radius vector would have the sign – for the present relative position of the planet and Uranus. But this analogy is worth little until it is supported by proper symbolic computations.

It seems strange (and the French were later indignant about this) that Airy did not mention Adams to Le Verrier at this point. Whewell was a Fellow of Trinity and Adams from the adjoining St Johns, so Airy could assume

389 The letter, in the Whewell papers in Trinity College, is quoted in Smith 'Cambridge and the Discovery of Neptune' *ISIS*, 1989, 80, 395–422. Smith assumes that this implies that at this time he thought his own telescope big enough – though this seems to read a lot into an 'off the cuff' remark.

they already knew each other. But he could make no such assumption about Le Verrier, and it is unclear why he did not at least mention Adams to him.

Before Airy had any reply, a meeting of the Board of Visitors of the Observatory took place on June 29th, at which John Herschel, James Challis and others were present. In the course of discussion Airy referred to the probability of shortly discovering a new planet, giving as his reason the very close coincidence between the results of Adams' and Le Verrier's positions of the supposed disturbing planet. Sir John Herschel then spoke in like confidence in an address in Southampton on September 10th.

Meantime, Le Verrier wrote back (28th June) assuring Airy that the errors in radius vector were well accounted for by his theory, and urging Airy to search for the planet.

Airy's 'Account' suggests that anyone reading this letter must be:

> … struck with its clearness of explanation, with the writer's extraordinary command, not only of the physical theories of perturbation, but also of the geometrical theories of the deduction of orbits from observation, and with his perception that his theory *ought* to explain all the phenomena, and his firm belief that it had done so. I had no longer any doubt upon the reality and general exactness of the prediction of the planet's place.

Why did Airy not instigate an immediate search at Greenwich? Grosser suggests one reason was some kind of irrational dread of any change in the observatory routine. A more likely version of this (which Allan Chapman suggests) is that he really did not think that this was the kind of work the observatory was for. This, indeed, was a view about which he was explicit, as we have seen. He also recognised that the largest telescope in his observatory at the time was the Sheepshanks equatorial

St John's Bridge

refractor with an aperture of only 6.7 inches. Airy himself had supervised the Cambridge Observatory's massive 11.75 inch Northumberland telescope (completed only recently in 1839). This would, in his view, be far more suitable, and finding a new planet was the kind of work in which a university telescope could and should be employed.

From June 10th Airy had been host to Peter Andreas Hansen, director of the Seeberg Observatory. On July 2nd Airy and Hansen visited Cambridge, and happened to meet John Couch Adams whilst crossing St John's Bridge. Airy had met Adams only once previously (in December 1845), in company with Challis, and on this occasion the encounter was very brief. Grosser complains at Airy's failure to introduce Adams to Hansen as the one who had calculated Neptune, and sarcastically suggests that Airy's 'otherwise excellent memory invariably failed him in matters involving Adams'. But Grosser's inference is unrealistic. If Airy was 'preoccupied and cool' this is not uncommon when one's mind is on other things and an encounter occurs out of the blue. Airy (who met hundreds of people) had received one short note from Adams, had no reply to his letter, and had met him only once – so probably barely recognised him. In any case, how exactly would Grosser expect Airy to introduce Adams? *'Oh Dr Hansen, this is John Adams – he sent me an inexplicitly derived set of results for a new planet some time ago, and failed to reply to my request for the derivation and information on Uranus's radius vector … '* Who knows what went through his mind, and how in hindsight he might have wished he had said something more? But his immediate reaction was both natural and understandable, and need imply no malice towards Adams.[390]

In any event, on July 6th he went to stay near Cambridge with another member of the Cambridge network, Dean George Peacock, who was Lowndean Professor of Geometry and Astronomy at Cambridge. Whether this stimulated him further we don't know, but on 9th July he wrote to Challis urging him to search the appropriate part of the sky:

> I have thought about the way of making such examination, but I am convinced that (for various reasons, of declination, latitude of place, feebleness of light, and regularity of superintendence)

---

[390] At the time of writing, in a web page www.uh.edu/engines/epi 1006.htm , based on an article in *American Scientist* March–April 1995, a Huston academic asserts: 'He wrote an angry letter to Challis, and he wouldn't even to speak to Adams.' Is this a fair analysis?

> there is no prospect whatever of its being made with any chance of success, except with the Northumberland telescope.
>
> Now I should be glad to ask you, in the first place, whether you could make such an examination?
>
> Presuming that your answer would be in the negative, I would ask, secondly, whether, supposing that an assistant were supplied to you for this purpose, you would superintend the examination.

Airy did not actually offer to provide an assistant (as often quoted) but asked whether the provision of one would enable the work. His motive (he later said) was because he knew how hard-pressed Challis and his assistants were, but we don't know what he had in mind to finance the help. On 13th July a second letter to Challis pressed:

> I can only add that, in my opinion, the importance of this inquiry exceeds that of any current work, which is of such a nature as not to be totally lost by delay.

Airy's suggestion was not centred on searching for a planetary disc, nor restricted to the exact spot Adams and Le Verrier had specified. It was based on making three sweeps of a belt 30° by 10° and looking for *motion*. When Challis began sweeps on July 29th, he used further calculations supplied by Adams.

Why Airy's urgency? In his 'Account' Airy explains that the planet would be in opposition in about six weeks, and so at the best point for observation. If it were as faint as he suspected it could be many years before such an opportunity recurred. Airy seems to have a fairly internationalist approach to science – and his urgency was probably not motivated by nationalistic desire for priority. As we have seen, he did not think his own observatory suited to the task by either purpose or equipment. The work should be done by a large privately operated telescope. It could be argued that he was at fault in not better informing other British astronomers (J. R. Hind in Regents Park, W. Lassell in Liverpool, and Lord Rosse and E. J. Cooper in Ireland had instruments which might have succeeded). Obviously, however, as the architect of the largest refractor in England at his Alma Mater, Airy would have been less than human had he not wished to see the honour fall there. Cambridge was his circle, and had provided his way from agricultural obscurity to position, fame, and marriage with the girl of his dreams! Other private establishments might not, in any case, have had staff to make the prolonged sweeps he thought were needed – but for Cambridge he may have had in mind some means to finance these.

At this time both Le Verrier and Adams were revising their estimates. On September 2nd 1846 Adams sent to Greenwich his sixth corrected solution. Airy was in Germany, and his assistant Robert Main replied offering Adams some more later data. Grosser thinks this 'intellectually emasculated' though one is not sure what he expected poor Main to do.

Adams, meanwhile, prepared an outline paper on his calculations (at last) but got to the British Association (in Southampton) too late to deliver it!

As Challis continued his search, Le Verrier, failing to enlist French observers (though they did mount a brief search[391]) finally persuaded Johann Gottfried Galle (1812–1910) to persuade in turn his superior at the Berlin observatory Johann Franz Encke (1791–1865) to allow a search. The planet was found on the first night, and confirmed the next day – September 25th 1846. Challis received a copy of Le Verrier's *Comptes Rendus* paper on 29th September, and on that night began to look for a disc – finding a candidate immediately which later turned out to be Neptune. On October 1st, Challis found out the planet had already been found, realising to his chagrin that he had actually seen it but had failed to spot either a motion or a disc shape.

On 10th August Airy had left with his family for an annual summer working holiday on the Continent. This year the holiday (spent mostly in Germany) was also convalescence from nervous exhaustion. Airy stated:

> We stayed for some time at Wiesbaden, as my nerves were shaken by work on the Railway Gauge Commission, and I wanted the Wiesbaden waters.[392]

He was staying with his friend Professor Hansen when he heard of the discovery of the new planet on 29th September. Chapman points out that Grosser wrongly states that Airy 'did not write to anyone about it for more than two weeks'. In fact, he wrote to both Challis at Oxford and Main in

---

[391] See Smith, op. cit. 408.

[392] Airy *Autobiography*, 183 quoted by Allan Chapman, op.cit. 129.

Greenwich the next day. The letters are entirely factual, and give no hint of any rising anxiety that he was about to be accused of all kinds of things. He arrived back only on 11th October – presumably to a mountain of backlogged mail. Chapman suggests that Airy had a genuinely internationalist view of science, 'patriotic issues were irrelevant in such matter, and I think he was astonished when his less impartial friends and colleagues, on both sides of the Channel, pointed accusing fingers …'

The Cambridge network had all been aware of Adams' work, and their reactions were complex. None of the circle had informed the French axis of Adams' work before the discovery or even immediately after it, and the French were (justifiably) annoyed when some of the Cambridge group later tried to claim credit for Adams. The main events unfolded as follows.

On 1st October John Herschel wrote to the *Athenaeum* (the letter being published 3rd October), referring to the 'remarkable calculations of M. Le Verrier' but also noting Adams' work. This aroused English interest, but not on the Continent where it was not immediately noticed.

Challis wrote on October 5th to the director of the Paris Observatory François Arago (1786–1853) saying he had been looking for the planet since 29th July, and the French assumed he had been using *Le Verrier's* data. When they later found that at the same time he was writing to British publications claiming to have been using *Adams'* figures they were somewhat upset, as we shall see.

On 14th October Airy wrote to Le Verrier:

> I do not know whether you are aware that collateral researches had been going on in England, and that they had led to precisely the same result as yours. I think that it probable that I shall be called on to give an account of these. If in this I shall give praise to others, I beg that you will not consider it as at all interfering with my acknowledgement of your claims. You are to be recognised as beyond doubt, the real predictor of the planet's place. I may add that the English investigations, as I believe, were not quite so extensive as yours. They were known to me earlier than yours.

Airy wrote the same day to Challis:

> Heartily do I wish that you had picked up the planet, I mean in the eyes of the public, because in my eyes you have done so. But these near misses are sometimes nearly unavoidable.

Grosser sees it as a 'change' that Airy should want to give Le Verrier full 'acknowledgement' but assert that Challis had 'really' picked it up. There is, however, no inconsistency here. For one thing, actually Adams' work is parallel to Le Verrier's, whilst Challis's is parallel to Galle's. For another, in any event, Challis is a 'near miss' – and the words that follow seem more designed to soothe poor Challis than to suggest making any public claim, since there is no doubt that in 'the eyes of the public' Challis will *not* be credited.

On October 17th Challis's detailed account of the British investigations appeared in the *Athenaeum,* and the meeting of the French Academy of Sciences on October 19th was a stormy one. Arago was particularly bitter, contrasting Challis's letter of 5th October, which did not mention Adams' work, with his *Athenaeum* article, which gave it central importance. What particularly incensed Arago was that Challis was apparently claiming his and Adams' right to *name* the new planet ('Oceanus') based on their unpublished work. Challis's motivation in this can only be guessed, but it incensed the French who saw this as the ultimate take-over bid. Arago, thundered:

> There exists only one rational and just way to write the history of science: it is to rely exclusively upon *publications* bearing a definite date; abandoning that, all is confusion and obscurity.

Arago had a point, but spoilt it with exaggeration, going on to claim that:

> Mr. Adams has no right to figure in the history of the discovery of the planet Le Verrier, neither by a detailed citation, nor by the slightest allusion.

The French press took off from this, becoming so hysterically detached from the facts as to induce public disavowals from both Arago and Le Verrier. Some of the English press were just as silly, suggesting a conspiracy of Airy to give Adams' calculations to Le Verrier and rob Adams of his 'just desserts'.

Airy was trying to reconcile the sides. A letter to Le Verrier of October 21st apologised for Challis's article, claiming it was only meant to make the

British aware of Adams' work, but the French Press continued vitriolic and often poorly informed attacks on both Airy and Challis.

On November 13th Airy, Challis and Adams all presented papers on the issue to the Royal Astronomical Society. Adams' was a technical paper, well received and admired. Challis's paper seemed to convince few. Airy had sought and obtained permission of his correspondents to produce letters in his 'Account' which basically set out events and defended his own role. Though modern scholars tend to view him more sympathetically, Airy continued to be abused both by the French, and by such British figures as David Brewster and James South. Even Professor Sedgwick, a close friend of Airy and friend of Challis, wrote to Airy on 3rd December not altogether convinced by his 'Account':

> Had the results communicated to you and Challis been sent to Berlin, I am told, they came so near the mark that to a certainty the new planet would have been made out in a very few weeks, perhaps a very few days, and the whole business settled in 1845 – Adams the sole, unadvised, unassisted discoverer. Is this true? Do Adams' results come so near the mark as to justify such language? If so, I must myself chime in with the pack of grumblers. To say the very least of it, a grand occasion has been thrown away.

This is a bit ingenuous. The planet was not in opposition in 1845, and Airy can hardly have been expected to send off to the Berlin observatory some unsupported statements about it without derivations, left for him by a previously unknown mathematician who did not reply to his request for further information. Since Galle was barely able to convince Encke to make a search based on Le Verrier's detailed calculations, he is hardly likely to have convinced him based on a summary from an unknown. The suggestion that *Challis* could have sent the results to Berlin is even less plausible – it would have been odd for Challis (who had himself a large suitable telescope) to do so. In his reply on 4th December, Airy told Sedgwick that he had not been aware that Adams (although a Fellow of Trinity) was still only a BA – he had assumed him to be an MA and had addressed his letter to 'Reverend W. J. Adams'. A Trinity MA should really know better than to ignore a prompt reply to an unsolicited and undated paper – and Airy might well have concluded that Adams had thought again about it. But as Chapman observes:

> On the other hand, one suspects that Airy, who was a great encourager of promising scientists, would have taken further initiatives to help had he been more fully acquainted with the circumstances.

Sedgwick in 1832

Sedgwick was a friend and a generous soul, but his letter to Lady Herschel on 19th December still reflected much of the British mood: 'We, some of us, grumble at our Astronomer [Challis] for not securing the new planet, after Adams had tied a noose tightly about its neck so early as September 1845.'[393] The complaint here is not that they didn't tell Berlin, but that Challis didn't find it himself. Sedgwick (with Sheepshanks) perhaps did more than any to forward the eventual recognition of Adams, but he was no astronomer! How far his criticism of Challis was justified we may consider later.

The central Cambridge figures faced assaults from French critics on one side and some British critics on the other. Unsurprisingly, their public pronouncements sometimes differed rather from their private reflections. Sheepshanks contended that Challis should be recognised for the optical discovery, but John Herschel wrote to Whewell:

John Herschel

> I do not call finding an object merely including it in a crowd of others (without knowing it is there, and rather suspecting, it *not* to be, with an *intention* of examining then at leisure to ascertain if it be among them or not) … Until the planet was actually seen and shown to be a planet – there was no discovery – except in so far

393 Clark & Hughes, *The Life and Letters of Adam Sedgwick* (1890) ii, 107. Standage (125) and also Baum & Sheehan (113) report Sedgwick's outburst of 'Curse their narcotic souls', but neither mention the good-natured laugh at his own intensity with which he followed it. Standage also suggests Sedwick's illegible handwriting in the letter showed he was 'incoherent with rage'. Actually, many of Sedgwick's letters were illegible – and any 'outbursts' were usually followed quickly by good-natured humour!

> as a successful physical hypothesis is one ...[394]

George Biddell Airy

This is obvious; otherwise we might say that Flamsteed 'discovered' Uranus in 1690. Herschel was also aware that French mathematics was generally the basis for the work, and that Le Verrier's analysis was much fuller than Adams'. Herschel had never sought to deny that the planet was in a sense the property of Le Verrier, but wanted to do justice to Adams' work. Chapman rightly suggests that for Airy too: 'In Airy's mind, scientific knowledge was, by definition, public, open, international and broadly useful'.[395]

Amongst scientists, all was not merely nationalistic. The Royal Society gave the Copley Medal, its highest award, to Le Verrier in November 1846, and the view that Le Verrier should have the priority was general. The *name* of the new planet was still controversial. Arago, for example, wanted Uranus named 'Herschel' and Neptune named 'Le Verrier' – though the names we now use today were gradually accepted.

In June 1847 the British Association met at Oxford. Adams and Le Verrier met with a cordial handshake, both were invited by John Herschel to his home in Collingwood, and they seemed to form an immediate friendship with no signs of jealousy. Sedgwick wrote, moreover, on 12th July 1847, of a royal visit to this BAAS meeting:

> When the Royal visitors entered the Physical and Mathematical Section, the great French Mathematician Le Verrier was on his legs discussing the orbit of a comet. When he sat down, Airy, Challis, Herschel, Adams, Sir W. Hamilton, and Sir David Brewster took part in a short discussion. In all Europe it would not have been possible to bring greater astronomical names together.

---

[394] Quoted in Smith, op. cit. 416.

[395] Chapman, op. cit. 131. Chapman gives other examples of misquoting and distortion in Grosser.

Airy's Transit Circle 1851

The business of science had to go on – recriminations apart.

Airy continued as Astronomer Royal until 1881. He continued to invent and add to the instruments in the observatory. He was involved in organising expeditions to observe the transits of Venus in 1874 and 1882, in studying tides, and on many scientific committees and advisory groups. He pioneered telegraphic time signals, and established a Spectroscopic department in 1874 (when aged 73!). He produced some 500 scientific papers and memoirs, a number of books, eventually accepted a knighthood (initially turned down because too expensive!), the Freedom of the City of London etc. He died in 1892 and was buried in the churchyard at Playford.

James Challis (1803–1882)

James Challis

Only a brief account of James Challis can be given here. He was born the fourth son of John Challis of Braintree, going to Mill Hill School just north of London. He entered Trinity College, Cambridge as a sizar in 1821, graduating as senior wrangler and first Smith prizeman in 1825. He became a Fellow of Trinity in 1826, was ordained and took a college living in 1830.

In 1831 he married, so having to vacate the Trinity Fellowship. When Airy went to Greenwich in 1835, Challis became Plumian Professor and Director of the Cambridge Observatory. Challis took up residence in 1836.

Cambridge Observatory

In 1844 Challis was in contact with Adams. On 12th February Adams' diary records that:

> Professor Challis brought one of the Notices of the Astronomical Society containing my results respecting the Comet.

This was the Comet of Faye, and in a one-page article Adams had computed the orbit using the data from the Northumberland telescope.[396] Perhaps Adams mentioned his work on Uranus at this time, but in any event on 13th February 1844 Challis wrote to Airy that: 'A young friend of mine, Mr Adams of St John's College, is working at the theory of Uranus'. He asked Airy to provide data on observations of Uranus, which were promptly sent. Adams' diary records that on February 16th 1844 'Professor Challis called with a note from Mr. Airy with the results of all the Greenwich observations of Uranus'.

In the autumn of 1844 a new comet (Vico's Comet) appeared, and, again from Challis's observations, Adams computed its orbit. This time, Challis wrote to him on October 7th:

> When you have satisfied yourself about the elliptic form of the orbit will it not be advisable to send a communication to *The Times* newspaper (the Astronomical Society is not sitting) in order that we may have the credit in England of first making the discovery.

Adams, at this point, was not even a Fellow (he was elected in November), yet we find Challis taking an interest and encouraging him to publish. This was followed by Airy replying within a day or so of getting the request for data and sending much more than asked. It would not be unnatural to suppose that Challis believed Adams to have got the general message – if you've got results then publish them! Adams' comet results were indeed published in *The Times* on October 15th, but Adams wrote home that he had found after his return to Cambridge that the French had earlier got 'very nearly the same results as myself, but earlier in time owing to their observations having been made earlier' .

In September 1845 Adams placed in Challis's hands (in Challis's own words):

> … a paper containing numerical values of the mean longitude at a given period of perihelion, eccentricity of orbit, mass and geometric longitude, September 30, of the supposed disturbing planet, which he calls by anticipation 'The New Planet', evidently

396 'Elements of the Comet of Faye', *Monthly Notices of the Royal Astronomical Society*, vi (1844).

> showing the conviction in his own mind of the reality of its existence.[397]

On 22nd September 1845 Challis gave Adams a letter of introduction to Airy:

> My friend Mr. Adams (who will probably deliver this note to you) has completed his calculations respecting the perturbation of the orbit of Uranus by a supposed ulterior planet, and has arrived at results which he would be glad to communicate to you personally, if you could spare him a few moments of your valuable time. His calculations are founded on the observations you were so good as to furnish him with some time ago; and from his character as a mathematician, and his practice in calculation, I should consider the deductions from his premises to be made in a trustworthy manner. If he should not have the good fortune to see you at Greenwich, he hopes to be allowed to write to you on this subject.

The version Adams sent the Astronomer Royal included (in the words of Challis) 'the addition of what was far more important' i.e. the residual errors of Uranus, which enabled one to see the accuracy of the theory. Challis differed from Airy in believing that if the observed errors were small then this must imply that the radius vector had been correct.

Challis's later account states:

> As the calculations rested on an assumption made according to Bode's law … without the above-mentioned numerical verification, no proof was given that the problem was solved or that the elements of the supposed planet were not mere speculative results. The earliest evidence of the complete solution of an inverse perturbation is to be dated from October 1845.[398]

The results were uncertain, and Adams was induced to try more calculations based on a reduced distance. Actually, the Bode's law figure would be 38.8 whereas the modern figure for Neptune is 30.06 AU.

---

[397] Challis 'Report to the Observatory Syndicate' 1846, in 'The Scientific Papers of John Couch Adams'.

[398] James Challis, 'Special Report of Proceedings in the Observatory relative to the new Planet', 12th December 1846.

Adams, apparently, set to work on this. But why did Challis not begin the search immediately?

> No one could have anticipated that the place of the unknown body was indicated with any degree of exactness by a theory of this kind. It might reasonably be supposed, without at all mistrusting the evidence which the theory gave of the *existence* of the new planet that its position was determined but roughly, and that search for it must necessarily be long and laborious. This was the view I took, and consequently I had no thought of commencing the search in 1845, the planet being considerably past opposition at the time Mr Adams completed his calculations. The succeeding interval to the midsummer of 1846 was a period of great astronomical activity … During this time I had little communication with Mr Adams respecting this new planet …

As it turned out the planet (although past opposition) *would* have been visible – but this is hindsight. What was Adams doing? Challis says that his new calculations and (at last) some figures on radius vector (which could as well have been calculated from the first theory) were finally sent to Airy only at the start of September 1846. Nothing at any time would have stopped Adams sending (say) a letter to *The Times.*

Northumberland Telescope

Meantime, at a meeting of the Greenwich Board of Visitors on June 29th 1846 Challis heard of Le Verrier's *Comptes Rendus* of June 1st, and on 9th July and 13th July Airy sent Challis the letters (quoted above) urging him to drop other work and pursue the planet. Challis got back from a holiday on 18th July, replied to Airy that he would start as soon as possible, and informed Adams who drew up a table giving the expected position of the planet during the period. Evidently both Airy and Challis expected Adams' (and Le Verrier's) predictions to be only approximate, and a band of sky was to be searched.

Northumberland Dome

Challis began his observation with the Northumberland telescope on 29th July 1846. He says he was unaware at the time of the Berlin star-maps, and 'consequently had to proceed on the principle of observations made at intervals'. On July 30th he made a sweep recording the stars, and did the same on August 12th. Later perusal showed that one object *had* moved – that object was in fact the planet. Challis explains:

> My time, however, was so occupied with comet reductions, and so little expectation had I of discovering the planet by a brief search, that I was only just preparing to map the places of the stars to see what success I had, when the announcement of the discovery reached me.

To Airy he later similarly explained his delay in comparing the July 30th and August 12th patterns:

> I delayed doing this partly because I thought the probability of discovery was very small till a much larger portion of the heavens was scrutinised, but chiefly because I was making a grand effort to reduce the vast numbers of comet observations which I have accumulated and this occupied the whole of my time.[399]

Meantime, Le Verrier had produced a third paper on 31st August 1846, refining further the position, and also predicting that it would be not less than about 3" in diameter and so observable as a disc. Galle, in Berlin, used this to find the disc-like planet on the first day of searching: 23rd September 1846.

On September 29th Challis saw for the first time Le Verrier's new figures and:

> By these I was induced to return again to the theoretical position of the planet, and to endeavour to detect it by the appearance of

[399] A letter of 12th October 1846.

> a disc. In fact, on the night of September 29th, out of a very large number of stars whose approximate places I recorded, I fixed upon one which appeared to me to have a disc, and which proved to be the planet. On October 1 I had intelligence of Dr Galle's discovery.

Poor old Challis! Expecting the planet to be too small to detect the *disc* (and his telescope, though big, was using a magnification of only 170) he was looking for *movement.* Expecting the search to take months, he did not hurry himself to check the movements in mid-August because he was preoccupied with comets. Hindsight is a wonderful thing! When he received notice that it should be observable as a disc, and that its position *was* fairly accurate, he (like Galle) found it the first night – but it was already too late by six days. Challis was unlucky – there is even a story that but for Mrs Challis keeping him and a friend Reverend Kingsley in for tea one cold night he might had found it sooner! But was he lazy, stupid, and uninterested in younger scientists as so many have suggested?

In final justification in his report Challis notes that:

> I was in quite a novel position: the history of astronomy does not afford a parallel instance of observations undertaken entirely in reliance upon deductions from theoretical calculations, and those too of a kind before untried.

Challis at this point was in some alarm. He realised with horror that the planet had been in his grasp, that Adams had given him a head-start, but that he had missed it. He wrote to the *Cambridge Chronicle* and then the *Athenaeum* explaining that he had been searching in the right area for the planet for *two months* (i.e. since *before* Le Verrier's third paper and based on Adams' figures not Le Verrier's), and that his efforts: 'though slow must eventually have been successful'. Challis gives to Adams such praise and assertion of priority that it is little surprise that the French took offence. Few would have found plausible his suggestion that:

> Some may be of the opinion that in placing before the first astronomer of the kingdom results which showed he had completed the problem, and by which he was, in a manner, pledged to the production of calculations, there was as much

> publication as was justifiable on the part of a mathematician whose name was not yet before the world.

Challis completed his 1846 report by saying that he was now diligently observing the planet. In a report of 1847 we do indeed find Challis observing the planet in communication with Adams, who was computing more details of its orbit from data of August 1846 observations supplied by Challis. The report carries further observation. Challis gives various figures as follows

- orbit eccentricity 'not more than 0.18 ... probably 0.06' (the modern figure is 0.009)
- mean distance of 30.35 (the modern figure is 30.06)
- sidereal period of 167 years (the modern figure is 164.8)

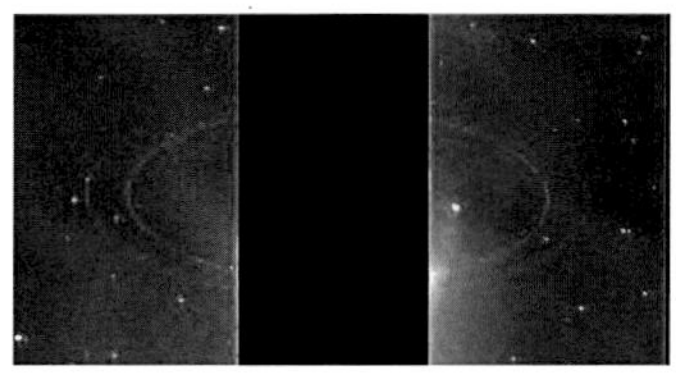

NASA - Neptune's Rings

The various communications between Challis and Airy were, naturally enough, a bit strained at times as each strove to ensure that he was not dumped on as some kind of scapegoat, though there seems not to have been a serious breakdown between them.

A final Neptune episode occurred when the Liverpool-based astronomer William Lassell (1799–1880) thought he had detected rings around Neptune, which Challis thought he could confirm.[400] Later both men changed their minds and it was decided that the apparent rings were a product of the telescopes used – though Lassell *did* find the Neptune moon Triton. Ironically, in the early 1980s a blink during occultation seemed to indicate there might actually *be* rings, and these were detected by Voyager II in 1989. The NASA website, however, asserts:

> The rings around Neptune are so faint that when Voyager's cameras captured this image, the brightness of Neptune nearly made them impossible to detect. The black box in the centre of the image is where Neptune was blocked out because no detail was visible given the long exposure time required to capture the

[400] See Robert W. Smith and Richard Baum, 'William Lassell and the Ring of Neptune' *Science History Publications*, 1984.

> almost invisible rings. The bright glow at the edges of the black box is some of the light reflected from Neptune. Two sharp rings are visible, Le Verrier and Adams, and one faint ring, Galle, is barely visible inside them.

Poor Challis didn't even get to have a ring named after him (!) – though it is unlikely that any observer really could see the rings at that time.

How are we to assess Challis? With hindsight obviously he should have dropped everything and looked for the planet – the discovery of which would have brought more applause than any routine work on comets. He was unlucky: he had made star comparisons of July 30th and August 12th but stopped just short of reaching Neptune, and he had *nearly* re-examined it looking for a disc. But decisions which seem 'obvious' afterwards are not always obvious when made in the hurly burly of day-to-day living in a busy life. Here are a couple of interesting quotes:

> Challis was a spectacular failure as a scientist, and ironically this failure has immortalised him … At a later time, or under less amiable circumstances, he would have been branded as a charlatan.[401]

> J.C. Adams … finished the calculations, and took them to the Professor of Astronomy at Cambridge. Unfortunately that particular professor did not happen to be very clever; sometimes there are professors who are not very clever, or are lazy, though you might not believe it, and it is hard luck on the students. However, this professor had sense enough to suggest that Adams should get help from someone else, and he recommended him to go to the Astronomer Royal (Airy) at Greenwich, and then he thought that he had done everything that could reasonably be expected of him and went peacefully to sleep … [later Airy got Le Verrier's paper]. So he woke up the professor at Cambridge and told him to begin searching. The professor set to work, but was still half asleep, so that

[401] Olin J. Eggen in *Dictionary of Scientific Biography*.

> though he looked straight at Neptune more than once, he did not recognise it ...[402]

The writer of the latter, H. H. Turner, was an *Oxford* professor himself and could with impunity be disparaging about one at 'the other place', but all this does a lot of violence to the truth. His book is written for young people, but it gives a quite misleading impression of the nature of science.

Some of the interesting general issues can be raised in our conclusions, but in the meantime we may note that this supposedly somnambulant 'spectacular failure' (Challis) contributed 225 papers on mathematics, physics and astronomy to scientific journals, and published 12 volumes of *Astronomical Observations Made at the Observatory at Cambridge* (1832–1864). Challis relinquished the observatory to Adams in 1861, but remained Plumian Professor until his death in 1882.

John Couch Adams

John Couch Adams c.1846

There are few historical figures about whom it is almost impossible to find anyone saying anything bad: John Couch Adams is one of them.

He was born in 1819 the eldest son of a family of seven born to Thomas and Tabitha Adams who were Cornish tenant farmers. Born in Lidcott Farm on the edge of the Laneast moor, John Couch Adams was baptised in the Wesleyan Chapel at Tregeare with which his whole family were connected. The family was loving and close-knit, the home happy though not affluent. Adams showed early promise at maths, and aged eleven he accompanied his dad to visit a relative Mr Pearse, who also had a precocious son. Adams won a friendly 'maths contest' against the lad, and Mr Pearse took Adams to match him against the local schoolmaster. The result led the schoolmaster to say to Adams' father: 'If he were my boy I should sell my hat off my head rather than not send him to College'. Adams showed as

[402] H. H. Turner in *A Voyage in Space* (1915).

little aptitude for farming as had Newton, and his parents resolved he should be educated. A better school at Devonport brought him within reach of a good library, and at the age of twelve he paid 2d a week to go on an astronomy course. In 1834 he received a copy of John Herschel's newly published *Astronomy* as a school prize, and the next year saw Halley's Comet.

St John's College Cambridge

From 1837 Adams was working on mathematics himself, and also tutoring sons of richer folk to supplement the family income. In Spring 1839 he began preparing for the sizarship examination of St John's College and in October started (in the middle of the night) his two-day coach trip to Cambridge to sit the exam.

Adams duly started at the college, and 'regularly repaired to the rooms of a Trinity Don, William Carus, whose religious and moral influence on the large number of undergraduates who frequented his rooms Sunday by Sunday is constantly referred to appreciatively by Adams'.[403] Carus had obtained his Fellowship in 1829, and was successor to the great evangelical figure Charles Simeon. He was also a friend of Trinity Fellow and Professor Adam Sedwick, whose Arminian evangelical faith was probably very like the Cornish Methodist background in which Adams had grown up. Adams must have felt at home in this group, devout but fun loving, and committed to the value of science; he moved easily into a specifically Anglican though deep piety that was common to his circle of Cambridge dons.[404] He was never ordained, but, according to his correspondence with

403 Smart, 'Occasional Notes' (1947), 45.

404 As well as scientists, the great biblical scholars F. B. Wescott (1825–1901) and J. B. Lightfoot (1828–1889) became Fellows of Trinity around the mid century, and Adams was also friendly with the slightly later Professor F. J. A. Hort (1733–1806). Charles Darwin had become friendly with the Sedgwick-Whewell-Henslow circle whilst at Christ's College 1828–1831, well *before* Adams' time, but had moved on.

Sedgwick, when he was offered a knighthood in 1847 he was still considering ordination.

St Johns College

Like Newton, Adams could sometimes be seen to be 'miles away' in a mathematical problem – though mercifully none of his biographers have suggested deep complexes! His interest in astronomy, alongside his 'proper' studies, still absorbed him during undergraduate days.

In the Easter vacation of 1841 he first went into the university observatory, and soon had a second visit to study the instruments. On June 26th 1841 he read Airy's 1832 'Report to the British Association on the state of Astronomical Science'. On 3rd July 1841 he wrote in his diary:

> Formed a design, in the beginning of this week, of investigating as soon as possible after taking my degree, the irregularities in the motion of Uranus which are yet unaccounted for; in order to find whether they may be attributed to the action of an undiscovered planet beyond it; and is possible thence to determine the elements of its orbit &c. approximately, which would probably lead to its discovery.

Obviously, at this time, he did not know Challis well, though with their mutual Trinity College connections they must have been acquainted. The fact, however, that he was being so affected by a nearly ten-year-old report indicates that he was not intimately in touch with current astronomical thinking.

John Couch Adams

That summer he was at home helping with the harvest but also (by his brother's account) absorbed in astronomical calculations. Studies continued, with astronomy always an interest. In January 1843 he sat the Mathematical Tripos (examinations which the Trinity group had helped reform). There was, of course, no specifically *science* degree at Cambridge until the Natural Science Tripos was introduced in the 1850s – and this was for the less able students!

Famously, Adams scored 4000 marks in his examinations – double that of his nearest rival, although the year was not a weak year. A modest and likeable man by all reports, Adams was not even sure of his success until the results – but then wrote home overjoyed to the family who had sacrificed so much to support him there. The First Smith's Prize followed two weeks later, and a College Fellowship soon after.

During 1843 Adams was taking pupils in term-time to help his own finances and also to be able to help the meagre family finances. As well during 1843, and particularly in the parlour at his family home in Lidcot during the vacation, he struggled on with the figures, and arrived at a first solution to the problem of the unknown planet.

A good and readable summary of Adams' approach in calculation is given in Standage *The Neptune File* chapter 5, but is omitted here for reasons of length.

In earlier sections we have noted the involvement of Adams with Challis and then with Airy. His famous note left for Airy on 21st October[405] gave various figures as follows [some estimated modern figures are in brackets]:

Mean Distance (assumed nearly in accordance with Bode's law)	38.4	[30.58]
Mean Sidereal Motion in 365.25 days	1° 30′.9	[2° 11′.1]
Mean Longitude, 1st October, 1845	323°34′	
Longitude of Perihelion	315 55	
Eccentricity	0.1610	[0.009]
Mass (that of the Sun being unity)	0.0001656	[0.0000522]

The note gave no calculations, but summarised the error between observation and theory. Flamsteed's 1690 Uranus observation has a massive error of +44".4 – and Adams says he decided 'not to use it in forming the equations of condition'. Airy is undisturbed by this in his response, as we noted above.

As we have seen, Airy responded quickly with a letter asking about the radius vector and for more detail. Adams' lack of response to this remains

[405] The full text is e.g. in Harrison, op. cit. and in Adams' scientific papers.

puzzling. He wrote of his regret to Airy on November 18th 1846 and added:

> I was not aware of the importance which you attached to my answer on this point, and I had not the smallest notion that you felt any difficulty on it, such as you subsequently mentioned to Mr. Le Verrier … the real angular motion of Uranus is considerably *slower* than that given by the tables. This appeared to me to show clearly that the tabular radius vector would be considerably increased by any theory which represents the motion in longitude … Hence it was that I was led to defer writing to you till I could find time to draw up an account of the method employed to obtain the results which I had communicated to you. More than once I commenced writing with this object, but unfortunately did not persevere. I was also much pained at not having been able to see you when I called at the Royal Observatory the second time, as I felt that the whole matter might be better explained by half an hour's conversation than by several letters, in writing which I have always experienced a strange difficulty.

Adams (like Le Verrier but unlike Airy) was totally convinced that only an exterior planet could account for the motion of Uranus, so the radius vector *must* be corrected if the planet's orbit worked. Airy, as noted, was more open-minded on the inverse square law itself, and so the double corroboration was important to him. However, Adams added:

> The only point which appeared to admit of any doubt was the assumption of the mean distance, and this I soon proceeded to correct. The work, however, went on very slowly as I had scarcely any time to give to these investigations except during the vacations.

In a letter of December 16th 1846 Sedgwick (a friend of both Airy and Adams) reported that Adams implied (though did not use the word) that he had been 'mortified' to find no message to have been left by Airy even if he were at dinner, but was later convinced that the servant had not passed on the message about his return. Answering Sedgwick's questions, Adams said he 'possibly might have' replied more readily otherwise to Airy's letter, but did not regard the radius vector as important, and also 'wanted to send my papers in good order to the Astronomer Royal' so was revising them throughout the summer. Adams apparently told Sedgwick that: 'I did think that the Astronomer Royal would have communicated my results among his correspondents. I took all that for granted, and I thought it a publication'. This was surely Adams' inexperience. When the Astronomer Royal had given so prompt a response asking for explicit information, Adams should not have assumed that his summary interim results would be circulated. Sedgwick added that Adams was 'anxious to have no misunderstanding with Airy … and expressed himself grieved at the ill-natured things that had been said'. Adams' disappointment was understandable, but he did not blame Airy whom he admired.

In the event, then, Adams was reworking his results and delayed any real publication or response to Airy. He had called on October 21st on his way back to Cambridge, and says he had little time 'except in the vacations' . This, with his admitted diffidence in writing (which Airy could have had no way of knowing), led to nothing further being done until he passed on the revised figures to Airy at the beginning of September 1846. By this time Airy had seen the 'double indication' he was looking for in the agreement of Adams' and Le Verrier's results, had a 'clear' letter back from Le Verrier on the calculations and Airy's question on the radius vector, and written twice to Challis to urge him to search urgently. Adams claims to Airy that he had decided to try to use the limited facility at St John's (an observatory which has since been demolished) 'if no one else took it up' – but he is vague about time scales.

As we have noted, the storm broke, Adams disliked the whole squabble, he made friends with Le Verrier at Oxford and Le Verrier visited Adams at Cambridge later that year. In the 1870s Adams was probably instrumental in an honorary Cambridge LLD being given to Le Verrier, as well as a second gold medal of the Royal Astronomical Society.

Adams himself was honoured, the Queen offering him a knighthood in 1847, which he turned down for pragmatic reasons (like Airy). A knighthood would have prevented possible ordination, restricted tutoring, restricted his choice of marriage partner, and seemed to him incongruous for a farmer's son. A biennial 'Adams Prize' was given at St John's from 1848.

In 1851 Adams became President of the Royal Astronomical Society.

Adams in old age

Adams did *not* become ordained and his Trinity Fellowship ceased in 1852, but he was given one at Pembroke College in 1853. In 1852–3 he was working on the lunar orbit – finally in 1853 succeeded in explaining it in Newtonian terms with the addition of an effect for tidal friction. His lunar theories, however, led to a prolonged dispute.

In autumn 1857 he became Professor of Mathematics at the University of St Andrews (where Brewster was Principal) but was appointed on 17th November 1858 as Lowndean Professor of Astronomy and Geometry (replacing Peacock) back at Cambridge. His younger brother William Grylls Adams graduated in 1859 (aged 23), going on to become a Professor of Natural Philosophy and to edit his brother's papers. In October 1861 Adams succeeded Challis at the Cambridge Observatory.

Adams enjoyed music and dancing, conversation, and made and kept friends easily. A kind of shy genius in mathematics, he was neither odd nor reclusive. Adams' friend Sedgwick (himself a bachelor!) had long been urging Adams to marry, and in a letter dated 30th December 1862 Adams writes with pleasure to tell him he is taking his advice. The letter has the kind of playful 'geological' references that were part of the general fun in letters between this group of men. The marriage was a happy one.

The Abbey memorial

During this whole period he was contributing papers – though still had a tendency to delay for more perfection and still showed a dislike for committing himself to writing. He turned down the post of Astronomer Royal in 1881. In this period Adams was associated with Girton College, active in promoting the admission of women to degrees at Cambridge, though he was conservative in his politics.

John Couch Adams died on 20th January 1892. He was buried in St Giles Cemetery in Cambridge, and a plaque was unveiled in Westminster Abbey in 1895.

Urbain Jean Joseph Le Verrier (1811–1877)

Urbain Le Verrier

Le Verrier was born in Normandy, and won a place at the prestigious Paris *École Polytechnique.* He graduated and started his academic career in research chemistry, though continued to have an interest in mathematics and astronomy. In 1837 two posts became available at the *École*, and since another candidate was thought better for the chemistry post Le Verrier was offered that in astronomy. He had published a paper on meteorites in 1832, but now looked for something better to further his ambitions. In 1840 he published studies of the mutual effects of the inner planets (Mercury, Venus, Earth and Mars), and then one on the outer planets (Jupiter, Saturn and Uranus). In 1844 he produced a paper on orbits of comets, and in particular Jupiter's great effect on them.

In 1845 the Director of the Paris Observatory, François Arago, suggested that the talented young mathematical astronomer should look at the problem of Uranus. Le Verrier's first paper on this was presented to the Academy of Sciences on 10th November 1845. This paper considered the effects of known planets on Uranus, and demonstrated that they alone certainly could not cause the observed orbit.

On 1st June 1846 his second paper, the *Comptes Rendus*, was presented. The first part of this considered whether the 19 'ancient' observations and 260 'modern' ones could be reconciled by readjusting the orbit. The answer was 'no'. An orbit could not be found which achieved this.

In the second part of the paper he considered other possibilities. One of these was that Newton's laws themselves might fail at greater distances – but this was a 'last resort'. He looked at the idea that a comet might have impacted and changed the course of Uranus around 1781 – and dismissed it along with the resistive fluid theory, etc. He concluded that *only* another planet could account for the perturbations, and asked 'Is it possible to work out the position that this planet would occupy in the sky?'

Like Adams, Le Verrier began with the assumption of Bode's law – though he did not actually use the name. Some distance had to be assumed, and the orbit could not be inside that of Uranus since this would affect other planets, nor too far away or its necessarily large mass would likewise affect other planets. Le Verrier's method (like that of Adams) is explained by Standage. The two methods differed, yet both arrived at a longitude on 1st January 1847 of 325°. It was this coincidence that (even without knowing that the methods were different) convinced Airy. However, Le Verrier was totally unaware of Adams, and Adams seems to have been unaware that Le Verrier was getting so near to his own results. Le Verrier was confident that his figure was fairly good, but was working on a more accurate figure.

Late in June Le Verrier received Airy's letter of 26th June asking about the radius vector, and replied promptly so that Airy received his detailed response on 1st July. Le Verrier, unlike Adams, was an established scientist and knew how to act. The British Astronomer Royal was an important scientific figure, and Le Verrier wrote:

> I am just about to finish the correction of the elements of the perturbing planet and to work out its position with great precision. If I might be allowed to hope that you will have enough confidence in my work to look for this planet in the sky, I will hasten, Sir, to send you its exact position as soon as I have obtained it.

Le Verrier also assured Airy that the radius vector 'is corrected on its own without having to be considered separately'. This alone (without the more detailed position promised) set Airy writing urgently to Challis.

In France, Arago's Paris Observatory made a brief search but gave up. Arago had presumably concluded that it would be a long job, and that (like Greenwich) this was not what his official observatory was for.

Few astronomers seemed at this point to be making serious efforts based on Le Verrier's predictions. He had, after all, said that they were likely to be accurate only to 10°, and this would therefore mean a lot of work. Only Challis knew that Adams had come up with the same figure, and he was looking but not really pulling out all the stops because he also thought it would be a long haul based on detecting movement. Was this, in fact, one reason why Airy and Challis kept Adams' work quiet at this stage? Was it in hope that they could reveal Adams' work in the double triumph of the first observation being made at Cambridge too?

Le Verrier did continue his calculations, and presented his third paper on 31st August – still unaware that Adams was working on the problem and in fact sent his revised figures to Airy (who was actually away in Germany) on 2nd September, together with the calculations and answers requested so long before. But Le Verrier was searching for someone to find his planet. One astronomer he wrote to (as we have noted) was Johann Gottfried Galle, an assistant at the Berlin Observatory, who received his letter on 23rd September. Flattered, Galle managed to persuade his boss Johann Enke (who was off to a birthday party), to let him search for the planet. Galle, together with an astronomy student Heinrich d'Arrest who had begged to be involved, searched for the planetary disc. They found nothing. Then d'Arrest suggested comparing that part of the sky with a new star atlas published by the Berlin Academy. They found the map, and as Galle read off star co-ordinates d'Arrest checked them on the map. Then one faint star at 327° longitude was read out and d'Arrest could not find it on the map. Encke was hurriedly fetched from his birthday party, and they studied the 'star' through the night. *Perhaps* it *did* have a kind of disc-like appearance - Encke apparently remarked 'A disc is only seen when it is known to exist'! *Perhaps* it had *moved* as well. They waited until the next night and checked – the object *had* moved, it must be Le Verrier's planet. They measured its diameter, and found it near to Le Verrier's predicted one.

Next day, Galle wrote to Le Verrier – the planet was found. Le Verrier was massively lionised in the French*Academy of Sciences* on 5th October, and apparently changed his mind about calling it 'Neptune' and induced Arago to suggest it be called 'Le Verrier'.

Then came a bombshell. Out of the blue they discovered the letter from the great English astronomer John Herschel in the *Athenaeum* of 3rd October. This described the 'remarkable calculations of M. Le Verrier' but also described the work of someone called 'Adams' (of whom none of the French had ever heard), whose earlier predictions had given Herschel confidence in those of Le Verrier. *Only this* had given Herschel confidence (he claimed) to announce a couple of weeks earlier that the new planet would soon be discovered:

> The remarkable calculations of M. Le Verrier, if uncorroborated by repetition of the numerical calculations by another hand, or by independent investigation from another quarter, would hardly justify so strong an assurance as that conveyed by my expressions above alluded to.

Mais! … Then appeared the material from James Challis. Challis, as we have seen, had been in some personal alarm at this point about possible criticism from home, and his pronouncements were designed to play down the 'loss' to British prestige by acknowledging Le Verrier's ownership but declaring 'English astronomers may lay claim to some merit'. Challis pressed Adams' priority and his own near-approach to the discovery based *not* on Le Verrier's but on *Adams'* figures. He had failed to actually spot it but:

> The planet was *secured*, and two positions of it recorded six weeks earlier here than in any other laboratory, and in a systematic search undertaken expressly for that purpose.

As a final straw, Challis even seemed to think they had a right to *name* the planet, suggesting 'Oceanus'. *Zut alors!*

Then Airy's letter of 14th October to Le Verrier arrived (as quoted above). Airy's attempts to reassure the increasingly incensed Le Verrier were accompanied by this same new English claim – all of them claimed to have known about and been acting on Adams' prior calculations, and yet none of them (even in Challis's recent letter of October 5th to Arago) had ever mentioned these to any French astronomer. *Quel horreur – c'est incroyable!*

The previous meeting of the Academy had been a celebration of Le Verrier, the one of October 19th was a tempest of anti-English feeling fired by the French papers which spoke of 'theft', 'false' claims etc. Two

(M. Adams découvrant la nouvelle planète dans le rapport de M. Leverrier)

(M. Adams cherchant la planète de M. Leverrier.)

much-reproduced cartoons of Adams show him looking in the wrong place and finding the planet only by looking at Le Verrier's calculations.[406] Finally, Le Verrier and Arago felt themselves that it had gone too far – and wrote distancing themselves from the press vitriol.

The French reaction was entirely understandable. Yet, as we have noted, Le Verrier received the Royal Society gold medal, and Le Verrier and Adams (who had made no claims throughout but maintained a dignified silence) became friends the next year. Adams was generally said to be modest and personable, Le Verrier is generally said to have been a 'difficult' person to deal with, and was seen to be arrogant. Quite the dynamics of the friendship are difficult to conclude, though Le Verrier seemed to relate better to foreign scientists than to colleagues or subordinates. In any event the Le Verrier–Adams friendship and mutual respect lasted throughout their lives.

Hard on the scientific turbulence came the 1848 revolution, and the short-lived Second French Republic. Arago took the Republican side, Le Verrier the side of authoritarian conservatism. When the conservative Louis-Napoleon seized power in 1851 he left Arago in his astronomical post, but

---

406 The tall hat Adams is wearing is *not*, as Standage states, a 'dunce's hat'. If we look closely at the cartoon Le Verrier is also wearing one – it is intended to convey an astronomer not a dunce.

Le Verrier was made a senator, and director of the Observatory when Arago died in 1853.

Arago had always been interested in the wider astronomical issues. William Herschel was one of his heroes, and physical astronomy fascinated him. Le Verrier seems to have (even more than Airy) been obsessed with order. The Paris Observatory had never been as clearly a utilitarian institution as Greenwich, but under his direction assistants were expected purely to compute, and he even dismissed an assistant for writing a book about plurality of worlds. Airy's staff seem to have been affectionately critical of his obsession for order and record-keeping. In contrast, Le Verrier's authoritarian ways and violent temper gradually alienated him from his staff, and mass resignation and total breakdown between Le Verrier and his appointed 'Board of Advisers' forced his resignation in 1870.[407]

We have seen that Newtonian physics triumphed in various planetary calculations culminating in the discovery of Neptune. Mercury, however, remained a problem. Its perihelion (which implied the axis of its ellipse) was advancing. Laboriously over the decade 1848–1858 Le Verrier founded the effects of all the known planets on this advance: He added them all up and they came to 527". Unfortunately, this was still 38" short of the observed advance. How could this be explained?

To Le Verrier the answer was obvious: there must be some as yet undetected body or bodies affecting Mercury as Neptune had affected Uranus.[408] The problem was that the body(s) had to have no appreciable effect on Venus or Earth. The obvious location was between Mercury and the Sun – but how come that any planet big enough had not been seen during a total eclipse?

> All these difficulties disappear if instead of a single planet, we invoke the existence of a series of small 'corpuscles' orbiting between Mercury and the Sun.[409]

His conclusion in September 1859 was that astronomers should be on the lookout for such bodies, seen as tiny dots in transit across the Sun. In

---

[407] Baum & Sheehan, *In Search of Planet Vulcan* (1997), gives good detail on this.

[408] This whole issue is detailed in N. R. Hanson 'Leverrier: The Zenith and Nadir of Newtonian Mechanics' *ISIS*, 1962, 53, 3, 173, 359–378.

[409] *Theorie* 105, quoted in Baum & Sheehan, op. cit. 139.

December an amateur astronomer Edmond Lescarbault (1814–1894) wrote to Le Verrier that he had observed just such a transit in March, moving in a line across the edge of the Sun. Le Verrier went to cross-examine the man, and emerged convinced that the new 'planet' existed. He announced it at the Academy on January 2nd 1860 – and this time there was no English ghost to haunt the feast as a French prediction and French observation were celebrated. Le Verrier was again lionised and Lescarbault given the Legion of Honour. Eventually the new planet was called Vulcan and Le Verrier calculated an orbit for it. Actually, the new planet did not solve Mercury's problems – one would have needed twenty Vulcans! Vulcan also proved elusive. One scientific enemy of Le Verrier (and he had many in France) claimed he had been observing at the time of the supposed transit and had seen nothing. Vulcan failed to materialise for repeat regular transits when predicted. By the late 1870s, Le Verrier was reduced to increasingly desperate attempts to calculate an orbit erratic enough for Vulcan to have escaped systematic searches for it. Nevertheless, in presenting him with the Gold Medal of the Royal Astronomical Society in 1876, Adams remarked that, bearing in mind the accuracy with which Mercury's orbit was now known:

> … the only way of accounting for it appears to be to suppose, with M. Le Verrier, the existence of several minor planets, or of a certain quantity of diffused matter circulating about the Sun within the orbit of *Mercury* …

To Adams, as to Le Verrier, Newton's laws seemed sacrosanct.

Le Verrier died of liver cancer in 1877 with the controversy still raging but amidst increasing scepticism. Vulcan (and various relatives) still continued to find advocates, but gradually its non-existence was accepted.[410]

Some Retrospects

Luck or Skill?

Challis's observations of Neptune in 1846–7 had led Adams to more accurate figures. Various other 'pre-sightings' were then later identified: Lalande in Paris (1795) Lamont in Munich (1845), John Herschel (1830) –

---

[410] Baum and Sheehan, op. cit. chart this progress, also Hanson op. cit.

and even Galileo (1612–13)! Using Lalande's records, the American astronomer Sears Cook Walker recomputed an orbit to compare with those of Le Verrier and Adams:

	Le Verrier	**Adams**	**Adams (May 47)**	**Walker**	***Modern***
Mean Distance	36.15	37.25	30.05	30.25	*30.58*
Period in years	217.387	227.3	(165.98)	166.381	*164.79*
Longitude 1.1.1847	326°32′	329°57′	328°13′54.5	328°7′57	
Eccentricity	0.10761	0.12062	0.0083835	0.00884	*0.009*
Mass (ratio to Sun)	0.000173	0.00010		0.00006	*0.0000522*

This led Benjamin Pierce of Harvard to claim that the Neptune discovered by Galle was not the planet computed, and its discovery near its reputed place was just a 'happy accident'. Pierce's arguments were repeated the following year by Jacques Babinet in France, who suggested that actually there were *two* perturbing planets, one still undiscovered. Le Verrier attempted a reply but Adams was silent. John Herschel pointed out that Neptune and Uranus were in conjunction late in 1821 so that the maximum mutual effect had allowed Adams and Le Verrier to find Neptune's longitude. Adams much later (1876) wrote in French:

> Il est vrai que, si nous voulions représenter les perturbations d'Uranus causées par un planète supérieure, pendant deux ou plusieurs périodes synodiques, cela ne pourrait se faire q'en adoptant une période approximativement vraie pour la planète perturbatrice; mais le cas est différent lorsque, comme ici, nous n'avons à représenter que les perturbations produites durant une fraction d'une période synodique.[411]

---

[411] From *Liouville's Journal de Mathematiques, II* (1976) in Adams' *Scientific Papers.* Translated this means: 'It is true that, if we wished to represent the perturbations of Uranus caused by a superior planet, during two or more synodic periods, that cannot be done except by adopting an approximately true period for the perturbing planet; but the situation is different when, as here, we only have to represent perturbations produced during a fraction of a synodic period.'

Actually, Adams and Le Verrier assumed greater orbital distance, but also greater mass for Neptune – the effects of which cancelled out. To be fair, Adams' further calculation assuming a shorter distance had effectively checked the robustness of the assumption about orbital distance. Two points, however, need conceding:

- Both Adams' and Le Verrier's orbits for Neptune would have increasingly diverged from its true one.
- Had they attempted locating Neptune in this way in (say) 1900 between two conjunctions with Uranus, they would probably have failed.

Adams and Le Verrier were lucky, in another sense Challis was unlucky, but this is not the same as saying that their work was a 'happy accident'.

Mercury and the 20th Century

Whether or not Vulcan existed, the perihelion of Mercury remained a problem. No viable solution could be found of particles or bodies to explain the missing arc seconds advance in this. The solution finally came after the publication of Einstein's general theory of relativity in 1915. This interprets concepts like mass, velocity, time and gravity as having meanings fundamentally different from those under Newtonian mechanics. The curvature of space-time in the presence of massive bodies is a different concept from inverse mutual attraction, though implications for observations of movements of bodies are very similar. For Mercury, however, the calculations for a small planet so close to the Sun made a difference – a difference of 43 arc seconds which was exactly the anomaly that existed! Einstein had developed a theoretical model to explain some apparent empirical anomalies (just as Adams and Le Verrier had done) – but in doing so had overturned the Newtonian mechanics which they assumed paradigmatic. On this issue Airy's original suspicion would have been right – it *was* Newton's dynamics that were at fault, they only worked approximately in certain conditions.

One final irony is raised by Michael Hoskin:

> It has recently been shown that the inner planets Mercury, Venus, Earth, and Mars, as well as the outer planet Pluto, provide instances of dynamical chaos … . From observation we can never know exactly – with unlimited precision – where any

> planet is; and for the inner planets and Pluto the initial range of uncertainty increases with time by leaps and bounds … . Systems subject to dynamical chaos are sensitive to chance perturbations: we live in a less certain world than Laplace imagined …[412]

Blame and Paradigm

The story of Neptune's discovery is more like an Elizabeth Gaskell than a Charles Dickens novel – there aren't any real villains! We have looked at four perspectives – each of them entirely reasonable even if some of them later regretted their decisions.

The story, however, raises some issues about the nature of science:

Firstly, as John Herschel[413] stated in words quoted above, seeing an object without recognising it is not 'discovering' it even if you are looking for it. Science should be essentially a public enterprise – publication *is* priority if this matters to you.

Secondly, science in practice involves *assumption*, and no laws (not even Newtonian dynamics) are sacrosanct. Airy was wrong and Le Verrier was right in assuming that Newtonian dynamics (and an extra planet) could explain Uranus, but for Mercury it was the other way around. Without hindsight it is often not possible to determine which assumption may prove valid and which invalid.

Thirdly, in practice scientists pursue research programmes they think may succeed. Professors tend to have their own research agenda – and are not always quick to abandon it for what could turn out to be a long, wild-goose chase. Not much has changed today – and if anything the UK pressure of the 'Research Assessment Exercise' or 'Research Excellence Framework' (which makes funding depend upon published papers) worsens this. All studies on creativity show that if success is too closely linked to reward, then people are less willing to take risks. With hindsight Challis *should* have dropped everything else – and Airy did at least reach a point where he was urging this – but had Challis later dropped everything to look for *Vulcan* then applause would have been less forthcoming.

---

412 Hoskin, *The Cambridge Illustrated History of Astronomy* (1997), 197.

413 John Herschel was interested in the philosophy of science, and had written a widely read book *Preliminary Discourse on the Study of Natural Philosophy* in 1831.

Fourthly, great scientists are lucky. Their hunches come off and their assumptions prove effective even if wrong. Their qualities are still manifest – but others with outstanding qualities may be less lucky. Fame, moreover, is fickle and seldom rational.

Questions

Here are some questions to ask as you read material on Neptune:

- Why has there been so great a divergence of 'blame' attached by different writers to Challis and/or Airy?
- How far did misunderstanding arise because of basic differences in paradigms and assumptions?
- Should nationalism (France vs. Britain) or institutional pride (the Cambridge network) have any part in science? Does priority matter? If not, why do we give Nobel prizes?
- What are the appropriate roles of individual brilliance vs. institutional research programmes in science?

References

Primary Sources

Vol 1 of W. G. Adams (ed.) *The Scientific Papers of John Couch Adams* (2 vols; 1896) is probably the most useful primary source. It has been reprinted in 2012 by *Forgottten Books.* Various publications of the Royal Astronomical Society also contain the reports and papers. Various autobiographies and 'Life and Letters' of involved parties could also be useful. Harrison's 'biography' (below) is also full of quoted primary sources. Over the period 2007–2010 various reprints have been issued of John Couch Adams work, for example: *The Scientific Papers of John Couch Adams* (2010), and *An Explanation of the Observed Irregularities in the Motion of Uranus: On the Hypothesis of Disturbance* (2009).

If you can read French the work *Recherches Sur Les Mouvements de La Planete Herschel* by Le Verrier was also reprinted in 2012.

Autobiography of Sir George Biddell Airy repr. CUP in 2010.

Secondary Sources:

For a general view, the book by Tom Standage *The Neptune Files* (2000) is fairly good, though in places seems still influenced by the anti-Airy hysteria. Richard Baum & William Sheehan *In Search of Planet Vulcan* (1997) gives a balanced summary on Neptune, and a more detailed account of the Le Verrier quest to find a similar solution for Mercury. Morton Grosser *The Discovery of Neptune* (1962) contains useful material but is written in a way so slanted against Airy that it has to be considered a distortion of history. Much of Grosser's commentary simply does not match even the primary material he quotes himself. Since Grosser also wrote the entry on Adams in the *Dictionary of Scientific Biography,* this is equally as biased against Airy.

On Adams, arising from the centenary year, there appeared in 1947 Howard Jones' classic booklet *John Couch Adams and the Discovery of Neptune.* There also appeared W. M. Smart's article of the same title in the 'Occasional Notes of the Royal Astronomical Society' (No 11, August 1947). The Astronomer Royal Jones[414] thought Professor Smart over-critical of Airy, and they traded letters in *Nature* later that year!

H. M. Harrison *Voyager in Time and Space: The Life of John Couch Adams Cambridge Astronomer* (1994) is billed as the first full biography of Adams. In fact, it really reads more like a commentated collection of documents from primary sources.

Older books can be useful, e.g. R. S. Ball *Great Astronomers* (1906) which contains sections on Airy, Le Verrier and Adams.

Books on Neptune can include useful material, e.g. Patrick Moore *The Planet Neptune* (1988).

Richard Baum's *In Search Of Planet Vulcan: The Ghost In Newton's Clockwork Universe* (2003) looks at this related issue.

Various articles are useful, especially:

Allan Chapman, 'Private Research and Public Duty: George Biddell Airy and the Search for Neptune' *Journal of the History of Astronomy* xix (1988), 121–139

[414] Jones actually points out the incredible workload of Airy – noted in Chapman's much later article but virtually ignored e.g. by Grosser. Smart denies in his response that he 'blames' Airy.

Robert W. Smith, 'The Cambridge Network in Action: The Discovery of Neptune' *ISIS,* 1989, 80, 393–422.

N. R. Hanson, 'Le Verrier: The Zenith and Nadir of Newtonian Mechanics' *ISIS,* 1962, 53, 359–378.

11. ET and the Plurality of Worlds

Astronaut and friend?

'Even if no UFOs hover in our heavens, belief in extraterrestrial beings has hovered in the human consciousness for dozens of decades. Although the Moon and Mars are as barren as giant bricks, moonlings and Martians long ago began to invade our culture and influence our thought, and they now occupy increasing roles in our cinematic and literary creations. Our extraterrestrials may no more exist than the gods of the Greeks, but their effects are no less indisputable.' Michael J. Crowe[415]

Throughout scientific history, and in particular over the last six centuries, the human race has wondered if the Earth is the only place in the universe to contain life, and whether life elsewhere may be self-conscious. The fascination continues today, with SETI, science fiction, and the various NASA exploration programmes. This, then, is a chapter about the 'Plurality of Worlds' debate (i.e. whether there are other inhabitable worlds besides the Earth and whether they have inhabitants). The amount of potential material on this is vast[416], so the present chapter focuses on two main aims. The first aim is to show how the debate relates to the issues of cosmology, and in particular in the thinking of the various astronomers/cosmologists we have met in previous chapters (to which reference should be made). Thus, although religious issues will inevitably come in, the focus is on the interaction with astronomy. The second aim is to consider how far observers, from Hevelius to William Herschel to

---

415 Michael J. Crowe, *The Extraterrestrial Life Debate 1750–1900*, (1986, 1999), Preface.

416 Crowe, op. cit. contains 675 pages, so read this if you want great detail!

Percival Lowell, saw what they wanted to see. The purpose of this is not so that we can feel smug, but to highlight general points about seeing, perception, and paradigms.

The Beginnings

The ancient Greeks differed on the issue of the plurality. The Epicurians and atomists took a very materialist view of reality. Mind was reducible to, and inseparable from, matter, and reality was an uncreated concourse of atoms randomly moving. This reached its culmination in the poetry of the Roman Titus Lucretius Carus (c100–55 BC), who wrote:

> In all dimensions alike, on this side or that, upward or downward throughout the universe, there is no end … . Granted, then, that empty space extends without limit in every direction and that seeds innumerable are rushing on countless courses through an unfathomable universe under the impulse of perpetual motion, it is in the highest degree unlikely that the Earth and sky is the only one to have been created and that all those particles of matter outside are accomplishing nothing. This follows from the fact that our world has been made by nature through the spontaneous and casual collision and the multifarious, accidental, random and purposeless congregation and coalescence of atoms …[417]

In an unlimited universe, accidental concourses of atoms would result in worlds and life elsewhere. Today we believe our own universe is big but finite; but the ancient idea is parallel to some forms of the modern 'anthropic principle' which argues that there are innumerable other universes most of which happen to be uninhabitable, as well as ours in which we have accidentally arisen because it happened to be inhabitable.

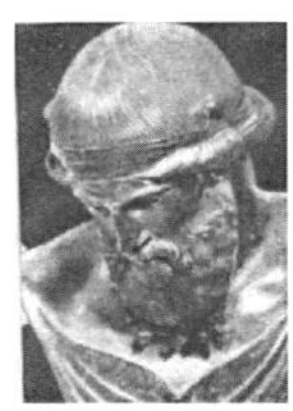
Plato

The Epicurean ideas ran counter to those of Plato and of Aristotle for different reasons. Plato typically worked from *a priori* rationalistic deductions:

> Are we right in saying that there is one world, or that they are many and infinite? There must be

[417] Lucretius, *The Nature of the Universe*, (trans. R. E. Latham), 1069.

> one only, if the created copy is to accord with the original … In order then that the world might be solitary, like the perfect animal, the creator made not two worlds or an infinite number of them; but there is and ever will be one only-begotten and created heaven.[418]

Aristotle

Since the world is a copy of the ideal in the divine mind, there can be only one. The argument (which is reflected in the 19th century Whewell as we shall see) does appear less than obvious – why should there not be one Creator with two different but perfect ideas, or who made two copies of the one idea? Aristotle, moreover, had a different view both of God and nature. His god is not a creator in any normal sense, but a part of an eternal reality that *includes* the material cosmos. Aristotle's physics was based on the idea of a radical distinction between super and sub-lunar motion, with sub-lunar based on 'natural place'.[419] There is no room in this for multiple universes. Moreover, the whole rotation in the universe and the Solar System is driven by god acting as an 'unmoved prime mover' outside it – and the notion of multiple unmoved prime movers seems unacceptable to reason and religion.[420]

In all these systems, of course, the link with actual observation is tenuous – the existence or non-existence of other worlds is a deduction from much more general ideas.

The Early Church

Augustine

Crowe suggests that early Christians reacted negatively to the plurality idea, and that Augustine of Hippo (354–430) 'did likewise'.[421] However, the passage of Augustine he cites[422] is really dealing with the Stoic arguments for an eternal recycling of the universe. Their objection that otherwise there would be no reason for God to start it at

---

418 See Plato *Timaeus*, 31–33.

419 See Aristotle *On the Heavens* and also chapter 2 above.

420 See Aristotle *Metaphysics*.

421 Crowe, op. cit. 6.

422 Augustine *City of God*, Bk 11 chap 5. Crowe also refers to Stanley Jaki's *Science and Creation*, 114f, which is also little concerned with the plurality issue.

one time rather than another, Augustine counters by pointing out that otherwise they would have to analogously accept the 'Epicurean dream' of the plurality of worlds (though based on creation not accident). Since Stoics and Epicureans were long-sworn enemies it is a good hit – but he is not really objecting (theologically or otherwise) to plurality. There seems no particular reason to suppose there was a settled early church view which rejected the notion of plurality as either impious or against Scripture.

Later figures like Albertus Magnus (1193–1280), Roger Bacon (1214–92), and Thomas Aquinas (1224–1274) strove in different ways to combine Aristotelianism with Christianity. They followed Aristotle's objections to plurality, though Aquinas was at pains to argue that this was not to limit God's omnipotence. Some theologians, however, were suspicious of Aristotelian arguments that apparently limited God, and in 1277 the Bishop of Paris, Etienne Tempier, issued a document that condemned any suggestion that 'the First Cause cannot make many worlds'.[423]

There may be an irony in the point that an insistence on the power of God actually led to more openness on the plurality issue. The next phase sees a close association between openness to a heliocentric planetary system and openness to plurality – both in a sense as criticisms of Aristotle. Obviously, if the Earth could be a local centre of 'natural place', then both heliocentricity and plurality became possible. The idea of a unique natural place was challenged in Paris by Jean Buridan (c 1295–1358) and in Oxford by William of Occam (c. 1280–1347), both open to plurality. Like Buridan, Nicole Oresme (1325–82) and Nicholas Cusanus (1401–1464) were open to heliocentricity, and again plurality. All these men were devout. Cusanus, for example, wrote:

> We will suppose that in every region there are inhabitants, differing in nature by rank and all owing their origin to God, who is the centre and circumference of all stellar regions ...[424]

Cusanus insisted that we could know little of such inhabitants, 'having no standards by which to appraise them'. There was no threat to Cusanus for holding such views, and eight years later he became a cardinal.

---

[423] Cited in Crowe, op. cit. 6.

[424] Cusanus *Of Learned Ignorance* (trans. Heron, 1954),114–5.

From Copernicus to the Victorians

Copernicus, of course, also addressed the 'natural place' issue in writing his heavily mathematical work, but he himself seems to have shown no interest in the plurality issue. Again, this is unlikely to be from any kind of 'fear' of church persecution – perhaps he was just not interested.

What was the situation in the generation after Copernicus?

Giordano Bruno

It has sometimes been suggested that the execution at the stake of Giodarno Bruno (1548–1600) was partly for his heliocentric and pluralist views. This seems highly unlikely, as neither touched any point of church dogma, and figures like Oresme and Cusanus had been highly respected churchmen. Kepler, moreover, was known by 1600 as a Copernican, and was involved in writing his work on a trip to the Moon – being persecuted neither by the Catholics nor his fellow Lutherans for such views. Sheila Rabin rightly writes in the *Stanford Encyclopaedia of Philosophy*:

> … in 1600 there was no official Catholic position on the Copernican system, and it was certainly not a heresy. When Giordano Bruno (1548–1600) was burned at the stake as a heretic, it had nothing to do with his writings in support of Copernican cosmology, and this is clearly shown in Finocchiaro's reconstruction of the accusations against Bruno (see also Blumenberg's part 3, chapter 5, titled 'Not a Martyr for Copernicanism: Giordano Bruno').[425]

Bruno, a Dominican Friar, was executed because he was a pantheist and denied the divinity of Jesus. Personally I disapprove of executing people for divergent theological beliefs (a practice which was initiated by St Augustine and done by both Catholics and branches of the Lutheran/Reformed faith[426]). But to present Bruno as some kind of martyr

---

[425] http://plato.stanford.edu/entries/copernicus/accessed September 13th 2013.

[426] We show this in the two volume *God's Strategy in Human History* (2013) by Roger Forster and Paul Marston.

for science or even for the plurality of worlds is historically inaccurate.[427]

Crowe claims that in 1550 Lutheran leader Phillip Melanchthon 'spoke out in opposition to the new cosmology [i.e. Copernicanism] including the tendency he saw in it to support the plurality of worlds'. However, in the passage Crowe then cites, Melanchthon simply says that Christ cannot have died and been resurrected in more than one place, nor 'in any other world without the knowledge of the Son of God, that men would be restored to eternal life'. This is not an attack on plurality, but an assertion of the all-sufficiency of the death of Christ.

One sometimes comes across an assumption that theology has generally opposed plurality in a belief that the universe was created just for human benefit. In reality, by far the majority of theologians and religious scientists who have written on the issue have favoured plurality. Those who have opposed it have very seldom done so dogmatically. The placing of the famous 1686 work by Fontenelle on, and off, and back on the Catholic index, was an odd exception, not a typical reaction.

Galileo, typically, tended to be extreme in whatever he wrote. In his 1613 *Letter on Sunspots* he regards as;

Galileo

> … false and damnable the view of those who would put inhabitants on Jupiter, Venus, Saturn and the Moon, meaning by 'inhabitants' animals like ours and men in particular.[428]

We should note, however, two things. Firstly, his concern is really about *men* elsewhere. Secondly (as Crowe's incomplete quotation does not quite show) it is part of a sideswipe at 'Appelles' who has argued that if there are inhabitants on the Moon there should be on sunspots – a 'deduction' which Galileo treats with customary sarcasm. The passage does not reveal any settled opposition to plurality.

---

427 Ironically, a visiting Nobel science prizewinner speaking at my university in 2013 did just this – having emphasised to us all that it was crucial only to believe things for which there was evidence!

428 op. cit. third letter, Drake *Discoveries and Opinions of Galileo* (1957), 137.

Kepler

The Lutheran Kepler, of course, wrote his famous work *The Dream*[429] around 1609, mentioning it in a letter of April 19th 1610 to Galileo about his *Sidereal Messenger*. Before reading this, Kepler had been filled with foreboding that Galileo had discovered other planetary systems – threatening to support a Bruno-like picture of an infinite universe with many suns. Why did Kepler object to this? There was no obvious Scriptural objection, and Crowe's suggestion of residual 'anthropocentricism' is not altogether convincing. Kepler's Solar System was a neo-Pythagorean/Platonic masterpiece of divine mathematical perfection with the Sun as the centrepiece and motive force. Perhaps the thought of this masterpiece endlessly repeated locally throughout the universe was too much for him. In the *Epitome* he argues empirically for our Sun being much brighter than the stars.[430] But was he against *any* form of pluralism?

The Dream was published only in 1634, with voluminous notes written in the 1620s. The problem with interpreting is that it is multi-layered, and is as full of symbolism (and joking allusions) as a T. S. Elliot poem. On one level it is an autobiography with Ducatus as an idealised Kepler and Fiolxhilde his mother. On another level it is a Platonic allegory – with the daemons as the philosophical specialisms enlightening the ignorance of Fiolxhilde. On another level it is the first work of science fiction. On another, a serious attempt to convey both the geography of the Moon and the implications of observational relativism in Copernicanism. Kepler had already argued pre-telescopically that the Moon had mountains and valleys etc. The telescope enabled him in the early 1620s to look in much greater detail at the lunar surface. In an appendix (a letter to the Jesuit Father Guldin) Kepler says that he will lay out 'theses' which he will 'demonstrate from phenomena which … have been suited to optical, physical and metaphysical axioms'[431] This was actually Kepler's whole approach to his astronomy – the Sun (we remember) was at the centre for physical and

---

429 This was briefly described in the chapter on Kepler. John Lear's translation (1965), contains all the notes, and a useful explanation (though he exaggerates Lutheran opposition to Copernicanism).

430 *Epitome* IV at the end of Part 1.

431 Lear, op. cit. 167.

metaphysical reasons. The whole system made sense of reality at every level. He proceeds to tie in all the various observations, for example of dark patches as seas, of craters as enhanced by the inhabitants as fortifications etc. This is one of the first instances of astronomical observation being interpreted as signs of intelligent life, and in turn stimulating further observation and research. How serious Kepler was is hard to say. In a 1623 letter he mentions a possibility of sending *The Dream* to a correspondent 'for fun' and in the appendix letter says 'these remarks are made in sport'.[432]

The works of Kepler and Galileo were background to an anonymous work of 1638: *The Discovery of a World in the Moone* … written by the young Reverend John Wilkins who became Master of Trinity and later Bishop of Chester.[433] This was one of the most influential popular works on astronomy of the century. A Copernican, Wilkins saw no problems with God creating intermediate creatures between humans and angels. In 1640 the third edition contained speculation on the possibility of travel to the Moon, and in the same year in his *Discourse Concerning a New Planet* Wilkins further argued (physically and metaphysically) for a Copernican system. The Moon, during the following couple of centuries, was the only heavenly body for which telescopes could make out detailed features. It is, therefore, little wonder that at the *empirical* level (rather than at a level of arguments from metaphysics or statistical considerations) it became the prime battleground for any controversy over actual evidence for extra terrestrials.

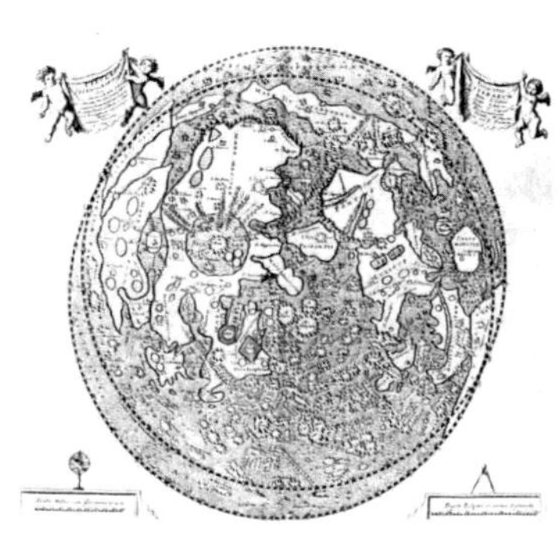

Hevelius Moon Map

The problem was, of course, that it depended on how you saw it! The best Moon maps of the time were those in *Selenographia* (1647) by Johannes Hevelius (1611–87), and *Almagestum Novum* (1651) by the Jesuit Giovanni Ricoli (1598–1671).[434] Both, of course,

432 Lear, op.cit. 77 & 167.

433 See Chapter 7 on Horrocks.

434 Crowe shows Moon pictures of Hevelius and Grimaldi, but that of Hevelius is a drawing not a map. His map (with seas etc. marked) is as illustrated above.

label some patches as 'sea' (*mare*) on the Moon, though many of the names differ. Hevelius believed that they really were seas and also believed in 'selenites' or lunar inhabitants, whereas Ricoli's map is marked *Nec Homines Lunum incolent* (no men live on the Moon) and (according to Crowe) he denied there was any water there.

Ricoli's fellow Catholic, René Descartes, saw no problem with plurality, though, like many figures of the period, held an open mind on whether there actually was or was not life elsewhere:

> I do not see at all that the mystery of the incarnation, and all the other advantages that God has brought forth for man obstruct him from having brought forth an infinity of other very great advantages for an infinity of other creatures. And, although I do not at all infer from this that there would be intelligent creatures in the stars or elsewhere, I also do not see that there would be any reason by which to prove that there were not; but I always leave undecided questions of this kind, rather than denying or affirming anything.[435]

This caution is not untypical of the times. What actually were the issues?

- Very few thought that plurality (even of intelligent life) was ruled out by the Bible. Genesis was not generally taken to teach that the universe was just for humankind. If other species needed redemption, then either Christ's redemption on Earth would be all-sufficient, or God would make some other provision.
- Copernicanism was increasingly accepted (by all Protestants and most Catholics). The decentralisation of the Earth brought little or no trauma, but it also implied a vastly extended universe, and the possibility of other local 'suns'.
- Some (e.g. Blaise Pascal) found the idea of vast empty spaces frightening. Some also found it wasteful or pointless, which tended to argue for other inhabitants if the universe was thought to have been designed with purpose. For atheists, if life had somehow arisen 'by chance' here, then surely also elsewhere in the vast universe?

---

[435] Cited in Crowe, op. cit. 16.

- The actual empirical *evidence,* was recognised as very minimal. Only the Moon could be seriously examined, and its surface was open to different interpretation. The only other arguments were suppositional.

The French priest Pierre Gassendi (1592–1655) insisted God could have created a plurality of worlds, but believed that in fact he had not done so. The Cambridge Platonists who influenced Newton, Henry More (1614–87) and Ralph Cudworth (1617–88) both attacked Epicurian atomism, and later rejected Cartesianism, but both were pluralists. In 1686 the famous *Entretiens sur la pluralite des mondes* was published by Bernard le Bovier de Fontenelle. The charming dialogue (placed on the Catholic index, removed in 1825 and reinserted in 1900!) became the most famous work on this since Wilkins, from whom Fontenelle had drawn inspiration. The popularity of his book, of course, was more because of the wit with which he populated the various planets than its 'serious philosophy', but Fontenelle lists the five main reasons for accepting plurality:

Bernard Le Bovier de Fontenelle

[1] The similarities of the planets to the Earth which is inhabited;

[2] the impossibility of imagining any other use for which they were made;

[3] the fecundity and magnificence of nature;

[4] the consideration she seems to show for the needs of their inhabitants as having given moons to planets distant from the Sun and more moons to those more remote; and

[5] that which is very important – all that which can be said on one side and nothing on the other.

These are all, of course, metaphysical rather than empirical arguments. Fontenelle, in turn, influenced Christiaan Huygens (1629–95) whose *Cosmotheoros* was published in 1698 containing the same five arguments. Was there any effect on observational astronomy? Like modern space programmes, finance can depend on other issues than 'pure research'. Astronomer Royal John Flamsteed

Christiaan Huygens

recommended Huygens' work to the vicar of Greenwich, Archdeacon Plume, and the latter's resulting fascination led him to bequeath money for an observatory and the Plumian Professorship of Astronomy at Cambridge.

Isaac Newton (1642–1727) became regarded, even in his lifetime, as an icon of science, and was deeply interested in metaphysics and religion. After an exchange of letters (later published) his friend (who later became Master of Trinity) Richard Bentley (1662–1742) published his *Confutation of Atheism* (1693). This joined Newtonianism, Christian apologetics, and pluralism. Newton himself did not take up the issue strongly, but in the 'General Scholium' of the 1713 edition of *Principia* mention is made of the possibility that stars 'are centres of other like systems' (i.e. of planets), but that these 'must be all subject to the dominion of One'. Crowe detects Bentley's influence on this.[436] There was actually a kind of circle of devout men interested in science and moving in Royal Society circles, who were concerned that some were seeing science as atheistic when in fact it tended to promote a view of the world as designed – so what else is new?! The devout Earl Robert Boyle (1627–1691) had written himself on this, and laid down finance for a series of lectures on the evidence from design, of which Bentley's was the first. Other writers of similar arguments from design included naturalist John Ray (1628–1705) *The Wisdom of God Manifested in the Works of Creation* (1691)and William Derham (1657–1735) *Astro-theology, or A Demonstration of the Being and Attributes of God from a Survey of the Heavens* (1714). All of this group tended to espouse or be open to pluralism. The Christian empiricist philosophers John Locke (1632–1704) who was influenced by Huygens' work, and George Berkeley (1685–1753), were also Christian apologists and also advocated pluralism. Likewise Newton's rival, the equally devout Willhelm Gottlieb Leibniz (1646–1716), suggested that in the vastness of the universe the sin and evil on the Earth may well pale into insignificance compared with other good things there may be elsewhere in it.

In the 18th century there were some who were either sceptical of plurality or who even opposed it.[437] In general, however, the views of both scientific

---

[436] Crowe notes several other non-committal mentions.

[437] See Crowe op.cit. for details.

and theological communities (which often overlapped) were that it was acceptable and quite likely.

William Herschel (1738–1822)

James Ferguson

In an earlier chapter we saw how Herschel's burgeoning interest in astronomy in the 1770s was stimulated by the works of James Ferguson (1710–1776). Ferguson was not original, but his *Astronomy Explained upon Sir Isaac Newton's Principles* (1756) not only went through many editions, but was adapted for the article in the 1771 launch of the *Encyclopaedia Britannica.* Ferguson's work stated that astronomy:

> … discovers to us … an inconceivable number of suns, systems, and Worlds, dispersed through boundless space … From what we know of our own system, it may be reasonably concluded that all the rest are with equal wisdom, contrived, situated and provided with accommodations for rational inhabitants …. Thousands of thousands of suns … attended by ten thousand times ten thousand Worlds … peopled with myriads of intelligent beings, formed for endless progression in perfection and felicity.[438]

This goes just a bit beyond the empirical base (!) but we remember that at this time also Thomas Wright (1711–1786) and Immanuel Kant (1724–1804) were developing ideas of the Milky Way as our galaxy, and possible galaxies beyond. Where Herschel is usually remembered today it is as 'That guy who discovered Uranus … oh and made telescopes and star maps'. But what was his real motivation? Here was a man in middle age, moving in elite Bath society and making a good living as a musician, able to express his creativity in composing music (a possible route to lasting fame). Science was not a career – even the Astronomer Royal post (itself inconceivable without an Oxbridge degree at least) required supplementary income (i.e. a parish). Herschel had no inkling he

William Herschel

[438]Ferguson, op. cit. 3–5.

could make a living selling telescopes (it came later as a great surprise to discover that his were better than anyone else's). He was not looking for more planets in our system – even when he found one he thought it was a comet! Herschel's real passion was not star maps, nor positional astronomy, but *astrophysics* – finding ways to explore the dynamics of a *developing* and *populated* universe.

For Herschel's times there was nothing in the least eccentric, unscientific, or irreligious in this – nor in his speculations about extraterrestrial life. It was mainstream. Crowe rightly suggests that pluralism was a core component of Herschel's research programme and 'many of his efforts make most sense when seen as an attempt to transform pluralism from being a delight of poets, a doctrine of metaphysicians, and a dogma of physicotheologians, into a demonstration of astronomers'.[439]

Herschel began his astronomy in the early 1770s, and in a May 28 1776 paper was observing the Moon through a newly acquired telescope when he saw:

> … something I had never observed before, which I ascribed to the power and distinctness of my Instrument, but which may perhaps be an optical fallacy … something which I immediately took to be growing substances. I will not call them Trees as from their size they can hardly come under that denomination, or if I do, it must be understood in that extended signification so as to take in any size how great soever … My attention was chiefly directed to Mare humorum, and this I now believe to be a forest, this word being also taken in its proper extended signification as consisting of such large growing substances. In the second figure (which is not drawn with any accuracy) there is a Wood which goes up to mount Gasendum. The different colours of the plain ground, of the Rocks and of the Shadows cast by high places are easily to be distinguished on the Moon. It has hitherto been supposed that those Seas as they are called consisted of a different kind of Soil, which reflected light less copiously than the hills & Mountains. I conclude them to be woods or Forests … Our tallest trees would vanish at that distance. It is not impossible but that the vegetable Creation (and indeed the

[439] Crowe, op. cit. 61–62.

> animals too) may be of a much larger size on the Moon than it is here; tho' perhaps not very likely. And I suppose that the borders of forests, to be visible, would require Trees at least 4, 5 or 6 times the height of ours. But the thought of Forests or Lawns and Pastures still remains exceedingly probable with me, as that will much better account for the different Colour, than different coloured soils will do.[440]

We can only conjecture as to what he was really seeing in his little 'not accurately drawn' sketch of his lunar 'forest'. Remember that he later said:

> Seeing is in some respects an art that must be learnt. To make a person see with such power is nearly the same as if I were asked to make him play one of Handel's fugues.

In this, however, we find Herschel already trying to interpret his telescope observations qualitatively. He is finding (in his mind) empirical evidence for the exciting population of the universe found in Ferguson.

By 1778 he thought he saw towns as well. This was, of course, an age in which human construction (at the start of the industrial revolution) was burgeoning:

> As upon the Earth several Alterations have been, and are daily, made of a size sufficient to be seen by the inhabitants of the Moon, such as building Towns, cutting canals for Navigation, making turnpike roads &c may we not expect something of a similar Nature on the Moon? – There is a reason to be assigned for circular-Buildings on the Moon, which is that, as the Atmosphere there is much rarer than ours and of consequence not so capable of refracting and (by means of clouds shining therein) reflecting the light of the Sun, it is natural enough to suppose that a Circus will remedy this deficiency, For in that shape of Building one half will have the direct and the other half the reflected light of the Sun ... Now if we could discover any new erection it is evident an exact list of those Towns that are already built will be necessary. But this is no easy undertaking to make out, and will require the observation of many a careful

[440] Quotes in Crowe ,op. cit. 63—64.

> Astronomer and the most capital Instruments that can be had. However this is what I will begin.

This, then, stimulates a telescopic research programme, in which Herschel himself is a participant.[441] On 17th June 1779 records observing 'a Cut or Canal that seems evidently to be the effect of Art rather than of Nature' and a month later identified a new spot in the Mare Crisium area as a 'city'.

Herschel's introduction to scientific society began in 1779. In May 1780 two of his papers were read to the Royal Society, the longer of which was 'Astronomical Observations Relating to the Mountains of the Moon'. Herschel's communications with Neville Maskelyne (1732–1811), in which this paper was based, contained a great deal of this lunar inhabitants material – although he prefaced it with a plea that Maskelyne would 'Promise not to call me a lunatic'. Maskelyne, anxious for the reputation both of Herschel and the Royal Society, managed to filter most of it out! From his viewpoint it seemed speculation, though from Herschel's own viewpoint was just a part of interpreting observation.

Herschel, of course, had a happy knack of ignoring inconvenient observations. By 1780 he knew that the sudden occultation of stars by the Moon made an atmosphere unlikely. In 1783, however, he managed to observe a star disappearing slowly as it went behind the Moon, indicating an atmosphere. In a letter of that year to Alexander Wilson, however, Herschel admits to having had little success over the last 5–6 years in detecting animation on the Moon. The highest power he has 'conveniently' been able to use is a magnification of 932, but he has not had much time and hopes to find more later and with improved instruments.[442].

Herschel did not claim lunar inhabitants in any published paper, and Crowe notes that in his lament in 1982 to Alexander Aubert he says of telescopes:

---

[441] It is hard not to see a parallel with e.g. Frank Drake (widely known for a strong belief in extraterrestrial intelligent life) an OZMA (looking for radio signals) and SETI (search for extra-terrestrial life). Hundreds of blanks – but 'certainty' of eventual discovery drives them on!

[442] Quoted in Crowe, op. cit. 65.

> These instruments have played me so many tricks that I have at last found them out in many of their humours … it would be hard if they had not been kind to me at last …

Just as we saw in the search for the planet Vulcan, observation is a funny thing. However, in his 1784 paper on Mars he still claims that it has 'a considerable but moderate atmosphere, so that its inhabitants probably enjoy a situation in many respects similar to ours' Saturn, Uranus etc. were likewise assumed inhabited. Again, although he admits that we will be unable to actually *observe* planetary systems around other stars, we have reason to believe that they exist and are inhabited. In 1795 he states:

> … since stars appear to be suns, and suns, according to common opinion are bodies that serve to enlighten, warm, and sustain a system of planets, we may have an idea of the numberless globes that serve for the habitation of living creatures …[443]

This is a mixture of astronomy and teleology – the assumption is that the Sun has a *purpose.*

This may also have fired Herschel's view of the Sun itself as inhabitable. In his 1795 solar paper he notes that he has observed a compressed star cluster so close that:

> … it will hardly be possible to assign any mutual distance to leave room for crowding in those planets, for whose support those stars have been or might be, supposed to exist. It would seem, therefore, highly probable that they exist for themselves; and are, in fact, only very capital, lucid, primary planets, connected together in one great system of mutual support.[444]

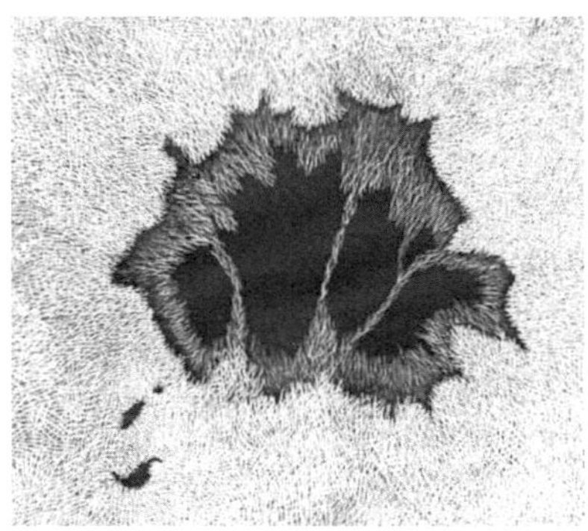

Sunspot July 1860 (shows structure)

[443] I, 330 – cited in Crowe. op. cit. 66.

[444] I, 482–483, quoted in Crowe, op. cit. 68.

Our own Sun likewise :

> … appears to be nothing else than a very eminent, large, and lucid planet, evidently the first, or in strictness of speaking the only primary one of our system … Its similarity to other globes of the solar system … leads us to suppose that it is most probably … inhabited … by beings whose organs are adapted to the peculiar circumstances of that vast globe.

Herschel, it should be noted, believed that his theories differed from fanciful and poetic views of the Sun as, for example, a place for exiling condemned souls. His system was based upon *astronomical principles.* It was becoming recognised that sunspots were not simply 'spots' but had more complex structures. Herschel's 'Sun' is actually a dynamical system. It consists of a cool, solid, spherical interior, above which an opaque layer of floating clouds shields the interior from the incandescent regions above and reflects the light outwards. These lower clouds generally intensify the apparent 'shining' but are themselves darker than the outer clouds because glowing by reflected light (this was illustrated by a photometric experiment). The luminous upper clouds have gaps through which we see the darkened interior, which can appear mottled. From the depths of the Sun's atmosphere gases float upwards through pores in the lower cloud region, and decompose/ignite generating the bright luminous clouds. When these clouds do separate, fiery vapours are heaped up around the 'openings' to constitute 'ridges' and 'nodules'. The lower clouds can also cut down the heat reaching the surface, and so its possible inhabitants. All this is a dynamical model to explain features of the Sun that include various aspects of sunspots.

Our modern version is, of course, very different, but is also a dynamic model with various solar layers and motions of materials up and down between these. The Sun is generating heat within its core by the nuclear fusion of hydrogen into helium. The energy produced by this is carried outward by convective currents in the outer 20–30% of the Sun. Complex magnetic fields are produced by fluid motions within and just below this convection zone. A sunspot arises because a strong magnetic field around that point (which extends from below the surface out into the corona) inhibits the transport of heat via convective motion in the Sun. Sunspots have concentrated magnetic fields, and are darker because about one third cooler (some 4000 degrees Kelvin) than the rest of the surface. Sunspots are made up of two parts: a dark central part (the umbra) and a lighter outer area (the penumbra). The area outside the sunspot has a granular appearance as a result of convection. The centre of each granule is hot material rising from the Sun's interior, while the edges are cooler material sinking downward.

Herschel's model was 'wrong' and 'premature'. He did not know enough physics, and his particular metaphysics (in particular the desire to populate the Sun) also misled him. But the idea of trying to find a dynamical model of the solar phenomena – fuelled as it was by the excitement of a programme that could ultimately identify extraterrestrials – was a fruitful one.

The Whewell–Brewster Debate

The first half of the 19th century saw little change in the general situation on plurality. The key evangelical Scottish theologian Thomas Chalmers (1780–1847) was widely admired and read for his eloquence and his knowledge. Two of his works were *Astronomical Discourses* (1817) and his Bridgewater Treatise *On the Wisdom, Power and Goodness of God* (1833). Chalmers, typically, asserts the rationality of believing that so great a creator (who created the vast universe) could be interested in humankind, and also reaffirms the likelihood of plurality. As, however, our present interest is not in comprehensive coverage, we are going to jump to the most famous plurality debate of the age, in the early 1850s.

William Whewell (1794–1866)

William Whewell

William Whewell was the son of a Lancaster master carpenter. Recognising his talent, Lancaster Grammar School gave him a free place, and he eventually went to Trinity College as a 'sub-sizar' with a scholarship in 1812. He passed out in 1816 as second Wrangler and second Smith's Prize man. He became a Fellow in 1817 and was ordained in 1826. He became Professor of Mineralogy in 1828, but resigned in 1832. In 1838 he became Professor of Moral Philosophy. Just after his marriage (to Cordelia Marshal) in 1841, he became Master of Trinity College, and was Vice-

Chancellor of Cambridge in 1842 and 1855. In 1848 he played a large part in establishing the new science degrees at the University, adding to earlier reforms of the Mathematical Tripos.

Whewell was the greatest Polymath of the age, though someone did remark 'Science was his forte, omniscience his foible!' He was an expert on the tides, but familiar with every branch of science. Influenced by Kant, his philosophy of science was the most profound of the century. He was a key figure in the early British Association for the Advancement of Science, and an FRS. He was well aware of the role of language in shaping ideas and invented words like 'scientist' and 'physicist' and technical terms like 'anode' and 'cathode' . He was a central member of the Cambridge network which included leading geologist Adam Sedgwick (1785–1873), astronomers John Herschel (1792–1871), George Biddell Airy (1801–1892) James Challis (1803–1882), and John Couch Adams (1819–1892) – these last three successively holding the professorship financed (as noted above) by ET enthusiast Archdeacon Plume!

Whewell's interests up to 1853 are shown from the following major works:

- (1831) Review of John Herschel's 'Preliminary Discourse on the Study of Natural Philosophy (1830)'. *Quarterly Review 90*: 374–407.
- (1833) *Astronomy and General Physics Considered With Reference to Natural Theology* (Bridgewater Treatise), Cambridge.
- (1837) *The History of the Inductive Sciences* (3 vols).
- (1840) *The Philosophy of the Inductive Sciences, Founded Upon Their History* (2 vols).
- (1844) 'On the Fundamental Antithesis of Philosophy', trans. *Camb. Phil. Soc.* 7, 2, 170–81.
- (1845) *The Elements of Morality, including Polity* (2 vols).
- (1846) *Lectures on Systematic Morality.*
- (1848) 'Second Memoir on the Fundamental Antithesis of Philosophy,' trans. *Camb. Phil. Soc.* 8, 5, 614–20.
- (1849) *Of Induction, With Especial Reference to Mr. J. Stuart Mill's System of Logic.*
- (1850) 'Mathematical Exposition of Some Doctrines of Political Economy: Second Memoir,' trans. *Camb. Phil. Soc.* 9, 128–49.

Whewell has been called a 'liberal Anglican'[445] but his sermons and other comments actually show a fairly conservative theology, not far removed from his friend Sedgwick's moderate evangelicalism.

In earlier decades, Whewell had been an advocate of plurality along the lines of Chalmers as evidenced in a set of sermons in 1827. His 1833 Bridgewater treatise assumes that natural theology cannot 'prove' God to unwilling atheists, but may encourage believers. It is very limited in what it can tell us of God, but actually science above all leads us to see God as 'incomprehensible, his attributes as unfathomable'. Whewell's view of God was not as exercising particular powers to control nature, but through the establishment of laws. The teleological argument from design to a Creator should be based on the evidence, design of natural laws for purpose – not on particular structures.[446] He therefore had no problem with the new 'nebular hypothesis' of a dynamic origin for the Solar System, seeing it only as a divine use of laws. He accepted that 'no one can resist the temptation' to assume that the other planets, analogous in their natures to our own, may also be inhabited. He accepted that other stars may have planetary systems, like ours inhabited by 'vegetable and animal and rational life'.

By 1850 Whewell was having doubts about this. He wrote an unpublished dialogue entitled 'Astronomy and Religion'. It begins from the same point as Chalmers: 'When I consider thy heavens, the work of thy fingers, the Moon and the stars which thou has ordained; what is man, that thou art mindful of him?' (Psalm 8:3) The sheer vastness of the universe and myriads of systems brought questions about the special-ness of mankind and the incarnation. If God did not take on the form of an angel when angels fell, would he be incarnated to save other fallen rational physical species?[447]

---

[445] John Hedley Brooke 'Natural Theology and the Plurality of Worlds: Observations on the Brewster-Whewell Debate' *Annals of Science* , 34, (1977), 221–286. Crowe cites this article, but Brooke himself has moved on since 1977 on this issue, and the heavy emphasis on 'liberal' vs 'evangelical' theology is implausible. Brewster was certainly more *Reformed* in theology than Whewell, but both were fairly conservative.

[446] In his *History of the Inductive Sciences* he suggests that for the appearance of new species geology 'says nothing but she points upward'. See also my *Reason, Science and Faith*, 350 etc.

[447] For further details of this dialogue see Crowe, op. cit. 278–281.

In 1853 he published anonymously *Of the Plurality of Worlds: An Essay.* In its preface he recognises that a scepticism on pluralism is unusual, and may be deemed 'blameable' but:

> Yet probably there are many who will be willing to see the question examined by all the light which modern science can throw upon it …[448]

This might lead us to expect a mainly empirical work, but actually it starts with Chalmers and Psalm 8:3 again. Whewell notes that the modern understanding of astronomy makes the whole physical universe incomparably larger than the Hebrews imagined, and in this context he asks:

> Can the earth be thus the centre of the moral and religious universe, when it has no claim to be the centre of the physical universe? (19)

Whewell has no quarrel with Chalmers' science, and no objection to a plurality of animal life – it is rational, moral and spiritual life he has a problem with. Animal life is essentially static, but rational creatures have *history* and progression in knowledge which needs 'special guidance and government' from God. We certainly have (as Chalmers said) no reason to assume that other rational creations require redemption of the kind we needed.

From chapter five he introduces geology. This shows thousands, probably millions of years before the arrival of the 'intellectual, moral, religious and spiritual being' humankind. This enables Whewell to argue (e.g. 102) that all the natural theological arguments for plurality fail:

- It cannot be 'unworthy' of God to leave vast spaces uninhabited by rational beings, for he has done this with vast earthly time tracts.
- It cannot be 'wasteful' of God for the same reasons.
- One cannot argue from the 'similarity' of other globes that inhabitability implies rational life, for the past Earth was likewise inhabitable.

---

[448] *Essay* Preface.p. iii.

From Chapter Seven he turns to astronomy. He first challenges assumptions that all nebulae are resolvable into stars, the Magellanic clouds, for example, are now deemed not to be. Many nebulae may just be 'vast masses of incoherent or gaseous matter' not yet forming Solar Systems. In Chapter Eight he challenges the assumption that each star resembles our own Sun which is unproven (citing John Herschel on this). They may be different sizes, rapidly changing, circling double stars with no stable planetary orbits etc. We have no actual evidence there are other planetary systems. Then (in Chapter Nine) he looks at the Solar System planets. Jupiter appears much bigger but its great oblateness indicates it may be mostly water – and Saturn has similar problems. Mars 'may have been judged worthy of inhabitants by his Creator' , but we need not discuss whether they are rational until we have some evidence of life there at all (188). He is dismissive of Venus and Mercury, which may be uninhabitable. For all we know, then, our Sun may be the 'largest sun among the stars' and the Earth the 'largest solid opaque globe in the solar system' (160). It is placed 'between the hot and fiery haze on one side, the cold watery vapour on the other' (203). We may, then, well be the only rational, moral, religious and spiritual life forms in the universe.

In Chapter Eleven Whewell outlines his own views of the argument from design. Of evolution, he has said there is currently (1853) no evidence – though he was well aware of Chambers' anonymous *Vestiges of the Natural History of Creation* published nearly a decade earlier. Interestingly, though, he adds:

> If … it should be made apparent by geological investigations of the extinct fossil creation, that the animal forms which have inhabited the earth, have gradually approached to that type in which the human form is included, passing from the most imperfect animal organizations, molluscs or even organic monads, to vertebrate animals, to warm blooded animals, to monkeys, and to men; still the evidences of design in the anatomy of man are not less striking than they were, when no such gradation was thought of. And … his moral and intellectual nature, his history and capacities, – stand where they stood before; nor is the vast chasm which separates man, as a being with such characters as these latter, from all other animals, at all filled up or bridged over (216).

Darwin's *Origin of Species* was published in 1859.

In a final section Whewell utilised some ideas of an old school fellow, the foremost anatomist of the day Richard Owen (1804–1892). Owen's idea was that the hierarchical structure and homologies of the animal kingdoms (however produced) represented archetypes in the mind of the creator. To Whewell, then, planets could be seen as reflecting an archetype that only in one case proved purposeful. Ironically, Owen (like most contemporaries) was a pluralist.

Why did Whewell change his mind on pluralism? He never said. His book credits no other anti-pluralists. It is unlikely to have been the influence of German philosophy, as Kant himself was a pluralist. It is unlikely to have been his 'nomological' emphasis on laws rather than specific structures as better indicating design – Whewell had *always* thought this. John Hedley Brooke suggests that Whewell was reacting to Chambers' anonymous 1844 work advocating evolution.[449] This is possible, but it is not obvious that a rejection of plurality scuppered Chambers, and the passage quoted above regards evolution even of man with equanimity. Any suggestions?

Whewell received little or no scientific support for his views, but the book caused a real storm of controversy. One of the most vitriolic reviews and attacks was by David Brewster, at whom we now look.

David Brewster (1781–1868)

David Brewster (1781–1868) was the son of a minister, licensed as a preacher though never ordained in the Church of Scotland, and a friend of Thomas Chalmers. From a child he built microscopes, telescopes and sundials, and earned a living through literary and scientific pursuits. He studied whilst still a child, though did not graduate, from Edinburgh University but later received honorary degrees. He was elected FRS (1815) and knighted in 1832. He edited various scientific journals, but was unable to obtain a

David Brewster

[449] *Vestiges of the Natural History of Creation* (1844) see J. H. Brooke 'Natural Theology and the Plurality of Worlds' *Annals of Science*, 34 (1977) 221–286.

professorship, and deplored the difficulties of making science a paid career in Britain. Like Whewell and Sedgwick, he was active in the BAAS from its beginning in 1831. In politics he was, like Sedgwick, as a Reform Whig. He went on to become principal and then Vice Chancellor of Edinburgh University in 1859.

In religion he was evangelical – although until the death of his wife in 1850 his faith seems to have been formal rather than fervent.[450] That death brought a crisis of faith (which may explain his passion to retain his natural theology modelled on Chalmers'), which he seems eventually to have resolved to find a deeper religious experience.

There were three major grounds where Brewster differed radically from Whewell. The first was his dissatisfaction with the university system (which made it hard to earn a living in science) and Brewster had clashed with Whewell after making some wild claims about the lack of research in British universities in the 1830s. The second issue was that Brewster (unlike Whewell) was passionately against the undulatory theory of light, preferring the corpuscular theory of his idol Newton. The third was that he was against 'scientific speculation', and was primarily an experimenter rather than a theoretician. He attacked Whewell's works on the history and philosophy of science as theoretical, anti-Scots etc. Whewell was irritated by the 'Scots grumble' but generally tried to be more gracious.

Brewster's reviews of the *Essay* were vitriolic and insulting: 'Why is he so savage?' Whewell wrote to Murchison. Brewster's *More Worlds Than One* (1854), noted the support of Bruno (!), Tycho, Kepler, Fontenelle, Huygens, etc, and proclaimed its intention to defend 'astronomical truth' against the recent *Essay* whose 'direct tendency is to ridicule and bring into contempt the grand discoveries in sidereal astronomy by which the last century has been distinguished' (7). It 'refutes' the *Essay* section by section.

Religious aspects begin with the startling conclusion that Psalm 8:3 makes sense only if the Psalmist knew there were extraterrestrials, for why otherwise would he be surprised at God's interest in man? Brewster takes Isaiah xiv.12, which says that God did not make the

---

[450] See E. O. Gordon *The home life of Sir David Brewster* (1869) 310–327.

Earth in vain but to be inhabited, to infer that since God could not have made other planets 'in vain' they too must have occupants (17). He also suggests that since the resurrected will have bodies and there is insufficient room for them here, 'we can scarcely doubt' that they must be intended for other planets whose occupants have by then died out' . This is a sample of the kind of 'logic' he used – so we may move to the astronomy!

Chapter Two describes the Solar System, with a mixture of poetry and Herschel. In Chapter Three he (like Whewell) moves to geology. The fundamental structure of geology (with progressive creation) he accepts, but claims there is no proof that it took as long as Whewell claimed. Chapter Four looks at the other planets, comparing them with Earth, and arguing for their inhabitability. Surprisingly (though we must remember that at that time no one had managed to 'boldly go' or discovered that most life forms spoke American and looked pretty humanoid) Brewster is pretty open about the outward forms that 'intelligent life' having an 'immortal soul' may take (65). Perhaps even (awesome to Brewster!) there might be a reason far above that of Newton? There may be new elements, new geologies, etc., so apparently adverse conditions are not a problem. Overall the analogies with the Earth '*taken together amount to a demonstration,* that in the economy of the material universe these globes must subserve the same purposes as the Earth' (79).

In Chapter Five Brewster considers the Sun and Moon. They have the obvious purpose of giving us light and seasons, but do they have inhabitants too? Brewster asserts that William Herschel (who had died 32 years earlier!) has 'made it highly probable, if not certain' that the light comes from outer luminous clouds, and this has now (claims Brewster) been further demonstrated by various discoveries of Arago. The Sun, then, is not a red-hot globe but has a cold nucleus. To be fair even John Herschel (as we shall see below) was still asserting the plausibility of this at that time. William Herschel is then also quoted to demonstrate the probability of the Moon being inhabited. Brewster hedges his bets by saying: 'We may reject this opinion, and yet still believe implicitly in a plurality of worlds' . He still, however, argues against the various objections made to Herschel's ideas. He accepts 'the Moon has no clouds or seas, but this is no reason why she may not have an atmosphere, and a precipitation of moisture upon her surface, sufficient for the support of vegetable life' (103). John Herschel is quoted to show: 'there are large regions perfectly level, and apparently of *a decided alluvial character*,' – so there must at one time have been a lunar atmosphere and flowing water. In the 1770s (Brewster claims) there were observed active lunar volcanoes, and William Herschel saw three in 1783. To John Herschel's blank denial there is a lunar atmosphere, Brewster brings observations of Cassini, Dunn and Schroeter. Lack of occultation of stars passing behind it is because the lunar atmosphere does not extend right up her mountains. Brewster's approach, it has to be said, is highly selective, rather credulous, and fairly teleological. Thus, for example, had the Moon been intended as nothing but a lamp for us, it would have been better 'a smooth sphere of lime or chalk'. Since it has mountains it must be for its inhabitants.

In Chapter Seven Brewster deals with religious objections to plurality, answering them in the manner of Wilkins, Chalmers & co.[451] In Chapter Eight Brewster confutes Whewell's claims about binary systems – in any case binary stars (like our Sun) may themselves be inhabited. In Chapter Nine he cites William Herschel's classification of nebulae, and gives reasons why a great number may turn out to be star clusters.

Chapter Ten is a summary, and in it Brewster discusses the validity of analogical reasoning. Actually, both Whewell and Brewster were using it heavily (since there was little or no direct evidence) – neither with more obvious logic than the other. Brewster then attacks the *Essay* explicitly, drawing on points that really he has already made. On geology, for example, he suggests that if God did indeed take a million years (say) to prepare the Earth for us, then presumably other planets are at a similar stage. Nebulae, and binary systems are also explicitly reprised.

Brewster, like Whewell, finishes with a look to the future. For Whewell, he thought that perhaps God would intervene again on

---

[451]On page 131 Brewster makes the startling suggestion that 'Men of lofty minds and of undoubted piety have regarded the existence of moral evil as,a necessary part – of the general scheme of the universe …'

Earth, as he had done in making mankind, to make some further super-race. Brewster looked forward to a bodily resurrection to be placed elsewhere in the universe. Brewster finishes with a plea that we must 'impregnate the popular mind with the truths of natural science; teaching them in every school, and recommending them, if not illustrating them, from every pulpit …'

So what are we to make of this debate? These were two key gladiators in the world of science and in the Royal Society and the BAAS. Both were profoundly Christian in outlook, and fairly conservative in theology. Both argued from existing astronomy (citing John Herschel) and other sciences in particular geology. Both argued from analogy. Both argued from natural theology. Yet they arrived at different conclusions – or did they rather start from different conclusions?

Interestingly, Adam Sedgwick, whose theology was not much different from these two protagonists, wrote in the margin of his copy of Whewell's book that the issue was purely empirical – the theological arguments did not convince either way.

Of Mars in Particular

Of interest is the 10th Edition (1869) of John Herschel's *Outlines of Astronomy*. In it we find that the Moon seems to have no atmosphere, but because we do not see its far side this may indicate a shape that gives a shallow atmosphere the other side, and so it may be inhabitable (365). The Sun, its spots, patterns etc., is described at length. It is admitted that it may be that the dark core is 'in a state of intense ignition', but 'It does not follow of necessity that it must be so'. William Herschel's model with layers of luminous and reflective clouds is described and evidence given for it. Figures are given (from Lord Kelvin as he later was) for the enormous heat loss (presumably from combustion), but John seems convinced (and this is only two years before his death in 1871) that his dad's model still works. The great puzzle, he finishes, is how such a great heat source can be kept up (332). On Mars we 'frequently discern, with perfect distinctness, the outlines of what may be continents and seas' (425). Its reddish colour is probably the

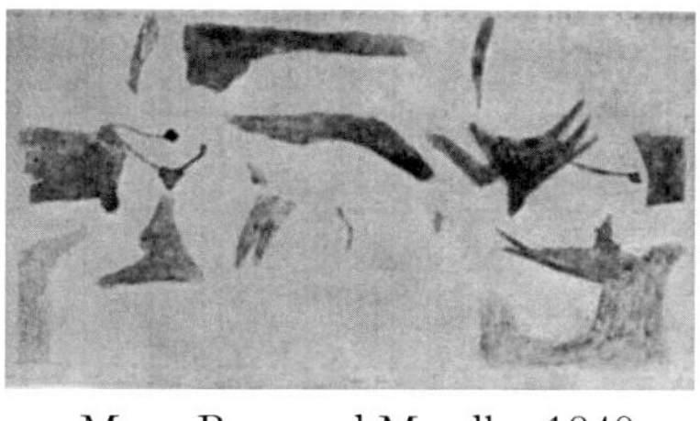

Mars: Beer and Maedler 1840

equivalent 'to the inhabitants of Mars' of red sandstone on Earth. The greenish 'seas', though not always seen, offer when visible 'forms considerably definite and highly characteristic' as shown in the charts of Wilhelm Beer and J. M. Madler. The observed variation in these spots may be due to 'the planet not being destitute of atmosphere and clouds' – something made more probable by brilliant white spots at its poles 'which have been conjectured, with some probability, to be snow, as they disappear when they have long been exposed to the sun …' (425).

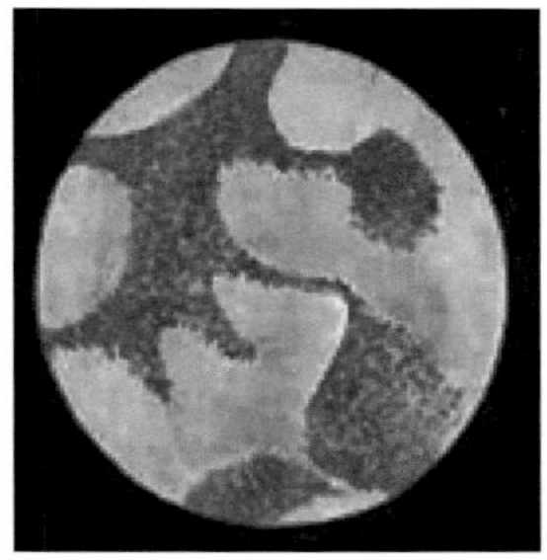
Mars: Secchi June 3 1858

In 1858 Father Pierre Angelo Secchi made some observations, showing mottled green patches on a pink background. In his 1863 colour map of the planet he labelled certain vague streak-like features he observed as 'canali' or 'channels'. This idea was picked up and exploded into controversy through the work of Giovanni Virginio Schiaparelli.

Giovanni Virginio Schiaparelli (1835–1910)

Giovanni Schiaparelli

Schiaparelli was an eminent Italian senator and astronomer. He had studied civil engineering at Turin University, and astronomy (1854–6) at Berlin with J. F. Encke and as assistant astronomer at Pulkovo (1856–1860) under Otto Struve. He became assistant (1860) and then the director (1862) in the Milan observatory.

In 1861 he discovered the asteroid Herperia, and in 1866 demonstrated that meteor swarms have comet-like orbits and may be cometary remains. He observed binary stars and Mercury, Venus and Mars – publishing some 250 papers overall and achieving a very high European reputation. In 1868 he got the Lalande prize, and in 1872 the RAS gave him a gold medal.

Pulkovo Observatory

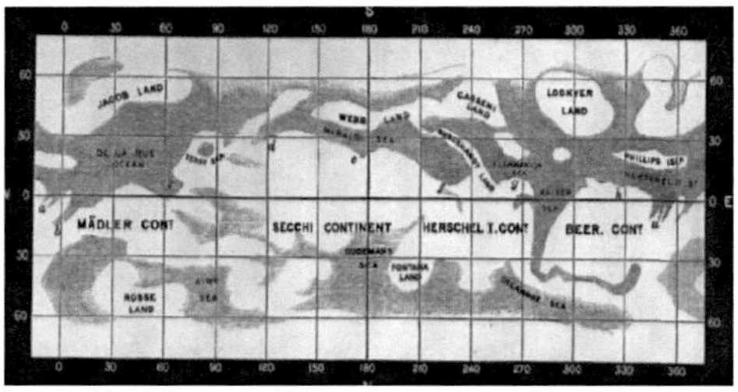

Mars: Nathaniel Green 1877

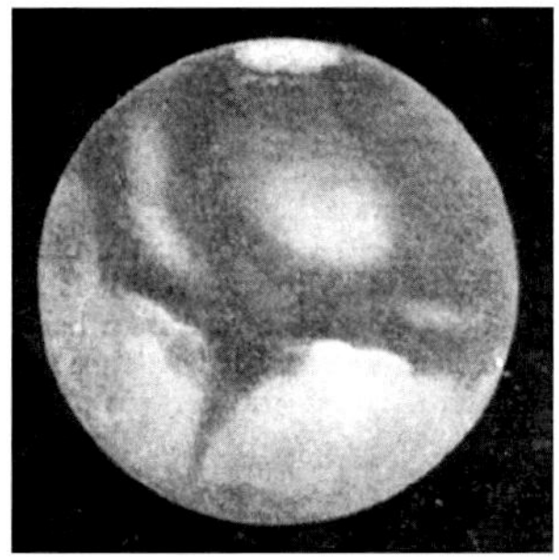
Mars: N Green 1877

In 1877 Mars came into opposition only 35m miles away. The English artist Nathaniel Green (1823–99), using a 13-inch reflector in Madeira, produced a tinted drawing and a map with a memoir which were published by the RAS.

Also in 1877 Schiaparelli produced the first of a series of Mars maps, which was published in a lengthy memoir beginning with a new determination of the axis of rotation of Mars.[452] This uses different names than Green (Schiaparelli's were eventually adopted), and he also (using only an 8¾-inch telescope in Milan) saw a vast intricate network of fine lines criss-crossing the reddish-ochre areas. He called these 'canali' after his countryman Secchi who, as we noted, had already used the term. This word in Italian is neutral, really meaning 'channels' without any implication of nature or artefact. Only in the English translation 'canals' was the definite implication of artefact implied.

In his 1877 map the canali are narrow winding streaks, irregular and not obviously like canals. In his successive maps (1879, 1881, 1884) the canali become straighter, finer, and as Lowell later commented 'in every way less natural'. According to Lowell, this showed that Schiaparelli 'started with no preconceived idea'. Lowell adds:

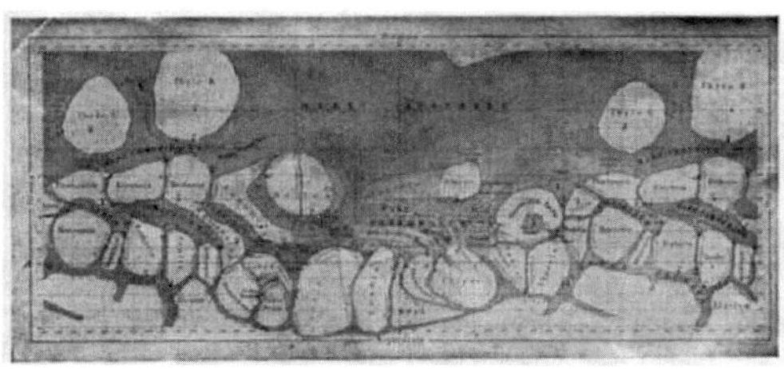
Mars: Giovanni Schiaparelli 1877

[452] See Crowe op. cit. if you really want the long title!

> … the canals did not change their characteristics from one opposition to another; the eye, it was, that learned to distinguish what it saw, and the brain made better report as it grew familiar with the messages sent it (1906, 29).

Actually (as T. W. Webb pointed out) Green was an artist and produced a *picture*, whilst Schiaparelli was colour blind and 'of micrometric vision' so commencing with 62 actual measured points produced a *chart.* Schiaparelli admitted his 1877 map was 'purely schematic' and in 1879 tried:

> … to better approach the true forms one actually sees on the planet, by representing with lines those features which have that appearance in the telescope and with different shades those which exhibit delicate gradations of tint … more pleasing to the eye, and more agreeable to the descriptions than the schema of pure lines produced in the (1877) memoir.[453]

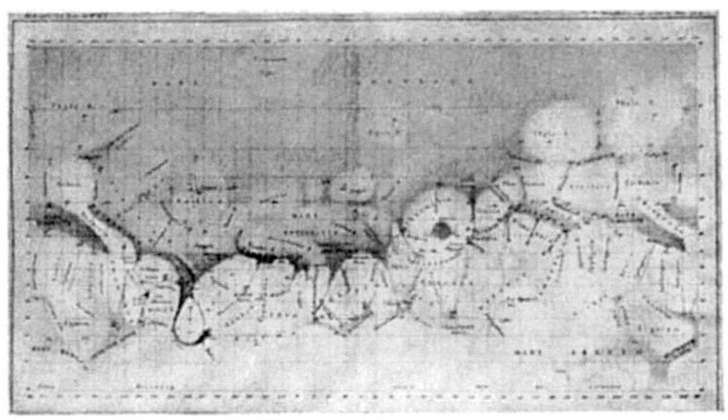

Mars: Giovanni Schiaparelli 1879

Reactions to his canali varied. *Nature* reported that at the RAS meeting on April 12th 1778 Green presented a letter and some drawings from Schiaparelli. Green suggested that the 'several dark channels' that Schiaparelli (but not himself) had noted might be:

1. Because they arose in changes on the planet after his own observation was complete.
2. Because of Schiaparelli's different drawing

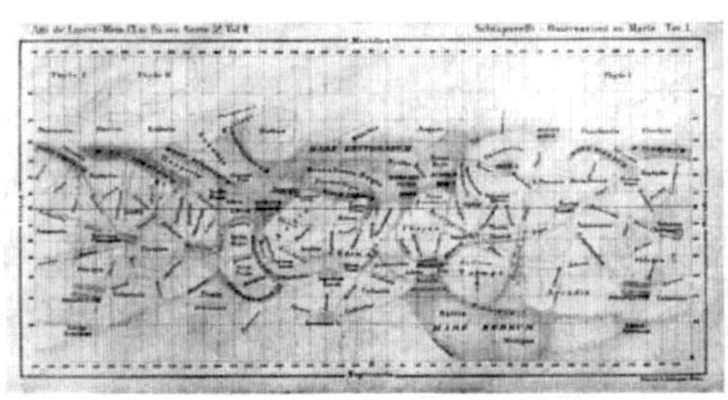

Mars: Giovanni Schiaparelli 1884

[453] Quoted in William Sheehan *The Planet Mars* ch 6.

techniques.

3. Because of a tendency of the eyepiece to 'elongate and develop dark points seen against a dark background'.

In December 1778 he added another possibility:

4. '… that the atmospheric vibrations have a tendency to cause a series of points in a line to appear connected together'.

In March 1880 he added two more possibilities:

5. 'some … may be the boundaries of faint tones of shade'.
6. '… they may be spaces between veil-like masses of atmosphere'.

When the Irish astronomer Charles E. Burton (1846–82) also 'saw' the canals, Green became convinced that 'it would be impossible to doubt their existence'. By 1882 he had noted that different observers seemed to see the canals differently, and veered back to caution and the possibility of (4) above.[454] Burton himself came round to 'strongly incline' to this view of Green and Maunder, though died soon after.

Lick Observatory (1880s)

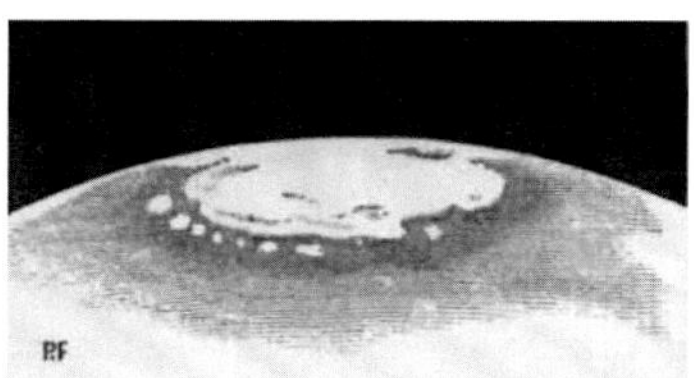

Mars South Pole (Chambers)

Reactions remained mixed. The FRAS Thomas William Webb (1807–85), in the fourth edition of his *Celestial Objects for Common Telescopes* (1881) used Burton's map for Mars – expressing his view that life existed there. Another FRAS George Chambers, in his fourth edition *Handbook of Descriptive and Practical Astronomy* (1889 3 vols), remarked that although the 'canals' had been seen by others:

> It cannot be said that their existence in the sharply defined forms suggested by Schiaparelli is generally recognisable.[455]

Chambers was not anti-pluralist. He quoted John Herschel's comment, which casually mentioned 'the inhabitants of Mars', and (after the style of

---

[454] These are in RAS Reports.

[455] George Chambers *A Handbook of Descriptive and Practical Astronomy* (1889) Vol 1, 152.

the devout Catholic Mivart) saw no conflict between an evolutionary origin for life and his Christian belief. The green patches he thought were seas, and the white poles were snow.

One sceptic about the canals was Edward Emerson Barnard at the Lick observatory in Hamilton, California, who complained in 1894 'to save my soul I can't believe in the canals as Schiaparelli draws them'. The Lick had the largest telescope in the world – not an 8.25 inch one! Its astronomers prevaricated (like most) but later provided a focus of opposition to the existence of canals.

E. W. Maunder

Another opponent was Edward Walter Maunder (1851–1928), a researcher at the Royal Observatory and founder of the British Astronomical Association. Maunder was an evangelical Wesleyan Charismatic and some have suspected a religious motive for his emphasis on the likelihood of rarity of life elsewhere and possible uniqueness of the Earth. Maunder, however, specifically asserted that religion was not relevant to deciding the issue of pluralism.[456] Maunder tended to Green's idea that apparent canals were edges of different colour tints.

Schiaparelli himself was cautious in the way he spoke of his canali, but was a pluralist. There were some (like A. R. Wallace the co-founder with Darwin of evolution by natural selection) who were anti-pluralist altogether, but the predominant view remained pluralist. It was not pluralism so much at issue, but whether it was evidenced on Mars by 'canali'. In 1878 he went to Rome to make a presentation of his discoveries to the Academy of Lynxes, and then the palace, stressing that with a better telescope (comparable, say, to that at Washington) he could get better results. On this occasion he said he had 'done a bit of a Flammarion' – an allusion to the flamboyant

Camille Flammarion

456 E. W. Maunder *Are the Planets Inhabited?* (1913), ch. 1.

French astronomer dismissed (though later reinstated) by Le Verrier for writing at age 19 an exuberant book on the plurality of worlds. Schiaparelli's stress on Mars as 'a world little different from our own' doubtless added force to his plea. The Academy, King and Senate enthused, and so in 1886 his observatory acquired a new 18-inch refractor. A whiff of extra terrestrials could do wonders for funding technical astronomy.

As the 1888 Mars opposition approached, various observatories had new big telescopes in readiness (including a massive 36-inch refractor at Lick). However at this, and the 1890 and excellent 1892 oppositions, divergences and controversy rumbled on. Some saw the canals and some didn't. Where there were big telescopes (e.g. at Lick), the weather might not be best, etc. There was, of course, also a problem that to be seen from Earth the canals would have to be 15–20 miles wide. Either construction was much easier up there or else what was being seen was canal-side cultivation.

In a widely read essay of Schiaparelli at this time (translated in abridgement by W. H. Pickering), we see how canals did 'make sense'. Since William Herschel the changing polar caps had been seen as ice. Actually it *had* been suggested by this time that they were mostly frozen carbon dioxide – but water seemed sensible enough to suppose. And if a large amount of water melted and refroze each year, what more natural than that it should form channels adapted by the inhabitants for irrigation?

There was also the factor noted by William Sheehan:

Percival Lowell

> For many observers the challenge of seeing the canals was irresistible; to fail to do so was to admit observational obtuseness. Under the circumstances, it is hardly surprising that more and more observers saw – or thought they saw – the canals, the whole process bearing a distinct analogy to the story of the emperor's new clothes.

Who will admit not seeing the emperor's new canals? Who, anyway, wants to be a spoilsport? Active Martians are Fun!

Percival Lowell (1855)

On a scene already buzzing with discussion about the Martian canals, there then came a figure who would rack it up just a bit higher. Percival Lowell had been born in Boston into a wealthy family. His upbringing mixed Puritan ethics with social Darwinism, and a good sprinkling of semi-benevolent capitalism. Returning from France to Boston in 1866, Percival continued a classic college prep education. By his own account, his serious interest in astronomy began at around age 15 when he began to observe Mars. He entered Harvard in 1872, studying mathematics (and also classics etc.), and graduating in 1876 with a short talk on the Laplacian nebular hypothesis (though heavily indebted to Herbert Spencer). After a graduation grand European tour, Lowell was involved in family business until 1883. Over the next decade he travelled the world, writing books about the Far East. One of these, *The Soul of the Far East* (1888) explains:

> All life, whether organic or inorganic, consists, as we know, in a change from a state of simple homogeneity to one of complex heterogeneity. The process is apparently the same in a nebula or a brachiopod, although much more intricate in the latter.

This is a kind of Spencerian social Darwinism, more Lamarckian than really Darwinian, with notions of an upward thrust of life leading ultimately to a higher form of society through enlightened capitalism. Consciousness was a higher development of matter, society of consciousness, and:

> … imagination, or the image-making faculty, may in a certain sense be said to be the creator of the world within … human progress is a function of the qualities of individuality and imagination.

Mars Hill

'Imagination', to Lowell, means 'image forming' rather than departing from reality. Naturally (although he appreciated the Japanese culture) the faculty is highest in the Europeans, and 'a lack of any fanciful ideas is one of the most salient traits of all

Far-Eastern races'. Lowell, also, later wrote (in his 1895 work) of two kinds of scientists: the plodding observers, and the imaginative theoreticians.

In December 1893 Lowell returned from a Far-East trip to receive Camille Flammarion's *La Planete Mars* as a Christmas gift. He realised that 1894 offered a great opportunity with Mars in close opposition. Presumably today he would have paid the Russians £17 million or so to fly him there, but the option for a capable, wealthy man in his era was more in the way of buying a telescope. So around January 17th 1894 he met with astronomer W. H. Pickering with whom he had been corresponding, and set in train events which led to him building his observatory in the clear air of Flagstaff, Arizona, on a place he called 'Mars Hill', starting in Spring 1894.

Lowell's profound commitment to pluralism was not an inevitable consequence of the nebular hypotheses (of which Whewell had been an early supporter) or evolution (of which A. R. Wallace was a pioneer). But it was associated with his Spencerian view of life moving on and up.

Lowell set out his objectives in an address to the Boston Scientific Society on May 22nd 1894. He was to study the Solar System:

> This may be put popularly as an investigation into the condition of life on other worlds, including last but not least their habitability by beings like [or] unlike man ... there is strong reason to believe that we are on the eve of pretty definite discovery in this matter.[457]

Lowell at 24-inch Telescope

To Lowell, the canali of Schiaparelli 'self-evidently' were 'the result of the work of some sort of intelligent beings' . Lowell did not feel some abstract call of science, but the thrill of a discoverer about to confirm the most exciting discovery of all – a civilisation on another world. He started observing in June 1794.

Various colour changes were noted over the next few weeks – by Lowell or his assistants – and interpretations were sought in terms

[457] Quoted in Sheehan op. cit.

of water and vegetation changes. The famous canals seemed to appear slowly over time.

Lowell's theory, in brief, was that Mars was losing water. To survive its intelligent inhabitants had developed a series of 'trigonometric to a degree' canals to carry melting water from the polar icecaps to irrigate oases in the desert.

Lowell had reasons why those with larger telescopes had not been able to see the canals – it was to do more with the air. He dashed off a series of articles and talks that irritated the co-editors of the *Astrophysical Journal* so much with apparent arrogance that they never published any of his articles. On a personal level, he was hospitable, entertaining at his observatory over the coming years even those who denied the canals altogether. Lowell, however, was a man of charisma and ability from a chiefly literary background, and his homespun approach could look amateurish in an age of increasing professionalism.

In 1895 he published his first work entitled just *Mars*. As we have noted, 'imagination' (by which he means the ability to erect images and construct theory) is expected to build a system of understanding from the basic empirical facts. Moreover:

> … proof is nothing but preponderance of probability … The law of gravitation … depends eventually … on a question of probability … All deduction rests ultimately upon the data derived from experience … the point at issue in any theory is not whether there be a possibility of its being false, but whether there be a probability of its being true … . The test of a theory is, first, that it shall not be directly contradicted by any facts, and, secondly, that the probabilities in its favour shall be sufficiently great.[458]

So this is the whole basis of his treatment. Over the previous few months, empirical observations have been amassed concerning the patterns to be observed on Mars. There is also a need to take into account the accepted theory of planetary development (the nebular hypothesis), and Spencerian evolutionary truths about organic development. Out of all this a system of

---

[458]Lowell*Mars* (1895), 6–7.

interpretation of patterns and structures seen on Mars can be constructed – as Lowell himself does in the book.

The motivation is also plain from the start. The Moon is close but dead, and so for all practical purposes (i.e. to search for other life) Mars is our 'nearest neighbour'. The search for intelligent life is the central issue – not, of course, 'human' life, but recognisably intelligent.

Lowell unexceptionally describes the Martian orbit etc., and then notes that two elements are needed for life: atmosphere and water. From various observations Lowell deduces that there is a thin and (generally though not absolutely always) cloudless atmosphere, and dust or ice particle induced hazes (he inclines to the latter). He also concludes: 'the climate of Mars appears to be astonishingly mild' (49). He argues also to a thin atmosphere from *a priori* reasons from the nebular hypothesis, gravity, etc. The polar ice cap is 'doubtless formed, not by the falling of snow, but by successive depositions of dew' (59).

Ch 3 argues for water based polar caps. On May 1st as the cap was melting, a 'dark blue band appeared surrounding it on all sides'. Lowell identifies this as water. He raises an idea that has been 'suggested, to that class of mind which likes to make of molehills of question mountains of doubt, the possibility that instead of ice we have here snow-caps of ... carbon dioxide' (80). Though superficially plausible, Lowell refutes the idea from physics. It has to be water.

Lowell spends some time on the basic Martian geography, and doubts that the 'seas' are really seas because they have 'every grade of tint' and show no polarisation of reflected light.

Mars is a smaller planet than Earth, further on its natural life cycle, and so at a stage where water is becoming ever scarcer. So what *are* the canals – given that at this distance an area of 30 miles would appear as just a dot? Lowell's observatory has seen four times as many as Schiaparelli:

> The lines appear either absolutely straight from one end to the other, or curved in an equally uniform manner. There is nothing haphazard in the look of any of them ... The result is that the whole of the great reddish-ochre portions of the planet is cut up into a series of spherical triangles of all possible sizes and shapes (131–5).

In Lowell's numerous diagrams this is exactly how they do look. His assistant Douglas's diagrams are a bit more fuzzy – looking as though he has used a crayon rather than a pencil! Lowell suggests that actually the pattern is one of 'straight lines and roundish spots' (179). All the spots are connected by at least two canals. Since the spots are round (not star shaped) they cannot be natural phenomena. They are usually 120–150 miles in diameter, the smallest about 75 miles. Both canals and spots are 'temporary phenomena' not permanent markings. All this points to artificially constructed or enhanced canals and oases for irrigation though:

> … all such evidence of design may be purely fortuitous, with about as much probability, as it has happily been put, as that a chance collection of numbers should take the form of a multiplication table (186).

Even more 'markedly unnatural' are the double canals. To see these 'all that is needed is a sufficiently steady air, a sufficiently attentive observer, and the suitable season of the Martian years … in good air the phenomenon is quite unmistakable' (188). Lowell neglects to mention a telescope but presumably one would come in handy! No one, says Lowell, who 'has seen the canals well … would ever have any doubt as to their seeming artificial …'

What we see, then, is 'not really the canal at all, but the strip of fertilized land bordering it – the thread of water in the midst of it, the canal itself, being far too small to be perceptible' (202). Since Mars is smaller the gravity is less, so the Martians can be built much bigger and with more muscle power. If a Martian were three times as large, he would be twenty seven times as strong – easily able to undertake such big constructions. As the Martians found water on their planet becoming scarcer, they arranged

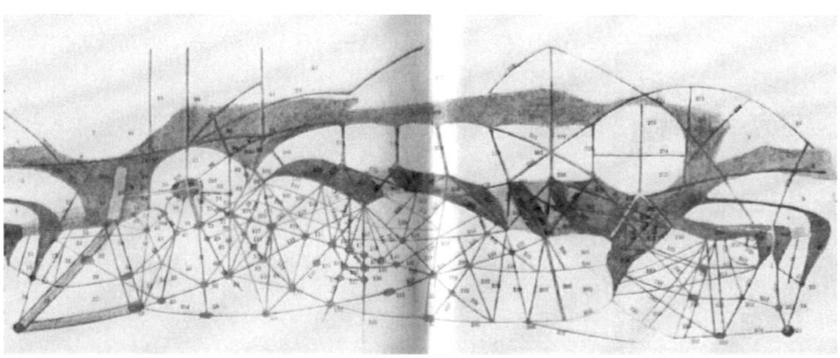

Lowell's 1895 Map of Mars on Mercator's Projection

this irrigation system to channel the water from their annually melting ice caps for irrigation. Lowell concludes:

> Man is merely this Earth's highest production up to date … He merely typifies in an imperfect way what is going on elsewhere, and what, to a mathematical certainty, is in some corners of the cosmos indefinitely excelled. If astronomy teaches anything, it teaches that man is but a detail in the evolution of the universe … he is destined to discover any number of cousins scattered through space (212 fin).

At the back of the book is a map, showing all the beautifully geometric canals and spots. We may wish to compare this (and earlier maps) with a modern photograph:

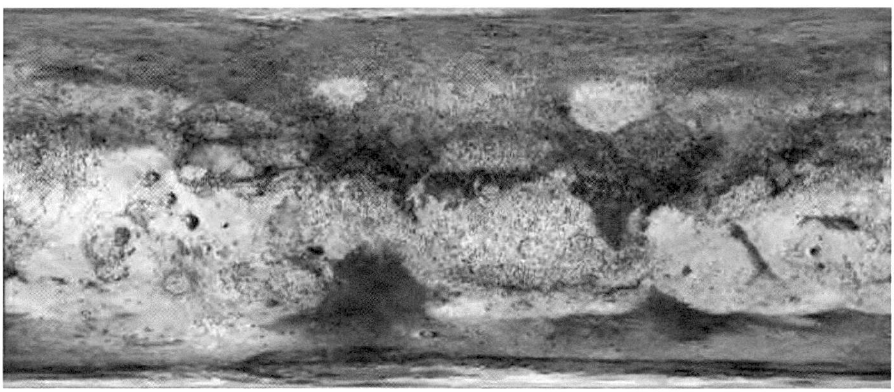

Modern Map of Mars photographically produced

Reactions to Lowell

Hoyt miraculously transforms Whewell's hesitant undogmatic dissent into the voice of orthodoxy, and implies that anti-plurality was common and dogmatic. In reality, it was not really about plurality (there were few against on principle, and virtually none of any significance who pronounced it irreligious) but about whether there were canals on Mars. In any event, speculation reached a fever pitch. H. G. Wells (1866–1946), then in a phase of Spencerian optimism which the bleaker winds of the 20th century later destroyed, serialised and then published *War of the Worlds* in 1898. Rewards were offered for means to communicate with the Martians. There was a near hysterical storm of public interest. Lowell's own magazine articles and lectures as well as his book were widely absorbed.

W. W. Campbell

Two basic centres of scientific scepticism emerged. One was around E. W. Maunder, as indicated above. The other on E. S. Holden and W. W. Campbell (1862–1938), who became director of the Lick observatory. One of the issues was that of spectroscopic reports (which will be looked at in the next chapter). Campbell basically doubted that there was any aqueous vapours on Mars, and so the whole machinery of Lowell. Campbell also questioned how the canals could apparently work from both poles, and why they would be geometric when any sensible canal maker would deviate around natural obstacles. Lowell, he claimed, was basing too much on too short a period of observation and gives 'many evidences of apparent lack of familiarity with the literature of the subject'.[459] Other astronomers, including even E. E. Bernard (who had recently been at Lick) were less hostile. In America, both the content and style of Lowell's work was controversial. The latter was, however, generally acknowledged to be literary and brilliant – which added to the effect of his ideas.

In 1895 Maunder published a comparative study of the 'Lactus Solis' region of Mars as drawn by many observers over the years. Ironically, his own conclusions, which involved complex changes in sea levels etc., probably fell into the same kinds of 'optical illusion' he had suggested explained the 'canals' in 1894. He had also, apparently retained a watery Mars although Campbell's main argument was that this was impossible.

All this goes to show that there was no single figure who was 'right' in his interpretation of Mars at that time.

Lowell Again

In 1896 Lowell commissioned a 13 ton, 26-inch refractor, which was to be set up in Mexico. Mars was observed from this observatory in Tacubaya in the

Tacubaya Observatory: Mexico

[459] Quoted in Hoyt, op. cit. 91.

winter of 1896–7. Another extraordinary event of this period was a claim by Lowell to have seen some 'surprisingly distinct' markings on Venus (a planet generally regarded as covered in opaque clouds). A chart drawn by Lowell appeared in the March 1897 *Monthly Notices of the Royal Astronomical Society*. This time, no one else could see the markings. In any event, Lowell collapsed from nervous exhaustion in April 1897, and took several years to recover. In summer 1901 a new spectrograph arrived at Flagstaff observatory. In 1903 Lowell claimed once again to have seen the markings on Venus, though since no one else saw them he did not emphasise the event in public. Ironically, in 1907 he referred to a critic's view that Venus was cloud covered as a hard-to-change 'preconceived opinion'![460]

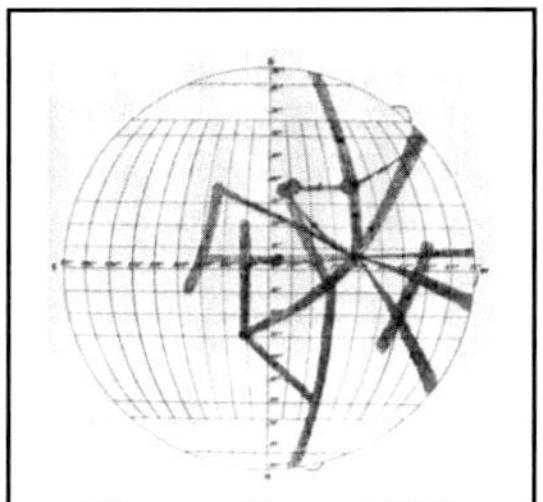

Venus Chart 1897

In 1903, also, E. W. Maunder did an experiment in which a group of boys in Greenwich were asked to copy a canal-expurgated picture of Mars, and they then drew the planet criss-crossed with lines. Maunder claimed that those who saw canals on Mars were not being deceptive but under an optical illusion. Flammarion then ran similar tests with French schoolboys, and as Lowell remarked 'not a boy of them drew an illusory line', and so suggested that 'it looks as if some leading questions had been put to the English schoolboys'. However, Lowell was putting leading questions to those he asked to confirm his 'lines', so if this was what it took to make them 'see' lines, then Maunder's claims were reasonable. In any event the British astronomical establishment decided against canals.

Lowell published two further major books on Mars. The first was *Mars and its Canals* (1906). This is a work with all the same basics, but much more detail, than the earlier one. The maps and charts are more 'line based' even than before. The climate is now proclaimed as lower than that on Earth, but above freezing point (87). Various projections on Mars are ascribed not to mountains but to occasional clouds.

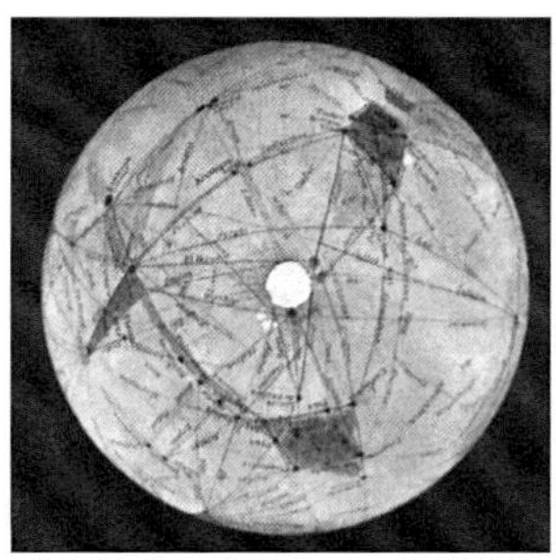

N. Polar Cap Lowell 1906

---

[460] Quoted in Hoyt, op. cit. 119.

This time, successive colour-tinted pictures of the *Mare Erythraeum* are produced in evidence that the glue-green areas are changing patterns of vegetation. Chapter 12 deals with terrestrial geology. In Part II we meet the canals, and various objections (e.g. the 'illusion theory') are considered and summarily dismissed. Again they are known to be canals because of:

1. Their straightness
2. Their individually uniform size
3. Their extreme tenuity
4. The dual character of some of them
5. Their position with regard to the planet's fundamental features
6. Their relation to the oases
7. The character of these spots
8. The systematic networking by both canals and spots of the whole surface of the plant.

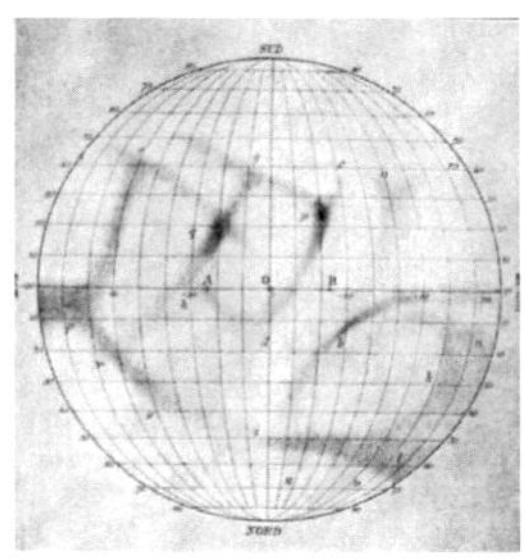
Schiaparelli's Mercury

The final Mars work, *Mars as the Abode of Life* appeared in 1908. This begins with its view of the whole process that links the nebular hypothesis to the Darwinian and traces the hypothetical life of a planet (whether Earth or Mars). Chapter I, then, is the origin of planets, Chapter II the evolution of life. 'There is now no more reason to doubt that plants grew out of chemical affinity than to doubt that stones did' (37). One novelty is the use of photographs of Mars – though actually the book seems to have a photograph of the camera used rather than of Mars. All the arguments (and the form of the diagrams) are as before – but now the whole is developed in terms of the general life cycles of planets. The Martians, then, are ahead of us, and their world will eventually dry up. Lowell does not really deal with the Whewellian problems of time spans here. If Mars is that much geologically ahead, one would have expected their technology to have developed to such a level that space travel would be common place. Why, then, have they not come to the Earth? Yet Lowell concludes that 'Mars at this moment is inhabited … these denizens are of an order whose acquaintance is

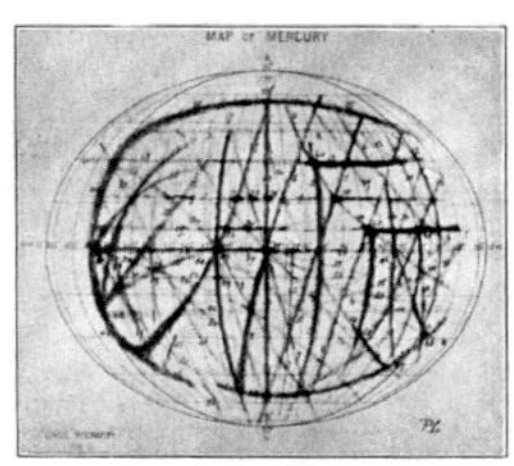
Lowell's Mercury

worth the making' (215).

In a final work in 1909 *The Evolution of Worlds,* Lowell looks at the development/evolution of all the planets in our system. Mars is now placed in a more general pattern of planetary life cycles. Beautiful photographs are given of Jupiter, Saturn and the Moon – oddly none of Mars, Venus or Mercury – on all of which Lowell had seen markings. A chart is produced, for example, of Mercury. Actually, even the best terrestrial telescopes can see only hazy markings on Mars. Schiaparelli had claimed to be able to map the markings and on this basis thought Mercury always had the same face to the Sun. Lowell's chart shows some quite distinct markings, though what they really were is a mystery. The Venus markings are reproduced – 'corroboration' has now apparently been made by: Miss Leonard (Lowell's secretary), Dr Slipher and Mr E. C. Slipher (all Lowell employees). No one else is mentioned – no one else could see them.

Modern Perspective

The 1960s spacecraft found no Martian canals, nor did Mariner 9 in the 1970s. Mars is now thought to have had a primordial atmosphere similar in density and pressure to that on Earth today, but has had its present form for some three billion years. The atmosphere today is thin, but dust storms periodically obscure the surface in a red haze. There are features that look like dried-up riverbeds, though since craters overlap them they are probably several billion years old. The present water is tied up in permafrost and in permanent polar caps, but the advancing and receding caps are due to a carbon dioxide frost. In June 2000 NASA's data led one scientist to comment:

> We see features that look like gullies formed by flowing water and the deposits of soil and rocks transported by these flows. The features appear to be so young that they might be forming today (*Science*, June 30, 2000.)

Since August 2012 NASA's 'Curiosity' rover has been moving on the planet's surface analysing samples. In 2013 this found evidence of clay on Mars, which could indicate that potentially life-supporting water was once present. It was also suggested that once Mars had a thicker and wetter atmosphere than Earth, but this was lost billions of years ago due to solar wind and a collision with a large Pluto-sized object. In August 2013 some scientists were suggesting that the presence of various mineral catalysts for life on Mars could even indicate that it formed there first and then came to Earth by meteorite.

Venus is, indeed, covered with highly reflective clouds and has little or no visible markings from Earth.

Mercury has only very hazy markings when seen from Earth.

Is there intelligent life elsewhere in the universe? Well the probability remains between zero and one depending on your starting assumptions! At present we have no serious detailed model to say how our incredibly complex DNA-based life originated on Earth, though there must be many planets in our universe where life would be possible, and even where life-conditions could last long enough for intelligent life to evolve. The work of Simon Conway Morris on convergence would indicate that, once started in suitable conditions, life forms similar to us would evolve. Maybe the humanoids in films like Star Trek and Avatar are not so unrealistic after all! What is less credible is that we should be able to contact them. The brief window in which intelligent life would reach our kind of level of science and technology before blowing itself into oblivion or being exterminated by their sun cycle is unlikely to coincide with ours – and if we one day decipher a message from deep space, the species that sent it are overwhelmingly like to be in oblivion. The fact that (according to a *You Gov* poll in September 2013) nearly half of Americans believe UFOs could indicate aliens, tells us more about Americans than about extra-terrestrials!

Conclusions on Martian Canals and ET

There are no canals on any other planets in the Solar System, though at one time Mars probably did have rivers. There has never been intelligent life on any other planet in our system either, though it is possible that there have been microbes.

The Martian canals episode is interesting in that it raises questions about the nature of observation and its relationship with theory. Lowell was no fool, and was thoughtful about the nature of observation. But, working at the limits of observation, he nevertheless saw what he wanted to see. His reasoning as to why more powerful telescopes and photography could not find these, look like ad hoc hypotheses to maintain his belief.

We began with a quotation from Crowe about the effects on human consciousness of the ideas of extra-terrestrials. Dan Goldin, long-time

Director of NASA, reputedly expressed similar views that 'no human endeavour or thought would be changed by that discovery'. Certainly the thought has stimulated astronomy, and the finance of astronomy, as well as drawing on the data of astronomy as the debate progressed. But it is doubtful whether major religions would see it as a threat, or people would be traumatised one way or the other.

In September 2013 apparently 200,000 people applied for the 'Mars One' programme – a one-way trip to Mars for reality TV. No one, however, should to go in hopes of meeting some of Lowell's canal engineers. The 'Emperor's new canals' really do not exist. The Jury is still out on whether there has been some kind of life there.

Questions

Here are some questions to ask as you think about plurality and ET:

- Can we assume on statistical grounds that the likelihood of intelligent life elsewhere in the universe is overwhelming?
- Should we take into account Whewell's point that actually we are in a brief window since the emergence of intelligent life here (possibly before we blow ourselves to oblivion) – and the chances of any other species being at just this point is remote? Brewster suggests that since we may suppose planets elsewhere to have been started at the same time, we may expect them to have reached a stage now fit for intelligent life. Which is more plausible now if we want to 'boldly go' on a SETI?
- How common are planets elsewhere? How precise are the conditions for the evolution not just of life but intelligence – which seem to require quite a long time of uninterrupted development!
- There are more specific questions still about local life. Do Martian meteorites show signs of bacterial life? Is there significant recent water activity on Mars? Is there some kind of life there now embedded in underground permafrost? Maybe *Curiosity* will help answer some of these questions.

References

Primary Sources:

Bernard Le Bovier Fontenelle *Conversations on the Plurality of Worlds* (trans. Gunning) has been reprinted in 2008.

William Whewell's *Plurality of Worlds: An Essay* (1853) repr.. by University of Chicago Press August 2001.David Brewster *More Worlds Than One: The Creed of the Philosopher and the Hope of the Christian Brewster's More Worlds Than One* (1854) repr. 2012 by Forgotten Books.

Lowell's main works on this are: *Mars* (1895), *Mars and Its Canals* (1906) and *Mars as the Abode of Life* (1908). The 1895 work is given complete on the web at http://www.wanderer.org/references/lowell/Mars. A. R. Wallace's book *Is Mars Habitable?* A Critical Examination of Professor Percival Lowell's Book *Mars and It's Canals* was reprinted in 2008. Lowell's: *Mars: Is There Life On Mars?* was reprinted in 2008 and there are several reprints of his Mars works.

Secondary Sources:

The most accessible and comprehensive work by a long way (if you can get it) is Michael J. Crowe's *The Extraterrestrial Life Debate 1750–1900* which was published in 1986 and reissued in Dover publications 1999.

On more recent ideas there is Steven Dick's *Life on Other Worlds: The Twentieth Century Extraterrestrial Life Debate* (Cambridge 1998).

Another general book is William Sheehan *The Planet Mars: A History of Observation and Discovery* (1996) also on www.uapress.arizona.edu/online.bks/mars/contents.htm

Biographies on Herschel have previously been listed.

Isaac Todhunter's original biography, *William Whewell D. D. Master of Trinity College Cambridge* is now available in several reprints.

Manachem Fish (1991) *William Whewell: Philosopher of Science*) (for £25–67 on Amazon at the time of writing) or the essays on Whewell edited by Manachem Fisch and Simon Schaeffer (1991).

On Brewster the classic *The Home Life of Sir David Brewster* by M. M. Gordon went through several 19th century editions and has been reprinted in 2012.

'Martyr of Science': Sir David Brewster 1781–1868 Eds A. D. Morrison-Low and J. R. R. Christie (1984) is a symposium.

Around now there should be a full run of Brewster's Edinburgh Journal issued for a mere £1495 (though at the time of writing I could not locate it)!

The classic account of Lowell is William Graves Hoyt's *Lowell and Mars* (Arizona 1976) but there is also the David Strauss *Percival Lowell* (Harvard 2001).

12. Birth of Astrophysics

NGC3603 Showing various stages of stellar life cycle[1]

'On the evening of August 29, 1864, I directed the telescope for the first time to a planetary nebula in Draco. The reader may now be able to picture … the feeling of excited suspense, mingled with a degree of awe, with which … I put my eye to the spectroscope. Was I not about to look into a secret place of creation? I looked into the spectroscope. No spectrum such only! … The light of the nebula was monochromatic … The riddle of the nebulae was solved … Not an aggregation of stars, but a luminous gas as I expected! A single bright line' William Huggins[1461]

The history of astronomy can be thought of as falling into three basic phases. In the first, it was purely positional. From the Greeks to the mid-16th century, the stellar sphere was assumed to be fixed, and the main puzzle was how to predict the motion of the planets. Even the heliocentricism of Oresme, Cusanus and Copernicus did not change this; their treatment of physics is really to get over the problems of falling objects, not to explain planetary motion. With Tycho and Kepler we enter a second phase. From 1577, of course, it is recognised that there can be new stars – the stellar sphere is not unchanging. Also, with Kepler forces of attraction (magnetism and gravity) are now suggested as part of a 'physics of the skies'. The issue is no longer simply to predict the *positions* of planets, but to relate their *orbits* to a physics that includes forces. The telescope also enables the estimation (albeit mostly speculative) of the relative sizes and masses of planets. All this culminates in Newton's system, with physics now explaining all the motions of the Solar System. Though Newton's *Optics* (as we shall see) sowed some key seeds, the next phase really awaited the 19th century. Kant, Laplace, Herschel and others

---

461*The Scientific Papers of Sir William Huggins* (eds. Sir William and Lady Margaret Huggins) (1909), 106.

then began speculating on the *evolution* of stars, nebulae and planets, as well as their internal composition and elements. New developments in physics and chemistry enabled properties of the celestial bodies to be examined from Earth: *astrophysics* was developed.

In this last chapter, therefore, we shall be looking at some of the key developments in astrophysics. In doing so we shall revisit some of the key figures met in previous sections, and will also look at the development of some key technologies and ideas in physics. The treatment will not be compendious, for other figures could also have been developed. Our cut-off point will be roughly 1900, leaving quantum theory, relativity, and much else as yet un-thought of.

Telescopes

In the chapter on Herschel we saw the various types of telescope, and noted the great increase in magnification that his instruments obtained. His '40-foot' telescope (with 4-foot mirror) at Slough was the largest so far (though it never worked very well). His ideas for mounting, however, as well as his ambitions for observation, were taken up by others.

Herschel's '40-Foot'

William Parsons – Earl of Rosse (1800–67)

William Parsons was born in York on June 17 1800, and was known as Lord Oxmantown until he succeeded to the Earldom on the death of his father in 1841. He went to university in Dublin and then in Oxford (obtaining a first in 1822). He was elected to the Commons from 1821–1834 (when he resigned), and represented Ireland in the House of Lords after 1841. He was an able administrator and economist, active in his country's affairs. William was especially interested, however, in mechanical pursuits and had both the engineering skills and the manual dexterity that befitted him for his life's work.

The Earl of Rosse

Birr Castle

A story is told that he once visited some large works in the North of England and the proprietor was so impressed with the knowledge of his visitor that he indicated that he would be pleased if he would consider the post of manager. Lord Rosse took no offence but produced his card and gently explained that he was not exactly the right man for the job, but he appreciated the compliment, and this led to a pleasant dinner and long friendship. His personal characteristics of charm and humility are well attested.

By his own account, when he found himself in possession of both leisure and great wealth, he 'deliberately cast around to think how that means and leisure could be most usefully employed'[462] It occurred to him that the making of great telescopes had seen no advance since Herschel, and that leisure, wealth, and his own engineering and mechanical skills could best be used for such a great project. Initially (around 1826) he tried working with the new Fraunhofer refractors, but concluded that only reflecting telescopes could achieve a really large aperture.

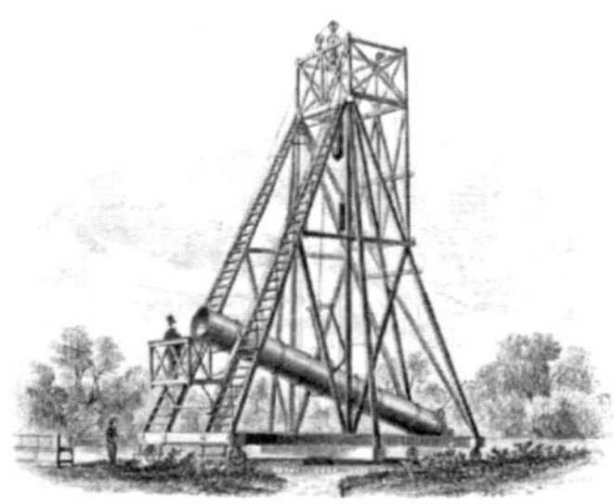

Rosse's '3-foot' Reflector

His first great reflector was based on a Herschel-type mounting, but had a 3-foot mirror that was twice the diameter of Herschel's 20-foot focal length one. After careful choice of alloy, he made it of 16 thin plates soldered to a brass framework. In 1840 he successfully cast a solid mirror of the same size.

---

[462] One account is from his friend Sir Robert Ball in *Great Astronomers* (1906), 274.

Mary Rosse

William also met, and married in July 1836, the twenty three year old Mary Field, who was the daughter of a wealthy Yorkshire landowner. Mary was a talented, active person, who designed her own furniture and was also a skilled blacksmith. One has the impression that she was far from overawed by, or subservient to, the man who was a 13 years her senior and an accomplished statesman and rising scientist. In 1842 William began an interest in the newly invented daguerrotype photography, and in the 1850s Mary also became involved in photographic methods, winning the first silver medal given by the Photographical Society of Ireland. In the terrible 1845–7 Irish famines, both William and Mary were very active in famine relief and providing employment for the impoverished populace.

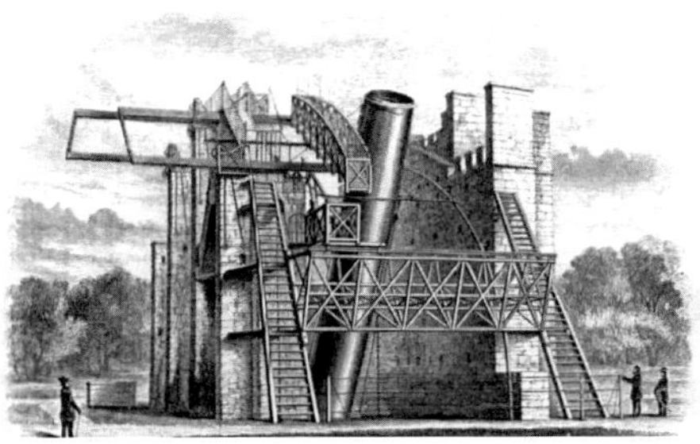

Also in 1842 was commenced the telescopic monster of all time in this conventional mode. After a number of setbacks Rosse was able to cast two 6-foot mirrors (each weighing about 4 tons) to mount in a monster tube of some 7-foot diameter. The mounting was fixed between two walls, with the intention of observing nebulae as they passed the meridian – assuming the Irish mist was missing that night! The nominal magnification was x6000.

The almost immediate success was to see as a spectacular spiral a nebula that John Herschel had previously seen as some rings and two discs. Rosse, then, drew the first spiral nebula. Even then, a number of people refused to believe in the existence of the spiral until eventually it was confirmed photographically.

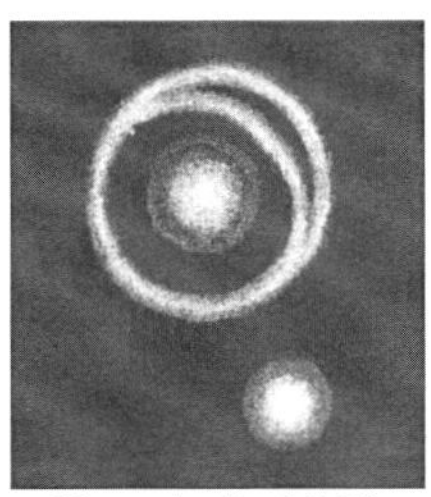

Herschel's M 71

Rosse's M 71

Lord Rosse was President of the BAAS in 1843, and of the Royal Society 1848–54. He also studied and named the great Crab Nebular, and made extensive and detailed studies of the Orion Nebula. Unfortunately he thought that he *had* resolved the Orion Nebula into stars (it actually *does* have stars, but embedded in a gaseous cloud from which stars are forming), and this led many to conclude that *all* nebulae might thus be resolved in time. Such studies of apparent nebulae could sometimes apparently resolve them into star clusters, and sometimes not. Obviously, however, the question always remained of whether a failure to resolve into clusters of individual stars was simply because no telescope was yet adequate to the task for that particular nebula. Whether, therefore, there really *were* different types of nebulae (e.g. some star clusters and some gaseous and non-resolvable clouds) was a question that had to be answered by other means. These are considered below.

Rosse's Crab Nebula

To round off this part on telescopes, however, we note that the optical telescope was still subject to improvement. One of the finest of the 19th century was that at the Lick Observatory. It was a refractor of three-foot aperture with a focal length of 57 feet. It was with this telescope that the observers affirmed the non-existence of Martian 'canals' – as we saw in the previous chapter. For a *reflecting* telescope larger than Lord Rosse's (which collapsed by 1909)[463], the world would have to await the one erected on Mount Wilson in 1917 – which is outside our present period of interest. By then, of course, the issue of the nature of nebulae had been decided by another technique entirely – spectroscopy.

Lick Telescope

[463] A working replica has now been erected at Birr Castle in the 1990s.

Physics and Spectroscopy

Before 1670 it was generally assumed that white light was the normal simple form of light, and this was *modified* to give coloured light. Isaac Newton showed in his 1672 paper[464] that a round beam of light was elongated into a spectrum when passed through a prism. He showed that white light was actually a mixture of colours separated by the prism, and seven basic colours visible to the human eye were noticeable in what he called the 'solar spectrum'.

Newton had tended to a corpuscular theory of light, though his *Queries* show a far from simple adherence to this idea. In 1801, however, the English physicist Thomas Young (1773–829) carried out a double-slit experiment. He passed a beam of light through two slits close together. Were light simply made up of particles, he reasoned, one should simply see two bright images on the screen the other side. In actual fact we see bands of light and dark – interference between the two beams of light, which seems to indicate waves. As we have noted, figures like David Brewster stuck to the Newtonian corpuscular theory – but in general the wave nature of light was accepted. If light was wave in form, then presumably different colours were different wavelengths, and since (logically enough) any length of wave should be possible, light should be infinitely variable in colour.

Around 1800, William Herschel[465] discovered the Infrared region and showed that Infrared rays are refracted according to the same laws as light. In 1801 J. W. Ritter discovered ultraviolet rays at the other end of the scale. It was recognised that visible light was just part of the whole spectrum.

We will now look at some of the key figures in the development of spectroscopy.

W. H. Wollaston

William Hyde Wollaston (1776–1828)

William Hyde Wollaston was the son of a clergyman who was a Fellow of the Royal Society and was interested in astronomy (he compiled a star catalogue). William's uncle was a Royal

---

[464] See the Chapter 8 above.

[465] See the Chapter 9 above.

Physician, and William (who was born in Norfolk) also went up to Caius College, Cambridge in 1782 to train as a physician. At this time Cambridge was seeing a rise in interest in observational science, spearheaded by a few figures (mostly Evangelical in their religion) such as Isaac Milner who was Jacksonian professor of chemistry. William was part of this set, interested in chemistry and astronomy. He graduated in 1787, and completed his medical studies in London. He became an FRS in 1793, but practised medicine until around 1800. In that year he suffered greatly impaired vision, and henceforth confined himself to research work in electrochemistry and optics.

Caius College

In 1802 Wollaston repeated Newton's prism experiment but this time used a slit of light instead of a round beam.[466] The idea was to cut down the amount that each colour of light overlapped with the next, and Wollaston observed in the resulting spectrum seven gaps or dark lines. This showed that the Sun did not send light of every degree of 'refrangibility'. He also produced experiments on the refractive index of Iceland spar (measured in different directions), showing that it gave support to Huygens' wave theory of light.

Wollaston was active in various areas of practical science, advising on issues of longitude, weights and measures etc. In 1802 he was awarded the Copley Medal of the Royal Society and became secretary in 1804 (he was briefly President in 1820). In 1807 he developed the *camera lucida* and in 1809 a 'reflecting goniometer' which he used to determine the geometrical form of crystals. He adopted the atomic theory of John Dalton (1766–1844), which was invented around 1803, and suggested in 1808 that knowledge of atoms in three dimensions would be useful. By 1813 his view of atoms had changed, and he sought to set up a scale showing proportions in which chemicals combined by weight. This was an attempt to be purely inductive, though it was over-simplifying the situation.

[466] *Phil. Trans.* cxii, 1802, 378.

Josef von Fraunhofer (1787–1826)

Josef von Fraunhofer

Josef von Fraunhofer (or Joseph Fraunhofer) was born in Bavaria in 1787, son of a poor master glazier who died when Joseph was 12.

He was then apprenticed to a glazier who offered him little hope of education or advancement until he miraculously escaped the physical collapse of his master's house in July 1801. This eventually led to his employment in a glass-making establishment in which he so impressed as to be made manager of the workshop in 1809 and director of the glassmaking in 1811.

The company produced first class telescopes and other optical instruments, and his ambition was to perfect the achromatic lens invented a century earlier. To do this necessitated knowing precisely the refractive indices of different glasses, and in 1814 he was working on this using two bright flame spectra as sources of monochromatic light. As he was comparing light from flame spectra with sunlight, his work with prisms led him to recognise that the Sun's spectrum contained some pronounced dark lines. This was more obvious as he magnified the resulting spectrum, effectively, creating the first 'spectroscope'. He found that the light from the Sun had literally hundreds (he counted 574) of dark lines in its spectrum.[467] The

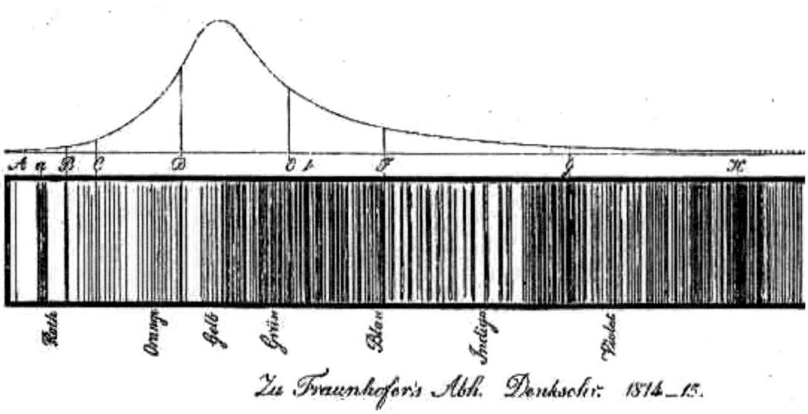

Josef von Fraunhofer's diagram of the solar spectrum: 1814-1815

darkest (called 'Fraunhofer Lines') he gave letters of the alphabet. Fraunhofer showed that these lines did not depend on the prism (i.e. the type of glass) used, so were a genuine feature of the sunlight. Fraunhofer noticed that the light from the Sun and planets seemed identical, but that from various bright stars (including the Sun itself, Sirius etc.) differed. All this was of great theoretical interest, though Fraunhofer's own interest were still in connection with its use in constructing the ideal achromatic telescope.

In 1821 and 1823 Fraunhofer published papers that related various diffraction phenomena in terms of the wave theory of light. The dark spectral lines were also found in spectra produced (1821–22) by reflection from a grating. He built in 1821 the first diffraction grating comprised of 260 close parallel wires, and used this (with the wave theory of light) to measure the wavelengths of specific colours and dark lines in the solar spectrum. He measured the values of some 300 of them. He also looked at the stars, and found that they had different spectral patterns, with different dark lines. Studying the spectrum emitted from his sodium lamp, he found it to have no dark lines, but he did note two bright lines in the orange where the two dark D lines are in the solar spectrum.

Refractor 1824

Fraunhofer remained a first-class instrument maker. Wilhelm Struve (1793–1864) used an 1824 9.5-inch refracting telescope and equatorial mounting made by Fraunhofer, and it was in 1838 that Friedrich Bessel (1784-1864) first measured a stellar parallax (of 61 Cygni) with a 6¼-inch heliometer at the Königsberg observatory.

Josef Fraunhofer never married, and died in 1826 from tuberculosis contracted the previous year.

In 1832 David Brewster (1781–1868), whom we met in the chapter on plurality of worlds, showed that when a continuous spectrum is passed through a gas a dark-line results in the spectrum.

There were various other minor observations, but the real progress awaited the 1850s. Professor W. H. Miller of Cambridge established by 1850 the coincidence of these lines with sodium as burned in the laboratory. George

Gabriel Stokes (1819–1903), who was Lucasian Professor at Cambridge from 1849, gave the explanation later given by Kirchoff. He suggested resonance as a mechanical explanation of the phenomenon, i.e. the sodium atom would have a frequency of vibration corresponding to the yellow light it emits, and so would absorb light of the same frequency. Stokes's friend, Sir William Thompson (later Lord Kelvin), taught from 1852 that sodium was a constituent of the Sun's atmosphere.[468]

Others were following this up, and in this period three kinds of terrestrial spectra were identified:

(1) The spectrum of an incandescent solid or liquid, which is nearly always continuous and without dark lines.

(2) The spectrum of a glowing gas, which (unless under great pressure) exhibits a characteristic mix of bright and dark lines.

(3) A spectrum that arises when an incandescent body is viewed through absorbent vapours, containing dark lines characteristic of the vapours.

The systematic development in spectroscopy came, however, with Kirchhoff.

Gustav Kirchhoff (1824–87)

Gustav Kirchhoff (1824–87)

Kirchoff was born in Königsberg which was then a part of Prussia. It became Kaliningrad under the U.S.S.R. in 1945, and is now a Russian oblast (region) sandwiched between Poland and independent Lithuania. Königsberg was famous as the birthplace of philosopher Immanuel Kant (1724–1804, mentioned below), who studied at the university and was Professor of logic and metaphysics from 1770. The also famous Friedrich Wilhelm Bessel became professor and the director of the observatory in 1810, and in 1838 (as noted above) was the first to measure a stellar parallax using a Fraunhofer instrument. Gustav Kirchhoff was the

---

468 *Report of the British Association* (1871), xcv.

son of a law councillor who was a part of the same social circle as the academics. He went to the local university (where Bessel was, of course, still director of the observatory) and (studying under Franz Neumann) worked on aspects of electricity and magnetism. In 1845 (still only 21) he announced 'Kirchhoff's laws' for the calculation of currents, voltages and resistances of electrical networks. Gustav graduated in 1847, marrying the daughter of one of the academics. In 1848 he obtained the right to lecture in Berlin University as a private lecturer, but in 1850 he became Professor of Physics in Breslau.

Heidelberg University

Kirchoff and Bunsen

Breslau is now Poland's fourth largest city (Wroclaw) and capital of Lower Silesia, some 160 kilometres from Germany. The university had been there from 1728, and was well established. The chemist Robert Bunsen (1811–99) came briefly to Breslau, and after moving to Heidelberg was instrumental in obtaining a professorship for the young Kirchhoff in 1854. Heidelberg University was founded in 1385, and had a long history with a chair of mathematics and physics from 1752. Bunsen's new chemical laboratory was completed in 1855.

In 1855 Bunsen improved Faraday's earlier invention to make the 'Bunsen burner' which gave a pure flame. Bunsen was then exploring its use to analyse salts on the basis of the distinctive colours produced in the pure flame. But how could he distinguish the colours? Bunsen was trying to compare them with coloured glass or solutions, but Kirchhoff pointed out that the use of spectra was clearly the most effective way to do this. Working together from 1859, the two were able to use pure salts and the Bunsen burner to indicate the association of particular spectral lines with particular elements. Their 1860 paper *Chemical Analysis by Observation of Spectra* showed their apparatus for their work with the following description:

> A is an internally blackened box with a trapezoidal bottom resting on three legs; the two oblique side walls, which form an angle of about 58° with each other, carry the two small telescopes B and C. The eyepiece of the first is removed and replaced by a plate in which a slit formed by two brass edges is adjusted at the focus of the objective lens. The lamp D is arranged before the slit so that the rim of the flame is on the axis of tube B. Somewhat below the spot where the axis meets the rim, there is the end of the loop formed in a fine platinum wire, which is held by arm E. The little pearl of the dry chlorine compound to be investigated is melted to this loop. Between the objective lenses of telescopes B and C is the hollow prism F of 60° refractive angle; it is filled with carbon disulphide. The prism rests on a brass plate that can be rotated on a vertical axis. This axis carries mirror G on its lower end and, above it, handle H by which prism and mirror can be rotated. A small telescope is directed toward the mirror so that the observer can see the

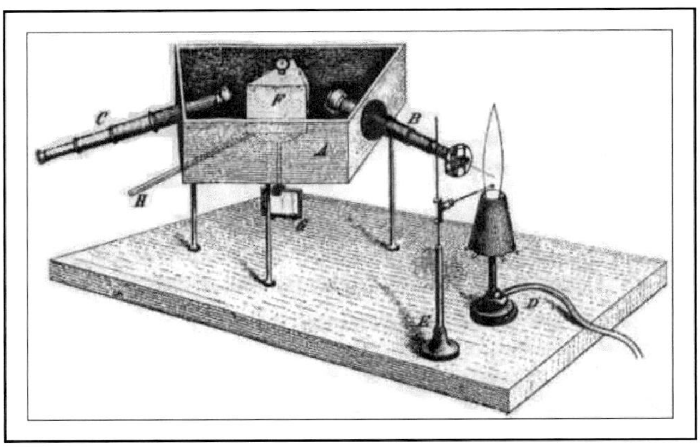

> horizontal scale mounted at a small distance. By rotating the prism, the entire spectrum of the flame can be brought before the hair line of telescope C … Every place in the spectrum corresponds to a reading to be made on the scale. If the spectrum is very weak, the hairline in C is illuminated with the aid of a lens that throws part of the rays of a lamp through a small opening in the side of the ocular tube of C.

They report spectra of various common materials, and that detection of the presence of sodium is very sensitive. Using this apparatus, Bunsen and Kirchhoff also discovered caesium (1860) and rubidium (1862), new elements identified by their spectral lines.

The 1860 article, however, also adds:

> Spectrum analysis, which, as we hope we have shown, offers a wonderfully simple means for discovering the smallest traces of certain elements in terrestrial substances, also opens to chemical research a hitherto completely closed region extending far beyond the limits of the earth and even of the solar system. Since in this analytical method it is sufficient to see the glowing gas to be analysed, it can easily be applied to the atmosphere of the Sun and the bright stars. However, a modification is here necessary, because of the light emitted by these stars. One of us in his work 'on the relationship between emission and absorption of bodies for heat and light' (Kirchhoff, these Ann. 109, 275) has proved theoretically that the spectrum of a glowing gas is reversed; i.e., the bright lines are converted into dark ones, in case it has behind it a light source of sufficient intensity and sending out a continuous spectrum. It can be concluded that the spectrum of the Sun with its dark lines is just a reversal of the spectrum which the atmosphere of the Sun would show by itself. Therefore, the chemical analysis of the Sun's atmosphere requires only the search for those substances that produce the bright lines that coincide with the dark lines of the solar spectrum.
>
> For example, the bright red line in the spectrum of a gas flame into which some lithium chloride has been brought changes into a black line when full sunlight is transmitted through the flame.

In an 1862 paper Kirchhoff adds:

> In order to test in the most direct manner possible the frequently asserted fact of the coincidence of the sodium lines with the D lines, I obtained a tolerably bright solar spectrum, and brought a flame coloured by sodium vapour in front of the slit. I then saw the dark D lines change into bright ones. The flame of a Bunsen's lamp threw the bright sodium lines upon the solar spectrum with unexpected brilliancy. In order to find out the extent to which the intensity of the solar spectrum could be increased without impairing the distinctness of the sodium lines, I allowed the full sun-light to shine through the sodium flame, and to my astonishment saw that the dark lines D appeared with an extraordinary degree of clearness.[469]

Kirchhoff also went on to use lime-light (an intense white incandescent light) to shine through a sodium flame, producing a kind of artificial solar spectrum (with the two D lines dark). The implication was that elements that gave off the light when incandescent could also reabsorb it. If more is absorbed than emitted by an intervening layer then dark lines will appear. Kirchhoff concluded that the Sun consists of a very hot nucleus, the surface of which (or 'photosphere') yielded a perfectly continuous spectrum. It was, however, surrounded by a less highly heated vapour high in sodium vapour in the glowing region around the Sun and this absorbed the sodium light leaving dark lines.

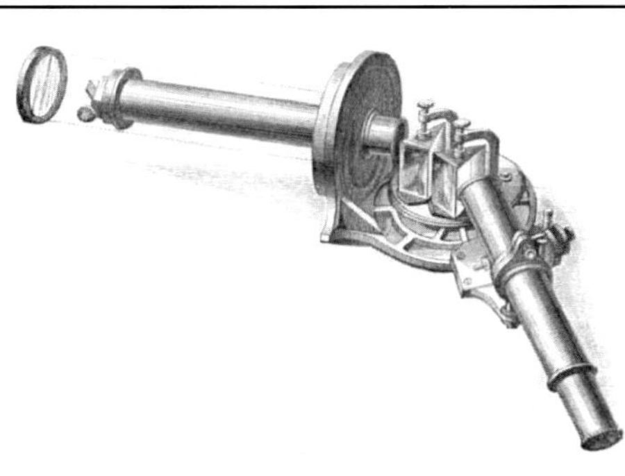

Simple Astronomical Spectroscope

Kirchhoff went on to look at issues of radiation, exploring the ratio of absorptive and emissive powers (which is a function of wavelength and temperature) and in 1862 establishing the idea of black-body radiation. Ironically, Kirchhoff was reluctant to follow atomic speculation (as in the explanation mentioned above by Stokes a decade

[469] *Untersuchungen über das Sonnenspectrum* (1862), 9.

earlier), which he considered premature and without inductive base.

In 1869 Kirchhoff's wife died, and he remarried in 1872. Sadly, Kirchhoff had met with an accident that left him using crutches or a wheelchair, though he is recorded as always of a cheerful disposition. In 1875, no longer able to continue experimentation, he accepted a chair in theoretical physics in Berlin.

Spectroscopes and Observations

From the start, opticians (in particular Fraunhofer) were involved in developing spectroscopes. In 1890 George Chambers FRAS (collaborating with E. W. Maunder who was mentioned in our previous chapter) wrote his 4th Edition *Handbook of Descriptive and Practical Astronomy*. His outline of spectroscopes is of interest. Chambers says:

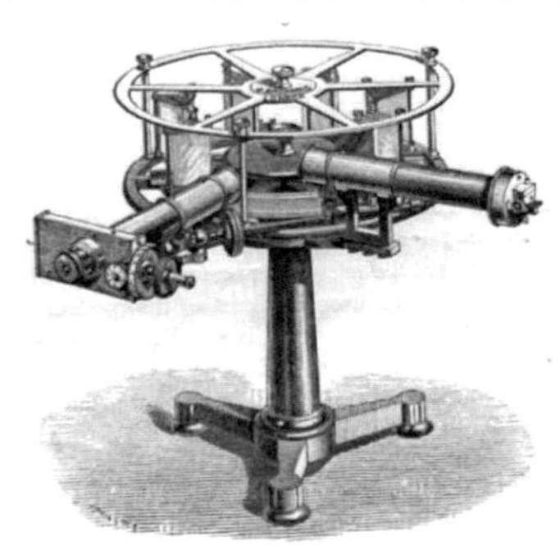

Automatic Spectroscope

> A spectroscope in its simplest conception consists of a narrow slit formed by a pair of knife edges, capable of being adjusted by means of a screw. The rays of light, admitted by this slit are received by a lens placed at its own focal distance from the slit. In passing through this lens the rays are rendered parallel. They are then allowed to fall on a prism of any transparent substance of high dispersive power, by reference one of flint glass. The spectrum produced by the passage of light through the prism is then viewed by means of a telescope furnished with a Huygenian eyepiece of low-power. To obtain the best definition, the prism should be placed … in such a position that the rays of light transversing the prism are equally inclined to its two faces. In the most powerful instruments a number of prisms, sometimes as many as 10 or 11, are arranged in a circle.

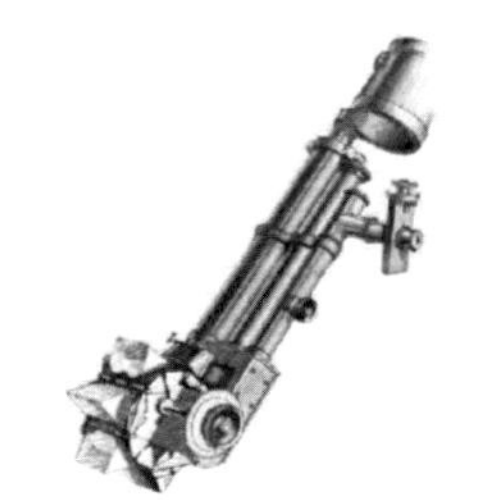

Young Spectroscope

In the simple illustration Chambers shows two

such prisms. With more complex systems, it was useful to have an instrument that adjusted all the different prisms simultaneously to fit one particular colour's deviation. Later also, the Princeton physicist/ astronomer C. A. Young (1834–1908), who made the first observations of the flash solar spectrum in the eclipses of 1869–70, invented an astronomical spectroscope which contained two half and four full prisms of 60 degree angle, making effectively a traverse of 10 prisms as the beam passes through twice.

Various important observations were made using these improving instruments, bringing knowledge of the *physical nature* of celestial bodies. One figure, William Huggins, epitomises the new approach.

William Huggins (1824–1910)

William Huggins

William Huggins was born in February 1824, the only surviving child of a successful London silk and cloth merchant. He was bright, and an interest in science manifested itself early in the acquisition of a microscope and a telescope at the age of 18. He had, however, to abandon plans to go to Cambridge, and from age 18 until 30 (1854) was responsible for his father's business and able to pursue science only in any spare time.

In 1854 Huggins joined the Royal Astronomical Society, and was able to divest himself of the business and move with his parents to Tulse Hill to pursue his scientific interests. In 1854 there was no real 'career' in science[470] – even Stokes, becoming Lucasian Professor at Cambridge in 1849, did not receive enough to live on and had to take up various other appointments to make ends meet. Figures like Rosse and Huggins as wealthy 'amateurs'[471] (though the word is anachronistic) were important to science in this time. Tulse Hill, where he built his observatory, is now a London suburb, but at that time was in the countryside where astronomical observation was unhindered by town lights and smoke.

---

[470] This was one of the real grievances of 'Darwin's bulldog' T. H. Huxley . As a non-Anglican he could not even take up a Cambridge professorship, and what few posts there were went on patronage rather than pure merit. (cf. Adrian Desmond, *Huxley* (1994)). His set (and the journal *Nature)* campaigned to change this state of affairs.

[471] Charles Darwin and Charles Lyell were similar wealthy 'amateurs' at this time.

The telescope he used from 1858 was an excellent eight-inch refractor. However, Huggins later wrote that:

> I soon became a little dissatisfied with the routine character of ordinary astronomical work, and in a vague way sought about in my mind for the possibility of research upon the heavens in a new direction or by new methods. It was just at this time … that the news reached me of Kirchhoff's great discovery of the true nature of the chemical constitution of the Sun from his interpretation of the Fraunhofer lines.
>
> This news was to me like a coming upon a spring of water in a dry and thirsty land. Here at last presented itself the very order of work for which in an indefinite way I was looking – namely, to extend his novel methods of research upon the sun to other heavenly bodies.[472]

Huggins's Telescope/Spectroscope

Huggins's Telescope

His problem was that, as he went on to note: 'The light received at the earth from a first magnitude star, e.g. Vega, is only about one forty thousand millionth part of that received from the sun' . Huggins worked with his friend the Cambridge Professor of Chemistry W. H. Miller (who had shown the relevance of the sodium lines as noted above), to design a spectroscope and attach a telescope to it. He was then able to compare spectral lines from celestial bodies with chemical spectra created in the laboratory. Huggins himself noted how this changed

[472] William Huggins, 'The New Astronomy: A Personal Retrospect' *The Nineteenth Century,* 41 (1897), 911 (also later published in his *Scientific Papers*).

the observatory, which now looked more like a chemical laboratory. His later spectroscope contained six prisms.

In January 1863, working with Miller, Huggins obtained photographic spectra of Sirius and Aldebaran. Huggins showed that stars are composed of elements that occur on the Sun and Earth. In 1864 he observed to his surprise that from an unresolved nebula in the constellation of Draco only a single bright line was observed. This indicated that this nebula was a cloud of luminous gas, not a star cluster. A physical way of determining whether or not *all* nebulae would be resolved into star clusters had been found – and the answer was 'no'. In 1866 he obtained a new spectroscope of greater power. He received a joint (with Miller) Royal Astronomical Society gold medal in 1867. By 1868 he had examined spectra from some seventy nebulae, one third of which appeared gaseous. To Huggins, this indicated something about the nebula hypothesis:

> … though the short span of human life is far too minute relatively to cosmical events for us to expect to see in succession any distinct steps in so august a process, the probability is indeed overwhelming in favour of an evolution in the past, and still going on, of the heavenly hosts.
>
> A time surely existed when the matter now condensed into the sun and planets filled the whole space occupied by the solar system, in the condition of gas, which then appeared as a glowing nebula, after the order, it may be, of some now appearing in the heavens. There remained no room for doubt that the nebulae, which our telescopes reveal to us, are the early stages of long processions of cosmical events, which correspond broadly to those required by the nebular hypothesis in one or other of its forms [i.e. of Herschel or Kant-Laplace].[473]

This is the classic approach of astrophysics – a combination of physics with astronomical observation, and an attempt to turn snapshots into evolutionary histories. In today's theory we do, indeed, see a glowing gas as a part of the development of a protostar, and the life cycle of stars is well explored.

---

[473] *The Scientific Papers of Sir William Huggins* (eds. Sir William and Lady Mary Huggins) (1909), 106.

From 1863 Huggins was attempting to photograph spectra – though a satisfactory technique was not developed until 1872 by Henry Draper.

In a nova observed in 1866 Huggins saw bright hydrogen lines, correctly concluding that the star was emitting a shell of hydrogen gas at a temperature greater than at the star's surface. In 1868 Huggins showed that comets emit the light of luminescent carbon gas. Christian Doppler (1803–53) had suggested in 1842 that the 'Doppler effect' seen in sound waves might operate on light. The overall colour shift is actually much too small to be detected by eye, but a shift in characteristic absorption lines was another matter. In 1868 Huggins was probably the first (after consulting Clerk Maxwell on some theory) to try to measure the radial velocity of stars (i.e. the velocity with which they appear to be receding from or approaching us) by the Doppler shift of their spectral lines. His figure for Sirius was 29.4 miles per second away from the Solar System (later amended to around 20 miles per second – the modern figure is around 5 miles per second). His apparatus was not accurate enough and it had to wait until the 1890s when the powerful telescopes such as that at the Lick observatory could make such measurements accurately.

In 1875 William Huggins married Margaret Lindsay Murray (1848–1915) of Dublin. Margaret had made drawings of star constellations and sunspots as a child, and had also made a small spectroscope from a plan in the magazine *Good Words*. She had also tried astrophotography. When they married he was 51, some twenty five years older than her – though early 50s marriage was not all that rare amongst academics. Margaret shared other interests with her husband, e.g. they were both musically gifted (he owned and played a Stradivarius violin). They worked together for over thirty years, and his obituary notes that 'Her name appears as joint author with his own on many of the scientific papers published by him since that date'.[474] This included their *magnum opus* entitled *An Atlas of Representative Stellar Spectra* in 1899. For women in those Victorian days making

Margaret L. Huggins

[474]*Report of the Council of the RAS to the Ninety-first Annual General Meeting,* LXXI, 4, February, 1911, 269.

any headway as scientists was even harder than for men – virtually no official positions were open to them. A sister (like Caroline Herschel) or wife could participate, particularly in astronomy.[475] In the 1890s, E. W. Maunder's equally talented wife, A. S. D. Maunder, actually edited the Journal of the British Astronomical Association (which she again did from 1917–1930), so Margaret was not a singular figure in her circles.[476] How one sees the balance between the husband–wife team depends on one's predilections. The *Dictionary of Scientific Biography* accords Margaret a role 'in a relation to her husband similar to that of Caroline Herschel to her brother William' – presumably largely running around at his bidding and direction, mostly on his agenda. The BBC online 'Local Heroes' page, in contrast, suggests that:

> the fact that she was the accomplished spectroscopist and photographer – and 25 years younger – strongly suggest that she was the driving force for much of the time.[477]

This is, to say the least, a bit OTT, given that poor old William had started his pioneering spectroscopic work with Miller (for which he later got a joint RAS gold medal and the Royal Society Royal Medal) when Margaret was ten. It seems, however, that in spite of her age and relative inexperience at the time of their marriage, the joint names on their work from that time indicates that William regarded her as a partner, not an assistant. When William was knighted in 1897 (by which, of course, she became 'Lady Huggins') she was cited as his 'gifted wife'. In 1890 William (who was comfortably off but not wealthy) was awarded a civil list pension of £150 p.a. in recognition of his work, and when he died in 1910 Margaret was given a pension of £100 p.a. in honour of her 'collaborative service to science'. Modern widows, alas, can sometimes be relatively worse off in pension terms when their husbands die!

Margaret herself, in a 1905 passage (cited by the BBC site) said:

---

475 See P. A. Kidwell 'Women Astronomers in Britain' *Isis,* 1984, 75, 534–45 for various others. To some extent Countess Mary Rosse could also be seen in this light, though her photographic interest was more parallel than identical.

476 Mary Bruck's *Agnes Mary Clerke and the Rise of Astrophysics* (2008) looks at another talented woman, a friend of the Huggins, and other figures.

477 http://www.bbc.co.uk/history/programmes/local_heroes/biogs/mlhuggins2.shtml

> I find that men welcome women scientists provided they have the proper knowledge. It is absurd to suppose that anyone can have useful knowledge of any subject without a great deal of study. When women have really taken the pains thoroughly to fit themselves to do original work, scientific men are willing to treat them as equals. It is a matter of sufficient knowledge.

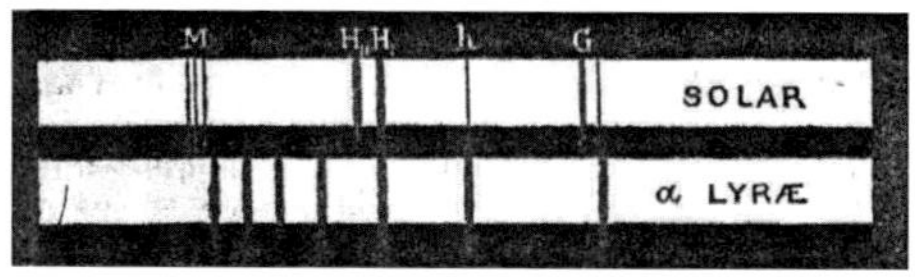

Huggins Vega and Solar Spectra 1877

Huggins regarded photographs of spectra as important. In 1877, for example, he says:

> With the most sensitive dry plates which have been prepared, a very bright star will impress its spectrum in fifteen minutes to half an hour. Stars that are less bright require an exposure of one to several hours … This photograph takes up the spectrum where eye observations fail. The first strong line coincident with the hydrogen line near G had been seen and compared with hydrogen. For the other lines we are indebted to photography.[478]

Huggins found this especially useful at the ultraviolet end of the spectrum, as the eye becomes less sensitive. The Huggins, then, continued their work, and were amongst the first to photograph the spectrum of a comet in 1881.

J. Norman Lockyer

During this time there was a difference of view with the astronomer J. Norman Lockyer (1836–1920). Lockyer was the son of a surgeon-apothecary, and had become recognised enough as an 'amateur' astronomer to obtain the directorship of the Solar Physics Observatory in Kensington. A more than nominal Anglican, he nevertheless wished to see *science* recognised as the most potent agent in the process of civilisation. In 1869 he founded the journal

---

[478] The RAS Monthly Review, 1877, 5–7. Huggins was at that time President of the RAS. Some comment on developments in stellar photography (e.g. dry plates) are in Hoskin, op. cit. 271.

Nature, which campaigned for this, and for the recognition that science should be a profession. Lockyer was especially interested in spectra during solar eclipses – either natural or by a method he found of simulating the effects using a dispersion large enough to weaken the spectrum of diffused atmospheric sunlight. Through a remarkable coincidence, Lockyer's results using this method reached the French Academy of Sciences within minutes of similar results from Jules Janssen (1824–1907) who had obtained his inspiration from a total eclipse in India.[479] This led in 1868 to Lockyer's discovery of the 'chromosphere' as a layer around the Sun which gave rise to red/lilac prominences visible during eclipses. A yellow line in this chromosphere was not reproduced in the laboratory, and he suggested that it was due to a new element which he called 'helium'.

In 1874 Lockyer published *Contributions to Solar Physics* showing the similarity of laboratory and astronomical spectra.[480] He was of a disposition less cautious and more speculative than the two Huggins's. Sometimes his speculations have turned out to have some aspect of truth, and sometimes not. Lockyer saw that the spectrum of an element varied with the intensity of the stimulus used to produce it. Locker speculated that a stimulus greater than that to break molecules into atoms would break up the atoms themselves and give sub-atoms with their own spectra.[481] The commonality of some sub-atoms from different elements might then explain apparently common lines. As it turns out there is truth in the dissociation, but not the commonality of lines.

Lockyer's striking ideas on stellar evolution will be dealt with below.

E. W. Maunder

Edward Walter Maunder (1851–1928)

Maunder attended King's College but did not graduate, and took a post as a photographic and spectroscopic assistant at the Greenwich Observatory. He found its director Airy fearsome,

[479] Michael Hoskin, *The Cambridge Illustrated History of Astronomy*, 268, gives a picture of the medal the French mint struck to commemorate this with both men's portraits on it.

[480] A nice colour version of this is in Michael Hoskin *The Cambridge Illustrated History of Astronomy*, 263.

[481] Though Chambers, op. cit. II, 325 suggests that Lockyer's theory may only imply 'a more complex condition of the molecules of the same substance'.

and Airy had little confidence in him as he had obtained the post by examination rather than personal selection! However Maunder was really the first professional UK astrophysicist! Maunder observed that when solar flares emanated from sunspots a day later a magnetic storm tended to hit the Earth. But why? As Clark says:

> Could the Sun be releasing a cannon ball of magnetism that lumbered across space before striking the Earth? Such a concept was science fiction to the Victorians, who thought that magnetism only surrounded a magnet and so could not be 'bottled' and transported elsewhere without moving the magnet itself (*TAnnie Schott Dill Russellhe, Sun Kings*, 143).

With his Wesleyan ideas of gender equality, Maunder had long lobbied for women to be treated equally – and when he founded the British Astronomical Association in 1890 entry was open equally to males and females. In 1891 Maunder obtained an assistant – a 'graduate'[482] from the Girton Ladies College, Cambridge (established 1869). Her mathematical skills supplemented his observational ones, and he regarded her as an equal partner in science. Clark comments:

> Together they discussed their joint belief in the Bible and the equality of the sexes. Eventually Annie Russell became Mrs Maunder on 28 December 1895.

The great Lord Kelvin opposed the idea of a connection of solar flares and magnetic storm. Maunder and Russell finally had a breakthrough when they realised that since the Sun rotated every 27 days, a tendency to 27 day gaps when magnetic storms occurred would show the link. He presented his paper in November 1904 to the RAS. Controversy raged, but Maunder's ideas prevailed, and a new slant was brought by the new Lucasian Professor Larmor that this was connected with the new idea of electron streams.

Observing Our Nearest Star

We have noted already spectral studies of the Sun, showing its similarity to other stars and identifying some of the layers it contained. But there were also continuing visual observations.

---

[482] Well she passed top in the Girton maths exams but was a woman so not given the BA.

Sunspots were amongst the first objects to be studied telescopically. In Galileo's day they had been shown to be on or near the Sun's surface, and to rotate with it. Heinrich Schwabe (1780–1875) brought some renewed interest in them. Actually, Schwabe was really searching for Vulcan – the elusive planet featured in Chapter Ten. But, although he failed to find Vulcan, he did have to record sunspots (to avoid confusing them with planets). With 17 years of his own observations, and others too, he noticed that sunspots seemed to have a ten-year cycle. His note in *Astronomische Nachrichten* in 1843 was actually brought to public attention by the naturalist and traveller Alexander von Humboldt (1769–1859) in 1851. Humboldt had also been interested in magnetic observations, and it had already been noted that there seemed to be about a ten-year cycle of what Humboldt called 'magnetic storms'. In 1852 Edward Sabine (1788–1883) noted correspondence between the sunspot cycle and the intensity of these magnetic storms. In September 1850 two astronomers R. C. Carrington (1826–1875)[483] and Richard Hodgson (1804–72) noted an outburst of light near a large spot, and this was concurrent with violent terrestrial magnetic storms and a spectacular auroral display. Some connection seemed highly probable, but the physics was not yet in place to explain this.

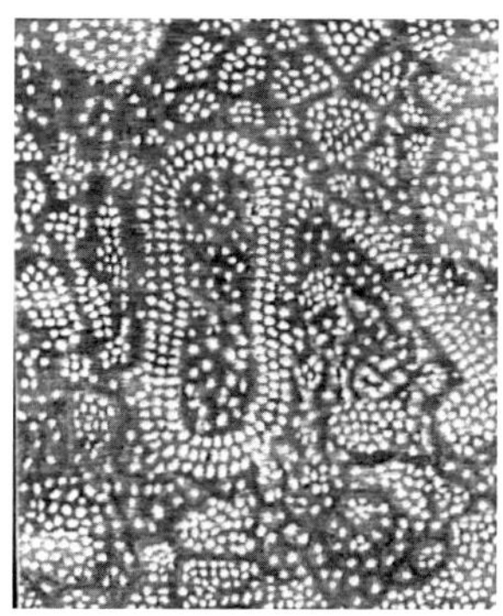

Huggins's Sun granules

Even in the days of William Herschel the grainy nature of edges of sunspots was noticed. In 1866 William Huggins summed up for the RAS[484] the fact that 'granules' are seen all over the Sun's face. He suggests that the Sun's surface is not uniformly level, the whole photosphere appears to be corrugated into ridges and vales and the granules are possibly masses of rather dense cloud-like matter floating about in the photosphere considered as composed of more aeriform matter. Later Huggins suggested that Janssen's 1877 photographs showed granules arranging themselves in spiral form. By this time, of course, the concentric layers of the Sun had been labelled:

---

483 In *The Sun Kings* Stuart Clark gives much detail on the tragic life of Richard Carrington – terming this observation of solar flare a 'tipping point'.

484 *RAS Monthly Notices* xxvi, 260.

1. Photosphere

The visible source of solar light – generally regarded as a shell of luminous clouds formed by cooling and condensing of vapours against the cold of space.

2. Chromosphere

A thin 'casing' or layer of self-luminous gaseous matter (chiefly hydrogen gas in an incandescent state) and the seat of solar prominences.

3. Corona

A vast shell of unknown vapours in a highly attenuated state, extending to some ½ degree from the Sun's visible edge.

William Herschel's cold-nucleus Sun now seemed unlikely. The spectral lines showed a highly luminous light source emitting a continuous spectrum which developed lines through passing through a cooler outer layer. Sunspots were also found to have different spectra, both from each other and at different points of the sunspot cycle.

In the last quarter of the 19th century, then, solar studies were well established – and spectral analysis was a major element of these.

There were also other issues of physics and the nature of the Sun. Estimates were made of the solar luminosity – the rate of emission of the Sun's heat. Figures including J. R. Mayer (1814–78) and Hermann von Helmholtz (1821–94) suggested that combustion could not explain the origin of the Sun's enormous radiated energy, so it must be because of the gravitational contraction of a large mass. Physicist William Thomson (1824–1907), later Lord Kelvin, was one of the greatest of 19th century scientists and the leading expert on heat and thermodynamics. On the basis of thermodynamic theory and Fourier's studies, Thomson estimated in 1862 that a million years ago the Sun's heat and temperature of the Earth must have been greatly different and unconducive to present life forms. He also estimated the probable age of the Earth from its own heat losses – putting this at around 100 million years (later reduced to some 20–40 million). This was of particular interest because geologists Charles Lyell (1897–1875) and Charles Darwin (1809–82)[485] were advocating vastly

---

[485]Darwin was, of course, regarded as a geologist prior to 1859.

greater ages for the Earth. Darwin's *Origin of Species* in 1859 had a theory of evolution that depended on vast ages for its plausibility. This brought Thomson (who did not believe evolution to be a rigorous theory) into confrontation with 'Darwin's Bulldog' Thomas Henry Huxley (1825–1895) and other pro-Darwin biologists. Actually the physicist–astronomers were 'right' in their criticisms based on existing knowledge. In a brilliant review of Darwin's work in 1860[486] Kelvin's associate Fleeming Jenkin (1833–85), who was a professor of engineering in London and then Edinburgh, showed how Darwin had little or no positive evidence for his theory. On the other hand, the calculations of the physicists are based on well-established laws.

> Looking on the Sun and planets as a certain complex physical combination, differing in degree but not in kind from those we can produce in the workshop by using similar materials subject to the same laws …

Can there be, he asks, some un-thought of source of heat in the Sun? How about, for example, clouds of interstellar dust? Jenkin speculates on various suggestions – but none of them are plausible. It should be noted that whilst both Thomson and Jenkin were Christians, this was not about biblical literalism, and Jenkin had no particular objection to the idea of God using some mechanism of evolution. But his conclusion, entirely rational in the context, is that Darwinian evolution is an interesting speculation, but presently stands against various inductively based calculations based on physics:

> A plausible theory should not be accepted while unproven; and if the arguments of this essay be admitted, Darwin's theory of the origin of species is not only without sufficient support from evidence, but is proved false by a cumulative proof.

This is often presented as an issue of 'astronomers vs. biologists', but this is a simplification. Whilst the later writings of Archibald Geikie elevated Charles Lyell and his uniformitarian view of geology as though it were mainstream, most leading geologists in 1859 (e.g. Professor Adam Sedgwick, 1785–1873) were sceptical of the possibility of estimating actual ages for the geological past because the assumption of uniformity in

---

486 'The North British Review', June 1867, 46: 277–318, reprinted in D. Hull's, *Darwin and His Critics* (1973), it is also on the web.

processes was gratuitous. The geological column had, of course, been effectively fully constructed by 1855 by men (including Lyell) who had rejected evolution – and the fossil record was more of a problem to Darwin than a help as he wrote his book. All this is of interest, however, in showing how the apparently secure results of one area of science can impinge upon another. The age of the Sun and Earth were issues of astrophysics, but impinged greatly on geology and biology.

Fortunately, Darwin, like most major innovative scientists, had a happy knack of simply ignoring inconvenient evidence. He took no notice and the conflict was kind-of resolved well after both were dead, with the discovery of nuclear energy. This, however, is outside our period of concern, so we may now return to matters more purely astrophysical.

Theory and Observation

Alongside the development of bigger telescopes, new physics and new observational techniques, there were various theories of stellar and planetary evolution. These were inevitably speculative, and those who put them forward were going well beyond any inductive base as more cautious scientists were not slow to point out.

Immanuel Kant

In the chapter on William Herschel we saw that philosopher Immanuel Kant (1724-1804) was developing ideas of Thomas Wright (1711–1786) on the Milky Way and the shape of the galaxy. Kant also, when aged only 31, wrote: *Universal Natural History and the Theory of the Heavens: An Essay on the Constitution and Mechanical Origin of the Whole Universe According to Newton's Principles* (1855). Unfortunately the publisher went bankrupt, and it was only in 1791 that the by then ageing and famous Kant allowed a reprint of part of it. Kant thought the fixed stars were a system that, in the Milky Way, resembled the planetary system in its disc-like structure. Nebulae, however, he saw as remote galactic systems. He suggested (very vaguely following Wright) that the entire universe was a system revolving about a common centre. Planetary systems formed by gravitational accretion of particles (under Newtonian gravity) with rotation as a key element driving the system into a disc from which planets in the same plane could evolve. It should be noted that Kant was contemptuous about the earlier 'reasoning of Epicurus, Leucippus and Democritus' the atomists who put forward apparently similar systems:

> The teachers of the mechanical production of the structure of the world derive all the order from mere chance … I find matter bound to necessary laws. Out of chaos I see a beautiful and orderly whole quite naturally developing itself … not by accident of chance … why did matter have laws aimed at order? … is this not undeniable proof of the community of their origin? … which must have been a Universal Supreme Intelligence …

Kant's system was strongly theistic, though he later questioned how far God could be rationally understood. He was not specifically *Christian* in more than a purely nominal sense, but the development of order from chaos could be seen as a theme in Genesis 1:2 (we may also remember Haydn's *Creation* in 1798) and Kant's model simply extended it cosmically.

Kant's model was purely qualitative, yet a modern work could write of it:

> Today we realise that Kant, by and large, got it right. Stars and their disks form in much the way he pictured, by the gravitational collapse of huge volumes of thinly dispersed interstellar gas and dust into appropriate nuclei.[487]

Two or three versions of this nebular hypothesis developed. One was due to Pierre-Simon de Laplace (1749–1827). In 1796 he published his *Exposition du système du monde* which made celestial mechanics available to a more popular audience. His five volume *Méchanique céleste* (1799–1825) showed his abilities as a mathematician. Famously, he was able to show that (contrary to what Newton had imagined) the Solar System was stable and did not need periodic divine readjustment. The 1796 work also suggested that the Solar System may have formed from a glowing nebulous mass as the innumerable tiny particles came together under Newtonian gravity. This would explain, for example, why the planets are all in roughly the same plane going in the same direction. Laplace himself was a nominal Catholic who was deeply critical of his church and a virtual atheist. But the system itself – and the removal necessity for occasional divine 'tinkering' which the deeply religious German philosopher Leibnitz had in any case

---

[487] John A. Wood in the *New Solar System* (4th edn 1999, ed. J K Beatty et al), 15.

found an obnoxious suggestion from Newton – was not necessarily regarded as atheistic. By the second quarter of the 19th century few if any theologians took the chronology in Genesis 1 etc. literally[488], and the vast time spans of a nebular hypothesis were no more threatening than those established for geology.

Pierre-Simon de Laplace

William Herschel's alternative system was outlined in Chapter Nine where we looked at his ideas of stellar evolution as evidenced by different nebula types.

Another who advocated the idea was philosopher Herbert Spencer (1820–1903) in 1858. Spencer held that nebulae are not further away than parts of our own galaxy, and are not collections of stars in the normal sense. His empirical reasons were: (i) nebulae seem to unaccountably avoid the plane of the Milky Way (ii) telescopes can sometimes resolve smaller but not larger ones (iii) he restated Whewell's objection in his 1853 *Essay* (cf. the previous chapter) based on John Herschel's views of the Magellanic clouds. It was Spencer's version of the nebular hypothesis, as we noted in the previous chapter, which was influential on Percival Lowell. But it was an idea that was very much around throughout the century.

Lockyer, as noted above, put forward another bold speculative system. In the beginning space contained a fairly uniform distribution of meteorites. Through rapid motions and chance collisions these, under gravity, gave rise to the various observed phenomena. Loose nebulae would eventually become stars. A star beginning as a meteorite swarm would rise in temperature until it condensed to a vaporised mass, and then cool by radiation. A very fast condensation would cause a nova. Original groupings too small to form nebulae could form comets, whilst isolated meteorites could reach the Earth. In its final state the universe would contain only cold dark bodies moving aimlessly. Lockyer tried to find spectral evidence for this theory, but most contemporaries were sceptical. Some of his ideas

[488] It is a demonstrable if persistent myth that Darwin, writing in 1859, challenged a 'literalist' view of Genesis. By that time no theologian – conservative or otherwise – believed it literal. Such literalism is a product of 20th century America (cf. *Reason, Science and Faith,* Paul Marston and Roger Forster, 1999).

do, in fact, resemble modern ideas of stellar evolution – but it is much more complex than he thought.

These various systems raise issues of inductive quantitative work vs. speculative models. Obviously, observation did impinge on theory. The demonstration from spectroscopy that there were gaseous nebulae gave more credence to a Kantian model than one based on meteorites – though ironically Lockyer was involved in spectroscopy whilst Kant put forward his model before spectroscopy was invented! Huggins thought Lockyer over-speculative, yet Huggins himself believed that his discoveries on the spectra of nebulae made some kind of nebular hypothesis likely (as we saw above). Scientists seldom if ever experiment without theory – the development of spectroscopic method illustrates this. But there are some scientists who are more inherently speculative (e.g. Laplace, Herschel and Lockyer), and some less (e.g. Fraunhofer, Maskelyne, and Huggins). Astrophysics owes much to both groups.

Questions

Here are some issues to think about on this subject:

- How far have the *motivations* for 'going into science' changed from the period covered by this book (i.e. pre-20th century) to the modern day?
- How much has the relationship between observational science and speculative models changed from the period of this course (i.e. pre-20th century) to the modern day?
- Do general world-views affect cosmologists today more, less, or about the same as they did in the former period?
- Does modern knowledge make the stars less awesome than formerly?

Some Final Retrospect

Any history of science that is simply a catalogue of 'discoveries' is not only boring but fails to understand the science of those involved. This book has not aimed at comprehensiveness, but at trying to get inside the thinking of some of the key figures in astronomical history up to the end of the 19th century. This has involved issues of contextual culture, religious world view, methodology, and an interaction with contemporary observations. Studying the history of science at other than a superficial level is a complex business. I hope that you have found it stimulating. It is sad that today in modern society so few seem actually to look up, and, if they do, the impact of the stars is muted by the reflected glare of artificial lighting. When, however, we do look up, it is hard not to share the curiosity that drove those astronomical pioneers – where did it all come from, where is it going, and what's it all about?

References

Primary Sources:

There are two versions of Kant's work: (i) *Kant's Cosmogony* (ed. Willy Ley, 1968) (ii) *Universal Natural History / The Theory of the Heavens* (ed. Stanley L Jaki, 1980). Michael J Crowe *Modern Theories of the Universe from Herschel to Hubble* (1994) is stimulating and contains some extracts from originals. There are, however, an increasing number of reprints now. Look on Amazon to find out what is available e.g.:

The Scientific papers of William Parsons, 3rd Earl of Rosse (repr. 2011).

The Monster Telescopes, Erected by the Earl of Rosse, Parsonstown: With an Account of the Manufacture of the Specula, and Full Descriptions of All the … (repr. 2010).

The Scientific Papers of Sir William Huggins (repr. 2010).

Gustrav Kirchoff Researches on the Solar Spectrum, and the Spectra of the Chemical Elements, 2 vols (repr. 2012).

Gustav Kirchoff (ed.), *The Laws of Radiation and Absorption: Memoirs by Prévost, Stewart, Kirchhoff, and Kirchhoff and Bunsen* (repr. 2010).

Obviously, however, much of such collected works are likely to be of less interest.

Secondary Sources

Michael Hoskin's *Cambridge Illustrated History of Astronomy* (1997) is a good general book covering much of this material – and with some nice pictures.

Owen Gingerich, *The General History of Astronomy: Volume 4, Astrophysics and Twentieth-Century Astronomy to 1950: Part A* (1984 repr. 2010) covers 1850–1950.

There is a hefty biography of Pierre-Simon Laplace, 1749–1827 by Charles Coulston Gillispie, Ivor Grattan-Guinness and Robert Fox (1997).

Most of the other figures are poorly served with biographies. Those which exist are usually themselves old and sometimes rare though now sometimes reprinted.

E. W. Maunder, *Sir William Huggins and spectroscopic astronomy* by (1913 repr. 2012).

John Montefiore, *A sketch of the life of Sir William Huggins* (1936).

Gerald Bayfield, *Dereham's forgotten scientist: William Hyde Wollaston* (1990).

Stuart Clark, *The Sun Kings* (2003) is detailed and informative on figures like Herschel, Carrington and Maunder.

A general history – Ian Glass (2005) *Revolutionaries of the Cosmos: The Astro-Physicists* , but only a small section is relevant.

Mary Bruck's *Agnes Mary Clerke and the Rise of Astrophysics* (2008) also looks at other figures in this period.

Arthur J. Meadows *Science and controversy: a biography of Sir Norman Lockyer* (1972 repr. 2011).

In July 2010 was published Lambert M. Surhone *William Hyde Wollaston* [but I was not disposed to pay £38 for a 140-page book, so I haven't read it! It now seems unavailable].

Barbara J. Becker *Unravelling Starlight: William and Margaret Huggins and the Rise of the New Astronomy* (2011) (prices start at £50 on Amazon).

Permissions

The black and white pictures in this book have mostly been taken by the author or friends, scanned from old publications on which copyright has lapsed, or taken from Wiki files which are in the public domain. Every effort has been made to identify the copyright holders, but if there are incorrect attributions, please let us know so that we can correct the information at reprint.

Copyrights for images in the colour plate section are as follows:

Epidaurus Theatre:© the author
Parthenon today: © Guillaume Piolle
http://commons.wikimedia.org/wiki/File:Parthenon_-_facade_ouest.jpg
Ptolemy: Public Domain
http://commons.wikimedia.org/wiki/File:Claudius_Ptolemaeus.jpg
Archiginnasio today:© the author
Frombork Cathedral: ©Schneider Ludwig
http://commons.wikimedia.org/wiki/File:Frombork_022.jpg?uselang=en-gb
Torun Cathedral Seen Across the Vistula: © Tilman Berger
http://commons.wikimedia.org/wiki/File:Torun01CenterWithWall.JPG?uselang=en-gb
Copernicus: Public Domain *(Original: District Museum, Torun, Poland)*
http://en.wikipedia.org/wiki/File:Nikolaus_Kopernikus.jpg
Map of Hven from copper etching of Blaeu Atlas 1663: Public Domain
http://en.wikipedia.org/wiki/File:Map_of_Hven_from_copper_etching_of_Blaeu_Atlas_1663.jpg
Stenborg Observatory
Donated by a student.
Prague Astronomical Clock: © the author
Tycho Brahe: Public Domain (*Original: Gavnø Castle, Denmark)*
http://en.wikipedia.org/wiki/File:Tycho_Brahe.JPG
Tycho's Great Quadrant: Public Domain
http://commons.wikimedia.org/wiki/File:Tycho-Brahe-Mural-Quadrant.jpg?uselang=en-gb
Graz: © Matthew Field
http://commons.wikimedia.org/wiki/File:Graz_Austria_pano_from_Schlossberg.jpg
Weil der Stadt *c.*1682: Public Domain
http://commons.wikimedia.org/wiki/File:Weil_der_Stadt,_Andreas_Kieser.png
Johannes Kepler: Public Domain *(Original: Fondation St-Thomas, Strasbourg)*
http://commons.wikimedia.org/wiki/File:Johannes_Kepler.jpeg
St Marks Square & Campanile: © the author
Doges Palace and Campanile: © the author
St Marks Astronomical Clock: © Waysider 1925
en.wikipedia.org/wiki/File:Venice_clocktower_in_Piazza_San_Marco_(torre_dell'orologio)_clockface.jpg
Galileo Galilei: Public Domain *(Original: National Maritime Museum, London)*
http://en.wikipedia.org/wiki/File:Justus_Sustermans_-_Portrait_of_Galileo_Galilei,_1636.jpg
Galileo Telescope: © Jim & Rhoda (Public Domain)
http://commons.wikimedia.org/wiki/File:Galileo_telescope_replica_%281%29.jpg?uselang=en-gb
Carr House: © the author
Much Hoole Church: © the author
Hoole Plate, Chaliceand Font: © the author
Toxteth Chapel: © the author
Newton's School: © the author
Woolsthorpe Manor: © the author
Colsterworth Parish Church: © the author
Trinity College: © the author
Tower of London and Mint: © Jillian (Public Domain)
http://upload.wikimedia.org/wikipedia/commons/3/30/Tower-of-london.JPG?uselang=en-gb **Principia:** © the author
Isaac Newton: Public Domain *(Origin: National Portrait Gallery)*
http://en.wikipedia.org/wiki/File:GodfreyKneller-IsaacNewton-1689.jpg
William Herschel: Public Domain *(Origin: National Portrait Gallery)*
http://commons.wikimedia.org/wiki/File:William_Herschel01.jpg
George Biddell Airy: Public Domain *(Origin: Royal Museums, Greenwich)*
http://commons.wikimedia.org/wiki/File:George_Biddell_Airy_%281801-1892%29,_by_John_Collier.jpg
John Couch Adams: St John's College Cambridge
Used by permission of the Master and Fellows of St John's College, Cambridge.
William Whewell: Public Domain
http://en.wikipedia.org/wiki/File:William_Whewell_portrait.jpg
William Huggins: Public Domain
http://en.wikipedia.org/wiki/File:Sir_William_Huggins_by_John_Collier.jpg
Percival Lowell © Lowell Observatory
Used by permission of Lowell Observatory.